MYSQL

IN A NUTSHELL

Other resources from O'Reilly

Related titles

Learning MySQL
Learning PHP & MySQL
Learning PHP 5
Learning Perl
Learning SQL
MySQL Cookbook
MySQL Pocket Reference
MySQL Stored Procedure Programming
PHP Cookbook™
PHP in a Nutshell
Programming PHP
Programming the Perl DBI
SQL Pocket Guide

oreilly.com

oreilly.com is more than a complete catalog of O'Reilly books. You'll also find links to news, events, articles, weblogs, sample chapters, and code examples.

oreillynet.com is the essential portal for developers interested in open and emerging technologies, including new platforms, programming languages, and operating systems.

Conferences

O'Reilly Media, Inc. brings diverse innovators together to nurture the ideas that spark revolutionary industries. We specialize in documenting the latest tools and systems, translating the innovator's knowledge into useful skills for those in the trenches. Visit *conferences.oreilly.com* for our upcoming events.

Safari Bookshelf (*safari.oreilly.com*) is the premier online reference library for programmers and IT professionals. Conduct searches across more than 1,000 books. Subscribers can zero in on answers to time-critical questions in a matter of seconds. Read the books on your Bookshelf from cover to cover or simply flip to the page you need. Try it today for free.

MYSQL

IN A NUTSHELL

Second Edition

Russell J.T. Dyer

O'REILLY®

Beijing • Cambridge • Farnham • Köln • Sebastopol • Taipei • Tokyo

MySQL in a Nutshell, Second Edition
by Russell J.T. Dyer

Printed in the United States of America.

Published by O'Reilly Media, Inc., 1005 Gravenstein Highway North, Sebastopol, CA 95472

O'Reilly books may be purchased for educational, business, or sales promotional use. Online editions are also available for most titles (*http://safari.oreilly.com*). For more information, contact our corporate/institutional sales department: (800) 998-9938 or *corporate@oreilly.com*.

Editor: Andy Oram
Copy Editor: Sarah Schneider
Production Editor: Sarah Schneider
Proofreader: Genevieve d'Entremont
Indexer: Ellen Troutman Zaig
Cover Designer: Karen Montgomery
Interior Designer: David Futato

Printing History:

April 2008: Second Edition
May 2005: First Edition

ISBN: 978-0-596-51433-4

[C] [1/09]

1230059843

To my friend Richard Stringer, for encouraging me in literature, liberalism, and writing, and for helping me to become the person I was meant to be.

Table of Contents

Part II. SQL Statements and Functions

Part III. MySQL Server and Client Tools

Part IV. APIs and Connectors

Part V. Appendixes

Preface

MySQL is the most popular open source database system available. Although it's free, it's still very dependable and fast, and is being employed increasingly in areas that used to be the province of Oracle or MS SQL Server. Thanks to a variety of utilities packaged with MySQL, administration is fairly effortless. With its several application programming interfaces (APIs), it's easy to develop your own software to interface with MySQL.

This book provides a quick reference to MySQL statements and functions, the administrative utilities, and the most popular APIs. The first few chapters are designed to help you to get started with MySQL. Each chapter on an API also starts with a tutorial.

When this book was written, version 5.0 of MySQL was generally available, and early releases of the development versions of 5.1 and 6.0 were available but not yet stable. As a result, you will find mostly features from version 5.0.*x* in this book. Features that appear only in newer versions are noted as such.

The Purpose of This Book

The purpose of this book is to provide a quick reference to:

- MySQL statements and functions
- Command-line options and configuration information for the MySQL server and utilities
- The most popular APIs used to access MySQL databases

Several chapters start with tutorials, but the central purpose of the book is to fill in the gaps for people who are already comfortable with relational databases.

The format that I've followed for a description of each statement or function is to move from curt memory-joggers to more leisurely explanations. If you know the statement or function that you're looking up, but can't quite remember the syntax, you'll find that first. If you need a bit more information to jog your memory or to clarify the possibilities available, you can find this in the first sentence or so of the explanation. If you require more clarification, you can continue with the slower-paced material that will follow a statement or function. Examples of usage are provided for almost all statements and functions.

In summary, the goal is to be brief but fairly complete, and to increase the level of detail as you read on.

How This Book Is Organized

This book is broken up into 14 chapters and 3 appendixes, as follows.

Part I, Introduction and Tutorials

Chapter 1, *Introduction to MySQL*, explains the major components of MySQL and useful guidelines for other information on MySQL.

Chapter 2, *Installing MySQL*, describes how to get MySQL running on common operating systems supported by MySQL AB. It is necessary to read this chapter only if your system does not already have MySQL installed.

Chapter 3, *MySQL Basics*, introduces SQL (Structured Query Language) and use of the `mysql` command-line interface. It's not a replacement for learning SQL and relational database design, but it can be useful to orient you to MySQL.

Part II, SQL Statements and Functions

Chapter 4, *Security and User Statements and Functions*, covers SQL statements and functions related to the management of user accounts and security.

Chapter 5, *Database and Table Schema Statements*, lists, explains, and provides examples of SQL statements and functions related to the creating, altering, and dropping of databases, tables, indexes, and views.

Chapter 6, *Data Manipulation Statements and Functions*, covers any SQL statements and functions that involve the manipulation of data—inserting, updating, replacing, or deleting.

Chapter 7, *Table and Server Administration Statements and Functions*, includes details and examples related to SQL statements and functions that might be used in the administration of databases, tables, or the server.

Chapter 8, *Replication Statements and Functions*, includes SQL statements that strictly relate to replication. This chapter also includes a tutorial and an explanation of the replication process. It also explains the replication states to help in solving problems.

Chapter 9, *Stored Routines Statements*, covers statements specifically related to events, stored procedures, triggers, and user-defined functions.

Chapter 10, *Aggregate Clauses, Aggregate Functions, and Subqueries*, combines aggregate clauses (i.e., `GROUP BY`) and functions that basically are only used with an aggregate clause. It also includes a tutorial on subqueries as they can be used to aggregate data.

Chapter 11, *String Functions*, covers any functions that are related to the manipulation of strings of data.

Chapter 12, *Date and Time Functions*, covers date and time related functions.

Chapter 13, *Mathematical Functions*, explains and gives examples of strictly mathematical related functions.

Chapter 14, *Flow Control Functions*, covers flow control functions such as `CASE` and `IF`.

Part III, MySQL Server and Client Tools

Chapter 15, *MySQL Server and Client*, covers the *mysqld* daemon and the *mysql* client and their options. It also explains scripts used to start the server (e.g., `mysqld_safe`).

Chapter 16, *Command-Line Utilities*, describes the utilities that can be used to administer the MySQL server and data. It also includes utilities such as **`mysqldump`** used for data backups.

Part IV, MySQL API

Chapter 17, *C API*, covers the functions provided by MySQL's basic C library.

Chapter 18, *Perl API*, presents the Perl DBI module, used to access MySQL databases from the programming language Perl.

Chapter 19, *PHP API*, presents the PHP functions used to query and manipulate MySQL databases.

Appendixes

Appendix A lists all the data types supported by MySQL.

Appendix B lists all MySQL operators, such as arithmetic signs and the `LIKE` and `IS NULL` comparison operators.

Appendix C lists the operating system's environment variables consulted by the MySQL server, client, and other utilities.

Conventions Used in This Book

The following typographical conventions are used in this book:

Plain text
: Indicates menu titles, menu options, menu buttons, and keyboard accelerators (such as Alt and Ctrl).

Italic
: Indicates new terms, URLs, email addresses, usernames, hostnames, filenames, file extensions, pathnames, and directories.

`Constant width`
: Indicates elements of code, configuration options, variables, functions, modules, databases, tables, columns, command-line utilities, the contents of files, or the output from commands.

`Constant width bold`
: Shows commands or other text that should be typed literally by the user.

`Constant width italic`
: Shows text that should be replaced with user-supplied values.

Using Code Examples

This book is here to help you get your job done. In general, you may use the code in this book in your programs and documentation. You do not need to contact us for permission unless you're reproducing a significant portion of the code. For example, writing a program that uses several chunks of code from this book does not require permission. Selling or distributing a CD-ROM of examples from O'Reilly books does require permission. Answering a question by citing this book and quoting example code does not require permission. Incorporating a significant amount of example code from this book into your product's documentation does require permission.

We appreciate, but do not require, attribution. An attribution usually includes the title, author, publisher, and ISBN. For example: "*MySQL in a Nutshell*, Second Edition, by Russell J.T. Dyer. Copyright 2008 Russell J.T. Dyer, 978-0-596-51433-4."

If you feel your use of code examples falls outside fair use or the permission given here, feel free to contact us at *permissions@oreilly.com*.

Request for Comments

Please address comments and questions concerning this book to the publisher:

O'Reilly Media, Inc.
1005 Gravenstein Highway North
Sebastopol, CA 95472
800-998-9938 (in the United States or Canada)

707-829-0515 (international or local)
707-829-0104 (fax)

The examples in this book are professionally written and have been tested, but that does not mean that they are guaranteed to be bug-free or to work correctly with your version and your platform's implementation of MySQL. If you have problems, find bugs, or have suggestions for future editions, please email them to:

bookquestions@oreilly.com

There's a web page for this book that lists errata, examples, and any additional information. You can access this page at:

http://www.oreilly.com/catalog/9780596514334

For more information about books, conferences, Resource Centers, and the O'Reilly Network, see the O'Reilly web site at:

http://www.oreilly.com

For more information about the author, go to his web site at:

http://russell.dyerhouse.com

Safari® Enabled

When you see a Safari® Enabled icon on the cover of your favorite technology book, that means the book is available online through the O'Reilly Network Safari Bookshelf.

Safari offers a solution that's better than e-books. It's a virtual library that lets you easily search thousands of top tech books, cut and paste code samples, download chapters, and find quick answers when you need the most accurate, current information. Try it for free at *http://safari.oreilly.com*.

Acknowledgments

Thanks to Andy Oram, my editor, for his guidance and editing, and for helping me to be the person fortunate enough to write this book yet again. I very much want to thank him and his family (his wife, Judy Lebow, and their children, Sonia and Sam) for taking me into their home for six weeks after my home town of New Orleans was devastated by Hurricane Katrina. I shall always appreciate their generosity.

Thanks also to Rick Rezinas, Judith Myerson, Bogdan Kecman, and others for reviewing the manuscript for technical accuracy. Their assistance was greatly appreciated. Thanks also to Isabel Kunkel (the assistant editor for the book) for her role in chasing me down to get chapters written and turned in. Special thanks to Kathryn Barrett (publicist for O'Reilly) for her moral support and advice over the past few years.

For the last three years I have been working at MySQL Inc. as the editor of its Knowledge Base. In that time I've learned a great deal more about MySQL software, and made many friends. It's a fabulous company and a caring community. When the hurricane chased me out of New Orleans in the summer of 2005, many of the people at MySQL assisted me in my recovery with funds they personally contributed, as well as emotional and moral support. Their assistance helped me establish a new home for myself and deal with the problems I encountered after the loss of my old home and community. And, of course, many of them helped with information and advice related to the writing of this book. From MySQL, I'd especially like to thank Ulf Sandberg (senior vice president) for always being supportive of me, and Rusty Osborne (my friend of 10 years and coworker in the KB) for her help and for continuing to listen to me through it all.

I

Introduction and Tutorials

This part of the book presents information that is useful to readers who need a basic introduction to MySQL. This part will probably not be sufficient for someone who is totally new to database programming and administration; a host of other introductory books exist for that reader. However, this part can provide the necessary background to someone who has some knowledge of other databases and wants to move to MySQL, who has used a MySQL database on a hosting service and wants to create a standalone server, or who has other gaps in introductory knowledge. Installation, basic configuration, and essential SQL are explained in this part of the book.

1

Introduction to MySQL

MySQL is an open source, multithreaded, relational database management system created by Michael "Monty" Widenius in 1995. In 2000, MySQL was released under a dual-license model that permitted the public to use it for free under the GNU General Public License (GPL); this caused its popularity to soar. The company that owns and develops MySQL is MySQL AB (the AB stands for *aktiebolag*, the Swedish term for stock company), which is now a subsidiary of Sun Microsystems. Currently, MySQL AB estimates that there are more than 6 million installations of MySQL worldwide, and reports an average of 50,000 downloads a day of MySQL installation software from its site and from mirror sites. The success of MySQL as a leading database is due not only to its price—after all, other cost-free and open source databases are available—but also its reliability, performance, and features.

The Value of MySQL

Many features contribute to MySQL's standing as a superb database system. Its speed is one of its most prominent features. In a comparison by *eWEEK* of several databases—including MySQL, Oracle, MS SQL, IBM DB2, and Sybase ASE—MySQL and Oracle tied for best performance and for greatest scalability (see *http://www.mysql.com/it-resources/benchmarks* for more details). MySQL is remarkably scalable, and is able to handle tens of thousands of tables and billions of rows of data. Plus, it manages small amounts of data quickly and smoothly.

The storage engine, which manages queries and interfaces between a user's SQL statements and the database's backend storage, is the critical software in any database management system. MySQL offers several storage engines with different advantages. Some are transaction-safe storage engines that allow for rollback of data. Additionally, MySQL has a tremendous number of built-in functions that are detailed in several chapters of this book. MySQL is also very well known for rapid and stable improvements. Each new release comes with speed and stability upgrades, as well as new features.

The MySQL Package

The MySQL package comes with several programs. Foremost is the MySQL server, represented by the *mysqld* daemon. The daemon listens for requests on a particular network port (3306 by default) by which clients submit queries. The standard MySQL client program is simply called *mysql*. With this text-based interface, a user can log in and execute SQL queries. This client can also accept queries from text files containing queries, and thereby execute them on behalf of the user or other software. However, most MySQL interaction is done by programs using a variety of languages. The interfaces for C, Perl, and PHP are discussed in this book.

A few wrapper scripts for *mysqld* come with MySQL. The `mysqld_safe` script is the most common way to start *mysqld*, because the script can restart the daemon if it crashes. This helps ensure minimal downtime for database services. The script `mysqld_multi` is used to start multiple sessions of `mysqld_safe`, and thereby multiple *mysqld* instances, for handling requests from different ports, and to make it easier to serve different sets of databases or to test different versions of MySQL.

MySQL also comes with a variety of utilities for managing a MySQL server. `mysqlaccess` is used for creating user accounts and setting their privileges. `mysqladmin` can be used to manage the MySQL server itself from the command line. This interaction includes checking a server's status and usage, and shutting down a server. `mysqlshow` may be used to examine a server's status, as well as information about databases and tables. Some of these utilities require Perl, or ActivePerl for Windows, to be installed on the server. See *http://www.perl.org* to download and install a copy of Perl on non-Windows systems, and see *http://www.activestate.com/Products/ActivePerl* to download and install a copy of ActivePerl on Windows systems.

MySQL also comes with a few utilities for importing and exporting data to and from MySQL databases. `mysqldump` is the most popular for exporting data and table structures to a plain-text file known as a *dump* file. This can be used for backing up data or for manually moving it between servers. The `mysql` client can be used to import the data back to MySQL from a dump file. See Chapter 16 for more on utilities.

Licensing

Although MySQL can be used for free and is open source, MySQL AB holds the copyrights to the source code. The company offers a dual-licensing program for its software: one allows cost-free use through the GPL under certain common circumstances, and the other is a commercial license bearing a fee. They're both the same software, but each has a different license and different privileges. See *http://www.fsf.org/licenses* for more details on the GPL.

MySQL AB allows you to use the software under the GPL if you use it without redistributing it, or if you redistribute it only with software licensed under the GPL. You can even use the GPL if you redistribute MySQL with software that you developed, as long as you distribute your software under the GPL as well.

However, if you have developed an application that requires MySQL for its functionality and you want to sell your software with MySQL under a nonfree license, you must purchase a commercial license from MySQL AB. There are other scenarios in which a commercial license may be required. For details on when you must purchase a license, see *http://www.mysql.com/company/legal/licensing*.

Besides holding the software copyrights, MySQL AB also holds the MySQL trademark. As a result, you cannot distribute software that includes MySQL in the name.

Mailing Lists

You can receive some assistance with problems that you may have with MySQL from the MySQL community at no charge through several listserv email systems hosted by MySQL AB. There is a main mailing list for MySQL (*mysql*) and several specialized mailing lists where anyone can post a message for help on a particular topic. One list covers questions about database performance (*benchmarks*). Another is for questions on the Windows versions of MySQL (*win32*). There are also lists for problems concerning the Java Database Connectivity™ (JDBC) drivers (*java*) and for the Perl DBI module (*perl*).

For a complete listing or to subscribe to one or more of these mailing lists, go to *http://lists.mysql.com*. On this mailing list page, you will find links for subscribing to each list. When you click a subscription link, you will see a very simple form on which to enter your email address. Incidentally, some subscribers like to use special email addresses and names representing their online personas. This allows anonymity and may make sorting emails easier. Others prefer to use their real names and contact information. After you enter your email address, you will receive an automated message to confirm your address. That email will have a link to the MySQL site with some parameters identifying your address. Click the link, and it will open your web browser and confirm your subscription.

The page from which you can subscribe to a list also has links for unsubscribing from lists, as well as links to archives of previous listserv messages for each list. You can search these archives for messages from others who are describing the same problem that you are trying to resolve. It's always a good idea to search archives before posting anything of your own, to find out whether your topic has been discussed before. If you can't find a solution in the documentation available to you or in the archives, you can post a message to a particular mailing list by sending an email to that list on *lists.mysql.com*. For example, if you have a problem with the Perl DBI module in relation to MySQL, you would send a message to *perl@lists.mysql.com*. Just be sure to send the message from the email account that is registered with the list to which you're submitting your question.

Books and Other Publications

Besides the mailing list archives mentioned in the previous section, MySQL AB provides extensive online documentation of the MySQL server and all of the other software it distributes. You can find the documentation at *http://dev.mysql.com/doc*. The documentation is now organized by version of MySQL. You can read the material online or download it in a few different formats (e.g., HTML or PDF). It is also available in hardcopy format: *MySQL Language Reference* and *MySQL Administrator's Guide*, both from MySQL Press.

In addition to this book, O'Reilly Media publishes a few other books on MySQL worth buying and reading. O'Reilly's mainline MySQL book is *Managing & Using MySQL* (2nd ed., 2002) by George Reese, Randy Jay Yarger, and Tim King (with Hugh E. Williams). George Reese has compiled a smaller version called *MySQL Pocket Reference* (2nd ed., 2007). For common practical problem solving, there's *MySQL Cookbook* (2nd ed., 2006) by Paul DuBois. For advice on optimizing MySQL and performing administrative tasks, such as backing up databases, O'Reilly has published *High Performance MySQL* (2004) by Jeremy D. Zawodny and Derek J. Balling.

O'Reilly also publishes several books with regard to the MySQL APIs. For PHP development with MySQL, there's *Web Database Applications with PHP and MySQL* (2nd ed., 2004) by Hugh E. Williams and David Lane. For interfacing with Perl to MySQL and other database systems, there's *Programming the Perl DBI* (2000) by Alligator Descartes and Tim Bunce. To interface to MySQL with Java, you can use the JDBC and JConnector drivers and George Reese's book, *Database Programming with JDBC and Java* (2nd ed., 2000).

In addition to the published books on MySQL, a few web sites offer brief tutorials on using MySQL topics. The O'Reilly Network often publishes articles on MySQL and the APIs for Perl, PHP, and Python in its online publication ONLamp.com (*http://www.onlamp.com/onlamp/general/mysql.csp*). Incidentally, I've contributed a few articles to that site and to several other publications on MySQL and related topics. MySQL AB also provides some in-depth articles on MySQL. You can find them in the DevZone section of its web site, *http://dev.mysql.com/tech-resources/articles*. Many of these articles deal with new products and features, making them ideal if you want to learn about using the latest releases available even while they're still in the testing stages. Developer Shed (*http://www.devarticles.com/c/b/MySQL*) is an additional educational resource. All of these online publications are subscription-free. If you are a MySQL Enterprise customer, though, you can get information about MySQL from its private Knowledge Base, of which I am currently the editor.

2
Installing MySQL

The MySQL database server and client software work on several different operating systems, notably Linux, FreeBSD, and a wide range of Unix systems: Sun Solaris, IBM AIX, HP-UX, and so on. MySQL AB has also developed a Mac OS X version, a Novell NetWare version, and several MS Windows versions. You can obtain a copy of the community version of MySQL from MySQL AB's site (*http://dev.mysql.com/downloads*).

This chapter briefly explains the process of installing MySQL on Unix, Linux, Mac OS X, NetWare, and Windows operating systems. For some operating systems, there are additional sections for different distribution formats. For any one platform, you can install MySQL by reading just three sections of this chapter: the next section on "Choosing a Distribution"; the section that applies to the distribution that you choose; and the section on "Postinstallation" at the end of the chapter.

Choosing a Distribution

Before beginning to download an installation package, you must decide which version of MySQL to install. The best choice is usually the latest stable version recommended by MySQL AB on its site. This is the GA (Generally Available) release. It's not recommended that you install a newer version unless you need some new feature that is contained only in one of the newer versions, such as the beta version or the RC (Release Candidate) version. It's also not recommended that you install an older version unless you have an existing database or an API application that won't function with the current version.

When installing MySQL, you also have the option of using either a source distribution or a binary distribution. It's easier, and recommended, for you to install a binary distribution. However, you may want to use a source distribution if you have special configuration requirements that must be set during the installation or at compile time. You may also have to use a source distribution if a binary distribution isn't available for your operating system.

Unix Source Distributions

The steps for installing MySQL on all Unix types of operating systems are basically the same. This includes Linux, Sun Solaris, FreeBSD, IBM AIX, HP-UX, etc. It's recommended that you install MySQL with a binary distribution, but as explained in the previous section, sometimes you may want to use a source distribution. To install a source distribution, you will need copies of GNU `gunzip`, GNU `tar`, GNU `gcc` (at least version 2.95.2), and GNU `make`. These tools are usually included in all Linux systems and in most Unix systems. If your system doesn't have them, you can download them from the GNU Project's site (*http://www.gnu.org*).

Once you've chosen and downloaded the source distribution files for MySQL, enter the following commands as *root* from the directory where you want the source files stored:

```
groupadd mysql
useradd -g mysql mysql
tar xvfz /tmp/mysql-version.tar.gz
cd mysql-version
```

The first command creates the user group `mysql`. The second creates the system user *mysql* and adds it to the group *mysql* at the same time. The next command uses the `tar` utility (along with `gunzip` via the `z` option) to unzip and unpack the source distribution file you downloaded. You should replace the word ***`version`*** with the version number—that is to say, you should use the actual path and filename of the installation file that you downloaded for the second argument of the `tar` command. The last command changes to the directory created by `tar` in the previous line. That directory contains the files needed to configure MySQL.

This brings you to the next step, which is to configure the source files to prepare them for building the binary programs. This is where you can add any special build requirements you may have. For instance, if you want to change the default directory from where MySQL is installed, use the **`--prefix`** option with a value set to equal the desired directory. To set the Unix socket file's path, you can use **`--with-unix-socket-path`**. If you would like to use a different character set from the default of *latin1*, use **`--with-charset`**. Here is an example of how you might configure MySQL with these particular options before building the binary files:

```
./configure --prefix=/usr/local/mysql \
            --with-unix-socket-path=/tmp \
            --with-charset=latin2
```

You can also enter this command on one line without the backslashes.

Several other configuration options are available. To get a complete and current listing of options permitted, enter the following from the command line:

```
./configure --help
```

You may also want to look at the latest online documentation for compiling MySQL at *http://dev.mysql.com/doc/mysql/en/compilation_problems.html*.

Once you've decided on any options that you want, run the configure script with these options. It will take quite a while to run, and it will display a great deal of information, which you can ignore usually if it ends successfully. After the configure script finishes, the binaries will need to be built and MySQL needs to be initialized. To do this, enter the following:

```
make
make install
cd /usr/local/mysql
./scripts/mysql_install_db
```


The first command builds the binary programs. If it's successful, you need to enter the second line to install the binary programs and related files in the appropriate directories. In the next line, you're changing to the directory where MySQL was installed. If you configured MySQL to be installed in a different directory, you'll have to use that one instead. The last command uses a script provided with the distribution to generate the initial privileges or grant tables.

All that remains now is to change the ownership of the MySQL programs and directories. You can do this by entering the following:

```
chown -R mysql /usr/local/mysql
chgrp -R mysql /usr/local/mysql
```

The first command changes ownership of the MySQL directories and programs to the mysql user. The second command changes the group owner of the same directory and files to mysql. These file paths may be different depending on the version of MySQL you installed and whether you configured MySQL for different paths.

With the programs installed and their file ownerships properly set, you can start MySQL. You can do this in several ways. To make sure that the daemon is restarted in the event that it crashes, enter the following from the command line:

```
/usr/local/mysql/bin/mysqld_safe &
```

This starts the *mysqld_safe* daemon, which will in turn start the MySQL server *mysqld*. If the *mysqld* daemon crashes, *mysqld_safe* will restart it. The ampersand at the end of the line instructs the shell to run the daemon in the background.

To have MySQL started at boot time, copy the *mysql.server* file, located in the *support-files* subdirectory of */usr/local/mysql*, to the */etc/init.d* directory. To do this, enter the following from the command line:

```
cp support-files/mysql.server /etc/init.d/mysql
chmod +x /etc/init.d/mysql
chkconfig --add mysql
```

The first line follows a convention of placing the startup file for the server in the server's initial daemons directory with the name *mysql*. You should change the file paths to the equivalent directory on your system. The second command makes the file executable. The third sets the run level of the service for startup and shutdown.

Now that MySQL is installed and running, you need to make some postinstallation adjustments that are explained in the last section of this chapter ("Postinstallation").

Unix Binary Distributions

Installing MySQL with a binary distribution is easier than using a source distribution and is the recommended choice if a binary distribution is available for your platform. The files are packaged together into an archive file and then compressed before being put on the Internet for downloading. Therefore, you will need a copy of GNU `tar` and GNU `gunzip` to be able to unpack the installation files. These tools are usually included on all Linux systems and most Unix systems. If your system doesn't have them, though, you can download them from the GNU Project's site (*http://www.gnu.org*).

Once you've chosen and downloaded the installation package, enter something like the following from the command line as *root* to begin the MySQL installation process:

```
groupadd mysql
useradd -g mysql mysql
cd /usr/local
tar xvfz /tmp/mysql-version.tar.gz
```

The first command creates the user group *mysql*. The second creates the user *mysql* and adds it to the group *mysql* at the same time. The next command changes to the directory where the MySQL files are about to be extracted. In the last command, you use the `tar` utility (along with `gunzip` via the `z` option) to unzip and unpack the source distribution file that you downloaded. The word ***`version`*** in the name of the installation file is replaced with the version number—that is to say, use the actual path and name of the installation file that you downloaded as the second argument of the `tar` command. For Sun Solaris systems, you should use `gtar` instead of `tar`.

After running the previous commands, you need to create a symbolic link to the directory created by *tar* in */usr/local*:

```
ln -s /usr/local/mysql-version /usr/local/mysql
```

This creates */usr/local/mysql* as a link to */usr/local/mysql-version*, where *mysql-version* is the actual name of the subdirectory that *tar* created in */usr/local*. The link is necessary because MySQL is expecting the software to be located in */usr/local/mysql* and the data to be in */usr/local/mysql/data* by default. It should be noted that for some versions of MySQL, a different directory is expected and used. So consult MySQL's online documentation to be sure.

At this point, MySQL is basically installed. Now you must generate the initial privileges or grant tables, and change the file ownership of the MySQL programs and datafiles. To do these tasks, enter the following from the command line:

```
cd /usr/local/mysql
./scripts/mysql_install_db

chown -R mysql /usr/local/mysql
chgrp -R mysql /usr/local/mysql
```

The first command changes to the directory containing MySQL's files. The second command uses a script provided with the distribution to generate the initial privileges or grant tables, which consist of the `mysql` database with MySQL's *root* user. The third command changes the ownership of the MySQL directories and programs to the *mysql* user. The last command changes the group owner of the same directory and files to *mysql*.

With the programs installed and their ownerships properly set, you can start MySQL. This can be done in several ways. To make sure that the daemon is restarted in the event that it crashes, enter the following from the command line:

```
/usr/local/mysql/bin/mysqld_safe &
```

The *mysqld_safe* daemon, started by this command, will in turn start the MySQL server *mysqld*. If the *mysqld* daemon crashes, *mysqld_safe* will restart it. The ampersand at the end of the line instructs the shell to run the command in the background.

To have MySQL started at boot time, copy the *mysql.server* file located in the *support-files* subdirectory of */usr/local/mysql* to the */etc/init.d* directory. To do this, enter the following from the command line:

```
cp support-files/mysql.server /etc/init.d/mysql
chmod +x /etc/init.d/mysql
chkconfig --add mysql
```

The first line follows a convention of placing the startup file for the server in the server's initial daemons directory with the name *mysql*. Set the file path according to your system, though. The second command makes the file executable. The third sets the run level of the service for startup and shutdown.

Now that MySQL is installed and running, you need to make some postinstallation adjustments that are explained in the last section of this chapter ("Postinstallation").

Linux RPM Distributions

If your server is running on a version of Linux that installs software through the RPM package format (where RPM originally stood for Red Hat Package Manager), it is recommended that you use a package instead of a source distribution. Currently, RPMs are provided based on only a couple of different Linux distributions: various versions of Red Hat Enterprise Linux and SuSE Linux Enterprise. For all other distributions of Linux, MySQL RPMs are based on the Linux kernel or the type of libraries installed on the server. For each version of MySQL, there are a few RPM files that you can download. The primary two contain the server and client files. Their naming scheme is *MySQL-server-version.rpm* and *MySQL-client-version.rpm*, where *version* is the actual version number. In addition to these main packages, you may also want to install some of the other RPM files that are part of a distribution. There's an RPM for client-shared libraries (*MySQL-shared-version.rpm*), another for libraries and C API include files for certain clients (*MySQL-devel-version.rpm*), and another for benchmarking and other MySQL performance tests (*MySQL-bench-version.rpm*).

To install RPM files after downloading them to your server, enter something like the following from the command line in the directory where they're located:

```
rpm -ivh MySQL-server-version.rpm \
         MySQL-client-version.rpm
```

If an earlier version of MySQL is already installed on the server, you will receive an error message stating this problem, and the installation will be canceled. If you want to upgrade an existing installation, you can replace the `i` option in the example with an uppercase `U`.

When the RPM files are installed, the *mysqld* daemon will be started or restarted automatically. Once MySQL is installed and running, you need to make some postinstallation adjustments that are explained in the last section of this chapter ("Postinstallation").

Macintosh OS X Distributions

On recent versions of Mac OS X, MySQL is usually installed already. However, in case it is not installed on your system or you want to upgrade your copy of MySQL by installing the latest release, directions are included here.

As of version 10.2 of Mac OS X and version 4.0.11 of MySQL, binary package (PKG) files are available for installing MySQL. If your server is using an older version of Mac OS X, you need to install MySQL using a Unix source or binary distribution, following the directions described earlier in this chapter for those particular packages. If your server is not running a graphical user interface (GUI) or a desktop manager, you can instead install MySQL on a Macintosh system with a TAR package. This can be downloaded from the download page on MySQL's web site. Explanation of that method of installation is included here.

If an older version of MySQL is already installed on your server, you will need to shut down the MySQL service before installing and running the newer version. You can do this with the *MySQL Manager Application*, which is a GUI application. It's typically installed on recent versions of Mac OS X by default. If your server doesn't have the MySQL Manager Application, enter the following from the command line to shut down the MySQL service:

```
mysqladmin -u root shutdown
```

Incidentally, if MySQL isn't already installed on your system, you may need to create the system user, *mysql*, before installing MySQL.

To install the MySQL package file, from the Finder desktop manager, double-click on the disk image file (the *.dmg* file) that you downloaded. This will reveal the disk image file's contents. Look for the PKG files; there will be at least two. Double-click on the one named *MySQL* followed by the version numbers. This will begin the installation program. The installer will take you through the installation steps from there. The default settings are recommended for most users and developers. You will need an administrator username and password. To have MySQL started at boot time, add a *StartupItem*. Within the disk image file that you downloaded, you should see an icon labeled *MySQLStartupItem.pkg*. Just double-click it, and it will create a *StartupItem* for MySQL.

To install the TAR package instead of the PKG package, download the TAR file from MySQL's site and move it to the */usr/local* directory, and then change to that directory. Next, untar and unzip the installation program like so:

```
cd /usr/local
tar xvfz mysql-version.tar.gz
```

In this example, change ***version*** to the actual version number. From here create a symbolic link for the installation directory. Then run the configuration program:

```
ln -s /usr/local/mysql-version /usr/local/mysql
cd /usr/local/mysql

./configure --prefix=/usr/local/mysql \
   --with-unix-socket-path=/usr/local/mysql/mysql_socket \
   --with-mysqld-user=mysql
```

Depending on your needs, you might provide other options than just these few. Next, you should set the ownership and group for the files and directories created to the *mysql* user and group, which should have been created by the installation program. For some systems, you may have to enable permissions for the hard drive or volume first. To do that, use the `vsdbutil` utility. If you want to check if permissions are enabled on the volume first, use the `-c` option; to just enable it, use the `-a` option for `vsdbutil`. You should also make a link to the *mysql* client and to *mysqladmin* from the */usr/bin* directory:

```
vsdbutil -a /Volumes/Macintosh\ HD/

sudo chgrp -R mysql /usr/local/mysql/.
sudo chown -R mysql /usr/local/mysql/.

ln -s /usr/local/mysql/bin/mysql /usr/bin/mysql
ln -s /usr/local/mysql/bin/mysqladmin /usr/bin/mysqladmin
```

Of course, change the name of the hard drive and its path to how it reads on your system. At this point, you should be able to start the daemon and log into MySQL. This is the same for both the TAR and the PKG method of installation on a Macintosh system:

```
sudo /usr/local/mysql/bin/mysqld_safe &

mysql -u root -p
```

Depending on the release of MySQL, the file path for a PKG installation may be different than shown here. An ampersand (`&`) sends the process to the background.

Once MySQL is installed and running, you need to make some postinstallation adjustments that are explained in the last section of this chapter ("Postinstallation").

Novell NetWare Distributions

If your server is using Novell NetWare 6.0 or later, and the required Novell support packs have been installed, you can install MySQL on it. For version 6.0 of NetWare, you need to have Support Pack 4 installed and updated along with the current version of LibC. For version 6.5 of NetWare, Support Pack 2 needs to be installed and updated along with the current version of LibC. You can obtain support packs from Novell's site (*http://support.novell.com*). You can find the latest version of LibC at *http://developer.novell.com/wiki/index.php/Libraries_for_C_(LibC)*. Another requirement for installing MySQL is that the MySQL server and data be installed on a Novell Storage Services (NSS) volume.

If an older version of MySQL is already installed and running on your server, you need to shut down the MySQL service before installing and running the newer version. You can do this from the server console like so:

```
mysqladmin -u root shutdown
```

Next, you need to log on to the server from a client that has access to the location (*SYS:MYSQL*) where MySQL is to be installed. Unpack the compressed binary package to that location. When the ZIP file has finished unpacking, you can establish a search path for the directory that holds the MySQL NetWare Loadable Modules (NLMs) by entering the following from the server console:

```
SEARCH ADD SYS:MYSQL\BIN
```

At this point, MySQL is basically installed. Now you need to generate the initial privileges or grant tables. You can do this by entering the following from the server console:

```
.\scripts\mysql_install_db
```

The `mysql_install_db` utility is a script provided with the distribution to generate the initial privileges or grant tables (i.e., the `mysql` database). Once this is done, MySQL is ready to be started. To do this, just enter the following from the server console:

```
mysqld_safe
```

To have MySQL started at boot time, you must add the following lines to the server's *autoexec.ncf* file:

```
SEARCH ADD SYS:MYSQL\BIN
MYSQLD_SAFE --autoclose --skip-external-locking
```

The first line establishes the search path for MySQL. The second line starts the *mysqld_safe* daemon at startup. The first option in this command instructs the server to close MySQL automatically when the server shuts down. The second option instructs the server not to allow external table locking. (External locks can cause problems with NetWare version 6.0.) Both of these options are recommended.

Once MySQL is installed and running, you will need to make some postinstallation adjustments that are explained in the last section of this chapter ("Postinstallation").

Windows Distributions

Installing MySQL on a server using Windows is fairly easy. If MySQL is already installed and running on your server and you want to install a newer version, you will need to shut down the existing one first. For server versions of MS Windows (e.g., Windows NT), MySQL is installed as a service. If it's installed as a service on your server, you can enter the following from a DOS command window to shut down the service and remove it:

```
mysqld -remove
```

If MySQL is running, but not as a service, you can enter the following from a DOS command window to shut it down:

```
msyqladmin -u root shutdown
```

MySQL AB's site (*http://dev.mysql.com/downloads/*) contains three installation packages: a Windows Essential package, a standard Windows package, and a standard Windows package without the installer. The Windows Essential package is the recommended format. It contains only the essential files for running MySQL. This includes the usual command-line utilities and the header files for the C API. The standard Windows package contains the essential files, as well as documentation, the *MySQL Administrator*, the embedded server, the benchmark suite, and a few other useful scripts. The standard Windows package without the installer contains the same binary files and other related files for MySQL, but not an installer. You'll need to extract and copy the files into the *c:\mysql* directory. Then, you must create a *my.ini* file in the *c:\windows* directory. Several examples showing different server usage come with the distribution package.

The Windows Essential package is a file called *MySQL-version.msi*. From the Windows desktop, just double-click this file's icon and the Windows Installer program will start.

The standard Windows installation package is a compressed file from which you have to extract the installation files. To do this, you need a utility such as WinZip (*http://www.winzip.com*) to uncompress the files. One of the files is named *setup.exe*. Double-click it to start the installer for this package. From this point, the installation process is pretty much the same for the packages that use the installer.

Once you've started the installer, a dialog box appears that offers you three general choices. The *Typical* choice is the recommended one, but it will omit the installation of C API include files and other client libraries. For the standard Windows package, this choice will also omit installation of the embedded server, the benchmark suite, and several other scripts. The *Complete* installation choice instructs the installer to install everything that's included in the distribution package that you downloaded. The *Custom* choice allows you to choose from a list of programs and libraries to install. On the same screen is a button labeled *Change* that lets you change the directory in which MySQL will be installed. Older versions of MySQL use *c:\mysql* as the default. Recent versions install MySQL by default in directories like *c:\Program Files\MySQL\MySQL Server version*, where the word *version* is replaced with the version number.

After you choose what to install and where, the files are installed. When the installer is finished, the MySQL Server Instance Configuration Wizard is started. It asks you a series of questions to create a server configuration file (*my.ini*), which, by default, is stored in *c:\windows*. The questions are based on the intended usage of the MySQL server, and your answers determine the contents of the configuration file. You will also be allowed to change the default location of the datafiles, the TCP/IP port used, and a couple of other settings.

To invoke the command-line utilities without having to enter the file path to the directory containing them, enter the following from the command line:

```
PATH=%PATH%;c:\Program Files\MySQL\MySQL Server version\bin
```

You should replace the word ***version*** with the version number—that is to say, you should enter the path to the MySQL installation. If you changed location when you installed MySQL, you need to use the path that you named. Older versions of Windows may not accept long directory names in the startup file. Therefore, you may need to abbreviate the line shown previously so that it looks something like this:

```
PATH=%PATH%;c:\Program~1\MySQL\MySQLS~1.1\bin
```

The characters `~1` are substitutes for the extra characters of a directory name that follow the first seven characters. An S is a substitute for any space that occurs in the first seven characters of a directory name. If the directory name ends in a dot and more characters, the last dot and characters are given. For example, a directory named "MySQL Server 4.1" would be entered as "MySQLS~1.1," as shown in the previous command. To make this new path available at boot time, you may want to add it to the *c:\autoexec.bat* file.

Once you've finished installing MySQL and you've set up the configuration file, the installer will start the MySQL server automatically. If you've installed MySQL manually without an installer, enter something like the following from a DOS command window:

```
mysqld --install
net start mysql
```

All that remains are some postinstallation adjustments that are explained in the next section.

Postinstallation

After you've finished installing MySQL on your server, you should perform a few tasks before allowing others to begin using the service. You may want to configure the server differently by making changes to the configuration file. At a minimum, you should change the password for the *root* user and add some nonadministrative users. Some versions of MySQL are initially set up with anonymous users. You should delete them. This section will briefly explain these tasks.

Although the MySQL developers have set the server daemon to the recommended configuration, you may want to set the daemon differently. For instance, you may want to turn on error logging. To do this, you will need to edit the main configuration file for MySQL. On Unix systems, this file is */etc/my.cnf*. On Windows systems, the main configuration file is usually either *c:\windows\my.ini* or *c:\my.cnf*. The configuration file is a simple text file that you can edit with a plain-text editor, not a word processor. The configuration file is organized into sections or groups under a heading name contained in square brackets. For instance, settings for the server daemon *mysqld* are listed under the group heading `[mysqld]`. Under this heading, you could add something like `log = /var/log/mysql` to enable logging and to set the directory for the log files to the one given. You can list many options in the file for a particular group. For a complete listing and explanation of these options, see Chapter 15.

You can change the password for the *root* user in MySQL in a few ways. One simple way is to log in to MySQL through the *mysql* client by entering the following from the command line:

```
mysql -u root -p
```

On a Windows system, you may have to add the path *c:\mysql\bin* to the beginning of this line, if you haven't added it to your command path. After successfully entering the command, you will be prompted for the *root* user's password. This is not the operating system's *root* user, but the *root* user for MySQL. Initially there is no password, so press Enter to leave it blank. If everything was installed properly and the *mysqld* daemon is running, you should get a prompt like this:

```
mysql>
```

This is the prompt for the *mysql* client interface. You should set the password for all *root* users. To get a list of users and their hosts for the server, execute the following command from the *mysql* client:

```
SELECT User, Host FROM mysql.user;

+------+-----------------------+
| User | Host                  |
+------+-----------------------+
| root | 127.0.0.1             |
| root | russell.dyerhouse.com |
| root | localhost             |
+------+-----------------------+
```

The results from my server are shown here. After installing, I have three user and host combinations. Although `127.0.0.1` and `localhost` translate to the same host, the password should be changed for both along with the one for my domain. To change the *root* user's password, enter the following at this prompt:

```
SET PASSWORD FOR 'root'@'127.0.0.1'=PASSWORD('password');

SET PASSWORD FOR 'root'@'russell.dyerhouse.com'=PASSWORD('password');

SET PASSWORD FOR 'root'@'localhost'=PASSWORD('password');
```

Replace the word ***`password`*** in quotes with the password that you want to use for *root*. On some systems, the wildcard `%` is used to allow *root* login from any host. After you change all of the root passwords, log out of the *mysql* client and log back in with the new password.

On some older systems or versions of MySQL, there are anonymous users. (Newer editions don't have them.) They will appear in the results of the `SELECT` statement shown earlier with blank fields for usernames. You should delete them by entering the following from the *mysql* client:

```
DELETE FROM mysql.user WHERE User='';
DELETE FROM mysql.db WHERE User='';
FLUSH PRIVILEGES;
```

The first two statements here delete any anonymous users from the `user` and `db` tables in the database called `mysql`—that's where the privileges or grant tables are stored. The last line resets the server privileges to reflect these changes.

The next step regarding users is to set up at least one user for general use. It's best not to use the *root* user for general database management. When you set up a new user, you should consider which privileges to allow her. If you want to set up a user who can view only data, you should enter something like the following from the *mysql* client:

```
GRANT SELECT ON *.* TO 'kerry'@'localhost' IDENTIFIED BY 'beck123';
```

In this line, the user is *kerry* from the localhost and her password is *beck123*. If you want to give a user more than viewing privileges, you should add additional privileges to the `SELECT` privilege, separated by commas. To give a user all privileges, replace `SELECT` with `ALL`. Here's another example using the `ALL` flag:

```
GRANT ALL ON db1.* TO 'kerry'@'localhost' IDENTIFIED BY 'beck123';
```

In this example, the user *kerry* has all basic privileges, but only for the `db1` database and only when logged in from the localhost, not remotely. This statement adds the user *kerry* to the table `user` in the `mysql` database, if there is already a row for her in it, but with no privileges. It will also add a row to the `db` table in the `mysql` database indicating that *kerry* has all privileges for the `db1` database. See the explanation of `GRANT` in Chapter 4 for more options.

If you have any existing MySQL datafiles from another system, you can copy the actual files to the directory where MySQL data is stored on your server—but this is not a recommended method. If you do this, be sure to change the ownership of the files to the *mysql* user and *mysql* group with the `chown` system command after you copy them to the appropriate directory. If your existing datafiles are dump files created by the `mysqldump` utility, see the explanation regarding that utility in Chapter 16. If your data needs to be converted from a text file, see the explanation of the `LOAD DATA INFILE` statement in Chapter 6. You probably should also check the online documentation (*http://dev.mysql.com/doc/mysql/en/Upgrade.html*) on upgrading from a previous version to a current one, especially if you are migrating across major versions. If you have existing data, always upgrade one release at a time. Don't skip any or you may have problems with tables, passwords, or any applications you've developed.

With the MySQL installation software downloaded and installed and all of the binary files and data in their places and properly set, MySQL is now ready to use. For an introduction to using MySQL, see the next chapter.

3
MySQL Basics

Although the bulk of this new edition of *MySQL in a Nutshell* contains reference information, which you can read in small segments as needed, this chapter presents a basic MySQL tutorial. It explains how to log in to the MySQL server through the *mysql* client, create a database, create tables within a database, and enter and manipulate data in tables.

This tutorial does not cover MySQL in depth. Instead, it's more of a sampler; it's meant to show you what's possible and to get you thinking about how to approach tasks in MySQL.

The mysql Client

There are various methods of interacting with the MySQL server to develop or work with a MySQL database. The most basic interface that you can use is the *mysql* client. With it, you can interact with the server from either the command line or within an interface environment.

If MySQL was installed properly on your server, *mysql* should be available for use. If not, see Chapter 2. On Unix-based systems, you can type `whereis mysql`. Windows, Macintosh, and other GUI-type systems have a program location utility for finding a program. If you used the default installation method, the *mysql* program probably resides at */usr/local/mysql/bin/mysql*. On Unix systems, if */usr/local/mysql/bin/* is in your default path (the `PATH` environment variable), you can specify `mysql` without the full pathname. If the directory is not in your path, you can add it by entering:

```
PATH=$PATH:/usr/local/mysql/bin
export PATH
```

Assuming that everything is working, you will need a MySQL username and password. If you're not the administrator, you must obtain these from her. If MySQL was just installed and the *root* password is not set yet, its password is blank. To learn how to set the *root* password and to create new users and grant them privileges, see Chapter 2 for starting points and Chapter 4 for more advanced details.

From a shell prompt, log in to MySQL like this:

```
mysql -h host -u user -p
```

If you're logging in locally—that is, from the server itself—either physically or through a remote login method, such as SSH (secure shell), you can omit the `-h host` argument. This is because the default host is *localhost*, which refers to the system you are on. In other circumstances, where your commands actually have to travel over a network to reach the server, replace the argument ***host*** with either a hostname that is translatable to an IP address or the actual IP address of the MySQL server. You should replace the argument ***user*** with your MySQL username. This is not necessarily the same as your filesystem username.

The `-p` option instructs *mysql* to prompt you for a password. You can also add the password to the end of the `-p` option (e.g., enter `-prover` where `rover` is the password); if you do this, leave no space between `-p` and the password. However, entering the password on the command line is not a good security practice, because it displays the password on the screen and transmits the password as clear text through the network, as well as making it visible whenever somebody gets a list of processes running on the server.

When you're finished working on the MySQL server, to exit *mysql*, type `quit` or `exit`, and press the Enter key.

Creating a Database and Tables

Assuming that you have all of the privileges necessary to create and modify databases on your server, let's look at how to create a database and then tables within a database. For the examples in this chapter, we will build a database for a fictitious bookstore:

```
CREATE DATABASE bookstore;
```

In this brief SQL statement, we have created a database called `bookstore`. You may have noticed that the commands or reserved words are printed here in uppercase letters. This isn't necessary; MySQL is case-insensitive with regard to reserved words for SQL statements and clauses. Database and table names are case-sensitive on operating systems that are case-sensitive, such as Linux systems, but not on systems that are case-insensitive, such as Windows. As a general convention, though, reserved words in SQL documentation are presented in uppercase letters and database names, table names, and column names in lowercase letters. You may have also noticed that the SQL statement shown ends with a semicolon. An SQL statement may be entered over more than one line, and it's not until the semicolon is entered that the client sends the statement to the server to read and process it. To cancel an SQL statement once it's started, enter `\c` instead of a semicolon.

With our database created, albeit an empty one, we can switch the default database for the session to the new database like this:

```
USE bookstore
```

This saves us from having to specify the database name in every SQL statement. MySQL by default will assume the current database, the one we last told it to use. No semicolon is given with the `USE` statement because it's a client-based SQL statement.

Next, we will create our first table, in which we will later add data. We'll start by creating a table that we'll use to enter basic information about books, because that's at the core of a bookstore's business:

```
CREATE TABLE books (
book_id INT,
title VARCHAR(50),
author VARCHAR(50));
```

This SQL statement creates the table `books` with three columns. Note that the entire list of columns is contained within parentheses.

The first column is a simple identification number for each record, which represents one book. You can specify the data type either as `INTEGER` or as `INT` like the example. The second and third columns consist of character fields of variable width, up to 50 characters each.

To see the results of the table we just created, enter a `DESCRIBE` statement, which displays a table as output:

```
DESCRIBE books;

+---------+-------------+------+-----+---------+-------+
| Field   | Type        | Null | Key | Default | Extra |
+---------+-------------+------+-----+---------+-------+
| book_id | int(11)     | YES  |     | NULL    |       |
| title   | varchar(50) | YES  |     | NULL    |       |
| author  | varchar(50) | YES  |     | NULL    |       |
+---------+-------------+------+-----+---------+-------+
```

Considering our bookstore a bit more, we realize that we need to add a few more columns for data elements: publisher, publication year, ISBN number, genre (e.g., novel, poetry, drama), description of book, etc. We also realize that we want MySQL to automatically assign a number to the `book_id` column so that we don't have to bother creating one for each row or worry about duplicates. Additionally, we've decided to change the `author` column from the actual author's name to an identification number that we'll join to a separate table containing a list of authors. This will reduce typing, and will make sorting and searching easier, as the data will be uniform. To make these alterations to the table that we've already created, enter the following SQL statement:

```
ALTER TABLE books
CHANGE COLUMN book_id book_id INT AUTO_INCREMENT PRIMARY KEY,
CHANGE COLUMN author author_id INT,
ADD COLUMN description TEXT,
```

```
ADD COLUMN genre ENUM('novel','poetry','drama'),
ADD COLUMN publisher_id INT,
ADD COLUMN pub_year VARCHAR(4),
ADD COLUMN isbn VARCHAR(20);
```

After the opening line of this SQL statement, notice that each clause in which we change or add a column is separated from the following one by a comma. On the second line here, we're changing the `book_id` column. Even though we are keeping the column name and the data type the same, we have to restate them. We're adding the `AUTO_INCREMENT` flag, which carries out the task mentioned in the previous paragraph, assigning a unique and arbitrary value to each book in the table. We're also making the column the `PRIMARY KEY` for indexing, which allows faster data retrieval.

The first `CHANGE` clause may look confusing because it lists the column name (`book_id`) twice. This makes sense when you understand the syntax of a `CHANGE` clause: the first `book_id` names the existing column you want to change, and the rest of the clause specifies the entire new column. To understand this better, examine the second `CHANGE` clause: it replaces the existing `author` column with a new `author_id` column. There will no longer be a column named `author`.

In the third line, we're changing the `author` column so that its label and data type align with the `authors` table that we'll create later. The `authors` table will have an indexed column to represent the author, just as the `books` table has an indexed column to represent the books. To figure out which author the `author_id` column in the `books` table is pointing to, we'll join the `books` table to the `authors` table in queries. Because the corresponding column in the `authors` table will have a data type of `INT`, so must this one.

The fourth line adds a column for each book's description. This has a data type of `TEXT`, which is a variable-length data type that can hold very large amounts of data, up to 64 kilobytes. There are other factors, though, that can limit a `TEXT` column further. See Appendix A for a list of data types, their limits, and other limiting factors.

For `genre`, we're enumerating a list of possible values to ensure uniformity. A blank value and a NULL value are also possible, although they're not specified.

Before moving on to adding data to our `books` table, let's quickly set up the `authors` table. This table will be what is known as a `reference table`. We need to enter data into the `authors` table, because when we enter data into the `books` table, we will need to know the identification number for the authors of the books:

```
CREATE TABLE authors
(author_id INT AUTO_INCREMENT PRIMARY KEY,
author_last VARCHAR(50),
author_first VARCHAR(50),
country VARCHAR(50));
```

This table doesn't require too many columns, although we might add other columns to it for an actual bookstore. As mentioned before, as needed, we'll join the `books` table to the `authors` table through the `author_id` in both tables.

In the `authors` table, we've separated the first and last name of each author into two columns so that we can easily sort and search on the last name. We've also added a column for the author's country of origin so that we can search for works by authors of a particular country when asked by customers. For production use, it might be better to use a country code and then have yet another reference table listing the full names of countries. But we're trying to keep this tutorial simple and include detail only when it has educational value.

Show Me

Let's take a moment to admire our work and see what we've done so far. To get a list of databases, use the `SHOW DATABASES` statement:

```
SHOW DATABASES;
```

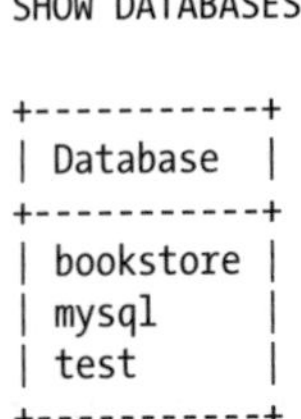

```
+-----------+
| Database  |
+-----------+
| bookstore |
| mysql     |
| test      |
+-----------+
```


The result of the `SHOW DATABASES` statement lists not only the database we've created, but also two others. One is the `mysql` database, which contains data about user privileges and was covered in Chapter 2. The third database is the `test` database, which is set up by default when MySQL is installed. It's there as a convenience for you to be able to add tables or run SQL statements for testing.

To see a list of tables in the `bookstore` database, once we select the `bookstore` database with the `USE` statement shown earlier, we would enter the following statement:

```
SHOW TABLES;

+---------------------+
| Tables_in_bookstore |
+---------------------+
| authors             |
| books               |
+---------------------+
```

The result of the `SHOW TABLES` statement provides a list containing our two tables, just as we expected. If you want to see a list of tables from another database while still using the `bookstore` database, add a `FROM` clause to the previous statement:

```
SHOW TABLES FROM mysql;
```

This displays a list of tables from the `mysql` database, even though the default database for the client session is the `bookstore` database.

Inserting Data

Now that we've set up our first two tables, let's look at how we can add data to them. We'll start with the simplest method: the `INSERT` statement. With the `INSERT` statement we can add one or more records. Before adding information about a book to our books table, because it refers to a field in our authors table, we need to add the author's information to the latter. We'll do this by entering these SQL statements through the *mysql* client:

```
INSERT INTO authors
(author_last, author_first, country)
VALUES('Greene','Graham','United Kingdom');

SELECT LAST_INSERT_ID( );

+------------------+
| LAST_INSERT_ID( ) |
+------------------+
|                1 |
+------------------+

INSERT INTO books
(title, author_id, isbn, genre, pub_year)
VALUES('The End of the Affair', 1,'0099478447','novel','1951');
```

Our first SQL statement added a record, or *row*, for Graham Greene, an author who wrote the book *The End of the Affair*. The standard INSERT syntax names the columns for which the values are to be inserted, as we're doing here. If you're going to enter values for all of the columns, you don't need to name the columns, but you must list the data in the same order in which the columns are listed in the table.

In the second SQL statement, we retrieved the identification number assigned to the row we just entered for the author by using the LAST_INSERT_ID( ) function. We could just as easily have entered SELECT author_id FROM authors;.

In the third SQL statement, we added data for a Graham Greene book. In that statement, we listed the columns in an order that's different from their order in the table. That's acceptable to MySQL; we just have to be sure that our values are in the same order.

Selecting Data

Now that we have one row of data in each of our two tables, let's run some queries. We'll use the SELECT statement to select the data that we want. To get all of the columns and rows from the books table, enter the following:

```
SELECT * FROM books;
```

The asterisk, which acts as a wildcard, selects all columns. We did not specify any criteria by which specific rows are selected, so all rows are displayed from the books table. To select specific columns, we name the columns we want. To select specific rows, we add a WHERE clause to the end of the SELECT statement:

```
SELECT book_id, title, description
FROM books
WHERE genre = 'novel';
```

This SQL statement displays just the book's identification number, the book's title, and the description of the book from the books table for all books where the genre column has a value of novel. The results will be more meaningful, of course, when we have data on more books in the database. So, let's assume that we've entered data for a few dozen more books, and proceed.

If we want to get a list of novels from the database along with the author's full name, we need to join the books table to the authors table. We can join the two tables with a JOIN clause like this:

```
SELECT book_id, title, pub_year,
CONCAT(author_first, ' ', author_last) AS author
FROM books
JOIN authors USING(author_id)
WHERE author_last = 'Greene';
```

In the FROM clause, we join the books table to the authors table using the author_id columns in both tables. If the columns had different labels, we would have to use a different clause or method in the JOIN clause to join the tables (e.g., ON (author_id = writer_id)). Notice in the second line of this SQL statement that we've employed a string function, CONCAT( ). With this function you can take bits of data and merge them together with text to form more desirable-looking output. In this case, we're taking the author's first name and pasting a space (in quotes) onto the end of it, followed by the author's last name. The results will appear in the output display as one column, which we've given a column heading of author. The keyword AS creates this column title with our chosen name, called an alias.

In the WHERE clause, we've specified that we want data on books written by authors with the last name *Greene*. If the books table did not contain books by Greene, nothing would be displayed. The results of the previous query are as follows:

```
+---------+-----------------------+----------+---------------+
| book_id | title                 | pub_year | author        |
+---------+-----------------------+----------+---------------+
|       1 | The End of the Affair | 1951     | Graham Greene |
|       2 | Brighton Rock         | 1937     | Graham Greene |
+---------+-----------------------+----------+---------------+
```

As you can see, a second book by Graham Greene was found and both have been displayed. The column heading was changed for the output of the author's name per the AS clause. We could change the column headings in the display for the other columns with the keyword AS as well. The author alias can be reused in a SELECT statement, but not in the WHERE clause, unfortunately. You can find more information on AS in Chapter 6.

Ordering, Limiting, and Grouping

For times when we retrieve a long list of data, it can be tidier to sort the data output in a specific order. To do this, we can use the ORDER BY clause. Suppose that we want a list of plays written by William Shakespeare from our database. We could enter

MySQL Basics

the following SQL statement to retrieve such a list and to sort the data by the play title:

```
SELECT book_id, title, publisher
FROM books
JOIN authors USING(author_id)
JOIN publishers USING(publisher_id)
WHERE author_last = 'Shakespeare'
AND genre = 'play'
ORDER BY title, pub_year;
```

The ORDER BY clause comes at the end, after the WHERE clause. Here the ORDER BY clause orders the data results first by the title column and then, within title, by the pub_year column, or the year that the particular printing of the play was published. By default, data is sorted in ascending alphanumeric order. If we want to order the results in descending order for the titles, we can just add a DESC flag immediately after the title column in the ORDER BY clause and before the comma that precedes pub_year:

```
...
ORDER BY title DESC, pub_year;
```

A large bookstore will have many editions of Shakespeare's plays, possibly a few different printings for each play. If we want to limit the number of records displayed, we could add a LIMIT clause to the end of the previous SQL statement:

```
SELECT book_id, title, publisher
FROM books
JOIN authors USING(author_id)
JOIN publishers USING(publisher_id)
WHERE author_last = 'Shakespeare'
AND genre = 'play'
ORDER BY title DESC, pub_year
LIMIT 20;
```

This addition limits the number of rows displayed to the first 20. The count starts from the first row of the result set after the data has been ordered according to the ORDER BY clause. If we want to retrieve the next 10, we would adjust the LIMIT clause to specify the number of rows to skip, along with the number of records to retrieve. So if we want to skip the first 20 rows and list the next 10 rows from our sort, we replace the LIMIT clause in the SQL statement with this one:

```
...
LIMIT 20, 10;
```

As you can see, in a two-argument LIMIT clause, the first argument specifies the number of rows to skip or the point to begin (i.e., 20) and the second argument states the number of rows to display (i.e., 10).

If we want to get just a list of titles by Shakespeare, and we are not concerned with which printing or publisher—that is to say, if we want one row for each title and are satisfied with the first row found for each—we could use the GROUP BY clause like this:

```
SELECT book_id, title
FROM books
JOIN authors USING(author_id)
```

```
WHERE author_last = 'Shakespeare'
GROUP BY title;
```

The result of this SQL statement is a list of titles by Shakespeare from the database, displaying the record identification number of the first one found for each title.

Analyzing and Manipulating Data

With MySQL you can not only retrieve raw data, but also analyze and format the data retrieved. For instance, suppose we want to know how many titles we stock by Leo Tolstoy. We could enter a SELECT statement containing a COUNT( ) function like this:

```
SELECT COUNT(*)
FROM books
JOIN authors USING(author_id)
WHERE author_last = 'Tolstoy';

+----------+
| COUNT(*) |
+----------+
|       12 |
+----------+
```


As another example, suppose that after setting up our database and putting it to use we have another table called orders that contains information on customer orders. We can query that table to find the total sales of a particular book. For instance, to find the total revenues generated from, say, William Boyd's book *Armadillo*, we would enter the following SQL statement in the *mysql* client:

```
SELECT SUM(sale_amount) AS 'Armadillo Sales'
FROM orders
JOIN books USING(book_id)
JOIN authors USING(author_id)
WHERE title = 'Armadillo'
AND author_last = 'Boyd';

+-----------------+
| Armadillo Sales |
+-----------------+
|          250.25 |
+-----------------+
```

Here we are joining three tables together to retrieve the desired information. MySQL selects the value of the sale_amount column from each row in the orders table that matches the criteria of the WHERE clause. Then it adds those numbers and displays the sum with the column heading given.

For columns that contain date or time information, we can decide on the format for displaying the data using a variety of functions. For instance, suppose that we want to extract from the orders table the date that a customer made a particular purchase, based on his receipt number (e.g., 1250), which in turn is the record identification number, or sale_id. We could simply enter the following statement and get the default format as shown in the last line of results:

```
SELECT purchase_date AS 'Purchase Date'
FROM orders
WHERE sale_id = '1250';

+---------------+
| Purchase Date |
+---------------+
| 2004-03-01    |
+---------------+
```

This format (year-month-day) is understandable. However, if we want the month displayed in English rather than numerically, we have to use some date functions:

```
SELECT CONCAT(MONTHNAME(purchase_date), ' ',
DAYOFMONTH(purchase_date), ', ',
YEAR(purchase_date)) AS 'Purchase Date'
FROM orders
WHERE sale_id = '1250';

+---------------+
| Purchase Date |
+---------------+
| March 1, 2004 |
+---------------+
```

To put the date together in the typical human-readable format used in the United States, we're using the CONCAT( ) function in conjunction with a few date functions. It may be a little confusing at first glance, because we're inserting a space between the month and the day at the end of the first line and a comma and a space after the day at the end of the second line. As for the date functions, the first one extracts the month from the purchase_date column and formats it so its full name is displayed. The second date function on the second line extracts just the day, after which we explicitly specify a comma. The third date function on the third line extracts just the year.

As you can see in the results, our combination of functions works. However, it's not the cleanest method by which the date can be assembled. We could use the DATE_FORMAT( ) function instead:

```
SELECT DATE_FORMAT(purchase_date, "%M %d, %Y")
AS 'Purchase Date'
FROM orders
WHERE sale_id = '1250';
```

This is a much more efficient method, and it provides the same output as the previous statement. You just have to know the formatting codes to be able to use this function properly. They're listed in Chapter 12, along with several more formatting codes and many more date and time functions.

Changing Data

You can change data in a table using a few different methods. The most basic and perhaps the most common method is to use the UPDATE statement. With this statement, you can change data for all rows or for specific records based on a WHERE clause.

Looking back on the results displayed from an earlier query, we can see that Graham Greene's book *Brighton Rock* has a copyright year of 1937. That's not correct; it should be 1938. To change or update that bit of information, we would enter the following SQL statement:

```
UPDATE books
SET pub_year = '1938'
WHERE book_id = '2';

Query OK, 1 row affected (0.00 sec)
Rows matched: 1  Changed: 1  Warnings: 0
```


First, we state the name of the table that's being updated. Next, we include the SET keyword with the column to change and its corresponding new value. If we wanted to change the values of more than one column, we would provide a comma-separated list of each column along with the equals sign operator and the new respective values. SET is given only once.

The preceding SQL statement has a WHERE clause limiting the rows that will be updated by specifying a condition the row must meet. In this case, our condition is for a specific value of a unique column, so only one row will be changed. The results of the query show that one row was affected, one row was matched, one row was changed, and there were no problems to generate warnings.

Sometimes inserting data into a table will cause a duplicate row to be created because a row for the data already exists. For instance, suppose that we want to run an SQL statement that inserts data on a few books into the books table and one of the books is already in the table. If we use INSERT, a duplicate row will generally be rejected. To prevent this, we can use the REPLACE statement, which inserts rows that are new and replaces existing rows with new data.

From MySQL's perspective, duplicates occur only when columns defined as unique contain the same value. Because the book_id column is assigned automatically, it's unlikely that we would duplicate it, because we wouldn't tend to assign its value when adding records. What's unique about each book in the book business is its ISBN number, which is the bar code number on the back of the book. To ensure that we do not have rows with the same ISBN number, we'll alter our books table again and change the isbn column to a UNIQUE column, a column that requires a unique value. This way we won't be able to enter data inadvertently on a book more than once:

```
ALTER TABLE books
CHANGE COLUMN isbn isbn VARCHAR(20) UNIQUE;
```

Now we're ready to insert data for more books without worrying about duplicate rows for books with the same ISBN number. Here is an example in which we attempt to add two more books by Graham Greene, one of which is already in the table:

```
REPLACE INTO books
(title, author_id, isbn, genre, pub_year)
VALUES('Brighton Rock',1,'0099478471','novel','1938'),
('The Quiet American',1,'0099478393','novel','1955');
```

The syntax for the REPLACE statement is the same as the INSERT statement. Notice that we've added two rows here in one statement. This is the same syntax that you would use if you want to add more than one row using INSERT. Just list each row's data within parentheses and separate them by commas, as shown. In this example, there is already a row for the book containing the ISBN number 0099478471 (i.e., *Brighton Rock*), so its data will be replaced and a new row will not be added. There is currently no row for Greene's book *The Quiet American*, though, so it will be added.

Deleting Data

To delete specific rows of data, you can use the DELETE statement. For example, if we want to delete all rows of data from our books table for the author J. K. Rowling, because we've decided not to carry Harry Potter books, we could issue the following statement:

```
DELETE FROM books
WHERE author_id =
   (SELECT authors.author_id FROM authors
    WHERE author_last = 'Rowling'
    AND author_first = 'J. K.');

DELETE FROM authors
WHERE author_last = 'Rowling'
AND author_first = 'J. K.';
```

Here, we're deleting only rows from the books table where the author identification number is whatever is selected from the authors table based on the specified author's last name and first name. That is to say, the author_id must be whatever value is returned by the SELECT statement, the subquery contained in the parentheses. This statement involves a subquery, so it requires version 4.1 or later of MySQL. To delete these same rows with an earlier version of MySQL, you would need to run the SELECT statement shown in parentheses here separately (not as a subquery), make note of the author's identification number, and then run the first DELETE statement, manually entering the identification number at the end instead of the parenthetical SELECT statement shown.

An alternative to the previous SQL statements would be to utilize user-defined variables. Here is the same example using variables:

```
SET @potter =
   (SELECT author_id FROM authors
    WHERE author_last = 'Rowling'
```

```
    AND author_first = 'J. K.');

DELETE FROM books
WHERE author_id = @potter;

DELETE FROM authors
WHERE author_id = @potter;
```

In the first part, we use the SET statement to establish a variable called @potter that will contain the results of the SELECT statement that follows in parentheses, another subquery. Incidentally, although this subquery is not available before version 4.1, user-defined variables are. The second SQL statement deletes the rows from books where the author identification number matches the value of the temporary variable. Next, we delete the data from the authors table, still making use of the variable. A user-defined variable will last until it's reset or until the MySQL session is closed.

Searching Data

Once our database is loaded with large amounts of data, it can be cumbersome to locate data simply by scrolling through the results of SELECT statements. Also, sometimes we don't have the exact or complete text for a column we're examining. For these situations, we can use the LIKE operator. Suppose that our books table now has thousands of entries. Suppose further that a customer says he's looking for a specific book. He can't remember the name of the author or the title of the book, but he does remember that the words *traveler* and *winter* are in the title. We could enter this SQL statement to search the database based on this minimal information:

```
SELECT book_id, title,
CONCAT(author_first, ' ', author_last) AS author
FROM books
JOIN authors USING(author_id)
WHERE title LIKE '%traveler%'
AND title LIKE '%winter%';

+---------+-----------------------------------+---------------+
| book_id | title                             | author        |
+---------+-----------------------------------+---------------+
|    1400 | If on a winter's night a traveler | Italo Calvino |
+---------+-----------------------------------+---------------+
```

With the LIKE operator, we use the percent sign wildcard twice to indicate that we're searching for all rows in which the title column's data contains the string traveler with zero or more characters before it (the preceding percent sign), and zero or more characters after it (the terminating percent sign). Put another way, the word *traveler* must be contained somewhere in the column's data to have a pattern match. The next part of the clause indicates that *winter* must also be found in the same column. Incidentally, the LIKE keyword is an operator like the equals sign.

If another customer asks us to search the database for a Graham Greene book with either the word *Stamboul* or the word *Orient* in the title, we could use OR within an expression like this:

```
SELECT book_id, title
FROM books
WHERE author_id = 1
AND title LIKE '%Stamboul%'
OR author_id = 1
AND title LIKE '%Orient%';
```

Since we already know the author's identification number, this statement is more succinct and includes only one table. Notice that we have to specify the `author_id` in each expression; otherwise we might get results by other authors that match the words for which we're searching. For more information on operators, see Appendix B. You can find more examples and possibilities for searching data in Chapter 6.

Importing Data in Bulk

Often, when setting up a new database, you will need to migrate data from an old database to MySQL. In the case of our bookstore, let's suppose that a vendor has sent us a disk with a list of all of their books in a simple text file. Each record for each book is on a separate line, and each field of each record is separated by a vertical bar. Here's what the fictitious vendor's data text file looks like:

```
ISBN|TITLE|AUTHOR LAST|AUTHOR FIRST|COPYRIGHT DATE|
067973452X|Notes from Underground|Dostoevsky|Fyodor|August 1994|
...
```

Obviously, an actual vendor file would contain more fields and records than are shown here, but this is enough for our example. The first line contains descriptions of the fields in the records that follow. We don't need to extract the first line; it's just instructions for us. So, we'll tell MySQL to ignore it when we enter our SQL statement.

As for the data, we must consider a few problems. First, the fields are not in the order that they are found in our tables. We'll have to tell MySQL the order in which the data will be coming so that it can make adjustments. The other problem is that this text table contains data for both our `books` table and our `authors` table. This is going to be a bit tricky, but we can deal with it. What we'll do is extract the author information only in one SQL statement, then we'll run a separate SQL statement to import the book information. Before starting, we've copied the vendor's file called *books.txt* to a temporary directory (e.g., */tmp*). Here we run a `LOAD DATA INFILE` statement from the *mysql* client:

```
LOAD DATA INFILE '/tmp/books.txt' REPLACE INTO TABLE authors
FIELDS TERMINATED BY '|' LINES TERMINATED BY '\r\n'
TEXT_FIELDS(col1, col2, col3, col4, col5)
SET author_last = col3, author_first = col4
IGNORE col1, col2, col5, 1 LINES;
```

First, I should point out that the `TEXT_FIELDS` and the `IGNORE` clause for columns are not available before version 4.1 of MySQL. The `IGNORE n LINES` clause has been around for a while, though. With `IGNORE 1 LINES`, the first line of the text file containing the column headings will be ignored. Going back to the first line in this SQL statement, we've named the file to load and the table in which to load the data.

The REPLACE flag has the effect of the REPLACE statement mentioned earlier. Of course, since the name fields aren't set to unique, there won't be any duplicates as far as MySQL is concerned. In a real-life situation, you would have to alter your table to prevent duplicates based on the author's name.

In the second line, we specify that fields are terminated by a vertical bar and that lines are terminated by a carriage return (\r) and a newline (\n). This is the format for an MS-DOS text file. Unix files have only a newline to terminate the line.

In the third line of the SQL statement, we create aliases for each column. In the fourth line, we name the table columns to receive data and set their values based on the aliases given in the previous line. In the final line, we tell MySQL to ignore the columns that we don't want, as well as the top line, because it doesn't contain data.

If you're using an older version of MySQL that isn't able to ignore unwanted columns, you will have to perform a couple of extra steps. There are a few different ways of doing this. One simple way, if the table into which we're loading data isn't too large, is to add three extra, temporary columns to authors that will take in the unwanted fields of data from the text file and drop them later. This would look like the following:

```
ALTER TABLE authors
ADD COLUMN col1 VARCHAR(50),
ADD COLUMN col2 VARCHAR(50),
ADD COLUMN col5 VARCHAR(50);

LOAD DATA INFILE '/tmp/books.txt' REPLACE INTO TABLE authors
FIELDS TERMINATED BY '|' LINES TERMINATED BY '\r\n'
IGNORE 1 LINES
(col1, col2, author_last, author_first, col5);

ALTER TABLE authors
DROP COLUMN col1,
DROP COLUMN col2,
DROP COLUMN col5;
```

These statements will work, but they're not as graceful as the more straightforward statement shown earlier. In the second SQL statement here, notice that the IGNORE clause specifies one line to be ignored. The last line of the same statement lists the columns in the authors table that are to receive the data and the sequence in which they will be imported. In the third SQL statement, having finished importing the data from the vendor's text file, we now delete the temporary columns with their unnecessary data by using a DROP statement. There's usually no recourse from DROP, no undo. So take care in using it.

Once we manage to copy the list of authors into the authors table from the text file, we need to load the data for the books and find the correct author_id for each book. We do this through the following:

```
LOAD DATA INFILE '/tmp/books.txt' IGNORE INTO TABLE books
FIELDS TERMINATED BY '|' LINES TERMINATED BY '\r\n'
TEXT_FIELDS(col1, col2, col3, col4, col5)
SET isbn = col1, title = col2,
pub_year = RIGHT(col5, 4),
```

```
author_id =
   (SELECT author_id
    WHERE author_last = col3
    AND author_first = col4)
IGNORE col3, col4, 1 LINES;
```

In this SQL statement, we've added a couple of twists to get what we need. On the fifth line, to extract the year from the copyright field—which contains both the month and the year—we use the string function `RIGHT( )`. It captures the last four characters of `col5` as specified in the second argument.

The sixth line starts a subquery that determines the `author_id` based on data from the `authors` table, where the author's last and first names match what is found in the respective aliases. The results of the column selected within the parentheses will be written to the `author_id` column.

Finally, we're having MySQL ignore `col3` and `col4`, as well as the column heading line. The `IGNORE` flag on the first line instructs MySQL to ignore error messages, not to replace any duplicate rows, and to continue executing the SQL statement. Doing this maneuver with earlier versions of MySQL will require temporary columns or a temporary table along the lines of the previous example. Actually, using a temporary table is still a prudent method for staging data. After you've verified it, you can execute an `INSERT...SELECT` statement (see Chapter 6).

Command-Line Interface

It's not necessary to open the *mysql* interface to enter SQL statements into the MySQL server. In fact, sometimes you may have only a quick query to make in MySQL, and you'd rather just do it from the shell or command line. For instance, suppose we have a table called `vendors` in our database, and we want to get a quick list of vendors in Louisiana and their telephone numbers. We could enter the following from the command line in Linux (or an equivalent operating system) to get this list:

```
mysql --user='paola' --password='caporale1017' \
-e "SELECT vendor, telephone FROM vendors \
    WHERE state='LA'" bookstore
```

We're still using the *mysql* client, but we're not entering the interface. As shown earlier, we provide the username *paola* and her password *caporale1017* as arguments to the command. This line ends with a backslash to let the Unix shell know that there are more parameters to come. Otherwise, we would need to put all of the information shown on one line.

On the second line, we use the `-e` option to indicate that what follows it in double quotes is to be executed by the *mysql* client. Notice that what's in double quotes is the same SQL statement with the same syntax as what we would enter if we were logged in to the interface. The syntax doesn't change because we're entering the SQL statement from the command line. We don't need a terminating semicolon, though, because the *mysql* client knows where the SQL statement ends.

Finally, after the SQL statement, we provide the name of the database to be used. We could eliminate this argument by adding the database name before the table name, separated by a dot (i.e., `bookstore.vendors`).

There are other command-line options with the *mysql* client. There are also other command-line utilities available for accessing and manipulating data in MySQL. You can use some of these utilities for backing up the database or for performing server maintenance and tuning. They are covered in Chapters 15 and 16.

Conclusion

Obviously, you can do plenty more with MySQL. This tutorial was designed to give you an idea of how to create a database and manage the data in some very basic ways. The remaining sections of this book provide details on MySQL statements, clauses, arguments, options, and functions. If you're new to MySQL, you can begin with the statements and clauses highlighted in this chapter, and refer to the chapters that follow for more options and to learn about other functions and features as needed.

II

SQL Statements and Functions

This part of the book is a complete reference for the version of the SQL language used by MySQL. It divides the SQL statements and functions by the basic functions (scheme design, data manipulation, replication, etc.). Examples use the *mysql* command-line client, but they are equally valid when issued from the programming APIs discussed in Part IV.

Some of the chapters in this part start with a list of statements grouped by type, as a quick reference. The statements are then listed in alphabetical order. For the more complex statements, to simplify their presentation, I've broken the syntax into several sections according to the different uses of the statement.

Here are some general elements of MySQL's SQL syntax:

- SQL statements may span multiple lines, but they must end with either a semicolon or `\G`, unless another character is specified with `DELIMITER`.
- When values are enclosed in parentheses, multiple values can usually be specified, separated by commas.
- Strings and dates must be specified within single or double quotes, unless a date is given as a numeric and is part of a date calculation.
- Elements of a statement's syntax are case-insensitive. However, on Unix-type systems, database and table names, as well as filenames, are case-sensitive.

The MySQL statements, clauses, and functions explained in Chapters 4 through 14 are grouped in each chapter, first by statements and clauses, then by functions. They are listed alphabetically within each group. Each statement is given with its syntax and an explanation. Optional clauses and flags are shown in square brackets.

Particular components, such as a database or table name, are shown in italics. The vertical bar is used to separate alternative choices and is not part of the statement syntax.

Some statements have alternative syntax structures. These alternatives are usually shown in complete form. The curly braces indicate that one of the choices is required. Examples show how a statement and the various clauses may be used for almost all statements.

To save space, some of the examples are shown without their results. Occasionally, when the results are shown, the typical ASCII table format is not shown because the statement is executed with a `\G` ending instead of the usual semicolon. In order to focus on the particulars of the statements and clauses, the statements are fairly straightforward and do not make much use of the many built-in functions available with MySQL. Explanations of any functions used, though, can be found in other chapters.

4
Security and User Statements and Functions

User access and privileges can be global (i.e., apply to all databases on the server), or they can be database-specific, table-specific, or column-specific. In version 5 of MySQL, users can also be limited to particular functions and procedures.

In addition to security-related SQL statements, users can be limited in their use of MySQL resources in order to prevent the monopolization of resources and the indirect denial of service to other users. Thus, you can limit the number of connections or the maximum resources per hour for a user.

The primary information regarding user access and privileges is stored in a set of regular MyISAM tables, known as the *grant tables*, that reside in the `mysql` database on the server. The tables are:

`user`
: Global privileges

`db`
: Database-specific privileges

`tables_priv`
: Table-specific privileges

`columns_priv`
: Column-specific privileges

Several other tables provide fine-tuning for user access and security. Execute `SHOW TABLES FROM mysql;` to get a list on your server. You can manipulate the data in these tables directly with standard SQL statements, such as `INSERT`, `UPDATE`, and `DELETE`, followed by the `FLUSH PRIVILEGES` statement to update the server's cache. However, it's recommended that you use specialized SQL statements to manage users and assign access rights:

`CREATE USER`
: To create new users

`GRANT`
: To create a user account, assigning privileges for a new user account, or assigning privileges to an existing user

`REVOKE`
: To remove privileges

`RENAME USER`
: To change a user's name

`SET PASSWORD`
: To change a password

`DROP USER`
: To delete a user's account

All of these statements are described in this chapter. This chapter also lists and explains MySQL functions related to user maintenance and several related to database and network security.

Statements and Functions

The following is a list of security and user statements that are covered in this chapter:

`CREATE USER`, `DROP USER`, `FLUSH`, `GRANT`, `RENAME USER`, `RESET`, `REVOKE`, `SET PASSWORD`, `SHOW GRANTS`, `SHOW PRIVILEGES`.

The following related functions are covered in this chapter as well. They are explained in detail after the SQL statements:

`AES_DECRYPT( )`, `AES_ENCRYPT( )`, `CURRENT_USER( )`, `DECODE( )`, `DES_DECRYPT( )`, `DES_ENCRYPT( )`,`ENCODE( )`, `ENCRYPT( )`, `MD5( )`, `OLD_PASSWORD( )`, `PASSWORD( )`, `SESSION_USER( )`, `SHA( )`, `SHA1( )`, `SYSTEM_USER( )`, `USER( )`.

SQL Statements in Alphabetical Order

The following is a list of MySQL statements and clauses in alphabetical order related to security and user account maintenance. The examples in this particular chapter have no theme to them and could be found in any organization using a MySQL database.

CREATE USER

```
CREATE USER 'user'[@'host']
[IDENTIFIED BY [PASSWORD] 'password'] [, ...]
```

This statement creates new user accounts on the MySQL server. The username is given within quotes, followed by the at sign (`@`) and a host IP address or hostname within quotes. For accessing MySQL locally, use the host of ***localhost***. The IP address is

127.0.0.1. Use the percent sign (%) wildcard as the host to allow a client with the specified username to connect from any host. If no host or @ is given, the percent sign is assumed.

The user password is given in plain text within quotes, preceded by the IDENTIFIED BY clause. You don't need to use the PASSWORD( ) function to encrypt the password; this is done automatically. However, if you wish to provide the hash value of the password, precede the password with IDENTIFIED BY PASSWORD. If the password clause is not given, a blank password is assumed and will be accepted. This is a potential security problem and should never be done. If you do this by mistake, use the SET PASSWORD statement to set the password.

Multiple user accounts may be specified in a comma-separated list.

The CREATE USER statement was introduced in version 5.0.2 of MySQL. For previous versions, use the GRANT statement. This new statement operates similarly to the GRANT statement, except that you cannot specify user privileges with the CREATE USER statement. As a result, the process is to create a user with the CREATE USER statement and then to grant the user privileges with the GRANT statement. This two-step process is a more logical process, especially to a newcomer to MySQL. However, you can still use just the GRANT statement to create and set privileges for a new user.

This statement requires CREATE USER privilege or INSERT privilege for the mysql database, which contains user account information and privileges. To remove a user, use the DROP USER statement and possibly also the REVOKE statement:

```
CREATE USER 'paola'@'localhost'
IDENTIFIED BY 'her_password',
'paola'@'caporale.com'
IDENTIFIED BY 'her_password';
```

In this example, two user accounts are created along with their passwords, but both are for the same person. The difference is that one allows the user to log into the server hosting the database and to run the mysql client or some other client on the server, the *localhost*. The other account allows the user to connect from a host named caporale.com using a client from that host. No other host will be allowed for this user.

DROP USER

DROP USER '*user*'@'*host*'

Use this statement to delete a user account for the MySQL server. As of version 5.0.2 of MySQL, this statement will delete the user account and its privileges from all grant tables. The username is given within quotes, followed by the at sign (@) and the host IP address or hostname within quotes. This statement requires a CREATE USER privilege or DELETE privilege for the mysql database, which contains user account information and privileges. Dropping a user account does not affect current sessions for the user account. It will take effect when any sessions opened by the user terminate. Use the KILL statement (explained in Chapter 7) to terminate an open client session for a user that has been dropped.

Some users may have more than one user account (i.e., user and host combinations). You should check the server's mysql.user table to be sure:

```
SELECT User,Host
FROM mysql.user
WHERE User LIKE 'paola';
```

```
+-------+--------------+
| User  | Host         |
+-------+--------------+
| paola | localhost    |
| paola | caporale.com |
+-------+--------------+

DROP USER 'paola'@'localhost',
'paola'@'caporale.com';
```

Prior to version 5.0.2 of MySQL, the `DROP USER` statement won't delete a user that has any privileges set to `'Y'`. To eliminate the user account's privileges, issue the `REVOKE` statement before using `DROP USER`:

```
REVOKE ALL ON *.* FROM 'paola'@'localhost';

DROP USER 'paola'@'localhost';
```

The `ALL` option is used to ensure revocation of all privileges. The `*.*` covers all tables in all databases. Prior to version 4.1.1 of MySQL, you would have to issue the following instead of a `DROP USER` statement:

```
DELETE FROM mysql.user
WHERE User='paola' AND Host='localhost';

FLUSH PRIVILEGES;
```

Notice that the `FLUSH PRIVILEGES` statement is necessary for the preceding `DELETE` statement to take effect immediately. It's not necessary after the `DROP USER` statement, though.

FLUSH

`FLUSH [LOCAL|NO_WRITE_TO_BINLOG] option[, ...]`

Options:

```
DES_KEY_FILE, HOSTS, LOGS, MASTER, PRIVILEGES, QUERY_CACHE,
STATUS, TABLE, TABLES, TABLES WITHOUT READ LOCK, USER_RESOURCES
```

Use this statement to clear and reload temporary caches in MySQL. It requires `RELOAD` privileges. To prevent this statement from writing to the binary log file, the `NO_WRITE_TO_BINLOG` flag or its `LOCAL` alias may be given. A particular cache to flush may be given as an option. Multiple options (see Table 4-1) may be given in a comma-separated list.

As of version 5.1 of MySQL, `FLUSH` cannot be used in stored functions and triggers, but can be used in stored procedures. As an alternative to the `FLUSH` statement, you can use the `mysqladmin` command (see Chapter 16).

Table 4-1. Options for FLUSH statement

Option	Explanation
`DES_KEY_FILE`	Reloads the DES encryption file, which is given with the `--des-key-file` option at startup or in the options file.

Option	Explanation
HOSTS	Clears the hosts cache, which is used to minimize host/IP address lookups. The hosts cache may need to be flushed if a host has been blocked from accessing the server.
LOGS	Used to close all of the log files and reopen them. If the server has binary logging enabled, it will change the binary log file to the next in numeric sequence. If the error log was enabled, it will rename the error log to the same name, but with the ending `-old`, and start a new error log. This option is not logged.
MASTER	This option is not logged and has been deprecated. Use the `RESET MASTER` statement instead.
PRIVILEGES	Reloads the grant tables for user privileges. This is necessary if the `user` table in the `mysql` database has been modified manually, without the GRANT statement.
QUERY CACHE	Instructs the server to defragment the query cache to improve performance. It doesn't remove queries from cache, though. Use the `RESET QUERY CACHE` statement to remove the queries.
SLAVE	This option is not logged and has been deprecated. Use the `RESET SLAVE` statement instead.
STATUS	Resets the session values and counters for key caches to 0. The current thread's session status variables are set to those of the global variables. The `max_used_conections` variable is set to the number of sessions open at the time.
TABLE[*table*, ...]	Followed by one or more table names, this option forces the given tables to be closed. This will terminate any active queries on the given tables. Specified without any tables, the option has the same effect as `TABLES`.
TABLES	Causes all tables to be closed, all queries to be terminated, and the query cache to be flushed. This is the same as `TABLE` with no table name.
TABLES WITH READ LOCK	Closes all tables and locks them with a global read lock. This will allow users to view the data, but not to update it or insert records. The lock will remain in place until the `UNLOCK TABLES` statement is executed. This option is not logged.
USER_RESOURCES	Resets all user resource values that are calculated on an hourly basis. These are the values for the columns `max_questions`, `max_updates`, and `max_connections` in the `user` table of the `mysql` database. Use this `FLUSH` option when users have been blocked because they exceed hourly limits. If these columns are missing, see Chapter 16 for the explanation of `mysql_fix_privilege_tables`.

GRANT

```
GRANT privilege[,...] [(column[,...])][, ...]
ON [TABLE|FUNCTION|PROCEDURE] {[{database|*}.{table|*}] | *}
TO 'user'@'host' [IDENTIFIED BY [PASSWORD] 'password'][, ...]

[REQUIRE NONE |
[{SSL|X509}] [CIPHER 'cipher' [AND]]
[ISSUER 'issue' [AND]]
```

```
GRANT

[SUBJECT 'subject']]

[WITH [GRANT OPTION |
       MAX_QUERIES_PER_HOUR count |
       MAX_UPDATES_PER_HOUR count |
       MAX_CONNECTIONS_PER_HOUR count |
       MAX_USER_CONNECTIONS count] ...]
```

This statement may be used to create new MySQL users, but its primary use is for granting user privileges. Privileges can be global (apply to all databases on the server), database-specific, table-specific, or column-specific. Users can now also be limited by functions and procedures. Additionally, users can be limited by number of connections or by a maximum of resources per hour.

The privileges to grant to a user are listed immediately after the `GRANT` keyword in a comma-separated list. To restrict a user to specific columns in a table, list those columns in a comma-separated list within parentheses. This is then followed by the `ON` clause in which the privileges granted may be limited to a database, table, function, or procedure. To limit the privileges to a function, use the `FUNCTION` keyword; to limit them to a procedure, use the `PROCEDURE` keyword.

For tables, the keyword `TABLE` is optional and the default. You can then specify the database to which the privileges relate in quotes, followed by a period (`.`) and the name of the table, function, or procedure in quotes. You may also use the asterisk wildcard (*) to specify all databases or all tables, functions, or procedures offered by the database.

In the `TO` clause, give the username (in quotes) and the IP address or host (also in quotes) for which the user account privileges are permitted, separated by an at sign (`@`). To provide the password for the user account, add the `IDENTIFIED BY` clause, followed by the user's password in plain text and enclosed in quotes. To provide the password in encrypted hash form, add the keyword `PASSWORD` just before the password given. You can use the `WITH` clause to grant the `GRANT OPTION` privilege to a user so that that user may execute this statement. The `GRANT` statement with the `IDENTIFIED BY` clause can be used to change a password for an existing user.

For an explanation of how to restrict user accounts based on types of connections, see the next section of this statement ("GRANT: Type of connection restrictions"). For information on how to restrict user accounts based on the amount of activity for a period of time or the number of connections permitted, see the last section of this statement ("GRANT: Time and number of connection limits"). To see the privileges for a given user, use the `SHOW GRANTS` statement described later in this chapter.

A large variety of privileges may be granted to a user, so a common set of privileges has been combined in the `ALL` keyword. Here is an example:

```
GRANT ALL PRIVILEGES ON *.*
TO 'evagelia'@'localhost'
IDENTIFIED BY 'papadimitrou1234'
WITH GRANT OPTION;
```

In this example, the user *evagelia* is created and granted all basic privileges because of the `ALL` keyword. This does not include the `GRANT` privilege, the ability to use the `GRANT` statement. To do that, the `WITH GRANT OPTION` clause is given, as shown here, explicitly to give that privilege to the user. It's not a good idea to give users this privilege unless they are MySQL server administrators. Table 4-2 later in this chapter lists and describes each privilege.

As mentioned before, a user's privileges can be refined to specific SQL statements and specific databases. A GRANT statement can also restrict a user to only certain tables and columns. Here is an example that leaves the user fairly limited:

```
GRANT SELECT ON workrequests.*
TO 'jerry'@'localhost' IDENTIFIED BY 'neumeyer3186';

GRANT SELECT,INSERT,UPDATE ON workrequests.workreq
TO 'jerry'@'localhost' IDENTIFIED BY 'neumeyer3186';
```

Assuming the user *jerry* does not already exist, the first statement here creates the user and gives him SELECT privileges only for the workrequests database for all of its tables. This will allow him to read from the various tables but not edit the data. The second SQL statement grants *jerry* the right to add and change data in the workreq table of the workrequests database. This will allow him to enter work requests and make changes to them. The first statement causes an entry to be made to the db table in the mysql database. The second affects the tables_priv table. An entry is also made to the user table showing the user *jerry*, but he has no global privileges. This is the equivalent of granting just the USAGE privilege.

Security & User Statements

GRANT: Type of connection restrictions

```
GRANT privilege[,...] [(column[,...])][, ...]
ON [TABLE|FUNCTION|PROCEDURE] {[{database|*}.{table|*}] | *}
TO 'user'@'host' [IDENTIFIED BY [PASSWORD] 'password'][, ...]

[REQUIRE NONE |
[{SSL|X509} [AND]]
[CIPHER 'cipher' [AND]]
[ISSUER 'issue' [AND]]
[SUBJECT 'subject']]

[time and number of connection limits] ...]
```

A user can also be restricted to certain types of connections with the REQUIRE clause. There are several options that may be given together with the keyword AND. Each option can be used only once in a statement. REQUIRE NONE is the default and indicates that no such restrictions are required. Encrypted and unencrypted connections from clients are permitted from the user that has been properly authenticated.

The REQUIRE SSL option restricts the user account to only SSL-encrypted connections. The *mysql* client of the user account would start the client with the --ssl-ca option, and also the --ssl-key and --ssl-cert options if necessary:

```
GRANT ALL PRIVILEGES ON workrequests.* TO 'rusty'@'localhost'
IDENTIFIED BY 'her_password'
REQUIRE SSL;
```

Use the REQUIRE X509 option to require the user account to have a valid CA certificate. This does not require any specific certificate, though. The *mysql* client would need to be started with the --ssl-ca, --ssl-key, and --ssl-cert options. To simplify handling of these options, the user can put them in a options file in her home directory on the server (e.g., *~/.my.cnf*). The following is a sample of what that options file would contain to conform to the user account restrictions:

```
[client]
ssl-ca=/data/mysql/cacert.pem
ssl-key=/data/mysql/rusty-key.pem
ssl-cert=/data/mysql/rusty-cert.pem
```

Use the `REQUIRE CIPHER` option to require that the user account use a given cipher method:

```
GRANT ALL PRIVILEGES ON workrequests.* TO 'rusty'@'localhost'
IDENTIFIED BY 'her_password'
REQUIRE CIPHER 'EDH-RSA-DES-CBC3-SHA';
```

`REQUIRE ISSUER` is used to require the user to supply a valid X.509 certificate issued by the given CA. Although the string given for an issuer may be lengthy, it must be written as one string without an embedded line break:

```
GRANT ALL PRIVILEGES ON workrequests.* TO 'rusty'@'localhost'
IDENTIFIED BY 'her_password'
REQUIRE ISSUER '/C=US/ST=Louisiana/L=New+20Orleans/O=WorkRequesters/CN=
   cacert.workrequests.com/emailAddress=admin@workrequests.com';
```

The `REQUIRE SUBJECT` option requires that the X.509 certificate used by the user account have the given subject:

```
GRANT ALL PRIVILEGES ON workrequests.* TO 'rusty'@'localhost'
IDENTIFIED BY 'her_password'
REQUIRE SUBJECT '/C=US/ST=Louisiana/L=New+20Orleans/O=WorkRequesters/CN=
   Rusty Osborne/emailAddress=rusty@workrequests.com';
```

GRANT: Time and number of connection limits

```
GRANT privilege[,...] [(column[,...])][, ...]
ON [TABLE|FUNCTION|PROCEDURE] {[{database|*}.{table|*}] | *}
TO 'user'@'host' [IDENTIFIED BY [PASSWORD] 'password'][, ...]

[type of connection restrictions]

[WITH [MAX_QUERIES_PER_HOUR count |
       MAX_UPDATES_PER_HOUR count |
       MAX_CONNECTIONS_PER_HOUR count |
       MAX_USER_CONNECTIONS count] ...]
```

You can use the `WITH` clause along with the `MAX_QUERIES_PER_HOUR` option to specify the maximum number of queries that a user account may execute per hour. The `MAX_UPDATES_PER_HOUR` option is used to give the maximum number of `UPDATE` statements that may be issued per hour by the user account. The maximum number of connections by a user account to the server per hour can be set with the `MAX_CONNECTIONS_PER_HOUR` option. The default values for these three options are all 0. This value indicates that there is no limit or restrictions for these resources. The `MAX_USER_CONNECTIONS` option is used to set the maximum number of simultaneous connections the given user account may have. If this value is not set or is set to 0, the value of the system variable `max_user_connections` is used instead. Here is an example of how a user might be limited in such a way:

```
GRANT SELECT ON catalogs.*
TO 'webuser'@'%'
```

```
WITH MAX_QUERIES_PER_HOUR 1000
MAX_CONNECTIONS_PER_HOUR 100;
```

This account is designed for large numbers of users running queries through a web server. The statement creates the *webuser* user and allows it to read tables from the `catalogs` database. The user may not run more than 1,000 queries in an hour and may establish only 100 connections in an hour.

To change an existing user account's resources without changing the account's existing privileges, you can use the `USAGE` keyword. Simply enter a statement like this:

```
GRANT USAGE ON catalogs.*
TO 'webuser'@'%'
WITH MAX_QUERIES_PER_HOUR 10000
MAX_CONNECTIONS_PER_HOUR 100;
```

In this example, the existing user account has been limited in resources without changing the user account's privileges. See Table 4-2 for a list of privileges.

Table 4-2. Privileges in GRANT and REVOKE

Privilege	Description
`ALL [PRIVILEGES]`	Grants all of the basic privileges. Does not include `GRANT OPTION`.
`ALTER`	Allows use of the `ALTER TABLE` statement.
`ALTER ROUTINE`	Allows the user account to alter or drop stored routines. This includes the `ALTER FUNCTION` and `ALTER PROCEDURE` statements, as well as the `DROP FUNCTION` and `DROP PROCEDURE` statements.
`CREATE`	Grants `CREATE TABLE` statement privileges.
`CREATE ROUTINE`	Allows the user account to create stored routines. This includes the `CREATE FUNCTION` and `CREATE PROCEDURE` statements. The user has `ALTER ROUTINE` privileges to any routine he creates.
`CREATE TEMPORARY TABLES`	Allows the `CREATE TEMPORARY TABLES` statement to be used.
`CREATE USER`	Allows the user account to execute several user account management statements: `CREATE USER`, `RENAME USER`, `REVOKE ALL PRIVILEGES`, and the `DROP USER` statements.
`CREATE VIEW`	Allows the `CREATE VIEW` statement. This was first enabled in version 5.0.1 of MySQL.
`DELETE`	Allows the `DELETE` statement to be used.
`DROP`	Allows the user to execute `DROP TABLE` and `TRUNCATE` statements.
`EVENT`	Allows the user account to create events for the event scheduler. As of version 5.1.12 of MySQL, this privilege allows the use of the `CREATE EVENT`, `ALTER EVENT`, and `DROP EVENT` statements.
`EXECUTE`	Allows the execution of stored procedures. This is available as of version 5 of MySQL.
`FILE`	Allows the use of `SELECT...INTO OUTFILE` and `LOAD DATA INFILE` statements to export from and import to a file.

Privilege	Description
GRANT OPTION	Allows the use of the GRANT statement to grant privileges to users. This option is specified with the WITH clause of the GRANT statement.
INDEX	Allows the use of CREATE INDEX and DROP INDEX statements.
INSERT	Allows the use of INSERT statements.
LOCK TABLES	Allows the use of LOCK TABLES statement for tables for which the user has SELECT privileges.
PROCESS	Allows the use of SHOW FULL PROCESSLIST statements.
REFERENCES	This is not used. It's for future releases.
RELOAD	Allows the use of FLUSH and RESET statements.
REPLICATION CLIENT	Allows the user to query master and slave servers for status information.
REPLICATION SLAVE	Required for replication slave servers. Allows binary log events to be read from the master server.
SELECT	Allows the use of the SELECT statement.
SHOW DATABASES	Permits the use of the SHOW DATABASES statement for all databases, not just the ones for which the user has privileges.
SHOW VIEW	Allows the use of the SHOW CREATE VIEW statement. This is for version 5.0.1 and above of MySQL.
SHUTDOWN	Allows the use of the shutdown option with the mysqladmin utility.
SUPER	Allows the use of CHANGE MASTER, KILL, PURGE MASTER LOGS, and SET GLOBAL statements, and the debug option with the command-line utility mysqladmin.
TRIGGER	Allows the user account to create and drop triggers: the CREATE TRIGGER and the DROP TRIGGER statements.
UPDATE	Allows the use of the UPDATE statement.
USAGE	Used to create a user without privileges, or to modify resource limits on an existing user without affecting the existing privileges.

RENAME USER

RENAME USER '*user*'[@'*host*'] TO '*user*'[@'*host*'][,...]

Use this statement to change the username or the host of an existing user account. It does not change the user privileges or necessarily migrate any privileges to specific databases, events, stored routines, tables, triggers, or views. Here is an example:

```
RENAME USER 'michaelzabalaoui'@'localhost' TO 'zabb'@'%',
'richardstringer'@'localhost' TO 'littlerichard'@'localhost';
```

The first user's name and host have been changed here, whereas the second user's name only was changed.

RESET

```
RESET [QUERY CACHE|MASTER|SLAVE]
```

Use this statement to reset certain server settings and log files. The RELOAD privilege is required to use this statement. The QUERY CACHE option clears the cache containing SQL query results.

Use the MASTER option to reset a master used for replication. This statement must be executed from the master itself. It will start a new binary log file, as well as delete the binary log file names from the index file and delete the contents of the binary log index file. The SLAVE option is used to reset a slave used for replication and must be executed from the slave itself. It will start a new relay log file and delete any existing ones, as well as delete its notation of its position in the master's binary log. See Chapter 8 on replication for more information on these two options.

REVOKE

```
REVOKE ALL PRIVILEGES, GRANT OPTION FROM user[, ...]

REVOKE privilege[,...] [(column[, ...])]
ON {[{database|*}.{table|*}] | *}
FROM 'user'@'host'[, ...]
```


Use this statement to revoke some or all privileges that were granted to a user with the GRANT statement. The first syntax is used to revoke all privileges from a user. Multiple users may be given in a comma-separated list. A list of users and their privileges are stored in the mysql database, in the user table in particular:

```
REVOKE ALL PRIVILEGES
ON *.*
FROM 'paola'@localhost';
```

To revoke only some privileges, use the second syntax structure, giving the specific privileges to be removed in a comma-separated list after the keyword REVOKE. For a list of privileges and their descriptions, see Table 4-2 under the description of the GRANT statement earlier in this chapter.

To revoke privileges for specific columns, list the columns within parentheses in a comma-separated list. Privileges that are granted based on columns are stored in the columns_priv table of the mysql database. Privileges may be revoked on a specific table for a specific database. To revoke privileges on all tables of a database, specify an asterisk as a wildcard for the table name. You can do the same for the database name to apply the statement to all databases. Table-specific privileges are stored in the tables_priv table, and database-specific privileges are stored in the db table.

SET PASSWORD

```
SET PASSWORD [FOR 'user'@'host'] = PASSWORD('password')
```

Use this statement to change the password for a user account. The username and host must be given. The change of password will apply only to the given combination of username and host. It won't apply to other hosts for the same user in the grant tables.

To get a list of user accounts on your server, enter the following SQL statement:

```
SELECT User, Host FROM mysql.user;
```

If the `FOR` clause is not given with the `SET PASSWORD` statement, the current user account is assumed. The `PASSWORD( )` function will encrypt the password given.

This statement does not need to be followed by a `FLUSH PRIVILEGES` statement. It will automatically update the privileges cache for the new password. If you updated your server from a version before 4.1 to a new version, you may have problems changing a user account's password and cause the user account's password to become invalid. You may need to run the `mysql_fix_privilege_tables` utility to change the `Password` column in the `user` table in the `mysql` database. See Chapter 16 for more information on this utility.

Here is an example of changing a user account's password:

```
SET PASSWORD FOR 'kenneth'@'localhost' = PASSWORD('his_password');
```

SHOW GRANTS

`SHOW GRANTS [FOR 'user'[@'host']]`

This SQL statement displays the `GRANT` statement for a given user. If the `FOR` clause is not given, the current user account is assumed. If the username is given without reference to a particular host, the wildcard `%` is assumed. Otherwise, the username should be followed by the host as shown here:

```
SHOW GRANTS FOR 'russell'@'localhost'\G

*************************** 1. row ***************************
Grants for russell@localhost:

GRANT ALL PRIVILEGES ON *.*
TO 'russell'@'localhost'
IDENTIFIED BY PASSWORD '57fa103a3c5c9f30'
WITH GRANT OPTION
```

The resulting statement is what would be entered to create the user *russell* for the host *localhost*, with the given privileges including the `WITH GRANT OPTION` flag.

SHOW PRIVILEGES

`SHOW PRIVILEGES`

This statement provides a list of privileges available, along with the context of each one (e.g., server administration) and a description. The output is not based on the user. Instead, it's a complete listing of the privileges that may be assigned to a user. This statement is available as of version 4.1 of MySQL.

Functions in Alphabetical Order

The following are MySQL functions in alphabetical order related to security and user account maintenance.

AES_DECRYPT( )

AES_DECRYPT(*string*, *password*)

This function decrypts text that was encrypted using the Advanced Encryption Standard (AES) algorithm with a 128-bit key length, reversing the AES_ENCRYPT( ) function. The function unlocks the encrypted string with the password given as the second argument. It returns NULL if one of the given parameters is NULL. This is available as of version 4.0.2 of MySQL. Here is an example:

```
SELECT AES_DECRYPT(personal, 'my_password') AS Personal
FROM teachers
WHERE teacher_id='730522';

+----------+
| Personal |
+----------+
| text     |
+----------+
```

In this example, the value for the personal column is decrypted using the password given. The result is just the plain text of the column.

AES_ENCRYPT( )

AES_ENCRYPT(*string*, *password*)

This function encrypts a given string using the AES algorithm with a 128-bit key length. It locks the encrypted string with the password given as the second argument. The function returns NULL if one of the given parameters is NULL. It's available as of version 4.0.2 of MySQL. The results of this function can be reversed with AES_DECRYPT( ). Here is an example:

```
UPDATE teachers
SET personal = AES_ENCRYPT('text', 'my_password')
WHERE teacher_id = '730522';
```

CURRENT_USER( )

CURRENT_USER( )

This function returns the username and the host that were given by the user for the current MySQL connection. There are no arguments for the function. It may not always return the same results as USER( ). Here is an example:

```
SELECT CURRENT_USER( ), USER( );

+-----------------+------------------+
| CURRENT_USER( ) | USER( )          |
+-----------------+------------------+
| ''@localhost    | russel@localhost |
+-----------------+------------------+
```

In this example, the user logged in to the *mysql* client with the username *russel* (missing one "l" in the name), but because there isn't an account for that user, the client logged in with the anonymous (i.e., '') account.

DECODE( )

`DECODE(string, password)`

This function decrypts a given string that was encrypted with a given password. See the `ENCODE( )` function later in this chapter:

```
SELECT ENCODE(pwd, 'oreilly')
FROM teachers
WHERE teacher_id = '730522';
```

This function decrypts the contents of the `pwd` column and unlocks it using the *oreilly* password, which was used to encrypt it originally using `ENCODE( )`.

DES_DECRYPT( )

`DES_DECRYPT(string, [key])`

This function decrypts text that was encrypted using the triple Data Encryption Standard (DES) algorithm with a 128-bit key length, reversing the `DES_ENCRYPT( )` function. It returns NULL if an error occurs. The function will work only if MySQL has been configured for Secure Sockets Layer (SSL) support. It is available as of version 4.0.1 of MySQL. Here is an example:

```
SELECT DES_DECRYPT(credit_card_nbr, 0)
FROM orders
WHERE order_nbr = '8347';
```

In this example, the value for the `credit_card_nbr` column is decrypted using the first key string in the key file. See the description of `DES_ENCRYPT( )` next for more information on key files.

DES_ENCRYPT( )

`DES_ENCRYPT(string, [key])`

This function returns encrypted text using the triple DES algorithm with a 128-bit key length. It returns NULL if an error occurs. The function is available as of version 4.0.1 of MySQL.

This function requires MySQL to be configured for SSL support. In addition, a key file must be created and the *mysqld* daemon must be started with the `--des-key-file` option. The key file should be set up with a separate key string on each line. Each line should begin with a single-digit number (0–9) as an index, followed by a space before the key string (e.g., `key_number des_string`).

The key given as the second argument to the function can either be the actual key to use for encryption or a number that refers to a key in the key file. If the second argument is omitted, the function uses the first key in the key file:

```
UPDATE orders
SET credit_card_nbr = DES_ENCRYPT('4011-7839-1234-4321')
WHERE order_nbr = '8347';
```

The results of this function can be reversed with `DES_DECRYPT( )`.

ENCODE( )

`ENCODE(string, password)`

This function encrypts a given string in binary format and locks it with the password. You should not use this function for the `password` column in the `user` table of the `mysql` database. Use `PASSWORD( )` instead. Here is an example:

```
UPDATE teachers
SET pwd = ENCODE('test', 'oreilly')
WHERE teacher_id = '730522';
```

The function here encrypts the word `test` and locks it with the *oreilly* password. The results are stored in the `pwd` column for the chosen teacher. To unlock the results, use the `DECODE( )` function with the same password.

ENCRYPT( )

`ENCRYPT(string[, seed])`

This function returns encrypted text using the C-language `crypt` function. A two-character string may be given in the second argument to increase the randomness of encryption. The resulting string cannot be decrypted. You should not use this function for the `password` column in the `user` table of the `mysql` database. Use `PASSWORD( )` instead. Here is an example:

```
UPDATE teachers
SET pwd = ENCRYPT('test', 'JT')
WHERE teacher_id = '730522';
```

MD5( )

`MD5(string)`

This function uses a Message-Digest algorithm 5 (MD5) 128-bit checksum to return a 32-character hash value of *string* from the Request for Comments (RFC) 1321 standard. Here is an example:

```
SELECT MD5('Test') AS 'MD5( ) Test';
+----------------------------------+
| MD5( ) Test                      |
+----------------------------------+
| 0cbc6611f5540bd0809a388dc95a615b |
+----------------------------------+
```

OLD_PASSWORD( )

`OLD_PASSWORD(string)`

This function encrypts a given string based on the password encryption method used prior to version 4.1 of MySQL. The result cannot be decrypted. Here is an example:

```
UPDATE teachers
SET pwd = OLD_PASSWORD('test')
WHERE teacher_id = '730522';
```

PASSWORD( )

PASSWORD(*string*)

This function encrypts a password given as an argument. The result cannot be decrypted. This function is used for encrypting data in the `password` column of the `user` table in the `mysql` database. Here is an example:

```
UPDATE teachers
SET pwd = PASSWORD('test')
WHERE teacher_id = '730522';
```

SESSION_USER( )

SESSION_USER( )

This function returns the username and the hostname for the current MySQL connection. The function takes no arguments. It's synonymous with `SYSTEM_USER( )` and `USER( )`.

SHA( )

SHA(*string*)

This function returns the Secure Hash Algorithm (SHA) 160-bit checksum for the given string. The result is a string composed of 40 hexadecimal digits. NULL is returned if the given string is NULL. This function is synonymous with `SHA1( )`. Here is an example:

```
SELECT SHA('test');

+------------------------------------------+
| SHA('test')                              |
+------------------------------------------+
| a94a8fe5ccb19ba61c4c0873d391e987982fbbd3 |
+------------------------------------------+
```

SHA1( )

SHA(*string*)

This function returns the SHA 160-bit checksum for the given string. The result is a string composed of 40 hexadecimal digits. NULL is returned if the given string is NULL. This function is synonymous with `SHA( )`.

SYSTEM_USER( )

SYSTEM_USER( )

This function returns the username and the hostname for the current MySQL connection. The function takes no arguments. It's synonymous with `SESSION_USER( )` and `USER( )`.

USER( )

```
USER( )
```

This function returns the username and the hostname for the current MySQL connection. The function takes no arguments. It's synonymous with `SESSION_USER( )` and with `SYSTEM_USER( )`. Here is an example:

```
SELECT USER( );

+-------------------+
| USER( )           |
+-------------------+
| russell@localhost |
+-------------------+
```

5
Database and Table Schema Statements

This chapter explains the SQL statements in MySQL related to database and table schema. These statements create, alter, and delete databases and tables, as well as display information related to databases, tables, and columns. The statements in this chapter pertain to information *about* these data structures, not the manipulation of data within them; statements that affect the data are covered in the next chapter. In essence, this chapter covers the SQL statements used when one is in the mode of creating database structures. This mode is a fairly distinct mindset and is sometimes the responsibility of different persons from those who manipulate the data itself.

This chapter covers the following SQL statements:

`ALTER DATABASE`, `ALTER SCHEMA`, `ALTER SERVER`, `ALTER TABLE`, `ALTER VIEW`, `CREATE DATABASE`, `CREATE INDEX`, `CREATE SCHEMA`, `CREATE SERVER`, `CREATE TABLE`, `CREATE VIEW`, `DESCRIBE`, `DROP DATABASE`, `DROP INDEX`, `DROP SERVER`, `DROP TABLE`, `DROP VIEW`, `RENAME DATABASE`, `RENAME TABLE`, `SHOW CHARACTER SET`, `SHOW COLLATION`, `SHOW COLUMNS`, `SHOW CREATE DATABASE`, `SHOW CREATE TABLE`, `SHOW CREATE VIEW`, `SHOW DATABASES`, `SHOW INDEXES`, `SHOW SCHEMAS`, `SHOW TABLE STATUS`, `SHOW TABLES`, `SHOW VIEWS`.

Statements and Clauses in Alphabetical Order

The following is a list of MySQL statements and clauses related to database and table schema, in alphabetical order. To understand how this book presents SQL syntax and describes SQL statements, as well as for information related to examples, please see the introduction to Part II. Many of the examples in this particular chapter involve the activities of the departments of a fictitious company: its human resources department and employee data, its sales department and client contact information, and its internal IT department with user work requests.

ALTER DATABASE

```
ALTER {DATABASE|SCHEMA} database
   [DEFAULT] CHARACTER SET character_set |
   [DEFAULT] COLLATE collation
```

Use this statement to alter settings for a database. Version 4.1.1 of MySQL introduced this function and added a file named *db.opt* containing the database settings to the database directory. Currently, two options are available: `CHARACTER SET` and `COLLATE`. Here are the contents of a typical *db.opt* file:

```
default-character-set=latin1
default-collation=latin1_swedish_ci
```

Although an administrator can edit the file manually, it may be more robust to use the `ALTER DATABASE` statement to change the file. It's synonymous with `ALTER SCHEMA` as of version 5.0.2 of MySQL. The `ALTER` privilege is necessary for this statement.

The `CHARACTER SET` option can set the first line shown, which specifies the default database character set that will be used. The `COLLATE` option can set the second line, which specifies the default database collation (how the character data is alphabetized). Here's an example of the use of this statement:

```
ALTER DATABASE human_resources
CHARACTER SET latin2_bin
COLLATE latin2_bin;
```

Notice that both options may be given in one SQL statement. The `DEFAULT` keyword is unnecessary, but it is offered for compatibility with other database systems. Beginning with version 4.1.8 of MySQL, if the name of the database is omitted from this SQL statement, the current database will be assumed. To determine the current database, use the `DATABASE( )` function:

```
SELECT DATABASE();

+--------------+
| DATABASE()   |
+--------------+
| workrequests |
+--------------+
```

See the explanations for the `SHOW CHARACTER SET` and `SHOW COLLATION` SQL statements later in this chapter for more information on character sets and collations.

ALTER SCHEMA

```
ALTER {DATABASE|SCHEMA} database
   [DEFAULT] CHARACTER SET character_set |
   [DEFAULT] COLLATE collation
```

This statement is synonymous with `ALTER DATABASE`. See the description of that statement previously for more information and examples.

ALTER SERVER

```
ALTER SERVER server
OPTIONS (
  { HOST host, |
    DATABASE database, |
    USER user, |
    PASSWORD password, |
    SOCKET socket, |
    OWNER character, |
    PORT port }
)
```

Use this SQL statement with the FEDERATED storage engine to change the connection parameters of a server created with `CREATE SERVER`. The values given are stored in the `server` table of the `mysql` database. Options are given in a comma-separated list. Option values must be specified as character or numeric literals (UTF-8; maximum length of 64 characters). This statement was introduced in version 5.1.15 of MySQL and requires `SUPER` privileges:

```
ALTER SERVER server1
OPTIONS (USER 'test_user', PASSWORD 'testing123', PORT 3307);
```

This example changes the values of an existing server, the username, the password, and the port to be used for connecting to the server.

ALTER TABLE

```
ALTER [IGNORE] TABLE table changes[, ...]
```

Use this statement to change an existing table's structure and other properties. A table may be altered with this statement in the following ways:

- Add a new column (see the "ALTER TABLE: ADD clauses for columns" subsection that follows)
- Add an index (see the "ALTER TABLE: ADD clause for standard indexes," "ALTER TABLE: ADD clause for FULLTEXT indexes," and "ALTER TABLE: ADD clause for SPATIAL indexes" subsections)
- Add a foreign key constraint (see the "ALTER TABLE: ADD clauses for foreign keys" subsection)
- Change an existing column (see the "ALTER TABLE: CHANGE clauses" subsection)
- Delete a column or index (see the "ALTER TABLE: DROP column clause" and "ALTER TABLE: DROP index clauses" subsections)
- Set other column and index factors (see the "ALTER TABLE: Miscellaneous clauses" subsection)
- Add and change table partitions (see the "ALTER TABLE: Partition altering clauses" and "ALTER TABLE: Partition administration clauses" subsections)
- Set table-wide options (see the "ALTER TABLE: Table options" subsection)

The `IGNORE` flag applies to all clauses and instructs MySQL to ignore any error messages regarding duplicate rows that may occur as a result of a column change. It will keep the first unique row found and drop any duplicate rows. Otherwise, the statement will be terminated and changes will be rolled back.

This statement requires the `ALTER`, `CREATE`, and `INSERT` privileges for the table being altered, at a minimum. While an `ALTER TABLE` statement is being executed, users will be able to read the table, but usually they won't be able to modify data or add data to a table being altered. Any `INSERT` statements using the `DELAYED` parameter that are not completed when a table is altered will be canceled and the data lost. Increasing the size of the `myisam_sort_buffer_size` system variable will sometimes make MyISAM table alterations go faster.

The syntax and explanation of each clause follows, with examples, grouped by type of clause. Multiple alterations may be combined in a single `ALTER TABLE` statement. They must be separated by commas and each clause must include the minimally required elements.

ALTER TABLE: ADD clauses for columns

```
ALTER [IGNORE] TABLE table
ADD [COLUMN] column definition [FIRST|AFTER column] |
ADD [COLUMN] (column definition,...)
```

These clauses add columns to a table. The same column definitions found in a `CREATE TABLE` statement are used in this statement. Basically, the statements list the name of the column followed by the column data type and the default value or other relevant components. The `COLUMN` keyword is optional and has no effect.

By default, an added column is appended to the end of the table. To insert a new column at the beginning of a table, use the `FIRST` keyword at the end of the `ADD COLUMN` clause. To insert it after a particular existing column, use the `AFTER` keyword followed by the name of the column after which the new column is to be inserted:

```
ALTER TABLE workreq
ADD COLUMN req_type CHAR(4) AFTER req_date,
ADD COLUMN priority CHAR(4) AFTER req_date;
```

In this example, two columns are added after the existing `req_date` column. The clauses are executed in the order that they are given. Therefore, `req_type` is placed after `req_date`. Then `priority` is added after `req_date` and before `req_type`. Notice that you can give more than one clause in one `ALTER TABLE` statement; just separate them with commas.

ALTER TABLE: ADD clause for standard indexes

```
ALTER [IGNORE] TABLE table
ADD {INDEX|KEY} [index] [USING index_type] (column,...)
```

Use the `ADD INDEX` clause to add an index to a table. If you omit the name of the index, MySQL will set it to the name of the first column on which the index is based. The type of index may be stated, but usually it's not necessary. The names of one or more columns for indexing must be given within parentheses, separated by commas.

Here is an example of how you can add an index using the `ALTER TABLE` statement, followed by the `SHOW INDEXES` statement with the results:

```
ALTER TABLE clients
ADD INDEX client_index
```

```
(client_name(10), city(5)) USING BTREE;

SHOW INDEXES FROM clients \G

*************************** 1. row ***************************
       Table: clients
  Non_unique: 0
    Key_name: PRIMARY
Seq_in_index: 1
 Column_name: client_id
   Collation: A
 Cardinality: 0
    Sub_part: NULL
      Packed: NULL
        Null:
  Index_type: BTREE
     Comment:
*************************** 2. row ***************************
       Table: clients
  Non_unique: 1
    Key_name: client_index
Seq_in_index: 1
 Column_name: client_name
   Collation: A
 Cardinality: NULL
    Sub_part: 10
      Packed: NULL
        Null: YES
  Index_type: BTREE
     Comment:
*************************** 3. row ***************************
       Table: clients
  Non_unique: 1
    Key_name: client_index
Seq_in_index: 2
 Column_name: city
   Collation: A
 Cardinality: NULL
    Sub_part: 5
      Packed: NULL
        Null: YES
  Index_type: BTREE
     Comment:
```

As you can see in the results, there was already an index in the table `clients` (see row 1). The index we've added is called `client_index`. It's based on two columns: the first 10 characters of the `client_name` column and the first 5 characters of the `city` column. Limiting the number of characters used in the index makes for a smaller index, which will be faster and probably just as accurate as using the complete column widths. The results of the `SHOW INDEXES` statement show a separate row for each column indexed, even though one of the indexes involves two rows.

The table in this example uses the MyISAM storage engine, which uses the `BTREE` index type by default, so it was unnecessary to specify a type. See Appendix A for more information about storage engines and available index types. Before MySQL version 5.1.10, the USING subclause could come either before or after the column list, but as of version 5.1.10, it must follow the column list.

ALTER TABLE: ADD clause for FULLTEXT indexes

```
ALTER [IGNORE] TABLE table
ADD FULLTEXT [INDEX|KEY] [index] (column,...) [WITH PARSER parser]
```

The ADD FULLTEXT clause adds an index to a TEXT column within an existing MyISAM table. A FULLTEXT index can also index CHAR and VARCHAR columns. This type of index is necessary to use the FULLTEXT functionality (the MATCH( ) AGAINST( ) function from Chapter 11). The INDEX and KEY keywords are optional as of MySQL version 5.

With this index, the whole column will be used for each column given. Although you can instruct it to use only the first few characters of a table, it will still use the full column for the index. The WITH PARSER clause may be used to give a parser plugin for a FULLTEXT index:

```
ALTER TABLE workreq
ADD FULLTEXT INDEX notes_index
(client_description, technician_notes);

SHOW INDEXES FROM workreq \G

*************************** 2. row ***************************
       Table: workreq
  Non_unique: 1
    Key_name: notes_index
Seq_in_index: 1
 Column_name: client_description
   Collation: NULL
 Cardinality: NULL
    Sub_part: NULL
      Packed: NULL
        Null: YES
  Index_type: FULLTEXT
     Comment:
*************************** 3. row ***************************
       Table: workreq
  Non_unique: 1
    Key_name: notes_index
Seq_in_index: 2
 Column_name: technician_notes
   Collation: NULL
 Cardinality: NULL
    Sub_part: NULL
      Packed: NULL
        Null: YES
  Index_type: FULLTEXT
     Comment:
```

I've eliminated the first row from these results because it relates to the primary index, not the one created here.

As of version 5.1 of MySQL, you can use the WITH PARSER clause to specify a parser plugin for a FULLTEXT index. This option requires that the plugin table be loaded in the mysql database. This table is part of the current installation of MySQL. If you've upgraded

MySQL and the plugin table is not in your system's `mysql` database, use the `mysql_upgrade` script to add it. Use the `SHOW PLUGINS` statement to see which plugins are installed.

ALTER TABLE: ADD clause for SPATIAL indexes

```
ALTER [IGNORE] TABLE table
ADD SPATIAL [INDEX|KEY] [index] (column,...)
```

This `ADD` clause is used to add a `SPATIAL` index. A `SPATIAL` index can index only spatial columns. A spatial index is used in a table that holds data based on the Open Geospatial Consortium (*http://www.opengis.org*) data for geographical and global positioning satellite (GPS) systems. For our purposes here, this clause is necessary to add an index for spatial extensions. For MyISAM tables, the `RTREE` index type is used. The `BTREE` is used by other storage engines that use nonspatial indexes of spatial columns. Here is an example:

```
ALTER TABLE squares
ADD SPATIAL INDEX square_index (square_points);

SHOW INDEXES FROM squares \G

*************************** 1. row ***************************
       Table: squares
  Non_unique: 1
    Key_name: square_index
Seq_in_index: 1
 Column_name: square_points
   Collation: A
 Cardinality: NULL
    Sub_part: 32
      Packed: NULL
        Null:
  Index_type: SPATIAL
     Comment:
```

Notice that when we created the table, we specified that the column `square_points` is NOT NULL. This is required to be able to index the column. See the `CREATE INDEX` statement for `SPATIAL` indexes in this chapter for an explanation and more examples related to spatial indexes.

ALTER TABLE: ADD clauses for foreign keys

```
ALTER [IGNORE] TABLE table
ADD [CONSTRAINT [symbol]] PRIMARY KEY [USING index_type] (column,...) |
ADD [CONSTRAINT [symbol]] UNIQUE [INDEX|KEY] index [USING index_type]
   (column,...) |
ADD [CONSTRAINT [symbol]] FOREIGN KEY [index] (column,...)
   [REFERENCES table (column,...)
   [ON DELETE {RESTRICT|CASCADE|SET NULL|NO ACTION|SET DEFAULT}]
   [ON UPDATE {RESTRICT|CASCADE|SET NULL|NO ACTION|SET DEFAULT}]]
```

These `ADD` clauses add foreign keys and references to InnoDB tables. A foreign key is an index that refers to a key or an index in another table. See the explanation of the `CREATE TABLE` statement later in this chapter for more information and for an example of an SQL statement involving the creation of foreign keys in a table. The various flags shown are also explained in the `CREATE TABLE` statement.

Here is an example:

```
CREATE TABLE employees
(emp_id INT AUTO_INCREMENT PRIMARY KEY,
tax_id CHAR(12),
emp_name VARCHAR(100))
ENGINE = INNODB;

CREATE TABLE employees_telephone
(emp_id INT,
tel_type ENUM('office','home','mobile'),
tel_number CHAR(25))
ENGINE = INNODB;

ALTER TABLE employees_telephone
ADD FOREIGN KEY emp_tel (emp_id)
REFERENCES employees (emp_id)
ON DELETE RESTRICT;
```

The first two SQL statements create InnoDB tables: one for basic employee information and the other for employee telephone numbers. Using the `ALTER TABLE` statement afterward, we add a foreign key restriction between the two. Let's look at the results using the `SHOW TABLE STATUS` statement, because the `SHOW INDEXES` statement won't show foreign key restraints:

```
SHOW TABLE STATUS FROM human_resources
LIKE 'employees_telephone' \G

*************************** 1. row ***************************
           Name: employees_telephone
         Engine: InnoDB
        Version: 10
     Row_format: Compact
           Rows: 0
 Avg_row_length: 0
    Data_length: 16384
Max_data_length: 0
   Index_length: 16384
      Data_free: 0
 Auto_increment: NULL
    Create_time: 2007-04-03 04:01:39
    Update_time: NULL
     Check_time: NULL
      Collation: latin1_swedish_ci
       Checksum: NULL
 Create_options:
        Comment: InnoDB free: 4096 kB; ('emp_id')
                 REFER 'human_resources'.'employees'('emp_id')
```

In the `Comment` field, we can see that we've created a restraint on the main table `employees` from `employees_telephone`. We're telling MySQL not to allow a row for an employee to be removed from the `employees` table without first removing the rows of data for the employee in the `employees_telephone` table.

In the following example, we first insert an employee in the `employees` table, then add her home telephone number to the second table, and then attempt to delete her from the first table:

```
INSERT INTO employees
VALUES(1000,'123-45-6789','Paola Caporale');

INSERT INTO employees_telephone
VALUES(1000,2,'+39 343-12-34-5678');

DELETE FROM employees WHERE emp_id = 1000;

ERROR 1451 (23000): Cannot delete or update a parent row:
a foreign key constraint fails
('human_resources'.'employees_telephone',
  CONSTRAINT 'employees_telephone_ibfk_1'
  FOREIGN KEY ('emp_id') REFERENCES 'employees' ('emp_id')
)
```

As you can see, we cannot delete the employee from the `employees` table and leave the stray row of data in the `employees_telephone` table. We have to delete the data in `employees_telephone` first, before deleting the related data from `employees`. See the explanation under `CREATE TABLE` in the "CREATE TABLE: Foreign key references" section later in this chapter for examples of the other options with foreign keys. Incidentally, you can't drop and add a foreign key in the same `ALTER TABLE` statement.

ALTER TABLE: CHANGE clauses

```
ALTER [IGNORE] TABLE table
ALTER [COLUMN] column {SET DEFAULT value|DROP DEFAULT} |
CHANGE [COLUMN] column column definition [FIRST|AFTER column] |
MODIFY [COLUMN] column definition [FIRST|AFTER column]
```

These three clauses are used to alter an existing column in a table. The first syntax structure is used either to set the default value of a column to a particular value or to reset it back to its default value for its column type (usually NULL or 0). The other two syntax structures are used primarily to change the column definitions. The `COLUMN` keyword is optional and has no effect.

To change the column's character set, add `CHARACTER SET` to the end of the column definition for the `CHANGE` or `MODIFY` clauses, followed by the character set name to use. Here's an example of the first clause:

```
ALTER TABLE clients
ALTER COLUMN city SET DEFAULT 'New Orleans';
```

This statement sets the default value of the `city` column in the `clients` table to a value of `New Orleans`, because that's where most of the clients are located.

The clauses that change column definitions are roughly synonymous; they follow the standards of different SQL systems for the sake of compatibility (e.g., `MODIFY` is used with Oracle). They can also be used to relocate the column within the table schema with the `FIRST` or the `AFTER` keywords. If a column's data type is changed, MySQL attempts to adjust the data to suit the new data type. If a column width is shortened, MySQL truncates the data and generates warning messages for the affected rows. Indexes related to changed columns will be adjusted automatically for the new lengths.

In the CHANGE clause, the current column name must be specified first, followed by either the same column name if the name is to remain the same, or a new column name if the name is to be changed. The full column definition for the column must be given as well, even if it's not to be changed.

The MODIFY clause cannot be used to change a column's name, so the column name appears only once with it.

The following SQL statement shows the columns in the clients table, where the column name begins with a c and contains an i to list the columns that begin with either client or city. After viewing these limited results, we change one column using each of the clauses for changing column definitions:

```
SHOW COLUMNS FROM clients LIKE 'c%i%';

+--------------+--------------+------+-----+---------+----------------+
| Field        | Type         | Null | Key | Default | Extra          |
+--------------+--------------+------+-----+---------+----------------+
| client_id    | int(11)      | NO   | PRI | NULL    | auto_increment |
| client_name  | varchar(255) | YES  | MUL | NULL    |                |
| city         | varchar(255) | YES  |     | NULL    |                |
| client_zip   | char(10)     | YES  |     | NULL    |                |
| client_state | char(2)      | YES  |     | NULL    |                |
+--------------+--------------+------+-----+---------+----------------+

ALTER TABLE clients
CHANGE COLUMN city client_city VARCHAR(100) CHARACTER SET 'latin2',
MODIFY COLUMN client_state CHAR(4) AFTER client_city;
```

After looking at the current columns, we've decided to change the name of the city column to client_city to match the other related columns, and to enlarge the client_state column and move it before the column for the postal ZIP code. To do this, the CHANGE clause is used to change the name of the city column, but not its column type and size. The second clause changes the column type and size and relocates the client_state column to a position after the client_city column.

When a column is changed, MySQL will attempt to preserve the data. If a column size is reduced, the data won't be completely deleted, but it may be truncated, in which case the results will show a number of warnings. Use the SHOW WARNINGS statement to view them.

ALTER TABLE: DROP column clause

```
ALTER [IGNORE] TABLE table
DROP [COLUMN] column
```

The DROP clause of the ALTER TABLE statement removes a given column from a table and deletes the column's data. A table must have at least one column, so this statement will fail if used on the only column in a table. Use the DROP TABLE statement to delete a table. If a dropped column is part of an index, the column will be removed automatically from the index definition. If all of the columns of an index are dropped, the index will automatically be dropped.

Here is an example including this clause:

```
ALTER TABLE clients
DROP COLUMN miscellaneous,
DROP COLUMN comments;
```

This statement drops two columns and deletes the data they contain without warning. Notice that multiple columns may be dropped by separating each clause by a comma. It's not possible to combine clauses. That is to say, `...DROP COLUMN (miscellaneous, comments)` is not permitted. Once a column has been deleted, you won't be able to recover its data from MySQL. Instead, you'll have to restore the table from a backup of your data if you made one.

ALTER TABLE: DROP index clauses

```
ALTER [IGNORE] TABLE table
DROP INDEX index |
DROP PRIMARY KEY |
DROP FOREIGN KEY foreign_key_symbol
```

These clauses are used to delete indexes. A standard index is fairly easy to eliminate with the first syntax shown. Here's an example of its use:

```
ALTER TABLE clients
DROP INDEX client_index;
```

The second syntax deletes the primary key index of a table. However, if the primary key is based on a column with an `AUTO_INCREMENT` type, you may need to change the column definition in the same statement so it is no longer `AUTO_INCREMENT` before you can drop the primary key. Here is an example in which we fail to change the indexed column first:

```
ALTER TABLE clients
DROP PRIMARY KEY;

ERROR 1075 (42000): Incorrect table definition;
there can be only one auto column and it must be defined as a key

ALTER TABLE clients
CHANGE client_id client_id INT,
DROP PRIMARY KEY;
```

The first SQL statement here causes an error in which MySQL complains that if we are going to have a column with `AUTO_INCREMENT`, it must be a key column. So using the `CHANGE` clause in the second SQL statement, we change the `client_id` column from `INT AUTO_INCREMENT` to just `INT`. After the `AUTO_INCREMENT` is removed, the `PRIMARY KEY` may be dropped. Before version 5.1 of MySQL, if a primary key doesn't exist, the first `UNIQUE` key is dropped instead. After version 5.1, an error is returned and no key is dropped.

To delete a foreign key, the third syntax is used. Here is an example that deletes a foreign index:

```
ALTER TABLE client
DROP FOREIGN KEY '0_34531';
```

In this example, the name of the index is not the name of any of the columns, but an index that was created by combining two columns and was given its own name. The name was changed by InnoDB automatically. To get a list of indexes for a table, use the `SHOW CREATE TABLE` statement.

ALTER TABLE: Miscellaneous clauses

```
ALTER [IGNORE] TABLE table
CONVERT TO CHARACTER SET charset [COLLATE collation] |
[DEFAULT] CHARACTER SET charset [COLLATE collation] |
DISABLE|ENABLE KEYS |
DISCARD|IMPORT TABLESPACE |
ORDER BY column [ASC|DESC][,...] |
RENAME [TO] table
```

You can use these miscellaneous clauses with the `ALTER TABLE` statement to change a variety of table properties. They are described here in the order that they are listed in the syntax.

Converting and setting character sets

The first two syntaxes shown may be used to change the character set and collation for a table. When a table is first created with the `CREATE TABLE` statement, unless a character set or collation is specified, defaults for these traits are used. To see the character set and collation for a particular table, use the `SHOW TABLE STATUS` statement. To convert the data, use the `CONVERT TO CHARACTER SET` clause. To set the table's default without converting the data, use the `DEFAULT CHARACTER SET` clause with the `ALTER TABLE` statement. The following example shows how to convert a table's character set:

```
SHOW TABLE STATUS LIKE 'clients' \G

*************************** 1. row ***************************
           Name: clients
         Engine: MyISAM
        Version: 10
     Row_format: Dynamic
           Rows: 632
 Avg_row_length: 12732
    Data_length: 1024512
Max_data_length: 281474976710655
   Index_length: 3072
      Data_free: 0
 Auto_increment: 1678
    Create_time: 2006-02-01 14:12:31
    Update_time: 2007-04-03 05:25:41
     Check_time: 2006-08-14 21:31:36
      Collation: latin1_swedish_ci
       Checksum: NULL
 Create_options: max_rows=1000
        Comment: This table lists basic information on clients.

ALTER TABLE clients
CONVERT TO CHARACTER SET latin2 COLLATE latin2_bin,
DEFAULT CHARACTER SET latin2 COLLATE latin2_bin;
```

The first clause in this example converts the data in the `clients` table from its default of `latin1_swedish_ci` to `latin2`. The second clause sets the new default for the table to `latin2`, as well. Be aware that the `CONVERT` clause may cause problems with the data. So be sure to make a backup copy before using this clause and check the converted data before finishing. If you have a column with a character set in which data might be lost in the conversion, you could first convert the column to a Binary Large Object (`BLOB`) data type, and then to the data type and character set that you want. This usually works fine because BLOB data isn't converted with a character set change.

Disabling and enabling keys

You can use the third clause (DISABLE and ENABLE) to disable or enable the updating of nonunique indexes on MyISAM tables. You will need ALTER, CREATE, INDEX, and INSERT privileges to execute this statement and clause. As of version 5.1.11 of MySQL, this clause will work on partitioned tables. When running a large number of row inserts, it can be useful to disable indexing until afterward:

```
ALTER TABLE sales_dept.catalog
DISABLE KEYS;

LOAD DATA INFILE '/tmp/catalog.txt'
INTO TABLE sales_dept.catalog
FIELDS TERMINATED BY '|'
LINES TERMINATED BY '\n';

ALTER TABLE sales_dept.catalog
ENABLE KEYS;
```

In this example, we've disabled the indexes of the catalog table in the sales_dept database so that we can more quickly import the new catalog data. If we had run the SHOW INDEXES statement at this point, we would have seen disabled in the Comment field of the results for all of the indexes except the PRIMARY key. In our example, we then reenabled the indexes for faster retrieval of data by users.

Discarding or importing tablespace

InnoDB tables use tablespaces instead of individual files for each table. A tablespace can involve multiple files and can allow a table to exceed the filesystem file limit as a result. You can use the TABLESPACE clauses in the ALTER TABLE statement to delete or import a tablespace:

```
ALTER TABLE workreq
IMPORT TABLESPACE;
```

This statement imports the *.idb* file if it's in the database's directory. Replacing the IMPORT keyword with DISCARD will delete the *.idb* file.

Reordering rows

You can use the next clause syntax structure, the ORDER BY clause, to permanently reorder the rows in a given table. Note that after an ALTER TABLE statement, any new rows inserted will be added to the end of the table and the table will not be reordered automatically. To enforce another order, you will need to run ALTER TABLE again with this clause. The only reason to use this clause is for tables that rarely change, because reordering sometimes improves performance. In most cases, instead of reordering the storage of the table, it's recommended you include an ORDER BY clause in your SELECT statements.

Here's an example with this clause:

```
ALTER TABLE clients
ORDER BY client_name;
```

It's possible to give more than one column name in the ORDER BY clause, separated by commas. Expressions cannot be used. You can, however, specify ascending (ASC, the default) or descending (DESC) order for each column.

Renaming a table

You can use the RENAME clause to change the name of an existing table. Here is an example of this clause:

```
ALTER TABLE client RENAME TO clients;
```

This statement renames the client table to clients. The TO keyword is not required; it's a matter of style preference and compatibility. A statement with this clause is equivalent to using the RENAME TABLE statement, except that the RENAME clause does not change user privileges from the old table name to refer to the new name of the table.

ALTER TABLE: Partition altering clauses

```
ALTER [IGNORE] TABLE table
PARTITION BY options |
ADD PARTITION (definition) |
COALESCE PARTITION number |
DROP PARTITION partition |
REORGANIZE PARTITION partition INTO (definition) |
REMOVE PARTITIONING
```

These table partition clauses for ALTER TABLE may be used to add or remove partitions in a table. They were added as of version 5.1.6 of MySQL. For partition clauses that analyze, check, optimize, rebuild, and repair partitions in a table, see the next subsection ("ALTER TABLE: Partition administration clauses"). Also, see the CREATE TABLE statement explanation for more information on table partitioning.

It should be noted that the execution of the partition clauses for ALTER TABLE is very slow. You may not want to use them with data that is in use if you can avoid it. Instead, you might deploy a method of locking the table to be partitioned for read-only activities, making a copy of the table, partitioning the new table, and switching the new table with the old one, but keeping the old table as a backup copy in case there are problems.

This section includes several examples of partitioning a MyISAM table. The partition clauses are explained as they are used in each example. Partitioning is visible at the filesystem level, so to start, let's look at a table's files:

```
ls -1 clients*

clients.frm
clients.MYD
clients.MYI
```

We used the ls command (because this server is running Linux) at the command line to get a directory listing of the files for the clients table, in the sales_dept database subdirectory, in the data directory for MySQL. You can see the usual three file types for a MyISAM table.

The PARTITION BY clause can be used to initially partition a table with the ALTER TABLE statement. Any partition options used with the same clause in the CREATE TABLE statement may be used in ALTER TABLE. See the definition of the CREATE TABLE statement later in this chapter for more options.

In the following example, we alter the table `clients` using this clause to create partitions:

```
ALTER TABLE clients
PARTITION BY KEY(client_id)
PARTITIONS 2;
```

In this statement, we are instructing MySQL to partition the given table by the `KEY` method using the `client_id` column. We further tell it to split the table into two partitions. Now, let's run the `ls` command again to see the results at the filesystem level:

```
ls -1 clients*

clients.frm
clients.par
clients#P#p0.MYD
clients#P#p0.MYI
clients#P#p1.MYD
clients#P#p1.MYI
```

As you can see, we now have a pair of index and datafiles for each partition, along with another file related to the partition schema (i.e., the *.par* file). The table schema file (i.e., the *.frm* file) remains unchanged.

The `ADD PARTITION` clause adds a new partition to a table in which partitions are determined based on a range of values. To demonstrate this, let's partition the `clients` table again, but this time we'll base the partitioning on a range of values for the `client_id` column, the primary key. If a table has a primary key, that key must be included in the basis of the partitions:

```
ALTER TABLE clients
ADD PARTITION (PARTITION p2);
```

The `REMOVE PARTITIONING` clause removes partitioning from a table. It shifts data back to one datafile and one index file. Here is an example of its use:

```
ALTER TABLE clients
REMOVE PARTITIONING;
```

For some situations, the `ADD PARTITION` clause discussed previously won't work. In particular, it won't work with a table in which the last partition was given the range of `MAXVALUE`:

```
ALTER TABLE clients
PARTITION BY RANGE (client_id) (
PARTITION p0 VALUES LESS THAN (400),
PARTITION p1 VALUES LESS THAN MAXVALUE);

ALTER TABLE clients
ADD PARTITION (PARTITION p2 VALUES LESS THAN (800));

ERROR 1481 (HY000):
VALUES LESS THAN value must be strictly increasing for each partition
```

Instead of `ADD PARTITION`, the `REORGANIZE PARTITION` clause can be used to split the data contained in the last partition into two separate partitions. This clause can be used to separate the data in an existing partition into multiple partitions based on their given partition definitions.

Here is an example of this clause using the partitions previously described:

```
ALTER TABLE clients
REORGANIZE PARTITION p1 INTO
(PARTITION p1 VALUES LESS THAN (800),
PARTITION p2 VALUES LESS THAN MAXVALUE);
```

When experimenting with an empty table, this SQL statement takes my server 10 seconds to execute. Consider this when using this clause or any partitioning clauses with ALTER TABLE.

The DROP PARTITION clause may be used to eliminate named partitions in an existing table and to delete the data contained in the dropped partitions. To reduce the number of partitions without loss of data, see the COALESCE PARTITION clause for this same SQL statement. For an example of the DROP PARTITION clause, if you have a table that has six partitions and you want to delete two of them, you could execute an SQL statement like the second one here:

```
CREATE TABLE clients
(client_id INT,
name VARCHAR(255))
PARTITION BY RANGE (client_id) (
PARTITION p0 VALUES LESS THAN (400),
PARTITION p1 VALUES LESS THAN (800),
PARTITION p2 VALUES LESS THAN (1000),
PARTITION p3 VALUES LESS THAN MAXVALUE);

ALTER TABLE clients
DROP PARTITION p1, p2;
```

Notice that the ALTER TABLE statement is dropping two middle partitions and not the last one. The data contained in the two dropped would be lost if they had any. Because of the MAXVALUE parameter of the last partition, any new rows of data that have a client_id of 400 or greater will be stored in the p3 partition. Partitions need to be in order, but not sequentially named.

The COALESCE PARTITION clause may be used to reduce the number of partitions in an existing table by the number given. For example, if you have a table that has four partitions and you want to reduce it to three, you could execute a statement like the ALTER TABLE one here:

```
CREATE TABLE clients
(client_id INT,
name VARCHAR(255))
PARTITION BY HASH( client_id )
PARTITIONS 4;

ALTER TABLE clients
COALESCE PARTITION 1;
```

Notice that the PARTITION keyword in this last SQL statement is not plural. Also notice that you give the number of partitions by which you want to reduce the partitions, not the total you want. If you give a value equal to or greater than the number of partitions in the table, you'll receive an error instructing you that you must use DROP TABLE instead.

See the CREATE TABLE statement explanation for more information about table partitioning.

ALTER TABLE: Partition administration clauses

```
ALTER [IGNORE] TABLE table
ANALYZE PARTITION partition |
CHECK PARTITION partition |
OPTIMIZE PARTITION partition |
REBUILD PARTITION partition |
REPAIR PARTITION partition
```

Because the `ANALYZE TABLE`, `CHECK TABLE`, `OPTIMIZE TABLE`, and `REPAIR TABLE` statements do not work with partitioned tables, you will have to use the clauses of `ALTER TABLE` in this subsection instead. They all follow the same syntax format: the clause is followed by a comma-separated list of partitions to be administered.

The `ANALYZE PARTITION` clause may be used to read and store the indexes of a partition:

```
ALTER TABLE clients
ANALYZE PARTITION p0, p1, p2;
```

To check a partition for corrupted data and indexes, use the `CHECK PARTITION` clause:

```
ALTER TABLE clients
CHECK PARTITION p0, p1, p2;
```

Use the `OPTIMIZE PARTITION` clause to compact a partition in which the data has changed significantly:

```
ALTER TABLE clients
OPTIMIZE PARTITION p0, p1, p2;
```

The `REBUILD PARTITION` clause defragments the given partitions:

```
ALTER TABLE clients
REBUILD PARTITION p0, p1, p2;
```

The `REPAIR PARTITION` clause attempts to repair corrupted partitions, similar to the `REPAIR TABLE` statement for tables:

```
ALTER TABLE clients
REPAIR PARTITION p0, p1, p2;
```

See the `CREATE TABLE` statement explanation for more information about table partitioning.

ALTER TABLE: Table options

```
ALTER TABLE table
[TABLESPACE tablespace_name STORAGE DISK]
   {ENGINE|TYPE} [=] {BDB|HEAP|ISAM|INNODB|MERGE|MRG_MYISAM|MYISAM} |
AUTO_INCREMENT [=] value |
AVG_ROW_LENGTH [=] value |
[DEFAULT] CHARACTER SET character_set |
CHECKSUM [=] {0|1} |
CONNECTION [=] 'string' |
COLLATE collation |
COMMENT [=] 'string' |
DATA DIRECTORY [=] '/path' |
ENGINE [=] engine |
INDEX DIRECTORY [=] '/path' |
INSERT_METHOD [=] {NO|FIRST|LAST } |
```

```
KEY_BLOCK_SIZE [=] value |
MAX_ROWS [=] value |
MIN_ROWS [=] value |
PACK_KEYS [=] {0|1|DEFAULT} |
DELAY_KEY_WRITE [=] {0|1} |
ROW_FORMAT [=] {DEFAULT|DYNAMIC|FIXED|COMPRESSED|REDUNDANT|COMPACT} |
RAID_TYPE = {1|STRIPED|RAID0} |
UNION [=] (table[,...])
```

This subsection lists all of the table options that can be set with the `ALTER TABLE` statement. The options are the same as those that can be specified for `CREATE TABLE` when a table is first created. (See the description of that statement in this chapter for more information about the options available.) You can give multiple options to `ALTER TABLE` in a comma-separated list.

To change the starting point for an `AUTO_INCREMENT` column, enter the following statement:

```
ALTER TABLE clients
AUTO_INCREMENT = 1000;
```

This statement sets the value of the primary key column to 1,000 so that the next row inserted will be 1,001. You cannot set it to a value less than the highest data value that already exists for the column.

For large tables, you may want to set the average row length for better table optimization by using the `AVG_ROW_LENGTH` option. The following example uses the `SHOW TABLE STATUS` statement to see the average row length for a table similar to the one we want to alter, to get an idea of what the average row length should be:

```
SHOW TABLE STATUS LIKE 'sales' \G

*************************** 1. row ***************************
           Name: sales
         Engine: MyISAM
        Version: 10
     Row_format: Dynamic
           Rows: 93
 Avg_row_length: 12638
    Data_length: 1175412
Max_data_length: 281474976710655
   Index_length: 706560
      Data_free: 0
 Auto_increment: 113
    Create_time: 2007-05-02 14:27:59
    Update_time: 2007-05-03 13:57:05
     Check_time: NULL
      Collation: latin1_swedish_ci
       Checksum: NULL
 Create_options:
        Comment:

ALTER TABLE clients
AVG_ROW_LENGTH = 12638;
```

In the second SQL statement we've set the average row length value of the `clients` table.

The CHARACTER SET option sets the character set to use for character data in the table. The DEFAULT flag is not required. This option is typically used along with the COLLATE option. These options do not affect columns for which the character set and collation are explicitly specified. Use the SHOW CHARACTER SET and SHOW COLLATION statements to see the character sets and collations available:

```
ALTER TABLE clients
DEFAULT CHARACTER SET 'latin2'
COLLATE 'latin2_general_ci';
```

The CHECKSUM option enables or disables a checksum for a table. Set the value to 0 to disable a checksum or 1 to enable checksum. If you upgrade a table that uses a checksum and was created prior to version 4.1 of MySQL, the table may be corrupted in the process. Try using REPAIR TABLE to recalculate the checksum for the table:

```
ALTER TABLE clients
CHECKSUM = 0;
```

The COLLATE option sets the collation to use with the data in the table (that is, how the character data is alphabetized). This option is typically used along with the CHARACTER SET option. These options do not affect columns for which the collation and character sets are explicitly specified. Use the SHOW CREATE TABLE statement to see the collation and character set for the table and its columns:

```
ALTER TABLE clients
COLLATE 'latin2_general_ci'
DEFAULT CHARACTER SET 'latin2';
```


With the COMMENT option, you can add notes for yourself or other table administrators regarding a table:

```
ALTER TABLE clients
MAX_ROWS = 1000,
COMMENT = 'This table lists basic information on clients.';

SHOW CREATE TABLE clients \G

*************************** 1. row ***************************
       Table: clients
Create Table: CREATE TABLE 'clients' (
  'client_id' int(11) NOT NULL AUTO_INCREMENT,
  'client_name' varchar(255) DEFAULT NULL, ...
  PRIMARY KEY ('client_id'),
  KEY 'client_index' ('client_name'(10),'city'(5)) USING BTREE
) ENGINE=MyISAM
AUTO_INCREMENT=1001
DEFAULT CHARSET=latin1 MAX_ROWS=1000
COMMENT='This table lists basic information on clients.'
```

I've shortened the results shown here to save space and to focus on the options. SHOW CREATE TABLE is the only method for viewing the table options in MySQL. They will not be shown with DESCRIBE.

The CONNECTION option is provided for tables that use the FEDERATED storage engine. Previously, you would use the COMMENT option to specify this option. The syntax for this option is:

```
CONNECTION='mysql://username:password@hostname:port/database/tablename'
```

The password and port are optional.

If you wish to federate an existing table with a remote table, you can alter the table on your system to specify the connection to the remote table like this:

```
ALTER TABLE clients
CONNECTION='mysql://russell:rover123@santa_clara_svr:9306/federated/clients';
```

The `DATA DIRECTORY` option is theoretically used to see the data directory path for the table. However, MySQL currently ignores the option:

```
ALTER TABLE clients
DATA DIRECTORY = '/data/mysql/clients';
```

Use the `ENGINE` option to change the storage engine (formerly known as the *table type*) for the table given. Be careful using this option as it may cause problems with data. Make a backup of your table and data before using it. As of version 5.1.11 of MySQL, this option cannot be used to change a table to the BLACKHOLE or MERGE storage engines:

```
ALTER TABLE clients
ENGINE = INNODB;
```

This statement changes the storage engine used for the given table to InnoDB. If a table has special requirements that the new engine cannot provide, you'll receive an error when trying to make this change and the statement will fail. For instance, a MyISAM table that has `FULLTEXT` indexes could not be changed to InnoDB since it doesn't support that kind of indexing. Instead, create a new table using the desired storage engine, migrate the data to the new table, and then drop the old table after verifying the integrity of the data.

The `INDEX DIRECTORY` option is theoretically used to see the directory path for the table indexes. However, MySQL currently ignores the option:

```
ALTER TABLE clients
INDEX DIRECTORY = '/data/mysql/clients_index';
```

To insert data into a `MERGE` table, you will need to specify the insert method it will use. To specify or change this method, use the `INSERT_METHOD` option with the `ALTER TABLE` statement. A value of `FIRST` indicates that the first table should be used; `LAST` indicates the last table should be used; `NO` disables inserts:

```
CREATE TABLE sales_national
(order_id INT, sales_total INT)
ENGINE = MERGE
UNION = (sales_east, sales_west)
INSERT_METHOD = LAST;

ALTER TABLE sales_national
INSERT_METHOD = FIRST;
```

In the first SQL statement here, we create the table `sales_national` based on two other tables and specify that inserts use the last table in the list of tables given. In the second SQL statement, we change the insert method.

To give the storage engine a hint of the size of index key blocks, use the `KEY_BLOCK_SIZE` option. Set the value to 0 to instruct the engine to use the default. This option was added in version 5.1.10 of MySQL:

```
ALTER TABLE clients
KEY_BLOCK_SIZE = 1024;
```

The MAX_ROWS and MIN_ROWS options are used to set the maximum and minimum rows of a table, respectively. Use the SHOW CREATE TABLE statement to see the results of these options:

```
ALTER TABLE clients
MIN_ROWS = 100,
MAX_ROWS = 1000;
```

For small MyISAM tables in which users primarily read the data and rarely update it, you can use the PACK_KEYS option to pack the indexes. This will make reads faster but updates slower. Set the value of this option to 1 to enable packing and 0 to disable it. A value of DEFAULT instructs the storage engine to pack CHAR or VARCHAR data type columns only:

```
ALTER TABLE clients
PACK_KEYS = 1;
```

The DELAY_KEY_WRITE option delays updates of indexes until the table is closed. It's enabled with a value of 1, disabled with 0:

```
ALTER TABLE clients
DELAY_KEY_WRITE = 1;
```

The ROW_FORMAT option instructs the storage engine how to store rows of data. With MyISAM, a value of DYNAMIC (i.e., variable length) or FIXED may be given. If you use the utility **myisampack** on a MyISAM table, the format will be set to a value of COMPRESSED. You can change a compressed MyISAM to uncompressed by giving a value of REDUNDANT. This is deprecated, though. InnoDB tables use the COMPACT method, but offer a REDUNDANT method to be compatible with a more wasteful format used in older versions of InnoDB:

```
ALTER TABLE clients
ROW_FORMAT = FIXED;
```

The RAID_TYPE option is used to specify the type of Redundant Arrays of Independent Disks (RAID) to be used. However, support for RAID has been removed from MySQL as of version 5.0. This SQL statement is also used to permit the options RAID_CHUNKS and RAID_CHUNKSIZE. They have been deprecated, as well.

For MERGE tables in which you want to change the tables that make up the merged table, use the UNION option:

```
ALTER TABLE sales_national
UNION = (sales_north, sales_south, sales_east, sales_west);
```

See the CREATE TABLE statement later in this chapter for more information and examples regarding many of the options for the ALTER TABLE statement.

ALTER VIEW

```
ALTER
  [ALGORITHM = {UNDEFINED|MERGE|TEMPTABLE}]
  [DEFINER = {'user'@'host'|CURRENT_USER}]
  [SQL SECURITY {DEFINER|INVOKER }]
VIEW view [(column, ...)]
```

Database & Table Schema

```
AS SELECT...
[WITH [CASCADED|LOCAL] CHECK OPTION]
```

Use this statement to change a view. Views are available as of version 5.0.1 of MySQL.

The statement is used primarily to change the SELECT statement that determines the view, which you can do simply by placing the new SELECT statement for the view after the AS keyword.

Change the column names provided by the view queries by providing the new column names in a comma-separated list within the parentheses following the view's name. Don't include either the old SELECT statement or the old column names in the statement.

The ALGORITHM parameter changes algorithmic methods to use for processing a view: the choices are MERGE or TEMPTABLE. TEMPTABLE prevents a view from being updatable.

The DEFINER clause can change the user account considered to be the view's creator. This clause is available as of version 5.1.2 of MySQL. The same version introduced the related SQL SECURITY clause. It instructs MySQL to authorize access to the view based on the privileges of either the user account of the view's creator (DEFINER) or the user account of the user who is querying the view (INVOKER). This can help prevent some users from accessing restricted views.

The WITH CHECK OPTION clause can change the restrictions on the updating of a view to only rows in which the WHERE clause of the underlying SELECT statement returns true. For a view that is based on another view, if you include the LOCAL keyword, this restriction will be limited to the view in which it's given and not the underlying view. If you specify CASCADED instead, underlying views will be considered as well.

Here is an example of this statement's use:

```
ALTER VIEW student_directory(ID, Name, Cell_Telephone, Home_Telephone)
AS SELECT student_id,
CONCAT(name_first, SPACE(1), name_last),
phone_dorm, phone_home
FROM students;
```

If you look at the example for CREATE VIEW later in this chapter, you'll see that we're adding an extra column to the view created in that example. The other settings remain unchanged.

You cannot change the name of an existing view. Instead, use the DROP VIEW statement and then create a new view with the CREATE VIEW statement.

CREATE DATABASE

CREATE {DATABASE|SCHEMA} [IF NOT EXISTS] *database* [*options*]

This statement creates a new database with the name given. As of version 5.0.2 of MySQL, the keyword DATABASE is synonymous with SCHEMA wherever used in any SQL statement. You can use the IF NOT EXISTS flag to suppress an error message when the statement fails if a database with the same name already exists.

A database name cannot be longer than 64 bytes (not characters) in size. The system uses Unicode (UTF-8), so any character that is part of the UTF-8 character set may be used. The name cannot be the ASCII value of 0 (0x00) or 255 (0xff)—these are reserved. Database names should not include single or double quotation marks or end with a space.

If you want a database name to include quotes, though, you will have to enable the SQL mode of `ANSI_QUOTES`. This can be done with the `--sql-mode` server option. As of version 5.1.6 of MySQL, database names can contain backslashes, forward slashes, periods, and other characters that may not be permitted in a directory name at the filesystem level. If you use a name that is a reserved word, you must always enclose it in quotes when referring to it.

Special characters in the name are encoded in the filesystem names. If you upgrade your system to a new version of MySQL and you have a database that has special characters in its name, the database will be displayed with a prefix of `#mysql50#`. For instance, a database named `human-resources` will be displayed as `#mysql50#human-resources`. You won't be able to access this database. Don't try to change the name from within MySQL, as you may destroy data. Instead, there are a couple of methods you can use. One is to shut down MySQL, go to the MySQL data directory, and rename the subdirectory that contains the database to a name without the unacceptable character (e.g., from `human-resources` to `human_resources`) and then restart MySQL. Another method would be to use the `mysqlcheck` utility, like so:

```
mysqlcheck --check-upgrade --fix-db-names
```

The `--fix-db-names` option was added in version 5.1.7 of MySQL. For more options with this utility, see Chapter 16.

As of version 4.1.1, a *db.opt* file is added to the filesystem subdirectory created for the database in the MySQL server's data directory. This file contains a couple of settings for the database. You can specify these settings as options to this SQL statement in a comma-separated list.

Currently, two options are available: `CHARACTER SET` and `COLLATE`. Here is an example of how you can create a database with both of these options:

```
CREATE DATABASE sales_prospects
CHARACTER SET latin1
COLLATE latin1_bin;
```

There is no equals sign before the value given for each option and no comma between the first and second option. Here are the contents of the *db.opt* file created for this statement:

```
default-character-set=latin1
default-collation=latin1_bin
```

For a list of character sets available on your system, use the `SHOW CHARACTER SET` statement. For a list of collation possibilities, use the `SHOW COLLATION` statement. MySQL occasionally adds new character sets and collations to new versions of MySQL. If you need one of the new ones, you'll have to upgrade your server to the new version.

Database & Table Schema

CREATE INDEX

```
CREATE [UNIQUE|FULLTEXT|SPATIAL] INDEX index
[USING type|TYPE type]
[USING type|TYPE type]
ON table (column [(length)] [ASC|DESC], ...)
```

Use this statement to add an index to a table after it has been created. This is an alias of the clause of the ALTER TABLE statement that adds an index. You can add indexes only to MyISAM, InnoDB, and BDB types of tables. You can also create these tables with indexes, as shown in the CREATE TABLE statement later in this chapter.

To prevent duplicates, add the UNIQUE flag between the CREATE keyword and INDEX. Only columns with CHAR, TEXT, and VARCHAR data types of MyISAM tables can be indexed with FULLTEXT indexes.

Creating UNIQUE indexes

CREATE UNIQUE INDEX *index*
ON *table* (*column*, ...)

After the INDEX keyword, the name of the index or key is given. This name can be the same as one of the columns indexed, or a totally new name.

You can specify the type of index with the USING keyword. For MyISAM and InnoDB tables, BTREE is the default, but RTREE is also available as of version 5.0 of MySQL. The TYPE keyword is an alias for USING.

For wide columns, it may be advantageous to specify a maximum number of characters to use from a column for indexing. This can speed up indexing and reduce the size of index files on the filesystem.

Although there is an ASC option for sorting indexes in ascending order and a DESC option for sorting in descending order, these are for a future release of MySQL. All indexes are currently sorted in ascending order. Additional columns for indexing may be given within the parentheses:

```
CREATE UNIQUE INDEX client_name
ON clients (client_lastname, client_firstname(4), rec_date);
```

In this example, an index is created called client_name. It is based on the last names of clients, the first four letters of their first names, and the dates that the records were created. This index is based on it being unlikely that a record would be created on the same day for two people with the same last name and a first name starting with the same four letters.

To see the indexes that have been created for a table, use the SHOW INDEXES statement. To remove an index, use the DROP INDEX statement.

Creating FULLTEXT indexes

CREATE FULLTEXT INDEX *index*
ON *table* (*column*, ...)

After the INDEX keyword, the name of the index or key is given. This name can be the same as one of the columns indexed or a totally new name.

You can specify the type of index with the USING keyword. For MyISAM and InnoDB tables, BTREE is the default, but RTREE is also available as of version 5.0 of MySQL. The TYPE keyword is an alias for USING.

For wide columns, it may be advantageous to specify a maximum number of characters to use from a column for indexing. This can speed up indexing and reduce the size of index files on the filesystem.

Although there is an ASC option for sorting indexes in ascending order and a DESC option for sorting in descending order, these are for a future release of MySQL. All indexes are currently sorted in ascending order. Additional columns for indexing may be given within the parentheses:

```
CREATE FULLTEXT INDEX client_notes
ON clients (business_description, comments);
```

In this example, an index is created called `client_notes`. It is based on two columns, both of which are TEXT columns.

To see the indexes that have been created for a table, use the SHOW INDEXES statement. To remove an index, use the DROP INDEX statement.

Creating SPATIAL indexes

```
CREATE SPATIAL INDEX index
ON table (column, ...)
```

SPATIAL indexes can index spatial columns only in MyISAM tables. This is available starting with version 4.1 of MySQL. Here is an example in which first a table and then a spatial index is created:

```
CREATE TABLE squares
(square_id INT, square_name VARCHAR(100),
square_points POLYGON NOT NULL);

CREATE SPATIAL INDEX square_index
ON squares (square_points);
```

Notice that when we create the table, we specify that the column square_points is NOT NULL. This is required to be able to index the column. Let's insert two rows of data:

```
INSERT INTO squares
VALUES(1000, 'Red Square',
(GeomFromText('MULTIPOLYGON(((0 0, 0 3, 3 3, 3 0, 0 0)))')) ),
(1000, 'Green Square',
(GeomFromText('MULTIPOLYGON(((3 3, 3 5, 5 5, 4 3, 3 3)))')) );
```

Here we added two squares by giving the five points of the polygon: the starting point (e.g., for the first row, x=0, y=0), the left top point (x=0, y=3), the right top point (x=3, y=3), the right bottom point (x=3, y=0), and the ending point (x=0, y=0) for good measure, which is the same as the starting point. So, the first row contains a square that is 3 × 3 in size, and the second contains a square that is 2 × 2 in size. Using the AREA( ) function we can find the area of each:

```
SELECT square_name AS 'Square',
AREA(square_points) AS 'Area of Square'
FROM squares;

+--------------+----------------+
| Square       | Area of Square |
+--------------+----------------+
| Red Square   |              9 |
| Green Square |              3 |
+--------------+----------------+
```


Database & Table Schema

If we want to find which square contains a given point on a Cartesian plane (e.g., x=1, y=2), we can use the `MBRContains( )` function like so:

```
SELECT square_name
FROM squares
WHERE
MBRContains(square_points, GeomFromText('POINT(1 2)'));

+-------------+
| square_name |
+-------------+
| Red Square  |
+-------------+
```

To see how the index we added is involved, we would run an `EXPLAIN` statement using the same `SELECT` statement:

```
EXPLAIN SELECT square_name
FROM squares
WHERE
MBRContains(square_points, GeomFromText('POINT(1 2)')) \G

*************************** 1. row ***************************
           id: 1
  select_type: SIMPLE
        table: squares
         type: range
possible_keys: square_index
          key: square_index
      key_len: 32
          ref: NULL
         rows: 1
        Extra: Using where
```

Notice that the SQL statement is using the `square_index` spatial index that we created.

CREATE SCHEMA

```
CREATE {DATABASE|SCHEMA} [IF NOT EXISTS] database [options]
```

This statement is synonymous with `CREATE DATABASE`. See the description of that statement earlier in this chapter for more information and examples.

CREATE SERVER

```
CREATE SERVER server
FOREIGN DATA WRAPPER wrapper
OPTIONS (
  { DATABASE database, |
    HOST host, |
    USER user, |
    PASSWORD password, |
    SOCKET socket, |
    OWNER character, |
```

```
    PORT port }
)
```

Use this SQL statement with the FEDERATED storage engine to set the connection parameters. The values given are stored in the mysql database, in the server table, in a new row. The server name given cannot exceed 63 characters, and it's not case-sensitive. The only wrapper permitted at this time is mysql. Options are given in a comma-separated list. You're not required to specify all options listed in the example syntax. If an option is not given, the default will be an empty string. To change options after a server has been created, use the ALTER SERVER statement, described earlier in this chapter. For option values, character or numeric literals (UTF-8; maximum length of 64 characters) must be given. This statement was introduced in version 5.1.15 of MySQL and requires SUPER privileges.

The host may be a hostname or an IP address. The username and password given are those that are required for accessing the server. Provide either the name of the socket or the port to use for connecting to the server. The owner is the filesystem username to use for accessing the server:

```
CREATE SERVER server1
FOREIGN DATA WRAPPER mysql
OPTIONS (USER 'russell', HOST 'dyerhouse.com', DATABASE 'db1', PORT 3306,
   OWNER 'root');

CREATE TABLE table1 (col1 INT)
ENGINE = FEDERATED CONNECTION='server1';
```

Database & Table Schema

CREATE TABLE

```
CREATE [TEMPORARY] TABLE [IF NOT EXISTS] table
{[(definition)][options]|[[AS] SELECT...]|[LIKE table]}
```

Use this statement to create a new table within a database. This statement has many clauses and options; however, when creating a basic table, you can omit most of them. The TEMPORARY keyword is used to create a temporary table that can be accessed only by the current connection thread and is not accessible by other users. The IF NOT EXISTS flag is used to suppress error messages caused by attempting to create a table by the same name as an existing one. After the table name is given, either the table definition is given (i.e., a list of columns and their data types) along with table options or properties, or a table can be created based on another table. The subsections that follow describe how to:

- Set column properties regarding NULL and default values (see the "CREATE TABLE: Column flags" subsection)
- Create an index for a table based on one or more columns (see the "CREATE TABLE: Index and key definitions" subsection)
- Reference a foreign key constraint (see the "CREATE TABLE: Foreign key references" subsection)
- Specify various table options (see the "CREATE TABLE: Table options" subsection)
- Create a table exactly like another table (see the "CREATE TABLE: Based on an existing table" subsection)

- Create a table with filesystem partitions (see the three subsections on partitioning: "CREATE TABLE: Partitioning," "CREATE TABLE: Partition definitions," and "CREATE TABLE: Subpartition definitions")

Here is a simple example of how you can use the `CREATE TABLE` statement:

```
CREATE TABLE clients
(client_id INT AUTO_INCREMENT PRIMARY KEY,
client_name VARCHAR(75),
telephone CHAR(15));
```

This creates a table with three columns. The first column is called `client_id` and may contain integers. It will be incremented automatically as records are created. It will also be the primary key field for records, which means that no duplicates are allowed and the rows will be indexed based on this column. The second column, `client_name`, is a variable-width, character-type column with a maximum width of 75 characters. The third column is called `telephone` and is a fixed-width, character-type column with a minimum and maximum width of 15 characters. To see the results of this statement, you can use the `DESCRIBE` statement. There are many column data types. They're all listed and described in Appendix A.

CREATE TABLE: Column flags

```
CREATE [TEMPORARY] TABLE [IF NOT EXISTS] table
(column type[(width)] [ASC|DESC] [NOT NULL|NULL] [DEFAULT value]
   [AUTO_INCREMENT] [[PRIMARY] KEY]|[[UNIQUE] KEY]
   [COMMENT 'string']
   [REFERENCES table [(column,...)]
      [MATCH FULL|MATCH PARTIAL|MATCH SIMPLE]
      [ON DELETE [RESTRICT|CASCADE|SET NULL|NO ACTION]]
      [ON UPDATE [RESTRICT|CASCADE|SET NULL|NO ACTION]] [,...]
   ]
[,...]) [options]
```

This is the syntax for the `CREATE TABLE` statement again, but detailing the column flags portion of the column definition. For some column types, you may need to specify the size of the column within parentheses after the column name and column type.

If a column is indexed, the keyword `ASC` or `DESC` may be given next to indicate whether indexes should be stored in ascending or descending order, respectively. By default, they are stored in ascending order. For older versions of MySQL, these flags are ignored. Adding the `NOT NULL` flag indicates the column may not be NULL. The `NULL` flag may be given to state that a NULL value is allowed. Some data types are NULL by default. For some, you don't have a choice whether a column may be NULL or not. To set a default value for a column, you can use the `DEFAULT` keyword. For some data types (e.g., `TIMESTAMP`), a default value is not allowed. The `AUTO_INCREMENT` option tells MySQL to assign a unique identification number automatically to a column. It must be designated as a `PRIMARY` or `UNIQUE` key column, and you cannot have more than one `AUTO_INCREMENT` column in a table. If a column is to be the basis of an index, either `PRIMARY KEY`, `UNIQUE KEY`, `UNIQUE`, or just `KEY` can be given. Just `KEY` indicates the column is a primary key.

To document what you're doing for an administrator or a developer, a comment regarding a column may be given. The results of a `SELECT` statement won't show it, but a `SHOW FULL COLUMNS` statement will reveal it. To add a comment, use the `COMMENT` keyword followed by a string within quotes. Here is an example using some of the flags and clauses mentioned here:

```
CREATE TABLE clients
(client_id INT NOT NULL AUTO_INCREMENT PRIMARY KEY,
client_name VARCHAR(75),
client_city VARCHAR(50) DEFAULT 'New Orleans',
telephone CHAR(15) COMMENT 'Format: ###-###-####');
```

In this example, the `client_id` column is a primary key. The `NOT NULL` option is included for completeness, even though it's not necessary, because a primary key must be unique and non-NULL. For the `client_city` column, the `DEFAULT` clause is used to provide the default value of the column. The default will be used during inserts when no value is given, although you can override the default by specifying an explicit blank value for the column. This statement also includes a comment regarding the typical format for entering telephone numbers in the `telephone` column. Again, this will be displayed only with the `SHOW FULL COLUMNS` statement.

For information on the `REFERENCES` column flag, see the "CREATE TABLE: Foreign key references" subsection later in this section.

CREATE TABLE: Index and key definitions

```
CREATE [TEMPORARY] TABLE [IF NOT EXISTS] table
(column, ..., index type[(width)] [ASC|DESC] |
[CONSTRAINT [symbol]] PRIMARY KEY [type] (column,...)
   [KEY_BLOCK_SIZE value|type|WITH PARSER parser] |
INDEX|[PRIMARY] KEY [index] [type] (column,...)
   [KEY_BLOCK_SIZE value|type|WITH PARSER parser] |
[CONSTRAINT [symbol]] UNIQUE [INDEX] [index] [type] (column,...)
   [KEY_BLOCK_SIZE value|type|WITH PARSER parser] |
[FULLTEXT|SPATIAL] [INDEX] [index] (column,...)
   [KEY_BLOCK_SIZE value|type|WITH PARSER parser] |
[CONSTRAINT [symbol]] FOREIGN KEY [index] (column,...)
    [reference_definition] |
CHECK (expression)]
[,...]) [options]
```

You can use one or more columns for an index, and a table can contain multiple indexes. Indexes can greatly increase the speed of data retrieval from a table. You can define an index involving multiple columns with this statement, or later with the `ALTER TABLE` statement or the `CREATE INDEX` statement. With the `CREATE TABLE` statement, though, indexes can be given after the definition of the columns they index.

A `KEY` (also called a `PRIMARY KEY`) is a particular kind of index obeying certain constraints. It must be unique, for instance. It is often combined in MySQL with the `AUTO_INCREMENT` keyword, and used for identifiers that appear as columns in tables. The general format is to specify the type of index, such as `KEY`, `INDEX`, or `UNIQUE`. This is followed by the index name. Optionally, the index type may be specified with the `USING` keyword. For most tables, there is only one type of index, so this is unnecessary.

Before version 5 of MySQL, `BTREE` is the only type for MyISAM tables. Beginning with version 5, the `RTREE` index type is also available, so you may want to specify the index type. After the index type, one or more columns on which the index is based are listed within parentheses, separated by commas. Before explaining the various possibilities, let's look at an example:

```
CREATE TABLE clients
(client_id INT AUTO_INCREMENT KEY,
name_last VARCHAR(50), name_first VARCHAR(50),
telephone CHAR(15),
INDEX names USING BTREE (name_last(5), name_first(5) DESC));
```

The client_id column here is a PRIMARY KEY, although that clause has been abbreviated to just KEY. This abbreviation is available as of version 4.1 of MySQL. There can be only one PRIMARY KEY but any number of other indexes. The table contains a second index using the first five characters of the two name columns. To specify a combination, the index definition is generally given at the end of the table's column definitions with the INDEX keyword. The index is named names in the example.

After the index name, the USING clause specifies the type of index to be used. Currently, this is unnecessary because BTREE is the default type for a MyISAM table.

Next, the two columns to index appear within parentheses. The name columns are variable-width columns and 50 characters in length, so to speed up indexing, only the first five characters of each column are used. The name_first column is supposed to be used in descending order per the DESC flag. However, this will be ignored for the current version of MySQL.

The syntax structures for the index clauses listed here vary depending on the type of table index to be created: PRIMARY KEY, INDEX, UNIQUE, FULLTEXT (or BLOB column types), or SPATIAL.

To create constraints on tables based on columns in another table, use the FOREIGN KEY index syntax structures. Foreign keys are used only to link columns in InnoDB tables. The CHECK clause is not used in MySQL but is available for porting to other database systems. Here is an example of how you can use foreign keys to create a table:

```
CREATE TABLE employees
(emp_id INT NOT NULL PRIMARY KEY,
name_last VARCHAR(25), name_first VARCHAR(25))
TYPE = INNODB;

CREATE TABLE programmers
(prog_id INT, emp_id INT,
INDEX (emp_id),
FOREIGN KEY (emp_id) REFERENCES employees(emp_id)
ON DELETE CASCADE)
TYPE=INNODB;
```

The first CREATE TABLE statement creates a table of basic employee information. The second CREATE TABLE statement creates a simple table of programmers. In the employees table, the key column emp_id will be used to identify employees and will be the foreign key for the programmers table. The programmers table sets up an index based on emp_id, which will be tied to the emp_id column in the employees table. The FOREIGN KEY clause establishes this connection using the REFERENCES keyword to indicate the employees table and the key column to use in that table. Additionally, the ON DELETE CASCADE clause instructs MySQL to delete the row in the programmers table whenever an employee record for a programmer is deleted from the employees table.

The next subsection, "CREATE TABLE: Foreign key references," gives the syntax for references to foreign keys and the meaning of each component.

At the end of both of these SQL statements, the storage engine is set to InnoDB with the TYPE clause. The ENGINE keyword could be used instead and would have the same effect.

To give the storage engine a hint of the size of index key blocks, use the KEY_BLOCK_SIZE option. Set the value to 0 to instruct the engine to use the default. This option was added in version 5.1.10 of MySQL.

The WITH PARSER clause may be used to give a parser plugin for an index. This is used only with FULLTEXT indexes.

CREATE TABLE: Foreign key references

```
CREATE [TEMPORARY] TABLE [IF NOT EXISTS] table
(column, ..., index type[(width)] [ASC|DESC]
[CONSTRAINT [symbol]] FOREIGN KEY [index] (column,...)
REFERENCES table [(column,...)]
   [MATCH FULL|MATCH PARTIAL|MATCH SIMPLE]
   [ON DELETE [RESTRICT|CASCADE|SET NULL|NO ACTION]]
   [ON UPDATE [RESTRICT|CASCADE|SET NULL|NO ACTION]]
[,...]) [options]
```

This subsection describes the REFERENCES options to the FOREIGN KEY clause, which creates a relationship between an index and another table. This information also applies to the REFERENCES column flag (see the earlier subsection "CREATE TABLE: Column flags").

The MATCH FULL clause requires that the reference match on the full width of each column indexed. In contrast, MATCH PARTIAL allows the use of partial columns. Partial columns can accelerate indexing when the first few characters of a column determine that a row is unique.

The ON DELETE clause instructs MySQL to react to deletions of matching rows from the foreign table according to the option that follows. The ON UPDATE clause causes MySQL to respond to updates made to the referenced table according to the options that follow it. You can use both clauses in the same CREATE TABLE statement.

The RESTRICT keyword option instructs MySQL not to allow the deletion or update (depending on the clause in which it's used) of the rows in the foreign table if rows in the current table are linked to them. The CASCADE keyword says that when deleting or updating the rows that are referenced in the parent table, delete or update the related rows in the child table accordingly (as in the last example of the previous subsection).

SET NULL causes MySQL to change the data contained in the related columns to a NULL value. For this to work, the column in the child table must allow NULL values. The NO ACTION setting has MySQL not react to deletions or updates with regard to the referencing table.

CREATE TABLE: Table options

```
CREATE [TEMPORARY] TABLE [IF NOT EXISTS] table
(column, ..., index type[(width)] [ASC|DESC]
[TABLESPACE tablespace_name STORAGE DISK]
   {ENGINE|TYPE} [=] {BDB|HEAP|ISAM|INNODB|MERGE|MRG_MYISAM|MYISAM} |
AUTO_INCREMENT [=] value |
AVG_ROW_LENGTH [=] value |
[DEFAULT] CHARACTER SET character_set |
```

```
CHECKSUM [=] {0|1} |
CONNECTION [=] 'string' |
COLLATE collation |
COMMENT [=] 'string' |
DATA DIRECTORY [=] '/path' |
DELAY_KEY_WRITE [=] {0|1} |
ENGINE [=] engine |
INDEX DIRECTORY [=] '/path' |
INSERT_METHOD [=] {NO|FIRST|LAST } |
KEY_BLOCK_SIZE [=] value |
MAX_ROWS [=] value |
MIN_ROWS [=] value |
PACK_KEYS [=] {0|1|DEFAULT} |
ROW_FORMAT [=] {DEFAULT|DYNAMIC|FIXED|COMPRESSED|REDUNDANT|COMPACT} |
RAID_TYPE = {1|STRIPED|RAID0} |
UNION [=] (table[,...])
```

This subsection lists all of the table options that can be set with the `CREATE TABLE` statement. The options are given after the closing parenthesis for the column definitions. To see the values for an existing table, use the `SHOW TABLE STATUS` statement. To change the values of any options after a table has been created, use the `ALTER TABLE` statement. Each option is explained in the following paragraphs in alphabetical order, as shown in the preceding syntax. Examples of each are also given.

`AUTO_INCREMENT`

This parameter causes MySQL to assign a unique identification number automatically to the column in each row added to the table. By default, the starting number is 1. To set it to a different starting number when creating a table, you can use the `AUTO_INCREMENT` table option. Here's an example using this option:

```
CREATE TABLE clients
(client_id INT AUTO_INCREMENT KEY,
client_name VARCHAR(75),
telephone CHAR(15))
AUTO_INCREMENT=1000;
```

This statement sets the initial value of the primary key column to 1000 so that the first row inserted will be 1001. There is usually no reason to set a starting number explicitly, because the key is used merely to distinguish different columns.

`AVG_ROW_LENGTH`

For large tables, you may want to set the average row length for better table optimization by using the `AVG_ROW_LENGTH` option:

```
CREATE TABLE clients
(client_id INT AUTO_INCREMENT KEY,
client_name VARCHAR(75),
telephone CHAR(15))
AVG_ROW_LENGTH = 12638;
```

`CHARACTER SET`

This option sets the character set used for character data in the table. The `DEFAULT` flag is not required. This option is typically used along with the `COLLATE` option. These options do not affect columns for which the character sets and collation are explicitly specified. Use the `SHOW CHARACTER SET` and `SHOW COLLATION` statements to see the character sets and collations available:

```
CREATE TABLE clients
(client_id INT AUTO_INCREMENT KEY,
client_name VARCHAR(75),
telephone CHAR(15))
DEFAULT CHARACTER SET 'latin2'
COLLATE 'latin2_general_ci';
```

`CHECKSUM`

This option enables or disables a checksum for a table. Set the value to 0 to disable the checksum or to 1 to enable a checksum on a table. If you are upgrading a table that uses a checksum and was created prior to version 4.1 of MySQL, the table may be corrupted in the process. Try using `REPAIR TABLE` to recalculate the checksum for the table:

```
CREATE TABLE clients
(client_id INT AUTO_INCREMENT KEY,
client_name VARCHAR(75),
telephone CHAR(15))
CHECKSUM = 0;
```

`COLLATE`

This option sets the collation (alphabetizing order) to use with character data in the table. This option is typically used along with the `CHARACTER SET` option. These options do not affect columns for which the collation and character sets are explicitly specified. Use the `SHOW CREATE TABLE` statement to see the collation and character set for the table and its columns:

```
CREATE TABLE clients
(client_id INT AUTO_INCREMENT KEY,
client_name VARCHAR(75),
telephone CHAR(15))
COLLATE 'latin2_general_ci'
DEFAULT CHARACTER SET 'latin2';
```

`COMMENT`

With this option, you can add notes for yourself or other table administrators regarding a table. Comments are shown only when the `SHOW CREATE TABLE` statement is executed:

```
CREATE TABLE clients
(client_id INT AUTO_INCREMENT KEY,
client_name VARCHAR(75),
telephone CHAR(15))
COMMENT = 'This table lists basic information on clients.';
```

`CONNECTION`

This option is provided for tables that use the FEDERATED storage engine. Previously, you would use the `COMMENT` option to specify this option. The syntax for this option is:

```
CONNECTION='mysql://username:password@hostname:port/database/tablename'
```

The password and port are optional.

If you want to federate an existing table with a remote table, you can alter the table on your system to specify the connection to the remote table like this:

```
CREATE TABLE clients
(client_id INT AUTO_INCREMENT KEY,
client_name VARCHAR(75),
telephone CHAR(15))
ENGINE = FEDERATED
CONNECTION='mysql://russell:rover123@santa_clara_svr:9306/federated/clients';
```

`DATA DIRECTORY`
: This option is theoretically used to see the data directory path for the table. As of version 5.1.23 of MySQL, this option is ignored for table partitions. Filesystem privileges for the path given are required to specify the option:

```
CREATE TABLE clients
(client_id INT AUTO_INCREMENT KEY,
client_name VARCHAR(75),
telephone CHAR(15))
DATA DIRECTORY = '/data/mysql/clients';
```

`DELAY_KEY_WRITE`
: This option delays index updates until the table is closed. It's enabled with a value of 1 and disabled with a value of 0:

```
CREATE TABLE clients
(client_id INT AUTO_INCREMENT KEY,
client_name VARCHAR(75),
telephone CHAR(15))
DELAY_KEY_WRITE = 1;
```

`ENGINE`
: Use this option to change the storage engine (formerly known as the *table type*) for the table given. Be careful using this option as it may cause problems with data. Make a backup of your table and data before using it. As of version 5.1.11 of MySQL, this option cannot be used to change a table to the BLACKHOLE or MERGE storage engines:

```
CREATE TABLE clients
(client_id INT AUTO_INCREMENT KEY,
client_name VARCHAR(75),
telephone CHAR(15))
ENGINE = MyISAM;
```

`INDEX DIRECTORY`
: This option is theoretically used to see the directory path for the table indexes. As of version 5.1.23 of MySQL, this option is ignored for table partitions. Filesystem privileges for the path given are required to specify the option:

```
CREATE TABLE clients
(client_id INT AUTO_INCREMENT KEY,
client_name VARCHAR(75),
telephone CHAR(15))
INDEX DIRECTORY = '/data/mysql/clients_index';
```

`INSERT_METHOD`
: To insert data into a MERGE table, you need to specify the insert method it will use. To set or change this method, use the `INSERT_METHOD` option with the `CREATE`

TABLE or ALTER TABLE statements. A value of FIRST indicates that the first table should be used; LAST indicates the last table should be used; NO disables insertions:

```
CREATE TABLE sales_national
(order_id INT, sales_total INT)
ENGINE = MERGE
UNION = (sales_east, sales_west)
INSERT_METHOD = LAST;
```

This SQL statement creates the table sales_national based on two other tables while specifying that insertions use the last table in the list of tables given.

KEY_BLOCK_SIZE

This option gives the storage engine a hint of the size of index key blocks. Set the value to 0 to instruct the engine to use the default. This option was added in version 5.1.10 of MySQL:

```
CREATE TABLE clients
(client_id INT AUTO_INCREMENT KEY,
client_name VARCHAR(75),
telephone CHAR(15))
KEY_BLOCK_SIZE = 1024;
```

MAX_ROWS, MIN_ROWS

These options are used to set the maximum and minimum rows of a table, respectively. Use the SHOW CREATE TABLE statement to see the results:

```
CREATE TABLE clients
(client_id INT AUTO_INCREMENT KEY,
client_name VARCHAR(75),
telephone CHAR(15))
MIN_ROWS = 100,
MAX_ROWS = 1000;
```


PACK_KEYS

For small MyISAM tables in which users primarily read the data and rarely update it, you can use the PACK_KEYS option to pack the indexes. This will make reads faster but updates slower. Set the value of this option to 1 to enable packing and 0 to disable it. A value of DEFAULT instructs the storage engine to pack CHAR or VARCHAR data type columns only:

```
CREATE TABLE clients
(client_id INT AUTO_INCREMENT KEY,
client_name VARCHAR(75),
telephone CHAR(15))
PACK_KEYS = 0;
```

RAID_TYPE

This option specifies the type of RAID to be used. However, support for RAID has been removed from MySQL as of version 5.0. This SQL statement also used to permit the options RAID_CHUNKS and RAID_CHUNKSIZE, but they have been deprecated as well.

ROW_FORMAT

This option tells the storage engine how to store rows of data. With MyISAM, a value of DYNAMIC (i.e., variable-length) or FIXED may be given. If you run the myisampack utility on a MyISAM table, the format will be set to a value of

COMPRESSED. You can uncompress a compressed MyISAM table by giving a value of REDUNDANT. This value is deprecated, though. InnoDB tables use the COMPACT method, but offer a REDUNDANT method to be compatible with a more wasteful format used in older versions of InnoDB:

```
CREATE TABLE clients
(client_id INT AUTO_INCREMENT KEY,
client_name VARCHAR(75),
telephone CHAR(15))
ROW_FORMAT = DYNAMIC;
```

UNION

To change the tables that make up a MERGE table, specify the full list of tables using this option:

```
CREATE TABLE sales_national
(order_id INT, sales_total INT)
ENGINE = MERGE
UNION = (sales_north, sales_south, sales_east, sales_west);
```

CREATE TABLE: Partitioning

```
CREATE [TEMPORARY] TABLE [IF NOT EXISTS] table
PARTITION BY
  [LINEAR] HASH(expression) |
  [LINEAR] KEY(columns) |
  RANGE(expression) |
  LIST(expression)
  [PARTITIONS number]
    [SUBPARTITION BY
      [LINEAR] HASH(expression) |
      [LINEAR] KEY(columns)
      [SUBPARTITIONS number]
    ]
  [PARTITION partition
        [VALUES {LESS THAN (expression)|MAXVALUE|IN (values)}]
        [[STORAGE] ENGINE [=] engine]
        [COMMENT [=] 'text' ]
        [DATA DIRECTORY [=] '/path']
        [INDEX DIRECTORY [=] '/path']
        [MAX_ROWS [=] number]
        [MIN_ROWS [=] number]
        [TABLESPACE [=] (tablespace)]
        [NODEGROUP [=] value]

        [(SUBPARTITION logical_name
           [[STORAGE] ENGINE [=] engine]
           [COMMENT [=] 'text' ]
           [DATA DIRECTORY [=] '/path']
           [INDEX DIRECTORY [=] '/path']
           [MAX_ROWS [=] number]
           [MIN_ROWS [=] number]
           [TABLESPACE [=] (tablespace)]
           [NODEGROUP [=] value]
        [, SUBPARTITION...])]
```

```
[, PARTITION...]]
]
```

These table partition clauses may be used in CREATE TABLE to create a table using partitions —that is, to organize data into separate files on the filesystem. This capability was added as of version 5.1.6 of MySQL. To add or alter partitions on an existing table, see the ALTER TABLE statement explanation earlier in this chapter. See that section also for comments on partitions in general. This subsection includes several examples of creating a MyISAM table with partitions.

The PARTITION BY clause is required when partitioning in order to explain how data is split and distributed among partitions. A table cannot have more than 1,024 partitions and subpartitions. The subclauses of PARTITION BY are explained in this subsection, whereas the PARTITION and SUBPARTITION clauses are explained in the next two subsections that cover this statement ("CREATE TABLE: Partition definitions" and "CREATE TABLE: Subpartition definitions"):

HASH
: This subclause creates a key/value pair that controls which partition is used for saving rows of data and for indexing data. The value of the hash consists of the specified columns. If a table has a primary key, that column must be used by the hash. Functions that return a numerical value (not a string) may be used within a hash specification:

```
CREATE TABLE sales_figures
(emp_id INT,
sales_date DATE,
amount INT)
PARTITION BY HASH(MONTH(sales_date))
PARTITIONS 12;
```

This creates 12 partitions, one for each month extracted from the sales_data.

By default, the HASH method and the KEY method (described next) use the modulus of the hash function's given value. The keyword LINEAR may be added in front of HASH or KEY to change the algorithm to a linear powers-of-two algorithm. For extremely large tables of data, the linear hash has higher performance results in processing data, but does not evenly spread data among partitions.

KEY
: This subclause functions the same as HASH except that it accepts only a comma-separated list of columns for indexing and distributing data among partitions. The LINEAR flag may be given to change the algorithm method used. See the previous description for HASH:

```
CREATE TABLE clients
(client_id INT AUTO_INCREMENT KEY,
client_name VARCHAR(75),
telephone CHAR(15))
PARTITION BY KEY (client_id)
PARTITIONS 4;
```

LIST
: This subclause can be used to give specific values for distributing data across partitions. The column and values must all be numeric, not strings:

```
CREATE TABLE sales_figures
(region_id INT, sales_date DATE, amount INT)
PARTITION BY LIST (region_id) (
   PARTITION US_DATA VALUES IN(100,200,300),
   PARTITION EU_DATA VALUES IN(400,500));
```

In this example, data is distributed between two partitions: one for the sales in the United States, which is composed of three regions, and a second partition for data for the two European regions. Notice that the names for the partitions given aren't in the usual naming convention (e.g., p0). Any name will do. It's a matter of preference.

RANGE

To instruct MySQL to distribute data among the partitions based on a range of values, use the RANGE subclause. Use the VALUES LESS THAN subclause to set limits for each range. Use VALUES LESS THAN MAXVALUE to set the limit of the final partition:

```
CREATE TABLE clients
(client_id INT AUTO_INCREMENT KEY,
client_name VARCHAR(75),
telephone CHAR(15))
PARTITION BY RANGE (client_id) (
   PARTITION p0 VALUES LESS THAN (500),
   PARTITION p1 VALUES LESS THAN (1000),
   PARTITION p3 VALUES LESS THAN MAXVALUE);
```

In this example, the data is distributed among the partitions based on the client_id values. The first partition will contain rows with a client identification number less than 500; the second will contain rows of values ranging from 501 to 1000; and the last partition will contain values of 1001 and higher. Values given for partitions must be in ascending order.

See the ALTER TABLE explanation for more information on table partitioning, especially modifying or removing partitioning.

CREATE TABLE: Partition definitions

```
CREATE [TEMPORARY] TABLE [IF NOT EXISTS] table
   PARTITION partition
      [VALUES {LESS THAN (expression) | MAXVALUE | IN (value_list)}]
      [[STORAGE] ENGINE [=] engine]
      [COMMENT [=] 'string' ]
      [DATA DIRECTORY [=] '/path']
      [INDEX DIRECTORY [=] '/path']
      [MAX_ROWS [=] number]
      [MIN_ROWS [=] number]
      [TABLESPACE [=] (tablespace)]
      [NODEGROUP [=] number]
      [(subpartition_definition[, subpartition_definition] ...)]
```

The subclauses described in this subsection define general parameters of partitions, such as their sizes and locations in the filesystems:

COMMENT

Use this subclause if you want to add a comment to a partition. The text must be contained within single quotes. Comments can be viewed only with the SHOW CREATE TABLE statement:

```
CREATE TABLE sales_figures
(region_id INT, sales_date DATE, amount INT)
PARTITION BY LIST (region_id) (
   PARTITION US_DATA VALUES IN(100,200,300)
   COMMENT = 'U.S. Data',
   PARTITION EU_DATA VALUES IN(400,500)
   COMMENT = 'Europe Data');
```

DATA DIRECTORY, INDEX DIRECTORY
: With these subclauses, you can specify file pathnames in order to fix the locations of partitions. The directories given must exist and you must have access privileges to the given directories:

```
CREATE TABLE clients
(client_id INT AUTO_INCREMENT KEY,
client_name VARCHAR(75),
telephone CHAR(15))
PARTITION BY RANGE (client_id) (
   PARTITION p0 VALUES LESS THAN (500)
   DATA DIRECTORY = '/data/mysql/old_clients/data'
   INDEX DIRECTORY = '/data/mysql/old_clients/index',
   PARTITION p1 VALUES LESS THAN MAXVALUE
   DATA DIRECTORY = '/data/mysql/new_clients/data'
   INDEX DIRECTORY = '/data/mysql/new_clients/index');
```

ENGINE
: This subclause specifies an alternative storage engine to use for the partition. However, at this time all partitions must use the same storage engine:

```
CREATE TABLE clients
(client_id INT AUTO_INCREMENT KEY,
client_name VARCHAR(75),
telephone CHAR(15))
PARTITION BY RANGE (client_id) (
   PARTITION p0 VALUES LESS THAN (500)
   ENGINE = InnoDB,
   PARTITION p1 VALUES LESS THAN MAXVALUE
   ENGINE = InnoDB);
```

MAX_ROWS, MIN_ROWS
: These subclauses suggest the maximum and minimum number of rows in a table partition, respectively. MySQL may deviate from these limits, though:

```
CREATE TABLE clients
(client_id INT AUTO_INCREMENT KEY,
client_name VARCHAR(75),
telephone CHAR(15))
PARTITION BY RANGE (client_id) (
   PARTITION p0 VALUES LESS THAN (500)
   MIN_ROWS = 10 MAX_ROWS = 1000,
   PARTITION p3 VALUES LESS THAN MAXVALUE
   MIN_ROWS = 10 MAX_ROWS = 500);
```

NODEGROUP
: This subclause can be used only with MySQL Cluster, and places a partition in the given node group. (MySQL clusters are divided into different node groups in order to let certain nodes manage the data nodes.)

`TABLESPACE`
: This subclause can be used only with MySQL Cluster, and specifies the tablespace to use with the partition.

`VALUES`
: This subclause specifies a range of values or a list of specific values for indexing and determining the disbursal of data among partitions. These are described earlier in the "CREATE TABLE: Partitioning" subsection.

CREATE TABLE: Subpartition definitions

```
CREATE [TEMPORARY] TABLE [IF NOT EXISTS] table
    SUBPARTITION partition
        [[STORAGE] ENGINE [=] engine]
        [COMMENT [=] 'string' ]
        [DATA DIRECTORY [=] '/path']
        [INDEX DIRECTORY [=] '/path']
        [MAX_ROWS [=] number]
        [MIN_ROWS [=] number]
        [TABLESPACE [=] (tablespace)]
        [NODEGROUP [=] number]
```

Only partitions distributed by the `RANGE` or `LIST` methods can be subpartitioned. The subpartitions can use only the `HASH` or `KEY` methods. The definitions for subpartitions are the same as for partitions, described earlier in the "CREATE TABLE: Partitioning" subsection. Here are some examples of subpartitioning:

```
CREATE TABLE ts (id INT, purchased DATE)
    PARTITION BY RANGE( YEAR(purchased) )
    SUBPARTITION BY HASH( TO_DAYS(purchased) )
    SUBPARTITIONS 2 (
        PARTITION p0 VALUES LESS THAN (1990),
        PARTITION p1 VALUES LESS THAN (2000),
        PARTITION p2 VALUES LESS THAN MAXVALUE
    );

CREATE TABLE sales_figures
(emp_id INT, sales_date DATE, amount INT)
PARTITION BY RANGE(YEAR(sales_date))
SUBPARTITION BY HASH(MONTH(sales_date))
SUBPARTITIONS 4 (
   PARTITION QTR1 VALUES LESS THAN (4),
   PARTITION QTR2 VALUES LESS THAN (7),
   PARTITION QTR3 VALUES LESS THAN (10),
   PARTITION QTR4 VALUES LESS THAN MAXVALUE);
```

Notice that although the subpartition uses `HASH`, the subpartitions are specified in ranges of values because it's a subpartition of a partition that uses the `RANGE` method.

CREATE TABLE: Based on an existing table

```
CREATE [TEMPORARY] TABLE [IF NOT EXISTS] table
LIKE table |
[IGNORE|REPLACE] [AS] SELECT...
```

These two syntaxes for the `CREATE TABLE` statement allow a new table to be created based on an existing table. With the `LIKE` clause, a table is created based on the structure of the existing table given. For example, suppose a database has a table called employees that contains information on full-time and part-time employees. Suppose further that it has been decided that information on part-time employees should be stored in a separate table. You could execute the following statement to create a new table for part-time employees with the same structure as the existing employees table:

```
CREATE TABLE part_time_employees
LIKE employees;
```

This statement results in a new table with the same structure but without any data. If the table that was copied has a primary key or any indexes, they won't be copied. You can use the CREATE INDEX statement to create an index. You would first have to do the following to copy the data over:

```
INSERT INTO part_time_employees
SELECT * FROM employees
WHERE part_time = 'Y';
```

To create a new table based on the structure of an existing table, and to copy some data from the old table to the new one, you can enter something like the following statement:

```
CREATE TABLE part_time_employees
SELECT *
FROM employees
WHERE part_time = 'Y';

CREATE INDEX emp_id ON part_time_employees(emp_id);
```

In this example, the table structure is copied and the data is copied for rows where the part_time column has a value of Y, meaning *yes*. You could follow this statement with a DELETE statement to delete the rows for part-time employees from the employees table. The second SQL statement in this example restores the index on emp_id. However, it doesn't make the column a primary key or an AUTO_INCREMENT one. For that, you would need to use ALTER TABLE instead.

You can use the IGNORE keyword before the SELECT statement to instruct MySQL to ignore any error messages regarding duplicate rows, to not insert them, or to proceed with the remaining rows of the SELECT statement. Use the REPLACE keyword instead if duplicate rows are to be replaced in the new table.

CREATE VIEW

```
CREATE
  [OR REPLACE]
  [ALGORITHM = {MERGE|TEMPTABLE|UNDEFINED}]
  [DEFINER = {'user'@'host'|CURRENT_USER}]
  [SQL SECURITY {DEFINER|INVOKER}]
VIEW view [(column, . . . )]
AS SELECT...
[WITH [CASCADED|LOCAL] CHECK OPTION]
```

Use this statement to create a view, which is a preset query stored in a database. In certain situations, a view can be useful for improved security. Views are available as of version 5.0.2 of MySQL.

The contents of a view are based on the SELECT statement given in the AS clause. Users can subsequently issue queries and updates to the view in place of a table; updates ultimately change the data in the tables that underlie the views.

The name of the view cannot be the same as a table in the database, because they share the same tablespace. A view can be based on other views, rather than directly based on a table. To label the column headings for the view's results set, column names may be given in a comma-separated list in parentheses after the view name. This SQL statement is available as of version 5.0.1 of MySQL.

A few parameters may appear between the CREATE and VIEW keywords. By default, attempts to create a view with the name of an existing view will fail, but the OR REPLACE parameter will overwrite a view with the same name if it exists and will create a new view otherwise. Also by default, the view's *definer* (used to determine access rights to the columns of the view) is the user who creates it, but another user can be specified with the DEFINER clause. This clause is available as of version 5.1.2 of MySQL. This version also introduced the related SQL SECURITY clause, which instructs MySQL to authorize access to the view based on the privileges of either the user account of the view's creator (DEFINER, the default) or the user account of the user who is querying the view (INVOKER). This can help prevent some users from accessing restricted views.

The ALGORITHM parameter selects one of the two types of algorithmic methods to use for processing a view: MERGE or TEMPTABLE. TEMPTABLE prevents a view from being updatable. The default of UNDEFINED leaves the choice to MySQL.

The WITH CHECK OPTION clause restricts updates to rows in which the WHERE clause of the underlying SELECT statement returns true. For a view that is based on another view, if you include the LOCAL keyword, this restriction will be limited to the view in which it's given and not the underlying view. Conversely, if you use the default choice of CASCADED, the WHERE clauses of underlying views will be considered as well.

If the mysqld server is started with the --updatable_views_with_limit option, updates that contain a LIMIT clause can update views only if the views contain all of the columns that are part of the primary keys of the underlying tables. If set to the default value of 1, only a warning is returned and updates are not restricted.

Here is an example of how you can use this statement:

```
CREATE DEFINER = 'russell'@'localhost'
SQL SECURITY INVOKER
VIEW student_directory(ID, Name, Telephone)
AS SELECT student_id,
CONCAT(name_first, SPACE(1), name_last), phone_home
FROM students;
```

This SQL statement creates a view that contains each student's identification number, the student's first and last name concatenated together with a space between, and the student's home telephone number. To retrieve this data, enter the following SQL statement:

```
SELECT * FROM student_directory
WHERE Name LIKE '%Tears';
```

```
+-----------+------------------+-----------+
| ID        | Name             | Telephone |
+-----------+------------------+-----------+
| 433342000 | Christina Tears  | 4883831   |
+-----------+------------------+-----------+
```

To save space in the output, the query includes a `WHERE` clause to retrieve a student with the last name of *Tears*. Notice that the column names are the ones named by the `CREATE VIEW` statement, not the underlying tables on which the view is based. This view will be available for all users who have `SELECT` privileges for the database in which it was created.

By default, a view is created in the default database at the time that the `CREATE VIEW` statement is entered. To create a view in a different database, simply add the database name and a dot as a separator in front of the view name in the `CREATE VIEW` statement.

To delete a view from a database, use the `DROP VIEW` statement. To see a list of existing views for the current database, run `SHOW FULL TABLES WHERE Table_type='VIEW';`.

DESCRIBE

`{DESCRIBE|DESC} *table* [*column*]`

This statement displays information about the columns of a given table. The `DESCRIBE` keyword can be abbreviated to `DESC`:

```
DESCRIBE workreq;

+--------------------+---------+------+-----+---------+----------------+
| Field              | Type    | Null | Key | Default | Extra          |
+--------------------+---------+------+-----+---------+----------------+
| req_id             | int(11) | NO   | PRI | NULL    | auto_increment |
| client_id          | int(11) | YES  |     | NULL    |                |
| client_description | text    | YES  | MUL | NULL    |                |
| technician_notes   | text    | YES  |     | NULL    |                |
+--------------------+---------+------+-----+---------+----------------+
```

For information on a specific column, supply only the column name. For information on multiple columns but not all columns, you can supply a name pattern within quotes and use the wildcard characters `%` and `_`. Quotes around the string aren't necessary unless the string contains spaces.

To list the columns in the `workreq` table that have names beginning with the characters *client*, enter the following:

```
DESCRIBE workreq 'client%';

+--------------------+---------+------+-----+---------+-------+
| Field              | Type    | Null | Key | Default | Extra |
+--------------------+---------+------+-----+---------+-------+
| client_id          | int(11) | YES  |     | NULL    |       |
| client_description | text    | YES  | MUL | NULL    |       |
+--------------------+---------+------+-----+---------+-------+
```

Database & Table Schema

Notice that the keyword LIKE is not used. The fields in the results have the following meanings:

Field
: Lists the name of each column in the table.

Type
: Shows the data type of each column.

Null
: Indicates whether the column in the table may contain a NULL value.

Default
: Shows the default value of the column.

Key
: Indicates what type of key the column is. If this field is empty, the column is not indexed. A value of PRI indicates a PRIMARY KEY column, UNI indicates a UNIQUE indexed column, and MUL means that multiple occurrences, or duplicate values, are permitted for the column. This is allowed because the column is only one of multiple columns making up an index.

Extra
: Lists any extra information particular to the column.

To understand how the options you use when creating or altering a table affect the output of DESCRIBE, let's look at the schema of the table shown in an earlier example:

```
SHOW CREATE TABLE workreq \G

*************************** 1. row ***************************
       Table: workreq
Create Table: CREATE TABLE 'workreq' (
  'req_id' int(11) NOT NULL AUTO_INCREMENT,
  'client_id' int(11) DEFAULT NULL,
  'client_description' text,
  'technician_notes' text,
  PRIMARY KEY ('req_id'),
  FULLTEXT KEY 'notes_index' ('client_description','technician_notes')
) ENGINE=MyISAM DEFAULT CHARSET=latin1
```

The results of this SHOW CREATE TABLE statement indicate that client_description is part of the index called notes_index. The other column that is part of that index is technician_notes. Notice in the results of the earlier DESCRIBE statement that only the first column of the index is marked MUL.

DROP DATABASE

DROP {DATABASE|SCHEMA} [IF EXISTS] *database*

Use this statement to delete a given database along with all of its tables and data. The addition of the IF EXISTS flag suppresses an error message if the database does not already exist. You must have the DROP privilege for the database to be able to delete it. Here is an example of this statement's use:

```
DROP DATABASE IF EXISTS test;
Query OK, 6 rows affected (0.42 sec)
```

The number of tables deleted is returned in the `rows affected` count. If the database doesn't exist or if there are other files in the database's filesystem directory, an error message will be displayed. The tables will be deleted if other files exist, but the foreign file and the directory for the database won't be removed. They will have to be deleted manually at the command line using a filesystem command such as `rm` in Unix or `del` in Windows. Here's an example in which a foreign file is found in the database directory when dropping a database:

```
DROP DATABASE IF EXISTS test;

ERROR 1010 (HY000):
Error dropping database (can't rmdir './test/', errno: 17)

SHOW TABLES FROM test;
Empty set (0.00 sec)

SHOW DATABASES LIKE 'test';

+-----------------+
| Database (test) |
+-----------------+
| test            |
+-----------------+
```

In this example, we attempt to drop the database, but we are unsuccessful because of a foreign file located in the database's directory at the filesystem level. The tables are all dropped as indicated from the results of the `SHOW TABLES` statement, but the database remains. After manually deleting the foreign file, we run the `DROP DATABASE` statement again:

```
DROP DATABASE IF EXISTS test;
Query OK, 0 rows affected (0.43 sec)

DROP DATABASE test;

ERROR 1008 (HY000): Can't drop database 'test';
database doesn't exist
```

This time the statement is successful, as indicated by our extra attempt without the `IF EXISTS` flag. No tables are dropped by the second attempt because they are all deleted on the first attempt, so the number of rows affected is 0.

If a database is dropped, any user privileges specific to the database (e.g., privileges listed in the `db` table of the `mysql` database) are not automatically deleted. Therefore, if a database is later created with the same name, those user privileges will apply to the new database, which is a potential security risk.

DROP INDEX

DROP INDEX *index* ON *table*

This statement deletes a given index from a table. It's synonymous with `ALTER TABLE...DROP INDEX...`. See the section on "ALTER TABLE: DROP index clauses" under `ALTER TABLE` earlier in this chapter for more details and options for dropping indexes from a table.

Database & Table Schema

To determine the name of a particular index, we'll use the `SHOW INDEXES` statement:

```
SHOW INDEXES FROM clients \G

*************************** 1. row ***************************
        Table: clients
   Non_unique: 0
     Key_name: PRIMARY
 Seq_in_index: 1
  Column_name: client_id
    Collation: A
  Cardinality: 0
     Sub_part: NULL
       Packed: NULL
         Null:
   Index_type: BTREE
      Comment:
*************************** 2. row ***************************
        Table: clients
   Non_unique: 1
     Key_name: client_index
 Seq_in_index: 1
  Column_name: client_name
    Collation: A
  Cardinality: NULL
     Sub_part: 10
       Packed: NULL
         Null: YES
   Index_type: BTREE
      Comment:
*************************** 3. row ***************************
        Table: clients
   Non_unique: 1
     Key_name: client_index
 Seq_in_index: 2
  Column_name: client_city
    Collation: A
  Cardinality: NULL
     Sub_part: 5
       Packed: NULL
         Null: YES
   Index_type: BTREE
      Comment:
```

The preceding results show three rows, but there are really only two indexes: the primary key based on the `client_id` column and the `client_index`, which is based on the `client_name` and the `client_city` columns combined. To delete `client_index`, use the `DROP INDEX` statement:

```
DROP INDEX client_index ON clients;

Query OK, 0 rows affected (0.06 sec)
Records: 0  Duplicates: 0  Warnings: 0
```

The `client_index` index is successfully dropped from the `clients` table. If you run `SHOW INDEXES` again, the results will list only the primary key.

DROP SERVER

```
DROP SERVER [IF EXISTS] server
```

This statement can be used with the FEDERATED storage engine to delete a given server that is created with `CREATE SERVER`. The `IF EXISTS` flag may be given to prevent an error from being generated if the server does not exist. Any tables created with a `CONNECTION` to a FEDERATED server will not be dropped or altered as a result of this statement. See the `CREATE SERVER` statement explanation earlier in this chapter for more information on this topic. This statement was introduced in version 5.1.15 of MySQL and requires `SUPER` privileges:

```
DROP SERVER server1;
```

DROP TABLE

```
DROP [TEMPORARY] TABLE [IF EXISTS] table[, ...]
     [RESTRICT|CASCADE]
```

Use this statement to delete a table from a database, including its data. You can delete multiple tables in the same statement by naming them in a comma-separated list. If some tables given exist and other don't, the ones that exist will be deleted and an error message will be generated for the nonexistent ones. The addition of the `IF EXISTS` flag prevents the error message from being displayed if a table doesn't exist. Instead, a `NOTE` is generated and not displayed, but can be retrieved with the `SHOW WARNINGS` statement. If the `TEMPORARY` flag is given, only temporary tables matching the table names given will be deleted. This statement will cause a commit of the current transaction, except when the `TEMPORARY` flag is used.

The `DROP` privilege is required for this statement. This privilege isn't checked when the `TEMPORARY` flag is used because the statement will apply only to temporary tables, and they are visible and usable only by the user of the current session who created them.

The `RESTRICT` and `CASCADE` flags are for future versions and are related to compatibility with other systems.

If a table is dropped, any specific user privileges for the table (e.g., privileges listed in the `tables_priv` table of the `mysql` database) are not automatically deleted. Therefore, if a table is later created with the same name, those user privileges will apply to the new table, a potential security risk:

```
DROP TABLE IF EXISTS repairs, clientss_old;
Query OK, 0 rows affected (0.00 sec)

SHOW WARNINGS;

+-------+------+-----------------------------+
| Level | Code | Message                     |
+-------+------+-----------------------------+
| Note  | 1051 | Unknown table 'clientss_old' |
+-------+------+-----------------------------+
```

In this example, we try to delete both the `repairs` and the `clients_old` tables, but we misspell `clients_old`. Because the `IF EXISTS` flag is included, the statement doesn't return an error message. Starting with version 4.1 of MySQL, a note is created that can be retrieved using the SHOW WARNINGS statement, as shown in this example. Notice that the number of tables deleted is not returned, although the **repairs** table is deleted.

DROP VIEW

```
DROP VIEW [IF EXISTS] view[, ...] [RESTRICT|CASCADE]
```

This statement deletes a view. Multiple views may be given in a comma-separated list. The IF EXISTS flag prevents error messages if one of the specified views doesn't exist. Instead, a note will be generated, which can be displayed afterward by executing the SHOW WARNINGS statement. Any other views given with the statements that do exist will be dropped.

The RESTRICT or CASCADE options are reserved for a future release of MySQL. This statement is available as of version 5.0.1 of MySQL and requires DROP privilege for the view being deleted.

RENAME DATABASE

```
RENAME {DATABASE|SCHEMA} database TO database[,...]
```

Use this statement to rename a given database to a new name, given after the TO keyword. While a database is being renamed, no other client can interact with the database involved. Tables that are currently locked or tables that are part of a transaction in progress cannot be renamed. Additional databases may be renamed in the same statement, given in a comma-separated list. This statement was added in version 5.1.7 of MySQL. As of version 5.0.2 of MySQL, the keyword DATABASE is synonymous with SCHEMA:

```
RENAME DATABASE personnel TO human_resources,
applicants TO human_resources_applicants;
```

In this example, the name of the database called **personnel** is changed to **human_resources**, and **applicants** is changed to **human_resources_applicants**, to coincide with a renaming of the department to which they relate. All of the tables and data are the same and continue to exist in the directories with the new database names.

RENAME TABLE

```
RENAME TABLE table TO table[,...]
```

Use this statement to rename a table to a new name, given after the TO keyword. Multiple tables may be specified in a comma-separated list, following the format *old_name* TO *new_name*. Multiple renames are performed left to right, and if any errors are encountered, all of the table name changes are reversed from right to left. While tables are being renamed, no other client can interact with the tables involved. Tables that are currently locked or tables that are part of a transaction in progress cannot be renamed.

Tables can be renamed and moved to databases on the same filesystem. If a trigger is associated with a table that is renamed and moved to a new database, the trigger will fail when used. You won't be warned of this possibility when renaming the table.

You can use this statement to rename a view, but you cannot use it to move the view to a different database.

This statement requires ALTER and DROP privileges for the table being renamed. CREATE and INSERT privileges are needed for the new table and database if the table is being moved.

As an example, suppose that users add data to a particular table during the course of the day, and each day the contents of the table are to be preserved. Suppose further that you want to reset the table to contain no data. Here's one way you might do that:

```
CREATE TABLE survey_new LIKE survey;

RENAME TABLE survey TO survey_bak,
survey_new TO survey;
```

In this example, a new table called survey_new is created based on the table structure of the old table called survey, but without the data. In the second SQL statement, the old table is renamed to survey_bak and the blank table, survey_new, is renamed to survey. If issued from an API program, the name of the backup copy could be generated based on the date (e.g., survey_2008dec07) so that each day's data could be preserved. As mentioned earlier, you can also change the database of a table in the process:

```
CREATE TABLE survey_new LIKE survey;

RENAME TABLE survey TO backup.survey_2008dec07,
survey_new TO survey;
```

In this example, the old table is renamed and moved into a database called backup.

SHOW CHARACTER SET

SHOW CHARACTER SET [LIKE '*pattern*'| WHERE *expression*]

This statement will show all of the character sets installed on the server. To be more selective, use a pattern with the LIKE clause and the wildcard characters (i.e., % and _). Or you may use the WHERE clause to refine the results set. For instance, to list all of the character sets beginning with the name *latin*, enter the following:

```
SHOW CHARACTER SET LIKE 'latin%'\G
*************************** 1. row ***************************
          Charset: latin1
      Description: ISO 8859-1 West European
Default collation: latin1_swedish_ci
           Maxlen: 1
*************************** 2. row ***************************
          Charset: latin2
      Description: ISO 8859-2 Central European
Default collation: latin2_general_ci
           Maxlen: 1
*************************** 3. row ***************************
          Charset: latin5
      Description: ISO 8859-9 Turkish
Default collation: latin5_turkish_ci
           Maxlen: 1
*************************** 4. row ***************************
          Charset: latin7
      Description: ISO 8859-13 Baltic
Default collation: latin7_general_ci
           Maxlen: 1
```

To see the default character set, use the SHOW VARIABLES statement. To change the client's character set, use the SET CHARACTER SET statement. The Default collation field in the results indicates the related collation for the character set. The Maxlen field gives the maximum number of bytes for storing one character of the character set. For European character sets, this value is usually 1; for Asian character sets, it's usually more than 1.

SHOW COLLATION

SHOW COLLATION [LIKE '*pattern*'| WHERE *expression*]

Use this statement to list all of the collation character sets. You can use the LIKE clause and the wildcard characters (% and _) to list character sets based on a naming pattern. Or you may use the WHERE clause to refine the results set. This statement is available as of version 4.1 of MySQL. Here is an example:

```
SHOW COLLATION LIKE '%greek%';

+-----------------+---------+----+---------+----------+---------+
| Collation       | Charset | Id | Default | Compiled | Sortlen |
+-----------------+---------+----+---------+----------+---------+
| greek_general_ci | greek  | 25 | Yes     | Yes      |       1 |
| greek_bin       | greek   | 70 |         | Yes      |       1 |
+-----------------+---------+----+---------+----------+---------+
```

In this example, character sets that contain the letters *greek* in their name are listed. These are Greek character sets. Under the Charset column is shown the character set for which the collation relates. Both are for the greek character set. Using SHOW CHARACTER SET, we can see information on this character set. Looking at the Default just shown (and the Default collation shown next), we can see that greek_general_ci is the default collation for the character set greek. This is indicated with the Yes value. The field Compiled in the results shown previously indicates that the character set was compiled in the MySQL server. The field Sortlen indicates the bytes needed when collating data:

```
SHOW CHARACTER SET LIKE 'greek';

+---------+-----------------+-------------------+--------+
| Charset | Description     | Default collation | Maxlen |
+---------+-----------------+-------------------+--------+
| greek   | ISO 8859-7 Greek | greek_general_ci |      1 |
+---------+-----------------+-------------------+--------+
```

SHOW COLUMNS

SHOW [FULL] COLUMNS FROM *table* [FROM *database*] [LIKE '*pattern*'|WHERE *expression*]

Use this statement to display the columns for a given table. If the table is not in the current default database, the FROM *database* clause may be given to specify another database. You can use the LIKE clause to list only columns that match a naming pattern given in quotes. Or you may use the WHERE clause to refine the results set. The FULL flag will return the name of the character set used for collating and the user privileges of the current session for the columns returned:

```
SHOW COLUMNS FROM clients FROM workrequests LIKE 'client%';
```

```
+-------------+-------------+------+-----+---------+-------+
| Field       | Type        | Null | Key | Default | Extra |
+-------------+-------------+------+-----+---------+-------+
| client_id   | varchar(4)  |      | PRI |         |       |
| client_name | varchar(50) | YES  |     | NULL    |       |
+-------------+-------------+------+-----+---------+-------+
```

In this example, only information for columns beginning with the name `client` is retrieved. The following example is just for the `client_id` column and uses the `FULL` flag along with the alternate display method (`\G`):

```
SHOW FULL COLUMNS FROM clients FROM workrequests
LIKE 'client_id'\G
*************************** 1. row ***************************
     Field: client_id
      Type: varchar(4)
 Collation: latin1_swedish_ci
      Null:
       Key: PRI
   Default:
     Extra:
Privileges: select,insert,update,references
   Comment:
```

Notice that the name of the collation used for the column (`latin1_swedish_ci`) and the user's privileges (`SELECT`, `INSERT`, `UPDATE`, and `REFERENCES`) with regard to the column are provided.

SHOW CREATE DATABASE

`SHOW CREATE {DATABASE|SCHEMA}` *`database`*

This statement displays an SQL statement that can be used to create a database like the one given. This statement is mostly useful for determining the default character set. It's available as of version 4.1 of MySQL. As of version 5.0.2, the keyword `SCHEMA` may be used instead of `DATABASE`:

```
SHOW CREATE DATABASE human_resources \G

*************************** 1. row ***************************
       Database: human_resources
Create Database: CREATE DATABASE `human_resources`
                 /*!40100 DEFAULT CHARACTER SET latin1 */
```

If you don't want the database name in the results to be quoted with backticks as shown here, you can set the server variable `SQL_QUOTE_SHOW_CREATE` to 0 instead of its default value of 1.

SHOW CREATE TABLE

`SHOW CREATE TABLE` *`table`*

This statement displays an SQL statement that can be used to create a table like the one named. The results may be copied and used with another database. You can also copy the results and modify the name of the table in order to use the CREATE statement on the same database. If you want a table exactly like an existing one, you might do better to use CREATE TABLE...LIKE... instead:

```
SHOW CREATE TABLE programmers \G

*************************** 1. row ***************************
Table: programmers
Create Table: CREATE TABLE 'programmers' (
              'prog_id' varchar(4) NOT NULL default '',
              'prog_name' varchar(50) NOT NULL default '',
              PRIMARY KEY ('prog_id')
              ) ENGINE=MyISAM DEFAULT CHARSET=latin1
```

Notice that the results include the table type and other default options.

As with the SHOW CREATE DATABASE statement, if you don't want the table name in the results to be quoted with backticks as shown here, you can set the server variable SQL_QUOTE_SHOW_CREATE to 0 instead of its default value of 1.

SHOW CREATE VIEW

SHOW CREATE VIEW *view*

Use this statement to display an SQL statement that can be used to create a view like the one named. The results may be copied and used with another database. You can also copy the results and modify the name of the view so that the statement may be used to create a similar or identical view on the same database. This statement is available as of version 5.0.1 of MySQL:

```
SHOW CREATE VIEW student_directory \G

*************************** 1. row ***************************
       View: student_directory
Create View: CREATE ALGORITHM=UNDEFINED
DEFINER='russell'@'localhost' SQL SECURITY INVOKER
VIEW 'student_directory'
AS SELECT 'students'.'student_id' AS 'ID',
CONCAT('students'.'name_first',
convert(repeat(_utf8' ',1) using latin1),
'students'.'name_last') AS 'Name',
'students'.'phone_home' AS 'Telephone'
FROM 'students'
```

This view is the same one created in the example given for the CREATE VIEW statement earlier. Notice that the database name (personnel) has been added to the end of the view name (employee_directory).

SHOW DATABASES

SHOW {DATABASES|SCHEMAS} [LIKE '*pattern*'| WHERE *expression*]

This statement displays the list of databases on the server. The keyword DATABASE is synonymous with SCHEMA as of version 5.0.2 of MySQL. Using the LIKE clause, a naming pattern may be given. Or you may use the WHERE clause to refine the results set.

For example, suppose that a server has a separate database for each customer of the organization and that the pattern for the names of the databases is `cust_number`, where the *number* is the customer account number. You could enter the following SQL statement to obtain a list of databases based on this pattern:

```
SHOW DATABASES LIKE 'cust%' LIMIT 1;

+------------------+
| Database (cust%) |
+------------------+
| cust_37881       |
+------------------+
```

The `SHOW DATABASES` privilege is necessary to see all databases. Otherwise, the user will see only the databases for which he has privileges. The `--skip-show-database` server option will disable this limitation.

The `mysqlshow` utility can be used at the command line to view the same information:

```
mysqlshow --user=user --password
```

The results from this utility are also limited by the user's privileges.

SHOW INDEXES

```
SHOW {INDEX|INDEXES|KEYS} FROM table [FROM database]
```

This SQL statement displays information about the indexes for a given table. A table from a different database can be specified either by preceding the table name with the database name and a dot (e.g., `database.table`) or by adding the `FROM` clause. The `INDEXES` keyword may be replaced with `INDEX` or `KEYS`—all three are synonymous:

```
SHOW INDEXES FROM contacts FROM sales_dept \G

*************************** 1. row ***************************
       Table: contacts
  Non_unique: 0
    Key_name: PRIMARY
Seq_in_index: 1
 Column_name: contact_id
   Collation: A
 Cardinality: 265
    Sub_part: NULL
      Packed: NULL
        Null:
  Index_type: BTREE
     Comment:
*************************** 2. row ***************************
       Table: contacts
  Non_unique: 0
    Key_name: contact_name
Seq_in_index: 1
 Column_name: name_last
   Collation: A
 Cardinality: NULL
    Sub_part: 10
      Packed: NULL
```

```
         Null: YES
   Index_type: BTREE
      Comment:
*************************** 3. row ***************************
        Table: contacts
   Non_unique: 0
     Key_name: contact_name
 Seq_in_index: 2
  Column_name: name_first
    Collation: A
  Cardinality: NULL
     Sub_part: 10
       Packed: NULL
         Null: YES
   Index_type: BTREE
      Comment:
```

Looking at these results, we can see that for each index the table name is given. This is followed by a field indicating whether the index is nonunique. A unique index is indicated by 0, a nonunique index by 1. The name of the index or key (i.e., `PRIMARY` or `contact_name` in the example) is shown next. For indexes that use only one column, the key name and the column name are often the same. For indexes that use more than one column, a row will be listed for each column, each row having the same table name and the same key name (i.e., `name_last` and `name_first` for `contact_name`).

The output gives the sequence of the columns in the index, where 1 is the first column. The name of the column (or columns) indexed is next, followed by the collation (how the column is sorted in the index). A value of `A` means ascending and `D` means descending. If the index is not sorted, the `Collation` field value is NULL.

The `Cardinality` field is based on the number of unique indexes contained in the column. The server consults this information to determine whether to use an index in a join. The higher the cardinality, the more likely it will be used.

The `Sub_part` field indicates the number of characters of the column that are indexed for partially indexed columns. This field is NULL if the NULL column is indexed.

The `Packed` field indicates how the key is packed. If the key is not packed, the field has a value of NULL. See the earlier subsection "ALTER TABLE: Table options" for a description of packed keys.

If the column may contain a NULL value, the `Null` field reads `Yes`; otherwise, it's empty. `Index_type` is the structure of the index, which can be `BTREE`, `HASH`, `FULLTEXT`, `RTREE` (as of version 5.0.1 of MySQL), or `SPATIAL`. The `Comments` field contains any comments associated with the index.

From the command line, the `mysqlshow` utility with the `--keys` option can be used to show the same information:

```
mysqlshow --user=user --password --keys database table
```

SHOW SCHEMAS

SHOW {DATABASES|SCHEMAS} [LIKE '*pattern*']

This statement is synonymous with `SHOW DATABASES`. See the description of that statement earlier in this chapter for more information and examples.

SHOW TABLE STATUS

SHOW TABLE STATUS [FROM *database*] [LIKE '*pattern*']

This statement displays status information on a set of tables from a database. To obtain the status of tables from a database other than the current default one, use the `FROM` clause. The results include information on all of the tables of the database, unless the `LIKE` clause is used to limit the tables displayed by a naming pattern:

```
SHOW TABLE STATUS FROM human_resources
LIKE 'employees' \G

*************************** 1. row ***************************
           Name: employees
         Engine: InnoDB
        Version: 10
     Row_format: Compact
           Rows: 122
 Avg_row_length: 16384
    Data_length: 1094812
Max_data_length: 281474976710655
   Index_length: 2048
      Data_free: 0
 Auto_increment: 1145
    Create_time: 2006-08-14 21:31:36
    Update_time: 2007-03-30 07:02:17
     Check_time: 2006-08-14 21:31:36
      Collation: latin1_swedish_ci
       Checksum: NULL
 Create_options: max_rows=1000
        Comment: InnoDB free: 4096 kB
```

In this example, the number of tables is limited to one because a specific table name is given in the `LIKE` clause without the `%` wildcard. You can change some of these variables or table options using the `ALTER TABLE` statement; see the "ALTER TABLE: Table options" subsection earlier in this chapter.

In the results of this statement, the name of the table is shown first, followed by a description of the table. The `Engine` field lists the type of storage engine used. The `Version` field gives the version number from the table's *.frm* file. `Row_format` can be `Compact`, `Compressed`, `Dynamic`, `Fixed`, or `Redundant`, unless it's an InnoDB table, in which case the possibilities are `Compact` or `Redundant`. The `Rows` field shows the number of rows of data contained in the table. Except for MyISAM tables, this number usually isn't accurate. The `Avg_row_length` field gives the average length of the rows in bytes. The `Data_length` field gives the size of the datafile in bytes. This is the same size shown at the filesystem level for the *.MYD* file. `Max_data_length` gives the maximum size allowed for the datafile of the table. `Index_length` is the size of the index file, the *.MYI* file. `Data_free` is the space that has been allocated for the datafile that is not in use at the moment; this is typically 0. The value of the `Auto_increment` field is the value of the column that uses `AUTO_INCREMENT` for the next row to be created. `Create_time` is the date and time the table was created; `Update_time` shows the time the table was last updated; and `Check_time` is the last date and time that the table was checked. This isn't always accurate. `Collation` names the collation used for sorting the table's data. `Checksum` provides the checksum value if there is one, NULL if not. The `Create_options` field lists any options, and the `Comment` field shows any comments that were given when the table was created or altered. For InnoDB tables, the free space is given under `Comment`.

From the command line, the utility `mysqlshow` with the `--keys` option can be used to show the indexes of a table:

```
mysqlshow --user=user --password --status database table
```

SHOW TABLES

```
SHOW [FULL|OPEN] TABLES [FROM database] [LIKE 'pattern'| WHERE expression]
```

This statement displays a list of tables and views (as of version 5.0.1 of MySQL). To distinguish between tables and views, add the `FULL` keyword. In the results, an extra column called `Table_type` will be displayed. A value of `BASE TABLE` indicates a table, and `VIEW` indicates a view. The tables shown will not include temporary tables and will be from the current database by default. To list tables from another database, add the `FROM` clause along with the name of the database. You can reduce the list of tables to those with a name meeting a given naming pattern with either the `LIKE` or the `WHERE` clause. For a list of all tables for all databases that are currently being used by queries, add the `OPEN` flag instead:

```
SHOW TABLES FROM workrequests LIKE 'work%';
```

This statement will list all of the tables and views with names that begins with the word "work" for the database `workrequests`. By default, only tables for which the user has privileges will be listed.

From the command line, the utility `mysqlshow` with the `--keys` option can be used to show the tables contained in a database:

```
mysqlshow --user=user --password database
```

SHOW VIEWS

There is no `SHOW VIEWS` statement at this time. To see a list of existing views for the current database, run `SHOW FULL TABLES WHERE Table_type='VIEW';`.

6
Data Manipulation Statements and Functions

This chapter explains SQL statements in MySQL related to data manipulation: adding, changing, and deleting data, as well as retrieving selected data. Statements that create and alter databases and tables are covered in the previous chapter. In essence, this chapter covers SQL statements used when manipulating the data itself, not when developing a database. The two modes involve fairly distinct mindsets and are sometimes conducted by different people.

Statements and Functions Grouped by Characteristics

The following SQL statements are covered in this chapter.

Data Manipulation Statements

Here is a list of SQL statements and clauses used in MySQL for data manipulation:

`DELETE`, `DO`, `EXPLAIN`, `HANDLER`, `HELP`, `INSERT`, `JOIN`, `LIMIT`, `LOAD DATA INFILE`, `REPLACE`, `SELECT`, `SET`, `SHOW ERRORS`, `SHOW WARNINGS`, `TRUNCATE`, `UNION`, `UPDATE`, `USE`.

Transaction Statements

Transactions are a set of SQL statements that the server has to execute as a unit: either all succeed or all fail. If the server detects that all have succeeded, it *commits* the transaction; if any statement fails, the server *rolls back* the previous statements. Transactions are supported by the InnoDB, BDB, and NDB Cluster storage engines, as well as some new storage engines for MySQL that are under development. Statements that manipulate transactions are ignored if executed against a storage engine that doesn't support transactions, notably MyISAM.

The following is a list of SQL statements that are specifically related to transactions. They work only with tables that use a transactional storage engine (e.g., InnoDB, BDB, and NDB Cluster):

BEGIN, COMMIT, RELEASE SAVEPOINT, ROLLBACK, ROLLBACK TO SAVEPOINT, SAVEPOINT, SET TRANSACTION, START TRANSACTION, XA.

Related Functions

The following functions are also covered in this chapter because they relate to data manipulation. They are explained at the end of this chapter:

ANALYSE( ), BENCHMARK( ), DATABASE( ), FOUND_ROWS( ), LAST_INSERT_ID( ), ROW_COUNT( ), SCHEMA( ).

Statements and Clauses in Alphabetical Order

The following is a list of MySQL statements and clauses related to data manipulation, in alphabetical order. To understand how this book presents SQL syntax and describes SQL statements, as well as for information related to examples, please see the introduction to Part II. Many of the examples in this chapter involve the activities of the departments of a fictitious company: its human resources department and employee data, its sales department and client contact information, and its internal IT department's work requests.

BEGIN

BEGIN [WORK]

Use this statement to start a transaction. Transaction statements are currently supported by the InnoDB, NDB Cluster, and BDB storage engines and are ignored if used with MyISAM tables. The WORK keyword is optional. Don't confuse the BEGIN statement with the BEGIN...END compound statement used in stored procedures and triggers (see Chapter 9). To eliminate confusion on this point, it's recommended you use the alias START TRANSACTION instead of BEGIN.

A transaction is permanently recorded when the session issues a COMMIT statement, starts another transaction, or terminates the connection. You can reverse a transaction by issuing a ROLLBACK statement if the transaction has not yet been committed. See the explanations of COMMIT and ROLLBACK later in this chapter for more information on transactions. The SAVEPOINT and ROLLBACK TO SAVEPOINT statements may also be useful.

Here is an example of the BEGIN statement's use in context:

```
BEGIN;

INSERT DATA INFILE '/tmp/customer_orders.sql'
INTO TABLE orders;

COMMIT;
```

In this example, if there is a problem after the batch of orders is inserted into the `orders` table, the `ROLLBACK` statement could be issued instead of the `COMMIT` statement shown here. `ROLLBACK` would remove the data imported by the `INSERT DATA INFILE` statement.

COMMIT

```
COMMIT [WORK] [AND [NO] CHAIN] [[NO] RELEASE]
```

Use this statement to commit transactions, which are SQL statements that have changed data and have been entered into MySQL but are not yet saved. Transaction statements are currently supported by the InnoDB, NDB Cluster, and BDB storage engines and are ignored if used with MyISAM tables.

If `AUTOCOMMIT` is enabled, it must be disabled for this statement to be meaningful. You can disable it explicitly with the statement:

```
SET AUTOCOMMIT = 0;
```

Normally, `AUTOCOMMIT` is disabled by a `START TRANSACTION` statement and reinstated with the `COMMIT` statement.

The `WORK` keyword is optional and has no effect on the results. It's available for compatibility with its counterpart, `BEGIN WORK`. Use the `AND CHAIN` clause to complete one transaction and start another, thus making it unnecessary to use `START TRANSACTION` again. Use the `AND RELEASE` clause to end the current client session after completing the transaction.

Add the keyword `NO` to indicate explicitly that a new transaction is not to begin (when used with `CHAIN`) or that the client session is not to end (when used with `RELEASE`). This is necessary only when the system variable `completion_type` is set so that the server assumes that a `COMMIT` statement indicates the start of another transaction or releases a session.

Here is a basic example of this statement:

```
START TRANSACTION;

LOCK TABLES orders WRITE;

INSERT DATA INFILE '/tmp/customer_orders.sql'
INTO TABLE orders;

SELECT ...;

COMMIT;

UNLOCK TABLES;
```

In this example, after inserting a batch of orders into the `orders` table, an administrator enters a series of `SELECT` statements to check the integrity of the data. They are omitted here to save space. If there is a problem, the `ROLLBACK` statement could be issued rather than the `COMMIT` statement shown here. `ROLLBACK` would remove the data imported by the `INSERT DATA INFILE` statement.

The following statements also cause a transaction to be committed: ALTER EVENT, ALTER FUNCTION, ALTER PROCEDURE, ALTER TABLE, BEGIN, CREATE DATABASE, CREATE EVENT, CREATE FUNCTION, CREATE INDEX, CREATE PROCEDURE, CREATE TABLE, DROP DATABASE, DROP EVENT, DROP FUNCTION, DROP INDEX, DROP PROCEDURE, DROP TABLE, LOAD DATA INFILE, LOCK TABLES, RENAME TABLE, SET AUTOCOMMIT=1, START TRANSACTION, TRUNCATE, and UNLOCK TABLES.

DELETE

```
DELETE [LOW_PRIORITY] [QUICK] [IGNORE] FROM table
       [WHERE condition]
       [ORDER BY column [ASC|DESC][,...]]
       [LIMIT row_count]

DELETE [LOW_PRIORITY] [QUICK] [IGNORE] table[, table]
       FROM table[,...]
       [WHERE condition]

DELETE [LOW_PRIORITY] [QUICK] [IGNORE] FROM table[, table]
       USING table[,...]
       [WHERE condition]
```

Use this statement to delete rows of data from a given table. Three basic syntax structures are allowed. The first one shown here is restricted to a single table, whereas the other two can handle multiple tables. For all three, the LOW_PRIORITY keyword instructs the server to wait until there are no queries on the table named before deleting rows. This keyword works only with storage engines that allow table-level locking (i.e., MyISAM, MEMORY, MERGE). The QUICK keyword can be used with MyISAM tables to make deletions faster by not merging leaves in the index's tree. The IGNORE keyword instructs MySQL to continue even if it encounters errors. You can retrieve error messages afterward with the SHOW WARNINGS statement.

Use the WHERE clause to specify which rows are to be deleted based on a given condition. You can use the DELETE statement in conjunction with the JOIN clause, which is explained later in this chapter.

Here is a simple example of this statement:

```
DELETE LOW_PRIORITY FROM workreq
WHERE client_id = '1076'
AND status <> 'DONE';
```

In this example, the client 1076 has closed its account, and management has decided just to delete all of its incomplete work requests. If a WHERE clause is not given, all of the rows for the table would be deleted permanently.

If you want to delete all of the data in a table, you can use this statement without the WHERE clause, but it's slow because deletions are performed one row at a time. The same result can be obtained faster with the TRUNCATE statement. However, the TRUNCATE statement doesn't return the number of rows deleted, so use DELETE if that's important to you.

To delete only a certain number of rows in a table, use the LIMIT clause to specify the number of rows to delete. To delete a specific number of rows for a particular range of column values, use the ORDER BY clause along with the LIMIT clause. For example, suppose an account executive informs the database administrator that the last four work requests she entered for a particular client (1023) need to be deleted. The database administrator could enter the following to delete those rows:

```
DELETE FROM workreq
WHERE client_id = '1023'
ORDER BY request_date DESC
LIMIT 4;
```

In this example, the rows are first ordered by the date of the work request, in descending order (latest date first). Additional columns may be given in a comma-separated list for the ordering. The `LIMIT` clause is used to limit the number of deletions to the first four rows of the results of the `WHERE` clause and the `ORDER BY` clause.

The second syntax for this statement allows other tables to be referenced. In the first example shown here, the database administrator wants to delete rows representing a particular client from the work request table, but she doesn't know the client account number. However, she knows the client's name begins with *Cole*, so she could enter the following to delete the records:

```
DELETE workreq FROM workreq, clients
WHERE workreq.client_id = clients.client_id
AND client_name LIKE 'Cole%';
```

In this example, the table in which rows will be deleted is given after the `DELETE` keyword. It's also given in the list of tables in the `FROM` clause, which specifies the table from which information will be obtained to determine the rows to delete. The two tables are joined in the `WHERE` clause on the client identification number column in each. Using the `LIKE` keyword, the selection of rows is limited to clients with a name beginning with *Cole*. Incidentally, if more than one client has a name beginning with *Cole*, the rows for all will be deleted from the work request table. You can delete rows in more than one table with a single statement by listing the tables in a comma-separated list after the `DELETE` keyword. For example, suppose that we decide to delete not only the work requests for the client, but also the row for the client in the `clients` table:

```
DELETE workreq, clients FROM workreq, clients
WHERE workreq.clientid = clients.clientid
AND client_name LIKE 'Cole%';
```

Notice that the only syntactical difference between this statement and the one in the previous example is that this statement lists both tables for which rows are to be deleted after the `DELETE` keyword and before the `FROM` clause. Deletions are permanent, so take care which tables you list for deletion.

The third syntax operates in the same way as the second one, but it offers a couple of keywords that may be preferred for clarity. If the previous example were entered with this third syntax, it would look like this:

```
DELETE FROM workreq USING workreq, clients
WHERE workreq.clientid = clients.clientid
AND client_name LIKE 'Cole%';
```

Notice that the table from which rows will be deleted is listed in the `FROM` clause. The tables that the statement will search for information to determine which rows to delete are listed in the `USING` clause. The results of statements using this syntax structure and those using the previous one are the same. It's just a matter of style preference and compatibility with other database systems.

Although MySQL will eventually reuse space allocated for deleted rows, you can compact a table that has had many rows deleted by using the `OPTIMIZE TABLE` statement or the `myisamchk` utility.

DO

DO *expression*[,...] | (*statement*)

This statement suppresses the display of an expression's results. Multiple expressions may be given in a comma-separated list. As of version 4.1 of MySQL, subqueries may be given. Here is an example:

```
DO (SET @company = 'Van de Lay Industries' );
```

This statement creates the `@company` variable with the value given, but without displaying any results.

EXPLAIN

EXPLAIN *table*

EXPLAIN [EXTENDED|PARTITIONS] SELECT...

Use this statement to display information about the columns of a given table or the handling of a `SELECT` statement. For the first usage, the statement is synonymous with the `DESCRIBE` and `SHOW COLUMNS` statements. For the latter usage, `EXPLAIN` shows which index the statement will use and, when multiple tables are queried, the order in which the tables are used. This can be helpful in determining the cause of a slow query. Here is an example involving a simple subquery in which we are retrieving a list of our top clients and counting the number of work request tickets they've generated, and then querying those results to order them by the number of tickets:

```
EXPLAIN
SELECT * FROM
   (SELECT client_name, COUNT(*) AS tickets
    FROM work_req
    JOIN clients USING(client_id)
    WHERE client_type = 1
    AND DATEDIFF(NOW(), request_date) < 91
    GROUP BY client_id) AS derived1
ORDER BY tickets DESC;

*************************** 1. row ***************************
           id: 1
  select_type: PRIMARY
        table: <derived2>
         type: ALL
possible_keys: NULL
          key: NULL
      key_len: NULL
          ref: NULL
         rows: 8
        Extra: Using filesort
```

```
*************************** 2. row ***************************
           id: 2
  select_type: DERIVED
        table: clients
         type: ALL
possible_keys: PRIMARY
          key: NULL
      key_len: NULL
          ref: NULL
         rows: 94
        Extra: Using where; Using temporary; Using filesort
*************************** 3. row ***************************
           id: 2
  select_type: DERIVED
        table: work_req
         type: ref
possible_keys: client_id,workreq_date_key
          key: workreq_date_key
      key_len: 5
          ref: company_database.clients.client_id
         rows: 1
        Extra: Using where; Using index
```

We can discern plenty from these results, such as which indexes were used, if any. For example, the `possible_keys` field in the third row lists the indexes that *might* have been used to find the data, whereas the `key` field indicates that the index `workreq_date_key` was actually used. (That index covers the `client_id` and `request_date` columns.) If the `possible_keys` field showed a value of NULL, then no index was used or could have been used. This would indicate that you should consider adding an index to the table.

Basically, this statement tells you what MySQL does when it executes the given SQL statement. It doesn't tell you what to do differently to improve performance. For that, you will need to use your judgment. See Table 6-1 for a list of possible `select_types`.

Table 6-1. select_type for EXPLAIN statement results

Type	General meaning
`SIMPLE`	Indicates a simple SELECT statement, without a subquery or a `UNION`.
`PRIMARY`	When using a subquery, this is the main `SELECT` statement.
`UNION`	When using a `UNION`, this is not the first `SELECT` statement.
`DEPENDENT UNION`	When using a `UNION`, this is not the first `SELECT` statement that is dependent on the main query.
`UNION RESULT`	The result of a `UNION`.
`SUBQUERY`	The first `SELECT` statement in a subquery.
`DEPENDENT SUBQUERY`	The first `SELECT` statement in a subquery that is dependent on the main query.
`DERIVED`	The table derived from the subquery.
`UNCACHEABLE SUBQUERY`	Indicates a subquery in which the results cannot be cached and therefore must be reevaluated for each row of the main query.

Type	General meaning
UNCACHEABLE UNION	The UNION of a subquery in which the results cannot be cached and therefore must be reevaluated for each row of the main query.

HANDLER

```
HANDLER table OPEN [AS handle]

HANDLER handle READ index { = | >= | <= | < } (value,...)
   [WHERE condition] [LIMIT ...]

HANDLER handle READ index {FIRST|NEXT|PREV|LAST}
   [WHERE condition] [LIMIT ...]

HANDLER handle READ {FIRST|NEXT}
   [WHERE condition] [LIMIT ...]

HANDLER handle CLOSE
```

A handle provides direct access to a table, as opposed to working from a results set. Handles can be faster than SELECT statements when reading large numbers of rows from a table. MyISAM and InnoDB tables currently support handlers.

A handle is usable only by the session (connection thread) that established it. The table is still accessible by other sessions, though, and is not locked by this statement. Because of this, and because the method provides direct table access, the data in the table can change and even be incomplete as the handler performs successive reads.

Create a handler by issuing a HANDLER statement with the OPEN clause to establish a handle for the table, much like a file handle in a programming language such as Perl. The AS clause and handle name are optional. If an alias is not given, the table name is used as the handler name for subsequent HANDLER statements.

You can then use HANDLER statement formats with READ clauses to read data from a table. Finish by issuing HANDLER with a CLOSE clause.

Here are a couple of basic examples of the HANDLER statement:

```
HANDLER clients OPEN AS clients_handle;
HANDLER clients_handle READ FIRST;
```

The first line creates the table handle called clients_handle, based on the clients table. The next SQL statement retrieves the first row of data from the table. The result of this statement is the same as running a SELECT to retrieve all columns of the table and then picking off the first row in the results set. To continue retrieving results in the same way as a results set from a SELECT, issue the following:

```
HANDLER clients_handle READ NEXT;
```

Every time the statement is run with the NEXT keyword, the pointer is advanced and the next row in the table is displayed until the end of the table is reached. To retrieve more than one row, you can use the LIMIT clause like this:

```
HANDLER clients_handle READ NEXT LIMIT 3;
```

This statement displays the next three rows from the table.

The WHERE clause may be used with a HANDLER...READ statement in the same way as with the SELECT statement. Here is an example:

```
HANDLER clients_handle READ FIRST
WHERE state = 'MA' LIMIT 5;
```

This statement displays the first five rows in which the client is located in the state of Massachusetts. Note that no ORDER BY clause is available for HANDLER...READ statements. Therefore, the first five rows are based on the order in which they are stored in the table.

To extract data based on an index, use one of the READ clauses that specify indexes. Here is an example like the previous one, but with the addition of an index:

```
HANDLER clients_handle READ cid PREV
WHERE state = 'MA' LIMIT 2;
```

This example retrieves two rows matching the condition of the WHERE clause; the rows come from the previous batch of rows displayed thanks to the PREV keyword. Performance could benefit from the use of the cid index, if it was based on the state column. To retrieve the next set of rows using this syntax, replace PREV with NEXT.

The LAST keyword searches for and retrieves rows starting from the last row of the table. Here is another example using an index:

```
HANDLER clients_handle READ name = ('NeumeyerGera');
```

The name index is a combination of the name_last and the name_first column, but only the first four characters of the first name are used by the index. Given the sample database used for this book, this statement displays the row for the client Gerard Neumeyer. The values for each column may be separated with commas (e.g., 'Neumeyer', 'Gera'), or spliced together as shown. This feature, a condition for a multicolumn index, would be a difficult contortion with a SELECT statement.

HELP

```
HELP [{'command | reserve_word'}]
```

You can use this statement to access built-in documentation. Enter HELP alone to display a list of MySQL commands for which you may display documentation. Typing HELP contents displays a table of contents for this internal documentation. For quick reference, you can also give an SQL statement or clause:

```
HELP SELECT;
```

This displays the syntax for the SELECT statement along with a brief description of some of the clauses. Similarly, entering HELP SHOW gives you a list of SQL statements beginning with SHOW.

INSERT

```
INSERT [LOW_PRIORITY|DELAYED|HIGH_PRIORITY] [IGNORE]
  [INTO] table
  SET column={expression|DEFAULT}, ...
  [ON DUPLICATE KEY UPDATE column=expression, ...]

INSERT [LOW_PRIORITY|DELAYED|HIGH_PRIORITY] [IGNORE]
```

```
INSERT
   [INTO] table [(column, ...)]
   VALUES ({expression|DEFAULT},...),(...),...
   [ON DUPLICATE KEY UPDATE column=expression, ...]

INSERT [LOW_PRIORITY|HIGH_PRIORITY] [IGNORE]
   [INTO] table [(column, ...)]
   SELECT...
   [ON DUPLICATE KEY UPDATE column=expression, ...]
```

Use this statement to add rows of data to a table. The first format shown can insert only one row of data per statement. The second format can handle one or more rows in a single statement. The columns and their order are specified once, but values for multiple rows may be given. Each row of values is to be contained in its own set of parentheses, separated by commas. The third format inserts columns copied from rows in other tables. Explanations of the specifics of each type of statement, their various clauses and keywords, and examples of their uses follow in the next three subsections of this SQL statement.

A few parameters are common to two formats, and a few are common to all formats.

You can use the `LOW_PRIORITY` keyword to instruct the server to wait until all other queries related to the table in which data is to be added are finished before running the `INSERT` statement. When the table is free, it is locked for the `INSERT` statement and will prevent concurrent inserts.

The `DELAYED` keyword is available for the first two syntaxes and indicates the same priority status, but it releases the client so that other queries may be run and so that the connection may be terminated. A `DELAYED` query that returns without an error message does not guarantee that the inserts will take place; it confirms only that the query is received by the server to be processed. If the server crashes, the data additions may not be executed when the server restarts and the user won't be informed of the failure. To confirm a `DELAYED` insert, the user must check the table later for the inserted content with a `SELECT` statement. The `DELAYED` option works only with MyISAM and InnoDB tables. It's also not applicable when the `ON DUPLICATE KEY UPDATE` clause is used.

Use the `HIGH_PRIORITY` keyword to override a **`--low-priority-updates`** server option and to disable concurrent inserts.

The `IGNORE` keyword instructs the server to ignore any errors encountered and suppress the error messages. In addition, for multiple row insertions, the statement continues to insert rows after encountering errors on previous rows. Warnings are generated that the user can display with the `SHOW WARNINGS` statement.

The `INTO` keyword is optional and only for compatibility with other database engines.

The `DEFAULT` keyword can be given for a column for the first two syntax formats to instruct the server to use the default value for the column. You can set the default value either with the `CREATE TABLE` statement when the table is created or with the `ALTER TABLE` statement for existing tables.

The `ON DUPLICATE KEY UPDATE` clause tells an `INSERT` statement how to handle an insert when an index in the table already contains a specified value in a column. With this clause, the statement updates the data in the existing row to reflect the new values in the given columns. Without this clause, the statement generates an error. An example appears in the next section.

Single-row insertion with the SET clause

```
INSERT [LOW_PRIORITY|DELAYED|HIGH_PRIORITY] [IGNORE]
  [INTO] table
  SET column={expression|DEFAULT}, ...
  [ON DUPLICATE KEY UPDATE column=expression, ...]
```

This variant of the INSERT statement allows only one row of data to be inserted into a table per SQL statement. The SET clause lists one or more column names, each followed by the value to which it is to be set. The value given can be a static value or an expression. Here is an example:

```
INSERT INTO clients
SET client_name =  'Geoffrey & Company',
city = 'Boston', state = 'MA';
```

This example lists three columns along with the values to be set in a row entry in the clients table. Other columns in the newly inserted row will be handled in a default manner. For instance, an AUTO_INCREMENT column will be set to the next number in sequence.

As mentioned earlier, the ON DUPLICATE KEY UPDATE clause allows an INSERT statement to handle rows that already contain specified values. Here is an example:

```
CREATE UNIQUE INDEX client_phone
ON clients(client_name,telephone);

ALTER TABLE clients
ADD COLUMN new_telephone TINYINT(1)
AFTER telephone;

INSERT INTO clients
SET client_name = 'Marie & Associates',
new_telephone = 0
telephone = '504-486-1234'
ON DUPLICATE KEY UPDATE
new_client = 1;
```

This example starts by creating an index on the client_phone column in the clients table. The index type is UNIQUE, which means that duplicate values for the combination of client_name and telephone columns are not allowed. With the second SQL statement, we add a column to flag new telephone numbers for existing clients. The INSERT statement tries to insert the specified client name and telephone number. But it indicates that if there is already a row in the table for the client, a new row is not to be added. Instead, the existing row is to be updated per the UPDATE clause, setting the original entry's telephone column to the value given in the SET clause. The assumption is that the new data being inserted either is for a new client or is an update to the existing client's telephone number. Instead of using a column value after the equals sign, a literal value or an expression may be given.

Multiple-row insertions

```
INSERT [LOW_PRIORITY|DELAYED|HIGH_PRIORITY] [IGNORE]
  [INTO] table [(column,...)]
  VALUES ({expression|DEFAULT},...), (...)
  [ON DUPLICATE KEY UPDATE column=expression,...]
```

This format of the INSERT statement allows one SQL statement to insert multiple rows. The columns in which data is to be inserted may be given in parentheses in a comma-separated list. If no columns are specified, the statement must include a value for each column in each row, in the order that they appear in the table. In the place reserved for an AUTO_INCREMENT column, specify NULL and the server will insert the correct next value in the column. To specify default values for other columns, use the DEFAULT keyword. NULL may also be given for any other column that permits NULL and that you wish to leave NULL. The VALUES clause lists the values of each row to be inserted into the table. The values for each row are enclosed in parentheses; each row is separated by a comma. Here is an example:

```
INSERT INTO clients (client_name, telephone)
VALUES('Marie & Associates', '504-486-1234'),
('Geoffrey & Company', '617-522-1234'),
('Kenneth & Partners', '617-523-1234');
```

In this example, three rows are inserted into the `clients` table with one SQL statement. Although the table has several columns, only two columns are inserted for each row here. The other columns are set to their default value or to NULL. The order of the values for each row corresponds to the order that the columns are listed.

Normally, if a multiple INSERT statement is entered and one of the rows to be inserted is a duplicate, an error is triggered and an error message is displayed. The statement is terminated and no rows are inserted. The IGNORE keyword, however, instructs the server to ignore any errors encountered, suppress the error messages, and insert only the non-duplicate rows. The results of this statement display like so:

```
Query OK, 120 rows affected (4.20 sec)
Records: 125  Duplicates: 5  Warnings: 0
```

These results indicate that 125 records were to be inserted, but only 120 rows were affected or successfully inserted. There were five duplicates in the SQL statement, but there were no warnings because of the IGNORE keyword. Entering the SHOW WARNINGS statement will display the suppressed warning messages.

Inserting rows based on a SELECT

```
INSERT [LOW_PRIORITY|HIGH_PRIORITY] [IGNORE]
  [INTO] table [(column,...)]
  SELECT...
  [ON DUPLICATE KEY UPDATE column=expression,...]
```

This method of the INSERT statement allows for multiple rows to be inserted in one SQL statement, based on data retrieved from another table by way of a SELECT statement. If no columns are listed (i.e., an asterisk is given instead), the SELECT will return the values of all columns in the order in which they are in the selected table and will be inserted (if possible without error) in the same order in the table designated for inserting data into. If you don't want to retrieve all of the columns of the selected table, or if the columns in both tables are not the same, then you must list the columns to retrieve in the SELECT statement and provide a matching ordered list of the columns of the table that data is to be inserted into.

For the following example, suppose that the `employees` table contains a column called `softball` to indicate whether an employee is a member of the company's softball team. Suppose further that it is decided that a new table should be created to store information about members of the softball team and that the team's captain will have privileges to this new table (`softball_team`), but no other tables. The employee names and telephone numbers need to be copied into the new table because the team's captain will not be allowed to do a query on the `employees` table to extract that information. Here are the SQL statements to set up the new table with its initial data:

```
CREATE TABLE softball_team
(player_id INT KEY, player_name VARCHAR(50),
 position VARCHAR(20), telephone CHAR(8));

INSERT INTO softball_team
(player_id, player_name, telephone)
  SELECT emp_id, CONCAT(name_first, ' ', name_last),
  RIGHT(telephone_home, 8)
  FROM employees
  WHERE softball = 'Y';
```

The first SQL statement creates the new table. The columns are very simple: one column as a row identifier, one column for both the first and last names of the player, another for the player's home telephone number, and yet another for the player's position, to be filled in later by the team's captain. Normally, we wouldn't include a column like the one for the player's name because that would be duplicating data in two tables. However, the team captain intends to change many of the player's names to softball nicknames (e.g., *Slugger Johnson*).

In the second SQL statement, the `INSERT` statement uses an embedded `SELECT` statement to retrieve data from the `employees` table where the `softball` column for the row is set to `'Y'`. The `CONCAT( )` function is used to put together the first and last names, separated by a space. This will go into the `name` column in the new table. The `RIGHT( )` function is used to extract only the last eight characters of the `telephone_home` column because all of the employees on the softball team are from the same telephone dialing area. See Chapter 11 for more information on these functions. Notice that we've listed the three columns that data is to go into, although there are four in the table. Also notice that the `SELECT` statement has three columns of the same data types but with different names.

Data Manipulation

JOIN

```
SELECT...|UPDATE...|DELETE...
table [INNER|CROSS] JOIN table [ON condition|USING (column[,...])] |
table STRAIGHT_JOIN table ON condition |
table LEFT [OUTER] JOIN table {ON condition|USING (column[,...])} |
table NATURAL [LEFT [OUTER]] JOIN table |
[OJ table LEFT OUTER JOIN table ON condition] |
table RIGHT [OUTER] JOIN table {ON condition|USING (column[,...])} |
table NATURAL [RIGHT [OUTER]] JOIN table
```

The `JOIN` clause is common to several SQL statements (`SELECT`, `UPDATE`, `DELETE`) and is complex; therefore, it is listed here as its own entry in the chapter. Use `JOIN` to link tables together based on columns with common data for purposes of selecting, updating, or deleting data. The `JOIN` clause is entered at the place in the relevant statement that specifies the tables to be referenced. This precludes the need to join the tables based on key columns in the `WHERE` clause.

The ON keyword is used to indicate the pair of columns by which the tables are to be joined (indicated with the equals sign operator). As an alternative method, the USING keyword may be given along with a comma-separated list of columns both tables have in common, contained within parentheses. The columns must exist in each table that is joined. To improve performance, you can also provide index hints to MySQL (see the last subsection of this clause definition, "Index hints").

Here is an example of a JOIN:

```
SELECT CONCAT(name_first, SPACE(1), name_last) AS Name
FROM employees
JOIN branches ON employees.branch_id = branches.branch_id
WHERE location = 'New Orleans';
```

This statement displays a list of employees from the employees table who are located in the New Orleans branch office. The problem solved by the JOIN is that the employees table doesn't indicate New Orleans by name as the branch; that table just has a numeric identifier. The branches table is used to retrieve the branch name for the WHERE clause. The location column is a column in the branches table. Nothing is actually displayed from the branches table here. Since the record identification column for branches is branch_id in both tables, the USING keyword can be used instead of ON to create the same join:

```
SELECT CONCAT(name_first, SPACE(1), name_last) AS Name
FROM employees
JOIN branches USING (branch_id)
WHERE location = 'New Orleans';
```

This will join the two tables on the branch_id column in each table. Since these tables have only one column in common, it's not necessary to specify that row; instead, you can use the NATURAL keyword. Here is the same statement with this change:

```
SELECT CONCAT(name_first, SPACE(1), name_last) AS Name
FROM employees
NATURAL JOIN branches
WHERE location = 'New Orleans';
```

Notice that the USING keyword and the column for linking are omitted. MySQL will assume that branch_id in both columns are the same and will naturally join the tables on them. The results of this SQL statement will be the same as those of the previous two.

When joining two tables in a simple join, as shown in the previous examples, if no rows in the second table match rows from the first table, no row will be displayed for the unmatched data. For example, if the branches table lists a branch office for which there are no employees listed in the employees table belonging to that branch, the results set would not show a row for that supposedly empty branch office. Sometimes, though, it can be useful to display a record regardless. In our example, this would tell us that something's wrong with the data: either one or more employees are marked with the wrong branch_id, or some employee records are missing from the employees table. Conversely, if an employee has a branch_id value that does not exist in the branches table, we would want to see it in the results so that we can correct the data.

To list a row for each employee including stray ones, the LEFT keyword may be given in front of the JOIN keyword to indicate that records from the first table listed on the left are to be displayed regardless of whether there is a matching row in the table on the right:

```
SELECT CONCAT(name_first, SPACE(1), name_last) AS Name,
location AS Branch
FROM employees
LEFT JOIN branches USING (branch_id)
ORDER BY location;
```

This SQL statement lists a row for each employee along with the employee's location. If a row for an employee has either a NULL value for the `branch_id`, or a branch number that is not in the `branches` table, the employee name will still be displayed but with the branch name reading as NULL. Again, this can be useful for spotting errors or inconsistencies in the data between related tables.

In contrast to `LEFT JOIN`, the `RIGHT JOIN` clause includes all matching entries from the table on the right even if there are no matches from the table on the left. Here is an example using a `RIGHT JOIN`:

```
SELECT CONCAT(name_first, SPACE(1), name_last) AS Name,
location AS Branch
FROM employees
RIGHT JOIN branches USING (branch_id)
ORDER BY location;
```

This example displays branches for which there are no matching employee records. For both the `LEFT` and `RIGHT JOIN` methods, the `OUTER` keyword is optional and has no effect on the results. It's just a matter of preference and compatibility with other database engines.

The `JOIN` clause has a few other options. The `STRAIGHT_JOIN` keyword explicitly instructs MySQL to read the tables as listed, from left to right. The keywords `INNER` and `CROSS` have no effect on the results, as of recent versions of MySQL. They cannot be used in conjunction with the keywords `LEFT`, `RIGHT`, or `NATURAL`. The syntax starting with the `OJ` keyword is provided for compatibility with Open Database Connectivity (ODBC).

You can use the `AS` keyword to introduce aliases for tables. Several examples of aliasing are provided earlier in the explanation of this clause.

Data Manipulation

Index hints

```
SELECT...|UPDATE...|DELETE...
table...JOIN table
USE {INDEX|KEY} [{FOR {JOIN|ORDER BY|GROUP BY}] ([index[,...]]) |
FORCE {INDEX|KEY} [{FOR {JOIN|ORDER BY|GROUP BY}] (index[,...]) |
IGNORE {INDEX|KEY} [{FOR {JOIN|ORDER BY|GROUP BY}] (index[,...])
```

When MySQL joins and searches tables, indexes can be used to increase the speed of the SQL statements. Use the `EXPLAIN` statement to analyze a joined SQL statement to see which indexes are being used and in which order, as well as whether there are other indexes available that aren't being used in the join. MySQL may not always choose the best index available. To hint to MySQL which index it should check first, and perhaps which index to ignore, or even to force it to use a particular index, you can employ *index hints*.

To tell MySQL to use a particular index, add the `USE INDEX` clause to the `JOIN` along with the names of the indexes in a comma-separated list, within parentheses. To present an example of this method, let's start with a `JOIN` statement that may execute in a suboptimal manner:

```
SELECT client_name, COUNT(*) AS tickets
FROM work_req
JOIN clients USING(client_id)
WHERE client_type = 1
AND DATEDIFF(NOW(), request_date) < 91
GROUP BY client_id
```

This statement retrieves a list of support clients and a count of the number of support tickets that they have created in the last 90 days. It gets the count of tickets from `work_req` and the client name from the `clients` table. To tweak the performance of the statement, let's examine the indexes for the `work_req` table:

```
SHOW INDEXES FROM work_req \G

*************************** 1. row ***************************
       Table: work_req
  Non_unique: 0
    Key_name: PRIMARY
Seq_in_index: 1
 Column_name: wr_id
   Collation: A
 Cardinality: 115
    Sub_part: NULL
      Packed: NULL
        Null:
  Index_type: BTREE
     Comment:
*************************** 2. row ***************************
       Table: work_req
  Non_unique: 1
    Key_name: workreq_date_key
Seq_in_index: 1
 Column_name: wr_id
   Collation: A
 Cardinality: 217337
    Sub_part: NULL
      Packed: NULL
        Null: YES
  Index_type: BTREE
     Comment:
*************************** 3. row ***************************
       Table: work_req
  Non_unique: 1
    Key_name: workreq_date_key
Seq_in_index: 2
 Column_name: request_date
   Collation: A
 Cardinality: 217337
    Sub_part: NULL
      Packed: NULL
        Null:
  Index_type: BTREE
     Comment:
```

The results show us that the table `work_req` has two indexes: a primary one based on the `wr_id` (see row 1) and a second one called `workreq_date_key` (see the `Key_name` field in rows 2 and 3) based on wr_id and request_date together. To suggest to MySQL in our JOIN statement that this second index should be used, enter the statement like so:

```
SELECT client_name, COUNT(*) AS tickets
FROM work_req
JOIN clients
USE INDEX FOR JOIN (workreq_date_key)
USING(client_id)
WHERE client_type = 1
AND DATEDIFF(NOW(), request_date) < 91
GROUP BY client_id;
```

The FORCE INDEX option instructs MySQL to attempt to limit its search to the specified index; others, however, will be used if the requested columns make it necessary:

```
SELECT client_name, COUNT(*) AS tickets
FROM work_req
JOIN clients
FORCE INDEX FOR JOIN (workreq_date_key)
USING(client_id)
WHERE client_type = 1
AND DATEDIFF(NOW(), request_date) < 91
GROUP BY client_id;
```

To instruct MySQL not to use certain indexes, list them with the IGNORE INDEX option in the same manner:

```
SELECT client_name, COUNT(*) AS tickets
FROM work_req
JOIN clients
IGNORE INDEX FOR JOIN (workreq_date_key)
USING(client_id)
WHERE client_type = 1
AND DATEDIFF(NOW(), request_date) < 91
GROUP BY client_id;
```

It's also permitted to use combinations of these three index hint clauses, separated only by a space.

LIMIT

```
...
LIMIT count |
LIMIT [offset,] count |
LIMIT count OFFSET offset
```

Use the LIMIT clause to limit the number of rows the server will process to satisfy the given SQL statement. For the SELECT statement, it limits the number of rows returned in the results set. In an UPDATE statement, it limits the number of rows changed. With the DELETE statement, it limits the number of rows deleted. The DELETE statement permits only the first syntax shown, whereas the other statements allow all three.

The LIMIT clause accepts only literal values, not expressions or variables. Nor will it accept a negative value. The most straightforward method of limiting the number of rows is to specify the maximum row count to be displayed, like this:

```
SELECT * FROM employees
LIMIT 5;
```

To begin listing rows after a specific number of records, an offset may be given, where the offset for the first row is 0. Two syntaxes accomplish this. One gives the amount of the offset, followed by a comma and then the maximum count of rows to display. The other specifies the count followed by the `OFFSET` keyword, followed by the amount of the offset. Here is an example of the first structure, which is preferred:

```
SELECT * FROM employees
LIMIT 10, 5;
```

In this example, after the 10th record is reached, the next 5 records will be returned—in other words, results 11 through 15 are returned. The offset and count for the `LIMIT` clause are based on the rows in the results set, not necessarily on the rows in the tables. So the amount of the offset is related to the order of the rows retrieved from the tables based on clauses, such as the `WHERE` clause and the `ORDER BY` clause.

LOAD DATA INFILE

```
LOAD DATA [LOW_PRIORITY|CONCURRENT] [LOCAL] INFILE '/path/file'
  [REPLACE|IGNORE] INTO TABLE table
  [CHARACTER SET character_set]
  [FIELDS [TERMINATED BY 'character']
  [[OPTIONALLY] ENCLOSED BY 'character'] [ESCAPED BY 'character']]

  [LINES [STARTING BY 'string'] [TERMINATED BY 'string']]

  [IGNORE count LINES]

  [(column,...)]

  [SET column = expression,...]
```

You can use this statement to import organized data from a text file into a table in MySQL. The file can be either on the server or on the client.

For a file on the server, if you use a bare filename (such as *input.txt*) or a relative path (such as *../*), the file is found relative to the directory of the database into which the data is to be imported. If the file is not located in the directory's database, the file permissions must be set so it can be read for all filesystem users.

For a file on the client, the `LOCAL` keyword must be given. This feature must be enabled on both the client and the server by using the startup option of `--local-infile=1`. See Chapter 15 for more information on server and client settings.

If a data text file contains rows of data duplicating some of the rows in the table into which it's being imported, an error will occur and the import may end without importing the remaining data. Duplicate rows are those that have the same values for key columns or other unique columns. To instruct the server to ignore any errors encountered and to continue loading other rows, use the `IGNORE` keyword. Use the `SHOW WARNINGS` statement to retrieve the error messages that would have been displayed. To instruct the server to replace any duplicate rows with the ones being imported, use the `REPLACE` keyword. This will completely replace the values of all columns in the row, even when the new record contains no data for a column and the existing one does.

Here is a basic example of `LOAD DATA INFILE`:

```
LOAD DATA INFILE '/tmp/catalog.txt'
INTO TABLE catalog
FIELDS TERMINATED BY '|'
LINES TERMINATED BY '\n';
```

In this example, the file to be loaded is in the */tmp* directory and is called *catalog.txt*. The data contained in the file is to be inserted into the `catalog` table in the current database in use. Each field in the text file is terminated with a vertical bar character. The rows of data in the text file are on separate lines. They are separated by a newline character (`\n`). This is the default for a Unix text file. For DOS or Windows systems, lines are usually terminated with `\n\r`, signifying a newline and a Return character. If the rows start with a special character, you can identify that character with the `LINES STARTED BY` clause.

This statement also offers the `ENCLOSED BY` clause to specify a character that can start and terminate a field, such as a quotation mark. You can use the `OPTIONALLY` keyword to indicate that the character is used for enclosing columns containing string data, but optional for numeric data. Numeric fields may then include or omit the given character. For example, if the optional character is an apostrophe (single quote), a numeric value for a field may be given as `'1234'` or `1234`, so MySQL should expect and accept both.

The `ESCAPED BY` clause indicates the character used in the input file to escape special characters. The backslash (\) is the default value.

Some data text files contain one or more lines of column headings that should not be imported. To omit these initial lines from the import, use the `IGNORE` *`count`* `LINES` clause, where *`count`* is the number of lines to ignore.

For some data text files, the fields of data are not in the same order as the columns of the receiving table. Sometimes there are fewer fields in the text file than in the table. For both of these situations, to change the order and number of columns, add a list of columns and their order in the text file to the end of the statement within parentheses. Here is an example of such a scenario:

```
LOAD DATA LOW_PRIORITY INFILE '/tmp/catalog.txt' IGNORE
INTO TABLE catalog
FIELDS TERMINATED BY '|'
LINES TERMINATED BY '\n'
IGNORE 1 LINES
(cat_id, description, price);
```

The first line of the text file contains column headings describing the data, but that line will not be imported because of the `IGNORE 1 LINES` clause here. The `catalog` table has several more columns than the three that are being imported, and they are in a different order. Finally, because this import is not critical, the `LOW_PRIORITY` keyword near the beginning of the statement instructs the server to handle other queries on the `catalog` table before running this statement. If this was replaced with `CONCURRENT`, the import would be performed even if other clients were querying the same table.

As of version 5.0.3 of MySQL, the list of fields can contain column names and user variables. Also, `SET` may be added to set or change the value to be imported. Here is an example:

```
LOAD DATA LOW_PRIORITY INFILE '/tmp/catalog.txt' IGNORE
INTO TABLE catalog
```

```
FIELDS TERMINATED BY '|'
LINES TERMINATED BY '\n'
IGNORE 1 LINES
(cat_id, @discarded, description, @mfg_price)
SET price = @mfg_price * .9;
```

In this example, the table receiving the data has five columns. The second one is to be ignored and stored in a `discarded` user variable. The third column is the `price`. Since the company sells the manufacturer's products at ten percent less than the manufacturer's suggested retail price, the statement receives the raw value in the user variable `@mfg_price` and then we use `SET` to adjust that value for the column when loaded.

RELEASE SAVEPOINT

`RELEASE SAVEPOINT` *identifier*

This statement instructs the server to release a savepoint named earlier with the `SAVEPOINT` statement for the current transaction. The statement does not commit the transaction, nor does it roll back the transaction to the savepoint. Instead, it merely eliminates the savepoint as a possible rollback point. See the `SAVEPOINT` statement for more information. Here is an example of `RELEASE SAVEPOINT`:

```
START TRANSACTION;

LOCK TABLES orders WRITE;

INSERT DATA INFILE '/tmp/customer_info.sql'
INTO TABLE orders;

SAVEPOINT orders_import;

INSERT DATA INFILE '/tmp/customer_orders.sql'
INTO TABLE orders;

SAVEPOINT orders_import1;

INSERT DATA INFILE '/tmp/customer_orders1.sql'
INTO TABLE orders;

SELECT...

RELEASE SAVEPOINT orders_import1;
```

In this example, the database administrator imports a customer information file and two files containing customer orders and sets up two savepoints. After running a few `SELECT` statements (not fully shown here), he decides that the results of the second batch of orders look all right and he releases the savepoint for that batch. He hasn't yet decided if the first batch was imported properly. If he decides that there was a problem, he can still roll back all of the orders imported, but he can no longer roll back just the second batch.

REPLACE

```
REPLACE [LOW_PRIORITY|DELAYED] [INTO] table [(column,...)]
  VALUES ({expression|DEFAULT},...)[, (...)]

REPLACE [LOW_PRIORITY|DELAYED] [INTO] table
  SET column={expression|DEFAULT}[, ...]

REPLACE [LOW_PRIORITY|DELAYED] [INTO] table [(column,...)]
  SELECT...
```

Use this statement to insert new rows of data and to replace existing rows where the `PRIMARY KEY` or `UNIQUE` index key is the same as the new record being inserted. This statement requires `INSERT` and `DELETE` privileges because it is potentially a combination of both.

The `LOW_PRIORITY` keyword instructs the server to wait until there are no queries on the table named, including reads, and then to lock the table for exclusive use by the thread so that data may be inserted and replaced. When the statement is finished, the lock is released, automatically. For busy servers, a client may be waiting for quite a while. The `DELAYED` keyword will free the client by storing the statement in a buffer for processing when the table is not busy. The client won't be given notice of the success of the statement, just that it's buffered. If the server crashes before the changes to the data are processed, the client will not be informed and the buffer contents will be lost. The `INTO` keyword is optional and is a matter of style preference and compatibility with other database engines.

The `REPLACE` statement has three basic formats. The first contains the values for each row in parentheses after the `VALUES` keyword. If the order and number of values do not match the columns of the table named, the columns have to be listed in parentheses after the table name in the order in which the values are arranged. Here is an example of the `REPLACE` statement using this syntax:

```
REPLACE INTO workreq (wr_id, client_id, description)
VALUES(5768,1000,'Network Access Problem'),
(5770,1000,'Network Access Problem');
```

Notice that this statement is able to insert two rows without the column names being listed twice. In this example, the first row already exists before this statement is to be executed. Once it's run, the row represented by the work request identifier 5768 is completely replaced with this data. Columns that are not included in the list of columns here are reset to their default values or to NULL, depending on the column.

The second syntax does not allow multiple rows. Instead of grouping the column names in one part of the statement and the values in another part, column names and values are given in a *`column=value`* pair. To enter the `REPLACE` statement from the preceding example in this format, you would have to enter the following two statements:

```
REPLACE INTO workreq
SET wr_id = 5768, client_id = 1000,
description = 'Network Access Problem';

REPLACE INTO workreq
SET wr_id = 5770, client_id = 1000,
description = 'Network Access Problem';
```

The third syntax involves a subquery, which is available as of version 4.1 of MySQL. With a subquery, data can be retrieved from another table and inserted into the table referenced in the main query for the statement. Here is an example:

```
REPLACE INTO workreq (wr_id, client_id, status)
SELECT wr_id, client_id, 'HOLD'
FROM wk_schedule
WHERE programmer_id = 1000;
```

Work requests assigned to a particular programmer are being changed to a temporarily on-hold status. The values for two of the columns are taken from the work schedule table, and the fixed string of `HOLD` is inserted as the value of the third column. Currently, the table for which replacement data is being inserted cannot be used in the subquery.

ROLLBACK

`ROLLBACK [WORK] [AND [NO] CHAIN] [[NO] RELEASE]`

Use this statement with transactional tables to reverse transactions that have not yet been committed. Transaction statements are currently supported by the InnoDB, NDB Cluster, and BDB storage engines and are ignored if used with MyISAM tables.

If `AUTOCOMMIT` is enabled, it must be disabled for this statement to be meaningful, which can be done as follows:

```
SET AUTOCOMMIT = 0;
```

`AUTOCOMMIT` is also disabled when a transaction is started with the `START TRANSACTION` statement. It is reinstated with the execution of the `COMMIT` statement, the ending of the current session, and several other statements that imply that a commit is desired. See the explanation of `COMMIT` earlier in this chapter for a list of statements that imply a commit.

The `WORK` keyword is optional and has no effect on the results. It's available for compatibility with its counterparts, `BEGIN WORK` and `COMMIT WORK`. Use the `AND CHAIN` clause to indicate that the transaction is to be rolled back and another is starting, thus making it unnecessary to execute the `START TRANSACTION` statement again. Use the `AND RELEASE` clause to end the current client session after rolling back the transaction. Add the keyword `NO` to indicate explicitly that a new transaction is not to begin (when used with `CHAIN`) or the client session is not to end (when used with `RELEASE`)—these are the default settings, though. It's necessary to specify `NO` only when the system variable `completion_type` is set to something other than the default setting.

Here is an example of this statement's use in context:

```
START TRANSACTION;

LOCK TABLES orders WRITE;

INSERT DATA INFILE '/tmp/customer_orders.sql'
INTO TABLE orders;

SELECT ...;

ROLLBACK;

UNLOCK TABLES;
```

In this example, after the batch of orders is inserted into the **orders** table, the administrator manually enters a series of `SELECT` statements (not shown) to check the integrity of the data. If everything seems all right, the `COMMIT` statement would be issued to commit the transactions, instead of the `ROLLBACK` statement shown here. In this case, a problem leads the administrator to issue `ROLLBACK` to remove the data imported by the `INSERT DATA INFILE` statement.

A rollback will not undo the creation or deletion of databases. It also cannot be performed on changes to table schema (e.g., `ALTER TABLE`, `CREATE TABLE`, or `DROP TABLE` statements). Transactions cannot be reversed with the `ROLLBACK` statement if they have been committed. Commits are caused by the `COMMIT` statement as well as several other implicit commit statements. See the explanation of `COMMIT` for a list of statements that imply a commit.

ROLLBACK TO SAVEPOINT

`ROLLBACK TO SAVEPOINT` *`identifier`*

This statement instructs the server to reverse SQL statements for the current transaction back to a point marked in the transaction by the `SAVEPOINT` statement. Any transactions for the session made after the savepoint are undone. This is in contrast to `ROLLBACK` by itself, which undoes all changes since the start of the transaction. Transaction statements are currently supported by the InnoDB, NDB Cluster, and BDB storage engines and are ignored if used with MyISAM tables. Multiple savepoints may be set up during a transaction. Here is an example:

```
START TRANSACTION;

LOCK TABLES orders WRITE;

INSERT DATA INFILE '/tmp/customer_info.sql'
INTO TABLE orders;

SAVEPOINT orders_import;

INSERT DATA INFILE '/tmp/customer_orders.sql'
INTO TABLE orders;

SELECT...

SAVEPOINT orders_import1;

INSERT DATA INFILE '/tmp/customer_orders1.sql'
INTO TABLE orders;

SELECT...

ROLLBACK TO SAVEPOINT orders_import1;
```

In this example, the database administrator has imported a customer information file and two files containing customer orders and has set up two savepoints. After running a few `SELECT` statements (not fully shown here), he decides that there was a problem loading the second batch of orders, so he rolls back the transaction to the savepoint, eliminating the data that was imported from the *customer_orders1.sql* file. If he wants, he can still roll back all of the orders imported, as well as the whole transaction. When

Data Manipulation

he's finished, he can commit the transactions by executing the COMMIT statement. See that statement earlier in this chapter for more information on committing transactions explicitly and implicitly.

SAVEPOINT

```
SAVEPOINT identifier
```

Use this statement to identify a point in a transaction to which SQL statements may potentially be undone later. It's used in conjunction with the ROLLBACK TO SAVEPOINT statement. It may be released with the RELEASE SAVEPOINT statement. You can use any unreserved word to identify a savepoint and can create several savepoints during a transaction. If an additional SAVEPOINT statement is issued with the same name, the previous point will be replaced with the new point for the name given. Here is an example:

```
START TRANSACTION;
LOCK TABLES orders WRITE;
INSERT DATA INFILE '/tmp/customer_info.sql'
INTO TABLE orders;
SAVEPOINT orders_import;
INSERT DATA INFILE '/tmp/customer_orders.sql'
INTO TABLE orders;
```

At this point in this example, the administrator can check the results of the orders imported before committing the transactions. If the administrator decides that the orders imported have problems (the */tmp/customer_orders.sql* file), but not the client information that was first imported (the */tmp/customer_info.sql* file), the following statement could be entered:

```
ROLLBACK TO SAVEPOINT orders_import;
```

If the administrator decides that the customer information that was imported also has problems, the ROLLBACK statement can be issued to undo the entire transaction.

As of version 5.0.17 of MySQL, if a stored function or trigger is used, a new savepoint level is set up and the previous savepoints are suspended. When the stored function or trigger is finished, any savepoints it created are released and the original savepoint level resumes.

SELECT

```
SELECT [flags] {*|column|expression}[, ...]
  FROM table[, ...]
  [WHERE condition]
  [GROUP BY {column|expression|position}[ASC|DESC], ...
     [WITH ROLLUP]]
  [HAVING condition]
  [ORDER BY {column|expression|position}[ASC|DESC] , ...]
  [LIMIT {[offset,] count|count OFFSET offset}]
  [PROCEDURE procedure(arguments)]
  options
```

Use this statement to retrieve and display data from tables within a database. It has many clauses and options, but for simple data retrieval many of them can be omitted. The basic syntax for the statement is shown. After the SELECT keyword, some keywords to control the whole operation may be given. Next comes an asterisk to retrieve all columns, a list of columns to retrieve, or expressions returning values to display, separated by commas.

Data can be retrieved from one or more tables, given in a comma-separated list. If multiple tables are specified, other clauses must define how the tables are joined. The remaining clauses may be called on to refine the data to be retrieved, to order it, and so forth. These various keywords, options, and clauses are detailed in subsections of this statement explanation. To start, here is a simple example of how you can use the `SELECT` statement:

```
SELECT name_first, name_last, telephone_home,
DATEDIFF(now( ), last_review)
AS 'Days Since Last Review'
FROM employees;
```

In this example, three columns and the results of an expression based on a fourth column are to be displayed. The first and last name of each employee, each employee's home telephone number, and the difference between the date of the employee's last employment review and the date now are listed. This last field has the addition of the `AS` keyword to set the column heading of the results set, and to name an alias for the field. An alias may be referenced in subsequent clauses of the same statement (e.g., the `ORDER BY` clause). To select all columns in the table, the wildcard * can be given instead of the column names.

SELECT statement keywords

```
SELECT
[ALL|DISTINCT|DISTINCTROW]
[HIGH_PRIORITY] [STRAIGHT_JOIN]
[SQL_SMALL_RESULT] [SQL_BIG_RESULT] [SQL_BUFFER_RESULT]
[SQL_CACHE|SQL_NO_CACHE] [SQL_CALC_FOUND_ROWS]
{*|column|expression}[, ...]
FROM table[, ...]
[WHERE condition] [other clauses] [options]
```

Between the initial `SELECT` keyword and list of columns and expressions, several keywords may be given. They are shown in the preceding syntax, with the other components of the statement abbreviated.

When a `WHERE` clause is used with the `SELECT` statement, rows in the results may contain duplicate data. If you want all rows that meet the selection conditions to be displayed, you may include the `ALL` keyword. This is the default, so it's not necessary to give this keyword. If you want to display only the first occurrence of a row, include the `DISTINCT` keyword or its synonym `DISTINCTROW`. Here is an example:

```
SELECT DISTINCT dept
FROM employees;
```

This statement will list the names of all departments for which we have employees listed in the `employees` table. Even though there are several employees in the same department, it will list only one row for each department.

By default, any `UPDATE` statements that are issued have priority over `SELECT` statements submitted by other client sessions at the same time; the updates are run first. To give a particular `SELECT` statement higher priority than any `UPDATE` statements, use the `HIGH_PRIORITY` keyword.

Multiple tables may be selected with the SELECT statement. The column on which they should be joined is given with the WHERE clause or the JOIN clause. The JOIN clause is described earlier in this chapter. For the purposes of this section, you just need to know that in order to optimize retrieval, MySQL might not join tables in the order that they are listed in the SQL statement. To insist on joining in the order given, you must use the STRAIGHT_JOIN keyword.

When you know that the results of a SELECT statement using the DISTINCT keyword or the GROUP BY clause (discussed later) will be small, you can use the SQL_SMALL_RESULT keyword. This will cause MySQL to use temporary tables, with a key based on the GROUP BY clause elements, to sort the results and possibly make for faster data retrieval. If you expect the results to be large, you can use the SQL_BIG_RESULT keyword. This will cause MySQL to use temporary tables on the filesystem. Regardless of whether you use DISTINCT or GROUP BY, the SQL_BUFFER_RESULT keyword may be given for any SELECT statement to have MySQL use a temporary table to buffer the results. You can use only one of the SQL_*_RESULT keywords in each statement.

If the MySQL server is not using the query cache by default, you can force its use by including the SQL_CACHE keyword. If the server does use the query cache by default, you can use the SQL_NO_CACHE to instruct MySQL not to use the cache for this particular SELECT statement. To determine whether the server uses query cache by default, enter SHOW VARIABLES LIKE 'query_cache_type';. A value of ON indicates that it is in use.

The last keyword available is SQL_CALC_FOUND_ROWS, which counts the number of rows that meet the conditions of the statement. This is not affected by a LIMIT clause. The results of this count must be retrieved in a separate SELECT statement with the FOUND_ROWS( ) function. See the end of this chapter for information on this function:

```
SELECT SQL_CALC_FOUND_ROWS
name_first, name_last, telephone_home,
DATEDIFF(now( ), last_review)
AS 'Days Since Last Review'
FROM employees
WHERE dept = 'sales'
ORDER BY last_review DESC
LIMIT 10;

SELECT FOUND_ROWS();
```

The first statement retrieves a list of sales people to review, limited to the 10 who have gone the longest without a performance review. The second gets a count of how many employees there are to review in the sales department.

Exporting SELECT results

```
SELECT [flags] {*|columns|expression}[, ...]
[INTO OUTFILE '/path/filename'
  [FIELDS TERMINATED BY 'character']
  [FIELDS ENCLOSED BY 'character']
  [ESCAPED BY 'character' ]
  [LINES [STARTING BY 'character'] [TERMINATED BY 'character']]
|INTO DUMPFILE '/path/filename'
|INTO 'variable'[, ...]
[FOR UPDATE|LOCK IN SHARE MODE]]
FROM table[, ...]
```

```
[WHERE condition]
[other clauses] [options]
```

The INTO clause is used to export data from a SELECT statement to an external text file or a variable. Only the results will be exported, not the column names or other information.

Various clauses set delimiter and control characters in the output:

`ESCAPED BY`
: Character used to escape special characters in the output. The default is a backslash.

`FIELDS ENCLOSED BY`
: Character to use before and after each field. By default, no character is used.

`FIELDS TERMINATED BY`
: Character with which to separate fields. The default is a tab.

`LINES STARTING BY`
: Character used to start each line. By default, no character is used.

`LINES TERMINATED BY`
: Character used to end each line. The default is a newline character.

FILE privilege is necessary to use the INTO clause of the SELECT statement. This statement and clause combination is essentially the counterpart of the LOAD DATA INFILE statement. See the explanation of that statement earlier in this chapter for more details on the options for this clause. Here is an example of this clause and these options:

```
SELECT * FROM employees
INTO OUTFILE '/tmp/employees.txt'
FIELDS TERMINATED BY '|'
LINES TERMINATED BY '\n'
ESCAPED BY '\\';
```

The text file created by this SQL statement will contain a separate line for each row selected. Each field will end with a vertical bar. Any special characters (e.g., an apostrophe) will be preceded by a backslash. Because a backslash is an escape character within an SQL statement, two backslashes are needed in the ESCAPE BY clause because the first escapes the second. To import the resulting data text file, use the FOUND_ROWS( ) statement.

The second syntax uses the clause INTO DUMPFILE and exports only one row into an external text file. It does not allow any field or line terminators like the INTO OUTFILE clause. Here is an example of its use:

```
SELECT photograph
INTO DUMPFILE '/tmp/bobs_picture.jpeg'
FROM employees
WHERE emp_id = '1827';
```

This statement exports the contents of the photograph column for an employee's record. It's a BLOB type column and contains an image file. The result of the exported file is a complete and usable image file.

You can also use the INTO clause to store a value in a user variable or a system variable for reuse. Here's an example:

```
SET @sales = 0;

SELECT SUM(total_order) AS Sales
INTO @sales
```

```
FROM orders
WHERE YEAR(order_date) = YEAR(CURDATE());
```

This example creates the user variable `@sales`. Then we calculate the total sales for the current year and store it into that variable for reuse in subsequent statements in the session.

Grouping SELECT results

```
SELECT [flags] {*|column|expression}[, ...]
FROM table[, ...]
[WHERE condition]
[GROUP BY {column|expression|position} [ASC|DESC], ...
  [WITH ROLLUP]]
[other clauses] [options]
```

A `SELECT` statement sometimes produces more meaningful results if you group together rows containing the same value for a particular column. The `GROUP BY` clause specifies one or more columns by which MySQL is to group the data retrieved. This is used with aggregate functions so that the values of numeric columns for the rows grouped will be aggregated.

For instance, suppose that a `SELECT` statement is to list the sales representatives for a business and their orders for the month. Without a `GROUP BY` clause, one line would be displayed for each sales representative for each order. Here's an example of how this might be resolved:

```
SELECT CONCAT(name_first, ' ', name_last) AS 'Sales Rep.',
SUM(total_order) AS 'Sales for Month'
FROM orders, employees
WHERE employees.emp_id = sales_rep
AND MONTH(order_date) = MONTH(CURDATE( ))
GROUP BY sales_rep;
```

This statement concatenates the first and last name of each sales representative who placed an order for a customer during the current month. The `GROUP BY` clause groups together the rows found for each sales representative. The `SUM( )` function adds the values of the `total_order` column for each row within each group. See Chapter 10 for more information on the `SUM( )` function and other aggregate functions.

You can specify multiple columns in the `GROUP BY` clause. Instead of stating a column's name, you can state its position in the table, where a value of 1 represents the first column in the table. Expressions may be given as well.

The `GROUP BY` clause does its own sorting and cannot be used with the `ORDER BY` clause. To set the sorting to ascending order explicitly for a column, enter the `ASC` keyword after the column in the clause that is to be set. This is not necessary, though, since it is the default setting. To sort in descending order, add `DESC` after each column that is to be sorted in reverse.

When grouping rows by one column, it may be desirable not only to have a total of the values for certain columns, but also to display a total for all of the grouped rows at the end of the results set. To do this, use the `WITH ROLLUP` keyword. Here is an example:

```
SELECT location AS Branch,
CONCAT(name_first, ' ', name_last) AS 'Sales Rep.',
SUM(total_order) AS 'Sales for Month'
```

```
FROM orders, employees, branches
WHERE sales_rep = employees.emp_id
AND MONTH(order_date) = MONTH(CURDATE( ))
AND employees.branch_id = branches.branch_id
GROUP BY Branch, sales_rep WITH ROLLUP;
```

```
+---------------+----------------+----------------+
| Branch        | Sales Rep.     | Sales for Month |
+---------------+----------------+----------------+
| Boston        | Ricky Adams    |           2472 |
| Boston        | Morgan Miller  |           1600 |
| Boston        | Morgan Miller  |           4072 |
| New Orleans   | Marie Dyer     |           1750 |
| New Orleans   | Tom Smith      |           6407 |
| New Orleans   | Simone Caporale |          5722 |
| New Orleans   | Simone Caporale |         13879 |
| San Francisco | Geoffrey Dyer  |            500 |
| San Francisco | Kenneth Dyer   |            500 |
| San Francisco | Kenneth Dyer   |           1000 |
| NULL          | Kenneth Dyer   |          18951 |
+---------------+----------------+----------------+
```

This statement groups and adds up the total for each sales representative. When there aren't any more sales representatives for a branch, a row in the display for the subtotal is generated. It displays the branch name and the name of the last representative. When there are no more branches, a row for the grand total of sales is generated. The branch shows NULL. For clarity, I've boldfaced the subtotals and the grand total in the results set.

Having SELECT results

```
SELECT [flags] {*|column|expression}[, ...]
FROM table[, ...]
[WHERE condition]
[GROUP BY condition]
[HAVING condition]
[other clauses] [options]
```

The `HAVING` clause is similar to the `WHERE` clause, but it is used for conditions returned by aggregate functions (e.g., `AVG( )`, `MIN( )`, and `MAX( )`). For older versions of MySQL, you must use aliases for aggregate functions in the main clause of the `SELECT` statement. Here is an example of how you can use this clause:

```
SELECT CONCAT(name_first, ' ', name_last) AS 'Name', total_order
FROM orders
JOIN employees ON sales_rep = emp_id
JOIN branches USING (branch_id)
WHERE location = 'New Orleans'
GROUP BY sales_rep
HAVING MAX(total_order);
```

This SQL statement retrieves from the `employees` table a list of employee names for all employees located in the New Orleans branch office. From this list, the statement refines the results by grouping the data for each representative together and determines the sum of each one's `total_order` column. Because of the `MAX( )` function, it displays data only

Data Manipulation

for the row with the maximum number. The JOIN clause is described in its own section earlier in this chapter.

Ordering SELECT results

```
SELECT [flags] {*|column|expression}[, ...]
FROM table[, ...]
[WHERE condition]
[ORDER BY {column|expression|position} [ASC|DESC], ...]
[other clauses] [options]
```

The results of a SELECT statement, by default, are displayed in the order in which the rows of data are found in the table, which may be the order in which they were entered into the table. To change the order of a results set, use the ORDER BY clause. As a basis for ordering the results, list one or more columns separated by commas. The order in which columns are listed is the order in which sorts will be conducted. You can also use aliases for columns, column combinations, or expressions that were established earlier in the same SELECT statement. Instead of stating a column's name, you can also state its position, where a value of 1 represents the first column in the table. Here is an example of a SELECT statement using the ORDER BY clause:

```
SELECT CONCAT(name_first, ' ', name_last) AS Name,
MONTH(birth_date) AS 'Birth Month', email_address
FROM employees
ORDER BY 'Birth Month' ASC, Name ASC;
```

Here a list of employees, the months in which they were born, and their email addresses are extracted. For the name, the CONCAT( ) function is used to put the first and last name together, separated by a space. The AS clause establishes an alias of *Name*. The MONTH( ) function is used to extract the month from the birth_date column, and the AS clause sets up the alias *Birth Month*. In the ORDER BY clause, the alias for the birth date is used for the initial sort and the name is used for the secondary sort. The result will be that all of the employees who have a birth date in the same month will be listed together and in alphabetical order by name. Both aliases are followed by the ASC keyword to indicate that the results should be sorted in ascending order. This is unnecessary, as ascending order is the default. However, to change an ordering method to descending, use the DESC keyword.

You can also order the results using expressions, which may be based on columns or aliases. Here is an example of a SELECT statement using an expression for ordering:

```
SELECT CONCAT(name_first, ' ', name_last) AS name,
pay_rate, hours
FROM employees
ORDER BY pay_rate * hours DESC;
```

In this example, the first and last names are selected and concatenated together under the name column heading in the results set. The pay_rate column lists the hourly dollar rate an employee is paid, and the hours column contains the typical number of hours a week that an employee works. In the ORDER BY clause, the product of the hourly pay rate and the number of hours is determined for the ordering of the results set. The rows are to be listed in descending order per the DESC keyword based on the expression.

Limiting SELECT results

```
SELECT [flags] {*|column|expression}[, ...]
FROM table[, ...]
[WHERE condition]
[other clauses]
[LIMIT {[offset,] count|count OFFSET offset}]
[PROCEDURE procedure(arguments)]
[FOR UPDATE|LOCK IN SHARE MODE]]
[other clauses] [options]
```

The `LIMIT` clause is used to limit the number of rows displayed by the `SELECT` statement. The most straightforward method of limiting the number of rows is to specify the maximum row count to be displayed, like this:

```
SELECT * FROM employees
LIMIT 5;
```

To begin listing rows after a specific number of records, an offset may be given. The offset for the first row is 0. Two formats accomplish this. One gives the amount of the offset, followed by a comma and then the maximum count of rows to display. The other syntax structure specifies the count, followed by the `OFFSET` keyword, followed by the amount of the offset. Here is an example of the first structure, which is preferred:

```
SELECT * FROM employees
LIMIT 10, 5;
```

In this example, after the 10th record is reached, the next 5 records will be displayed—in other words, results 11 through 15 are returned. The offset and count for the `LIMIT` clause are based on the rows in the results set, not necessarily on the rows in the tables. So the amount of the offset is related to the order of the rows retrieved from the tables based on clauses, such as the `WHERE` clause and the `ORDER BY` clause. See the description of the `LIMIT` clause earlier in this chapter for more details.

Other SELECT clauses and options

```
SELECT [flags] {*|column|expression}[, ...]
FROM table[, ...]
[WHERE condition]
[other clauses]
[PROCEDURE procedure(arguments)]
[LOCK IN SHARE MODE|FOR UPDATE]
```

To send the results of a `SELECT` statement as standard input to a procedure, use the `PROCEDURE` clause. The `PROCEDURE` keyword is followed by the name of the procedure, which can be followed by parentheses containing parameters to be passed to the procedure. Here is an example:

```
SELECT * FROM employees
PROCEDURE ANALYSE(10, 225);
```

In this statement, the results of the `SELECT` statement are sent to the built-in function `ANALYSE( )` along with two numeric parameters. See `ANALYSE( )` near the end of this chapter for more information on this function.

To lock the rows that are being selected from a table, `LOCK IN SHARE MODE` may be given at the end of the `SELECT` statement. This prevents other clients from changing the data while the `SELECT` statement is running. The `FOR UPDATE` option instructs MySQL to invoke a temporary write lock on the rows being selected. Both of these locks will be terminated when the statement is finished running.

SET

```
SET [GLOBAL|@@global.|SESSION|@@session.] variable = expression
```

Use this statement to set a system or user variable for global or session use. System variables can be either *global variables*, which makes them visible to all users, or *session variables* (also called *local variables*), which are available only to the connection thread that creates the variable. To make a system variable global, use the `GLOBAL` keyword or precede the variable name by `@@global`. System variables are limited to the current session by default, but you can document that behavior by using the `SESSION` keyword or preceding the variable name with `@@session` or just `@@` (or use the synonyms `LOCAL` and `@@local`). To mark a user variable, place a single `@` in front of the variable name. Here is an example of creating a user variable:

```
SET @current_quarter = QUARTER(CURDATE( ));
```

This statement uses the `CURDATE( )` function to determine the current date. It's wrapped in the `QUARTER( )` function, which determines the quarter for the date given. The result is a number from one to four depending on the date. The number is stored in the user variable, `@current_quarter`. For examples involving system variables, see the explanation of the `SET` statement in Chapter 7.

Here's a more complete example of how this statement and a user variable may be used:

```
SET @row = 0;

SELECT @row := @row + 1 AS Row,
client_name AS Client
FROM clients
ORDER BY client_id LIMIT 3;

+------+--------------------+
| Row  | Client             |
+------+--------------------+
|    1 | Geoffrey & Company |
|    2 | Kenneth & Partners |
|    3 | Marie & Associates |
+------+--------------------+
```

In this example, the user variable `@row` is set to 0 and then used in a `SELECT` statement with the `:=` operator to increment the value by 1 with each row retrieved. This gives us a nice row numbering in the results.

SET TRANSACTION

```
SET [GLOBAL|SESSION] TRANSACTION ISOLATION LEVEL
{READ UNCOMMITTED|READ COMMITTED|REPEATABLE READ|SERIALIZABLE}
```

Use this statement to set an isolation level for the current transaction, for a transaction that's about to be started, or globally. Use the keyword `SESSION` to set the level for the current session. Use `GLOBAL` to set it for all subsequent transactions (this does not affect existing ones). If neither of these two keywords is included, the level is set for the next transaction of the current session. This statement applies only to InnoDB tables at this time.

The level `READ UNCOMMITTED` is known as a dirty read because `SELECT` statements are executed in a nonlocking manner. Thus, queries by one transaction can be affected by ongoing, uncommitted updates in another transaction, or old data may be used, thus making the results inconsistent. `READ COMMITTED` is a more consistent read, similar to Oracle's isolation level. However, changes that are committed in one transaction will be visible to another. The result is that the same query in the same transaction could return different results.

`REPEATABLE READ` is the default. It makes all reads consistent for a transaction.

In the safest level, `SERIALIZABLE`, changes are not allowed in other transactions if a transaction has executed a simple `SELECT` statement. Basically, queries are performed with `LOCK IN SHARE MODE`.

Here is an example of how you can use this statement:

```
SET SESSION TRANSACTION ISOLATION LEVEL READ COMMITTED;
START TRANSACTION;
...
```

SHOW ERRORS

```
SHOW ERRORS [LIMIT [offset,] count]

SHOW COUNT(*) ERRORS
```

Use this statement to display error messages. The results are only for the previous statement that has been executed. To see the number of error messages generated by an SQL statement, use `COUNT(*)`. To limit the number of error messages displayed, use the `LIMIT` clause. An offset can be given along with the count to specify a starting point for displaying error messages.

This statement is available as of version 4.1 of MySQL. It will not display warnings or notes—just error messages. Use `SHOW WARNINGS` to get all three types of messages.

Here are a couple of examples of this statement, which were entered after an `INSERT` statement was entered and encountered a problem:

```
SHOW COUNT(*) ERRORS;

+-----------------------+
| @@session.error_count |
+-----------------------+
|                     1 |
+-----------------------+
```

Data Manipulation

```
SHOW ERRORS;

+-------+------+---------------------------------------------+
| Level | Code | Message                                     |
+-------+------+---------------------------------------------+
| Error | 1136 | Column count doesn't match value count at row 2 |
+-------+------+---------------------------------------------+
```

The first statement returns the number of error messages generated by the `INSERT` statement. Notice that the results are stored in the session variable `error_count`, which is updated by each statement issued in the session. The second statement displays the error messages. This statement is perhaps more meaningful when used with an API program in which you would like to capture the error messages for a specific purpose or analysis.

SHOW WARNINGS

SHOW WARNINGS [LIMIT [*offset*,] *count*]

SHOW COUNT(*) WARNINGS

Use this statement to display warning messages, error messages, and notes for previous SQL statements for the current session. This statement is available as of version 4.1 of MySQL. To find out the number of such messages generated by the previous statement in the session, use `COUNT(*)`. Use the `LIMIT` clause to limit the number of messages displayed. An offset can be given along with the limit to specify a starting point for displaying messages. Here are a couple of examples of how you can use this statement:

```
INSERT INTO clients (client_name, telephone)
VALUES('Marie & Associates', '504-486-1234');
Query OK, 1 row affected, 1 warning (0.00 sec)

SHOW COUNT(*) WARNINGS;

+-------------------------+
| @@session.warning_count |
+-------------------------+
|                       1 |
+-------------------------+

SHOW WARNINGS;

+---------+------+----------------------------------------------+
| Level   | Code | Message                                      |
+---------+------+----------------------------------------------+
| Warning | 1265 | Data truncated for column 'client_name' at row 1 |
+---------+------+----------------------------------------------+
```

In this example, we enter the name of a client and her telephone number in the table `clients`, but in the results we see that one warning is issued. The second statement returns the number of messages; of course, the last line of the results from the `INSERT` already told us this. Notice that the results are stored in the session variable `warning_count`. The third SQL statement displays the warning message. These statements are perhaps more meaningful when used with an API program in which you would like to capture the number of errors generated or the error messages for a specific purpose or analysis.

START TRANSACTION

```
START TRANSACTION [WITH CONSISTENT SNAPSHOT]
```

Use this statement to start a transaction. Transaction statements are currently supported by the InnoDB, NDB Cluster, and BDB storage engines and are ignored if used with MyISAM tables. The purpose of a transaction is to be able to undo SQL statements if need be. You can reverse a transaction if you have not yet committed it with a `COMMIT` statement, implicitly by starting another transaction, or by terminating the connection. In earlier versions of MySQL, `BEGIN` or `BEGIN WORK` were used instead of `START TRANSACTION`. See the explanations of the `COMMIT` and `ROLLBACK` statements earlier in this chapter for more information on transactions. The `SAVEPOINT` statement and the `ROLLBACK TO SAVEPOINT` statement may also be useful.

Here is an example of this statement's use in context:

```
START TRANSACTION;

INSERT DATA INFILE '/tmp/customer_orders.sql'
INTO TABLE orders;

COMMIT;
```

In this example, after the batch of orders is inserted into the `orders` table, the user decides everything went properly and issues the `COMMIT` statement to actually enter the data in the database and to end the transaction started with the `START TRANSACTION` statement. If there had been a problem, the `ROLLBACK` statement could be issued instead of `COMMIT`. `ROLLBACK` would remove the data imported by the `INSERT DATA INFILE` statement.

The `WITH CONSISTENT SNAPSHOT` clause initiates a consistent read. It does not change the current transaction isolation level. Therefore, it provides consistent data only if the current isolation level allows consistent reading (i.e., `REPEATABLE READ` or `SERIALIZABLE`). At this time, it only works with InnoDB tables. See the `SET TRANSACTION` statement earlier in this chapter for more information on isolation levels.

TRUNCATE

TRUNCATE [TABLE] *table*

Use this statement to delete the contents of a table rapidly. It's similar to the `DELETE` statement in that it will delete all of the data contained in a given table. The `TRUNCATE` statement does its job by dropping the table and then recreating it without data. As a result, it does not report the number of rows deleted. Another drawback is that the value for an `AUTO_INCREMENT` column will be lost along with the data. The statement does preserve file partitions and partition parameters if the table was originally partitioned.

This statement is not transaction-safe. As of version 5.1.16 of MySQL, `DROP` privileges are required for this statement. Previously, `DELETE` privileges were required.

UNION

```
SELECT... UNION [ALL|DISTINCT] SELECT...[, UNION...]
```

The `UNION` keyword unites the results of multiple `SELECT` statements into one results set. The `SELECT` statements can retrieve data from the same table or from different tables. If different tables are used, the results set generated by each SQL statement should match in column count and the order of column types. The column names do not need to be the same, but the data sent to the respective fields in the results set needs to match.

Don't confuse this statement with the `JOIN` clause or a subquery, which are used to merge columns of data from multiple tables into rows in the results of a `SELECT` statement. In contrast, the `UNION` clause is used to merge together the results tables of separate and distinct `SELECT` statements into one results table.

Here is an example of a `UNION` used to merge the results of two `SELECT` statements:

```
SELECT CONCAT(name_first, SPACE(1), name_last) AS Name,
telephone_work AS Telephone
FROM employees
UNION
SELECT location, telephone FROM branches
ORDER BY Name;
```

This statement presents a list of employees and branch office locations in one column, with the telephone number for each in the second. The column headings used for the results set will be the ones used for the first `SELECT` statement. Because of the `ORDER BY` clause, the results will be sorted by the values for the alias *Name*. Otherwise, the names of employees would be listed before the names of offices. The example shown merges the results of only two `SELECT` statements. You can merge several `SELECT` statements, entering the `UNION` keyword before each additional `SELECT` statement.

If the results set is to be sorted based on a column, the table name must not be specified in the `ORDER BY` clause (i.e., `table.column` is not accepted). To resolve ambiguity, use an alias for the columns to order by. If an alias has been given for a column that is to be part of the `ORDER BY` clause, that alias must be used instead of the column name. The use of column position has been deprecated.

The keyword `DISTINCT` indicates that any duplicated rows (rows where all of the data of all columns is the same as a previous row) are not included in the results. This is the default, so it's not necessary to include the keyword `DISTINCT`. Including the keyword `ALL`, though, will instruct MySQL to include all rows, including duplicates.

To limit the results of a union, add the `LIMIT` clause to the end of the SQL statement:

```
SELECT CONCAT(name_first, SPACE(1), name_last) AS Name,
telephone_work AS Telephone
FROM employees
UNION
SELECT location, telephone FROM branches
ORDER BY Name
LIMIT 10;
```

To limit the results of one table in a union and not the final results set, put parentheses around the individual `SELECT` statements and add the `LIMIT` clause to the end of the `SELECT` statement or statements that you want to limit:

```
( SELECT CONCAT(name_first, SPACE(1), name_last) AS Name,
telephone_work AS Telephone FROM employees LIMIT 10 )
UNION
( SELECT location, telephone FROM branches )
ORDER BY Name;
```

This statement limits the results to only 10 employees, but allows all of the branches to be displayed. You can put limits on each SELECT statement if you want, and limit the final results by adding the LIMIT clause to the end of the full SQL statement.

UPDATE

```
UPDATE [LOW_PRIORITY] [IGNORE] table
SET column=expression[, ...]
[WHERE condition]
[ORDER BY {column|expression|position} [ASC|DESC], ...]
[LIMIT {[offset,] count|count OFFSET offset}]

UPDATE [LOW_PRIORITY] [IGNORE] table_reference
     SET column=expression[, ...]
     [WHERE condition]
```

This statement changes existing rows of data in a table. The first syntax shown updates only one table per statement. The second syntax can be used to update or reference data in multiple tables from one statement. Explanations of both types of statements and examples of their use follow.

Single table UPDATE

```
UPDATE [LOW_PRIORITY] [IGNORE] table
SET column=expression[, ...]
[WHERE condition]
[ORDER BY {column|expression|position} [ASC|DESC], ...]
[LIMIT {[offset,] count|count OFFSET offset}]
```

This syntax changes a single table. The SET clause specifies each column that should change and the value to which it is to be set, separated by an equals sign. The value can be a static value or an expression. If a column in a table is defined as NOT NULL, and if an UPDATE statement then sets its value to NULL, the default value for the column will be used if it is available; otherwise, an error is generated.

The LOW_PRIORITY keyword may be used to instruct the server to wait until all other queries related to the table in which data is to be added are completed before running the UPDATE statement. When the table is free, it will be locked for the UPDATE statement and thereby prevent concurrent data updates or inserts.

Normally, if one of the updates would create a duplicate row (a row that shares the same value as an existing row in a column declared to be unique), the statement reports an error. The statement is then terminated and no more rows are updated. If the table is InnoDB, BDB, or NDB, the entire transaction is reversed or rolled back; if not, the rows that were updated before the error will remain updated. However, if the IGNORE keyword is used, the server ignores any errors encountered, suppresses error messages, and continues updating nonduplicate rows.

The results of such a statement will display like this:

```
Query OK, 120 rows affected (4.20 sec)
Records: 125 Duplicates: 5 Warnings: 0
```

Notice that only 120 rows were updated, although 125 would have been updated if there had been no duplication problem.

Here is an example of the UPDATE statement using this syntax:

```
UPDATE clients
SET client_name = 'Geoffrey & Company',
city = 'Boston', state = 'MA'
WHERE client_name LIKE 'Geoffrey%';
```

This example sets the values of two columns for any rows (probably only one in this case) that meet the condition of the WHERE clause using the LIKE operator. Only these two columns will be updated in the matching rows. If there are several rows with the column client_name containing a starting value of *Geoffrey*, all of them will be changed.

The number of rows that are updated can be limited by using the LIMIT clause. As of version 4.0.13 of MySQL, the LIMIT clause is based on the number of rows matched, not necessarily the number changed. Starting with version 4.0.0 of MySQL, you can also choose to UPDATE only the first few rows found in a certain order by using the ORDER BY clause. See the SELECT statement earlier in this chapter for details about the ORDER BY and the LIMIT clauses. Here is an example of an UPDATE statement using both of these clauses:

```
UPDATE clients
SET client_terms = client_terms + 15
WHERE client_city = 'Boston'
AND YEAR(date_opened) < 2005
ORDER BY date_opened
LIMIT 50;
```

This example indicates that we've decided to somewhat arbitrarily upgrade the client terms (i.e., allow 15 additional days to pay their invoices) for any clients located in Boston who opened an account before the year 2005, but only for the first 50 clients based on the date order in which their account was opened. Notice that the value of the column client_terms is set with an expression that refers to the value of the column before the UPDATE statement is executed. Expressions are calculated from left to right, so the results of one expression could affect the results of those that follow within the same statement.

Multiple table UPDATE

```
UPDATE [LOW_PRIORITY] [IGNORE] table_reference
SET column=expression[, ...]
[WHERE condition]
```

This syntax of the UPDATE statement, available as of version 4.0.4 of MySQL, allows for multiple tables to be updated or referenced in one SQL statement. A SET clause specifies each column that should change and the value to which it is to be set, separated by an equals sign. The value can be a static value or an expression. The keywords LOW_PRIORITY and IGNORE are handled the same way as in the first syntax for the UPDATE statement. The ORDER BY and the LIMIT clauses are not available with the multiple-table syntax.

The columns by which tables are joined may be given in the WHERE clause (e.g., WHERE clients.branch_id=branches.client_id), or with the JOIN clause.

Here is an example using the JOIN clause:

```
UPDATE clients JOIN branches USING (branch_id)
SET client_terms = client_terms + 60
WHERE location = 'New Orleans';
```

In this example, only one table is being changed, but two are joined to determine which clients belong to the New Orleans branch in order to be able to give them 60 additional days to pay their bills due to a recent hurricane. See the JOIN clause earlier in this chapter for details on joining tables.

USE

USE *database*

This statement sets the default database that MySQL is to use for the current session. This allows the name of the default database to be omitted from statements. For instance, db1.table1 can be written as just table1, and db1 is assumed.

```
USE company_database;
```

The semicolon may be omitted from the statement since it's *mysql* client-related. You can specify a default database at startup with the --database or --D option.

XA

XA {START|BEGIN} '*identifier*' [JOIN|RESUME]

XA PREPARE '*identifier*'

XA COMMIT '*identifier*' [ONE PHASE]

XA ROLLBACK '*identifier*'

XA RECOVER

XA END '*identifier*' [SUSPEND [FOR MIGRATE]]

This statement is used for XA distributed transactions. These are transactions in which multiple, separate transactional resources may be involved in a global transaction. In MySQL, this is currently available only with InnoDB tables.

The XA START statement starts an XA transaction, assigning an identifier to be used in subsequent statements, and puts the transaction into an ACTIVE state. Implicit commits cannot be made while the transaction is in ACTIVE state. This statement is synonymous with XA BEGIN. The JOIN and RESUME keywords are not supported.

Once you've entered all of the SQL statements for a particular session, mark the transaction as PREPARED by executing an XA PREPARE. XA RECOVER lists all transactions in a prepared state. Use the XA COMMIT ONE PHASE statement to mark the XA transaction just given as prepared and committed. XA COMMIT without the ONE PHASE keyword will commit and end the entire transaction. Use XA ROLLBACK to undo the specified XA transaction and terminate it. XA END ends the specified transaction and puts it into an IDLE state.

Functions in Alphabetical Order

This section describes special functions that are closely related to the data manipulation SQL statements in this chapter. Functions for the formatting and retrieval of column data are covered in other chapters.

ANALYSE( )

ANALYSE([*maximum_elements*[, *maximum_memory*]])

This function returns an analysis of a results table from a SELECT statement. Use this function only as part of a PROCEDURE clause. The first parameter is the maximum number of unique values that may be analyzed for each column; the default is 256. The second parameter is the maximum memory that should be allocated for each column during analysis; the default is 8,192 bytes (8 MB). Here is an example:

```
SELECT col1
FROM table1
PROCEDURE ANALYSE( ) \G
*************************** 1. row ***************************
             Field_name: table1.col1
              Min_value: 1
              Max_value: 82
             Min_length: 1
             Max_length: 2
       Empties_or_zeros: 0
                  Nulls: 0
Avg_value_or_avg_length: 42.8841
                    Std: 24.7600
      Optimal_fieldtype: TINYINT(2) UNSIGNED NOT NULL
```

BENCHMARK( )

BENCHMARK(*number, expression*)

Use this function to evaluate the performance of a MySQL server. The expression given as the second argument of the function is repeated the number of times given in the first argument. The results are always 0. It's the processing time reported that is meaningful. This function is meant to be used from within the *mysql* client. Here is an example:

```
SELECT BENCHMARK(1000000,PI( ));

+--------------------------+
| BENCHMARK(1000000,PI( )) |
+--------------------------+
|                        0 |
+--------------------------+
1 row in set (0.04 sec)
```

DATABASE( )

DATABASE( )

This function returns the name of the database currently in use for the session. There are no arguments. If no database has been set to default yet, it returns NULL; prior to version 4.1.1 of MySQL, it returns an empty string. Here is an example:

```
SELECT DATABASE( );

+--------------------+
| DATABASE( )        |
+--------------------+
| company_database   |
+--------------------+
```

As of version 5.0.2 of MySQL, `SCHEMA( )` has been introduced as a synonym for `DATABASE( )`.

FOUND_ROWS( )

FOUND_ROWS( )

Use this function in conjunction with the `SQL_CALC_FOUND_ROWS` option of a `SELECT` statement to determine the number of rows an SQL statement using a `LIMIT` clause would have generated without the limitation. There are no arguments for the function. It's available as of version 4 of MySQL. Here is an example:

```
SELECT SQL_CALC_FOUND_ROWS
name_first, name_last, telephone_home,
DATEDIFF(now( ), last_review)
AS 'Days Since Last Review'
FROM employees
WHERE dept = 'sales'
ORDER BY last_review DESC
LIMIT 10;

SELECT FOUND_ROWS();
```

In the first statement, we retrieve a list of sales people to review, limited to the 10 who have gone the longest without a performance review. In the second SQL statement, we're getting a total count of how many employees there are to review in the sales department.

LAST_INSERT_ID( )

LAST_INSERT_ID([*expression*])

This function returns the identification number of the last row inserted using the MySQL connection. The identification number for rows inserted by other clients will not be returned. Identification numbers that are set manually when rows are inserted, without the aid of `AUTO_INCREMENT`, won't register and therefore won't be returned by `LAST_INSERT_ID( )`. If multiple rows are inserted by one SQL statement, `LAST_INSERT_ID( )` returns the identification number for the first row inserted.

Here is an example:

```
SELECT LAST_INSERT_ID( );

+-------------------+
| LAST_INSERT_ID( ) |
+-------------------+
|              1039 |
+-------------------+
```

As of version 5.1.12 of MySQL, an expression may be given to adjust the results. For instance, if you insert multiple rows of data, the result would be the value of the first row inserted, not the last. By giving an expression to include adding the number of rows, the results will be for the last row.

ROW_COUNT( )

ROW_COUNT( )

This function returns the number of rows changed by the previous SQL statement executed. If the previous statement was not one that could potentially change data rows—in other words, it wasn't an INSERT, UPDATE, DELETE, or other such statement—this function will return –1. Here is an example:

```
SELECT ROW_COUNT();

+-------------+
| ROW_COUNT() |
+-------------+
|           4 |
+-------------+
```

The results here show that four rows were changed.

SCHEMA( )

SCHEMA( )

This function returns the name of the database currently in use for the session. There are no arguments. If no database has been set as the default, it returns NULL. Here is an example:

```
SELECT SCHEMA( );

+--------------------+
| DATABASE( )        |
+--------------------+
| company_database   |
+--------------------+
```

Introduced in version 5.0.2 of MySQL, SCHEMA( ) is a synonym for DATABASE( ).

7
Table and Server Administration Statements and Functions

The following SQL statements are covered in this chapter:

`ALTER SERVER`, `ANALYZE TABLE`, `BACKUP TABLE`, `CACHE INDEX`, `CHECK TABLE`, `CHECKSUM TABLE`, `CREATE SERVER`, `FLUSH`, `KILL`, `LOAD INDEX INTO CACHE`, `LOCK TABLES`, `OPTIMIZE TABLE`, `REPAIR TABLE`, `RESET`, `RESTORE TABLE`, `SET`, `SHOW ENGINE`, `SHOW ENGINES`, `SHOW OPEN TABLES`, `SHOW PLUGINS`, `SHOW PROCESSLIST`, `SHOW STATUS`, `SHOW TABLE STATUS`, `SHOW VARIABLES`, `UNLOCK TABLES`.

The following functions are also covered in this chapter as they relate to data manipulation:

`CONNECTION_ID( )`, `GET_LOCK( )`, `IS_FREE_LOCK( )`, `IS_USED_LOCK( )`, `RELEASE_LOCK( )`, `UUID( )`, `VERSION( )`.

Statements and Clauses in Alphabetical Order

The following is a list of MySQL statements and clauses related to table and server administration, in alphabetical order. To understand how this book presents SQL syntax and describes SQL statements, as well as for information related to examples, please see the introduction to Part II. The examples in this chapter involve a fictitious database for a computer consulting firm that maintains work requests for computer maintenance. Some examples involve a fictitious database of a vendor.

ALTER SERVER

```
ALTER SERVER server
   OPTIONS
    ({ HOST host
     | DATABASE database
     | USER user
     | PASSWORD password
     | SOCKET socket
     | OWNER owner
     | PORT port_number }, ...)
```

Use this statement to change the settings for a server created for a FEDERATE storage engine. Servers are created with the `CREATE SERVER` statement. See the description of that statement later in this chapter for more information on the options. The `SUPER` privilege is required to be able to use this statement. Here is an example:

```
ALTER SERVER testing
OPTIONS(USER 'test_user2');
```

ANALYZE TABLE

```
ANALYZE [LOCAL|NO_WRITE_TO_BINLOG] TABLE table[, ...]
```

Use this statement to store information that can be useful later when the MySQL optimizer chooses the order for consulting indexes during a query. Multiple tables can be specified in a comma-separated list. The statement works on MyISAM and InnoDB tables. Unless the `NO_WRITE_TO_BINLOG` option is given, the statement is written to the binary log file and will be executed by slaves if using replication. The `LOCAL` option is synonymous with this option. For MyISAM tables, this statement places a read lock on the tables; for InnoDB, a write lock. This statement requires `SELECT` and `INSERT` privileges. Here is an example:

```
ANALYZE TABLE workreq;

+----------------------+---------+----------+----------+
| Table                | Op      | Msg_type | Msg_text |
+----------------------+---------+----------+----------+
| workrequests.workreq | analyze | status   | OK       |
+----------------------+---------+----------+----------+
```

The message type in the results can be `status`, `error`, `info`, or `warning`. If the table hasn't changed since it was last analyzed, the message text will read, "Table is already up to date" and the table won't be analyzed.

This statement is equivalent to using `myisamchk --analyze` at the command line for MyISAM tables. To analyze all tables (MyISAM and InnoDB), you can use the `mysqlcheck` utility from the command line like so:

```
mysqlcheck --user=russell -p --analyze --all-databases
```

If you want to see the stored key distribution that the `ANALYZE TABLE` statement creates, execute the `SHOW INDEXES` statement.

BACKUP TABLE

```
BACKUP TABLE table[, ...] TO '/path'
```

This statement makes a backup copy of a MyISAM table. However, it has been deprecated because it does not work reliably. It's recommended that you use `mysqlhotcopy` (see Chapter 16) until this statement is replaced.

You can specify additional tables in a comma-separated list. The absolute path to the directory to which MySQL is to copy files appears within quotes after the `TO` keyword.

The statement copies each table's *.frm* file and *.MYD* file, which contain the table structure and the table data, respectively. The *.MYI* file containing the index is not copied, but it will be rebuilt with the `RESTORE TABLE` statement when restoring the table. Here is an example:

```
BACKUP TABLE clients TO '/tmp/backup';

+----------------------+--------+----------+----------+
| Table                | Op     | Msg_type | Msg_text |
+----------------------+--------+----------+----------+
| workrequests.clients | backup | status   | OK       |
+----------------------+--------+----------+----------+
```

If the backup succeeds, the results will look like the preceding output and two files will be created for each table backed up: a *.frm* file and a *.MYD* file. If MySQL does not have the filesystem privileges necessary to write to the backup directory, or if a file with the same name is already in the directory, the backup will fail. In that case, the results set will include one row with an error message type and another with a status type and the message text stating, "Operation failed."

CACHE INDEX

```
CACHE INDEX table[[INDEX|KEY] (index, ...), ...] IN cache
```

This statement tells MySQL to cache the given indexes to a specific index cache, which can be created with the `SET GLOBAL` statement. This statement is used only on MyISAM tables. Multiple tables may be listed in a comma-separated list. To specify only certain indexes of a table, give them in a comma-separated list in parentheses after the table name. The `INDEX` or `KEY` keyword may be given for clarity and compatibility with other database products. Note that the naming of specific indexes for a table is ignored in the current versions of MySQL; the option is for a future release. For now, all indexes are assigned to the named cache, which is the same as specifying no indexes.

To create an additional cache, issue a `SET GLOBAL` statement with the `key_buffer_size` variable like this:

```
SET GLOBAL my_cache.key_buffer_size = 100*1024;

CACHE INDEX workreq, clients IN my_cache \G

*************************** 1. row ***************************
   Table: workrequests.workreq
      Op: assign_to_keycache
Msg_type: status
Msg_text: OK
```

```
*************************** 2. row ***************************
   Table: workrequests.clients
      Op: assign_to_keycache
Msg_type: status
Msg_text: OK
```

In this example, the first line creates a cache called *my_cache* with a buffer size of 100 megabytes. The second line assigns the indexes for the two tables named to *my_cache*. As long as this cache exists, all queries by all users will use this cache. If you attempt to create a cache index without setting the global variable first, you will receive an error stating that it's an *unknown key cache*. If the key cache is eliminated for any reason, the indexes will be assigned back to the default key cache for the server.

CHECK TABLE

CHECK TABLE *table*[, ...] [CHANGED|QUICK|FAST|MEDIUM|EXTENDED|FOR UPGRADE]

Use this statement to check tables for errors; as of version 5.1.9 of MySQL, it works with the MyISAM, InnoDB, ARCHIVE, and CSV storage engines. If errors are discovered, you should run the REPAIR TABLE statement to repair the table. Multiple tables may be given in a comma-separated list. This statement requires SELECT privileges.

There are several ways to control checking, specified after the list of tables:

CHANGED
: Checks only tables that have been changed since the last check.

QUICK
: Checks tables for errors, but won't scan individual rows for linking problems.

FAST
: Checks only tables that have not been closed properly.

MEDIUM
: Determines the key checksum for the rows and compares the results against the checksum for the keys. This option also checks rows to ensure that links were deleted properly.

EXTENDED
: Thoroughly checks each row for errors. It takes a long time to complete.

FOR UPGRADE
: Checks a table against the version of MySQL in use. If the table was created from an earlier version and there have been changes to the new version that make the table incompatible, the statement will then begin the EXTENDED method to thoroughly check the table. If it's successful, it will note that the table has already been checked so that future checks can avoid the time-consuming check. This option is available starting with version 5.1.7 of MySQL.

Here is an example of how you can use this statement:

```
CHECK TABLE workreq MEDIUM;

+---------------------+-------+----------+----------+
| Table               | Op    | Msg_type | Msg_text |
+---------------------+-------+----------+----------+
```

```
| workrequests.workreq | check | status   | OK       |
+----------------------+-------+----------+----------+
```

If an error is found with an InnoDB table, the server is shut down to prevent more problems. Check the error log for details to resolve the problem.

CHECKSUM TABLE

```
CHECKSUM TABLE table[, ...] [QUICK|EXTENDED]
```

This statement returns a MyISAM table's live checksum value, a value that can be optionally maintained to improve a table's repairability. To enable live checksum for a table, use the `CREATE TABLE` or `ALTER TABLE` statements with a table option of `CHECKSUM=1`.

Multiple tables may be given in a comma-separated list. If the `QUICK` option is employed, the live table checksum will be returned, if available. If not, NULL will be returned. Normally one would use the `QUICK` option when the table is probably fine. The `EXTENDED` option instructs the server to check each row. You should use this option only as a last resort. If no option is specified, the `QUICK` option is the default, if available. If not, the `EXTENDED` option is the default. The checksum value can be different if the row format changes, which can happen between versions of MySQL. Here is an example of this statement's use and its results:

```
CHECKSUM TABLE workreq;

+----------------------+-----------+
| Table                | Checksum  |
+----------------------+-----------+
| workrequests.workreq | 195953487 |
+----------------------+-----------+
```

CREATE SERVER

```
CREATE SERVER 'server'
   FOREIGN DATA WRAPPER mysql
   OPTIONS
    ({ HOST host
     | DATABASE database
     | USER user
     | PASSWORD password
     | SOCKET socket
     | OWNER owner
     | PORT port_number }, ...)
```

This statement creates a server for use by the FEDERATED storage engine. The server created is registered in the `server` table in the `mysql` database. The server name given cannot exceed 63 characters and is case-insensitive. The only acceptable wrapper name is `mysql`. Multiple options may be given, separated by commas. The `PORT` option requires a numeric literal, whereas the other options require character literals. So don't put the port number within quotes. `SUPER` privilege is required to be able to use this statement. Here is an example of this statement:

```
CREATE SERVER testing
FOREIGN DATA WRAPPER mysql
OPTIONS (USER 'test_user', HOST '10.1.1.100',
```

```
DATABASE 'test', PORT 3307);

SELECT * FROM mysql.servers
WHERE Server_name = 'testing' \G

*************************** 1. row ***************************
Server_name: testing
       Host: 10.1.1.100
         Db: test
   Username: test_user
   Password:
       Port: 3307
     Socket:
    Wrapper: mysql
      Owner:

CREATE TABLE table1 (col_id INT, col_1 VARCHAR(25))
ENGINE=FEDERATED CONNECTION='testing';
```

A server created with this statement can be altered with the ALTER SERVER statement. Once created, servers can be accessed by setting the ENGINE clause in either the CREATE TABLE statement or the same clause of the ALTER TABLE statement for existing tables.

FLUSH

```
FLUSH [LOCAL|NO_WRITE_TO_BINLOG] option[, ...]
```

Options:

```
DES_KEY_FILE, HOSTS, LOGS, PRIVILEGES, QUERY_CACHE,
STATUS, TABLE, TABLES, TABLES WITH READ LOCK, USER_RESOURCES
```

Use this statement to clear temporary caches in MySQL. It requires RELOAD privileges. Multiple options may be given in a comma-separated list.

To prevent this statement from writing to the binary log file, include the NO_WRITE_TO_BINLOG keyword or its alias, LOCAL. The DES_KEY_FILE option reloads the DES encryption file. HOSTS clears the hosts cache, which is used to minimize host/IP address lookups. The hosts cache may need to be flushed if a host has been blocked from accessing the server. LOGS is used to close all of the log files and reopen them. The PRIVILEGES option reloads the grant table for users. This is necessary if the user table in the mysql database is modified manually, without a GRANT statement. QUERY CACHE instructs the server to defragment the query cache. The STATUS option resets the status variables that report information about the caches.

The TABLE option, followed by one or more table names, forces the given tables to be closed. This will terminate any active queries on the given tables. The TABLES option, without any table names listed, causes all tables to be closed, all queries to be terminated, and the query cache to be flushed. This option is actually the same as TABLE with no table name.

Use the TABLES WITH READ LOCK option to close all tables and lock them with a global read lock. This should be considered when dealing with transactional tables and implicit commits of changes. This option will allow users to view the data, but not to update it or to insert records. The lock will remain in place until the `UNLOCK TABLES` statement is executed.

`USER_RESOURCES` resets all user resources. You can use this when users have been locked out due to exceeding usage limits.

The *mysqladmin* utility may be used to execute this statement with several of its options. See Chapter 16 for information on this utility.

Two options for this statement have been deprecated: `MASTER` and `SLAVE`. `RESET MASTER` and `RESET SLAVE` should be used instead.

As of version 5.1 of MySQL, the `FLUSH` statement cannot be called by a stored function or a trigger, although it can be included in a stored procedure.

KILL

`KILL [CONNECTION|QUERY]` *`thread`*

Use this statement to terminate a client connection to MySQL. You can use the `SHOW PROCESSLIST` statement to obtain a connection thread identifier for use in this statement. As of version 5 of MySQL, you can use `CONNECTION` or `QUERY` keywords to distinguish between terminating a connection or terminating just the current query associated with the given connection.

Some processes cannot be terminated immediately. Instead, this statement flags the process for termination. The system may not check the flag until the process is completed. This will occur with statements such as `REPAIR TABLE`. Besides, you shouldn't attempt to terminate the execution of the `REPAIR TABLE` or the `OPTIMIZE TABLE` statements. That will corrupt a MyISAM table. The utility `mysqladmin` with the options `processlist` and `KILL` may be used from the command line to execute these related statements.

Here is an example of the `SHOW PROCESSLIST` and the `KILL` statements used together:

```
SHOW PROCESSLIST \G
...
     Id: 14397
   User: reader
   Host: localhost
     db: russell_dyer
Command: Query
   Time: 7
  State: Sending data
   Info: SELECT COUNT(*) AS hits
           FROM apache_log
           WHERE SUBDATE(NOW(), INT....

KILL QUERY 14397;
```

The results of the `SHOW PROCESSLIST` are truncated. Using the thread identifier 14397 from the results, the `KILL` statement is used with the `QUERY` keyword to terminate the SQL statement that's running, without terminating the client connection. If the `CONNECTION` keyword or no keyword is given, the entire connection is terminated. In that case, if the client attempts to issue another SQL statement, it receives a 2006 error message stating that the MySQL server has gone away. Then it typically will try to reconnect to the server, establish a new thread, and run the requested query.

LOAD INDEX INTO CACHE

```
LOAD INDEX INTO CACHE
  table [[INDEX|KEY] (index[, ...)] [IGNORE LEAVES]
  [, ...]
```

Use this statement to preload a table's index into a given key cache for a MyISAM table. The syntax allows one or more indexes to be specified in a comma-separated list in parentheses, in order to preload just the specified indexes, but presently MySQL simply loads all the indexes for the table into the cache. The keywords `INDEX` and `KEY` are interchangeable and optional; they do not affect the results. The `IGNORE LEAVES` clause instructs MySQL not to preload leaf nodes of the index. Here is an example of how you can use this statement:

```
LOAD INDEX INTO CACHE workreq;

+----------------------+--------------+----------+----------+
| Table                | Op           | Msg_type | Msg_text |
+----------------------+--------------+----------+----------+
| workrequests.workreq | preload_keys | status   | OK       |
+----------------------+--------------+----------+----------+
```

LOCK TABLES

```
LOCK TABLES table [AS alias]
   {READ [LOCAL]|[[LOW_PRIORITY] WRITE]} [, ...]
```

Use this statement to lock the given tables for exclusive use by the current connection thread. A `READ` lock allows the locked tables to be read by all threads, but it does not allow writes to the tables, even by the thread that locked them. A `READ LOCAL` lock allows all threads to read the tables that are locked while the locking connection can execute `INSERT` statements. Until the lock is released, though, direct data manipulation by command-line utilities should be avoided. A `WRITE` lock prohibits other threads from reading from or writing to locked tables, but it permits reads and writes by the locking thread. SQL statements for tables that are locked with the `WRITE` option have priority over statements involving tables with a `READ` lock. However, the `LOW_PRIORITY` keyword may be given before the `WRITE` to instruct the server to wait until there are no queries on the tables being locked.

Only locked tables may be accessed by a locking thread. Therefore, all tables to be used must be locked. To illustrate this, assume a new programmer has been hired. The programmer's information must be added to the `programmers` table. The `wk_schedule` table that contains the records for scheduling work also needs to be adjusted to assign work to the new programmer and away from others. Here is how you might lock the relevant tables:

```
LOCK TABLES workreq READ, programmers READ LOCAL,
  wk_schedule AS work LOW_PRIORITY WRITE;
```

In this example, the `workreq` table is locked with a `READ` keyword so that no new work requests may be added while the table for the programmers' work schedules is being updated, but the work requests may still be viewed by other users. The `programmers` table is locked for writing with the `READ LOCAL` keyword, because one record needs to be inserted for the new programmer's personal information. The `wk_schedule` table is locked for exclusive use by the current thread.

For convenience, you can give a table an alias with the `AS` keyword. In the example, the `wk_schedule` table is referred to as `work` for subsequent SQL statements until the tables are unlocked. During this time, the thread can refer to the table only by this name in all other SQL statements.

You can release locks with the `UNLOCK TABLES` statements. A `START TRANSACTION` statement also unlocks tables, as does the issuing of another `TABLE LOCKS` statement. Therefore, all tables to be locked should be named in one statement. Additional tables can be added to the end of the `TABLE LOCKS` statement in a comma-separated list.

You can lock all tables with a `FLUSH TABLES WITH READ LOCK` statement. You can use the `GET_LOCK( )` and `RELEASE_LOCK( )` functions as alternatives to the `LOCK TABLES` and `UNLOCK TABLES` covered in this chapter.

OPTIMIZE TABLE

```
OPTIMIZE [LOCAL|NO_WRITE_TO_BINLOG] TABLE table[, ...]
```

Use this statement to optimize the data contained in a table. Optimization is useful when many rows have been deleted from a table. It's also useful to run this statement periodically with a table that contains several variable-character-width columns (i.e., `VARCHAR`, `BLOB`, and `TEXT` columns). This statement generally works only with MyISAM, BDB, and InnoDB tables. It may work on other tables, however, if the *mysqld* daemon is started with the `--skip-new` option or the `--safe-mode` option. See Chapter 15 for more information on setting server startup options.

This statement also repairs some row problems and sort indexes. It temporarily locks the tables involved while optimizing. Multiple tables can be listed for optimization in a comma-separated list. To prevent the activities of this statement from being recorded in the binary log file, use the `NO_WRITE_TO_BINLOG` keyword or its alias, `LOCAL`. Here is an example of the statement's use:

```
OPTIMIZE LOCAL TABLE workreq, clients;

+----------------------+----------+----------+----------+
| Table                | Op       | Msg_type | Msg_text |
+----------------------+----------+----------+----------+
| workrequests.workreq | optimize | status   | OK       |
| workrequests.clients | optimize | status   | OK       |
+----------------------+----------+----------+----------+
```

Here, two tables are optimized successfully and the activity is not written to the binary log file.

REPAIR TABLE

```
REPAIR [LOCAL|NO_WRITE_TO_BINLOG] TABLE
    table[, ...] [QUICK] [EXTENDED] [USE_FRM]
```

Use this statement to repair corrupted MyISAM tables. Multiple tables may be given in a comma-separated list. To prevent this statement from recording its activities in the binary log file, give the NO_WRITE_TO_BINLOG keyword or its LOCAL alias. The QUICK keyword instructs MySQL to repair the table indexes only. The EXTENDED keyword rebuilds the indexes one row at a time. This option takes longer, but it can be more effective, especially with rows containing duplicate keys.

Before running this statement, make a backup of the table. If a table continues to have problems, there may be other problems (e.g., filesystem problems) that you should consider. Here is an example of this statement:

```
REPAIR TABLE systems QUICK EXTENDED;

+----------------------+--------+----------+----------+
| Table                | Op     | Msg_type | Msg_text |
+----------------------+--------+----------+----------+
| workrequests.systems | repair | status   | OK       |
+----------------------+--------+----------+----------+
```

In this example, the repair is successful. This is indicated by the OK in the Msg_text field. If it is unsuccessful, you could try the USE_FRM option with this statement. That option will create a new index file (*.MYI*) using the table schema file (*.frm*). It won't be able to determine the current value for AUTO_INCREMENT columns or for DELETE LINK, so it shouldn't be used unless the original *.MYI* file is lost. Incidentally, if the MySQL server dies while the REPAIR TABLE statement is running, you should run the statement again as soon as the server is back up, before running any other SQL statements.

RESET

```
RESET {MASTER|SLAVE|QUERY CACHE}[, ...]
```

Use this statement to reset certain server settings and files. It's similar to the FLUSH statement, but more powerful for its specific uses. The RELOAD privilege is required to use it. Multiple options may be given in a comma-separated list. Currently, you can reset the MASTER, QUERY CACHE, and SLAVE options. See the RESET MASTER and the RESET SLAVE statements in Chapter 8 for detailed explanations of each option. The QUERY CACHE option clears the cache containing SQL query results.

RESTORE TABLE

```
RESTORE TABLE table[, ...] FROM '/path'
```

This statement restores a table that was saved to the filesystem by the BACKUP TABLE statement. Multiple tables may be given in a comma-separated list. The absolute path to the directory containing the backup files must appear within quotes. If the tables already exist in the database, an error message will be generated and the restore will fail. If it's successful, the table indexes will be built automatically. This is necessary because the BACKUP TABLE statement doesn't back up the index files. Here is an example of this statement:

```
RESTORE TABLE clients, programmers FROM '/tmp/backup';
```

```
+--------------------------+---------+----------+----------+
| Table                    | Op      | Msg_type | Msg_text |
+--------------------------+---------+----------+----------+
| workrequests.clients     | restore | status   | OK       |
+--------------------------+---------+----------+----------+
| workrequests.programmers | restore | status   | OK       |
+--------------------------+---------+----------+----------+
```

In this example, the statement is successful in restoring the *.frm* and *.MYD* files located in the backup directory and regenerating the *.MYI* files.

SET

`SET [GLOBAL|@@global.|SESSION|@@session.] variable = expression`

This statement sets a system or user variable for global or session use. Global variables relate to all users. Session variables are available only to the connection thread that creates the variable. For system variables to be recognized as global, the `GLOBAL` keyword is used. Alternatively, the variable can be preceded by `@@global.` to signify that it is global. For system variables that are limited to the current session, use the `SESSION` keyword, or place `@@session` or just `@@` immediately in front of the variable name. The default for variables is to limit them to the session, making them local. `LOCAL` and `@@local` are aliases for `SESSION` and `@@session`, respectively. Here are a couple of examples involving system variables, one using the keyword method and the other using the variable prefix method:

```
SET GLOBAL concurrent_insert =  1;
SET @@session.interactive_timeout=40000;
```

The first statement disables concurrent inserts without having to restart the server. The second statement changes the interactive timeout to a higher value than normal. This setting is for the current client connection only. For other clients, this variable will still contain the default value.

To see a list of system variables and their values, use the `SHOW VARIABLES` statement. For a description of these variables, see Appendix C. For examples involving user variables, see the description of the `SET` statement in Chapter 6.

SHOW ENGINE

`SHOW ENGINE engine {STATUS|MUTEX}`

Use this statement to display details of the status of a given storage engine. This statement provides information on table and record locks for transactions, waiting locks, pending requests, buffer statistics and activity, and logs related to the engine.

Currently, the engines that may be given are `INNODB`, `NDB`, and `NDBCLUSTER`. These last two keywords are interchangeable. Prior to version 5.1.12 of MySQL, the option of `BDB` was permitted. In later versions, the BDB engine is not supported and a warning message is generated when it is used with this statement. The `MUTEX` option is available only for the InnoDB engine. For the NDB engine, an empty results set is returned if there are no operations at the time.

SHOW ENGINES

SHOW [STORAGE] ENGINES

This statement lists the table types or storage engines available for the version of MySQL running on the server. It states which are disabled on the server and which are enabled, as well as which is the default type. It also provides comments on each type. The STORAGE keyword is optional and has no effect on the results. This SQL statement replaces SHOW TABLE TYPES, which produced the same results, but is deprecated. Here is an example of this statement:

```
SHOW ENGINES \G

*************************** 1. row ***************************
      Engine: ndbcluster
     Support: DISABLED
     Comment: Clustered, fault-tolerant tables
Transactions: YES
          XA: NO
  Savepoints: NO
*************************** 2. row ***************************
      Engine: MRG_MYISAM
     Support: YES
     Comment: Collection of identical MyISAM tables
Transactions: NO
          XA: NO
  Savepoints: NO
*************************** 3. row ***************************
      Engine: BLACKHOLE
     Support: YES
     Comment: /dev/null storage engine (anything you write to it disappears)
Transactions: NO
          XA: NO
  Savepoints: NO
*************************** 4. row ***************************
      Engine: CSV
     Support: YES
     Comment: CSV storage engine
Transactions: NO
          XA: NO
  Savepoints: NO
*************************** 5. row ***************************
      Engine: MEMORY
     Support: YES
     Comment: Hash based, stored in memory, useful for temporary tables
Transactions: NO
          XA: NO
  Savepoints: NO
*************************** 6. row ***************************
      Engine: FEDERATED
     Support: YES
     Comment: Federated MySQL storage engine
Transactions: YES
          XA: NO
  Savepoints: NO
```

```
*************************** 7. row ***************************
      Engine: ARCHIVE
     Support: YES
     Comment: Archive storage engine
Transactions: NO
          XA: NO
  Savepoints: NO
*************************** 8. row ***************************
      Engine: InnoDB
     Support: YES
     Comment: Supports transactions, row-level locking, and foreign keys
Transactions: YES
          XA: YES
  Savepoints: YES
*************************** 9. row ***************************
      Engine: MyISAM
     Support: DEFAULT
     Comment: Default engine as of MySQL 3.23 with great performance
Transactions: NO
          XA: NO
  Savepoints: NO
9 rows in set (0.00 sec)
```

SHOW OPEN TABLES

`SHOW OPEN TABLES [FROM` *database*`] [LIKE '`*pattern*`'|WHERE` *expression*`]`

Use this statement to display a list of tables that are open, i.e., that are in the table cache. The list does not include any temporary tables. The `LIKE` clause can be used to limit the tables displayed by a naming pattern. Similarly, the `WHERE` clause may be used to refine the results set. Here is an example of this statement:

```
SHOW OPEN TABLES
FROM college LIKE '%student%';

+----------+--------------------+--------+-------------+
| Database | Table              | In_use | Name_locked |
+----------+--------------------+--------+-------------+
| college  | student_surveys    |      0 |           0 |
| college  | students           |      0 |           0 |
| college  | student_exams      |      0 |           0 |
| college  | student_exams_past |      0 |           0 |
+----------+--------------------+--------+-------------+
```


SHOW PLUGINS

`SHOW PLUGINS`

Use this statement to display a list of plugins on the server. This statement is available as of version 5.1.5 of MySQL, but with the name `SHOW PLUGIN`. It was changed to `SHOW PLUGINS` as of version 5.1.9. Here is an example:

```
SHOW PLUGINS;
```

```
+------------+--------+----------------+---------+---------+
| Name       | Status | Type           | Library | License |
+------------+--------+----------------+---------+---------+
| binlog     | ACTIVE | STORAGE ENGINE | NULL    | GPL     |
| partition  | ACTIVE | STORAGE ENGINE | NULL    | GPL     |
| ARCHIVE    | ACTIVE | STORAGE ENGINE | NULL    | GPL     |
| BLACKHOLE  | ACTIVE | STORAGE ENGINE | NULL    | GPL     |
| CSV        | ACTIVE | STORAGE ENGINE | NULL    | GPL     |
| FEDERATED  | ACTIVE | STORAGE ENGINE | NULL    | GPL     |
| MEMORY     | ACTIVE | STORAGE ENGINE | NULL    | GPL     |
| InnoDB     | ACTIVE | STORAGE ENGINE | NULL    | GPL     |
| MyISAM     | ACTIVE | STORAGE ENGINE | NULL    | GPL     |
| MRG_MYISAM | ACTIVE | STORAGE ENGINE | NULL    | GPL     |
| ndbcluster | ACTIVE | STORAGE ENGINE | NULL    | GPL     |
+------------+--------+----------------+---------+---------+
```

SHOW PROCESSLIST

```
SHOW [FULL] PROCESSLIST
```

This statement displays a list of connection threads running on the MySQL server. The statement requires `SUPER` privileges to be able to see all threads. Otherwise, only threads related to the current connection are shown. The `FULL` keyword shows the full text of the information field. Here is an example:

```
SHOW PROCESSLIST\G
*************************** 1. row ***************************
     Id: 1
   User: root
   Host: localhost
     db: workrequests
Command: Query
   Time: 0
  State: NULL
   Info: SHOW PROCESSLIST
```

You can use this statement to determine a thread identification number to be used with the `KILL` statement.

SHOW STATUS

```
SHOW [GLOBAL|LOCAL|SESSION] STATUS [LIKE 'pattern'|WHERE expression]
```

This statement displays status information and variables from the server. You can reduce the number of variables shown with the `LIKE` clause, based on a naming pattern for the variable name. Similarly, the `WHERE` clause may be used to refine the results set. Here is an example of how you can use this statement with the `LIKE` clause:

```
SHOW STATUS LIKE '%log%';

+----------------------------+-------+
| Variable_name              | Value |
+----------------------------+-------+
| Binlog_cache_disk_use      | 0     |
| Binlog_cache_use           | 0     |
```

```
| Com_show_binlog_events           | 0     |
| Com_show_binlogs                 | 0     |
| Com_show_engine_logs             | 0     |
| Innodb_log_waits                 | 0     |
| Innodb_log_write_requests        | 0     |
| Innodb_log_writes                | 1     |
| Innodb_os_log_fsyncs             | 3     |
| Innodb_os_log_pending_fsyncs     | 0     |
| Innodb_os_log_pending_writes     | 0     |
| Innodb_os_log_written            | 512   |
| Tc_log_max_pages_used            | 0     |
| Tc_log_page_size                 | 0     |
| Tc_log_page_waits                | 0     |
+----------------------------------+-------+
```

The results show any system variable in which the variable name has the word *log* in it. This is a new server installation, so the results have small or zero values. If we wanted to eliminate the InnoDB logs from the results, we could use the `WHERE` clause like so:

```
SHOW STATUS
WHERE Variable_name LIKE '%log%'
AND Variable_name NOT LIKE '%Innodb%';

+------------------------+-------+
| Variable_name          | Value |
+------------------------+-------+
| Binlog_cache_disk_use  | 0     |
| Binlog_cache_use       | 0     |
| Com_show_binlog_events | 0     |
| Com_show_binlogs       | 0     |
| Com_show_engine_logs   | 0     |
| Tc_log_max_pages_used  | 0     |
| Tc_log_page_size       | 0     |
| Tc_log_page_waits      | 0     |
+------------------------+-------+
```

Notice that when using the `WHERE` clause, the field name in the results must be given. In this case, the field name `Variable_name` is given. You could also give the field name `Value` to limit the results to entries of a certain value or range of values:

```
SHOW GLOBAL STATUS
WHERE Variable_name LIKE '%log%'
AND Variable_name LIKE '%Innodb%'
AND Value > 100;

+-----------------------+-------+
| Variable_name         | Value |
+-----------------------+-------+
| Innodb_os_log_written | 512   |
+-----------------------+-------+
```

In this example, we are looking for log entries for InnoDB with values over 100. The results consist of just one entry.

You can change many variables at server startup using options for the MySQL server daemon. See Chapter 15 for more details. You can change some of them while the daemon is running with the SET statement, without having to restart the server. That statement is covered earlier in this chapter.

SHOW TABLE STATUS

SHOW TABLE STATUS [FROM *database*] [LIKE '*pattern*'|WHERE *expression*]

This statement displays status information on a set of tables from a database. To obtain the status of tables from a database other than the current default one, use the FROM clause. The results will include information on all of the tables of the database unless the LIKE clause is used to limit the tables displayed by a naming pattern. Similarly, the WHERE clause may be used to refine the results set. As an alternative to this statement, you can use the utility mysqlshow with the --status option, as described in Chapter 16. Here's an example of this statement using the LIKE clause:

```
SHOW TABLE STATUS FROM workrequests LIKE 'workreq'\G

*************************** 1. row ***************************
           Name: workreq
         Engine: MyISAM
        Version: 7
     Row_format: Dynamic
           Rows: 543
 Avg_row_length: 983
    Data_length: 534216
Max_data_length: 4294967295
   Index_length: 6144
      Data_free: 120
 Auto_increment: 5772
    Create_time: 2002-04-23 14:41:58
    Update_time: 2004-11-26 16:01:46
     Check_time: 2004-11-28 17:21:20
      Collation: latin1_swedish_ci
       Checksum: NULL
 Create_options:
        Comment:
```

This example shows results for only one table because a specific table name is given in the LIKE clause without the % wildcard. To find a group of tables, but to limit the results more, you can use the WHERE clause. Here is an example:

```
SHOW TABLE STATUS FROM workrequests
WHERE Rows > 1000;
```

This example lists all tables from the given database that contain more than 1,000 rows of data. Notice that we're using the field name Rows from the results set to limit the results. Any field name can be used in this way and multiple fields may be given, separated by the AND parameter of the WHERE clause.

As for the results themselves, most are obvious from their field names. The Row_format field can have a value of Compact, Compressed, Dynamic, Fixed, or Redundant. InnoDB tables are either Compact or Redundant. The Rows field gives an accurate count with MyISAM tables, but not with InnoDB.

The Data_length field gives the size of the datafile associated with the table. Max_data_length is the maximum size allowed for the datafile. These two values are estimates for MEMORY tables. The `Auto_increment` value shows the value for the column that uses `AUTO_INCREMENT`.

When used with views, this statement returns NULL values for almost all fields.

You can change some of these variables or table options using the `ALTER TABLE` statement in Chapter 5.

SHOW VARIABLES

SHOW [GLOBAL|LOCAL|SESSION] VARIABLES [LIKE '*pattern*'|WHERE *expression*]

This statement displays the system variables for the MySQL server. The `SESSION` keyword displays values for current sessions or connections. This is the default and is synonymous with `LOCAL`. The `GLOBAL` keyword shows variables that relate to new connections. You can limit the variables with the `LIKE` clause and a naming pattern for the variables. Similarly, the `WHERE` clause can be used to refine the results set. Here is an example of this statement with the `LIKE` clause:

```
SHOW GLOBAL VARIABLES LIKE 'version%';

+-------------------------+-----------------------------+
| Variable_name           | Value                       |
+-------------------------+-----------------------------+
| version                 | 5.1.16-beta                 |
| version_comment         | MySQL Community Server (GPL) |
| version_compile_machine | i686                        |
| version_compile_os      | pc-linux-gnu                |
+-------------------------+-----------------------------+
```

In this example, the variables shown are limited to global variables whose names begin with the word *version*. Suppose that we wanted to see only the two variables of these results that contain a numeric value. We could do this by using the `WHERE` clause like so:

```
SHOW GLOBAL VARIABLES
WHERE Variable_name LIKE 'version%'
AND Value REGEXP '[0-9]';

+-------------------------+-------------+
| Variable_name           | Value       |
+-------------------------+-------------+
| version                 | 5.1.16-beta |
| version_compile_machine | i686        |
+-------------------------+-------------+
```

Notice that, for the `WHERE` clause, we specify the field names of the results set: `Variable_name` and `Value`. In this case, we're also using the `LIKE` and `REGEXP` string comparison functions to narrow the results.

You can change many of the variables at server startup with options for the MySQL server daemon. See Chapter 15 for more details. You can change some of them while the daemon is running with the `SET` statement, without having to restart the server. That statement is covered earlier in this chapter.

UNLOCK TABLES

```
UNLOCK TABLES
```

Use this statement to unlock tables that were locked by the current connection thread with the `LOCK TABLES` statement or by `FLUSH TABLES WITH READ LOCK`. `UNLOCK TABLES` implicitly commits any active transactions if any tables were locked with `LOCK TABLES`. When performing a large amount of changes to data in MyISAM tables, it can be useful and faster to lock the tables first. This way the key cache isn't flushed after each SQL statement. Instead, the server flushes the key cache when executing `UNLOCK TABLES`. Here is an example:

```
UNLOCK TABLES;
```

Functions in Alphabetical Order

The following is a list of MySQL functions related to the tasks in this chapter, in alphabetical order.

CONNECTION_ID( )

```
CONNECTION_ID( )
```

This function returns the MySQL connection or thread identification number for the MySQL session. There are no arguments. Connection identifiers are unique. Here is an example:

```
SELECT CONNECTION_ID( );

+------------------+
| CONNECTION_ID( ) |
+------------------+
|           11266  |
+------------------+
```

GET_LOCK( )

```
GET_LOCK(string, seconds)
```

This function attempts to get a lock on the name given in the first argument. The number of seconds to attempt the lock is given in the second argument. If successful, it returns 1. If the function is unsuccessful because the attempt times out, it returns 0. If the lock fails due to an error of any kind, NULL is returned. The function `RELEASE_LOCK( )` may be used to release a lock. A lock is also released when the same client issues another `GET_LOCK( )` or when the client's connection is terminated. Here is an example:

```
SELECT GET_LOCK('my_lock', 10);

+-------------------------+
| GET_LOCK('my_lock', 10) |
+-------------------------+
|                       1 |
+-------------------------+
```

IS_FREE_LOCK( )

IS_FREE_LOCK(*string*)

Use this function to determine whether the name of the lock given in parentheses is free and available as a lock name. The function returns 1 if the lock name is free, and 0 if it's not (because it is in use by another client). The function returns NULL if there is an error. Locks are created by `GET_LOCK( )`. This function is available as of version 4.0.2 of MySQL. Here is an example:

```
SELECT IS_FREE_LOCK('my_lock');

+-------------------------+
| IS_FREE_LOCK('my_lock') |
+-------------------------+
|                       0 |
+-------------------------+
```

The results here indicate that the lock is not free.

IS_USED_LOCK( )

IS_USED_LOCK(*string*)

This function determines whether the name given is already in use as a lock name. If the lock name is in use, it returns the connection identifier of the client holding the lock. It returns NULL if it is not in use. Locks are created by `GET_LOCK( )`. This function is available as of version 4.1.0 of MySQL. Here is an example:

```
SELECT IS_USED_LOCK('my_lock');

+-------------------------+
| IS_USED_LOCK('my_lock') |
+-------------------------+
|                       1 |
+-------------------------+
```

The results here indicate that the lock is in use and the connection identifier of the client is 1.

RELEASE_LOCK( )

RELEASE_LOCK(*string*)

This function releases a lock created by `GET_LOCK( )`. The name of the lock is given in parentheses. If successful, 1 is returned; if unsuccessful, 0 is returned. If the lock specified does not exist, NULL is returned. Here is an example:

```
SELECT RELEASE_LOCK('my_lock');

+-------------------------+
| RELEASE_LOCK('my_lock') |
+-------------------------+
|                       1 |
+-------------------------+
```

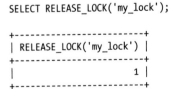

As an alternative to using SELECT, you can use the DO statement. In this case, no results are returned, but the lock is released:

```
DO RELEASE_LOCK('my_lock');
```

UUID( )

UUID( )

This function returns a Universal Unique Identifier (UUID), a 128-bit number composed of five hexadecimal numbers. This number is intended to be unique per invocation and is based on values that are both temporal and spatial. There are no arguments for the function. It's available as of version 4.1.2 of MySQL. Here is an example:

```
SELECT UUID( );

+--------------------------------------+
| UUID( )                              |
+--------------------------------------+
| '8bde367a-caeb-0933-1031-7730g3321c32' |
+--------------------------------------+
```

The first three hexadecimal sets of numbers are based on the date and time of the execution of the statement. The fourth set is based on time regardless of daylight saving time. The last set is a unique number, an IEEE 802 node number related to the computer generating the number. For instance, for some operating systems it could be the network card's Media Access Control (MAC) address.

VERSION( )

VERSION( )

This function returns the MySQL server version. There are no arguments for the function. Here is an example:

```
SELECT VERSION( );

+-------------+
| VERSION( )  |
+-------------+
| 5.1.16-beta |
+-------------+
```

8
Replication Statements and Functions

This chapter includes a tutorial on setting up and using replication, a list of SQL statements and functions used specifically with replication, and an explanation of replication states that will be useful for checking whether replication is operating as needed. The replication SQL statements and functions covered in this chapter are:

`CHANGE MASTER TO`, `LOAD DATA FROM MASTER`, `LOAD TABLE...FROM MASTER`, `MASTER_POS_WAIT( )`, `PURGE MASTER LOGS`, `RESET MASTER`, `RESET SLAVE`, `SET GLOBAL SQL_SLAVE_SKIP_COUNTER`, `SET SQL_LOG_BIN`, `SHOW BINARY LOGS`,`SHOW MASTER LOGS`, `SHOW BINLOG EVENTS`, `SHOW MASTER STATUS`, `SHOW SLAVE HOSTS`, `SHOW SLAVE STATUS`, `START SLAVE`, `STOP SLAVE`.

Merits of Replication

One of the difficulties of maintaining a large and active MySQL database is making clean backups without having to bring down the server. Performing a backup while a server is running can slow down a system considerably. Additionally, backups made on active servers can result in inconsistent data because a related table may be changed while another is being copied. Taking down the server ensures consistency of data, but it interrupts MySQL service to users. Sometimes this is necessary and unavoidable, but daily server outages for backing up data may be an unacceptable choice. A simple alternative is to set up replication of MySQL, so that one or more redundant servers maintain a consistent and continuous copy of the main MySQL server's databases, and can be taken down for backups while the main server continues serving the users.

Typically, replication is primarily a matter of configuring multiple servers to the one where users submit their updates, known in this context as a *master* server, which houses the data and handles client requests. The server logs all data changes to a binary log, locally. The master in turn informs another MySQL server (a *slave* server), which contains a copy of the master's databases, and of any additions to its binary log. The slave in turn makes these same changes to its databases. The slave can either reexecute the master's SQL statements locally, or just copy over changes to the master's databases. There are other uses for replication (such as load balancing), but the concern of this tutorial is using replication for data backups and resiliency. Also, it's easy to set up multiple slaves for each server, but one is probably enough if you're using replication only for backups.

As a backup method, you can set up a separate server to be a slave, and then once a day (or however often you prefer) turn off replication to make a clean backup of the slave server's databases. When you're finished making the backup, replication can then be restarted and the slave will automatically query the master for changes to the master's data that the slave missed while it was offline.

Replication is an excellent feature built into the MySQL core. It doesn't require you to buy or install any additional software. You just physically set up a slave server and configure MySQL on both servers appropriately to begin replication. Then it's a matter of developing a script to routinely stop the replication process, make a backup of the slave's data, and restart replication.

To understand how to make replication efficient and robust in a particular environment, let's look in detail at the steps that MySQL goes through to maintain a replicated server. The process is different depending on the version of MySQL your servers are using. This chapter applies primarily to version 4.0 or higher of MySQL. There were some significant improvements made in version 4.0 related to how replication activities are processed, making it much more dependable. Therefore, it is recommended that you upgrade your servers if they are using an older version. You should upgrade one release at a time, and use the same version of MySQL on both the master and all the slave servers. Otherwise, you may experience problems with authenticating the servers, incompatible table schemas, and other such problems.

Replication Process

When replication is running, SQL statements that change data are recorded in a binary log (*bin.log*) on the master server as it executes them. Only SQL statements that change the data or the schema are logged. This includes data-changing statements such as `INSERT`, `UPDATE`, and `DELETE`, and schema-manipulation statements such as `CREATE TABLE`, `ALTER TABLE`, and `DROP TABLE`. This also includes actions that affect data and schema, but that are executed from the command line by utilities such as `mysqladmin`. This does not include `SELECT` statements or any statements that only query the server for information (e.g., `SHOW VARIABLES`).

Along with the SQL statements, the master records a log position identification number. This is used to determine which log entries the master should relay to the slave. This is necessary because the slave may not always be able to consistently receive information from the master. We've already discussed one situation where an administrator deliberately introduces a delay: the planned downtime for making a backup of the slave. In addition, there may be times when the slave has difficulty staying connected to the master due to networking problems, or it may simply fall behind because the master has a heavy load of updates in a short period of time. However, if the slave reconnects hours or even days later, with the position identification number of the last log entry received, it can tell the master where it left off in the binary log and the master can send the slave all of the subsequent entries it missed while it was disconnected. It can do this even if the entries are contained in multiple log files due to the master's logs having been flushed in the interim.

To help you better understand the replication process, I've included—in this section especially, and throughout this chapter—sample excerpts from each replication log and index file. Knowing how to sift through logs can be useful in resolving server problems, not only with replication but also with corrupt or erroneously written data.

Here is a sample excerpt from a master binary log file:

```
/usr/local/mysql/bin/mysqlbinlog /var/log/mysql/bin.000007 >
   /tmp/binary_log.txt
tail --lines=14 /tmp/binary_log.txt

# at 1999
#081120 9:53:27 server id 1 end_log_pos 2158 Query thread_id=1391
   exec_time=0 error_code=0
USE personal;
SET TIMESTAMP=1132502007;
CREATE TABLE contacts2 (contact_id INT AUTO_INCREMENT KEY, name VARCHAR(50),
   telephone CHAR(15));

# at 2158
#081120  9:54:53 server id 1  end_log_pos 2186  Intvar
SET INSERT_ID=1;

# at 2186
#081120  9:54:53 server id 1 end_log_pos 2333 Query thread_id=1391
   exec_time=0 error_code=0
SET TIMESTAMP=1132502093;
INSERT INTO contacts2 (name, telephone) VALUES ('Rusty Osborne',
   '001-504-838-1234');
```

As the first line shows, I used the command-line utility `mysqlbinlog` to read the contents of a particular binary log file. (MySQL provides `mysqlbinlog` to make it possible for administrators to read binary log files.) Because the log is extensive, I have redirected the results to a text file in the */tmp* directory using the shell's redirect operator (>). On the second line, I used the `tail` command to display the last 14 lines of the text file generated, which translates to the last 3 entries in this case. You could instead pipe (|) the contents to `more` or `less` on a Linux or Unix system if you intend only to scan the results briefly.

After you redirect the results of a binary log to a text file, it may be used to restore data on the master server to a specific point in time. Point-in-time recovery methods are an excellent recourse when you have inadvertently deleted a large amount of data that has been added since your last backup.

The slave server, through an input/output (I/O) thread, listens for communications from the master that inform the slave of new entries in the master's binary log and of any changes to its data. The master does not transmit data unless requested by the slave, nor does the slave continuously harass the master with inquiries as to whether there are new binary log entries. Instead, after the master has made an entry to its binary log, it looks to see whether any slaves are connected and waiting for updates. The master then pokes the slave to let it know that an entry has been made to the binary log in case it's interested. It's then up to the slave to request the entries. The slave will ask the master to send entries starting from the position identification number of the last log file entry the slave processed.

Looking at each entry in the sample binary log, you will notice that each starts with the position identification number (e.g., 1999). The second line of each entry provides the date (e.g., 081120 for November 20, 2008), the time, and the replication server's identification number. This is followed by the position number expected for the next entry. This number is calculated from the number of bytes of text that the current entry required. The rest of the entry provides stats on the thread that executed the SQL statement. In some of the entries, a `SET` statement is provided with the `TIMESTAMP` variable so that when the binary log entry is used, the date and time will be adjusted on the slave server to match the date and time of the entry on the master. The final line of each entry lists the SQL statement that was executed.

The excerpt begins with a `USE` statement, which is included to be sure that the slave makes the subsequent changes to the correct database. Similarly, notice that the second entry sets the value of `INSERT_ID` in preparation for the `INSERT` statement of the following entry. This ensures that the value to be used for the column `contact_id` on the slave is the same. Nothing is left to chance or assumed, if possible.

The master server keeps track of the names of the binary log files in a simple text file (*bin.index*). Here is an excerpt from the binary index file:

```
/var/log/mysql/bin.000001
/var/log/mysql/bin.000002
/var/log/mysql/bin.000003
/var/log/mysql/bin.000004
/var/log/mysql/bin.000005
/var/log/mysql/bin.000006
/var/log/mysql/bin.000007
```

This list of binary log files can also be obtained by entering the `SHOW MASTER LOGS` statement. Notice that the list includes the full pathname of each binary log file in order, reflecting the order in which the files were created. The master appends each name to the end of the index file as the log file is opened. If a slave has been offline for a couple of days, the master will work backward through the files to find the file containing the position identification number given to it by the slave. It will then read that file from the entry following the specified position identification number to the end, followed by the subsequent files in order, sending SQL statements from each to the slave until the slave is current or disconnected. If the slave is disconnected before it can become current, the slave will make another request when it later reconnects with the last master log position identification number it received.

After the slave is current again, the slave will go back to waiting for another announcement from the master regarding changes to its binary log. The slave will make inquiries only when it receives another nudge from the master or if it is disconnected temporarily. When a slave reconnects to the master after a disconnection, it makes inquiries to ensure it didn't miss anything while it was disconnected. If it sits idle for a long period, the slave's connection will time out, also causing it to reconnect and make inquires.

When the slave receives new changes from the master, the slave doesn't update its databases directly. Direct application of changes was tried in versions of replication prior to MySQL 4.0 and found to be too inflexible to deal with heavy loads, particularly if the slave's databases are also used to support user read requests (i.e., the slave helps with load balancing). For example, tables in its replicated databases may be busy when the slave is attempting to update the data. A `SELECT` statement could be executed with the `HIGH_PRIORITY` flag, giving it priority over `UPDATE` and other SQL statements that change data and are not also specifically entered with the `HIGH_PRIORITY` flag. In this case, the replication process would be delayed by user activities. On a busy server, the replication process could be delayed for several minutes. If the master server crashes during such a lengthy delay, this could mean the loss of many data changes of which the slave is not informed because it's waiting to access a table on its own system.

By separating the recording of entries received and their reexecution, the slave is assured of getting all or almost all transactions up until the time that the master server crashes. This is a much more dependable method than the direct application method used in earlier versions of MySQL.

Currently, the slave appends the changes to a file on its filesystem named *relay.log*. Here is an excerpt from a relay log:

```
/*!40019 SET @@session.max_insert_delayed_threads=0*/;
/*!50003 SET @OLD_COMPLETION_TYPE=@@COMPLETION_TYPE,COMPLETION_TYPE=0*/;

# at 4
#081118  3:18:40 server id 2  end_log_pos 98
   Start: binlog v 4, server v 5.0.12-beta-standard-log created 051118
      3:18:40

# at 98
#700101  1:00:00 server id 1  end_log_pos 0 Rotate to bin.000025 pos: 4

# at 135
#080819 11:40:57 server id 1  end_log_pos 98
   Start: binlog v 4, server v 5.0.10-beta-standard-log created 050819
      11:40:57 at startup
ROLLBACK;

# at 949
#080819 11:54:49 server id 1  end_log_pos 952
    Query thread_id=10 exec_time=0 error_code=0
SET TIMESTAMP=1124445289;
CREATE TABLE prepare_test (id INTEGER NOT NULL, name CHAR(64) NOT NULL);

# at 952
#080819 11:54:49 server id 1  end_log_pos 1072
```

```
   Query thread_id=10 exec_time=0 error_code=0
SET TIMESTAMP=1124445289;
INSERT INTO prepare_test VALUES ('0','zhzwDeLxLy8XYjqVM');
```

This log is like the master's binary log. Notice that the first entry mentions the server's ID number, 2, which is the slave's identification number. There are also some entries for server 1, the master. The first entries have to do with log rotations on both servers. The last two entries are SQL statements relayed to the slave from the master.

A new relay log file is created when replication starts on the slave and when the logs are flushed (i.e., the `FLUSH LOGS` statement is issued). A new relay log file is also created when the current file reaches the maximum size as set with the `max_relay_log_size` variable. The maximum size can also be limited by the `max_binlog_size` variable. If these variables are set to 0, there is no size limit placed on the relay log files.

Once the slave has made note of the SQL statements relayed to it by the master, it records the new position identification number in its master information file (*master.info*) on its filesystem. Here is an example of the content of a master information file on a slave server:

```
14
bin.000038
6393
master_host
replicant
my_pwd
3306
60
0
```

This file is present primarily so the slave can remember its position in the master's binary log file even if the slave is rebooted, as well as the information necessary to reconnect to the master. Each line has a purpose as follows:

1. The first line contains the number of lines of data in the file (14). Although fewer than 14 lines are shown here, the actual file contains blank lines that make up the rest.
2. The second line shows the name of the last binary log file on the master from which the slave received entries. This helps the master respond more quickly to requests.
3. The third line shows the position identification number (6393) in the master's binary log.
4. The next few lines contain the master's host address, the replication username, the password, and the port number (3306). Notice that the password is not encrypted and is stored in clear text. Therefore, be sure to place this file in a secure directory. You can determine the path for this file in the configuration file, as discussed later in this chapter.
5. The next to last line (60) lists the number of attempts the slave should make when reconnecting to the master before stopping.

6. The last line here is 0 because the server from which this master information file came does not have the SSL feature enabled. If SSL was enabled on the slave and allowed on the master, there would be a value of 1 on this line. It would also be followed by 5 more lines containing values related to SSL authentication, completing the 14 lines anticipated on the first line.

Take note of how the values in the master information file match the following excerpt from a `SHOW SLAVE STATUS` statement executed on the slave:

```
SHOW SLAVE STATUS \G

*************************** 1. row ***************************
Slave_IO_State: Waiting for master to send event
Master_Host: master_host
Master_User: replicant
Master_Port: 3306
Connect_Retry: 60
Master_Log_File: bin.000038
Read_Master_Log_Pos: 6393
Relay_Log_File: relay.000002
Relay_Log_Pos: 555
Relay_Master_Log_File: bin.000011
Slave_IO_Running: Yes
Slave_SQL_Running: No
Replicate_Do_DB: test
Replicate_Ignore_DB:
Replicate_Do_Table:
Replicate_Ignore_Table:
Replicate_Wild_Do_Table:
Replicate_Wild_Ignore_Table:
Last_Errno: 1062
Last_Error: Error 'Duplicate entry '1000' for key 1' on query.'
Skip_Counter: 0
Exec_Master_Log_Pos: 497
Relay_Log_Space: 22277198
Until_Condition: None
Until_Log_File:
Until_Log_Pos: 0
Master_SSL_Allowed: No
Master_SSL_CA_File:
Master_SSL_CA_Path:
Master_SSL_Cert:
Master_SSL_Cipher:
Master_SSL_Key:
Seconds_Behind_Master: NULL
```

Notice the labels for the additional SSL variables at the end of this excerpt. The master information file contains lines for them, whether they are empty or populated. Also note that, for tighter security, the command does not return the password.

After noting the new position number and other information that may have changed, the slave uses the same I/O thread to resume waiting for more entries from the master.

When the slave server detects any change to its relay log, through a different thread, the slave uses an SQL thread to execute the new SQL statement recorded in the relay log to the slave's databases. After the new entry is recorded in the slave's relay log, the new relay log position identification number is recorded in its relay log information file (*relay-log.info*) through the slave's SQL thread. Here is an excerpt from a relay log information file:

```
/var/log/mysql/relay.000002
555
bin.000011
497
```

The first line lists the file path and name of the current relay log file (`Relay_Log_File` in the `SHOW SLAVE STATUS` command). The second value is the SQL thread's position in the relay log file (`Relay_Log_Pos`). The third contains the name of the current binary log file on the master (`Relay_Master_Log_File`). The last value is the position in the master log file (`Exec_Master_Log_Pos`). These values can also be found in the results of the `SHOW SLAVE STATUS` statement shown earlier in this section.

When the slave is restarted or its logs are flushed, it appends the name of the current relay log file to the end of the relay log index file (*relay-log.index*). Here is an example of a relay log index file:

```
/var/log/mysql/relay.000002
/var/log/mysql/relay.000003
/var/log/mysql/relay.000004
```

This process of separating threads keeps the I/O thread free and dedicated to receiving changes from the master. It ensures that any delays in writing to the slave's databases on the SQL thread will not prevent or slow the receiving of data from the master. With this separate thread method, the slave server naturally has exclusive access to its relay log file at the filesystem level.

As an additional safeguard to ensure accuracy of data, the slave compares the entries in the relay log to the data in its databases. If the comparison reveals any inconsistency, the replication process is stopped and an error message is recorded in the slave's error log (*error.log*). The slave will not restart until it is told to do so. After you have resolved the discrepancy that the slave detected in the data, you can then instruct the slave to resume replication, as explained later in this chapter.

Here is an example of what is recorded on a slave server in its error log when the results don't match:

```
020714 01:32:03  mysqld started
020714  1:32:05  InnoDB: Started
/usr/sbin/mysqld-max: ready for connections
020714  8:00:28  Slave SQL thread initialized, starting replication in log
'server2-bin.035' at position 579285542, relay log './db1-relay-bin.001'
position: 4
020714  8:00:29  Slave I/O thread: connected to master
'...@66.216.68.90:3306',  replication started in log 'server2-bin.035' at
position 579285542 ERROR: 1146  Table 'test.response' doesn't exist
020714  8:00:30  Slave: error 'Table 'test.response' doesn't exist' on query
'INSERT INTO response SET connect_time=0.073868989944458,
```

```
page_time=1.53695404529572, site_id='Apt'', error_code=1146
020714  8:00:30  Error running query, slave SQL thread aborted. Fix the
problem, and restart the slave SQL thread with "SLAVE START". We stopped at
log 'server2-bin.035' position 579285542
020714  8:00:30  Slave SQL thread exiting, replication stopped in log
'server2-bin.035' at position 579285542
020714  8:00:54  Error reading packet from server:  (server_errno=1159)
020714  8:00:54  Slave I/O thread killed while reading event
020714  8:00:54  Slave I/O thread exiting, read up to log 'server2-bin.035',
position 579993154
020714  8:01:58  /usr/sbin/mysqld-max: Normal shutdown

020714  8:01:58  InnoDB: Starting shutdown...
020714  8:02:05  InnoDB: Shutdown completed
020714  8:02:06  /usr/sbin/mysqld-max: Shutdown Complete

020714 08:02:06  mysqld ended
```

In the first message, I have boldfaced an error message showing that the slave has realized the relay log contains entries involving a table that does not exist on the slave. The second boldfaced comment gives a message informing the administrator of the decision and some instructions on how to proceed.

The replication process may seem very involved and complicated at first, but it all occurs quickly; it's typically not a significant drain on the master server. Also, it's surprisingly easy to set up: it requires only a few lines of options in the configuration files on the master and slave servers. You will need to copy the databases on the master server to the slave to get the slave close to being current. Then it's merely a matter of starting the slave for it to begin replicating. It will quickly update its data to record any changes made since the initial backup copied from the master was installed on the slave. From then on, replication will keep it current—theoretically. As an administrator, you will have to monitor the replication process and resolve problems that arise occasionally.

Before concluding this section, let me adjust my previous statement about the ease of replication: replication is deceptively simple. When it works, it's simple. Before it starts working, or if it stops working, the minimal requirements of replication make it difficult to determine why it doesn't work. Now let's look at the steps for setting up replication.

The Replication User Account

There are only a few steps to setting up replication. The first step is to set up user accounts dedicated to replication on both the master and the slave. It's best not to use an existing account for security reasons. To set up the accounts, enter an SQL statement like the following on the master server, logged in as *root* or a user that has the `GRANT OPTION` privilege:

```
GRANT REPLICATION SLAVE, REPLICATION CLIENT ON *.*
TO 'replicant'@'slave_host' IDENTIFIED BY 'my_pwd';
```

These two privileges are all that are necessary for a user to replicate a server. The REPLICATE SLAVE privilege permits the user to connect to the master and to receive updates to the master's binary log. The REPLICATE CLIENT privilege allows the user to execute the SHOW MASTER STATUS and the SHOW SLAVE STATUS statements. In this SQL statement, the user account *replicant* is granted only what is needed for replication. The username can be almost anything. Both the username and the hostname are given within quotes. The hostname can be one that is resolved through */etc/hosts* (or the equivalent on your system), or it can be a domain name that is resolved through DNS. Instead of a hostname, you can give an IP address:

```
GRANT REPLICATION SLAVE, REPLICATION CLIENT ON *.*
TO 'replicant'@'12.127.17.72' IDENTIFIED BY 'my_pwd';
```

If you upgraded MySQL on your server to version 4.x recently, but you didn't upgrade your mysql database, the GRANT statement shown won't work because these privileges didn't exist in the earlier versions. For information on fixing this problem, see the section on mysql_fix_privilege_tables in Chapter 16.

Now enter the same GRANT statement on the slave server with the same username and password, but with the master's hostname or IP address:

```
GRANT REPLICATION SLAVE, REPLICATION CLIENT ON *.*
TO 'replicant'@'master_host' IDENTIFIED BY 'my_pwd';
```

There is a potential advantage of having the same user on both the master and the slave: if the master fails and will be down for a while, you can redirect users to the slave with DNS or by some other method. When the master is back up, you can then use replication to get the master up-to-date by temporarily making it a slave to the former slave server. This is cumbersome, though, and is outside the scope of this book. For details, see *High Performance MySQL* (O'Reilly). You should experiment with and practice such a method with a couple of test servers before relying on it with production servers.

To see the results of the first GRANT statement for the master, enter the following:

```
SHOW GRANTS FOR 'replicant'@'slave_host' \G

*************************** 1. row ***************************
Grants for replicant@slave_host:

GRANT REPLICATION SLAVE, REPLICATION CLIENT ON *.*
TO 'replicant'@'slave_host'
IDENTIFIED BY PASSWORD '*60115BF697978733E110BA18B3BC31D181FFCG082'
```

Note, incidentally, that the password has been encrypted in the output. If you don't get results similar to those shown here, the GRANT statement entry failed. Check what you typed when you granted the privileges and when you executed this statement. If everything was typed correctly and included in both statements, verify that you have version 4.0 of MySQL or higher, a version that supports these two new privileges. Enter SELECT VERSION( ); on each server to determine the versions they are using.

Configuring the Servers

Once the replication user is set up on both servers, you will need to add some lines to the MySQL configuration file on the master and on the slave server. Depending on the type of operating system, the configuration file will probably be called either *my.cnf* or *my.ini*. On Unix types of systems, the configuration file is usually located in the */etc* directory. On Windows systems, it's usually located in *c:* or in *c:\Windows*. If the file doesn't exist on your system, you can create it. Using a plain text editor (e.g., vi or *Notepad.exe*)—one that won't add binary formatting—add the following lines to the configuration file of the master under the `[mysqld]` group heading:

```
[mysqld]
server-id = 1
log-bin = /var/log/mysql/bin.log
...
```

The server identification number is an arbitrary number used to identify the master server in the binary log and in communications with slave servers. Almost any whole number from 1 to 4294967295 is fine. Don't use 0, as that causes problems. If you don't assign a server number, the default server identification number of 1 will be used. The default is all right for the master, but a different one should be assigned to each slave. To keep log entries straight and avoid confusion in communications between servers, it is very important that each slave have a unique number.

In the configuration file excerpt shown here, the line containing the `log-bin` option instructs MySQL to perform binary logging to the path and file given. The actual path and filename is mostly up to you. Just be sure that the directory exists and that the user *mysql* is the owner, or at least has permission to write to the directory. By default, if a path is not given, the server's data directory is assumed as the path for log files. To leave the defaults in place, give `log-bin` without the equals sign and without the file pathname. This example shows the default pathname. If you set the log file name to something else, keep the suffix *.log* as shown here. It will be replaced automatically with an index number (e.g., `.000001`) as new log files are created when the server is restarted or the logs are flushed.

These two options are all that is required on the master. They can be put in the configuration file or given from the command line when starting the *mysqld* daemon each time. On the command line, add the required double dashes before each option and omit the spaces around the equals signs.

For InnoDB tables, you may want to add the following lines to the master's configuration file:

```
innodb_flush_log_at_trx_commit = 1
sync-binlog = 1
```

These lines resolve problems that can occur with transactions and binary logging.

For the slave server, we will need to add several options to the slave's configuration file, reflecting the greater complexity and number of threads on the slave. You will have to provide a server identification number, information on connecting to the master server, and more log options. Add lines similar to the following to the slave's configuration file:

```
[mysqld]
server-id = 2

log-bin = /var/log/mysql/bin.log
log-bin-index = /var/log/mysql/log-bin.index
log-error = /var/log/mysql/error.log

relay-log = /var/log/mysql/relay.log
relay-log-info-file = /var/log/mysql/relay-log.info
relay-log-index = /var/log/mysql/relay-log.index

slave-load-tmpdir = /var/log/mysql/
skip-slave-start
...
```

At the top, you can see the server identification number is set to 2. The next stanzas set the logs and related index files. If these files don't exist when the slave is started, it will automatically create them.

The second stanza starts binary logging like on the master server, but this time on the slave. This is the log that can be used to allow the master and the slave to reverse roles as mentioned earlier. The binary log index file (*log-bin.index*) records the name of the current binary log file to use. The `log-error` option establishes an error log. Any problems with replication will be recorded in this log.

The third stanza defines the relay log that records each entry in the master server's binary log, along with related files mentioned earlier. The `relay-log-info-file` option names the file that records the most recent position in the master's binary log that the slave recorded for later execution (not the most recent statement actually executed by the slave), while the relay log index file in turn records the name of the current relay log file to use for replication.

The `slave-load-tmpdir` option is necessary only if you expect the `LOAD DATA INFILE` statement to be executed on the server. This SQL statement is used to import data in bulk into the databases. The `slave-load-tmpdir` option specifies the temporary directory for those files. If you don't specify the option, the value of the `tmpdir` variable will be used. This relates to replication because the slave will log `LOAD DATA INFILE` activities to the log files with the prefix `SQL_LOAD-` in this directory. For security, you may not want those logs to be placed in a directory such as */tmp*.

The last option, `skip-slave-start`, prevents the slave from replicating until you are ready. The order and spacing of options, incidentally, are a matter of personal style.

To set variables on the slave related to its connection with the master (e.g., the master's host address), it is recommended that you use the `CHANGE MASTER TO` statement to set the values on the slave. You could provide the values in the configuration file. However, the slave will read the file only the first time you start up the slave for replication. Because the values are stored in the *master.info* file, MySQL just relies on that file during subsequent startups and ignores these options in the main MySQL configuration file. The only time it adjusts the *master.info* file contents is when you tell it to explicitly through a CHANGE MASTER TO statement. You could edit the *master.info* file and other replication information files directly, but you might cause more problems in doing so. It's best to use the CHANGE MASTER TO statement to make changes. Here is an example:

```
CHANGE MASTER TO MASTER_HOST = 'master_host';
CHANGE MASTER TO MASTER_PORT = 3306;
CHANGE MASTER TO MASTER_USER = 'replicant';
CHANGE MASTER TO MASTER_PASSWORD = 'my_pwd';
```

This set of SQL statements provides information about the master server. The first statement gives the hostname (or the IP address) of the master. The next one provides the port for the connection. Port 3306 is the default port for MySQL, but another could be used for performance or security considerations. The next two lines set the username and password for logging into the master server. After you run these SQL statements, their values are stored in the *master.info* file and you shouldn't need to rerun the statements upon subsequent startups.

At this point, the servers should be configured properly. Next, you will need to get the slave's data current by making a backup on the master server and copying it manually to the slave. This is described in the following section. If the master and slave are new servers and the master has no data yet, you can skip the next section and proceed to "Starting Replication."

Copying Databases and Starting Replication

If you're setting up replication with an existing server that already contains data, you will need to make an initial backup of the databases and copy the backup to the slave server. I'll list the recommended method first, followed by some alternatives and their limitations.

To get a snapshot of the database in a consistent state, you need to shut down the server while you make a copy of the data, or at least prevent users from changing data. Considering that once you set up replication you may never have to shut down your master server for backups again, explain to management that it's worth inconveniencing the users this one time to get a clean, consistent backup. The following sections will explain how to lock the tables. Note that you can allow users to make changes as soon as your copy is made. If they make changes before replication starts, MySQL can easily recognize and incorporate those changes into the slave.

Using mysqldump

This utility, described in Chapter 16, creates a file of SQL statements that can later be executed to recreate databases and their contents. For the purposes of setting up replication, use the following options while running the utility from the command line on the master server:

```
mysqldump --user=root --password=my_pwd \
   --extended-insert --all-databases  \
   --ignore-table=mysql.users --master-data > /tmp/backup.sql
```

The result is a text file (*backup.sql*) containing SQL statements to create all of the master's databases and tables and insert their data. Here is an explanation of some of the special options shown:

`--extended-insert`
: This option creates multiple-row `INSERT` statements and thereby makes the resulting dump file smaller. It also allows the backup to run faster.

`--ignore-table`
: This option is used here so that the usernames and passwords won't be copied. This is a good security precaution if the slave will have different users, and especially if it will be used only for backups of the master. Unfortunately, there is no easy way to exclude the entire `mysql` database containing user information. You could list all the tables in that database to be excluded, but they have to be listed separately, and that becomes cumbersome. The only table that contains passwords is the `users` table, so it may be the only one that matters. However, it depends on whether you set security on a database, table, or other basis, and therefore want to protect that user information.

`--master-data`
: This option locks all of the tables during the dump to prevent data from being changed, but allows users to continue reading the tables. This option also adds a few lines like the following to the end of the dump file:

```
-- --
Position to start replication from --

CHANGE MASTER TO MASTER_LOG_FILE='bin.000846';
CHANGE MASTER TO MASTER_LOG_POS=427;
```

When the dump file is executed on the slave server, these lines will record the name of the master's binary log file and the position in the log at the time of the backup, while the tables were locked. When replication is started, these lines will provide this information to the master so it will know the point in the master's binary log to begin sending entries to the slave. This is meant to ensure that any data that changes while you set up the slave server isn't missed.

To execute the dump file and thereby set up the databases and data on the slave server, copy the dump file generated by `mysqldump` to the slave server. The MySQL server needs to be running on the slave, but not replication. Run the *mysql* client through a command such as the following on the slave:

```
mysql --user=root --password=my_pwd < /tmp/backup.sql
```

This will execute all of the SQL statements in the dump file, creating a copy of the master's databases and data on the slave.

Alternative Methods for Making Copies

If you peruse MySQL documentation, you might get the idea that the `LOAD DATA FROM MASTER` statement is ideal for making a copy, but it is actually not very feasible. First, it works only on MyISAM tables. Second, because it performs a global read lock on the master while it is making a backup, it prevents the master from serving users for some time. Finally, it can be very slow and depends on good network connectivity (so it can time out while copying data). Basically, the statement is a nice idea, but it's not very practical or dependable in most situations. It has been deprecated by MySQL AB and will be removed from future releases.

A better alternative is to drop down to the operating system level and copy the raw files containing your schemas and data. To leave the server up but prevent changes to data before you make a copy of the MySQL data directory, you could put a read-only lock on the tables by entering the following command:

```
FLUSH TABLES WITH READ LOCK;
```

This statement will commit any transactions that may be occurring on the server, so be careful and make sure the lock is actually in place before you continue. Then, without disconnecting the client that issued the statement, copy the data directory to an alternative directory. Once this is completed, issue an `UNLOCK TABLES` statement in the client that flushed and locked the tables. After that, the master responds to updates as usual, while you need only transfer the copy of the data directory to the slave server, putting it into the slave server's data directory. Be sure to change the ownership of all of the files and directories to `mysql`. In Linux, this is done by entering the following statement as *root*:

```
chown -R mysql:mysql /path_to_data
```

You will run into a complication with this method of copying the data directory if you have InnoDB tables in your databases, because they are not stored in the data directory. Also, if you don't have administrative access to the filesystem to be able to manually copy the data directory, you won't be able to use this method. This is why `mysqldump` remains the recommended method for copying the master's data.

Starting Replication

After you create the replication user accounts, configure the servers properly, and load the backed-up databases onto the slave server, you're ready to begin replication. Execute the following SQL statement while logged in as *root* or a user with `SUPER` privileges on the slave:

```
START SLAVE;
```

After this statement is run, the slave should connect to the master and get the changes it missed since the backup. From there, it should stay current by continuously interacting with the master, as outlined in the "Replication Process" section earlier in this chapter.

If everything is configured correctly on the slave, it will most likely start without a problem and return no message when `START SLAVE` is executed. However, when the slave tries to connect to the master, the connection may fail. Or when the SQL thread begins processing entries received from the master, it may fail. For whatever reason, if a slave fails after it is started, the client that started the slave will not be informed of the failure, nor will it be informed of the subsequent termination of the slave thread. For that information, you will have to read the slave's error logs. To confirm a slave is running, you can execute the SHOW SLAVE STATUS statement and check the results to see what state the slave is in, if any. We will describe the various slave states later in this chapter.

By default, the START SLAVE statement starts both the I/O thread and the execution thread as described earlier in the "Replication Process" section. You can specify which slave thread to start if you don't want to start both. You can also specify a particular master binary log file and the position in the log in which to *stop* replicating. You shouldn't need to make these distinctions when first starting a slave. These extra options for START SLAVE are useful when debugging a problem with a slave log, and especially when attempting to restore data to a particular position in the log because a user entered an erroneous statement and you want to revert to an earlier point in the database.

Here is an example of these possibilities:

```
START SLAVE SQL_THREAD
UNTIL MASTER_LOG_FILE = 'relay.0000052',
MASTER_LOG_POS = 254;
```

You can also control the processing of the relay log file with this syntax, but using the RELAY_LOG_FILE and the RELAY_LOG_POS parameters. You cannot specify a master log position and a relay log position in the same statement, though.

The UNTIL clause will be ignored if the SQL thread is already running. It will also be ignored if a slave already doing replication is shut down and restarted, or if the STOP SLAVE statement is executed followed by a START SLAVE statement without the UNTIL clause. Therefore, to use these options for fine-grained control, restart the slave server with the --skip-slave-start option in the configuration file.

Backups with Replication

With replication running, it's an easy task to make a backup of the data. You just need to temporarily stop the slave server from replicating by entering the following SQL statement while logged onto the slave server as *root* or as a user with SUPER privileges:

```
STOP SLAVE;
```

The slave server knows the position where it left off in the binary log of the master server and will record that information in the *master.info* file. So, you can take your time making a backup of the replicated databases on the slave server. You can use any backup utility or method you prefer. The only complication is if the slave also assists in handling user requests for load balancing, in which case STOP SLAVE throws the burden back on the master or on other slaves.

If the slave is used only for backups and has no users accessing the data, you could simply copy the data directory. I prefer to use mysqldump because it's fairly straightforward and works with all table types. To make a backup with mysqldump, enter something like the following:

```
mysqldump --user=root --password=my_pwd --lock-all-tables \
 --all-databases > /backups/mysql/backup.sql
```

When the backup is finished, enter the following SQL statement as *root* on the slave server to restart replication:

```
START SLAVE;
```

After entering this statement, there should be a flurry of activity on the slave as it executes the SQL statements that occurred while it was down. After a very short period of time, though, it should be current.

SQL Statements and Functions in Alphabetical Order

Several SQL statements apply directly to replication. One function, `MASTER_POS_WAIT( )`, also applies to replication, and it is listed here with the statements.

CHANGE MASTER TO

```
CHANGE MASTER TO
[MASTER_HOST = 'host' |
MASTER_USER = 'user' |
MASTER_PASSWORD = 'password' |
MASTER_PORT = port |
MASTER_CONNECT_RETRY = count |
MASTER_LOG_FILE = 'filename' |
MASTER_LOG_POS = position |
RELAY_LOG_FILE = 'filename' |
RELAY_LOG_POS = position |
MASTER_SSL = {0|1} |
MASTER_SSL_CA = 'filename' |
MASTER_SSL_CAPATH = 'path' |
MASTER_SSL_CERT = 'filename' |
MASTER_SSL_KEY = 'filename' |
MASTER_SSL_CIPHER = 'list' |
MASTER_SSL_VERIFY_SERVER_CERT = {0|1}], [,...]
```

This statement changes the settings on a slave server related to the master server and replication. Some of the variables relate to connecting to the master server, and some relate to master log files and the current position in the log files. This statement is run from the slave.

If the slave is engaging in replication, it may be necessary to use the `STOP SLAVE` statement before using this statement and the `START SLAVE` statement afterward. These options can be set from the server's options file, but it's much better to use this SQL statement to set replication options. `MASTER_SSL_VERIFY_SERVER_CERT` is available as of version 5.1.18 of MySQL and is comparable to the `--ssl-verify-server-cert` option. See Chapter 15 for more information on this client option.

Multiple option and value pairs may be given in one `CHANGE MASTER TO` statement, as long as the pairs are separated by commas. For example, the following SQL statement sets several properties for this slave:

```
CHANGE MASTER TO
   MASTER_HOST='mysql.company.com',
   MASTER_PORT=3306,
   MASTER_USER='slave_server',
   MASTER_PASSWORD='password',
   MASTER_CONNECT_RETRY=5;
```

The clauses related to log files name the master log files and provide the slave with the current position of the master log files. This may be necessary when first setting up a new slave or when a slave has been disabled for a while. Use the `SHOW MASTER STATUS` statement to determine the current position of the master log files, and the `SHOW SLAVE STATUS` statement to confirm a slave's position for the related files. Here is an example using the clauses related to log files:

```
CHANGE MASTER TO
   MASTER_LOG_FILE= 'log-bin.000153',
   MASTER_LOG_POS = 79,
   RELAY_LOG_FILE = 'log-relay.000153',
   RELAY_LOG_POS = 112;
```

The remaining clauses set various SSL variables. These values are saved to the *master.info* file. To see the current values for these options, use the `SHOW SLAVE STATUS` statement.

Relay log options are available as of version 4.1.1 of MySQL. The `MASTER_SSL` variable is set to 0 if the master does not allow SSL connections, and 1 if it does. The `MASTER_SSL_CA` variable holds the name of the file that contains a list of trusted certificate authorities (CAs). `MASTER_SSL_CAPATH` contains the absolute path to that file. The `MASTER_SSL_CERT` variable specifies the name of the SSL certificate file for secure connections, and `MASTER_SSL_KEY` specifies the SSL key file used to negotiate secure connections. Finally, `MASTER_SSL_CIPHER` provides a list of acceptable cipher methods for encryption.

LOAD DATA FROM MASTER

```
LOAD DATA FROM MASTER
```

This statement has been deprecated and will be removed from future releases of MySQL. It never worked very well. It was meant to make a copy of all the databases on the master server (except the `mysql` database) and copy them to the slave servers. It gets a global read lock on all tables while it takes a snapshot of the databases, and releases the lock before copying them to the slaves. The `MASTER_LOG_FILE` and the `MASTER_LOG_POS` variables will be updated so that the slave knows where to begin logging.

This statement works only with MyISAM tables. The user for the connection must have `RELOAD`, `SELECT`, and `SUPER` privileges on the master server. The user must also have `CREATE` and `DROP` privileges on the slave server. For large databases, increase the values of the `net_read_timeout` and `net_write_timeout` variables with the `SET` statement. To load a specific table from the master server, use the `LOAD TABLE...FROM MASTER` statement.

Again, this statement does not work very well: it's not dependable and usually has problems with properly copying data from the master to the slave. Instead, use a utility such as `mysqldump` to copy the data on the master and then transfer the resulting file to the slave, as described in detail in the tutorial section at the start of this chapter.

LOAD TABLE...FROM MASTER

```
LOAD TABLE table FROM MASTER
```

This statement has been deprecated and will be removed from future releases of MySQL because it has many problems. It was meant to copy a MyISAM table from the master server to a slave server. The user for the connection must have `RELOAD` and `SUPER` privileges as well as `SELECT` privileges for the table on the master server. The user must also have `CREATE` and `DROP` privileges on the slave server.

Instead of using this statement, use a utility such as **`mysqldump`** to copy the data from the master. This method is described in detail in the tutorial section at the start of this chapter.

MASTER_POS_WAIT( )

```
MASTER_POS_WAIT(log_filename, log_position[, timeout])
```

This function is useful to synchronize MySQL master and slave server logging. The function causes the master to wait until the slave server has read and applied all updates to the position (given in the second argument) in the master log (named in the first argument). You can specify a third argument to set the number of seconds the master will wait. A value of 0 or a negative amount is given to instruct the function not to time out and to keep trying.

The function returns the number of log entries that were made by the slave while the master was waiting. If all is set properly, you should receive these results rapidly. However, if there is an error, NULL is returned. NULL is also returned if the slave's SQL thread is not started, if the slave's master options are not set, or if the parameters given with this function are not correct. If you give the timeout parameter and the amount of time is exceeded, –1 is returned.

PURGE MASTER LOGS

```
PURGE {MASTER|BINARY} LOGS {TO 'log_filename'|BEFORE 'date'}
```

This statement deletes the binary logs from a master server. The keywords `MASTER` and `BINARY` are synonymous and one is required for the statement. Log files are deleted sequentially from the starting log file to the one named with the `TO` clause, or up until (but not including) the date named with the `BEFORE` clause. Here is an example of each method:

```
PURGE MASTER LOGS TO 'log-bin.00110';
PURGE MASTER LOGS BEFORE '2004-11-03 07:00:00';
```

Before running this statement, it would be prudent to make a backup of the logs. Then use `SHOW SLAVE STATUS` on each slave to determine which logs the slaves are reading, and run `SHOW BINARY LOGS` on the master server to get a list of log files. The oldest log file in the list is the one that will be purged. If the slaves are current, they shouldn't be reading this log file. If they still are, you might not want to purge it. If you find that your log files aren't being rotated very often, you can set the system variable `expire_logs_days` to shorten the amount of time before new log files are created and old ones archived.

RESET MASTER

```
RESET MASTER
```

This statement deletes all the binary log files on the master server. Binary log files are located in the directory indicated by the value of the `--log-bin` option of *mysqld* (see Chapter 15). The log files are typically named *log-bin.n*, where *n* is a six-digit numbering index. Use the `SHOW MASTER LOGS` statement to get a list of log files to be sure.

This statement will delete all of the master log files and begin numbering the new file at 000001. To get the slave servers in line with the reset master, run the `RESET SLAVE` statement. You can run the `MASTER` and `SLAVE` options together in a comma-separated list like so:

```
RESET MASTER, SLAVE;
```

This is a recommended method for ensuring consistency.

RESET SLAVE

```
RESET SLAVE
```

Use this statement within or after the `RESET MASTER` statement that sets the binary logging index back to 1. This statement will delete the *master.info* file, the *relay-log.info* file, and all of the relay log files on the slave server. It will delete the relay log files regardless of whether the SQL thread has finished executing its contents. A new *.info* file will be created with the default startup values.

SET GLOBAL SQL_SLAVE_SKIP_COUNTER

```
SET GLOBAL SQL_SLAVE_SKIP_COUNTER = number
```

This statement skips the given number of events from the master. It is used for fine-tuning a recovery. It returns an error if the slave thread is running. Here is an example:

```
SET GLOBAL SQL_SLAVE_SKIP_COUNTER=10;
```

SET SQL_LOG_BIN

```
SET SQL_LOG_BIN = {0|1}
```

This statement enables or disables binary logging of SQL statements for the current connection. It does not affect logging for the activities of other threads and is reset to the default value when the connection is closed. The statement requires `SUPER` privileges. A value of 0 disables binary logging; 1 enables it. Here is an example:

```
SET SQL_LOG_BIN = 0;
```

SHOW BINLOG EVENTS

```
SHOW BINLOG EVENTS [IN 'log_filename']
   [FROM position] [LIMIT [offset,] count]
```

This statement displays the events in a binary log file. Use the `IN` clause to specify a particular log file. If the `IN` clause is omitted, the current file is used. To obtain a list of binary log files, use the `SHOW MASTER LOGS` statement. Here is an example of how you can use this statement and typical results:

```
SHOW BINLOG EVENTS IN 'log-bin.000161'\G
*************************** 1. row ***************************
     Log_name: log-bin.000161
          Pos: 4
   Event_type: Start
    Server_id: 1
 Orig_log_pos: 4
         Info: Server ver: 4.1.7-standard-log, Binlog ver: 3
1 row in set (0.00 sec)
```

This log file has only one row of data because the SQL statement was run shortly after the server was started. For a larger log file recording many rows of events, the results take a long time and drain system resources significantly. To minimize this, you can focus and limit the results with the `FROM` and `LIMIT` clauses. In the results, notice the `Pos` label with a value of 4. In a large log file, that number might be in the thousands. The results displayed could be focused only on rows starting from a particular position in the log with the `FROM` clause. You can limit the number of rows of events displayed with the `LIMIT` clause. In the `LIMIT` clause, you can also set the starting point of the output based on the number of rows in the results set and limit them to a certain number of rows. Here is an example of both of these clauses:

```
SHOW BINLOG EVENTS IN 'log-bin.000160'
FROM 3869 LIMIT 2,1\G
*************************** 1. row ***************************
     Log_name: log-bin.000160
          Pos: 4002
   Event_type: Intvar
    Server_id: 1
 Orig_log_pos: 4002
         Info: INSERT_ID=5
```

In this example, the retrieval of log events is to begin from position 3869 as set by the `FROM` clause. The results set contains several rows, although only one is shown here. The display is limited to one row, starting from the third one in the results set per the `LIMIT` clause. The number of skipped records is the sum of the `FROM` argument and the first `LIMIT` argument.

As an alternative to using this statement when working with large binary log files, you might try using the `mysqlbinlog` utility and redirecting the results to a text file that you can read in a text editor when it's finished. Besides, this utility will provide you more information than `SHOW BINLOG EVENTS`.

SHOW BINARY LOGS

```
SHOW BINARY LOGS
```

This statement displays a list of binary logs created by the master MySQL server in the filesystem directory. It's synonymous with `SHOW MASTER LOGS`. To delete logs, see the description of the `PURGE MASTER LOGS` statement earlier in this chapter. For information on enabling logs, see Chapter 16. Here is an example:

```
SHOW BINARY LOGS;
```

SHOW MASTER LOGS

```
SHOW MASTER LOGS
```

This statement displays a list of binary logs created by the master MySQL server in the filesystem directory. It's synonymous with `SHOW BINARY LOGS`. To delete logs, see the description of the `PURGE MASTER LOGS` statement earlier in this chapter. For information on enabling logs, see Chapter 16.

SHOW MASTER STATUS

```
SHOW MASTER STATUS
```

This statement displays information on the status of the binary log file that is being used currently on the master MySQL server:

```
SHOW MASTER STATUS;

+----------------+----------+--------------+------------------+
| File           | Position | Binlog_Do_DB | Binlog_Ignore_DB |
+----------------+----------+--------------+------------------+
| log-bin.000141 |     1123 |              |                  |
+----------------+----------+--------------+------------------+
```

SHOW SLAVE HOSTS

```
SHOW SLAVE HOSTS
```

This statement displays a list of slave servers for the master server. Slaves must be started with the `--report-host=slave` option in order to be shown. Here is an example:

```
SHOW SLAVE HOSTS;

+-----------+----------+------+-----------+
| Server_id | Host     | Port | Master_id |
+-----------+----------+------+-----------+
|         2 | slave2   | 3306 |         1 |
|         3 | slave3   | 3306 |         1 |
+-----------+----------+------+-----------+
```

Four fields are in the results:

`Server_id`
: The server identification number for the slave server, which is set by the `--server-id` option (preferably in the slave's options file).

`Host`
: The hostname of the slave server, which is set by the `--report-host` option on the slave.

`Port`
: The port on which the slave is listening for replication. This defaults to 3306, but can be set with the `CHANGE MASTER TO` statement, described earlier in this chapter.

`Master_id`
: The server identification number of the master. It's set on the master with `--server-id` and conversely on the slave with the `CHANGE MASTER TO` statement.

SHOW SLAVE STATUS

```
SHOW SLAVE STATUS
```

This statement displays information on the slave thread. Here is an example of this statement and its results:

```
SHOW SLAVE STATUS\G
*************************** 1. row ***************************
             Slave_IO_State: Waiting for master to send event
                Master_Host: localhost
                Master_User: root
                Master_Port: 3306
              Connect_Retry: 5
            Master_Log_File: log-bin.000154
        Read_Master_Log_Pos: 159
             Relay_Log_File: log-relay-bin.154
              Relay_Log_Pos: 694
      Relay_Master_Log_File: log-bin.154
           Slave_IO_Running: Yes
          Slave_SQL_Running: Yes
            Replicate_Do_DB:
        Replicate_Ignore_DB:
                 Last_Errno: 0
                 Last_Error:
               Skip_Counter: 0
        Exec_Master_Log_Pos: 159
            Relay_Log_Space: 694
            Until_Condition: None
             Until_Log_File:
              Until_Log_Pos: 0
         Master_SSL_Allowed: Yes
         Master_SSL_CA_File: ssl_ca.dat
         Master_SSL_CA_Path: /data/mysql/ssl_ca
            Master_SSL_Cert: ssl_cert.dat
          Master_SSL_Cipher:
             Master_SSL_Key:
      Seconds_Behind_Master: 3
```

You can set some of these values at startup with the MySQL server daemon (*mysqld*). See Chapter 15 for more information on setting server variables at startup. You can also set some of these variables with the `SET` statement, and you can adjust others for particular tables with the `ALTER TABLE` statement. You can reset some of the log file variables with the `RESET MASTER` and `RESET SLAVE` statements.

START SLAVE

```
START SLAVE [IO_THREAD|SQL_THREAD]

START SLAVE [SQL_THREAD]
   UNTIL MASTER_LOG_FILE = 'log_filename', MASTER_LOG_POS = position
START SLAVE [SQL_THREAD]
   UNTIL RELAY_LOG_FILE = 'log_filename', RELAY_LOG_POS = position
```

Use this statement to start a slave server. In the first syntax, you can start just the I/O thread or just the SQL thread by using the respective keyword. You can start both by listing both keywords, separated by a comma. The default is to start both. The I/O thread reads SQL queries from the master server and records them in the relay log file. The SQL thread reads the relay log file and then executes the SQL statements. See the "Replication Process" section earlier in this chapter for details.

The second syntax limits the reading of the threads to a specific point, given with `MASTER_LOG_POS`, in the master log file named with the `MASTER_LOG_FILE` parameter. The `UNTIL` clause stops processing of the given log files when the given position is reached. The third syntax specifies the relay log file and limits its reading and execution. If the `SQL_THREAD` keyword is given in either the second or third syntaxes, the reading will be limited to the SQL thread.

The starting of a slave thread isn't always dependable. Run the `SHOW SLAVE STATUS` statement to confirm that the thread began and remained running.

STOP SLAVE

```
STOP SLAVE [IO_THREAD|SQL_THREAD]
```

This statement stops the slave server threads. To stop a specific type of slave thread, specify one or both of the thread types. Both may be given in a comma-separated list. The default is to stop both. The statement requires `SUPER` privileges. You can start slave threads with the `START SLAVE` statement.

Replication States

In order to be able to monitor replication effectively, you need to know and understand the various states that the master and slave can occupy. Server states can be displayed by using the `SHOW PROCESSLIST` statement on the master and the slave. At least one line of the results will be related to the replication activities for the user account associated with replication. Following the examples of this chapter, the account is *replicant* on the master and *system user* on the slave. In the `Command` column, on the master the value will be `Binlog Dump`, meaning a binary log thread; on the slave the value will be `Connect`. The results will also contain a field called `State`, in which the state of the thread will be given. Here is an example from a slave:

```
SHOW PROCESSLIST \G
*************************** 1. row ***************************
 Id: 16
 User: system user
 Host:
 db: NULL
 Command: Connect
 Time: 119255
 State: Waiting for master to send event
 Info: NULL
```

These results show only one thread, the I/O thread waiting on the master. If the server were processing entries from the master's binary log, there would probably be another row shown in the results for the SQL thread. What follows is a list of all of the possible server states that you may see on master and slave servers, along with descriptions of each. In addition to understanding these traits, you may want to develop a script to check that replication is running on the slave and not stalled and to notify you if it's not running. Replication on MySQL is very stable, but if it does stop, it's very quiet about it. Fortunately, it's very good about rapidly catching up once you restart it.

Master BinLog Dump Thread States

Here is an overview of master server replication states that can be reported for binary log threads (`Binlog Dump`):

Has sent all binlog to slave; waiting for binlog to be updated
: This is the most common status message you should see for a slave connection on the master. In this state, the master is basically doing nothing regarding replication. It has sent the slave all entries requested and is now waiting for another event to occur that will cause its binary log to be updated. Notice that it says it is waiting for the binary log to be updated. It doesn't say it's waiting for the databases to be updated. That's handled by a different component of MySQL. The thread lives only to provide information about the binary log to the slave.

Sending binlog event to slave
: After the binary log has been updated, the master informs the slave that one or more new entries have been made. If the slave requests the entries, the master enters this state, indicating that it is in the process of sending a slave entries or information on pertinent database events. There are obviously other states in between, but they are so fast and short-lived that they are not registered and therefore will not show up in the results of `SHOW PROCESSLIST`.

Finished reading one binlog; switching to next binlog
: If a slave has been offline for a while, the master may have flushed its logs in the interim. Whenever the master does this, it will start a new log file, saving the previous ones. When a slave requests log entries that span more than one log file as the master switches from one file to the next, it enters this state.

Waiting to finalize termination
: Once the master has completed the process of updating a slave, the master shows this status as it's closing the binary log file and winding down the communication with the slave. When it is finished, the master will return to the first thread state (*Has sent all binlog to slave; waiting for binlog to be updated*) in which it is waiting for more changes to the binary log.

Slave I/O Thread States

Here is a list of replication states that can be found on the slave server for I/O threads:

Connecting to master
: This state indicates that the slave I/O thread is attempting to connect to the master. If it can't connect, it may stay in this state for a while as it retries.

Checking master version
: After the slave connects to the master, it compares versions of MySQL with the master to ensure compatibility. This is very quick.

Registering slave on master
: After the slave connects to the master, it registers itself with the master as a replication slave server. During this process, it will be in this state. On the master side of the connection, the `Binlog Dump` state will be *Has sent all binlog to slave; waiting for binlog to be updated*, as described previously.

Requesting binlog dump
: When the slave has been informed of changes to the master binary log, it enters this state to request the new entries. Also, when it first connects to a server—either for the first time or after having been disconnected for a while—it enters this state briefly to request all entries since the last master binary log position that it gives the master. If no changes have occurred, none are returned. If there are new entries, the entries starting from the position given until the end of the master's binary log will be transmitted to the slave. On the master side, you will see the state *Sending binlog event to slave* as a result of the request.

Waiting to reconnect after a failed binlog dump request
: If the request for new entries mentioned in the previous state fails to be received from the master, the slave enters this state as it waits to be able to connect to the master periodically. This timeout period is configured using the `--master-connect-retry` and defaults to 60 seconds. The number of retries it will make can be found in the *master.info* file shown earlier in this chapter. Each time the slave attempts to reconnect, it will enter the next state.

Reconnecting after a failed binlog dump request
: If the slave failed to stay connected to the master while trying to retrieve entries to the master's binary log (as mentioned in the previous state description), this state indicates that the slave is trying to reconnect. If it fails again, it will go back to the previous state and wait to retry. By default, it will try 60 times before stopping. You can change the number of retries with the `--master-connect-retry` option.

Waiting for master to send event
: This state is the most common that you will see, unless your server is very busy. The SQL thread is currently connected to the master and is waiting for the master to send it binary log updates. If there is no activity after a while, the connection will time out. The number of seconds that will elapse before timeout is reached can be found in the variable `slave_net_timeout` (previously `slave_read_timeout`). A timeout is the same as a lost connection for the slave. Therefore, it will become active and attempt to reconnect to the master, then inquire about any changes to the master's binary log, before entering this state again.

Queueing master event to the relay log
: This state occurs when the slave I/O thread has received changes to the master's binary log from the master and is writing the SQL statements and the related information to the slave's relay log. Once it's done, the slave's SQL thread will

read the relay log and execute the new SQL statements written to the log. On the SQL thread, this is the *Reading event from the relay log* state described in the next section.

Waiting to reconnect after a failed master event read
: If the connection to the slave failed while reading an event (represented by an entry in the master's binary log), the slave will wait in this state for a certain amount of time before attempting to reconnect to the master. The number of seconds that the slave will wait before retrying is found in the `master-connect-retry` variable on the slave. When the slave attempts to reconnect, it enters the next state.

Reconnecting after a failed master event read
: This state occurs after the slave I/O thread loses its connection to the master while receiving an entry from the master binary log.

Waiting for the slave SQL thread to free enough relay log space
: If the SQL thread isn't processing the entries in the relay log fast enough, and the backlog has caused the relay log files to become too large, the I/O thread will enter this state. In this state, it's waiting for the SQL thread to process enough of the entries in the relay log so that the I/O thread can delete some of the older content of the log. The maximum amount of space allocated for the relay log files is found in the `relay_log_space_limit` variable. The slave SQL thread automatically deletes relay log files. The `FLUSH LOGS` statement, though, causes the slave to rotate log files and to consider deleting old files.

Waiting for slave mutex on exit
: When the I/O thread has been terminated, it enters this state as it closes. The term *mutex* stands for mutual exclusion. The SQL thread gets the mutex to prevent any other slave replication activities so that replication can be shut down without loss of data or file corruption.

Slave SQL Thread States

Here is a list of replication states that can be found on the slave server for SQL threads:

Has read all relay log; waiting for the slave I/O thread to update it
: Because replication is so fast, you will usually see the slave's SQL thread in this state unless you have a very busy database system with data constantly being updated. This state indicates that the slave's SQL thread has read all of the entries in its relay log and has executed all of the SQL statements that it contains. It has no further updates to make to its databases and is waiting for the slave's I/O thread to add more entries to the relay log file. As mentioned in the similar state for the master, each thread acts somewhat independently and focuses only on the activities of its purview. Messages related to each thread's state reflect this.

Replication

Reading event from the relay log
: When an entry has been made to the relay log by the slave's I/O thread, the slave's SQL thread enters this state. In this state it is reading the current relay log file and is executing the new SQL statements that it contains. Basically, the SQL thread is busy updating the slave's databases.

Waiting for slave mutex on exit
: When the SQL thread has finished updating the slave's databases,it enters this state while it's closing the relay log file and terminating communications with the slave server. The SQL thread gets the mutex to prevent any other slave replication activities so that replication can be shut down without loss of data or file corruption. This is a very minimal state. However, if there is a problem with closing the relay log file or ending the activities of the slave server, this state is displayed so that you know the thread is locked. This could be caused by a table or log file being corrupted. If you see this state, you may want to run `myisamchk` or a similar utility, or the `REPAIR TABLE` statement on the tables that accessed at the time of the lockup. You'll have to look in the relay log file and the error log file on the slave to determine which tables might need checking.

9

Stored Routines Statements

MySQL allows sets of SQL statements, known as *routines*, to be stored in the database for easier and more consistent use. You can create your own functions based on existing SQL statements and built-in functions, allowing a user to pass values to these user-defined functions as well as receive values in return. This can make complex tasks simpler for end users, as well as allow database administrators to control or enhance the functions available to users. Additionally, MySQL provides SQL statements related to *events*. Events are internal methods to schedule the execution of SQL statements or stored procedures. These are the SQL statements covered in this chapter:

`ALTER EVENT`, `ALTER FUNCTION`, `ALTER PROCEDURE`, `ALTER TRIGGER`, `BEGIN...END`, `CALL`, `CLOSE`, `CREATE EVENT`, `CREATE FUNCTION`, `CREATE PROCEDURE`, `CREATE TRIGGER`, `DECLARE`, `DELIMITER`, `DROP EVENT`, `DROP FUNCTION`, `DROP PREPARE`, `DROP PROCEDURE`, `DROP TRIGGER`, `EXECUTE`, `FETCH`, `OPEN`, `PREPARE`, `SHOW CREATE EVENT`, `SHOW CREATE FUNCTION`, `SHOW CREATE PROCEDURE`, `SHOW EVENTS`, `SHOW FUNCTION CODE`, `SHOW FUNCTION STATUS`, `SHOW PROCEDURE CODE`, `SHOW PROCEDURE STATUS`, `SHOW TRIGGERS`.

Statements in Alphabetical Order

This section is an alphabetical listing of MySQL statements related to events, stored procedures, triggers, and user-defined functions. For an explanation of the method of presenting syntax and describing the SQL statements, as well as for information related to examples, please see the introduction to Part II. Many of the examples in this particular chapter involve the activities of a fictitious college.

ALTER EVENT

```
ALTER EVENT
[DEFINER = {'user'@'host'|CURRENT_USER}]
event
ON SCHEDULE
AT timestamp [+ INTERVAL count interval] |
EVERY count interval
   [STARTS timestamp [+ INTERVAL count interval]]
   [ENDS timestamp [+ INTERVAL count interval]]
[ON COMPLETION [NOT] PRESERVE]
[ENABLE|DISABLE|DISABLE ON SLAVE]
[COMMENT 'comment']
DO statement
```

Use this statement to alter an existing scheduled MySQL event. The statement can be used to change the time when the scheduled SQL statement will execute or other aspects of its upcoming execution. The `event` parameter has to be the name of an event that was already scheduled but has not yet been completed, or was completed but preserved by the server. It isn't possible within MySQL to change the name of an event. Instead, use the `DROP EVENT` statement to delete an existing event and then create it again with a new name using `CREATE EVENT`. You can use the `SHOW CREATE EVENT` statement to be sure that all other parameters are the same.

To change the MySQL user and host through which MySQL executes the event, use the `DEFINER` clause. As of version 5.1.12 of MySQL, a user that has `EVENT` privilege can change an event. Unless the definer is specified with the `DEFINER` clause, the user that changes an event becomes the new definer.

To change the time and date that form the basis for running the event, use the `ON SCHEDULE AT` clause and give the new time in the `timestamp` format (*yyyy-mm-dd hh:mm:ss*). The time given can be a string, a time function, or just `CURRENT_TIMESTAMP`. You can also specify a time relative to the timestamp given by adding a plus sign followed by the keyword `INTERVAL`, the number of intervals (e.g., `1`), and then the interval increment (e.g., `HOUR`). For *`interval`*, use one of the allowable intervals shown in the description of the `CREATE EVENT` statement later in this chapter.

To make the event a recurring one, add the `EVERY` clause, using the same syntax and format. You can also give starting and ending times for a recurring event with the `STARTS` and `ENDS` clauses.

If an event is not yet completed, you can keep the server from dropping it by adding the `ON COMPLETION` clause with the `PRESERVE` keyword. If you already did this when you created the event, you can change your mind and set the server to `NOT PRESERVE` the event.

If you created an event that you need to temporarily disable for some reason, you can do so with this statement by using the `DISABLE` keyword. An event that has been disabled can be enabled with the `ENABLE` keyword. The `DISABLE ON SLAVE` keyword prevents the event from running on slave servers.

With the `COMMENT` clause, you can add or change a comment describing the event for future reference. The `DO` clause can include any SQL statement to be executed. A stored procedure can be used to easily execute a set of SQL statements.

Here is an example using this statement to change a periodic event:

```
ALTER EVENT students_copy
ON SCHEDULE EVERY 1 DAY
STARTS '2007-12-10 01:30:00'
ON COMPLETION PRESERVE;
```

If you look at the example for `CREATE EVENT` later in this chapter, you'll see that our only change is to move the time from 2:30 A.M. to 1:30 A.M. here. The starting time and date given are not only for the time we want, but since this statement is run on December 9, the date of December 10 is given. When an event's time is altered or when an event is first created, it must be for a future time. The `EVERY` clause is included because `STARTS` is part of it and not a separate clause of its own. So that the `ON COMPLETION PRESERVE` isn't set back to the default of `ON COMPLETION NOT PRESERVE`, we stipulate it again here.

ALTER FUNCTION

```
ALTER FUNCTION stored_procedure
  [{CONTAINS SQL|NO SQL|READS SQL DATA|MODIFIES SQL DATA} |
   SQL SECURITY {DEFINER|INVOKER} |
   COMMENT 'string']
```

This statement changes the characteristics of an existing user-defined function. You cannot change the function itself with it. To do that, you need to delete the function with `DROP FUNCTION` and create a new procedure with `CREATE FUNCTION`. See the description of `CREATE FUNCTION` later in this chapter for an explanation of each characteristic.

There are three types of characteristics you can set or change with this statement: the types of interaction with the server, the user recognized for SQL security, and a comment. Each type may be given in a space-separated list, in any order. See `CREATE FUNCTION` later in this chapter for a discussion of the characteristics. The `COMMENT` clause replaces any existing comment. To clear a comment without inserting another, give two quotes with nothing between them.

This statement requires the `CREATE ROUTINE` privilege. The `ALTER ROUTINE` and `EXECUTE` privileges are granted to the user and host account that creates or alters a function, by default.

Here is an example using this statement, in which a function shown in the example for the `CREATE FUNCTION` statement is altered:

```
ALTER FUNCTION date_reformatted
SQL SECURITY INVOKER
COMMENT "Converts a string date like 'Dec. 7, 2007' to standard format.";
```

ALTER PROCEDURE

```
ALTER PROCEDURE stored_procedure
  [{CONTAINS SQL|NO SQL|READS SQL DATA|MODIFIES SQL DATA}]
  [SQL SECURITY {DEFINER|INVOKER}]
  [COMMENT 'string']
```

This statement changes the characteristics of an existing stored procedure. You cannot change the procedure itself with it. To do that, you need to delete the procedure with

DROP PROCEDURE and create a new procedure with CREATE PROCEDURE. See the description of CREATE PROCEDURE later in this chapter for an explanation of each characteristic.

There are three types of characteristics that you can set or change with this statement: the types of interaction with the server, the user recognized for SQL security, and a comment. Each type may be given in a space-separated list, in any order. See CREATE PROCEDURE later in this chapter for a discussion of the characteristics. The COMMENT clause replaces any existing comment. To clear a comment without inserting another, give two quotes with nothing between them.

This statement requires the CREATE ROUTINE privilege. The ALTER ROUTINE and EXECUTE privileges are granted to the user and host account that creates or alters a stored procedure, by default.

Here is an example of this statement:

```
ALTER PROCEDURE students_copy_proc
SQL SECURITY INVOKER
COMMENT 'Copies data from students table to students_backup.
Add a comment with @ref_note.'
```

If you look at the example for CREATE PROCEDURE later in this chapter, you'll see that the example here is changing the procedure created in that example. We're only adding that the user account to be used for executing the procedure will be the invoker, and we're adding a comment about the procedure—we didn't include one when we created the procedure.

ALTER TRIGGER

There is not an ALTER TRIGGER statement at this time. Instead, use the DROP TRIGGER statement and then CREATE TRIGGER again with the new, adjusted trigger.

BEGIN...END

```
BEGIN...END
```

Use this combination of statements to start and end the steps that are part of a stored procedure or trigger. In essence, BEGIN marks the beginning of a compound SQL statement and END marks the end of it. Multiple SQL statements can be included between them.

Traditionally, as you know from using the *mysql* client, each SQL statement must end with a semicolon. However, semicolons must be used within CREATE PROCEDURE and CREATE TRIGGER statements to separate the internal statements that form the procedure or trigger. So as not to confuse the parser in the client and server, include a DELIMITER command to change the default delimiter to another character before entering BEGIN, and then to set it back to a semicolon again after entering END. For examples of these statements, see the CREATE PROCEDURE and CREATE TRIGGER statements later in this chapter.

CALL

```
CALL stored_procedure[([parameter[, ...]])]
```

Use this statement to call a stored procedure. Parameters to be passed to the stored procedure may be given within the parentheses. If the keyword of `INOUT` is used, values may be given to the stored procedure and returned to the SQL statement that called it. For an example of this statement, see the `CREATE PROCEDURE` statement later in this chapter.

CLOSE

```
CLOSE cursor
```

This statement closes a cursor that has been declared within the current routine and has been opened using the `OPEN` statement. See the descriptions of the `DECLARE` and `FETCH` statements later in this chapter for more information on cursors.

CREATE EVENT

```
CREATE [DEFINER = {'user'@'host'|CURRENT_USER}] EVENT
[IF NOT EXISTS] event
ON SCHEDULE
AT timestamp [+ INTERVAL count interval] |
EVERY count interval
   [STARTS timestamp [+ INTERVAL count interval]]
   [ENDS timestamp [+ INTERVAL count interval]]
[ON COMPLETION [NOT] PRESERVE]
[ENABLE|DISABLE|DISABLE ON SLAVE]
[COMMENT 'comment']
DO statement
```

Use this statement to schedule the execution of an SQL statement at a specific time and date. Events may also be recurring. Although there are many options, the basic syntax is:

```
CREATE EVENT event ON SCHEDULE AT timestamp DO statement
```

The event name you give may be any nonreserved word and is case-insensitive. The `DO` clause can include any SQL statement to be executed. A stored procedure can be passed here to conveniently execute a set of SQL statements.

With the `DEFINER` clause, you can specify the MySQL user and host to be used by MySQL for the event. This means that the event may be created by a user with `SUPER` privileges but executed by another user account in which privileges are limited for security reasons. The `IF NOT EXISTS` clause may be given to prevent errors from being returned if the event has already been created.

For the required `ON SCHEDULE AT` clause, include a specific time and date in the `timestamp` format (*yyyy-mm-dd hh:mm:ss*). The time given can be a string, a time function, or just `CURRENT_TIMESTAMP`. You can also specify a time relative to the timestamp given by adding a plus sign followed by the keyword `INTERVAL`, the number of intervals (e.g., `1`), and then the interval increment (e.g., `HOUR`). For *`interval`*, use one of the allowable intervals: `SECOND`, `MINUTE`, `MINUTE_SECOND`, `HOUR`, `HOUR_SECOND`, `HOUR_MINUTE`, `DAY`, `DAY_SECOND`, `DAY_MINUTE`, `DAY_HOUR`, `WEEK`, `MONTH`, `QUARTER`, `YEAR`, or `YEAR_MONTH`.

Stored Routines Statements

To make the event a recurring one, add the EVERY clause, using the same syntax and format. You can also give starting and ending times for a repeating event with the STARTS and ENDS clauses.

Once an event is completed, it will be dropped automatically. However, you can drop it manually before completion with the DROP EVENT statement. You can also keep the server from dropping an event by adding the ON COMPLETION clause with the PRESERVE keyword. The NOT PRESERVE keyword instructs the server not to retain the event when completed; this is the server's default behavior.

When creating an event, you may want to create it with the DISABLE parameter so that it won't begin to execute until you enable it. Then use the ALTER EVENT statement to enable it later. The DISABLE ON SLAVE keyword will disable the event from running on slave servers. By default, an event runs on the master and all slaves.

With the COMMENT clause, you can add a comment describing the event for future reference. This comment is displayed only when SHOW CREATE EVENT is executed for the event.

Here is an example using this statement. It schedules a procedure that is created in the example under the CREATE PROCEDURE statement later in this chapter:

```
CREATE EVENT students_copy
ON SCHEDULE EVERY 1 DAY
STARTS '2007-11-27 02:30:00'
ON COMPLETION PRESERVE
COMMENT 'Daily copy of students table to students_backup'
DO CALL students_copy_proc();
```

In this example, the event will be run once a day starting from the time given and then every day afterward at the same time (2:30 A.M.). It's set to be recurring, but in case someone ever changes that aspect of it, MySQL will preserve the event upon completion. We've added a comment to explain the purpose of the event. Use ALTER EVENT to change an event and SHOW EVENTS to get a list of events.

CREATE FUNCTION

```
CREATE
[DEFINER = {'user'@'host'|CURRENT_USER}]
FUNCTION function ([parameter data_type[,...]])
RETURNS data_type
  [LANGUAGE SQL]
  [[NOT] DETERMINISTIC]
  [{CONTAINS SQL|NO SQL|READS SQL DATA|MODIFIES SQL DATA}]
  [COMMENT 'string']
  [SQL SECURITY {DEFINER|INVOKER}]
RETURN routine
```

A user-defined function is essentially a set of SQL statements that may be called as a unit, processing any data it's given in its parameters and returning a value to the caller of the function. This is similar to a stored procedure, except that a function returns a value and a stored procedure does not. A stored procedure normally places the values it generates in user variables that can then be retrieved in various ways.

The basic, minimum syntax is something like this:

```
CREATE FUNCTION function_name (parameter) RETURNS INT RETURN routine
```

The function name given can be any nonreserved name; don't use the name of a built-in function. The name is case-insensitive. Within parentheses, give a comma-separated list of the parameters. For each parameter, specify the data type to be used (`INT`, `CHAR`, etc.). The keyword `RETURNS` is followed by the data type of the value that will be returned by the function. At the end comes the keyword `RETURN` followed by the routine to perform.

You may provide special parameters to indicate the characteristics of the function. Several may be given in any order, in a space-separated list. You can specify the language used as SQL with the `LANGUAGE SQL` parameter, but this is the default and usually unnecessary.

A function that returns the same results each time for the same given parameters is considered *deterministic*. You can save processing time on the server by specifying this property through the `DETERMINISTIC` parameter. `NOT DETERMINISTIC` is the default.

The following keywords may be used to tell the server how the function will interact with it, allowing the server to optimize the function. The server does not enforce the restrictions on the function, however:

`CONTAINS SQL`
: The function executes SQL statements, but does not read from or write to a table; one example is a function that queries server status. This is the default.

`NO SQL`
: The function does not contain any SQL statements.

`READS SQL DATA`
: The function might read data from at least one table, but it doesn't write data to any tables.

`MODIFIES SQL DATA`
: The function might write data to at least one table, as well as potentially read data from tables.

With the `COMMENT` clause, you can add a comment describing the function for future reference.

This statement requires the `CREATE ROUTINE` privilege. The `ALTER ROUTINE` and `EXECUTE` privileges are granted to the user and host account that creates or alters a routine, by default. With the `DEFINER` clause, you can specify the MySQL user and host to be used by MySQL for the function. Related to this clause is `SQL SECURITY` keyword, which instructs MySQL to use either the user account of the creator (`DEFINER`) of the function or the account that's calling the function (`INVOKER`). This can help to prevent some users from accessing restricted functions.

Here is an example using this statement:

```
CREATE FUNCTION date_reformatted (new_date VARCHAR(13))
RETURNS DATE
RETURN STR_TO_DATE(REPLACE(new_date, '.', ''), '%b %d, %Y');

SELECT date_reformatted('Dec. 7, 2007')
AS proper_date;

+-------------+
| proper_date |
+-------------+
```

```
| 2007-12-07  |
+-------------+
```

This function simply uses the STR_TO_DATE( ) function to convert a string to a particular date format (i.e., yyyy-mm-dd) based on a common string that users may give. It expects the data given to be no more than 13 characters long. Because some users may include a period after the abbreviated month name and some may not, the function uses the REPLACE( ) function to remove the period. A function like this one can be used in any type of statement (e.g., an UPDATE statement to set a column value).

To change an existing user-defined function, use the ALTER FUNCTION statement. The DROP FUNCTION statement removes a user-defined function. You cannot change standard, built-in functions.

CREATE PROCEDURE

```
CREATE
[DEFINER = {'user'@'host'|CURRENT_USER}]
PROCEDURE stored_procedure ([[IN|OUT|INOUT] parameter data_type[,...]])
  [LANGUAGE SQL]
  [NOT] DETERMINISTIC]
  [{CONTAINS SQL|NO SQL|READS SQL DATA|MODIFIES SQL DATA}]
  [COMMENT 'string']
  [SQL SECURITY {DEFINER|INVOKER}]
routine
```

A *procedure*, also known as a *stored procedure*, is a set of SQL statements stored on the server and called as a unit, processing any data it's given in its parameters. A procedure may communicate results back to the user by placing the values it generates in user variables that can then be retrieved in various ways.

The basic, minimum syntax is something like this:

```
CREATE PROCEDURE procedure_name (IN parameter INT) SQL_statements
```

The procedure name given can be any nonreserved name, and is case-insensitive. Within parentheses, give a comma-separated list of the parameters that will take data in (IN), return data (OUT), or do both (INOUT). For each parameter, specify the data type to be used (INT, CHAR, etc.).

You may provide special parameters to indicate the characteristics of the stored procedure. Several may be given in any order, in a space-separated list. You can specify the language used as SQL with the LANGUAGE SQL parameter, but this is the default and usually unnecessary.

A procedure that returns the same results each time for the same given parameters is considered *deterministic*. You can save processing time on the server by specifying this property through the DETERMINISTIC parameter. NOT DETERMINISTIC is the default.

The following keywords may be used to tell the server how the procedure will interact with it, allowing the server to optimize the procedure. The server does not enforce the restrictions on the procedure, however:

CONTAINS SQL
: The procedure executes SQL statements, but does not read from or write to a table; one example is a procedure that queries server status. This is the default.

`NO SQL`
: The procedure does not contain any SQL statements.

`READS SQL DATA`
: The procedure might read data from at least one table, but it doesn't write data to any tables.

`MODIFIES SQL DATA`
: The procedure might write data to at least one table, as well as potentially read data from tables.

With the `COMMENT` clause, you can add a comment describing the procedure for future reference.

This statement requires the `CREATE ROUTINE` privilege. The `ALTER ROUTINE` and `EXECUTE` privileges are granted to the user and host account that creates or alters a routine, by default. With the `DEFINER` clause, you can specify the MySQL user and host to be used by MySQL for the procedure. Related to this clause is the `SQL SECURITY` keyword, which instructs MySQL to use either the user account of the creator (`DEFINER`) of the procedure or the account that's executing the procedure (`INVOKER`). This can help prevent some users from accessing restricted procedures.

In the following example, we create a simple procedure that copies all of the data from the `students` table to a backup table with the same schema. The table also includes an extra column in which the user can add a comment or reference note:

```
DELIMITER |

CREATE PROCEDURE students_copy_proc (IN ref_note VARCHAR(255))
BEGIN
REPLACE INTO students_backup
SELECT *, ref_note FROM students;
END|

DELIMITER ;

SET @ref_note = '2008 Spring Roster';

CALL students_copy_proc(@ref_note);
```

The first statement changes the terminating character for an SQL statement from its default, a semicolon, to a vertical bar. See the `BEGIN...END` statement earlier in this chapter for the reasons this is necessary.

Inside the procedure, the `REPLACE` statement selects all columns from `students` along with the value of the `ref_note` variable. Thus, every row of `students` is inserted, along with the value of the variable, into a new row in `students_backup`.

After the procedure is defined and the delimiter is changed back to a semicolon, the example sets a variable called `ref_note` that contains a note the user wants added to each row of data in the new table. This variable is passed to the `CALL` statement that runs the procedure.

To change an existing stored procedure, use the `ALTER PROCEDURE` statement. The `DROP PROCEDURE` statement removes a procedure.

CREATE TRIGGER

```
CREATE
[DEFINER = {'user'@'host'|CURRENT_USER}]
TRIGGER trigger {AFTER|BEFORE}
{DELETE|INSERT|UPDATE}
ON table FOR EACH ROW statement
```

Only one of each trigger timing and trigger event combination is allowed for each table. For example, a table cannot have two `BEFORE INSERT` triggers, but it can have a `BEFORE INSERT` and an `AFTER INSERT` trigger.

To specify that the trigger be executed immediately before the associated user statement, use the parameter `BEFORE`; to indicate that the trigger should be executed immediately afterward, use `AFTER`.

At this time, only three types of SQL statements can cause the server to execute a trigger: insertions, deletions, and updates. Specifying `INSERT`, however, applies the trigger to `INSERT` statements, `LOAD DATA` statements, and `REPLACE` statements—all statements that are designed to insert data into a table. Similarly, specifying `DELETE` includes both `DELETE` and `REPLACE` statements because `REPLACE` potentially deletes rows as well as inserting them.

Triggers are actions to be taken when a user requests a change to data. Each trigger is associated with a particular table and includes definitions related to *timing* and *event*. A trigger timing indicates when a trigger is to be performed (i.e., `BEFORE` or `AFTER`). A trigger event is the action that causes the trigger to be executed (i.e., a `DELETE`, `INSERT`, or `UPDATE` on a specified table).

After specifying the trigger event, give the keyword `ON` followed by the table name. This is followed by `FOR EACH ROW` and the SQL statement to be executed when the trigger event occurs. Multiple SQL statements to execute may be given in the form of a compound statement using `BEGIN...END`, which is described earlier in this chapter.

There is no `ALTER TRIGGER` statement at this time. Instead, use the `DROP TRIGGER` statement and then reissue `CREATE TRIGGER` with the new trigger.

To show how a trigger may be created, suppose that for a college database, whenever a student record is deleted from the `students` table, we want to write the data to another table to preserve that information. Here is an example of how that might be done with a trigger:

```
DELIMITER |

CREATE TRIGGER students_deletion
BEFORE DELETE
ON students FOR EACH ROW

BEGIN
INSERT INTO students_deleted
(student_id, name_first, name_last)
VALUES(OLD.student_id, OLD.name_first, OLD.name_last);
END|

DELIMITER ;
```

The first statement changes the terminating character for an SQL statement from its default, a semicolon, to a vertical bar. See the BEGIN...END statement earlier in this chapter for the reasons this is necessary.

Next, we create a trigger to stipulate that, before making a deletion in the students table, the server must perform the compound SQL statement given. The statements between BEGIN and END will write the data to be deleted to another table with the same schema.

To capture that data and pass it to the INSERT statement, we use the OLD table alias provided by MySQL coupled with the column names of the table where the row is to be deleted. OLD refers to the table in the trigger's ON clause, before any changes are made by the trigger or the statement causing the trigger. To save space, in this example we're capturing the data from only three of the columns. OLD.* is not allowed, so we have to specify each column. To specify the columns after they are inserted or updated, use NEW as the table alias.

The statement to be executed by the trigger in the previous example is a compound statement. It starts with BEGIN and ends with END and is followed by the vertical bar (|) that we specified as the delimiter. The delimiter is then reset in the last line back to a semicolon.

DECLARE

```
DECLARE variable data_type [DEFAULT value]

DECLARE condition CONDITION FOR
{SQLSTATE [VALUE] value |  error_code]

DECLARE cursor CURSOR FOR SELECT...

DECLARE {CONTINUE|EXIT|UNDO} HANDLER FOR
  {[SQLSTATE [VALUE] value]
   [SQLWARNING]
   [NOT FOUND]
   [SQLEXCEPTION]
   [error_code]
   [condition]}
SQL_statement
```

This statement declares local variables and other items related to routines. It must be used within a BEGIN...END compound statement of a routine, after BEGIN and before any other SQL statements. There are four basic uses for DECLARE: to declare local variables, conditions, cursors, and handlers. Within a BEGIN...END block, variables and conditions must be declared before cursors and handlers, and cursors must be declared before handlers.

The first syntax shows how to declare variables. It includes the data type and, optionally, default values. A variable declared with this statement is available only within the routine in which it is declared. If the default is a string, place it within quotes. If no default is declared, NULL is the default value.

A condition is generally either an SQLSTATE value or a MySQL error code number. The second syntax is used for declaring a condition and associating it with an SQLSTATE or an error code. When declaring a condition based on an SQLSTATE, give the `SQLSTATE VALUE` clause followed by the state. Otherwise, give the error code number.

The third syntax declares a cursor, which represents—within a procedure—a results set that is retrieved one row at a time. Give a unique, nonreserved word for the cursor's name. This is followed by `CURSOR FOR` and then a `SELECT` statement. It must not have an `INTO` clause. To call or open a cursor, use the `OPEN` statement within the same routine in which the declaration was made. To retrieve data from a cursor, which is done one row at a time, use the `FETCH` statement. When finished, use the `CLOSE` statement to close an open cursor.

The last syntax for this statement declares a handler. With a handler, you can specify an SQL statement to be executed given a specific condition that occurs within a routine. Three types of handlers are allowed: `CONTINUE`, `EXIT`, and `UNDO`. Use `CONTINUE` to indicate that the routine is to continue after the SQL statement given is executed. The `EXIT` parameter indicates that the `BEGIN...END` compound statement that contains the declaration should be exited when the condition given is met. `UNDO` is meant to instruct MySQL to undo the compound statement for which it is given. However, this parameter is not yet supported by MySQL.

The handler's `FOR` clause may contain multiple conditions in a comma-separated list. There are several related to the SQLSTATE: you can specify a single SQLSTATE code number, or you can list `SQLWARNING` to declare any SQLSTATE code starting with 01, `NOT FOUND` for any SQLSTATE code starting with 02, or `SQLEXCEPTION` for all states that don't start with 01 or 02. Another condition you can give is a MySQL error code number. You can also specify the name of a condition you previously created with its own `DECLARE` statement.

DELIMITER

```
DELIMITER character
```

This statement changes the delimiter (terminating character) of SQL statements from the default of a semicolon to another character. This is useful when creating a stored procedure or trigger, so that MySQL does not confuse a semicolon contained in the procedure or trigger as the end of the `CREATE PROCEDURE` or `CREATE TRIGGER` statement. This statement is also used to restore the default delimiter. Don't use the backslash as the delimiter, as that is used to escape special characters. Examples of this statement appear in the `CREATE PROCEDURE` and `CREATE TRIGGER` statements earlier in this chapter.

DROP EVENT

```
DROP EVENT [IF EXISTS] event
```

This statement deletes an event. The `IF EXISTS` keyword prevents error messages when the event doesn't exist. Instead, a note will be generated, which can be displayed afterward by executing the `SHOW WARNINGS` statement. As of version 5.1.12 of MySQL, this statement requires the `EVENT` privilege.

DROP FUNCTION

```
DROP FUNCTION [IF EXISTS] function
```

Use this statement to delete a user-defined function. The `IF EXISTS` keyword prevents error messages when the function doesn't exist. Instead, a note will be generated, which can be displayed afterward by executing the `SHOW WARNINGS` statement. This statement requires the `ALTER ROUTINE` privilege for the function given, which is automatically granted to the creator of the function.

DROP PREPARE

```
{DROP|DEALLOCATE} PREPARE statement_name
```

This statement deletes a prepared statement. The syntax of `DROP PREPARE` and `DEALLOCATE PREPARE` are synonymous. For an example, see the `PREPARE` statement later in this chapter.

DROP PROCEDURE

```
DROP PROCEDURE [IF EXISTS] procedure
```

This statement deletes a stored procedure. The `IF EXISTS` keyword prevents error messages when the stored procedure doesn't exist. Instead, a note will be generated, which can be displayed afterward by executing the `SHOW WARNINGS` statement. This statement requires the `ALTER ROUTINE` privilege for the stored procedure given, which is automatically granted to the creator of the stored procedure.

DROP TRIGGER

```
DROP TRIGGER [IF EXISTS] [database.]trigger
```

This statement deletes a trigger. The `IF EXISTS` keyword prevents error messages when the trigger doesn't exist. Instead, a note will be generated, which can be displayed afterward by executing the `SHOW WARNINGS` statement. You may specify the database or schema with which the trigger is associated. If not given, the current default database is assumed. As of version 5.1.6 of MySQL, this statement requires the `TRIGGER` privilege for the table related to the trigger given. Previously, it required `SUPER` privilege. When upgrading from version 5.0.10 or earlier of MySQL, be sure to drop all triggers because there's a problem with using or dropping triggers from earlier versions.

EXECUTE

```
EXECUTE statement_name [USING @variable[, ...] ...]
```

This statement executes a user-defined prepared statement. If the prepared statement contains placeholders so that you can pass parameters to it, these parameters must be given in the form of user-defined variables. Multiple variables may be given in a comma-separated list. You can use the `SET` statement to set the value of a variable. See the `PREPARE` statement later in this chapter for an example of the `EXECUTE` statement's use.

FETCH

```
FETCH cursor INTO variable[, ...]
```

A cursor is similar to a table or a view: it represents, within a procedure, a results set that is retrieved one row at a time using this statement. You first establish a cursor with the DECLARE statement. Then you use the OPEN statement to initialize the cursor. The FETCH statement retrieves the next row of the cursor and places the data retrieved into one or more variables. There should be the same number of variables as there are columns in the underlying SELECT statement of the cursor. Variables are given in a comma-separated list. Each execution of FETCH advances the pointer for the cursor by one row. Once all rows have been fetched, an SQLSTATE of 02000 is returned. You can tie a condition to this state through a DECLARE statement and end fetches based on the condition. Use the CLOSE statement to close a cursor.

OPEN

```
OPEN cursor
```

This statement opens a cursor that has been declared within the current routine. Data selected with the cursor is accessed with the FETCH statement. The cursor is closed with the CLOSE statement. See the descriptions of the DECLARE and FETCH statements earlier in this chapter for more information on cursors.

PREPARE

```
PREPARE statement_name FROM statement
```

This statement creates a prepared statement. A prepared statement is used to cache an SQL statement, so as to save processing time during multiple executions of the statement. This can potentially improve performance. Prepared statements are local to the user and session; they're not global. The name given can be any nonreserved name and is case-insensitive. The statement given within quotes can be any type of SQL statement.

If you want to include a value that will be changed when the statement is executed, give a question mark as a placeholder within ***statement***. When the prepared statement is executed later with the EXECUTE statement, the placeholders will be replaced with the values given. The values must be user variables (set with the SET statement) and must be passed to the EXECUTE statement in the order that the placeholders appear in the prepared statement. Here is a simple example using these statements:

```
PREPARE state_tally
FROM 'SELECT COUNT(*)
      FROM students
      WHERE home_city = ?';

SET @city = 'New Orleans';
EXECUTE state_tally USING @city;

SET @city = 'Boston';
EXECUTE state_tally USING @city;
```

In this example, the query within the prepared statement will return a count of the number of students from the city given. By setting the value of the user-defined variable

`@city` to another city, we can execute the prepared statement `state_tally` again without having to reenter the `PREPARE` statement. The results will probably be different, of course. To remove a prepared statement from the cache, use the `DROP PREPARE` statement.

SHOW CREATE EVENT

`SHOW CREATE EVENT` *`event`*

This statement displays an SQL statement that can be used to create an event like the one given. It's mostly useful for displaying any comments associated with the event because they're not included in the results of the `SHOW EVENTS` statement.

Here is an example showing an event that was created with the `CREATE EVENT` statement earlier in this chapter:

```
SHOW CREATE EVENT students_copy \G

*************************** 1. row ***************************
       Event: students_copy
    sql_mode:
Create Event: CREATE EVENT `students_copy` ON SCHEDULE
EVERY 1 DAY ON COMPLETION PRESERVE ENABLE
COMMENT 'Daily copy of students table to students_backup'
DO CALL students_copy_proc()
```

SHOW CREATE FUNCTION

`SHOW CREATE FUNCTION` *`function`*

This statement displays an SQL statement that can be used to create a function like the one given. It's useful for displaying the SQL statements that are performed by the function.

Here is an example of a function that was created with the `CREATE FUNCTION` statement earlier in this chapter:

```
SHOW CREATE FUNCTION date_reformatted \G

*************************** 1. row ***************************
       Function: date_reformatted
       sql_mode:
Create Function: CREATE DEFINER=`root`@`localhost`
FUNCTION `date_reformatted`(new_date VARCHAR(12))
RETURNS date
SQL SECURITY INVOKER
COMMENT 'Converts a string date like ''Dec. 7, 2007'' to standard format.'
RETURN STR_TO_DATE(REPLACE(new_date, '.', ''), '%b %d, %Y')
```

SHOW CREATE PROCEDURE

`SHOW CREATE PROCEDURE` *`procedure`*

This statement displays an SQL statement that can be used to create a stored procedure like the one given. It's useful for displaying the SQL statements that are performed by the stored procedure.

Here is an example of a procedure that was created with the CREATE PROCEDURE statement earlier in this chapter:

```
SHOW CREATE PROCEDURE students_copy_proc \G

*************************** 1. row ***************************
       Procedure: students_copy_proc
        sql_mode:
Create Procedure: CREATE DEFINER=`root`@`localhost`
PROCEDURE `students_copy_proc`(IN ref_note VARCHAR(255))
BEGIN
REPLACE INTO students_backup
SELECT *, ref_note FROM students;
END
```

SHOW EVENTS

SHOW EVENTS [FROM *database*] [LIKE '*pattern*'|WHERE *expression*]

This statement displays a list of scheduled events on the server. The results can also include events that have been completed but were preserved. The database to which events are related may be given in the FROM clause; the default is the current database. The LIKE or WHERE clauses can be used to list events based on a particular naming pattern. With the WHERE clause, you can use the names of fields in the results to create an expression that sets a condition determining the results returned. An example of this follows. See CREATE EVENT earlier in this chapter for more information on events:

```
 SHOW EVENTS FROM college
WHERE Definer='russell@localhost' \G

*************************** 1. row ***************************
            Db: college
          Name: students_copy
       Definer: russell@localhost
          Type: RECURRING
    Execute at: NULL
Interval value: 1
Interval field: DAY
        Starts: 2007-11-27 02:30:00
          Ends: NULL
        Status: ENABLED
```

SHOW FUNCTION CODE

SHOW FUNCTION CODE *function*

This statement displays the internal code of a function. It requires that the MySQL server be built with debugging. This statement was introduced in version 5.1.3 of MySQL.

SHOW FUNCTION STATUS

```
SHOW FUNCTION STATUS [LIKE 'pattern'|WHERE expression]
```

This statement displays information on user-defined functions. The `LIKE` or `WHERE` clauses can be used to list functions based on a particular naming pattern. With the `WHERE` clause, you can use the names of fields in the results to create an expression that sets a condition determining the results returned. Here is an example using this statement:

```
SHOW FUNCTION STATUS
WHERE Name='date_reformatted' \G

*************************** 1. row ***************************
           Db: college
         Name: date_reformatted
         Type: FUNCTION
      Definer: root@localhost
     Modified: 2007-11-27 11:55:00
      Created: 2007-11-27 11:47:37
Security_type: INVOKER
      Comment: Converts a string date like 'Dec. 7, 2007' to standard format.
```

SHOW PROCEDURE CODE

```
SHOW PROCEDURE CODE stored_procedure
```

This statement displays the internal code of a stored procedure. It requires that the MySQL server be built with debugging. This statement was introduced in version 5.1.3 of MySQL.

SHOW PROCEDURE STATUS

```
SHOW PROCEDURE STATUS [LIKE 'pattern'|WHERE expression]
```

This statement displays information on stored procedures. The `LIKE` or `WHERE` clauses can be used to list stored procedures based on a particular naming pattern. With the `WHERE` clause, you can use the names of fields in the results to create an expression that sets a condition determining the results returned. Here is an example using this statement:

```
SHOW PROCEDURE STATUS
WHERE Name='students_copy_proc' \G

*************************** 1. row ***************************
           Db: college
         Name: students_copy_proc
         Type: PROCEDURE
      Definer: russell@localhost
     Modified: 2007-11-27 09:27:42
      Created: 2007-11-27 09:27:42
Security_type: DEFINER
      Comment:
```

Note that for the `WHERE` clause we use the field name to get the specific stored procedure.

SHOW TRIGGERS

```
SHOW TRIGGERS STATUS [FROM database]
[LIKE 'pattern'|WHERE expression]
```

This statement displays a list of triggers on the server. The database to which triggers are related may be given in the `FROM` clause; the default is the current database. The `LIKE` or `WHERE` clauses can be used to list triggers based on a particular naming pattern. The `LIKE` clause includes the name of the table with which the trigger is associated or a pattern for the table name that includes wildcards (`%`). With the `WHERE` clause, you can use the names of fields in the results to create an expression that sets a condition determining the results returned. Here is an example using this statement:

```
SHOW TRIGGERS LIKE 'students' \G

*************************** 1. row ***************************
  Trigger: students_deletion
    Event: DELETE
    Table: students
Statement: BEGIN
INSERT INTO students_deleted
(student_id, name_first, name_last)
VALUES(OLD.student_id, OLD.name_first, OLD.name_last);
END
   Timing: BEFORE
  Created: NULL
 sql_mode:
  Definer: root@localhost
```

See `CREATE TRIGGER` earlier in this chapter for more information on triggers and to see how the trigger shown was created.

10
Aggregate Clauses, Aggregate Functions, and Subqueries

MySQL has many built-in functions that you can use in SQL statements for performing calculations on combinations of values in databases; these are called *aggregate functions*. They include such types of basic statistical analysis as counting rows, determining the average of a given column's value, finding the standard deviation, and so forth. The first section of this chapter describes MySQL aggregate functions and includes examples of most of them. The second section provides a tutorial about subqueries. It includes several examples of subqueries in addition to the ones shown in the first section and in various examples throughout this book. Subqueries are included in this chapter because they are often used with `GROUP BY` and aggregate functions and because they're another method for grouping selected data.

The following functions are covered in this chapter:

`AVG( )`, `BIT_AND( )`, `BIT_OR( )`, `COUNT( )`, `GROUP_CONCAT( )`, `MAX( )`, `MIN( )`, `STD( )`, `STDDEV( )`, `STDDEV_POP( )`, `STDDEV_SAMP( )`, `SUM( )`, `VAR_POP( )`, `VAR_SAMP( )`, `VARIANCE( )`.

Aggregate Functions in Alphabetical Order

This section describes each aggregate function. Many of the examples use a subquery. For detailed information about subqueries, see the "Subqueries" section later in this chapter.

A few general aspects of aggregate functions include:

- Aggregate functions return NULL when they encounter an error.
- Most uses for aggregate functions include a `GROUP BY` clause, which is specified in each description. If an aggregate function is used without a `GROUP BY` clause it operates on all rows.

AVG( )

AVG([DISTINCT] *column*)

This function returns the average or mean of a set of numbers given as the argument. It returns NULL if unsuccessful. The DISTINCT keyword causes the function to count only unique values in the calculation; duplicate values will not factor into the averaging.

When returning multiple rows, you generally want to use this function with the GROUP BY clause that groups the values for each unique item, so that you can get the average for that item. This will be clearer with an example:

```
SELECT sales_rep_id,
CONCAT(name_first, SPACE(1), name_last) AS rep_name,
AVG(sale_amount) AS avg_sales
FROM sales
JOIN sales_reps USING(sales_rep_id)
GROUP BY sales_rep_id;
```

This SQL statement returns the average amount of sales in the sales table made by each sales representative. It will total all values found for the sale_amount column, for each unique value for sales_rep_id, and divide by the number of rows found for each of those unique values. If you would like to include sales representatives who made no sales in the results, you'll need to change the JOIN to a RIGHT JOIN:

```
SELECT sales_rep_id,
CONCAT(name_first, SPACE(1), name_last) AS rep_name,
FORMAT(AVG(sale_amount), 2) AS avg_sales
FROM sales
RIGHT JOIN sales_reps USING(sales_rep_id)
GROUP BY sales_rep_id;
```

Sales representatives who made no sales will show up with NULL in the avg_sales column. This version of the statement also includes an enhancement: it rounds the results for avg_sales to two decimal places by adding the FORMAT( ) function.

If we only want the average sales for the current month, we could add a WHERE clause. However, that would negate the effect of the RIGHT JOIN: sales people without orders for the month wouldn't appear in the list. To include them, first we need to run a subquery that extracts the sales data that meets the conditions of the WHERE clause, and then we need to join the subquery's results to another subquery containing a tidy list of the names of sales reps:

```
SELECT sales_rep_id, rep_name,
IFNULL(avg_sales, 'none') as avg_sales_month
FROM
  (SELECT sales_rep_id,
   FORMAT(AVG(sale_amount), 2) AS avg_sales
   FROM sales
   JOIN sales_reps USING(sales_rep_id)
   WHERE DATE_FORMAT(date_of_sale, '%Y%m') =
         DATE_FORMAT(CURDATE(), '%Y%m')
   GROUP BY sales_rep_id) AS active_reps
RIGHT JOIN
  (SELECT sales_rep_id,
   CONCAT(name_first, SPACE(1), name_last) AS rep_name
   FROM sales_reps) AS all_reps
```

```
    USING(sales_rep_id)
    GROUP BY sales_rep_id;
```

In the first subquery here, we are determining the average sales for each sales rep that had sales for the current month. In the second subquery, we're putting together a list of names of all sales reps, regardless of sales. In the main query, using the `sales_rep_id` column as the joining point of the two results sets derived from the subqueries, we are creating a results set that will show the average sales for the month for each rep that had some sales, or (using `IFNULL( )`) the word *none* for those who had none.

BIT_AND( )

`BIT_AND(`*`expression`*`)`

This function returns the bitwise `AND` for all bits for the expression given. Use this in conjunction with the `GROUP BY` clause. The function has a 64-bit precision. If there are no matching rows, before version 4.0.17 of MySQL, –1 is returned. Newer versions return 18446744073709551615, which is the value of 1 for all bits of an unsigned `BIGINT` column.

BIT_OR( )

`BIT_OR(`*`expression`*`)`

This function returns the bitwise `OR` for all bits for the expression given. It calculates with a 64-bit precision (`BIGINT`). It returns 0 if no matching rows are found. Use it in conjunction with the `GROUP BY` clause.

BIT_XOR( )

`BIT_XOR(`*`expression`*`)`

This function returns the bitwise `XOR` (exclusive `OR`) for all bits for the expression given. It calculates with a 64-bit precision (`BIGINT`). It returns 0 if no matching rows are found. Use it in conjunction with the `GROUP BY` clause. This function is available as of version 4.1.1 of MySQL.

COUNT( )

`COUNT([DISTINCT]` *`expression`*`)`

This function returns the number of rows retrieved in the `SELECT` statement for the given column. By default, rows in which the column is NULL are not counted. If the wildcard * is used as the argument, the function counts all rows, including those with NULL values. If you want only a count of the number of rows in the table, you don't need `GROUP BY`, and you can still include a `WHERE` to count only rows meeting specific criteria. If you want a count of the number of rows for each value of a column, you will need to use the `GROUP BY` clause. As an alternative to using `GROUP BY`, you can add the `DISTINCT` keyword to get a count of unique non-NULL values found for the given column. When you use `DISTINCT`, you cannot include any other columns in the `SELECT` statement. You can, however, include multiple columns or expressions within the function. Here is an example:

```
SELECT branch_name,
COUNT(sales_rep_id) AS number_of_reps
FROM sales_reps
JOIN branch_offices USING(branch_id)
GROUP BY branch_id;
```

This example joins the `sales_reps` and `branch_offices` tables together using the `branch_id` contained in both tables. We then use the `COUNT( )` function to count the number of sales reps found for each branch (determined by the `GROUP BY` clause).

GROUP_CONCAT( )

```
GROUP_CONCAT([DISTINCT] expression[, ...]
   [ORDER BY {unsigned_integer|column|expression}
   [ASC|DESC] [,column...]]
   [SEPARATOR character])
```

This function returns non-NULL values of a group concatenated by a `GROUP BY` clause, separated by commas. The parameters for this function are included in the parentheses, separated by spaces, not commas. The function returns NULL if the group doesn't contain non-NULL values.

Duplicates are omitted with the `DISTINCT` keyword. The `ORDER BY` clause instructs the function to sort values before concatenating them. Ordering may be based on an unsigned integer value, a column, or an expression. The sort order can be set to ascending with the `ASC` keyword (default), or to descending with `DESC`. To use a different separator from a comma, use the `SEPARATOR` keyword followed by the preferred separator.

The value of the system variable `group_concat_max_len` limits the number of elements returned. Its default is 1024. Use the `SET` statement to change the value. This function is available as of version 4.1 of MySQL.

As an example of this function, suppose that we wanted to know how many customers order a particular item. We could enter an SQL statement like this:

```
SELECT item_nbr AS Item,
GROUP_CONCAT(quantity) AS Quantities
FROM orders
WHERE item_nbr = 100
GROUP BY item_nbr;

+------+------------+
| Item | Quantities |
+------+------------+
|  100 | 7,12,4,8,4 |
+------+------------+
```

Notice that the quantities aren't sorted—it's the item numbers that are sorted by the `GROUP BY` clause. To sort the quantities within each field and to use a different separator, we would enter something like the following instead:

```
SELECT item_nbr AS Item,
GROUP_CONCAT(DISTINCT quantity
  ORDER BY quantity ASC
  SEPARATOR '|')
AS Quantities
```

```
FROM orders
WHERE item_nbr = 100
GROUP BY item_nbr;

+------+------------+
| Item | Quantities |
+------+------------+
|  100 | 4|7|8|12   |
+------+------------+
```

Because the results previously contained a duplicate value (4), we're eliminating duplicates here by including the DISTINCT keyword.

MAX( )

MAX(*expression*)

This function returns the highest number in the values for a given column. It's normally used in conjunction with a GROUP BY clause specifying a unique column, so that values are compared for each unique item separately.

As an example of this function, suppose that we wanted to know the maximum sale for each sales person for the month. We could enter the following SQL statement:

```
SELECT CONCAT(name_first, SPACE(1), name_last) AS rep_name,
MAX(sale_amount) AS biggest_sale
FROM sales
JOIN sales_reps USING(sales_rep_id)
WHERE DATE_FORMAT(date_of_sale, '%Y%m') =
      DATE_FORMAT(CURDATE(), '%Y%m')
GROUP BY sales_rep_id DESC;
```

We've given sale_amount as the column for which we want the largest value returned for each sales rep. The WHERE clause indicates that we want only sales for the current month. Notice that the GROUP BY clause includes the DESC keyword. This will order the rows in descending order for the values of the biggest_sale field: the biggest sale at the top, the smallest at the bottom.

Here's an example of another handy but less obvious use of this function: suppose we have a table in which client profiles are kept by the sales people. When a sales rep changes a client profile through a web interface, instead of updating the existing row, the program we wrote creates a new entry. We use this method to prevent sales people from inadvertently overwriting data and to keep previous client profiles in case someone wants to refer to them later. When the client profile is viewed through the web interface, we want only the latest profile to appear. Retrieving the latest row becomes a bit cumbersome, but we can do this with MAX( ) and a subquery as follows:

```
SELECT client_name, profile,
MAX(entry_date) AS last_entry
FROM
  (SELECT client_id, entry_date, profile
   FROM client_profiles
   ORDER BY client_id, entry_date DESC) AS profiles
JOIN clients USING(client_id)
GROUP BY client_id;
```

In the subquery, we retrieve a list of profiles with the date each has in its entry in the table `client_profiles`; the results contain the duplicate entries for clients. In the main query, using `MAX( )`, we get the maximum (latest) date for each client. The associated `profile` is included in the columns selected by the main query. We join the results of the subquery to the `clients` table to extract the client's name.

The subquery is necessary so that we get the latest date instead of the oldest. The problem is that the `GROUP BY` clause orders the fields based on the given column. Without the subquery, the `GROUP BY` clause would use the value for the `entry_date` of the first row it finds, which will be the earliest date, not the latest. So we order the data in the subquery with the latest entry for each client first. `GROUP BY` then takes the first entry of the subquery results, which will be the latest entry.

MIN( )

`MIN(`*`expression`*`)`

This function returns the lowest number in the values for a given column. It's normally used in conjunction with a `GROUP BY` clause specifying a unique column, so that values are compared for each unique item separately. Here is an example:

```
SELECT CONCAT(name_first, SPACE(1), name_last) AS rep_name,
MIN(sale_amount) AS smallest_sale,
MAX(sale_amount) AS biggest_sale
FROM sales
JOIN sales_reps USING(sales_rep_id)
GROUP BY sales_rep_id;
```

In this example, we retrieve the smallest sale and largest sale made by each sales representative. We use `JOIN` to join the two tables to get the sales rep's name. Because `MAX( )` is very similar, see the examples in its description earlier in this chapter for *additional* ways to use `MIN( )`.

STD( )

`STD(`*`expression`*`)`

This function returns the population standard deviation of the given column. This function is an alias for `STDDEV( )`; see the description of that function for an example of its use.

STDDEV( )

`STDDEV(`*`expression`*`)`

This function returns the population standard deviation of the given column. It's normally used in conjunction with a `GROUP BY` clause specifying a unique column, so that values are compared for each unique item separately. It returns NULL if no matching rows are found. Here is an example:

```
SELECT CONCAT(name_first, SPACE(1), name_last) AS rep_name,
SUM(sale_amount) AS total_sales,
COUNT(sale_amount) AS total_tickets,
AVG(sale_amount) AS avg_sale_per_ticket,
STDDEV(sale_amount) AS standard_deviation
```

```
FROM sales
JOIN sales_reps USING(sales_rep_id)
GROUP BY sales_rep_id;
```

This statement employs several aggregate functions. We use `SUM( )` to get the total sales for each sales rep, `COUNT( )` to retrieve the number of orders for the each, `AVG( )` to determine the average sale, and `STDDEV( )` to find out how much each sale made by each sales rep tends to vary from each one's average sale. Incidentally, statistical functions return several decimal places. To return only two decimal places, you can wrap each function in `FORMAT( )`.

STDDEV_POP( )

`STDDEV_POP(`*`expression`*`)`

This function returns the population standard deviation of the given column. It was added in version 5.0.3 of MySQL for compliance with SQL standards. This function is an alias for `STDDEV( )`; see the description of that function earlier in this chapter for an example of its use.

STDDEV_SAMP( )

`STDDEV_SAMP(`*`expression`*`)`

This function returns the sample standard deviation of the given column. It's normally used in conjunction with a `GROUP BY` clause specifying a unique column, so that values are compared for each unique item separately. It returns NULL if no matching rows are found. It was added in version 5.0.3 of MySQL for compliance with SQL standards. Here is an example:

```
SELECT CONCAT(name_first, SPACE(1), name_last) AS rep_name,
AVG(sale_amount) AS avg_sale_per_ticket,
STDDEV_POP(sale_amount) AS population_std_dev,
STDDEV_SAMP(sale_amount) AS sample_std_dev
FROM sales
JOIN sales_reps USING(sales_rep_id)
GROUP BY sales_rep_id;
```

This SQL statement uses several aggregate functions: `AVG( )` to determine the average sale for each sales rep; `STDDEV_POP( )` to determine how much each sale made by each sales rep tends to vary from each rep's average sale; and `STDDEV_SAMP( )` to determine the standard deviation from the average based on a sample of the data.

SUM( )

`SUM([DISTINCT]` *`expression`*`)`

This function returns the sum of the values for the given column or expression. It's normally used in conjunction with a `GROUP BY` clause specifying a unique column, so that values are compared for each unique item separately. It returns NULL if no matching rows are found. The parameter `DISTINCT` may be given within the parentheses of the function to add only unique values found for a given column. This parameter was added in version 5.1 of MySQL. Here is an example:

```
SELECT sales_rep_id,
SUM(sale_amount) AS total_sales
FROM sales
WHERE DATE_FORMAT(date_of_sale, '%Y%m') =
      DATE_FORMAT(SUBDATE(CURDATE(), INTERVAL 1 MONTH), '%Y%m')
GROUP BY sales_rep_id;
```

This statement queries the sales table to retrieve only sales made during the last month. From these results, SUM( ) returns the total sale amounts aggregated by the sales_rep_id (see "Grouping SELECT results" under the SELECT statement in Chapter 6).

VAR_POP( )

VAR_POP(*expression*)

This function returns the variance of a given column, based on the rows selected as a population. It's synonymous with VARIANCE and was added in version 5.0.3 of MySQL for compliance with SQL standards. See the description of VAR_SAMP( ) for an example of this function's use.

VAR_SAMP( )

VAR_SAMP(*expression*)

This function returns the variance of a given column, based on the rows selected as a sample of a given population. It's normally used in conjunction with a GROUP BY clause specifying a unique column, so that values are compared for each unique item separately. To determine the variance based on the entire population rather than a sample, use VAR_POP( ). Both of these functions were added in version 5.0.3 of MySQL for compliance with SQL standards. Here is an example of both:

```
SELECT CONCAT(name_first, SPACE(1), name_last) AS rep_name,
AVG(sale_amount) AS avg_sale,
STDDEV_POP(sale_amount) AS population_std_dev,
STDDEV_SAMP(sale_amount) AS sample_std_dev,
VAR_POP(sale_amount) AS population_variance,
VAR_SAMP(sale_amount) AS sample_variance
FROM sales
JOIN sales_reps USING(sales_rep_id)
GROUP BY sales_rep_id;
```

This SQL statement uses several aggregate functions: AVG( ) to determine the average sale for each sales rep; STDDEV_POP( ) to determine how much each sale made by each sales rep tends to vary from each rep's average sale; and STDDEV_SAMP( ) to determine the standard deviation from the average based on a sample of the data. It also includes VAR_POP( ) to show the variances based on the population, and VAR_SAMP( ) to return the variance based on the sample data.

VARIANCE( )

VARIANCE(*expression*)

The *variance* is determined by taking the difference between each given value and the average of all values given. Each of those differences is then squared, and the results are totaled. The average of that total is then determined to get the variance. This function returns the variance of a given column, based on the rows selected as a population. It's normally used in conjunction with a GROUP BY clause specifying a unique column, so that values are compared for each unique item separately. This function is available as of version 4.1 of MySQL. Here is an example:

```
SELECT CONCAT(name_first, SPACE(1), name_last) AS rep_name,
AVG(sale_amount) AS avg_sale,
STDDEV_POP(sale_amount) AS standard_deviation,
VARIANCE(sale_amount) AS variance
FROM sales
JOIN sales_reps USING(sales_rep_id)
GROUP BY sales_rep_id;
```

This SQL statement uses a few aggregate functions: AVG( ) to determine the average sale for each sales rep; STDDEV_POP( ) to determine how much each sale made by each sales rep tends to vary from each rep's average sale; and VARIANCE( ) to show the variances based on the population. To comply with SQL standards, VAR_POP( ) could have been used instead of VARIANCE( ).

Subqueries

A subquery is a SELECT statement nested within another SQL statement. This feature became available as of version 4.1 of MySQL. Although the same results can be accomplished by using the JOIN clause or UNION, depending on the situation, subqueries are a cleaner approach that is sometimes easier to read. They make a complex query more modular, which makes it easier to create and to troubleshoot. Here is a simple example of a subquery:

```
SELECT *
FROM
  (SELECT col1, col2
   FROM table1
   WHERE col_id = 1000) AS derived1
ORDER BY col2;
```

In this example, the subquery or *inner* query is a SELECT statement specifying two column names. The other query is called the *main* or *outer* query. It doesn't have to be a SELECT. It can be an INSERT, a DELETE, a DO, an UPDATE, or even a SET statement. The outer query generally can't select data or modify data from the same table as an inner query, but this doesn't apply if the subquery is part of a FROM clause. A subquery can return a value (a scalar), a field, multiple fields containing values, or a full results set that serves as a derived table.

You can encounter performance problems with subqueries if they are not well constructed. One problem occurs when a subquery is placed within an IN( ) clause as part of a WHERE clause. It's generally better to use the = operator for each value, along with AND for each parameter/value pair.

When you see a performance problem with a subquery, try reconstructing the SQL statement with JOIN and compare the differences using the BENCHMARK( ) function. If the performance is better without a subquery, don't give up on subqueries. Only in some situations is performance poorer. For those situations where there is a performance drain, MySQL AB is working on improving MySQL subqueries. So performance problems you experience now may be resolved in future versions. You may just need to upgrade to the current release or watch for improvements in future releases.

Single Field Subqueries

The most basic subquery is one that returns a scalar or single value. This type of subquery is particularly useful in a WHERE clause in conjunction with an = operator, or in other instances where a single value from an expression is permitted.

As an example of this situation, suppose that at our fictitious college one of the music teachers, Sonia Oram, has called us saying that she wants a list of students for one of her classes so that she can call them to invite them to a concert. She wants the names and telephone numbers for only the students in her first period Monday morning class.

The way most databases store this data, the course number would be a unique key and would make it easy to retrieve the other data without a subquery. But Sonia doesn't know the course number, so we enter an SQL statement like this:

```
SELECT CONCAT(name_first, ' ', name_last) AS student,
phone_home, phone_dorm
FROM students
JOIN course_rosters USING (student_id)
WHERE course_id =
  (SELECT course_id
   FROM course_schedule
   JOIN teachers USING (teacher_id)
   WHERE semester_code = '2007AU'
   AND class_time = 'monday_01'
   AND name_first = 'Sonia'
   AND name_last = 'Oram');
```

Notice in the subquery that we're joining the `course_schedule` table with `teachers` so we can give the teacher's first and last name in the WHERE clause of the subquery. We're also indicating in the WHERE clause a specific semester (Autumn 2007) and time slot (Monday, first period). The results of these specifics should be one course identification number because a teacher won't teach more than one class during a particular class period. That single course number will be used by the WHERE clause of the main query to return the list of students on the class roster for the course, along with their telephone numbers.

If by chance more than one value is returned by the subquery in the previous example, MySQL will return an error:

```
ERROR 1242 (ER_SUBSELECT_NO_1_ROW)
SQLSTATE = 21000
Message = "Subquery returns more than 1 row"
```

Despite our supposition, it is possible that a teacher might teach more than one class at a time: perhaps the teacher is teaching one course in violin and another in viola, but each class had so few students that the department head put them together. In such a situation, the teacher would want the data for both course numbers. To use multiple fields derived from a subquery in a WHERE clause like this, we would have to use something other than the = operator, such as IN. For this kind of situation, see the next section on "Multiple Fields Subqueries."

Multiple Fields Subqueries

In the previous section, we discussed instances where one scalar value was obtained from a subquery in a WHERE clause. However, there are times when you may want to match multiple values. For those situations you will need to use the subquery in conjunction with an operator or a clause: ALL, ANY, EXISTS, IN, or SOME.

As an example of a multiple fields subquery—and specifically of a subquery using IN (or using ANY or SOME)—let's adapt the example from the previous section to a situation where the teacher wants the contact information for students in all of her classes. To do this, we can enter the following SQL statement:

```
SELECT CONCAT(name_first, ' ', name_last) AS student,
phone_home, phone_dorm
FROM students
JOIN course_rosters USING (student_id)
WHERE course_id IN
  (SELECT course_id
   FROM course_schedule
   JOIN teachers USING (teacher_id)
   WHERE semester_code = '2007AU'
   AND name_first = 'Sonia'
   AND name_last = 'Oram');
```

In this example, notice that the subquery is contained within the parentheses of the IN clause. Subqueries are executed first, so the results will be available before the WHERE clause is executed. Although a comma-separated list isn't returned, MySQL still accepts the results so that they may be used by the outer query. The criteria of the WHERE clause here does not specify a specific time slot as the earlier example did, so multiple values are much more likely to be returned.

Instead of IN, you can use ANY or SOME to obtain the same results by the same methods. (ANY and SOME are synonymous.) These two keywords must be preceded by a comparison operator (e.g., =, <, >). For example, we could replace the IN in the SQL previous statement with = ANY or with = SOME and the same results will be returned. IN can be preceded with NOT for negative comparisons: NOT IN(...). This is the same as != ANY (...) and != SOME (...).

Let's look at another subquery returning multiple values but using the ALL operator. The ALL operator must be preceded by a comparison operator (e.g., =, <, >). As an example of this usage, suppose one of the piano teachers provides weekend seminars for students. Suppose also that he heard a few students are enrolled in all of the seminars he has scheduled for the semester and he wants a list of their names and telephone numbers in advance. We should be able to get that data by entering an

SQL statement like the following (though currently it doesn't work, for reasons to be explained shortly):

```
SELECT DISTINCT student_id,
CONCAT(name_first, ' ', name_last) AS student
FROM students
JOIN seminar_rosters USING (student_id)
WHERE seminar_id = ALL
  (SELECT seminar_id
   FROM seminar_schedule
   JOIN teachers ON (instructor_id = teacher_id)
   WHERE semester_code = '2007AU'
   AND name_first = 'Sam'
   AND name_last = 'Oram');
```

In this example, a couple of the tables have different column names for the ID we want, and we have to join one of them with `ON` instead of `USING`, but that has nothing to do with the subquery. What's significant is that this subquery returns a list of seminar identification numbers and is used in the `WHERE` clause of the main query with `= ALL`. Unfortunately, although this statement is constructed correctly, it doesn't work with MySQL at the time of this writing and just returns an empty set. However, it should work in future releases of MySQL, so I've included it for future reference. For now, we would have to reorganize the SQL statement like so:

```
SELECT student_id, student
FROM
  (SELECT student_id, COUNT(*)
     AS nbr_seminars_registered,
   CONCAT(name_first, ' ', name_last)
     AS student
   FROM students
   JOIN seminar_rosters USING (student_id)
   WHERE seminar_id IN
     (SELECT seminar_id
      FROM seminar_schedule
      JOIN teachers
      ON (instructor_id = teacher_id)
      WHERE semester_code = '2007AU'
      AND name_first = 'Sam'
      AND name_last = 'Oram')
   GROUP BY student_id) AS students_registered
WHERE nbr_seminars_registered =
   (SELECT COUNT(*) AS nbr_seminars
   FROM seminar_schedule
   JOIN teachers
   ON (instructor_id = teacher_id)
   WHERE semester_code = '2007AU'
   AND name_first = 'Sam'
   AND name_last = 'Oram');
```

This is much more involved, but it does work with the latest release of MySQL.

The first subquery is used to get the student's name. This subquery's `WHERE` clause uses another subquery to retrieve the list of seminars taught by the professor for the semester, to determine the results set from which the main query will draw its ultimate data. The third subquery counts the number of seminars that the same professor is teaching for the semester. This single value is used with the WHERE clause of the main query. In essence, we're determining the number of seminars the professor is teaching and which students are registered for all of them.

The last possible method for using multiple fields in a subquery uses EXISTS. With EXISTS, in order for it to return meaningful or desired results, you need to stipulate in the WHERE clauses of the subquery a point in which it is joined to the outer query. Using the example from the previous section involving the teacher Sonia Oram, let's suppose that we want to retrieve a list of courses that she teaches:

```
SELECT DISTINCT course_id, course_name
FROM courses
WHERE EXISTS
  (SELECT course_id
   FROM course_schedule
   JOIN teachers USING (teacher_id)
   WHERE semester_code = '2007AU'
   AND name_first = 'Sonia'
   AND name_last = 'Oram'
   AND courses.course_id = course_schedule.course_id);
```

As you can see here, we've added EXISTS to the WHERE clause with the subquery in parentheses, similar to using IN. The significant difference is that we added `courses.course_id = course_schedule.course_id` to the end. Without it, a list of all courses would be returned regardless of the criteria of the WHERE clause in the subquery. Incidentally, if we specified NOT EXISTS instead, we would get all courses *except* for the ones taught by the teacher given.

Results Set Subqueries

A subquery can be used to generate a results set, which is a table from which an outer query can select data. That is, a subquery can be used in a FROM clause as if it were another table in a database. It is a *derived table*. Along these lines, each derived table must be named. This is done with AS following the parentheses containing the subquery. A subquery contained in a FROM clause generally cannot be a correlated subquery—that is, it cannot reference the same table as the outer query. The exception is if it's constructed with a JOIN.

In the following example, let's consider the subquery separately as though it were a plain query and not a subquery. It will generate a results set containing the student's ID and the student's average exam score for a specific course taught during a specific semester. The query uses AVG( ), which requires a GROUP BY clause. The problem with GROUP BY is that it will order data only by the columns by which it's given to group data. In this case, it will order the data by `student_id` and not list the results by any other, more useful column. If we want to order the data so that the highest student average is first, descending in order to the lowest student average, we have to turn our query into a subquery and have the outer query re-sort the results:

```
SELECT CONCAT(name_first, ' ', name_last) AS student,
student_id, avg_grade
```

```
FROM students
JOIN
  (SELECT student_id,
   AVG(exam_grade) AS avg_grade
   FROM exams
   WHERE semester_code = '2007AU'
   AND course_id = 1489
   GROUP BY student_id) AS grade_averages
USING(student_id)
ORDER BY avg_grade DESC;
```

The results set (the derived table generated by the subquery in the `FROM` clause) is named `grade_averages`. Notice that although the column `student_id` exists in the derived table, in the table from which it gets its data (i.e., `exams`) and in the primary table used in the main query (i.e., `students`), there is no ambiguity. No error is generated. However, if we wanted to specify that the data be taken from the derived table, we could put `grade_averages.student_id` in the `SELECT` of the outer query.

This subquery is a correlated subquery, which is generally not permitted in a `FROM` clause. It's allowed in this example because we are using a `JOIN` to join the results set to the table referenced in the outer query.

11
String Functions

MySQL has several built-in functions for formatting, manipulating, and analyzing strings, both user-specified and within columns of data. This chapter lists these string functions, provides the syntax of each, and gives examples of their use. The examples in this chapter use a fictitious database for a college.

String functions do not change their inputs; the functions' return values contain the changes.

String Functions Grouped by Type

The list of string functions is quite long, but many perform similar roles. The following list groups the functions by these roles.

Character Sets and Collation

CHARSET( ), COALESCE( ), COERCIBILITY( ), COLLATION( ).

Converting

ASCII( ), BIN( ), BINARY, CAST( ), CHAR( ), COMPRESS( ), CONVERT( ), EXPORT_SET( ), HEX( ), MAKE_SET( ), ORD( ), SOUNDEX( ), UNCOMPRESS( ), UNHEX( ).

Formatting

CONCAT( ), CONCAT_WS( ), LCASE( ), LENGTH( ), LOWER( ), LPAD( ), LTRIM( ), OCTET_LENGTH( ), QUOTE( ), RPAD( ), RTRIM( ), SPACE( ), TRIM( ), UCASE( ), UPPER( ).

Expressions

BIT_LENGTH( ), CRC32( ), CHAR_LENGTH( ), CHARACTER_LENGTH( ), ELT( ), FIELD( ), FIND_IN_SET( ), INSTR( ), INTERVAL( ), LOCATE( ), MATCH( ) AGAINST( ), POSITION( ), STRCMP( ), UNCOMPRESSED_LENGTH( ).

Extracting

LEFT( ), LOAD_FILE( ), MID( ), RIGHT( ), SUBSTR( ), SUBSTRING( ), SUBSTRING_INDEX( ).

Manipulating

INSERT( ), REPEAT( ), REPLACE( ), REVERSE( ).

String Functions in Alphabetical Order

The rest of this chapter lists the string functions in alphabetical order.

ASCII( )

ASCII(*string*)

This function returns the numeric code corresponding to the first character of a given string. If the given string is empty, 0 is returned. Despite the function's name, it works for characters outside the ASCII set (that is, characters that correspond to values above 127) and is probably most useful for such characters.

As an example of this function's use, suppose that for a college we had a table listing the names of fraternities with their Greek letters. For easier manipulation of the data contained in a column, we might want to convert the Greek letters to a numeric code with this function:

```
SELECT greek_id,
CONCAT_WS('-',
   ASCII( SUBSTR(greek_id, 1, 1) ),
   ASCII( SUBSTR(greek_id, 2, 1) ),
   ASCII( SUBSTR(greek_id, 3, 1) )
) AS 'ASCII Values'
FROM fraternities WHERE frat_id = 101;

+----------+--------------+
| greek_id | ASCII Values |
+----------+--------------+
| ΔΣΠ      | 196-211-208  |
+----------+--------------+
```

In this example, we use the SUBSTR( ) function to extract each letter so we can then convert each one individually to its numeric equivalent with the ASCII( ) function. Then, using CONCAT_WS( ), we insert hyphens between each number returned. We can use this number to more easily manage the data related to this fraternity. See the descriptions of CHAR( )

and `CONVERT( )` later in this chapter for more information on this function and for more details related to this example.

BIN( )

`BIN(number)`

This function returns a binary number for a given integer. It returns NULL if the input is NULL:

```
SELECT BIN(1), BIN(2), BIN(3);

+--------+--------+--------+
| BIN(1) | BIN(2) | BIN(3) |
+--------+--------+--------+
| 1      | 10     | 11     |
+--------+--------+--------+
```

For the number 1 in a base 10 system, the first position in a binary system is *on*, or 1. For the number 2, the first position from the right is *off* and the second is *on*. For 3, the first and the second positions are *on*.

BINARY

`BINARY string`

Use this function to treat strings in their binary state. This function is useful for making SQL statements case-sensitive. Notice that the syntax does not call for parentheses:

```
SELECT student_id, name_last
FROM students
WHERE BINARY LEFT(UCASE(name_last), 1) <>
   LEFT(name_last, 1);

+------------+-----------+
| student_id | name_last |
+------------+-----------+
|  433302000 | dyer      |
|  434016005 | de Vitto  |
+------------+-----------+
```

This statement checks for any student whose last name starts with a lowercase letter. Each student's last name is converted to uppercase letters, and then the first letter starting from the left is extracted to be compared with the first letter of the last name without case conversion. The results show one record that is probably a typing error and a second that is probably correct. Notice that the `BINARY` keyword is specified before the comparison is made between the strings, and is applied to both strings.

BIT_LENGTH( )

`BIT_LENGTH(string)`

This function returns the number of bits in a given string. The following example uses the default character set, where one character requires 8 bits:

```
SELECT BIT_LENGTH('a') AS 'One Character',
BIT_LENGTH('ab') AS 'Two Characters';

+---------------+----------------+
| One Character | Two Characters |
+---------------+----------------+
|             8 |             16 |
+---------------+----------------+
```

CAST()

CAST(*expression* AS *type* [CHARACTER SET *character_set*])

Use this function to convert a value from one data type to another. This function is available as of version 4.0.2 of MySQL. The data type given as the second argument can be BINARY, CHAR, DATE, DATETIME, SIGNED [INTEGER], TIME, or UNSIGNED [INTEGER]. BINARY converts a string to a binary string.

CHAR conversion is available as of version 4.0.6 of MySQL. This function is similar to CONVERT( ). Optionally, you can add CHARACTER SET to use a different character set from the default for the value given. The default is drawn from the system variables character_set_connection and collation_connection.

As an example, suppose we want to retrieve a list of courses for the current semester (Spring) and their locations, sorting them alphabetically by their building name. Unfortunately, the building names are in an ENUM( ) column because we're at a small college. Since they're not in alphabetical order in the column definition, they won't be sorted the way we want. Instead, they will be sorted in the lexical order of the column definition, that is, the order they are listed in the ENUM( ) column of the table definition. Using CAST( ) in the WHERE clause can resolve this:

```
SELECT course_id, course_name,
CONCAT(building, '-', room_num) AS location
FROM courses
WHERE year = YEAR(CURDATE())
AND semester = 'spring'
ORDER BY CAST(building AS CHAR);
```

By using the CAST( ) function to treat the values of building as a CHAR data type, we make sure the results will be ordered alphabetically.

CHAR()

CHAR(*ascii*[, ...] [USING *character_set*])

This function returns a string corresponding to the numeric code passed as the argument. This is the reverse of ASCII( ), described earlier in this chapter. You can optionally give the USING parameter to specify a different character set to use in relation to the string given. If you give it a value greater than 255, it assumes the amount over 255 is another character. So, CHAR(256) is equivalent to CHAR(1,0).

As an example of this function's use, suppose that a college database has a table for fraternities on campus and that the table has a column to contain the Greek letters for each fraternity's name. To create a table with such a column, we would at a minimum enter something like the following:

```
CREATE TABLE fraternities (
frat_id INT(11),
greek_id CHAR(10) CHARACTER SET greek);
```

Notice that for the column `greek_id` we're specifying a special character set to be used. This can be different from the character set for other columns and for the table. With this minimal table, we enter the following `INSERT` statement to add one fraternity and then follow that with a `SELECT` statement to see the results:


```
INSERT INTO fraternities
VALUES(101,
   CONCAT(CHAR(196 USING greek),
   CHAR(211 USING greek),
   CHAR(208 USING greek)));

SELECT greek_id
FROM fraternities
WHERE frat_id = 101;

+----------+
| greek_id |
+----------+
| ΔΣΠ      |
+----------+
```

Using the `CHAR( )` function and looking at a chart showing the Greek alphabet, we figure out the ASCII number for each of the three Greek letters for the fraternity Delta Sigma Pi. If we had a Greek keyboard, we could just type them. If we used a chart available online in a graphical browser, we could just copy and paste them into our *mysql* client. Using the `CONCAT( )` function, we put the results of each together to insert the data into the column in the table.

CHAR_LENGTH( )

`CHAR_LENGTH(`*`string`*`)`

This function returns the number of characters in a given string. This is synonymous with `CHARACTER_LENGTH( )`. A multiple-byte character is treated as one character. Use `LENGTH( )` if you want each byte to be counted. Here is an example:

```
SELECT course_id,
   CASE
   WHEN CHAR_LENGTH(course_desc) > 30
   THEN CONCAT(SUBSTRING(course_desc, 1, 27), '...')
   ELSE course_desc
   END AS Description
FROM courses;
```

In this example, a `CASE` control statement is used to specify different display results based on a condition. Using the `CHAR_LENGTH( )` function, MySQL determines whether the content of `course_desc` is longer than 30 characters. If it is, the `SUBSTRING( )` function extracts the first 27 characters and the `CONCAT( )` function adds ellipsis points to the end of the truncated data to indicate that there is more text. Otherwise, the full contents of course_desc are displayed. See the CHARACTER_LENGTH( ) description next for another example of how CHAR_LENGTH( ) may be used.

CHARACTER_LENGTH( )

CHARACTER_LENGTH(*string*)

This function returns the number of characters of a given string. A multiple-byte character is treated as one character. It's synonymous with CHAR_LENGTH( ).

As another example of how this function or CHAR_LENGTH( ) might be used, suppose that in a college's table containing students names we notice that some of the names appear garbled. We realize this is happening because we weren't prepared for non-Latin characters. We could enter an SQL statement like the following to find students with the names containing multibyte characters:

```
SELECT student_id,
CONCAT(name_first, SPACE(1), name_last) AS Name
FROM students
WHERE CHARACTER_LENGTH(name_first) != LENGTH(name_first)
OR CHARACTER_LENGTH(name_last) != LENGTH(name_last);
```

In this example, in the WHERE clause we're using CHARACTER_LENGTH( ) to get the number of bytes and LENGTH( ) to get the number of characters for each name, and then we're comparing them with the != operator to return only rows where the two methods of evaluation don't equal.

CHARSET( )

CHARSET(*string*)

This function returns the character set used by a given string. It's available as of version 4.1.0 of MySQL. Here is an example:

```
SELECT CHARSET('Rosá')
AS 'Set for My Name';

+-----------------+
| Set for My Name |
+-----------------+
| utf8            |
+-----------------+
```

COALESCE( )

COALESCE(*column*[, ...])

This function returns the leftmost non-NULL string or column in a comma-separated list. If all elements are NULL, the function returns NULL. Here is an example:

```
SELECT CONCAT(name_first, ' ', name_last)
  AS Student,
COALESCE(phone_dorm, phone_home, 'No Telephone Number')
  AS Telephone
FROM students;
```

In this example, the results will show the student's dormitory telephone number if there is one (i.e., if the student lives in the dormitory). If not, it will show the student's home telephone number (i.e., maybe his parent's house). Otherwise, it will return the string given, indicating that there is no telephone number for the student.

COERCIBILITY( )

`COERCIBILITY(string)`

This function returns an arbitrary value known as the *coercibility* of a given string or other item, showing how likely that item is to determine the collation used in an expression. MySQL sometimes needs to choose which collation to use when results of an SQL statement involve different types of data. Here are possible return values from this function:

0
: Collation has been explicitly specified (e.g., a statement using `COLLATE`).

1
: The argument merges values of different collations.

2
: The argument has an implicit collation (e.g., a column is given).

3
: The argument is a system constant, such as a system variable or a function that returns something similar.

4
: The argument is a literal string.

5
: The argument is NULL or an expression derived from a NULL value.

Lower coercibility levels take precedence over higher ones when the server is determining which collation to use. This function is available as of version 4.1.1 of MySQL. Here is an example:

```
SELECT COERCIBILITY('Russell')
AS 'My State';

+----------+
| My State |
+----------+
|        4 |
+----------+
```

COLLATION( )

`COLLATION(string)`

This function returns the collation for the character set of a given string. This function is available as of version 4.1.0 of MySQL. Here is an example:

```
SELECT COLLATION('Rosá');
```

```
+--------------------+
| COLLATION('Rosá')  |
+--------------------+
| utf8_general_ci    |
+--------------------+
```

COMPRESS( )

`COMPRESS(string)`

This function returns a given string after compressing it. It requires MySQL to have been compiled with a compression library (e.g., `zlib`). If it wasn't, a NULL value will be returned. This statement is available as of version 4.1 of MySQL. Here is an example:

```
UPDATE students_records
SET personal_essay =
(SELECT COMPRESS(essay)
 FROM student_applications
 WHERE applicant_id = '7382') AS derived1
WHERE student_id = '433302000';
```

If you want to store a value that was compressed with this function, it's best to store it in a `BLOB` column, since the results are binary. Use `UNCOMPRESS( )` to uncompress a string that was compressed with this function.

CONCAT( )

`CONCAT(string, ...)`

With this function, strings or columns can be concatenated or pasted together into one resulting field. Any number of strings may be specified, with each argument separated by a comma. If any of the values given are NULL, a NULL value is returned. Here is an example:

```
SELECT CONCAT(name_first, ' ', name_last) AS Student
FROM students WHERE name_last = 'Dyer';

+-------------------+
| Student           |
+-------------------+
| Kenneth Dyer      |
| Geoffrey Dyer     |
| Marie Dyer        |
| NULL              |
+-------------------+
```

In this example, the database contained four students with the last name *Dyer*, but one of them had a NULL value in the `name_first` column. Within the parentheses of the function, notice that a space is given within quotes as the second element so that the results show a space between each student's first and last name.

Another use for `CONCAT( )` is to convert numeric values of a given column to strings. This may be useful when working with an API such as Perl and when using `UNION` to mix data from two different data types.

Here is an example:

```
SELECT CONCAT(type_id) AS id, type AS title
  FROM types
UNION
SELECT topic_id AS id, topic AS title
  FROM topics;
```

In this example, the column `type_id` is an `INT`, whereas the column `topic_id` is a `CHAR` column. In MySQL, the results can be mixed. However, if this SQL statement is used to create a hash of data in Perl or another API language, you may encounter problems retrieving data. In order that the data in the columns agree, the `CONCAT( )` function is used to convert the numeric values to their string equivalents.

CONCAT_WS( )

CONCAT_WS(*separator*, *string*, ...)

This function combines strings of text and columns, separated by the string specified in the first argument. Any number of strings may be specified after the first argument, with each argument separated by a comma. Null values are ignored. Here is an example:

```
SELECT CONCAT_WS('|', student_id, name_last, name_first)
AS 'Dyer Students'
FROM students
WHERE name_last='Dyer';

+------------------------+
| Dyer Students          |
+------------------------+
| 433342000|Dyer|Russell |
| 434892001|Dyer|Marie   |
+------------------------+
```

Here, the vertical bar is used to separate the columns. This function can be useful for exporting data to formats acceptable to other software. You could incorporate something like this into an API program, or just execute it from the command line using the *mysql* client like this:

```
mysql -u root -p \
-e "SELECT CONCAT_WS('|', student_id, name_last, name_first)
AS '# Dyer Students #' FROM testing.students
WHERE name_last='Dyer';" > dyer_students.txt

cat dyer_students.txt

# Dyer Students #
433342000|Dyer|Russell
434892001|Dyer|Marie
```

The `-e` option in the *mysql* client instructs it to execute what is contained in quotes. The entire `mysql` statement is followed by a `>` sign to redirect output to a text file. Afterward, the `cat` command shows the contents of that file. Notice that the usual ASCII table format is not included. This makes the file easy to import into other applications.

CONVERT( )

`CONVERT([_character_set]string USING character_set)`

Use this function to convert the character set of a given string to another character set specified with the `USING` keyword. This function is available as of version 4.0.2 of MySQL. The function has some similarities to `CAST( )`. If the character set for the given string is not the same as the default, you can specify its character set by listing it immediately before the string and preceded by an underscore:

```
UPDATE students SET name_first =
CONVERT(_latin1'Rosá' USING utf8)
WHERE student_id = 433342000;
```

In this example, we're converting the student's first name with the accented character into a format usable by the column that uses UTF-8. Notice that the character set given for the string is preceded by an underscore and there are no spaces before the quotation mark for the string.

CRC32( )

`CRC32(string)`

This function returns the given string's cyclic redundancy check (CRC) value as a 32-bit unsigned value. It's available as of version 4.1 of MySQL. It returns NULL if given a NULL value. Even if a numeric value is given, it treats the value as a string:

```
SELECT CRC32('test');

+---------------+
| CRC32('test') |
+---------------+
|    3632233996 |
+---------------+
```

ELT( )

`ELT(index, string, ...)`

This function returns the `index` element from the list of strings given, where the list is numbered starting with 1. If the number given is less than 1 or if the number of elements is less than the number given, this statement returns NULL:

```
SELECT student_id,
CONCAT(name_first, SPACE(1), name_last)
   AS Name,
ELT(primary_phone, phone_dorm, phone_home, phone_work)
   AS Telephone
FROM students;
```

In this SQL statement, we're using the value of the `primary_phone` column to provide the index for `ELT( )`. This column is an `ENUM` column that records which of the three telephone columns is the student's primary telephone number. The function will return the value for the column selected based on the index. As a result, the SQL statement will give a list of students and their primary telephone numbers.

EXPORT_SET( )

EXPORT_SET(*number*, *on*, *off*[, *separator*,[*count*]])

This function returns a series of strings in order that represent each bit of a given *number*. The second argument specifies a string to represent bits that are 1 (an *on* bit), and the third argument specifies a string to represent bits that are 0 (an *off* bit). The fourth argument may specify a separator, and the last argument may specify a number of bit equivalents to display. The default separator is a comma. Here is an example:

```
SELECT BIN(4) AS 'Binary Number',
EXPORT_SET(4, 'on', 'off', '-', 8)
AS 'Verbal Equivalent';

+---------------+-------------------------------+
| Binary Number | Verbal Equivalent             |
+---------------+-------------------------------+
| 100           | off-off-on-off-off-off-off-off |
+---------------+-------------------------------+
```

Notice that the lowest-order bit is displayed first, so the conversion of the binary equivalent of 4 is displayed by EXPORT_SET( ) in what one might consider reverse order, from right to left: not 100, but 001 (or, as part of 8 bits, 00100000).

FIELD( )

FIELD(*string*, *string*[, ...])

This function searches for the first string given in the following list of strings, and returns the numeric position of the first string in the list that matches. The first element is 1 among the arguments being searched. If the search string is not found or is NULL, 0 is returned.

As an example of this function, suppose that in a table containing telephone numbers of students at a college, there are three columns for telephone numbers (dormitory, home, and work numbers). Suppose further that another column is used to indicate which column contains the primary telephone number of the student. However, we realize that for many rows this primary_phone column is NULL. So, we decide to make a guess as to which is the primary telephone number by using the FIELD( ) function along with a subquery:

```
UPDATE students
JOIN
  (SELECT student_id,
   FIELD(1, phone_dorm IS TRUE,
            phone_home IS TRUE,
            phone_work IS TRUE)
   AS first_phone_found
   FROM students
   WHERE primary_phone IS NULL) AS sub_table
   USING (student_id)
SET primary_phone = first_phone_found;
```

Notice that in the subquery, within the FIELD( ) function, we're looking for a value of 1 (the first parameter of the function). For the other parameters given, each telephone column will be examined using the `IS TRUE` operator: it will return true (or rather 1) if the column is not NULL. The `FIELD( )` function will return the number of the element in the list that returns 1 (meaning it exists). So if `phone_dorm` is NULL but `phone_home` has a telephone number in it, the subquery will return a value of 2—even if `phone_work` also contains a number. The `JOIN` uses the results to update each student record that has a NULL value for `primary_phone` with the value of the `first_phone_found` field in the results of the subquery.

FIND_IN_SET( )

`FIND_IN_SET(`*`string, string_list`*`)`

This function returns the location of the first argument within a comma-separated list that is passed as a single string in the second argument. The first element of the list is 1. A 0 is returned if the string is not found in the set or if the string list is empty. It returns NULL if either argument is NULL.

As an example of how this function might be used, suppose that a table in our college application contains the results of a survey that students took on the college's web site. One of the columns, `favorite_activities`, contains a list of activities each student said is her favorite in the order that she likes them, her favorite being first. The text of the column comes from a web form on which students entered a number to rank each activity they like; they left blank the ones they don't take part in. So, each column has text separated by commas and spaces (e.g., *bike riding, reading, swimming*). Here's how this function could be used to order a list of students who said that *reading* is one of their favorite activities:

```
SELECT student_id,
FIND_IN_SET('reading',
   REPLACE(favorite_activities, SPACE(1), '') )
   AS reading_rank
FROM student_surveys
WHERE survey_id = 127
AND favorite_activities LIKE '%reading%'
ORDER BY reading_rank;
```

We use the `WHERE` clause to choose the correct survey and the `LIKE` operator to select only rows where the column `favorite_activities` contains the value *reading*. This will eliminate those students who didn't rank reading as a favorite activity from the results. `FIND_IN_SET( )` won't allow spaces because they confuse the function, so we need to remove spaces from the text in the `favorite_activities` column. Thus, we slip in a call to `REPLACE( )` to replace any space found with an empty string. With that done, `FIND_IN_SET( )` will return the ranking each student gave for *reading*. The `ORDER BY` clause orders those results by `reading_rank`—the alias given for the second field with the `AS` clause.

HEX( )

`HEX(`*`string`*`)`

The first version of this function accepts a string and returns its numerical value, in hexadecimal, as it is represented in the underlying character set. The second version accepts a decimal integer and returns the hexadecimal equivalent. The function returns NULL if given a NULL value.

For an example, suppose that a college has conducted a student survey through an application that has somehow saved a number of formatting characters as strings containing their hexadecimal equivalents. For instance, a tab appears as `09`, and we want to replace each instance with an actual tab. Although we could do this with a straight replacement function, we'd like to use a slightly more abstract solution that can be used with many different characters that suffer from this problem in a particular column.

One solution, changing all instances in the column **`student_surveys`**, is as follows:

```
UPDATE student_surveys
SET opinion = REPLACE(opinion, HEX('\t'), UNHEX(HEX('\t')))
WHERE survey_id = 127;
```

In this SQL statement, `HEX( )` is used to return the hexadecimal value of tab, represented by `\t`. That value is given to `REPLACE( )` as the string for which it is to replace. Then, using `HEX( )` again but wrapped in `UNHEX( )` to return the binary character for tab, we're providing `REPLACE( )` with the replacement value.

INSERT( )

`INSERT(`*`string, position, length, new_string`*`)`

This function inserts the string from the final argument into the string specified by the first argument, at the specified position. If *`length`* is greater than 0, the function overwrites that number of characters, so the new string replaces part of the original. The function returns NULL if any of the arguments are NULL. The first position is 1. Don't confuse this function with the SQL `INSERT` statement. Here is an example of this function:

```
UPDATE courses
SET course_name =
INSERT(course_name, INSTR(course_name, 'Eng.'), 4, 'English')
WHERE course_name LIKE "%Eng.%";
```

In this example, some course names have the word *English* abbreviated as *Eng*. This SQL statement overwrites any such occurrences with the word *English*. It uses the `INSTR( )` function to find the starting point of the abbreviation. The number value it returns is used as the position argument for the `INSERT( )` function. If it's not found, the course name will not be changed because a value of 0 will be returned by `INSTR( )`, and the `INSERT( )` function ignores any request in which *`position`* lies outside the length of the original string.

INSTR( )

`INSTR(`*`string, substring`*`)`

This function returns the starting position of the first occurrence of the substring in the string given as the first argument. The index of the first position is 1. This function is case-insensitive unless one of the arguments given is a binary string. For an example of this function, see the description of `INSERT( )` previously in this chapter. `INSTR( )` is similar to one of the syntaxes of `LOCATE( )`, but the parameters are given in a different order.

INTERVAL( )

INTERVAL(*search_value, ordered_value, ...*)

This function returns the position in which *search_value* would be located in a comma-separated list of *ordered_value* arguments. In other words, the function returns the first *ordered_value* that is less than or equal to *search_value*. All arguments are treated as integers, and the caller must list the *ordered_value* arguments in increasing order. If *search_value* would be located before the first ordered value, 0 is returned. If *search_value* would be located after the last ordered value, the position of that value is returned.

For example, suppose that a professor at our fictitious college has given the same few exams every semester for the last four semesters. Suppose that he has a table containing a row for each semester, and a column for each exam that contains the average of student grades for the semester. Now the professor wants to know how the average score for the same exam for the current semester compares against the previous semesters: he wants to know how the students on average rank by comparison. We could find this answer by running the following SQL statement:

```
SELECT INTERVAL(
   (SELECT AVG(exam1) FROM student_exams),
   S1,S2,S3,S4) AS Ranking
FROM
  (SELECT
    (SELECT exam1_avg FROM student_exams_past
       ORDER BY exam1_avg LIMIT 0,1) AS S1,
    (SELECT exam1_avg FROM student_exams_past
       ORDER BY exam1_avg LIMIT 1,1) AS S2,
    (SELECT exam1_avg FROM student_exams_past
       ORDER BY exam1_avg LIMIT 2,1) AS S3,
    (SELECT exam1_avg FROM student_exams_past
       ORDER BY exam1_avg LIMIT 3,1) AS S4) AS exam1_stats;
```

In this complex example, we're running four subqueries to get the average exam score stored (*S1*, *S2*, *S3*, and *S4*) in the same column for the four semesters for which we have data. Then we're putting each of these values into one row of a derived table (`exam1_stats`). We will then select each column of that limited derived table for the strings to compare against in the `INTERVAL( )` function. For the first parameter of that function, though, we're running yet another subquery to determine the average grades of students for the same exam for the current semester. The results will be a number from 0 to 4, depending on how this semester's average compares.

LCASE( )

LCASE(*string*)

This function converts a string given to all lowercase letters. It's an alias of `LOWER( )`. Here is an example:

```
SELECT teacher_id,
CONCAT(LEFT(UCASE(name_last), 1),
SUBSTRING(LCASE(name_last), 2))
AS Teacher
FROM teachers;
```

In this example, we're using a combination of LEFT( ) paired with UCASE( ) and SUBSTRING( ) paired with LCASE( ) to ensure that the first letter of the teacher's name is displayed in uppercase and the rest of the name is in lowercase letters.

LEFT( )

LEFT(*string*, *length*)

This function returns the first *length* characters from a string. If you want to extract the end of the string instead of the beginning, use the RIGHT( ) function. Both are multibyte-safe. Here is an example:

```
SELECT LEFT(phone_home, 3) AS 'Area Code',
COUNT(*)
FROM students
GROUP BY LEFT(phone_home, 3);
```

Using the LEFT( ) function, this statement extracts the first three digits of phone_home for each row, which is the telephone area code (i.e., city code). It then groups the results, using the same function in the WHERE clause. This returns a count of the number of students living in each telephone area code.

LENGTH( )

LENGTH(*string*)

This function returns the number of bytes contained in a given string. It is not aware of multibyte characters, so it assumes there are eight bits to a byte and one byte to a character. OCTET_LENGTH( ) is an alias. If you want to get the length of characters regardless of whether a character is multibyte or not, use CHARACTER_LENGTH( ).

As an example, suppose that we notice in an online survey that some odd binary characters have been entered into the data through the web interface—probably from a spam program. To narrow the list of rows, we can enter the following statement to find the rows that have binary characters in three columns that have the bad data:

```
SELECT respondent_id
FROM survey
WHERE CHARACTER_LENGTH(answer1) != LENGTH(answer1)
OR CHARACTER_LENGTH(answer2) != LENGTH(answer2)
OR CHARACTER_LENGTH(answer3) != LENGTH(answer3)
survey_id = 127;
```

In this example, the WHERE clause invokes CHARACTER_LENGTH( ) to get the number of bytes, and LENGTH( ) to get the number of characters for each column containing a respondent's answers to the survey questions. We then compare them with the != operator to return only rows in which the two methods of evaluation are not equal. The LENGTH( ) will return a greater value for multibyte characters, whereas CHARACTER_LENGTH( ) will return 1 for each character, regardless of whether it's a multibyte character.

LOAD_FILE( )

LOAD_FILE(*filename*)

This function reads the contents of a file and returns it as a string that may be used in MySQL statements and functions. The user must have FILE privileges in MySQL, and the file must be readable by all users on the filesystem. It returns NULL if the file doesn't exist, if the user doesn't have proper permissions, or if the file is otherwise unreadable. The file size in bytes must be less than the amount specified in the system variable max_allowed_packet. Starting with version 5.1.6 of MySQL, the system variable character_set_filesystem is used to provide filenames in the character set recognized by the underlying filesystem. Here is an example:

```
UPDATE applications
SET essay = LOAD_FILE('/tmp/applicant_7382.txt'),
student_photo = LOAD_FILE('/tmp/applicant_7382.jpeg')
WHERE applicant_id = '7382';
```

In this example, an essay written by someone who is applying for admission to the college is loaded into the *essay* column (which is a TEXT data type) of the row for the applicant in the applications table. The entire contents of the file, including any binary data (e.g., hard returns and tabs), are loaded from the file into the table. Additionally, an image file containing the student's photograph is loaded into another column of the same table, but in a BLOB column.

LOCATE( )

LOCATE(*substring, string[, start_position]*)

This function returns the numeric starting point of the first occurrence of a substring in the string supplied as a second argument. A starting position for searching may be specified as a third argument. It's not case-sensitive unless one of the strings given is a binary string. The function is multibyte-safe.

As an example of this function's potential, suppose that a table for a college contains a list of courses and one of the columns (course_desc) contains the description of the courses. A typical column starts like this:

```
Victorian Literature [19th Cent. Engl. Lit.]: This course covers Engl.
   novels and Engl. short-stories...
```

We want to replace all occurrences of the abbreviation Engl. with English except in the beginning of the strings where the abbreviation is contained in square brackets, as shown here. To do this, we could enter an SQL statement like this:

```
UPDATE courses
SET course_desc =
INSERT(course_desc, LOCATE('Engl.', course_desc, LOCATE(']', course_desc)),
   5, 'English')
WHERE course_desc LIKE '%Engl.%';
```

In this statement, we use the LOCATE( ) function to locate the first occurrence of the closing square bracket. From there, we use LOCATE( ) again to find the first occurrence of Engl.. With the INSERT( ) function (not the INSERT statement), we remove the five characters starting from that point located after the closing square bracket and inserting the text English. This is a bit complex, but it generally works. However, it replaces only one occurrence of the text we're trying to replace, whereas in the sample text shown there are at least two occurrences of Engl. after the brackets. We could keep running that SQL statement until we replace each one. A better method would be to run this SQL statement instead:

```
UPDATE courses
SET course_desc =
CONCAT(
   SUBSTRING_INDEX(course_desc, ']', 1),
   REPLACE( SUBSTR(course_desc, LOCATE(']', course_desc)),
   'Engl.', 'English')
)
WHERE course_desc LIKE '%Engl.%';
```


In this statement, we use SUBSTRING_INDEX( ) to extract the opening text until the first closing bracket. We then use LOCATE( ) to locate the closing bracket, SUBSTR( ) to extract the text from that point forward, and then REPLACE( ) to replace all occurrences of Engl. in that substring. Finally, CONCAT( ) pastes the opening text that we preserved and excluded from the replacement component together with the cleaned text.

LOWER( )

LOWER(*string*)

This function converts a given string to all lowercase letters. It is an alias of LCASE( ):

```
SELECT course_id AS 'Course ID',
LOWER(course_name) AS Course
FROM courses;
```

This statement displays the name of each course in all lowercase letters.

LPAD( )

LPAD(*string*, *length*, *padding*)

This function adds ***padding*** to the left end of ***string***, stopping if the combination of ***string*** and the added padding reach ***length*** characters. If ***length*** is shorter than the length of the string, the string will be shortened starting from the left to comply with the length constraint. The padding can be any character. Here is an example:

```
SELECT LPAD(course_name, 25, '.') AS Courses
FROM courses
WHERE course_code LIKE 'ENGL%'
LIMIT 3;

+---------------------------+
| Courses                   |
+---------------------------+
| .........Creative Writing |
| .....Professional Writing |
| ......American Literature |
+---------------------------+
```

In this example, a list of three courses is retrieved and the results are padded with dots to the left of the course names.

LTRIM( )

`LTRIM(string)`

This function returns the given string with any leading spaces removed. When used with an SQL statement such as `UPDATE`, rows that do not contain leading spaces will not be changed. This function is multibyte-safe. To trim trailing spaces, use `RTRIM( )`. To trim both leading and trailing spaces, use `TRIM( )`. Here is an example:

```
UPDATE students
SET name_last = LTRIM(name_last);
```

In this example, the last names of several students have been entered inadvertently with a space in front of the names. This SQL statement removes any leading spaces from each name retrieved that contains leading spaces and then writes the trimmed text over the existing data.

MAKE_SET( )

`MAKE_SET(bits, string1, string2, ...)`

This function converts the decimal number in ***bits*** to binary and returns a comma-separated list of values for all the bits that are set in that number, using ***string1*** for the low-order bit, ***string2*** for the next lowest bit, etc. Here is an example:

```
SELECT BIN(9) AS 'Binary 9',
MAKE_SET(100, 'A','B','C','D')
AS Set;

+----------+------+
| Binary 9 | Set  |
+----------+------+
| 1001     | A,D  |
+----------+------+
```

The binary equivalent of 9 is 1001. The first bit starting from the right of the binary number shown is 1 (or *on*), so the first string in the list is put into the results. The second and third bits of the binary number are 0, so the second and third strings (`'B'` and `'C'`) are left out of the results. The fourth bit counting from the right is 1, so the fourth string of the list is added to the results.

MATCH( ) AGAINST( )

`MATCH(column[, ...]) AGAINST (string)`

This function is used only for columns indexed by a `FULLTEXT` index, and only in `WHERE` clauses. In these clauses, it can be a condition used to search columns for a given string. Text in the string containing spaces is parsed into separate words, so a column matches if it contains at least one word. Small words (three characters or less) are ignored. Here is an example:

```
SELECT applicant_id
FROM applications
WHERE MATCH (essay) AGAINST ('English');
```

This SQL statement searches the table containing data on people applying for admission to the college. The `essay` column contains a copy of the applicant's admission essay. The column is searched for applicants who mention the word `English`, so that a list of applicants who have voiced an interest in the English program will be displayed.

MID( )

`MID(`*`string`*`, `*`position`*`[, `*`length`*`])`

This function returns the characters of a given string, starting from the position specified in the second argument. The first character is numbered 1. You can limit the length of the string retrieved by specifying a limit in the third argument. This function is similar to `SUBSTRING( )`.

As an example of this function, suppose that a table of information about teachers contains a column listing their home telephone numbers. This column's entries are in a format showing only numbers, no hyphens or other separators (e.g., `50412345678`). Suppose further that we decide to add the country code and hyphens in a typical U.S. format (e.g., `+1-504-123-45678`) because although all our teachers live in the U.S., we're about to acquire a small school in a different country. We could make these changes like so:

```
UPDATE teachers
SET phone_home =
CONCAT_WS('-', '+1',
   LEFT(phone_home, 3),
   MID(phone_home, 4, 3),
   MID(phone_home, 7) );
```

This convoluted SQL statement extracts each component of the telephone number with the `LEFT( )` and `MID( )` functions. Using `CONCAT_WS( )`, the data is merged back together along with the country code at the beginning. Components in the return value are separated with a hyphen, which is given as its first parameter.

OCTET_LENGTH( )

`OCTET_LENGTH(`*`string`*`)`

This function returns the number of bytes contained in the given string. It does not recognize multibyte characters, so it assumes there are eight bits to a byte and one byte to a character. An *octet* is synonymous with *byte* in most contexts nowadays, so this function is an alias of `LENGTH( )`. See the description of that function earlier in this chapter for examples of its use.

ORD( )

`ORD(`*`string`*`)`

This function returns an ordinal value, the position of a character in the ASCII character set of the leftmost character in a given string. For multibyte characters, it follows a formula to determine the results: byte1 + (byte2 * 256) + (byte3 *256^2)....

Here is an example:

```
SELECT ORD('A'), ORD('a');

+----------+----------+
| ORD('A') | ORD('a') |
+----------+----------+
|       65 |       97 |
+----------+----------+
```

POSITION( )

`POSITION(substring IN string)`

This function returns an index of the character in *string* where *substring* first appears. The first character of *string* is numbered 1. This function is like `LOCATE( )`, except that the keyword `IN` is used instead of a comma to separate the substring and the containing string. Also, this function does not provide a starting point to begin the search; it must begin from the leftmost character. Here is an example:

```
UPDATE courses
SET course_name =
INSERT(course_name, POSITION('Eng.' IN course_name), 4, 'English')
WHERE course_name LIKE "%Eng.%";
```

In this example, some course names have the word `English` abbreviated as `Eng.` This SQL statement overwrites any such occurrences with the word `English`. It uses the `POSITION( )` function to find the starting point of the abbreviation. The numerical value it returns is then used as the position argument for the `INSERT( )` function (not the `INSERT` statement). If it's not found, the course name will not be changed, because a value of 0 will be returned by `POSITION( )`, and the `INSERT( )` function ignores any request in which *position* lies outside the length of the original string.

QUOTE( )

`QUOTE(string)`

This function accepts a string enclosed in single quotes and returns a string that is safe to manipulate with SQL statements. Single quotes, backslashes, ASCII NULLs, and Ctrl-Zs contained in the string are escaped with a backslash. This is a useful security measure when accepting values from a public web interface. Here is an example:

```
SELECT QUOTE(course_name) AS Courses
FROM courses
WHERE course_code = 'ENGL-405';

+---------------------+
| Courses             |
+---------------------+
| 'Works of O\'Henry' |
+---------------------+
```

Notice in the results that because of the `QUOTE( )` function, the string returned is enclosed in single quotes, and the single quote within the data returned is escaped with a backslash.

REPEAT( )

REPEAT(*string*, *count*)

This function returns the string given in the first argument of the function as many times as specified in the second argument. It returns an empty string if *count* is less than 1. It returns NULL if either argument is NULL. Here is an example:

```
SELECT REPEAT('Urgent! ', 3)
AS 'Warning Message';
```

REPLACE( )

REPLACE(*string*, *old_element*, *new_element*)

This function goes through the first argument and returns a string in which every occurrence of the second argument is replaced with the third argument. Here is an example:

```
UPDATE students,
REPLACE(title, 'Mrs.', 'Ms.');
```

This SQL statement will retrieve each student's title and replace any occurrences of "Mrs." with "Ms." UPDATE will change only the rows where the replacement was made.

REVERSE( )

REVERSE(*string*)

This function returns the characters of *string* in reverse order. It's multibyte-safe. Here is an example:

```
SELECT REVERSE('MUD');

+----------------+
| REVERSE('MUD') |
+----------------+
| DUM            |
+----------------+
```

RIGHT( )

RIGHT(*string*, *length*)

This function returns the final *length* characters from a string. If you want to extract the beginning of the string instead of the end, use the LEFT( ) function. Both are multibyte-safe. Here is an example:

```
SELECT RIGHT(soc_sec, 4)
FROM students
WHERE student_id = '43325146122';
```

This statement retrieves the last four digits of the student's Social Security number as an identity verification.

RPAD( )

`RPAD(string, length, padding)`

This function adds *padding* to the right end of *string*, stopping if the combination of *string* and the added padding reach *length* characters. If the length given is shorter than the length of the string, the string will be shortened to comply with the length constraint. The padding can be any character. Here is an example:

```
SELECT RPAD(course_name, 25, '.') AS Courses
FROM courses
WHERE course_code LIKE 'ENGL%'
LIMIT 3;

+---------------------------+
| Courses                   |
+---------------------------+
| Creative Writing......... |
| Professional Writing..... |
| American Literature...... |
+---------------------------+
```

This statement presents a list of three course names that are retrieved. Each row of the results is padded with dots to the right.

RTRIM( )

`RTRIM(string)`

This function returns the given string with any trailing spaces removed. When used with an SQL statement such as `UPDATE`, rows that do not contain trailing spaces will not be changed. This function is multibyte-safe. To trim leading spaces, use `LTRIM( )`. To trim both leading and trailing spaces, use `TRIM( )`. Here is an example:

```
UPDATE students
SET name_last = RTRIM(name_last);
```

In this example, the last names of several students have been entered inadvertently with a space at the end of the names. This SQL statement removes any trailing spaces from each name retrieved that contains trailing spaces and then writes the trimmed text over the existing data.

SOUNDEX( )

`SOUNDEX(string)`

This function returns the results of a classic algorithm that can be used to compare two similar strings. Here is an example:

```
SELECT IF(SOUNDEX('him') = SOUNDEX('hymm'),
'Sounds Alike', 'Does not sound alike')
AS 'Sound Comparison';

+------------------+
| Sound Comparison |
+------------------+
```

```
| Sounds Alike      |
+-------------------+
```

SOUNDEX( ) was designed to allow comparisons between fuzzy inputs, but it's rarely used.

SPACE( )

SPACE(*count*)

This function returns a string of spaces. The number of spaces returned is set by the argument. Here is an example:

```
SELECT CONCAT(name_first, SPACE(1), name_last)
AS Name
FROM students LIMIT 1;

+-------------------+
| Name              |
+-------------------+
| Richard Stringer  |
+-------------------+
```

Although this example requires a lot more typing than just placing a space within quotes, it's more apparent when glancing at it that a space is to be inserted. For multiple or variable spaces, you could substitute the count with another function to determine the number of spaces needed based on data from a table, the length of other inputs, or some other factor.

STRCMP( )

STRCMP(*string*, *string*)

This function compares two strings to determine whether the first string is before or after the second string in ASCII sequence. If the first string precedes the second string, –1 is returned. If the first follows the second, 1 is returned. If they are equal, 0 is returned. This function is often used for alphanumeric comparisons, but it is case-insensitive unless at least one of the strings given is binary. Here is an example:

```
SELECT * FROM
(SELECT STRCMP(
   SUBSTR(pre_req, 1, 8),
   SUBSTR(pre_req, 10, 8))
AS Comparison
FROM courses) AS derived1
WHERE Comparison = 1;
```

In this example, because course codes are all eight characters long, we use SUBSTR( ) to extract the first two course code numbers. Using STRCMP( ), we compare the two course codes to see if they're in sequence. To see only the results where the courses are out of sequence, we use a subquery with a WHERE clause to return only rows for which the STRCMP( ) returns a –1 value, indicating the two strings are not in sequence.

The problem with this statement is that some courses have more than two prerequisites. We would have to expand this statement to encompass them. However, that doesn't resolve the problem either; it provides only more indications of what we know. To reorder the data, it would be easier to create a simple script using one of the APIs to extract, reorder, and then replace the column values.

SUBSTR( )

```
SUBSTRING(string, position[, length])
SUBSTRING(string FROM position FOR length)
```

This function is an alias of `SUBSTRING( )`. See its description next for details and an example of its use.

SUBSTRING( )

```
SUBSTRING(string, position[, length])
SUBSTRING(string FROM position[ FOR length])
```

This function returns the characters of a given string, starting from the position given. The first character is numbered 1. You can restrict the length of the string retrieved by specifying a limit. The function is similar to `MID( )`. Here is an example:

```
SELECT CONCAT_WS('-',
   SUBSTRING(soc_sec, 1, 3),
   SUBSTRING(soc_sec FROM 4 FOR 2),
   SUBSTRING(soc_sec FROM 6)
)
AS 'Social Security Nbr.'
FROM students LIMIT 1;

+----------------------+
| Social Security Nbr. |
+----------------------+
| 433-12-3456          |
+----------------------+
```

This example shows the two syntaxes of `SUBSTRING( )` for reformatting a Social Security number (the U.S. federal tax identification number) stored without dashes. It uses `CONCAT_WS( )` to put the three pieces of data together, separated by the hyphen given.

SUBSTRING_INDEX( )

```
SUBSTRING_INDEX(string, delimiter, count)
```

This function returns a substring of ***string***, using ***delimiter*** to separate substrings and ***count*** to determine which of the substrings to return. Thus, a ***count*** of 1 returns the first substring, 2 returns the second, and so on. A negative number instructs the function to count from the right end. Here is an example:

```
SELECT SUBSTRING_INDEX(pre_req, '|', -1)
AS 'Last Prerequisite',
pre_req AS 'All Prerequisites'
FROM courses WHERE course_id = '1245';

+-------------------+---------------------------+
| Last Prerequisite | All Prerequisites         |
+-------------------+---------------------------+
```

```
| ENGL-202           | ENGL-101|ENGL-201|ENGL-202 |
+--------------------+---------------------------+
```

In this example, the `pre_req` column for each course contains prerequisite courses separated by vertical bars. The statement displays the last prerequisite, because –1 was entered for the count.

TRIM( )

`TRIM([[BOTH|LEADING|TRAILING] [padding] FROM] string)`

This function returns the given string with any trailing or leading padding removed, depending on which is specified. If neither is specified, `BOTH` is the default, causing both leading and trailing padding to be removed. The default padding is a space if none is specified. The function is multibyte-safe.

As an example, in a table containing the results of a student survey we notice that one of the columns that lists each student's favorite activities contains extra commas at the end of the comma-separated list of activities. This may have been caused by a problem in the web interface, which treated any activities that a student didn't select as blank values separated by commas at the end (e.g., `biking,reading,,,,`):

```
UPDATE student_surveys
SET favorite_activities =
TRIM(LEADING SPACE(1) FROM TRIM(TRAILING ',' FROM favorite_activities));
```

In this example, we're using `TRIM( )` twice: once to remove the trailing commas from the column `favorite_activities` and then again on those results to remove leading spaces. Since the functions are part of an `UPDATE` statement, the double-trimmed results are saved back to the table for the row for which the data was read. This is more verbose than it needs to be, though. Because a space is the default padding, we don't have to specify it. Also, because we want to remove both leading and trailing spaces and commas from the data, we don't have to specify `LEADING` or `TRAILING` and can allow the default of `BOTH` to be used. Making these adjustments, we get this tighter SQL statement:

```
UPDATE student_surveys
SET favorite_activities =
TRIM(TRIM(',' FROM favorite_activities));
```

If we suspected that the faulty web form also added extra commas between the text (not just at the end), we could wrap these concentric uses of `TRIM( )` within `REPLACE( )` to replace any occurrences of consecutive commas with a single comma:

```
UPDATE student_surveys
SET favorite_activities =
REPLACE(TRIM(TRIM(',' FROM favorite_activities)), ',,', ',');
```

UCASE( )

`UCASE(string)`

This function converts a given string to all uppercase letters. It's an alias of `UPPER( )`. Here is an example:

```
SELECT course_id AS 'Course ID',
UCASE(course_name) AS Course
FROM courses LIMIT 3;
```

```
+-----------+---------------------+
| Course ID | Course              |
+-----------+---------------------+
|      1245 | CREATIVE WRITING    |
|      1255 | PROFESSIONAL WRITING |
|      1244 | AMERICAN LITERATURE  |
+-----------+---------------------+
```

UNCOMPRESS( )

UNCOMPRESS(*string*)

This function returns the uncompressed string corresponding to the compressed string given, reversing the results of the COMPRESS( ) function. It requires MySQL to have been compiled with a compression library (e.g., zlib). It returns NULL if the string is not compressed or if MySQL wasn't compiled with zlib. This function is available as of version 4.1.1 of MySQL. Here is an example:

```
SELECT UNCOMPRESS(essay)
FROM applications_archive
WHERE applicant_id = '1748';
```

UNCOMPRESSED_LENGTH( )

UNCOMPRESSED_LENGTH(*string*)

This function returns the number of characters contained in the given compressed string before it was compressed. You can compress strings using the COMPRESS( ) function. This function is available as of version 4.1 of MySQL. Here is an example:

```
SELECT UNCOMPRESSED_LENGTH(COMPRESS(essay))
FROM student_applications
WHERE applicant_id = '1748';
```

UNHEX( )

UNHEX(*string*)

This function converts hexadecimal numbers to their character equivalents. It reverses the results of the HEX( ) function and is available as of version 4.1.2 of MySQL.

To illustrate its use, suppose that in a table we have a column with a binary character in the data; specifically, tabs were entered through a web interface using an API. However, the column is a VARCHAR data type. The problem is that when the data is retrieved, we want to line up all the results in our display by counting the length of each column, and a tab keeps the display from lining up vertically. So we want to fix the data. We can use UNHEX( ) to locate rows containing the binary character and then replace it with spaces instead:

```
UPDATE students
SET comments = REPLACE(comments, UNHEX(09), SPACE(4))
WHERE LOCATE(UNHEX(09), comments);
```

We've looked at an ASCII chart and seen that a tab is represented by the hexadecimal number `09`. Knowing that bit of information, in the `WHERE` clause we're passing that value to `UNHEX( )` to return the binary character for a tab, yielding the search string with which `LOCATE( )` will search the column `comments`. If it doesn't find a tab in the column for a row, it will return 0. Those rows will not be included in the search results. The ones that do contain tabs will have a value of 1 or greater and therefore will be included in the results. Using `UNHEX( )` along with `REPLACE( )` in the `SET` clause, we replace all tabs found with four spaces.

UPPER( )

`UPPER(`*`string`*`)`

This function converts a given string to all uppercase letters. It's an alias of `UCASE( )`. See that function's description earlier in this chapter for an example.

12

Date and Time Functions

By using temporal data type columns, you can use several built-in functions offered by MySQL. This chapter presents those functions. Currently, five temporal data types are available: `DATE`, `TIME`, `DATETIME`, `TIMESTAMP`, and `YEAR`. You would set a column to one of these data types when creating or altering a table. See the descriptions of `CREATE TABLE` and `ALTER TABLE` in Chapter 6 for more details. The `DATE` column type can be used for recording just the date. It uses the *`yyyy-mm-dd`* format. The `TIME` column type is for recording time in the *`hhh:mm:ss`* format. To record a combination of date and time, use `DATETIME`: *`yyyy-mm-dd hh:mm:ss`*. The `TIMESTAMP` column is similar to `DATETIME`, but it is more limited in its range of allowable time: it starts at the Unix epoch time (i.e., 1970-01-01) and stops at the end of 2037. Plus, it has the distinction of resetting its value automatically when the row in which it is contained is updated, unless you specifically instruct MySQL otherwise. Finally, the `YEAR` data type is used only for recording the year in a column. For more information on date and time data types, see Appendix B.

Any function that calls for a date or a time data type will also accept a combined datetime data type. MySQL requires that months range from 0 to 12 and that days range from 0 to 31. Therefore, a date such as February 30 would be accepted prior to version 5.0.2 of MySQL. Beginning in version 5.0.2, MySQL offers more refined validation that would reject such a date. However, some date functions accept 0 for some or all components of a date, or incomplete date information (e.g., 2008-06-00). As a general rule, the date and time functions that extract part of a date value usually accept incomplete dates, but date and time functions that require complete date information return NULL when given an incomplete date. The descriptions of these functions in this chapter indicate which require valid dates and which don't, as well as which return 0 or NULL for invalid dates.

The bulk of this chapter consists of an alphabetical listing of date and time functions, with explanations of each. Each of the explanations include an example of the function's use, along with a resulting display, if any. For the examples in this chapter, I used the scenario of a professional services firm (e.g., a law firm or an investment advisory firm) that tracks appointments and seminars in MySQL. For help locating the appropriate function, see the next section or the index at the end of this book.

Date and Time Functions Grouped by Type

Following are lists of date and time functions, grouped according to their purpose: to retrieve the date or time, to extract an element from a given date or time, or to perform calculations on given dates or times.

Determining the Date or Time

CURDATE( ), CURRENT_DATE( ), CURRENT_TIME( ), CURRENT_TIMESTAMP( ), CURTIME( ), LOCALTIME( ), LOCALTIMESTAMP( ), NOW( ), SYSDATE( ), UNIX_TIMESTAMP( ), UTC_DATE( ), UTC_TIME( ), UTC_TIMESTAMP( ).

Extracting and Formatting the Date or Time

DATE( ), DATE_FORMAT( ), DAY( ), DAYNAME( ), DAYOFMONTH( ), DAYOFWEEK( ), DAYOFYEAR( ), EXTRACT( ), GET_FORMAT( ), HOUR( ), LAST_DAY( ), MAKEDATE( ), MAKETIME( ), MICROSECOND( ), MINUTE( ), MONTH( ), MONTHNAME( ), QUARTER( ), SECOND( ), STR_TO_DATE( ), TIME( ), TIME_FORMAT( ), TIMESTAMP( ), WEEK( ), WEEKDAY( ), WEEKOFYEAR( ), YEAR( ), YEARWEEK( ).

Calculating and Modifying the Date or Time

ADDDATE( ), ADDTIME( ), CONVERT_TZ( ), DATE_ADD( ), DATE_SUB( ), DATEDIFF( ), FROM_DAYS( ), FROM_UNIXTIME( ), PERIOD_ADD( ), PERIOD_DIFF( ), SEC_TO_TIME( ), SLEEP( ), SUBDATE( ), SUBTIME( ), TIME_TO_SEC( ), TIMEDIFF( ), TIMESTAMPADD( ), TIMESTAMPDIFF( ), TO_DAYS( ).

Date and Time Functions in Alphabetical Order

The rest of the chapter lists each function in alphabetical order.

ADDDATE( )

ADDDATE(*date*, INTERVAL *value type*)
ADDDATE(*date*, *days*)

This function adds the given interval of time to the date or time provided. This is a synonym for DATE_ADD( ); see its definition later in this chapter for details and interval types. The second, simpler syntax is available as of version 4.1 of MySQL. This shorthand syntax does not work, though, with DATE_ADD( ). Here is an example:

```
UPDATE seminars
SET seminar_date = ADDDATE(seminar_date, INTERVAL 1 MONTH)
WHERE seminar_date = '2007-12-01';
```

```
UPDATE seminars
SET seminar_date = ADDDATE(seminar_date, 7)
WHERE seminar_date = '2007-12-15';
```

The first SQL statement postpones a seminar that was scheduled for December 1, 2007 to a month later (January 1, 2008). The second statement postpones the seminar on December 15 to December 22, seven days later.

ADDTIME( )

`ADDTIME(`*`datetime, datetime`*`)`

This function returns the date and time for a given string or column (in *time* or *datetime* format), incremented by the time given as the second argument. If a negative number is given, the time is subtracted. In this case, the function is the equivalent of `SUBTIME( )`. This function is available as of version 4.1.1 of MySQL. Here is an example:


```
SELECT NOW( ) AS Now,
ADDTIME(NOW( ), '1:00:00.00') AS 'Hour Later';

+---------------------+---------------------+
| Now                 | Hour Later          |
+---------------------+---------------------+
| 2007-01-11 23:20:30 | 2007-01-12 00:20:30 |
+---------------------+---------------------+
```

Notice that the hour is increased by one, and because the time is near midnight, the function causes the date to be altered by one day as well. To increase the date, add the number of days before the time (separated by a space) like so:

```
SELECT NOW( ) AS Now,
ADDTIME(NOW( ), '30 0:0:0') AS 'Thirty Days Later';

+---------------------+---------------------+
| Now                 | Thirty Days Later   |
+---------------------+---------------------+
| 2007-01-11 23:20:30 | 2007-02-10 23:20:30 |
+---------------------+---------------------+
```

CONVERT_TZ( )

`CONVERT_TZ(`*`datetime, time_zone, time_zone`*`)`

This function converts a given date and time from the first time zone given to the second. It requires time zone tables to be installed in the `mysql` database. If they are not already installed on your system, go to MySQL AB's web site (*http://dev.mysql.com/downloads/timezones.html*) to download the tables. Copy them into the *mysql* subdirectory of the *data* directory of MySQL. Change the ownership to the *mysql* system user and change the user permissions with system commands such as `chown` and `chmod`, and restart the server. This function is available as of version 4.1.3 of MySQL. Here is an example:

```
SELECT NOW() AS 'New Orleans',
CONVERT_TZ(NOW(), 'US/Central', 'Europe/Rome')
e')
```

```
AS Milan;

+---------------------+---------------------+
| New Orleans         | Milan               |
+---------------------+---------------------|
| 2007-03-12 20:56:15 | 2007-03-13 02:56:15 |
+---------------------+---------------------+
```

This example retrieves the current time of the server, which for the sake of this example is located in New Orleans, and converts this time to the time in Milan. Notice that we're using the named time zone of `Europe/Rome`. There's isn't a `Europe/Milan` choice. If a named time zone that doesn't exist is given, a NULL value is returned for that field. To find the named time zones available, check the `time_zone_name` table in the `mysql` database:

```
SELECT Name
FROM mysql.time_zone_name
me
WHERE Name LIKE '%Europe%';
```

This will list all of the time zone names for Europe. From here, you can scan the list for one in the same zone and close to the city that you want. Incidentally, if you're converting times with this function for tables you've locked, the `time_zone_name` table will need to be locked, too.

CURDATE( )

```
CURDATE( )
```

This function returns the current system date in *yyyy-mm-dd* format. It will return the date in a *yyyymmdd* format (a numeric format) if it's used as part of a numeric calculation. You can use the function in `SELECT` statements as shown here, in `INSERT` and `UPDATE` statements to set a value, or in a `WHERE` clause. `CURDATE( )` is synonymous with `CURRENT_DATE( )`; see its definition next for more details. Here is an example:

```
SELECT CURDATE() AS Today,
CURDATE() + 1 AS Tomorrow;
ow;

+------------+----------+
| Today      | Tomorrow |
+------------+----------+
| 2007-01-15 | 20070116 |
+------------+----------+
```

Because the second use of the function here involves a numeric calculation, tomorrow's date is displayed without dashes. If you only want to convert a date to the numeric format, just add 0. To keep the format the same, use this function together with a function such as `ADDDATE( )`.

CURRENT_DATE( )

```
CURRENT_DATE( )
```

This function returns the current date. The usual parentheses are not required. It's synonymous with `CURDATE( )`. You can use either in `SELECT` statements, as well as `INSERT` and `UPDATE` statements to dynamically set values, or in `WHERE` clauses. Here is an example:

```
UPDATE appointment
SET appt_date = CURRENT_DATE( )
WHERE appt_id = '1250';
```

This statement changes the appointment date for a client who came in today unexpectedly.

CURRENT_TIME( )

CURRENT_TIME( )

This function returns the current time in *hh:mm:ss* format. It will return the time in the *hhmmss* format (numeric format) if it's used as part of a numeric calculation. The parentheses are not required. It's synonymous with `CURTIME( )`. Here is an example:

```
INSERT INTO appointments
(client_id, appt_date, start_time)
VALUES('1403', CURRENT_DATE( ), CURRENT_TIME);
```

In this example, we're logging an unscheduled appointment that has just begun so that we can bill the client later. Of course, it's easy enough to use one `datetime` column with the `NOW( )` function for inserting data, and use other functions for extracting separate components later.

CURRENT_TIMESTAMP( )

CURRENT_TIMESTAMP( )

This function returns the current date and time in *yyyy-mm-dd hh:mm:ss* format. It will return the time in a *yyyymmddhhmmss* format (numeric format) if it's used as part of a numeric calculation. Parentheses aren't required. It's a synonym of `NOW( )`. Here is an example:

```
SELECT CURRENT_TIMESTAMP() AS Now,
CURRENT_TIMESTAMP() + 10000 AS 'Hour Later';
r';

+---------------------+----------------+
| Now                 | Hour Later     |
+---------------------+----------------+
| 2008-01-12 16:41:47 | 20080112174147 |
+---------------------+----------------+
```

By adding 10,000 to the current time, the hour is increased by 1 and the minutes and seconds by 0 each, and the time is displayed in the second field without dashes. This is in line with the *yyyymmddhhmmss* format involved in numeric calculations, with the numbers right-justified.

CURTIME( )

CURTIME( )

This function returns the current system time in *hh:mm:ss* format. It will return the time in an *hhmmss* format (numeric format) if it's used as part of a numeric calculation. This is an alias for CURRENT_TIME( ). Here is an example:

```
SELECT CURTIME() AS Now,
CURTIME() + 10000 AS 'Hour Later';
r';

+----------+------------+
| Now      | Hour Later |
+----------+------------+
| 16:35:43 |     163543 |
+----------+------------+
```

By adding 10,000 to the current time, this statement increases the hour by 1 and the minutes and seconds by 0 each. This is in keeping with the *yyyymmddhhmmss* format previously mentioned.

DATE( )

DATE(*expression*)

This function returns the date from a given string, value, or expression that is submitted in a date or datetime format. This function is available as of version 4.1.1 of MySQL. Here is an example:

```
SELECT appointment, DATE(appointment)
FROM appointments
WHERE client_id = '8639' LIMIT 1;

+---------------------+-------------------+
| appointment         | DATE(appointment) |
+---------------------+-------------------+
| 2008-01-11 14:11:43 | 2008-01-11        |
+---------------------+-------------------+
```

In this SQL statement, the value of the appointment column, which is a DATETIME type column, is shown first. The second field is the date extracted by the function from the same column and row.

DATE_ADD( )

DATE_ADD(*date*, INTERVAL *number type*)

Using the date or datetime given, this function adds the number of intervals specified. It's fairly synonymous with the ADDDATE( ) function. If none of the parameters include datetime or time factors, the results will be returned in date format. Otherwise, the results will be in datetime format. See Table 12-1 for a list of intervals permitted. Here is an example:

```
UPDATE appointments
SET appt_date = DATE_ADD(appt_date, INTERVAL 1 DAY)
WHERE appt_id='1202';
```

In this example, the appointment date is changed to its current value plus one additional day to postpone the appointment by a day. If we changed the 1 to –1, MySQL would subtract a day instead. This would make the function the equivalent of `DATE_SUB( )`.

If you leave out some numbers in the second argument, MySQL assumes that the leftmost interval factors are 0 and are just not given. In the following example, although we're using the interval `HOUR_SECOND`, we're not giving the number of hours and the function still works—assuming we don't mean 5 hours and 30 minutes later. MySQL assumes here that we mean `'00:05:30'` and not `'05:30:00'`:

```
SELECT NOW( ) AS 'Now',
DATE_ADD(NOW( ), INTERVAL '05:30' HOUR_SECOND)
AS 'Later';

+---------------------+---------------------+
| Now                 | Later               |
+---------------------+---------------------+
| 2007-03-14 10:57:05 | 2007-03-14 11:02:35 |
+---------------------+---------------------+
```


When adding the intervals `MONTH`, `YEAR`, or `YEAR_MONTH` to a date, if the given date is valid but the results would be an invalid date because it would be beyond the end of a month, the results are adjusted to the end of the month:

```
SELECT DATE_ADD('2009-01-29', INTERVAL 1 MONTH)
AS 'One Month Later';

+-----------------+
| One Month Later |
+-----------------+
| 2009-02-28      |
+-----------------+
```

Table 12-1 shows the intervals that may be used and how the data should be ordered. For interval values that require more than one factor, a delimiter is used and the data must be enclosed in quotes. Other delimiters may be used besides those shown in the table. For example, *'hh|mm|ss'* could be used for `HOUR_SECOND`. In case you hadn't noticed, the names for intervals involving more than two time factors use the name of the first and last factor (e.g., `DAY_MINUTE` and not `DAY_HOUR_MINUTE`). Keep that in mind when trying to remember the correct interval.

Table 12-1. DATE_ADD( ) intervals and formats

INTERVAL	Format for given values
DAY	*dd*
DAY_HOUR	*'dd hh'*
DAY_MICROSECOND	*'dd.nn'*
DAY_MINUTE	*'dd hh:mm'*
DAY_SECOND	*'dd hh:mm:ss'*

INTERVAL	Format for given values
HOUR	*hh*
HOUR_MICROSECOND	'*hh.nn*'
HOUR_MINUTE	'*hh:mm*'
HOUR_SECOND	'*hh:mm:ss*'
MICROSECOND	*nn*
MINUTE	*mm*
MINUTE_MICROSECOND	'*mm.nn*'
MINUTE_SECOND	'*mm:ss*'
MONTH	*mm*
QUARTER	*qq*
SECOND	*ss*
SECOND_MICROSECOND	'*ss.nn*'
WEEK	*ww*
YEAR	*yy*
YEAR_MONTH	'*yy-mm*'

DATE_FORMAT( )

DATE_FORMAT(*date*, '*format_code*')

This function returns a date and time in a desired format, based on formatting codes listed within quotes for the second argument of the function. Here is an example:

```
SELECT DATE_FORMAT(appointment, '%W - %M %e, %Y at %r')
AS 'Appointment'
FROM appointments
WHERE client_id = '8392'
AND appointment > CURDATE( );

+--------------------------------------+
| Appointment                          |
+--------------------------------------+
| Monday - June 16, 2008 at 01:00:00 PM |
+--------------------------------------+
```

Using the formatting codes, we're specifying in this example that we want the name of the day of the week (`%W`) followed by a dash and then the date of the appointment in a typical U.S. format (`%M %e, %Y`), with the month name and a comma after the day. We're ending with the word "at" followed by the full nonmilitary time (`%r`). The results are returned as a binary string.

As of MySQL version 5.1.15, a string is returned along with the character set and collation of the string, taken from the `character_set_connection` and the `collation_connection` system variables. This allows the function to return non-ASCII characters. Here is an example of this function:

```
SELECT NOW( ),
DATE_FORMAT(NOW( ), '%M') AS 'Month in Hebrew';

+---------------------+-----------------+
| Now                 | Month in Hebrew |
+---------------------+-----------------+
| 2008-03-14 12:00:24 | מרץ             |
+---------------------+-----------------+
```

In this example, of course, the client and server were set to display Hebrew characters. Also, the server variable `lc_time_names` was set to Hebrew (`he_IL`) so as to return the Hebrew word for March. See MySQL's documentation page on *MySQL Server Locale Support* (*http://dev.mysql.com/doc/refman/5.1/en/locale-support.html*) for a list of locale values available for time names.

Table 12-2 contains a list of all the formatting codes you can use with `DATE_FORMAT( )`. You can also use these codes with `TIME_FORMAT( )` and `EXTRACT( )`.

Table 12-2. DATE_FORMAT( ) format codes and resulting formats

Code	Description	Results
%%	A literal '%'	
%a	Abbreviated weekday name	(Sun...Sat)
%b	Abbreviated month name	(Jan...Dec)
%c	Month, numeric	(1...12)
%d	Day of the month, numeric	(00...31)
%D	Day of the month with English suffix	(1st, 2nd, 3rd, etc.)
%e	Day of the month, numeric	(0...31)
%f	Microseconds, numeric	(000000...999999)
%h	Hour	(01...12)
%H	Hour	(00...23)
%i	Minutes, numeric	(00...59)
%I	Hour	(01...12)
%j	Day of the year	(001...366)
%k	Hour	(0...23)
%l	Hour	(1...12)
%m	Month, numeric	(01...12)
%M	Month name	(January...December)
%p	A.M. or P.M.	A.M. or P.M.
%r	Time, 12-hour	(hh:mm:ss [AM|PM])
%s	Seconds	(00...59)
%S	Seconds	(00...59)
%T	Time, 24-hour	(hh:mm:ss)

Code	Description	Results
%u	Week, where Monday is the first day of the week	(0...52)
%U	Week, where Sunday is the first day of the week	(0...52)
%v	Week, where Monday is the first day of the week; used with %x	(1...53)
%V	Week, where Sunday is the first day of the week; used with %X	(1...53)
%w	Day of the week	(0=Sunday...6=Saturday)
%W	Weekday name	(Sunday...Saturday)
%x	Year for the week, where Monday is the first day of the week, numeric, four digits; used with %v	(yyyy)
%X	Year for the week, where Sunday is the first day of the week, numeric, four digits; used with %V	(yyyy)
%y	Year, numeric, two digits	(yy)
%Y	Year, numeric, four digits	(yyyy)

DATE_SUB( )

`DATE_SUB(`*`date`*`, INTERVAL `*`number type`*`)`

Use this function to subtract from the results of a date or time data type column. See Table 12-1, under the description of `DATE_ADD( )`, for a list of interval types. Here is an example of this function:

```
SELECT NOW( ) AS Today,
DATE_SUB(NOW( ), INTERVAL 1 DAY)
AS Yesterday;

+---------------------+---------------------+
| Today               | Yesterday           |
+---------------------+---------------------+
| 2007-05-14 14:26:54 | 2007-05-13 14:26:54 |
+---------------------+---------------------+
```

Notice in this example that the time remains unchanged, but the date was reduced by one day. If you place a negative sign in front of the value 1, the reverse effect will occur, giving a result of May 15 in this example. Any intervals that can be used with `DATE_ADD( )` can also be used with `DATE_SUB( )`.

DATEDIFF( )

`DATEDIFF(`*`date`*`, `*`date`*`)`

This function returns the number of days of difference between the two dates given. Although a parameter may be given in date and time format, only the dates are used for determining the difference. This function is available as of version 4.1.1 of MySQL. Here is an example:

```
SELECT CURDATE( ) AS Today,
DATEDIFF('2008-12-25', NOW( ))
AS 'Days to Christmas';
```

```
+------------+-------------------+
| Today      | Days to Christmas |
+------------+-------------------+
| 2008-03-14 |               286 |
+------------+-------------------+
```

DAY( )

DAY(*date*)

This function returns the day of the month for a given date. It's available as of version 4.1.1 of MySQL and is synonymous with the DAYOFMONTH( ) function, described later. Here is an example:

```
SELECT DAY('2008-12-15')
AS 'Day';

+-------+
| Day   |
+-------+
|    15 |
+-------+
```

This function is more meaningful when applied to a date column where the date is unknown before entering the SQL statement.

DAYNAME( )

DAYNAME(*date*)

This function returns the name of the day for the date provided. As of MySQL version 5.1.15, the lc_time_names system variable will be consulted to determine the actual set of names to use. Use the SET statement to change this variable. See MySQL's documentation page on *MySQL Server Locale Support* (*http://dev.mysql.com/doc/refman/5.1/en/locale-support.html*) for a list of locale values available for time names. Here is an example:

```
SELECT appt_date AS Appointment,
DAYNAME(appt_date) AS 'Day of Week'
FROM appointments
WHERE appt_id = '1439';

+---------------------+-------------+
| Date of Appointment | Day of Week |
+---------------------+-------------+
| 2008-03-14          | Friday      |
+---------------------+-------------+

SET lc_time_names = 'it_IT';

SELECT appt_date AS Appointment,
DAYNAME(appt_date) AS ''Day of Week in Italian'
FROM appointments
WHERE appt_id = '1439';
```

```
+---------------------+-----------------------+
| Date of Appointment | Day of Week in Italian |
+---------------------+-----------------------+
| 2008-03-14          | venerdì               |
+---------------------+-----------------------+
```

For this example, I have set `character_set_client`, `character_set_connection`, and `character_set_results` to `utf8`, and set my terminal program to UTF-8 characters. Incidentally, the day of the week here is in lowercase because this is how it's written in Italian.

DAYOFMONTH( )

DAYOFMONTH(*date*)

This function returns the day of the month for the date given. If the day for the date is beyond the end of the month (e.g., '2008-02-30'), the function returns NULL along with a warning that can be retrieved with SHOW WARNINGS. Here is an example:

```
SELECT DAYOFMONTH('2008-02-28') AS 'A Good Day',
DAYOFMONTH('2008-02-30') AS 'A Bad Day';

+------------+-----------+
| A Good Day | A Bad Day |
+------------+-----------+
|         28 |      NULL |
+------------+-----------+
1 row in set, 1 warning (0.00 sec)

SHOW WARNINGS;

+---------+------+----------------------------------------------+
| Level   | Code | Message                                      |
+---------+------+----------------------------------------------+
| Warning | 1292 | Truncated incorrect datetime value: '2008-02-30' |
+---------+------+----------------------------------------------+
```

Prior to MySQL version 5.0.2, invalid dates such as this were permitted. The function would have returned 30 for a value of '2008-02-30'. If you wish to allow invalid dates, start your server with this line in your options file:

```
sql_mode = 'TRADITIONAL,ALLOW_INVALID_DATES'
```

DAYOFWEEK( )

DAYOFWEEK(*date*)

This function returns the numerical day of the week for a given date. Sunday returns a value of 1, and Saturday returns a value of 7. Here is an example:

```
SELECT DAYOFWEEK('2008-11-03') AS 'Day of Week',
DAYNAME('2008-11-03') AS 'Name of Day';

+-------------+-------------+
| Day of Week | Name of Day |
+-------------+-------------+
```

```
|            2 | Monday      |
+-------------+-------------+
```

DAYOFYEAR( )

`DAYOFYEAR(`*`date`*`)`

This function returns the day of the year. January 1 would give a value of 1, and December 31 would normally be 365, except in leap years, when it would be 366. Here is an example:

```
SELECT DAYOFYEAR('2008-03-01') AS 'FirstDate',
DAYOFYEAR('2008-02-28') AS 'SecondDate',
(DAYOFYEAR('2008-03-01') - DAYOFYEAR('2008-02-28')) AS 'Days Apart',
DAYOFYEAR('2008-12-31') AS 'Last Day of Year';

+------------+-------------+------------+------------------+
| First Date | Second Date | Days Apart | Last Day of Year |
+------------+-------------+------------+------------------+
|         61 |          59 |          2 |              366 |
+------------+-------------+------------+------------------+
```

In the third field, we are using the function to calculate the number of days from the first date to the second date. Since 2008 is a leap year, the result is 2 and the last field shows 366 for the last day of the year.

EXTRACT( )

`EXTRACT(`*`type`*` FROM `*`expression`*`)`

This function extracts date or time information from a date or a datetime expression in the format type requested. The acceptable types are the same as the intervals for `DATE_ADD( )`. See Table 12-1 earlier in this chapter under that function for a list of intervals permitted. Here is an example:

```
SELECT NOW( ) AS 'Time Now',
EXTRACT(HOUR_MINUTE FROM NOW( )) AS "Now in 'hhmm' format";

+---------------------+----------------------+
| Time Now            | Now in 'hhmm' format |
+---------------------+----------------------+
| 2008-03-14 20:36:04 |                 2036 |
+---------------------+----------------------+
```

FROM_DAYS( )

`FROM_DAYS(`*`value`*`)`

This function returns the date based on the number of days given, which are from the beginning of the currently used standard calendar. Problems occur for dates before 1582, when the Gregorian calendar became the standard. The opposite of this function is `TO_DAYS( )`. Here is an example:

```
SELECT FROM_DAYS((365.25*2008))
AS 'Start of 2008?', FROM_DAYS(366);
```

```
+-----------------+
| Start of 2008?  |
+-----------------+
| 2008-01-16      |
+-----------------+
```

Assuming that there are 365.25 days in a year on average (allowing for the leap year), you would think that multiplying that factor by 2008 would give a result of January 1, 2008, but it doesn't because of the calendar change centuries ago. This function is possibly useful for comparing dates and displaying the results in a readable format. However, since there are many other functions available in MySQL, its usefulness is fairly diminished. Here is an example:

```
SELECT CURDATE( ) As 'Now',
TO_DAYS(NOW( )) AS 'Days since Day 0',
FROM_DAYS(TO_DAYS(NOW( )) + 7) AS '7 Days from Now',
ADDDATE(CURDATE( ), 7) AS 'Simpler Method';

+------------+------------------+-----------------+----------------+
| Now        | Days since Day 0 | 7 Days from Now | Simpler Method |
+------------+------------------+-----------------+----------------+
| 2007-03-14 |           733114 | 2007-03-21      | 2007-03-21     |
+------------+------------------+-----------------+----------------+
```

FROM_UNIXTIME( )

`FROM_UNIXTIME(`*`unix_timestamp`*`[, `*`format`*`])`

This function returns the date based on Unix time, which is the number of seconds since January 1, 1970, Greenwich Mean Time (GMT), with 12:00:01 being the first second of Unix time (the epoch). The second, optional argument formats the results using the formatting codes from `DATE_FORMAT( )`. The function returns the date and time in the *yyyy-mm-dd hh:mm:ss* format, unless it's part of a numeric expression. Then it returns the data in the *yyyymmdd* format. Here is an example:

```
SELECT FROM_UNIXTIME(0) AS 'My Epoch Start',
UNIX_TIMESTAMP( ) AS 'Now in Unix Terms',
FROM_UNIXTIME(UNIX_TIMESTAMP( )) AS 'Now in Human Terms';

+---------------------+-------------------+---------------------+
| My Epoch Start      | Now in Unix Terms | Now in Human Terms  |
+---------------------+-------------------+---------------------+
| 1969-12-31 18:00:00 |        1173928232 | 2007-03-14 22:10:32 |
+---------------------+-------------------+---------------------+
```

Here we're selecting the date based on zero seconds since the start of Unix time. The results are off by six hours because the server's not located in the GMT zone. This function is typically used on columns whose values were derived from `UNIX_TIMESTAMP( )`, as shown in the third field of the example.

GET_FORMAT( )

`GET_FORMAT(`*`data_type, standard`*`)`

This function returns the format for a given data type, based on the standard given as the second argument. The format codes returned are the same codes used by the DATE_FORMAT( ) function. The data type may be DATE, TIME, DATETIME, or TIMESTAMP, and the format type may be EUR, INTERNAL, ISO, JIS, or USA. This function is available as of version 4.1.1 of MySQL. The TIMESTAMP data type isn't acceptable until version 4.1.4.

Here's an example using the function that returns the USA format:

```
SELECT GET_FORMAT(DATE, 'USA') AS 'US Format',
GET_FORMAT(DATE, 'EUR') AS 'European Format';

+-----------+-----------------+
| US Format | European Format |
+-----------+-----------------+
| %m.%d.%Y  | %d.%m.%Y        |
+-----------+-----------------+
```

I wouldn't say that using the period as the separator is very American, but the order of day followed by month is in keeping with American standards, and the day preceding the month is European. You can hand off the results of the function to DATE_FORMAT( ) to format the value of a date column like so:

```
SELECT appointment,
DATE_FORMAT(appointment, GET_FORMAT(DATE, 'USA'))
AS 'Appointment'
WHERE apt_id = '8382';

+-------------+-------------+
| appointment | Appointment |
+-------------+-------------+
| 2008-03-15  | 03.15.2008  |
+-------------+-------------+
```

Table 12-3 lists the results for the different combinations. The ISO standard refers to ISO 9075. The data type of TIMESTAMP is not listed because the results are the same as DATETIME.

Table 12-3. DATE_FORMAT arguments and their results

Combination	Results
DATE, 'EUR'	%d.%m.%Y
DATE, 'INTERNAL'	%Y%m%d
DATE, 'ISO'	%Y-%m-%d
DATE, 'JIS'	%Y-%m-%d
DATE, 'USA'	%m.%d.%Y
TIME, 'EUR'	%H.%i.%S
TIME, 'INTERNAL'	%H%i%s
TIME, 'ISO'	%H:%i:%s
TIME, 'JIS'	%H:%i:%s
TIME, 'USA'	%h:%i:%s %p
DATETIME, 'EUR'	%Y-%m-%d-%H.%i.%s

Combination	Results
DATETIME, 'INTERNAL'	%Y%m%d%H%i%s
DATETIME, 'ISO'	%Y-%m-%d %H:%i:%s
DATETIME, 'JIS'	%Y-%m-%d %H:%i:%s
DATETIME, 'USA'	%Y-%m-%d-%H.%i.%s

HOUR( )

HOUR(*time*)

This function returns the hour for the time given. For columns containing the time of day (e.g., DATETIME), the range of results will be from 0 to 23. For TIME data type columns that contain data not restricted to day limits, this function may return values greater than 23. Here is an example:

```
SELECT appt_id, appointment,
HOUR(appointment) AS 'Hour of Appointment'
FROM appointments
WHERE client_id = '3992'
AND appointment > CURDATE( );

+---------+---------------------+---------------------+
| appt_id | appointment         | Hour of Appointment |
+---------+---------------------+---------------------+
| 8393    | 2008-03-15 13:00:00 |                  13 |
+---------+---------------------+---------------------+
```

This statement is selecting the upcoming appointment for a particular client. The hour is returned in military time (i.e., 13 is 1 P.M.).

LAST_DAY( )

LAST_DAY(*date*)

This function returns the date of the last day of the month for a given date or datetime value. NULL is returned for invalid dates. It's available as of version 4.1.1 of MySQL. Here is an example:

```
SELECT LAST_DAY('2008-12-15')
AS 'End of Month';

+--------------+
| End of Month |
+--------------+
| 2008-12-31   |
+--------------+
```

There is no FIRST_DAY( ) function at this time. However, you can use LAST_DAY( ) in conjunction with a couple of other functions to return the first day of the month:

```
SELECT CURDATE( ) AS 'Today',
ADDDATE(LAST_DAY(SUBDATE(CURDATE(), INTERVAL 1 MONTH)), 1)
AS 'First Day of Month';
```

```
+------------+-------------------+
| Today      | First Day of Month |
+------------+-------------------+
| 2008-06-18 | 2008-06-01         |
+------------+-------------------+
```

In this example, we are subtracting one month from the results of CURDATE( ) to get the same day last month. From there, we're using LAST_DAY( ) to find the last day of last month. Then ADDDATE( ) is employed to add one day to the results, to find the first day of the month after last month, that is to say, the current month. This method adjusts for dates in January that would involve a previous year.

LOCALTIME( )

LOCALTIME( )

This function returns the current system date in *yyyy-mm-dd hh:mm:ss* format. When part of a calculation, the results are in the numeric format of *yyyymmddhhmmss.nnnnnn*, which has placeholders for macroseconds. The parentheses are not required. It's available as of version 4.0.6 of MySQL and is synonymous with LOCALTIMESTAMP( ) and NOW( ). Here is an example:

```
SELECT LOCALTIME( ) AS 'Local Time',
LOCALTIME( ) + 0 AS 'Local Time as Numeric';

+---------------------+-----------------------+
| Local Time          | Local Time as Numeric |
+---------------------+-----------------------+
| 2007-03-15 01:53:16 | 20070315015316.000000 |
+---------------------+-----------------------+
```

LOCALTIMESTAMP( )

LOCALTIMESTAMP( )

This function returns the current system date in *yyyy-mm-dd hh:mm:ss* format. When part of a calculation, the results are in the numeric format of *yyyymmddhhmmss.nnnnnn*, which has placeholders for macroseconds. It's synonymous with LOCALTIMESTAMP( ) and NOW( ). Here is an example:

```
UPDATE appointments
SET end_time = LOCALTIME( )
WHERE appt_id = '8839';
```

MAKEDATE( )

MAKEDATE(*year*, *days*)

This function determines the date requested from the start of the given year, by adding the number of days given in the second argument. It returns the date in the *yyyy-mm-dd* format. It returns NULL if a value given for *days* is not greater than 0. It will accept more than a year's worth of days, though. It just returns a date into the next year or whatever year is appropriate, based on however many days the result is from the beginning of the year given. This function is available as of version 4.1.1 of MySQL. Here is an example:

```
SELECT MAKEDATE(2009, 1) AS 'First Day',
MAKEDATE(2009, 365) AS 'Last Day',
MAKEDATE(2009, 366) AS 'One More Day';

+------------+------------+--------------+
| First Day  | Last Day   | One More Day |
+------------+------------+--------------+
| 2009-01-01 | 2009-12-31 | 2010-01-01   |
+------------+------------+--------------+
```

MAKETIME( )

`MAKETIME(`*`hour, minute, second`*`)`

This function converts a given hour, minute, and second to *hh:mm:ss* format. It returns NULL if the value for the *minute* or the *second* values are greater than 59. It will accept an hour value greater than 24, though. This function is available as of version 4.1.1 of MySQL. Here is an example:

```
SELECT MAKETIME(14, 32, 5)
AS Time;

+----------+
| Time     |
+----------+
| 14:32:05 |
+----------+
```

MICROSECOND( )

`MICROSECOND(`*`time`*`)`

This function extracts the microseconds value of a given time. It displays the resulting number in six characters, padded with zeros to the right. When a date or datetime is given that does not include a specific value for microseconds, a value of zero microseconds is assumed. Therefore, 000000 is returned. This function is available as of version 4.1.1 of MySQL. Here is an example:

```
SELECT MICROSECOND('2008-01-11 19:28:45.82')
AS 'MicroSecond';

+-------------+
| MicroSecond |
+-------------+
|      820000 |
+-------------+
```

MINUTE( )

`MINUTE(`*`time`*`)`

This function returns the minute value (0–59) of a given time. Here is an example:

```
SELECT CONCAT(HOUR(appointment), ':',
MINUTE(appointment)) AS 'Appointment'
FROM appointments
WHERE client_id = '3992'
AND appointment > CURDATE( );

+-------------+
| Appointment |
+-------------+
|       13:30 |
+-------------+
```

This statement is using the string function `CONCAT( )` to paste together the hour and the minute, with a colon as a separator. Of course, a function such as `DATE_FORMAT( )` would be a better choice for such a task. If an invalid time is given (e.g., minutes or seconds in excess of 59), NULL is returned and a warning issued:

```
SELECT MINUTE('13:60:00') AS 'Bad Time',
MINUTE('13:30:00') AS 'Good Time';

+----------+-----------+
| Bad Time | Good Time |
+----------+-----------+
|     NULL |        30 |
+----------+-----------+
1 row in set, 1 warning (0.00 sec)

SHOW WARNINGS;

+---------+------+------------------------------------------+
| Level   | Code | Message                                  |
+---------+------+------------------------------------------+
| Warning | 1292 | Truncated incorrect time value: '13:60:00' |
+---------+------+------------------------------------------+
```

MONTH( )

`MONTH(`*`date`*`)`

This function returns the numeric value of the month (0–12) for the date provided. Since a date column can contain a zero value (e.g., `'0000-00-00'`), the function will return 0 for those situations. However, for nonzero invalid dates given, NULL is returned. Here is an example:

```
SELECT appointment AS 'Appointment',
MONTH(appointment) AS 'Month of Appointment'
FROM appointments
WHERE client_id = '8302'
AND appointment > CURRDATE( );

+-------------+----------------------+
| Appointment | Month of Appointment |
+-------------+----------------------+
| 2008-06-15  |                    6 |
+-------------+----------------------+
```

This SQL statement is retrieving the month of any appointments after the current date for a particular client. There's only one appointment, and it's in June.

MONTHNAME( )

MONTHNAME(*date*)

This function returns the name of the month for the date provided. As of version 5.1.15 of MySQL, the `lc_time_names` system variable is used to determine the actual set of names to use. Use the `SET` statement to change this variable. See the MySQL documentation page on *MySQL Server Locale Support* (*http://dev.mysql.com/doc/refman/5.1/en/locale-support.html*) for a list of locale values available for time names. Here is an example:

```
SELECT appointment AS 'Appointment',
MONTHNAME(appointment) AS 'Month of Appointment'
FROM appointments
WHERE client_id = '8302'
AND appointment > NOW( );

+-------------+----------------------+
| Appointment | Month of Appointment |
+-------------+----------------------+
| 2008-03-15  | March                |
+-------------+----------------------+

SET lc_time_names = 'it_IT';

+-------------+----------------------+
| Appointment | Month of Appointment |
+-------------+----------------------+
| 2008-03-15  | marzo                |
+-------------+----------------------+
```

In this example, the client has only one appointment after the current date, and it's in March. After setting the `lc_time_names` variable to `'it_I''` (i.e., italian, Italy), the results returned for the same SQL statement are given in Italian. You can use this function in conjunction with a function such as `CONCAT( )` to paste the results into other text or to create a style you prefer:

```
SELECT CONCAT('Il tuo appuntamento è in ', MONTHNAME(appointment), '.')
AS 'Reminder'
FROM appointments
WHERE client_id = '8302'
AND appointment > NOW( );

+--------------------------------+
| Reminder                       |
+--------------------------------+
| Il tuo appuntamento è in marzo. |
+--------------------------------+
```

NOW()

NOW( )

This function returns the current date and time. The format returned is *yyyy-mm-dd hh:mm:ss.nnnnnn*, unless the function is used in a numeric calculation. Then it will return the data in a *yyyymmdd* format. It's synonymous with LOCALTIME() and LOCALTIMESTAMP( ). Here is an example:

```
SELECT NOW( ) AS Now,
NOW( ) + 105008 AS '1 hour, 50 min., 8 sec. Later';

+---------------------+-----------------------------+
| Now                 | 1 hour, 50 min., 8 sec. Later |
+---------------------+-----------------------------+
| 2007-03-18 20:08:30 |        20070318305838.000000 |
+---------------------+-----------------------------+
```

By adding 105,008 to the current time, the hour is increased by 1, the minutes by 50, and the seconds by 8, and the time is displayed in the second field without dashes. Notice that the results show the hours to be 30 now and not 6, and the date wasn't adjusted. Raw adding of time is usually not a good alternative to functions such as DATE_ADD( ) or TIME_ADD( ).

The NOW( ) function is similar to the SYSDATE() function in that they both return the current datetime in the same format. However, the NOW( ) function returns the time the SQL statement began, whereas SYSDATE( ) returns the time the function was invoked. This can lead to differences when long triggers or stored procedures run; an embedded SYSDATE( ) will then reflect a later time than NOW( ). For this reason, there are potential problems using SYSDATE( ) with regard to replication. See the description of SYSDATE() later in this chapter for more information:

```
SELECT NOW( ) AS 'Start',
SLEEP(5) AS 'Pause',
NOW( ) AS 'Middle But Same',
SYSDATE( ) AS 'End';

+---------------------+-------+---------------------+---------------------+
| Start               | Pause | Middle But Same     | End                 |
+---------------------+-------+---------------------+---------------------+
| 2008-06-15 11:02:41 |     0 | 2008-06-15 11:02:41 | 2008-06-15 11:02:46 |
+---------------------+-------+---------------------+---------------------+
1 row in set (5.27 sec)
```

MySQL executes the elements of a SELECT statement from left to right, so the Start field is determined first. The SLEEP( ) function instructs the server to pause the execution of the SQL statement by the amount of seconds given. After this, the third element is executed. As you can see, the results for that third field are the same as the first because NOW( ) returns the starting time. However, in the fourth field, SYSDATE( ) returns the time it was executed, five seconds after the start. This may not seem like much of a difference between the functions, but there may be situations where it matters. In particular, it may matter with SQL statements, triggers, or stored procedures that take a long time to finish executing.

PERIOD_ADD( )

PERIOD_ADD(*yearmonth*, *number*)

This function adds a specified number of months to a period, which is a string containing only the year and month in either *yyyymm* or *yymm* format. Here is an example:

```
SELECT CURDATE( ),
EXTRACT(YEAR_MONTH FROM CURDATE( ))
AS 'Current Period',
PERIOD_ADD(EXTRACT(YEAR_MONTH FROM CURDATE( )), 1)
AS 'Next Accounting Period';

+------------+----------------+------------------------+
| CURDATE( ) | Current Period | Next Accounting Period |
+------------+----------------+------------------------+
| 2008-12-15 |         200812 |                 200901 |
+------------+----------------+------------------------+
```

Functions such as this one are particularly useful when you are building a program and need to design an SQL statement that will account for accounting periods that roll into the following year.

PERIOD_DIFF( )

PERIOD_DIFF(*yearmonth*,*yearmonth*)

This function returns the number of months between the periods given. The periods given must be in string format and contain only the year and month, in either *yyyymm* or *yymm* format. Here is an example:

```
SELECT appointment AS 'Date of Appointment',
CURDATE( ) AS 'Current Date',
PERIOD_DIFF(
   EXTRACT(YEAR_MONTH FROM appointment),
   EXTRACT(YEAR_MONTH FROM CURDATE( ))
) AS 'Accounting Periods Apart';

+------------------+--------------+----------------------------+
| Last Appointment | Current Date | Accounting Periods Ellapsed |
+------------------+--------------+----------------------------+
| 2008-11-15       | 2009-01-15   |                          -2 |
+------------------+--------------+----------------------------+
```

This SQL statement determines that it has been two months since the client's last appointment. If you want the results not to contain a negative, either switch the order of the periods or wrap the PERIOD_DIFF( ) within ABS( ). The PERIOD_DIFF( ) function takes into account that the periods are in different years. But it doesn't work on standard date columns, so you have to put them into the proper string format as shown here with a function such as EXTRACT( ).

QUARTER( )

QUARTER(*date*)

This function returns the number of the quarter (1–4) for the date provided. The first quarter (i.e., the first three months) of each year has a value of 1. Here is an example:

```
SELECT COUNT(appointment)
AS 'Appts. Last Quarter'
FROM appointments
WHERE QUARTER(appointment) = (QUARTER(NOW( )) - 1)
AND client_id = '7393';

+---------------------+
| Appts. Last Quarter |
+---------------------+
|                  16 |
+---------------------+
```

Date and Time Functions

In this example, MySQL calculates the total number of appointments for a particular client that occurred before the current quarter. The flaw in this SQL statement is that it doesn't work when it's run during the first quarter of a year. In the first quarter, the calculation on the fourth line would produce a quarter value of 0. This statement also doesn't consider appointments in previous quarters of previous years. To solve these problems, we could set up user-defined variables for the values of the previous quarter and for its year:

```
SET @LASTQTR:=IF((QUARTER(CURDATE( ))-1) = 0, 4, QUARTER(CURDATE( ))-1);

SET @YR:=IF(@LASTQTR = 4, YEAR(NOW( ))-1, YEAR(NOW( )));

SELECT COUNT(appointment) AS 'Appts. Last Quarter'
FROM appointments
WHERE QUARTER(appointment) = @LASTQTR
AND YEAR(appointment) = @YR
AND client_id = '7393';
```

In the first SQL statement here, we use an `IF` statement to test whether reducing the quarter by 1 would yield a 0 value. If so, we'll set the user variable for the last quarter to 4. In the second statement, we establish the year for the last quarter based on the value determined for `@LASTQTR`. The last SQL statement selects rows and counts them where the `QUARTER( )` function yields a value equal to the `@LASTQTR` variable and where the `YEAR( )` function yields a value equal to the `@YR` variable based on the appointment date, and where the client is the one for which we are running the statement.

SEC_TO_TIME( )

`SEC_TO_TIME(`*`seconds`*`)`

This function returns the period for a given number of seconds in the format *hh:mm:ss*. It will return the time in *hhmmss* format if it's used as part of a numeric calculation. Here is an example:

```
SELECT SEC_TO_TIME(3600) AS 'Time Format',
SEC_TO_TIME(3600) + 0 AS 'Numeric Format';

+-------------+----------------+
| Time Format | Numeric Format |
+-------------+----------------+
```

```
| 01:00:00    |     10000.000000 |
+-------------+------------------+
```

We've given a value of 3,600 seconds, which the function formats to show as 1 hour in the first field. The next field shows the same results, but in numeric format and with microseconds included. If the number of seconds exceeds 86,400, or 1 day's worth, the value for hours will result in an amount greater than 23 and will not be reset back to 0.

SECOND( )

`SECOND(`*`time`*`)`

This function returns the seconds value (0–59) for a given time. Here is an example:

```
SELECT NOW( ), SECOND(NOW( ));

+---------------------+----------------+
| NOW( )              | SECOND(NOW( )) |
+---------------------+----------------+
| 2009-05-09 14:56:11 |             11 |
+---------------------+----------------+
```

The first field generated shows the time that this statement was entered, using the `NOW( )` function. The second field displays only the seconds value for the results of `NOW( )`.

SLEEP( )

`SLEEP(`*`seconds`*`)`

This function pauses the execution of an SQL statement in which it is given for the number of seconds given. It returns 0 in the results if successful; 1 if not. This function became available as of version 5.0.12 of MySQL. It's not exactly a time and date function, but it's included here due to it's true time aspects. Here is an example:

```
SELECT SYSDATE( ) AS 'Start',
SLEEP(5) AS 'Pause',
SYSDATE( ) AS 'End';

+---------------------+-------+---------------------+
| Start               | Pause | End                 |
+---------------------+-------+---------------------+
| 2008-07-16 13:50:20 |     0 | 2008-07-16 13:50:25 |
+---------------------+-------+---------------------+
1 row in set (5.13 sec)
```

The `SYSDATE( )` function returns the time it is executed, not necessarily the time the statement started or finished. You can see that the time in the first field is different by five seconds from the results in the third field due to the use of `SLEEP( )`. Notice also that the statement took a little over five seconds to execute.

If you type Ctrl-C one time before an SQL statement containing `SLEEP( )` is completed, it will return 1 for the `SLEEP( )` field and MySQL will then go on to execute the rest of the SQL statement. In that case, the third field in the previous example would show less than a five-second difference from the first.

STR_TO_DATE( )

`STR_TO_DATE(datetime, 'format_code')`

This function returns the date and time of a given string for a given format. The function takes a string containing a date or time, or both. To specify the format of the string returned, a formatting code needs to be provided in the second argument. The formatting codes are the same codes used by the `DATE_FORMAT( )` function; see its definition for a list of those formats. This function is available as of version 4.1.1 of MySQL. Here is an example:

```
SELECT STR_TO_DATE(
'January 15, 2008 1:30 PM',
'%M %d, %Y %h:%i %p'
) AS Anniversary;

+---------------------+
| Anniversary         |
+---------------------+
| 2008-01-15 13:30:00 |
+---------------------+
```

To retrieve a return value suitable for insertion into a date or time column, use `'%Y-%m-%d'` for a date column and `'%h:%i:%s'` for a time column.

SUBDATE( )

`SUBDATE(date, INTERVAL value type)`
`SUBDATE(date days)`

Use this function to subtract a date or time interval from the results of a `DATE` or `TIME` data type column. It's an alias for `DATE_SUB( )`. If a negative value is given, the interval specified is added instead of subtracted. This is the equivalent of `ADDDATE( )`. See Table 12-1 under `DATE_ADD( )` earlier in this chapter for a list of intervals permitted. Here is an example:

```
SELECT SUBDATE(NOW( ), 1) AS 'Yesterday',
SUBDATE(NOW( ), INTERVAL -1 DAY) AS 'Tomorrow';

+---------------------+---------------------+
| Yesterday           | Tomorrow            |
+---------------------+---------------------+
| 2008-05-09 16:11:56 | 2008-05-11 16:11:56 |
+---------------------+---------------------+
```

As of version 4.1 of MySQL, when subtracting days you can just give the number of days for the second argument (i.e., just `1` instead of `INTERVAL 1 DAY`).

SUBTIME( )

`SUBTIME(datetime, datetime_value)`

This function returns the date and time for the given string or column decreased by the time given as the second argument (*d hh:mm:ss*). If a negative number is given, the time is added and the function is the equivalent of `ADDTIME( )`. This function is available as of version 4.1.1 of MySQL. Here is an example:

```
SELECT NOW( ) AS Now,
SUBTIME(NOW( ), '1:00:00.000000') AS 'Hour Ago';

+---------------------+---------------------+
| Now                 | Hour Ago            |
+---------------------+---------------------+
| 2008-01-12 00:54:59 | 2008-01-11 23:54:59 |
+---------------------+---------------------+
```

Notice that the hour is decreased by one, and because the time is just after midnight, the function causes the date to be altered by one day as well. If either argument is given with a microsecond value other than all zeros, the results will include microseconds. To decrease the date, give the number of days before the time (separated by a space) like so:

```
SELECT NOW( ) AS Now,
SUBTIME(NOW( ), '30 0:0.0') AS 'Thirty Days Ago';

+---------------------+---------------------+
| Now                 | Thirty Days Ago     |
+---------------------+---------------------+
| 2008-01-12 00:57:04 | 2007-12-13 00:57:04 |
+---------------------+---------------------+
```

SYSDATE( )

`SYSDATE( )`

This function returns the system date at the time it is executed. It will return the date and time in the *yyyy-mm-dd hh:mm:ss* format, but will return the data in the *yyyymmddhhmmss* format if it's used as part of a numeric calculation. It will display the microseconds value if the calculation involves a microseconds value. Here is an example:

```
SELECT SYSDATE( ),
SYSDATE( ) + 0 AS 'Numeric Format';

+---------------------+----------------+
| SYSDATE( )          | Numeric Format |
+---------------------+----------------+
| 2008-03-15 23:37:38 | 20080315233738 |
+---------------------+----------------+
```

This function is similar to the `NOW( )` function in that they both return the current datetime and in the same format. However, the `NOW( )` function returns the time when the SQL statement began, whereas `SYSDATE( )` returns the time the function was invoked. See the definition of `NOW( )` earlier in this chapter for an example of this situation and its significance.

If you're using replication, the binary log will include `SET TIMESTAMP` entries, so if you restore a database from the binary log, values from `NOW( )` will be adjusted to the same times as when the original SQL statements were executed. `SYSDATE( )` entries are unaffected by these `SET TIMESTAMP` entries:

```
SET @yesterday = UNIX_TIMESTAMP(SUBDATE(SYSDATE( ), 1));

SELECT FROM_UNIXTIME(@yesterday);
```

```
+---------------------------+
| FROM_UNIXTIME(@yesterday) |
+---------------------------+
| 2008-03-17 00:19:17       |
+---------------------------+

SET TIMESTAMP = @yesterday;

SELECT NOW( ), SYSDATE( );

+---------------------+---------------------+
| NOW( )              | SYSDATE( )          |
+---------------------+---------------------+
| 2008-03-17 00:19:17 | 2008-03-16 00:22:53 |
+---------------------+---------------------+
```


These statements are more involved than necessary, but they help illustrate my point. In the first SQL statement, we use the `SET` statement to set up a user variable to hold the date and time of yesterday. To change the `TIMESTAMP` variable, we need the new datetime in the Unix time format, so we use `UNIX_TIMESTAMP( )`. Within that function, we use `SUBDATE( )` to get the datetime for one day before. The second statement is just so we can see the value of the user variable. With the third statement, we set the system variable to the value of the user variable we created. The result is that when we run the last SQL statement—the `SELECT( )` with both `NOW( )` and `SYSDATE( )`—we can see that the results are different by the one day and also a few seconds. The difference is that the value for `NOW( )` is locked because we set the `TIMESTAMP` variable.

If you're replicating, you may not want to use `SYSDATE( )` for setting values, as their results won't be replicated if you restore the data later. It is possible to resolve this problem by starting the server with the `--sysdate-is-now` option. This will cause `SYSDATE( )` to function the same as `NOW( )`.

TIME( )

`TIME(`*`time`*`)`

This function returns the time from a given string or column containing date and time data. It's available as of version 4.1.1 of MySQL. Here is an example:

```
SELECT NOW( ), As Now,
TIME(NOW( )) AS 'Time only';

+---------------------+-----------+
| Now                 | Time only |
+---------------------+-----------+
| 2008-03-17 00:19:17 | 00:19:17  |
+---------------------+-----------+
```

TIME_FORMAT( )

`TIME_FORMAT(`*`time, format_code`*`)`

This function returns the time value of the time element provided and formats it according to formatting codes given as the second argument. See Table 12-1 under the

DATE_FORMAT( ) function earlier in this chapter for formatting codes, but only those related to time values. This function will return NULL or 0 for nontime formatting codes. Here is an example:

```
SELECT TIME_FORMAT(appointment, '%l:%i %p')
AS 'Appt. Time' FROM appointments
WHERE client_id = '8373'
AND appointment > SYSDATE( );

+------------+
| Appt. Time |
+------------+
|  1:00 PM   |
+------------+
```

TIME_TO_SEC( )

TIME_TO_SEC(*time*)

This function returns the number of seconds that the given time represents. It's the inverse of SEC_TO_TIME( ). Here is an example:

```
SELECT TIME_TO_SEC('01:00')
AS 'Seconds to 1 a.m.';

+-------------------+
| Seconds to 1 a.m. |
+-------------------+
|              3600 |
+-------------------+
```

Here, we calculate the number of seconds up until 1 A.M. (i.e., 60 seconds times 60 minutes), or one hour into the day.

TIMEDIFF( )

TIMEDIFF(*time*, *time*)

This function returns the time difference between the two times given. Although the arguments may be given in time or datetime format, both arguments must be of the same data type. Otherwise, NULL will be returned. Microseconds may be included in the values given. They will be returned when given and if the result is not zero microseconds. This function is available as of version 4.1.1 of MySQL. Here is an example:

```
SELECT appointment AS Appointment,
NOW( ) AS 'Time Now',
TIMEDIFF(appointment, NOW( )) AS 'Time Remaining'
FROM appointments
WHERE rec_id='3783';

+-------------------+-------------------+----------------+
| Appointment       | Time Now          | Time Remaining |
+-------------------+-------------------+----------------+
| 2008-01-11 10:30:00| 2008-01-10 22:28:09| 12:01:51      |
+-------------------+-------------------+----------------+
```

TIMESTAMP( )

`TIMESTAMP(`*`date, time`*`)`

This function merges the date and time from given strings or columns that contain date and time data separately; the result is returned in *yyyy-mm-dd hh:mm:ss* format. If only the date or only the time is given, the function will return zeros for the missing parameter. It's available as of version 4.1.1 of MySQL. Here is an example:

```
SELECT TIMESTAMP(appt_date, appt_time) AS 'Appointment'
FROM appointments LIMIT 1;

+---------------------+
| Appointment         |
+---------------------+
| 2008-07-16 11:13:41 |
+---------------------+
```


TIMESTAMPADD( )

`TIMESTAMPADD(`*`interval, number, datetime`*`)`

This function adds the given number of intervals of time to the given date or time. Intervals that are accepted by this function are: `FRAC_SECOND`, `SECOND`, `MINUTE`, `HOUR`, `DAY`, `WEEK`, `MONTH`, `QUARTER`, and `YEAR`. For compatibility with other systems, you can add the `SQL_TSI_` prefix to these interval names (e.g., `SQL_TSI_YEAR` for `YEAR`). This function is available as of version 5.0.0 of MySQL and is similar to `DATE_ADD( )`, but the list of intervals accepted is not exactly the same. Here is an example:

```
UPDATE appointments
SET appointment = TIMESTAMPADD(HOUR, 1, appointment)
WHERE appt_id = '8930';
```

In this example, an appointment is set to an hour later.

TIMESTAMPDIFF( )

`TIMESTAMPDIFF(`*`interval, datetime, datetime`*`)`

This function returns the time difference between the two times given, but only for the interval being compared. The intervals accepted are the same as those accepted for `TIMESTAMPADD( )`. This function is available as of version 5.0.0 of MySQL. Here is an example:

```
SELECT NOW( ) AS Today,
TIMESTAMPDIFF(DAY, NOW( ), LAST_DAY(NOW( )))
AS 'Days Remaining in Month';

+---------------------+-------------------------+
| Today               | Days Remaining in Month |
+---------------------+-------------------------+
| 2008-01-12 02:19:26 | 19                      |
+---------------------+-------------------------+
```

This SQL statement retrieves the current date and time and uses the `LAST_DAY( )` function to determine the date of the last day of the month. Then the `TIMESTAMPDIFF( )` function determines the difference between the day of the date now and the day of the date at the end of the month.

TO_DAYS( )

TO_DAYS(*date*)

This function returns the date based on the number of days given, which are from the beginning of the currently used standard calendar. Problems occur for dates before 1582, when the Gregorian calendar became the standard. The opposite of this function is FROM_DAYS( ). Here is an example:

```
SELECT CURDATE( ) AS 'Today',
TO_DAYS('2008-12-31'),
TO_DAYS(CURDATE( )),
(TO_DAYS('2008-12-31') -
TO_DAYS(CURDATE( )))
AS 'Days to End of Year' \G

*************************** 1. row ***************************
                Today: 2008-11-03
TO_DAYS('2007-12-31'): 733772
  TO_DAYS(CURDATE( )): 733714
  Days to End of Year: 58
```

In this example, the TO_DAYS( ) function is used to calculate the difference in the number of days between the two dates, the number of days from the current date until the year's end. I've used the \G ending instead of the semicolon so as to save space horizontally.

UNIX_TIMESTAMP( )

UNIX_TIMESTAMP([*datetime*])

This function returns the number of seconds since the start of the Unix epoch (January 1, 1970, Greenwich Mean Time). Without a given time, this function will return the Unix time for the current date and time. Optionally, a date and time value (directly or by way of a column value) may be given for conversion to Unix time with this function. Here is an example:

```
SELECT UNIX_TIMESTAMP( ) AS 'Now',
UNIX_TIMESTAMP('2008-05-09 20:45:00') AS 'Same Time from String';

+------------+-----------------------+
| Now        | Same Time from String |
+------------+-----------------------+
| 1210383900 |            1210383900 |
+------------+-----------------------+
```

The first column uses the function to determine the Unix time for the moment that the statement was entered. The second column uses the same function to determine the Unix time for the same date and time provided in a common, readable format.

UTC_DATE( )

UTC_DATE( )

This function returns the current Universal Time, Coordinated (UTC) date in *yyyy-mm-dd* format, or in *yyyymmdd* format if it's used as part of a numeric calculation. It's available as of version 4.1.1 of MySQL. The parentheses are optional. Here is an example:

```
SELECT UTC_DATE( ),
UTC_DATE( ) + 0 AS 'UTC_DATE( ) Numeric';

+-------------+---------------------+
| UTC_DATE( ) | UTC_DATE( ) Numeric |
+-------------+---------------------+
| 2008-12-07  |            20081207 |
+-------------+---------------------+
```


UTC_TIME( )

UTC_TIME( )

This function returns the current UTC time in *hh:mm:ss* format, or in *hhmmss* format if it's used as part of a numeric calculation. As a numeric, the microseconds are included in the results. It's available as of version 4.1.1 of MySQL. The pair of parentheses is optional. Here is an example:

```
SELECT UTC_TIME( ),
UTC_TIME( ) + 0 AS 'UTC_TIME( ) Numeric';

+-------------+-------------------- +
| UTC_TIME( ) | UTC_TIME( ) Numeric |
+-------------+---------------------+
| 22:01:14    |       220114.000000 |
+-------------+---------------------+
```

UTC_TIMESTAMP( )

UTC_TIMESTAMP( )

This function returns the current UTC date and time in *yyyy-mm-dd hh:mm:ss* format. It will return the UTC date and time in a *yyyymmddhhmmss* format if it's used as part of a numeric calculation. As a numeric, the microseconds are included in the results. This statement is available as of version 4.1.1 of MySQL. The parentheses are optional. Use UTC_TIME( ) is you want only the UTC time, and UTC_DATE( ) if you want only the UTC date. Here is an example:

```
SELECT UTC_TIMESTAMP( ),
UTC_TIMESTAMP( ) + 0 AS 'UTC_TIMESTAMP( ) Numeric';

+---------------------+--------------------------+
| UTC_TIMESTAMP( )    | UTC_TIMESTAMP( ) Numeric |
+---------------------+--------------------------+
| 2008-12-07 22:08:24 |    20081207220824.000000 |
+---------------------+--------------------------+
```

WEEK( )

`WEEK(date[, value])`

This function returns the number of the week starting from the beginning of the year for the date provided. This may seem simple enough. However, it's complex because there are one or two more days in a year beyond 52 weeks (i.e., 52 × 7 = 364); the first day of the year usually isn't the first day of a week. When a year starts on a Sunday—if you consider Sunday to be the first day of the week—January 1 is definitely the first week of the year. In that case, the function should return 0 or 1 depending on whether you think of 0 as the first number or 1. If you consider Monday the first day of the week, though, then if January 1 is a Sunday, the question is whether you want that day to be considered as part of the last week of the previous year, or just as week 0 of this year and make 1 represent the first full week of the current year. All of these possibilities for MySQL to consider when executing `WEEK( )` are represented by the mode you specify as its second parameter.

The range of values accepted for the function's second parameter is 0 to 7. Even numbers indicate that Sunday is the first day of the week; odd values indicate Monday is the first day of the week. Codes 0, 1, 4, and 5 return results ranging from 0 to 53; codes 2, 3, 6, and 7 return results ranging from 1 to 53. Codes 0, 2, 5, and 7 determine results of the date given with regard to the year that holds the first day of the week of the week that the first day of the year given is in. Here is an example:

```
SELECT DAYNAME('2006-01-01') AS 'Day',
WEEK('2006-01-01', 0) AS '0(S,0)', WEEK('2006-01-01', 1) AS '1(M,0)',
WEEK('2006-01-01', 2) AS '2(S,1)', WEEK('2006-01-01', 3) AS '3(M,1)',
WEEK('2006-01-01', 4) AS '4(S,0)', WEEK('2006-01-01', 5) AS '5(M,0)',
WEEK('2006-01-01', 6) AS '6(S,1)', WEEK('2006-01-01', 7) AS '7(M,1)'
   UNION ...
```

```
+-----------+--------+--------+--------+--------+--------+--------+--------+--------+
| Day       | 0(S,0) | 1(M,0) | 2(S,1) | 3(M,1) | 4(S,0) | 5(M,0) | 6(S,1) | 7(M,1) |
+-----------+--------+--------+--------+--------+--------+--------+--------+--------+
| Sunday    |      1 |      0 |      1 |     52 |      1 |      0 |      1 |     52 |
| Monday    |      0 |      1 |     53 |      1 |      1 |      1 |      1 |      1 |
| Tuesday   |      0 |      1 |     52 |      1 |      1 |      0 |      1 |     53 |
| Wednesday |      0 |      1 |     52 |      1 |      1 |      0 |      1 |     52 |
| Thursday  |      0 |      1 |     52 |      1 |      0 |      0 |     53 |     52 |
| Friday    |      0 |      0 |     52 |     53 |      0 |      0 |     52 |     52 |
| Saturday  |      0 |      0 |     52 |     52 |      0 |      0 |     52 |     52 |
+-----------+--------+--------+--------+--------+--------+--------+--------+--------+
```

This results set is created with the `SELECT` statement shown repeated six times, joined together using `UNION` to merge the results into one results table. The year is adjusted for each `SELECT` statement, ranging from 2006 to 2011, and 2014 used in the middle for the Wednesday due to leap year. This chart shows the results of `WEEK( )` for seven different dates (one for each day of the week), all the first day of their respective years. For each date, each row shows the results for each parameter possibility for the `WEEK( )` function. The column headings specify the parameter used, along with whether the parameter considers Sunday or Monday (indicated by S or M, respectively) to be the first day of the week. The 0 just after the S or M indicates that results can range from 0 to 53 weeks; 1 indicates a range of 1 to 53. It's a complex chart, but the subject is complex and it's hoped that seeing all of the possibilities will make it easier to understand. Table 12-4 may also be useful in choosing the mode that you want.

If no mode is specified with the WEEK( ) function, the default is used. The default value is stored in the system variable default_week_format. It can be changed with the SET statement:

```
SHOW VARIABLES LIKE 'default_week_format';

+---------------------+-------+
| Variable_name       | Value |
+---------------------+-------+
| default_week_format | 0     |
+---------------------+-------+

SET default_week_format = 1;
```

As an alternative to WEEK( ), you can use YEARWEEK( ). It's synonymous with WEEK( ), but with the mode of 3 only.

Table 12-4. WEEK( ) modes

Mode	Beginning of week	Range of weeks	Determining if week 1 is first week
0	Sunday	0–53	First day of week considered
1	Monday	0–53	
2	Sunday	1–53	First day of week considered
3	Monday	1–53	
4	Sunday	0–53	
5	Monday	0–53	First day of week considered
6	Sunday	1–53	
7	Monday	1–53	First day of week considered

WEEKDAY( )

WEEKDAY(*date*)

This function returns the number for the day of the week. Monday is considered the first day of the week for this function and returns a value of 0; a Sunday returns 6. Here is an example:

```
SELECT appt_id, client_id
FROM appointments
WHERE WEEKDAY(appt) > 4 AND
EXTRACT(YEAR_MONTH FROM appt) = EXTRACT(YEAR_MONTH FROM NOW( ));
```

This SQL statement, based on the WHERE clause, retrieves a list of appointments that are on the weekends of the current month.

WEEKOFYEAR( )

`WEEKOFYEAR(date)`

This function returns the calendar week of the year for a given date. It was added in version 4.1.1 of MySQL and is synonymous with `WEEK( )`, but with the mode of 3 for that function only. There's no way to change the mode for this function. Here is an example:

```
SELECT CURDATE( ) AS Date,
WEEKOFYEAR(CURDATE( )) AS Week;

+------------+------+
| Date       | Week |
+------------+------+
| 2005-01-11 |    2 |
+------------+------+
```

YEAR( )

`YEAR(date)`

This function returns the year of the date provided. It returns values from 1,000 to 9,999, and returns 0 for a zero date. Here is an example:

```
SELECT YEAR('2008-01-01')
AS 'Year';

+------+
| Year |
+------+
| 2008 |
+------+
```

YEARWEEK( )

`YEARWEEK(date[, value])`

This function returns the year coupled with the number of the week into the year: *yyyyww*. By default, the first day of the week is Sunday and is the basis of the calculation. Optionally, you can set Monday as the first day of the week by entering a value of 1 for the second argument. This function is somewhat synonymous with `WEEK( )`, but with the year appended to the results and the mode of 2 for that function. If you set the second parameter of this function to 1, it becomes similar to `WEEK( )` with the mode of 3. Here is an example:

```
SELECT YEARWEEK('2008-01-07')
AS 'YearWeek';

+----------+
| YearWeek |
+----------+
|   200801 |
+----------+
```

This function can be useful in conjunction with the `PERIOD_ADD( )` and `PERIOD_DIFF( )` functions.

13 Mathematical Functions

MySQL has many built-in mathematical functions that you can use in SQL statements for performing calculations on values in databases. Each function accepts either numbers or numeric columns for parameter values. All mathematical functions return NULL on error.

The following functions are covered in this chapter:

`ABS( )`, `ACOS( )`, `ASIN( )`, `ATAN( )`, `ATAN2( )`, `BIT_COUNT( )`, `CEIL( )`, `CEILING( )`, `CONV( )`, `COS( )`, `COT( )`, `DEGREES( )`, `EXP( )`, `FLOOR( )`, `FORMAT( )`, `GREATEST( )`, `INET_ATON( )`, `INET_NTOA( )`, `LEAST( )`, `LN( )`, `LOG( )`, `LOG2( )`, `LOG10( )`, `MOD( )`, `OCT( )`, `PI( )`, `POW( )`, `POWER( )`, `RADIANS( )`, `RAND( )`, `ROUND( )`, `SIGN( )`, `SIN( )`, `SQRT( )`, `TAN( )`, `TRUNCATE( )`.

Functions in Alphabetical Order

The following is a list of MySQL mathematical functions in alphabetical order, along with descriptions of each and examples of their use.

ABS( )

`ABS(`*`number`*`)`

This function returns the absolute value of a given number. Here is an example:

```
SELECT ABS(-10);

+----------+
| ABS(-10) |
+----------+
|       10 |
+----------+
```

ACOS( )

ACOS(*number*)

This function returns the arc cosine, in radians, of a given number. For input greater than 1 or less than –1, NULL is returned. Here is an example:

```
SELECT ACOS(.5), ACOS(1.5);

+----------+-----------+
| ACOS(.5) | ACOS(1.5) |
+----------+-----------+
| 1.047198 |      NULL |
+----------+-----------+
```

ASIN( )

ASIN(*number*)

This function returns the arcsine, in radians, of a given number. For input greater than 1 or less than –1, NULL is returned. Here is an example:

```
SELECT ASIN(1);

+----------+
| ASIN(1)  |
+----------+
| 1.570796 |
+----------+
```

ATAN( )

ATAN(*number*[, ...])

This function returns the arctangent, in radians, of a given number. To determine the arctangent of two numbers (Y and X), add the optional second argument to the function or use ATAN2( ). The value of Y for a Cartesian plane is given as the first argument and X as the second. Here is an example:

```
SELECT ATAN(2);

+----------+
| ATAN(2)  |
+----------+
| 1.107149 |
+----------+
```

ATAN2( )

ATAN2(*number*, *number*)

This function returns the arctangent, in radians, of X and Y for a point on a Cartesian plane. The value for Y is given as the first argument and X as the second. The reverse function is TAN( ). Here is an example:

```
SELECT ATAN2(10, 5);

+--------------+
| ATAN2(10, 5) |
+--------------+
|     1.107149 |
+--------------+
```

BIT_COUNT( )

`BIT_COUNT(`*`number`*`)`

This function returns the number of bits set in the argument, which is an integer that the function treats as a binary number.

```
SELECT BIT_COUNT(10), BIT_COUNT(11);

+---------------+---------------+
| BIT_COUNT(10) | BIT_COUNT(11) |
+---------------+---------------+
|             2 |             3 |
+---------------+---------------+
```

CEIL( )

`CEIL(`*`number`*`)`

This function rounds a given floating-point number up to the next higher integer. It's an alias to `CEILING( )`.

```
SELECT CEIL(1), CEIL(1.1);

+---------+-----------+
| CEIL(1) | CEIL(1.1) |
+---------+-----------+
|       1 |         2 |
+---------+-----------+
```

CEILING( )

`CEILING(`*`number`*`)`

This function rounds a given floating-point number up to the next higher integer. It's an alias to `CEIL( )`. This function can be particularly useful when you want a numeric value for a time function, but without the decimal places (the microseconds) in the results:

```
SELECT NOW(), NOW() + 0, CEILING(NOW() + 0);

+---------------------+-----------------------+--------------------+
| NOW()               | NOW() + 0             | CEILING(NOW() + 0) |
+---------------------+-----------------------+--------------------+
| 2007-07-16 00:07:14 | 20070716000714.000000 |     20070716000714 |
+---------------------+-----------------------+--------------------+
```

CONV( )

CONV(*number*, *from_base*, *to_base*)

This function converts a number from one numeric base system to another. The number to convert is given in the first argument, the base from which to convert the number in the second, and the base to which to convert the number in the third. The minimum base allowed is 2 and the maximum is 36. Here is an example:

```
SELECT CONV(4, 10, 2) AS 'Base-10 4 Converted',
CONV(100, 2, 10) AS 'Binary 100 Converted';

+---------------------+----------------------+
| Base-10 4 Converted | Binary 100 Converted |
+---------------------+----------------------+
| 100                 | 4                    |
+---------------------+----------------------+
```

Here, the number 4 under the base 10 system is converted to the base 2 or binary equivalent and back again.

COS( )

COS(*number*)

This function returns the cosine of ***number***, where ***number*** is expressed in radians. Here is an example:

```
SELECT COS(2 * PI( ));

+----------------+
| COS(2 * PI( )) |
+----------------+
|              1 |
+----------------+
```

COT( )

COT(*number*)

This function returns the cotangent of a number. Here is an example:

```
SELECT COT(1);

+------------+
| COT(1)     |
+------------+
| 0.64209262 |
+------------+
```

DEGREES( )

DEGREES(*number*)

This function converts radians to degrees.

```
SELECT DEGREES(PI( ));

+-----------------+
| DEGREES(PI( ))  |
+-----------------+
|      180.000000 |
+-----------------+
```

EXP( )

`EXP(number)`

This function returns the value of the natural logarithm base number *e* to the power of the given number.

```
SELECT EXP(1);

+----------+
| EXP(1)   |
+----------+
| 2.718282 |
+----------+
```

FLOOR( )

`FLOOR(number)`

This function rounds a given floating-point number down to the next lower integer. It's a counterpart to `CEILING( )`.

```
SELECT CEILING(1.1), FLOOR(1.1);

+--------------+------------+
| CEILING(1.1) | FLOOR(1.1) |
+--------------+------------+
|            2 |          1 |
+--------------+------------+
```

FORMAT( )

`FORMAT(number, decimal)`

This function returns the given floating-point ***number*** with a comma inserted between every three digits and a period before the number of decimal places specified in the second argument.

```
SELECT FORMAT(1000.375, 2)
AS Amount;

+----------+
| Amount   |
+----------+
| 1,000.38 |
+----------+
```

Notice that the function rounds the number given to two decimal places.

GREATEST( )

`GREATEST(value, value, ...)`

This function compares two or more values, returning the greatest value. In an `INTEGER` data type context, all values are treated as integers for comparison. In a `REAL` data type context, all values are treated as `REAL` values for comparison. If any parameter contains a case-sensitive string (i.e., with a `BINARY` keyword), all values are compared as case-sensitive strings. Here is an example:

```
SELECT GREATEST(col1, col2, col3);
```

INET_ATON( )

`INET_ATON(IP_address)`

This function converts an Internet Protocol (IP) address in dot-quad notation to its numeric equivalent. The function `INET_NTOA( )` can be used to reverse the results. Here is an example:

```
SELECT INET_ATON('12.127.17.72')
AS 'AT&T';

+-----------+
| AT&T      |
+-----------+
| 209654088 |
+-----------+
```

This function is useful in sorting IP addresses that lexically might not sort properly. For instance, an address of 10.0.11.1 would come after 10.0.1.1 and before 10.0.2.1 under normal sort conditions in an `ORDER BY` clause.

INET_NTOA( )

`INET_NTOA(IP_address)`

This function converts the numeric equivalent of an IP address to its dot-quad notation. The function `INET_ATON( )` can be used to reverse the results.

```
SELECT INET_NTOA('209654088')
AS 'AT&T';

+--------------+
| AT&T         |
+--------------+
| 12.127.17.72 |
+--------------+
```

LEAST( )

`LEAST(value, value, ...)`

Use this function to compare two or more values and return the smallest value. In an `INTEGER` datatype context, all values are treated as integers for comparison. In a `REAL` data type context, all values are treated as REAL values for comparison. If any parameter contains a case-sensitive string (i.e., with a BINARY keyword), all values are compared as case-sensitive strings. Here is an example:

```
SELECT LEAST(col1, col2, col3);
```

LN()

LN(*number*)

This function returns the natural logarithm of its input. Here is an example:

```
SELECT LN(5);

+----------+
| LN(5)    |
+----------+
| 1.609438 |
+----------+
```

LOG()

LOG(*number*[, *base*])

This function returns the logarithm of the first argument to the base indicated by the second argument. This is the same as using LOG(*number*)/LOG(*base*). If the function is called with only the first argument, its natural logarithm is returned; the function is equivalent to LN in that case. Here is an example:

```
SELECT LOG(5,4);

+------------+
|   LOG(5,4) |
+------------+
| 1.16096405 |
+------------+
```

LOG2()

LOG2(*number*)

This function returns the base 2 logarithm of a given number.

LOG10()

LOG10(*number*)

This function returns the base 10 logarithm of a given number.

MOD()

MOD(*number*, *number*)
number MOD *number*

This function returns the remainder of a number given in the first argument when divided by the number given in the second argument, the modulo. The function works the same as using the % operator between two given numbers. The second syntax shown is available as of version 4.1 of MySQL. Starting with version 4.1.7, fractional values may be given. Here is an example:

```
SELECT MOD(10, 3);

+------------+
| MOD(10, 3) |
+------------+
|          1 |
+------------+
```

Here's an example of the alternate syntax:

```
SELECT 10 MOD 3;

+----------+
| 10 MOD 3 |
+----------+
|        1 |
+----------+
```

OCT( )

`OCT(number)`

This function returns the octal, or base 8, numeric system value of the given number. It returns NULL if the argument is NULL. Here is an example:

```
SELECT OCT(1), OCT(9), OCT(16);

+--------+--------+---------+
| OCT(8) | OCT(9) | OCT(16) |
+--------+--------+---------+
| 10     | 11     | 20      |
+--------+--------+---------+
```

PI( )

`PI( )`

This function returns by default the first five decimal places of the number *pi*. You can adjust it to include more decimal places by adding a mask to the end of the function. There is no argument within the parentheses of the function. Here is an example:

```
SELECT PI( ), PI( ) + 0.0000000000;

+----------+----------------------+
| PI( )    | PI( ) + 0.0000000000 |
+----------+----------------------+
| 3.141593 |         3.1415926536 |
+----------+----------------------+
```

POW( )

`POW(number, exponent)`

This function returns the result of raising the number given in the first argument to the exponent given in the second argument. It's an alias of `POWER( )`. Here is an example:

```
SELECT POW(2, 4);

+-----------+
| POW(2, 4) |
+-----------+
| 16.000000 |
+-----------+
```

POWER( )

`POWER(number, exponent)`

This function returns the result of raising the number given in the first argument to the power of the number given in the second argument. It's an alias for `POW( )`.

RADIANS( )

`RADIANS( )`

This function converts degrees to radians. Here is an example:

```
SELECT RADIANS(180);

+-----------------+
| RADIANS(180)    |
+-----------------+
| 3.1415926535898 |
+-----------------+
```

RAND( )

`RAND([seed])`

This function returns a random floating-point number from 0 to 1. A seed number may be passed as an argument to start the sequence of random numbers at a different point. Here is an example:

```
SELECT RAND( ), RAND( );

+------------------+------------------+
| RAND( )          | RAND( )          |
+------------------+------------------+
| 0.29085519843814 | 0.45449978900561 |
+------------------+------------------+
```

Note that rerunning this statement with the same seed will produce the same results. This type of sequence is properly known as a pseudorandom number generator, and is generally not considered strong enough for security purposes, but it is adequate for making random choices among a set of alternatives.

ROUND( )

ROUND(*number*[, *precision*])

This function rounds a number given in the first argument to the nearest integer. The number may be rounded to the number of decimal places given in the second argument. Here is an example:

```
SELECT ROUND(2.875), ROUND(2.875, 2);

+--------------+-----------------+
| ROUND(2.875) | ROUND(2.875, 2) |
+--------------+-----------------+
|            3 |            2.88 |
+--------------+-----------------+
```

SIGN( )

SIGN(*number*)

This function returns –1 if the given number is a negative, 0 if it is zero, and 1 if it is positive. Here is an example:

```
SELECT SIGN(-5);

+----------+
| SIGN(-5) |
+----------+
|       -1 |
+----------+
```

SIN( )

SIN(*number*)

This function returns the sine of the number given, where ***number*** is expressed in radians. Here is an example:

```
SELECT SIN(.5 * PI( ));

+-----------------+
| SIN(.5 * PI( )) |
+-----------------+
|               1 |
+-----------------+
```

SQRT( )

SQRT(*number*)

This function returns the square root of its input, which must be a positive number. Here is an example:

```
SELECT SQRT(25);
```

```
+----------+
| SQRT(25) |
+----------+
| 5.000000 |
+----------+
```

TAN( )

`TAN(number)`

This function returns the tangent of an angle, where ***number*** is expressed in radians. It's the reverse of `ATAN2( )`. Here is an example:

```
SELECT ATAN2(1), TAN(0.785398);

+----------+---------------+
| ATAN2(1) | TAN(0.785398) |
+----------+---------------+
| 0.785398 |      1.000000 |
+----------+---------------+
```

TRUNCATE( )

`TRUNCATE(number, number)`

This function returns a number equivalent to its first argument, removing any digits beyond the number of decimal places specified in the second argument. The function does not round the number; use the `ROUND( )` function instead. If 0 is given for the second argument, the decimal point and the fractional value are dropped. If a negative number is given as the second argument, the decimal point and the fractional value are dropped, and the number of positions given is zeroed out in the remaining integer. Here is an example:

```
SELECT TRUNCATE(321.1234, 2) AS '+2',
TRUNCATE(321.1234, 0) AS '0',
TRUNCATE(321.1234, -2) AS '-2';

+--------+-----+-----+
| +2     | 0   | -2  |
+--------+-----+-----+
| 321.12 | 321 | 300 |
+--------+-----+-----+
```

Notice that for the first field in the results, the last two decimal places are dropped. For the second field, the decimal point and all of the fractional value are dropped. For the third field, the decimal point and the fractional value are dropped, and because the second parameter is –2, the two least significant digits (starting from the right) of the integer are changed to zeros.

14
Flow Control Functions

MySQL has a few built-in flow control functions that you can use in SQL statements for more precise and directed results. This chapter provides the syntax of function and gives examples of their use. For the examples in this chapter, a fictitious database for a stock broker is used.

The following functions are covered in this chapter:

`CASE`, `IF( )`, `IFNULL( )`, `ISNULL( )`, `NULLIF( )`.

Functions in Alphabetical Order

The following are the MySQL flow control functions listed alphabetically.

CASE

```
CASE value
  WHEN [value] THEN result
    . . .
  [ELSE result]
END

CASE
  WHEN [condition] THEN result
    . . .
 [ELSE result]
END
```

This function produces results that vary based on which ***condition*** is true. It is similar to the `IF( )` function, except that multiple conditions and results may be strung together. In the first syntax shown, the ***value*** given after `CASE` is compared to each `WHEN` value. If a match is found, the ***result*** given for the `THEN` is returned. The second syntax tests each condition independently, and they are not based on a single value. For both syntaxes, if no match is found and an `ELSE` clause is included, the result given for the `ELSE` clause is returned. If there is no match and no `ELSE` clause is given, NULL is returned.

If the chosen *result* is a string, it is returned as a string data type. If *result* is numeric, the result may be returned as a decimal, real, or integer value.

Here's an example of the first syntax shown:

```
SELECT CONCAT(name_first, SPACE(1), name_last) AS Client,
telephone_home AS Telephone,
CASE type
  WHEN 'RET' THEN 'Retirement Account'
  WHEN 'REG' THEN 'Regular Account'
  WHEN 'CUS' THEN 'Minor Account'
END AS 'Account Type'
FROM clients;
```

This SQL statement retrieves a list of clients and their telephone numbers, along with a description of their account types. However, the account type is a three-letter abbreviation, so CASE( ) is used to substitute each type with a more descriptive name.

This example uses the syntax in which a common parameter is evaluated to determine the possible result. The following SQL statement utilizes the other syntax for the function:

```
SELECT CONCAT(name_last, SPACE(1), name_first) AS Prospect,
CASE
  WHEN YEAR(NOW( )) - YEAR(birth_date) ≤ 17 THEN 'Minor'
  WHEN YEAR(NOW( )) - YEAR(birth_date) > 17 < 26 THEN 'Too Young'
  WHEN YEAR(NOW( )) - YEAR(birth_date) > 60 THEN 'Elderly'
  ELSE home_telephone;
END
AS Telephone
FROM prospects;
```

In this example, the SQL statement analyzes a table containing a list of people that the broker might call to buy an investment. The table contains the birth dates and the telephone numbers of each prospect. The SQL statement provides the telephone numbers only for prospects aged 26 to 60 because anyone younger or older would not be suitable for this particular investment. However, a message for each prospect that is disqualified is given based on the clauses of the CASE( ) statement.

When using a CASE statement within a stored procedure, it cannot be given a NULL value for the ELSE clause. Also, a CASE statement ends with END CASE.

IF( )

IF(*condition*, *result*, *result*)

This function returns the *result* given in the second argument if the *condition* given in the first argument is met (i.e., the *condition* does not equal 0 or NULL). If the condition does equal 0 or NULL, the function returns the *result* given in the third argument. Note that the value of *condition* is converted to an integer. Therefore, use a comparison operator when trying to match a string or a floating-point value. The function returns a numeric or a string value depending on its use. As of version 4.0.3 of MySQL, if the second or the third argument is NULL, the type (i.e., string, float, or integer) of the other non-NULL argument will be returned:

```
SELECT clients.client_id AS ID,
CONCAT(name_first, SPACE(1), name_last) AS Client,
telephone_home AS Telephone, SUM(qty) AS Shares,
IF(
   (SELECT SUM(qty * price)
    FROM investments, stock_prices
    WHERE stock_symbol = symbol
    AND client_id = ID )
    > 100000, 'Large', 'Small') AS 'Size'
FROM clients, investments
WHERE stock_symbol = 'GT'
AND clients.client_id = investments.client_id
GROUP BY clients.client_id LIMIT 2;

+------+----------------+-----------+--------+-------+
| ID   | Client         | Telephone | Shares | Size  |
+------+----------------+-----------+--------+-------+
| 8532 | Jerry Neumeyer | 834-8668  |  200   | Large |
| 4638 | Rusty Osborne  | 833-8393  |  200   | Small |
+------+----------------+-----------+--------+-------+
```

This SQL statement is designed to retrieve the names and telephone numbers of clients who own Goodyear stock (the stock symbol is *GT*) because the broker wants to call them to recommend that they sell it. The example utilizes a subquery (available as of version 4.1 of MySQL) to tally the value of all the clients' stocks first (not just Goodyear stock), as a condition of the `IF( )` function. It does this by joining the **`investments`** table (which contains a row for each stock purchase and sale) and the **`stock_prices`** table (which contains current prices for all stocks). If the sum of the value of all stocks owned by the client (the results of the subquery) is more than $100,000, a label of `Large` is assigned to the `Size` column. Otherwise, the client is labeled `Small`. The broker wants to call her large clients first. Notice in the results shown that both clients own the same number of shares of Goodyear, but one has a large portfolio.

Note that the `IF` statement used in stored procedures has a different syntax from the `IF( )` function described here. See Chapter 17 for more information on the `IF` statement.

IFNULL( )

`IFNULL(`*`condition`*`, `*`result`*`)`

This function returns the results of the ***`condition`*** given in the first argument of the function if its results are not NULL. If the condition results are NULL, the results of the expression or string given in the second argument are returned. It will return a numeric or a string value depending on the context:

```
SELECT CONCAT(name_first, SPACE(1), name_last) AS Client,
telephone_home AS Telephone,
IFNULL(goals, 'No Goals Given') AS Goals
FROM clients LIMIT 2;
```

```
+----------------+-----------+----------------+
| Client         | Telephone | Goals          |
+----------------+-----------+----------------+
| Janice Sogard  | 835-1821  | No Goals Given |
| Kenneth Bilich | 488-3325  | Long Term      |
+----------------+-----------+----------------+
```

This SQL statement provides a list of clients and their telephone numbers, along with their investment goals. If the client never told the broker of an investment goal (i.e., the `goals` column is NULL), the text "No Goals Given" is displayed.

ISNULL( )

`ISNULL(column)`

Use this function to determine whether the value of the argument given in parentheses is NULL. It returns 1 if the value is NULL and 0 if it is not NULL. Here is an example:

```
SELECT CONCAT(name_first, SPACE(1), name_last) AS Client,
telephone_work AS 'Work Telephone'
FROM clients
WHERE ISNULL(telephone_home);
```

In this example, after realizing that we don't have home telephone numbers for several of our clients, we use the `ISNULL( )` function in the `WHERE` clause of a `SELECT` statement to list client names and their work telephone numbers so that we can call them to get their home telephone numbers. Only rows in which the `home_telephone` column is NULL will result in a value of 1 and will therefore be shown in the results.

NULLIF( )

`NULLIF(condition1, condition2)`

This function returns NULL if the two arguments given are equal. Otherwise, it returns the value or results of the first argument. Here is an example:

```
SELECT clients.client_id AS ID,
CONCAT(name_first, SPACE(1), name_last) AS Client,
telephone_home AS Telephone,
NULLIF(
  (SELECT SUM(qty * price)
   FROM investments, stock_prices
   WHERE stock_symbol = symbol
   AND client_id = ID ), 0)
AS Value
FROM clients, investments
WHERE clients.client_id = investments.client_id
GROUP BY clients.client_id;
```

In this example, NULL is returned for the `Value` column if the value of the client's stocks is 0 (i.e., the client had stocks but sold them all). If there is a value to the stocks, however, the sum of their values is displayed.

MySQL Server and Client Tools

This part of the book shows you how to invoke the programs associated with MySQL: the main *mysqld* server, various wrappers for that server, the *mysql* command-line client, and useful administrative utilities. These programs are controlled by options that can be included on the command line or in the MySQL configuration file (*my.cnf* or *my.ini*, depending on your system).

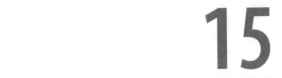

15 MySQL Server and Client

The primary executable file making up the MySQL server is the *mysqld* daemon, which listens for requests from clients and processes them. The general-purpose client provided with MySQL is the *mysql* program. This chapter presents the many options available for both the *mysqld* MySQL server and the *mysql* client. A few scripts provided with MySQL that are used to start the server (`mysqld_multi` and `mysqld_safe`) are also explained. The daemons and scripts are listed in alphabetical order.

mysql Client

mysql

`mysql` *`options`* `[`*`database`*`]`

The `mysql` client can be used to interact with MySQL in terminal or monitor mode. To enter monitor mode, enter something like the following from the command line:

```
mysql -u russell -p
```

If the MySQL server is running, the client will prompt the user for a password (thanks to the `-p` option). Once in monitor mode, you can enter SQL statements to view or to change data as well as the status of the server.

As an alternative to monitor mode, when performing straightforward tasks in MySQL, you can still use the `mysql` client from the command line. For instance, to execute a batch file that contains several SQL statements that will insert data into a database, you could do something like this:

```
mysql -u russell -pmy_pwd db1 < stuff.sql
```

In this example, the password is given so that the user isn't prompted. It's entered immediately after the `-p` option without a space in between. Although including the password on the command line poses a security risk for interactive use, it's a valuable feature for using `mysql` in scripts.

Next, the database name `db1` is given. The Unix redirect (the less-than sign) tells the shell to input the test file *stuff.sql* to the command. When the client has finished processing the text file, the user is returned to the command prompt.

To handle even smaller tasks, you can execute a single SQL command against the database by running `mysql` with the `--execute` or `-e` option.

Several options may be given when calling the `mysql` client at the command line. They can also be included in the options file (*my.cnf* or *my.ini*, depending on your system) under the group heading of `[client]`. If used in the options file, the leading double-dashes are not included. The options are listed alphabetically here:

`--auto-rehash`
: This option generates a hash of table and column names to complete the names for users when typing in monitor mode; users invoke autocompletion by pressing the Tab key after having entered the first few letters of the name.

`--batch, -B`
: This option causes the client to display data selected with fields separated by tabs and rows by carriage returns. The client won't prompt the user, won't display error messages to the `stdout`, and won't save to the history file.

`--character-sets-dir=`*`path`*
: This option specifies the local directory containing character sets for the client to use.

`--column-names`
: This option instructs the client to return the names of columns in a results set. This is more relevant when executing SQL statements from the command line.

`--column-type-info, -m`
: This option instructs the client to return the metadata for columns in a results set. This option is available as of version 5.1.14 of MySQL; the short form is available as of version 5.1.21.

`--compress, -C`
: This option instructs the client to compress data passed between it and the server if supported.

`--database=database, -D database`
: This option sets the default database for the client to use. This is equivalent to executing the `USE` statement.

`--debug[=options], -#[options]`
: This option instructs the client to record debugging information to the log file specified. The set of flags used by default is `d:t:o,logname`. See Table 16-1 at the end of the list of options for `mysqldump` in the next chapter for an explanation of these flags and others that may be used.

`--debug-check`
: This option causes the client to display debugging information when finished. This option is available as of version 5.1.21 of MySQL.

`--debug-info, -T`
: This option adds debugging, CPU usage, and memory usage information to the log when the utility ends.

`--default-character-sets-dir=`*`path`*
: This option specifies the local directory that contains the default character sets for the client to use. Enter `SHOW CHARACTER SET;` on the server for a list of character sets available.

`--defaults-group-suffix=`*`value`*
: The client looks for options in the options file under the group headings of `[mysql]` and `[client]`. Use this option to specify option groups that the client is to use, based on their suffixes. For instance, the value given might be just `_special` so that groups such as `[mysql_special]` and `[client_special]` will be included.

`--delimiter=`*`string`*`, -F `*`string`*
: This option use this option to specify the delimiter used to terminate each SQL statement when entered into the client. By default, the client expects a semicolon.

`--execute='`*`statement`*`', -e '`*`statement`*`'`
: This option executes the SQL statement contained in single or double quotes, then terminates the client.

`--force, -f`
: This option makes the client continue executing or processing a statement even if there are SQL errors.

`--help, -?`
: This option displays basic help information.

`--hostname=`*`host`*`, -h `*`host`*
: This option specifies the hostname or IP address of the MySQL server. The default is *localhost*, which connects to a server on the same system as the client.

`--html, -H`
: This option instructs the client to return results in an HTML format when executing an SQL statement at the command line or from a file containing SQL statements.

`--ignore-spaces, -i`
: This option instructs the client to ignore spaces after function names (e.g., `CUR_DATE( )`) when executing SQL statements at the command line or from a text file containing SQL statements.

`--line-numbers`
: When the client is accepting SQL statements from an input file, this option instructs the client to display the line number of an SQL statement that has returned an error. This is the default option; use `--skip-line-numbers` to disable this option.

`--local-infile[={0|1}]`
: The SQL statement `LOAD DATA INFILE` imports data into a database from a file. That file could be located on the server or on the computer in which the client is running (i.e., locally). To indicate that a file is local, you would add the `LOCAL` flag to that statement. This option sets that flag: a value of 1 enables the `LOCAL`, whereas a value of 0 indicates that the file is on the server. If the server is set so it imports data only from files on the server, this option will have no effect.

`--named-commands, -G`
: This option permits named commands on the client. See the next section for this client program for a description of commands. Enter `help` or `\h` from the *mysql* client to get a list of them. This option is enabled by default. To disable it, use the `--skip-named-commands` option.

`--no-auto-rehash`, `-A`
: Automatic rehashing is normally used to let the user complete table and column names when typing in monitor mode by pressing the Tab key after having entered the first few letters of the name. This option disables autocompletion and thereby decreases the startup time of the client. This option is deprecated as of version 4 of MySQL.

`--no-beep`
: This option instructs client not to emit a warning sound for errors.

`--no-named-commands`
: This option disables named commands on the client, except when at the start of a line (i.e., named commands cannot appear in the middle of an SQL statement). This option is enabled by default. See the description of the `--named-commands` option and the following section for more information.

`--no-tee`
: This option instructs the client not to write results to a file.

`--one-database`, `-o`
: This option instructs the client to execute SQL statements only for the default database (set by the `--database` option) and to ignore SQL statements for other databases.

`--pager[=`*`utility`*`]`
: With this option, on a Unix type of system, you can pipe the results of an SQL statement executed from the command line to a pager utility (e.g., `more`) that will allow you to view the results one page at a time and possibly scroll up and down through the results. If this option is given without specifying a particular pager utility, the value of the environment variable `PAGER` will be used. This option is enabled by default. Use the `--skip-pager` option to disable it.

`--password[=`*`password`*`]`, `-p[`*`password`*`]`
: This option provide the password to give to the MySQL server. No spaces are allowed between the `-p` and the password. If this option is entered without a password, the user will be prompted for one.

`--port=`*`port`*, `-P` *`port`*
: This option specifies the socket port to use for connecting to the server. The default is 3306. If you run multiple daemons for testing or other purposes, you can use different ports for each by setting this option.

`--prompt=`*`string`*
: This option sets the prompt for monitor mode to the given string. By default, it's set to `mysql>`.

`--protocol=`*`protocol`*
: This option specifies the protocol to use when connecting to the server. The choices are `TCP`, `SOCKET`, `PIPE`, and `MEMORY`.

`--quick`, `-q`
: This option causes the client to retrieve and display data one row at a time instead of buffering the entire results set before displaying data. With this option, the history file isn't used and it may slow the server if the output is suspended.

`--raw, -r`
: For data that may contain characters that would normally be converted in batch mode to an escape-sequence equivalent (e.g., newline to `\n`), this option may be used to have the client print out the characters without converting them.

`--reconnect`
: This option instructs the client to attempt to reconnect to the server if the connection is lost. The client tries only once, though. This is enabled by default. To disable it, use `--skip-reconnect`. To make the client wait until the server is available, use `--wait`.

`--safe-updates, -U`
: This option helps prevent inadvertent deletion of multiple and possibly all rows in a table. It requires that when the `DELETE` or `UPDATE` statements are used, a `WHERE` clause be given with a key column and value. If this option is included in the options file, using it at the command line when starting the client will disable it.

`--secure-auth`
: This option prevents authentication of users with passwords created prior to version 4.1 of MySQL or connecting to servers that permit the old format.

`--set-variable` *`var=value`*, `-o` *`var=value`*
: This option sets a server variable. Enter **`mysql --help`** for the current values for a particular server's variables.

`--show-warnings`
: This option instructs the client not to suppress warning messages, but to display them after an SQL statement is executed in which a warning is generated, even if there was no error.

`--silent, -s`
: This option suppresses all messages except for error messages. Enter the option multiple times to further reduce the types of messages returned.

`--skip-column-names`
: This option instructs the client not to return column names in the results.

`--skip-line-numbers`
: When the client is accepting SQL statements from an input file, this option instructs the client not to display the line number of an SQL statement that has returned an error. This disables `--line-numbers`, the default.

`--skip-named-commands`
: This option disables named commands on the client. See the description of the `--named-commands` option and the following section for more information.

`--skip-pager`
: This option disables paged results on Unix types of systems. See the `--pager` option for more information.

`--skip-reconnect`
: This option instructs the client not to attempt to reconnect to the server if the connection is lost. It disables the default option `--reconnect`.

`--skip-ssl`
: This option specifies that an SSL connection should not be used, if SSL is enabled by default.

`--socket=`*socket*, `-S` *socket*
: This option provides the path and name of the server's socket file on Unix systems, or the named pipe on Windows systems.

`--ssl`
: This option specifies that an SSL connection should be used. It requires the server to have SSL enabled. If this option is enabled on the utility by default, use `--skip-ssl` to disable it.

`--ssl-ca=`*pem_file*
: This option specifies the name of the file (i.e., the *pem* file) containing a list of trusted SSL CAs.

`--ssl-capath=`*path*
: This option specifies the path to the trusted certificates file (i.e., the *pem* file).

`--ssl-cert=`*filename*
: This option specifies the name of the SSL certificate file to use for SSL connections.

`--ssl-cipher=`*ciphers*
: This option gives a list of ciphers that may be used for SSL encryption.

`--ssl-key=`*filename*
: This option specifies the SSL key file to use for secure connections.

`--ssl-verify-server-cert`
: This option verifies the client's certificate against the server's certificate for the client at startup. It is available as of version 5.1.11 of MySQL.

`--table`, `-t`
: This option displays results from a query in ASCII format, which is the format normally used in monitor mode. The alternative is the `--xml` option.

`--tee=`*filename*
: This option instructs the client to write results to the given file. You can include an absolute or relative pathname, or a simple filename. This option doesn't work in batch mode.

`--unbuffered`, `-n`
: This option flushes the memory buffer after each query is performed.

`--user=`*user*, `-u` *user*
: This option instructs the client to access MySQL with a username different from the current system user.

`--verbose`, `-v`
: This option displays more information. Use `-vv` or `-vvv` to increase verbosity.

`--version`, `-V`
: This option displays the version of the utility.

`--vertical`
: This option displays results in a vertical format instead of putting each row of data on a single line. This is similar to using the end of `\G` of an SQL statement in monitor mode.

`--wait`, `-w`
: If the client cannot connect to the server, this option tells the client to wait and retry repeatedly until it can connect.

`--xml`, `-X`
: This option exports results in an XML format.

mysqld Server

mysqld

`mysqld [options]`

When *mysqld* starts, various options can be used to alter the server's behavior. Although you don't need to know all of the server options available or use them—quite often the default settings are fine—as a database administrator, it's useful to know what options exist for various categories that may be related to your needs.

Options may be given at the command line when starting or restarting the server. However, it's common practice to enter them into a configuration file. On Unix-based systems, the main configuration file typically is */etc/my.cnf*. For Windows systems, the main file is usually either *c:\systems\my.ini* or *c:\my.conf*. Options are entered on separate lines and follow a `variable=value` format. Some options are binary and can be enabled by just including the option at the command line when starting the server or in the options file with no value (or an equals sign followed by no value).

Within the options file, options are grouped under headings contained within square brackets. The *mysqld* daemon reads options from the configuration file under the headings of `[mysqld]` and `[server]` as it's started. For more recent versions of the MySQL server, the group `[mysqld-5.0]` is also read. Groups are read in the order mentioned here, and the last setting for an option read is the one used. To get a list of options that *mysqld* is using on a particular server, enter the following line from the command line (results follow):

```
$ mysqld --print-defaults
/usr/libexec/mysqld would have been started with the following arguments:
--datadir=/data/mysql --socket=/var/lib/mysql/mysql.sock
--old-passwords=1
```

As the resulting message indicates, the `--print-defaults` options draws information from the options files and indicates the options and what their values would be if the MySQL server were restarted. However, if the options files were changed since MySQL was started, or if MySQL was started from the command line or with command-line options from a script on the server, this output will not reflect those options. Basically, the results of `--print-defaults` do not reflect the current settings, just the options it finds in the options files for the relevant server groups. To determine the current server options that have been used—other than the default options—while a server is running, you can enter the following command from a Unix system (sample results follow):

```
$ ps aux | grep mysql

mysql 27670 0.2 3.2 124252 17296 ? Sl Aug21 25:06
/usr/libexec/mysqld --defaults-file=/etc/my.cnf --basedir=/usr
--datadir=/data/mysql --user=mysql --pid-file=/var/run/mysqld/mysqld.pid
--skip-locking --socket=/var/lib/mysql/mysql.sock
```

If you see an option that you don't see in your default options file, it may be coming from a different options file. You may even be running a different installation of `mysqld` than you think. In such a situation, you would have to specify the path to the `mysqld` you want to use when starting the server.

In the following sections of this chapter, options are grouped by their use:

Location
: These options specify where the server can find files and directories it needs.

Security and connection
: These options are related to user and database security, limits on connections, and how clients connect to the server.

Global
: These options affect server behavior, and are stored in global variables.

Logs
: These options relate to server logs.

Performance optimization
: This section contains several options that could be included in other categories, but they are worth considering together because they can affect the speed of the database.

Replication
: These options are strictly related to replication.

Storage engine specific options
: These options concerning storage engines (formerly known as table types) are grouped into subsections based on the specific storage engines to which they relate.

Some options are listed in more than one section because they have more than one use relative to the sections listed.

The options are shown as they would be entered from the command line. If an option is used in a configuration file, the long form should be used and the double-dash prefix should be omitted. For example, `--basedir=/data/mysql` would be entered from the command line. However, in a configuration file the same option would read as `basedir=/data/mysql` on its own separate line.

The syntax for listing options is as follows:

`--option=value`
: An option that requires a value

`--option[=value]`
: An option that can take a value, but does not require one

`--option[=value]`
: A binary option that is to be given without a value

A few options have single-letter abbreviations, also called short forms. The short form is shown in parentheses after the long form.

As new versions of MySQL are released, more options may be added. To get a list for your version, type `mysqld --verbose --help` from the command line on the server host.

For many of the options, there is a system variable with the same name as the option, but without the leading double-dashes. For some options, the dashes within the name will need to be changed to underscores (e.g., the variable associated with `--setting-example` would be `setting_example`). Before changing the value or the setting of a variable, it's often a good idea to see what the variable is set to. You can do this by entering a statement like this:

```
SHOW VARIABLES LIKE 'setting_example';
```

Location

Some `mysqld` options allow you to instruct MySQL where files are located and what network settings should be used when clients connect to it remotely. An alphabetical list of these options follows, along with the syntax and an explanation of each. This list does not include storage system specific options related to file paths. See the section for the particular storage engine's options later in this chapter:

`--basedir=`*`path`*, `-b` *`path`*
: If you've installed more than one version of MySQL on your server or if you have moved the binary files for MySQL, you will need to specify the base directory for the MySQL installation. This option is particularly necessary if you're using `mysqld_safe` to keep the *mysqld* daemon running; list this option under the `[mysqld_safe]` group heading.

`--character-sets-dir=`*`path`*
: This option specifies the absolute path to the directory containing character sets. By default, this directory is in the subdirectory *charsets* in the directory where MySQL is installed (e.g., */usr/share/mysql/charsets/*).

`--datadir=`*`path`*, `-h` *`path`*
: If you want to put your datafiles for MySQL (i.e., database directories and table files) in a different directory from the default, you need to use this option. This is useful especially if you want the data on a different hard drive. Within the directory that you name, MySQL will create subdirectories for each database. If you use this option, be sure that the *mysql* user on the filesystem has permissions to read and write to the directory. Generally, you would make it the owner of the directory.

`--init-file=`*`filename`*
: If you have a set of SQL commands that you must execute every time you restart the server, rather than enter them manually you could put them in a file and use this option to tell MySQL to execute them for you at startup. Each SQL statement in the file must be on a separate line. Unfortunately, you cannot include comments in the file. You could put them in a separate text file in the same directory, perhaps with a similar same filename (e.g., *init.sql* and *init.txt*).

`--secure-file-priv=`*`path`*
: Use this option to restrict the importing of files to the given path. This is related to the `SELECT...INTO OUTFILE` and `LOAD DATA` statements, as well as the `LOAD_FILE( )` function. This option is available as of version 5.1.17 of MySQL.

`--pid-file=`*`filename`*
: Instead of starting `mysqld` directly, the common method used lately is to start the script `mysqld_safe`. It will in turn start `mysqld` and make sure it keeps running. Thus, if `mysqld` crashes, `mysqld_safe` will automatically restart it. To keep track of the system process for `mysqld`, the `mysqld_safe` program will record the process identification number in a file called *mysqld.pid*. With this option, you can tell MySQL where to put that file.

`--plugin-dir=`*`path`*
: This option sets the directory where plugins on the server are placed. It's available as of version 5.1.2 of MySQL.

`--skip-symbolic-links`
: This option is used to disable symbolic links. The reverse is to enable them through `--symbolic-links`. Prior to version 4.0.3 of MySQL, this option was `--skip-symlink`.

`--slave-load-tmpdir=`*`value`*
: This option specifies the directory where a slave server stores temporary files when the `LOAD DATA INFILE` statement is executed.

`--slow-query-log-file=`*`filename`*
: See the "Performance optimization" section later in this chapter.

`--socket=`*`filename`*
: Socket files are used on Unix systems. With this option, you may specify the path and filename of the socket file. If you don't use this option, recent versions of MySQL place the socket file in the data directory of MySQL. On Windows systems, this option may be used to provide the pipe name (*MySQL* by default) for local connections. Just as with the `--port` option, the `--socket` option may be used for multiple instances of MySQL. You could issue one `mysqld_safe` command with the default socket file and another with an option such as `--socket=mysqld_test.sock` to indicate a test server. A second server that you assign to the same socket file will refuse to start because otherwise the daemons would conflict with each other. Incidentally, it's not necessary to specify a separate port and socket file, but most administrators do it all the same.

`--symbolic-links`, `-s`
: This option enables symbolic links at the filesystem level for database directories and table files. MySQL expects to find the files in its data directory, but if you want to store the data in other directories in order to find more space or spread reads and writes around, this option allows you to create links in the data directory that point to where the data actually is stored. On Windows systems, this allows you to create shortcuts to databases (e.g., `database.sym`). On Unix systems with MyISAM tables, this option allows you to specify a different directory for a table's location with the `DATA DIRECTORY` or `INDEX DIRECTORY` options of both the `ALTER TABLE` and `CREATE TABLE` SQL statements. When the table is renamed or deleted, the related files that are symbolically linked will be renamed or deleted, respectively.

`--sync-frm`
: This option instructs the server to synchronize the *.frm* files with the filesystem when a table is created. This slows down table creation slightly, but is more stable than leaving it in memory only.

`--temp-pool`
: This option instructs the server to utilize a small set of names for temporary filenaming rather than unique names for each file.

`--tmpdir=`*`path`*, `-t` *`path`*
: If you want to control where MySQL places its temporary files, specify this option. You can give multiple file paths in a colon-separated list. When you're using a storage engine such as InnoDB to create tablespaces over multiple files and you're working with huge tables of data that would exceed the filesystem limits, this option is useful for working around those limits. For instance, if you have a system with a

file or directory size limit of 4 MB, you can provide two directories with the `--tmpdir` option and thereby double your physical table limitations to 8 MB. The directories could even be on separate filesystems that your operating system mounts.

Security and connections

These `mysqld` server options relate to security, user-related settings, and the network connections clients make to the server:

`--allow-suspicious-udfs[={0|1}]`
: As of version 5.0.3 of MySQL, the server requires user-defined functions to be named with an acceptable suffix—*`function_name`*`_add( )`, *`function_name`*`_clear( )`, *`function_name`*`_deinit( )`, *`function_name`*`_init( )`, *`function_name`*`_reset( )`, etc.—and won't load functions that fail to adhere to that standard. However, you can disable that security protection by giving this option a value of 0. A value of 1 enables it and is the default.

`--automatic-sp-privileges[={0|1}]`
: By default, this option is set to 1 and therefore gives users the `ALTER ROUTINE` and the `EXECUTE` privileges for any stored routine that the user has created, as long as the user and those routines exist. If you set this option to 0, the user does not get those privileges and therefore cannot alter or execute routines. However, you can explicitly grant users those privileges, as with other MySQL privileges.

`--back-log=`*`value`*
: When the primary thread of the MySQL server gets many connection requests simultaneously, they are backlogged while the server begins new threads. Use this option to set the number of connections that may be backed up. The number cannot exceed the system value for TCP/IP connections related to the `listen( )` system function.

`--bind-address=`*`address`*
: This option specifies the IP address the server binds to. It's used to restrict network access on a host with multiple IP addresses.

`--bootstrap`
: This option isn't normally used by administrators. It's used by the `mysql_install_db` script to create the necessary privileges tables without the *mysqld* daemon running.

`--character-set-client-handshake`
: Use this option at the command line only (not available in the options file) to instruct the server not to ignore strange characters that it receives (perhaps due to a character set mismatch) from the client. Use `--skip-character-set-client-handshake` to disable this option because it's set by default.

`--chroot=`*`path`*
: This option runs the daemon with `chroot( )` from the filesystem so as to start it in a closed environment for additional security. This is a recommended security measure.

`--connect-timeout=`*`value`*
: This option may be used to change the number of seconds that the server should wait for a connection packet before terminating the connection and returning *Bad Handshake*. As of version 5.1.23, the related variable is set to five seconds by default.

If clients display messages saying that they lost the connection to the server, you might try increasing this value.

`--des-key-file=`*`filename`*
: This option instructs the server to obtain the default keys from the given file when the MySQL functions `DES_ENCRYPT( )` or `DES_DECRYPT( )` are used.

`--enable-named-pipe`
: This option enables support for named pipe connections with the `mysqld-nt` and `mysqld-max-nt` servers, which support them. It's used only with Windows NT, 2000, XP, and 2003 systems; do not use it on non-Windows systems (e.g., Linux or Mac OS X). Use the `--socket` option with this one to specify the path and name of the pipe.

`--init-connect='`*`string`*`'`
: This option specifies one or more SQL statements, all combined in a single *`string`*, that are to be executed each time a client connects to the server. It will not allow SQL statements to be executed for users with the `SUPER` privilege.

`--init-file=`*`filename`*
: This option indicates a file containing SQL statements that are to be executed when the server is started. This option will not work if the `--disable-grant-options` option is enabled. SQL statements need to be on separate lines, and comments are not permitted in the file.

`--interactive-timeout=`*`value`*
: For interactive clients (clients using `mysql_real_connect( )` with the `CLIENT_INTERACTIVE` flag), this option sets the number of seconds of inactivity allowed before closing the connection.

`--local-infile[={0|1}]`
: The SQL statement `LOAD DATA INFILE` can import data from a file on either the server's host or the client's host. By adding the `LOCAL` option, the client instructs the server to import locally from the client machine. This has the potential to be a security problem, though, because the file being loaded could have malicious code. Therefore, some administrators for public servers want to prevent clients from being able to import files local to the client, while still allowing them to import files located on the server. Use this option and set it to 0 to disable importing files local to the client. By default this is set to 1.

`--max-allowed-packet=`*`value`*
: See the "Performance optimization" section later in this chapter.

`--max-connect-errors=`*`value`*
: If the client has problems connecting and the number of attempts exceeds the value of the MySQL variable `max_connect_errors` (10 by default), the host address for the client will be blocked from further attempts. Use this option to change that value of that variable. To reset blocked hosts, run the `FLUSH HOSTS` statement on the server.

`--max-connections=`*`value`*
: Clients are not permitted to have more connections than the number specified by the variable `max_connections`. By default it's either 100 or 150, depending on your version. Use this option to change that value.

`--max-user-connections=value`
: This option limits the number of connections per user account. Set the value to 0 to disable the limit and thereby allow a single user to create as many connections as MySQL and the operating system allow.

`--net-buffer-length=value`
: Memory is allocated by MySQL for each thread's connection and results. The amount initially allocated for each of these buffers is controlled by the variable `net_buffer_length`. You can use this option to change the value, but you normally shouldn't. Each buffer can expand as needed until it reaches the limit specified in `max_allowed_packet`, but when each thread finishes its work, the buffers contract again to their initial sizes.

`--net-read-timeout=value`
: This option sets the number of seconds the server will wait for a response from the client while reading from it before terminating the connection. Use `--net-write-timeout` to set the amount of time the server should wait when writing to a client before terminating. The timeouts apply only to TCP/IP connections and not to connections made through a socket file, a named pipe, or shared memory.

`--net-retry-count=value`
: If the connection to the client is interrupted while the server is reading, the server will try to reestablish the connection a number of times. That number can be set with this option.

`--net-write-timeout=value`
: This option sets the number of seconds the server will wait for a response from the client while writing to it before terminating the connection. Use `--net-read-timeout` to set the amount of time the server should wait when reading from a client before terminating. The timeouts apply only to TCP/IP connections and not to connections made through a socket file, a named pipe, or shared memory.

`--old-passwords`
: This option permits clients to continue to use passwords that were created before version 4.1 of MySQL, along with the old, less secure encryption method in use in earlier versions.

`--old-protocol, -o`
: This option has the server use version 3.20 protocol of MySQL for compatibility with older clients.

`--old-style-user-limits`
: Prior to version 5.0.3 of MySQL, user resource limits were based on each combination of user and host. Since then, user resources are counted based on the user regardless of the host. To continue to count resources based on the old method, use this option.

`--one-thread`
: This option instructs the server to run only one thread, which is needed when debugging a Linux system using older versions of the *gdb* debugger.

`--port=port, -P port`
: This option specifies the port on which the server will listen for client connections. By default, MySQL uses port 3306. However, if you want to use a separate port, you may specify one with this option. This feature can be useful if you are running more than one instance of MySQL on your server. For example, you might use port 3306

for your regular MySQL server and port 3307 for a particular department's databases, as well as 3308 for testing a new version of MySQL.

`--port-open-timeout=`*`value`*
: As of version 5.1.5 of MySQL, this option may be used to set the number of seconds the server should wait for a TCP/IP port to become available. This usually comes into play when the server has been restarted.

`--safe-show-database`
: This option hides database names that a user does not have permission to access.

`--safe-user-create`
: This option prevents a user from creating new users without the `INSERT` privilege for the `user` table in the `mysql` database.

`--secure`
: This option enables reverse host lookup of IP addresses, which provides some defense against spoofing domain names but adds overhead to each remote connection.

`--secure-auth`
: This option prevents authentication of users with passwords created prior to version 4.1 of MySQL.

`--secure-file-priv=`*`path`*
: See the "Location" section earlier in this chapter.

`--skip-automatic-sp-privileges`
: This option disables the `--automatic-sp-privileges` option, which is related to users automatically being granted `ALTER ROUTINE` and `EXECUTE` privileges on stored procedures that they create.

`--skip-character-set-client-handshake`
: This option disables the `--character-set-client-handshake` option.

`--skip-grant-tables`
: This option instructs the server not to use the grants table and thus give all users full access. This option presents a security risk. It may be used if the *root* password is lost so that you may log in without it and then reset the password. Restart the server without this option or run the `FLUSH PRIVILEGES` statement from the monitor to reenable privileges.

`--skip-host-cache`
: This option disables the use of the internal host cache, which requires a DNS lookup for each new connection.

`--skip-name-resolve`
: This option requires a client's IP address to be named in the privileges tables for tighter security and faster connections.

`--skip-networking`
: This option prevents network connections of clients and allows only local connections.

`--skip-show-database`
: This option prevents the `SHOW DATABASES` statement from being executed by users without the specific privilege.

`--skip-ssl`
: This option specifies that an SSL connection should not be used, if SSL is enabled by default.

`--ssl`
: This option specifies the use of SSL-protected connections. It requires the server to be SSL-enabled. If this option is enabled on the utility by default, use `--skip-ssl` to disable it.

`--ssl-ca=`*`pem_file`*
: This option specifies the file (i.e., the *pem* file) that provides a list of trusted SSL CAs.

`--ssl-capath=`*`path`*
: This option specifies a directory of files that provide trusted SSL certificates (i.e., *pem* files).

`--ssl-cert=`*`filename`*
: This option specifies the SSL certificate file for SSL connections.

`--ssl-cipher=`*`ciphers`*
: This option gives a list of ciphers that may be used for SSL encryption.

`--ssl-key=`*`filename`*
: This option specifies the SSL key file for secure connections.

`--ssl-verify-server-cert`
: This option has the client verify its certificate with the server during an SSL connection. It is available as of version 5.1.11 of MySQL.

`--standalone`
: If MySQL is running Windows NT, this option instructs the server not to run as a service.

`--thread-handling={one-thread|one-thread-per-connection}`
: This option specifies the thread handling model that the server is to use. The `one-thread` option is basically used for debugging; `one-thread-per-connection` is the default. This option is available as of version 5.1.17 of MySQL.

`--user=`*`user`*`, -u `*`user`*
: This option instructs the client to access MySQL under a username different from the current system user.

Global

Following is a list of global server options related to the server's behavior:

`--ansi, -a`
: This option instructs the server to use standard American National Standards Institute (ANSI) SQL syntax instead of MySQL syntax.

`--auto-increment-increment[=`*`value`*`]`
: This option and the `--auto-increment-offset` option are used when replicating a master to a master server. They determine the amount by which an `AUTO_INCREMENT` column is increased with each new row inserted into any table in the system. By default, the variable associated with this option is set to 1. Each can be set to a value from 1 to 65535. If either option is set to 0, they both will be set back to 1. If either is set to a non-integer value, it will remain unchanged. If either is set to a negative value or a value in excess of 65535, they both will then be set to 65535. Don't use these options with MySQL Cluster, as they cause problems.

`--auto-increment-offset[=value]`
This option sets the starting number for `AUTO_INCREMENT` columns on all tables on the server. Each successive row inserted into tables will be incremented by the value of the `auto-increment-increment` system variable. If that variable is set to a number lower than the value set by this option, the value of the `auto-increment-offset` system variable (set by this option) will be ignored. See the description of the `--auto-increment-increment` option previously for more restrictions on this option.

`--character-set-server=set, -C`
This option makes the server use a particular character set by default for its calculations. It's available as of version 4.1.3 of MySQL.

`--character-set-filesystem=value`
This option specifies the character set that the filesystem uses. It was added in version 5.1.6 of MySQL.

`--completion-type=[=0|1|2]`
The SQL statements `COMMIT` and `ROLLBACK` support an optional `AND CHAIN` parameter that automatically begins a new transaction at the same isolation level after the end of the transaction completed by these statements. If this option is set to 1, this chaining effect will be the default setting for those SQL statements. Similarly, if this option is set to 2, the default setting for the statements will be `RELEASE`, which causes the server to disconnect after each transaction is terminated. A value of 0, which is the default, does nothing.

`--console`
On Windows systems, this option has the server display error messages to `stdout` and `std.err` even if `--log-error` is enabled.

`--core-file`
This option instructs the server to create a core file if the daemon dies. Some systems require the `--skip-stack-trace` option to be set as well. Some systems also require the `--core-file-size` option when using `mysqld_safe`. On Solaris systems, if the `--user` option is used also, the server will not create the core file.

`--date-format=value`
The variable associated with this option is not yet implemented. It's expected to be used to set the default date format for the MySQL server.

`--datetime-format=value`
The variable associated with this option is not yet implemented. It's expected to be used to set the default datetime format for the MySQL server.

`--default-week-format=value`
The variable associated with this option is not yet implemented. It's expected to be used to set the default format for the days of the week on the MySQL server.

`--debug[=options], -# options]`
This option is used to get a trace file of the daemon's activities. The debug options are typically `d:t:o,filename`. See Table 16-1 at the end of the list of options for the `mysqldump` utility later in this chapter for an explanation of these flags and others that may be used. MySQL has to be compiled for debugging using the `--with-debug` option when configuring.

`--default-character-set=character_set`
This option is used to specify the default character set. This option is deprecated as of version 4.1.3 of MySQL. Use the `--character-set-server` option instead.

`--default-collation=collation`
: This option specifies the collation to use as the default. This option is deprecated as of version 4.1.3 of MySQL. Use the `--collation-server` option instead.

`--default-time-zone=zone`
: This option specifies the default time zone for the server. The filesystem time zone is used by default.

`--div-precision-increment=value`
: This option sets the number of decimal places to show in the results of dividing numbers. The variable associated with this option (`div_precision_increment`) has a default value of 4. You can set it from 0 to 30.

`--enable-pstack`
: This option instructs the server to print a symbolic stack trace if the server fails and exits.

`--exit-info[=flags], -T [flags]`
: This option displays debugging information when the server exits.

`--external-locking`
: This option allows system locking. Be careful when using it on a platform with problems with `lockd`, such as Linux, because the *mysqld* daemon may deadlock and require rebooting the server to unlock it. This option was previously called `--enable-locking`.

`--flush`
: This option flushes all changes to disk after each SQL statement instead of waiting for the filesystem to do the writes at regular intervals.

`--flush-time=seconds`
: This option sets the `flush_time` variable, which specifies the number of seconds a table can remain open before it's closed and flushed to free resources and to synchronize data. For current operating systems, this option shouldn't be used because it will slow the server. A value of 0 disables it and is the default.

`--gdb`
: This option is recommended when debugging the MySQL daemon. It enables a handler for `SIGINT`, which is necessary for the server daemon to be stopped with Ctrl-C at debugging breakpoints. It also disables core file handling as well as stack tracing.

`--group-concat-max-len=value`
: This option sets the maximum length of a value created by the `GROUP_CONCAT( )` function.

`--language=[language|pathname]`
: This option specifies the language the daemon should use to display messages. It can be the name of a language or a pathname to the language file.

`--lower-case-table-names[=0|1|2]`
: If this option is set to 1, database and table names will be saved in lowercase letters on the server, and MySQL will not consider case when given database and table names. A value of 2 causes databases and tables to be stored on the filesystem in filenames with uppercase and lowercase based on what it is given when they are created. However, they will be treated as lowercase. A value of 0 disables these

features, but you shouldn't set it to 0 if using a case-insensitive filesystem, such as Windows.

`--max-error-count=value`
: When errors, warnings, and notes are generated, they are stored by the server to be displayed when the `SHOW ERRORS` or `SHOW WARNINGS` statements are executed. This option limits the number of messages that will be stored. The default value is 64.

`--max-join-size=value`
: This option sets the maximum number of rows in a join. By default, this option is set very high. You may want to lower it if you suspect abuse from users. To reset it to the default value, enter a value of `DEFAULT`. If you set this option to any other value, it causes the system variable `SQL_BIG_SELECTS` to be set to 0. If the `SQL_BIG_SELECTS` variable is then set to another value, this option's setting is ignored.

`--max_length_for_sort_data=value`
: This option sets the maximum size of data that can be sorted with the `ORDER BY` clause.

`--max_prepared_stmt_count=value`
: This option sets the maximum number of prepared statements allowed on the server. Values from 0 to 1000000 (one million) are accepted; the default is 16382. If you set the value lower than the current number of prepared statements, existing ones will be unaffected. But when they are removed, new ones cannot be added until the total count falls below the value given with this option. This option is available as of version 5.1.10 of MySQL.

`--new, -n`
: At the time of this writing, this option is used to test queries before upgrading from version 4.0 to 4.1.

`--open_files_limit=value`
: This option specifies the maximum number of files the daemon can keep open, which may require it to close tables more often than is optimal.

`--help, -?`
: This option displays basic help information. It displays more information when combined with the `--verbose` option.

`--read_only`
: If this option is used, users cannot add, change, or delete data on the server, unless they have `SUPER` privileges. The other exception is that updates from slave threads are allowed. This option does not carry to the slaves. It can be set on slaves independently from the master and may be useful to keep slaves synchronized properly.

`--safe-mode=value`
: This option disables some optimizations at startup.

`--set-variable variable = value, -O variable = value`
: This option sets a server variable. Enter `mysqld --verbose --help` to see the current values for particular server variables.

`--skip-external-locking`
: Previously called `--skip-locking`, this option prevents system locking.

`--skip-locking`
: This option disables system locking of the server.

`--skip-new`
: This option instructs the server not to use new options—i.e., options that are enabled by default but are still in beta testing mode.

`--sql-mode=`*`value`*
: This option covers a number of possible ways of interpreting SQL statements, mostly for compatibility with other database engines. Multiple values may be given in a comma-separated list.

`--sql_auto_is_null={0|1}`
: If you enable this option by setting it to 1, you can give the name of a column that uses `AUTO_INCREMENT` in `WHERE` clauses with a condition of NULL to find the last inserted row. For example, `SELECT...WHERE client_id IS NULL;` will return the row that was last inserted into a table where `client_id` is the primary key. A value of 0 for this option will disable it. The option is useful when interfacing with ODBC applications (e.g., MS Access).

`--sql_big_selects={0|1}`
: Disable (set to 0) this option to prevent large `SELECT` statements from being executed. Large statements are defined as joins whose results would exceed the maximum number of rows set by the `--max_join_size` option. The default value of 1 enables large SQL statements. Setting the `--max_join_size` option to something other than `DEFAULT` will reset this option back to 0.

`--sql_buffer_result={0|1}`
: If this option is set to 1, the results of `SELECT` statements will be sent to a buffer before being returned to the client. This slows the results, but unlocks the associated tables faster for the use of other clients. The default setting of 0 disables this option.

`--sql-safe-updates={0|1}`
: This option, when set to 1, is useful in helping to prevent inadvertent deletion of multiple and possibly all rows in a table. It requires that `DELETE` and `UPDATE` statements contain a `WHERE` clause with a key column and value. The default value of 0 disables the option.

`--sql_select_limit={`*`value`*`|DEFAULT}`
: This option limits the number of rows returned from a `SELECT` statement when the `LIMIT` clause hasn't been given. The value of `DEFAULT` means that there is no limit.

`--sysdate-is-now`
: The `SYSDATE( )` function returns the date and time in which the function was executed by MySQL within an SQL statement. It doesn't return the time that the SQL statement started, as the `NOW( )` function does. If you want `SYSDATE( )` to return the same time as `NOW( )`, use this option. See the description of `SYSDATE( )` in Chapter 12 for an example.

`--tc-heuristic-recover={COMMIT|ROLLBACK}`
: This option is not yet implemented by MySQL. It will relate to the heuristic recovery process when it is implemented.

`--time_format=`*`value`*
: The variable associated with this option is not yet implemented. It's expected to be used to set the default time format for the MySQL server.

`--transaction-isolation=`*`option`*
: This option sets the default transaction isolation level. The available levels are `READ-UNCOMMITTED`, `READ-COMMITTED`, `REPEATABLE-READ`, or `SERIALIZABLE`.

`--updatable_views_with_limit={0|1}`
: Set this option to 1 to prevent updates to views that do not contain all of the columns of the primary key of the underlying table; the option applies only when the SQL statement contains a `LIMIT` clause. If set to the default value of 1, only a warning is returned and the update is not prevented.

`--version`
: This option displays the version of MySQL that is running on the server.

`--version_compile_machine`
: This option displays the type of machine on which MySQL was compiled.

`--version_compile_os`
: This option displays the type of operating system on which MySQL was compiled.

Logs

These `mysqld` server options relate to general logs created by MySQL. For storage engine specific logs, see the "Storage engine specific options" section later in this chapter.

`--binlog-do-db=`*`value`*
: This option limits the binary log to entries created by SQL statements executed against the database given, and only when it is the default database. If the user sets the default database to another database, but executes SQL statements affecting the database given with this option, those statements will not be written to the binary log. Additional databases may be specified with multiple instances of this option. Despite this option, though, `ALTER DATABASE`, `CREATE DATABASE`, and `DROP DATABASE` statements for the given database will be logged regardless of the default database setting.

`--binlog-ignore-db=`*`value`*
: This option omits entries from the binary log for SQL statements executed against the database given, but only when it is the default database. So when the user sets the default database to another database, but executes SQL statements affecting the database given with this option, those statements will be written to the binary log. Additional databases may be specified with multiple instances of this option. Despite this option, though, `ALTER DATABASE`, `CREATE DATABASE`, and `DROP DATABASE` statements for the given database will be logged regardless of the default database setting.

`--log[=`*`filename`*`], -l [`*`filename`*`]`
: This option instructs the server to log connection information and queries to the given file, or to the default (*host.log*) if none is given.

`--log-bin[=`*`filename`*`]`
: This option records database changes to a binary log to the filename given. If a filename isn't provided, the default name of ***`host-bin.index`*** will be used, where ***`host`*** is the hostname of the server and ***`index`*** is a numeric count.

`--log-bin-trust-function-creators[={0|1}]`
: By default, if binary logging is enabled, when creating a stored procedure you have to state whether the function is deterministic and whether it will modify data. If this option is specified without a value or with a value of 1, this requirement is disabled. If set to 0, which is the default setting, the requirement is enabled.

`--log-error[=filename]`
: This option activates logging of error messages and server startup messages to the filename given. The default name for the log if none is specified is *host.err*, where *host* is the server's hostname.

`--log-long-format, -0`
: This option instructs the server to be more verbose in logs. This is the default setting as of version 4.1 of MySQL. Use the `--log-short-format` option to disable this option.

`--log-short-format`
: This option instructs the server to be less verbose in logs. It is available as of version 4.1 of MySQL.

`--log-queries-not-using-indexes`
: See "Performance optimization" later in this chapter.

`--log-slave-updates`
: This option is used on a slave server to instruct it to write to its own binary log any updates to data made from SQL threads. The option requires that the `--log-bin` option be used on the slave. With this method, it's possible to have a slave act as master to a slave under it.

`--log-slow-admin-statements`
: See "Performance optimization."

`--log-slow-queries[=filename]`
: See "Performance optimization."

`--log-tc=filename`
: This option specifies the filename of the memory-mapped transaction coordinator log. The default filename is *tc.log*, located in the data directory for MySQL.

`--log-tc-size=size`
: This option specifies the size of the memory-mapped transaction coordinator log. The default is 24 KB.

`--log-update[=filename]`
: Activates logging of updates to the filename given. This feature is deprecated in favor of binary logging.

`--log-warnings, -W`
: This option activates logging of warning messages. Prior to version 4.0 of MySQL, this option was invoked with the `--warnings` option. After version 4.1.2, this option is enabled by default and can be disabled with the `--skip-log-warnings` option.

`--long_query_time=value`
: See "Performance optimization."

`--max-binlog-dump-events`
: This option is used by the MySQL test suite for testing and debugging replication.

`--relay-log=filename`
: See "Replication" later in this chapter.

`--relay-log-index=filename`
: See "Replication" later in this chapter.

`--relay-log-info-file=filename`
: See "Replication" later in this chapter.

`--relay-log-purge[={0|1}]`
: See "Replication" later in this chapter.

`--relay-log-space-limit=value`
: See "Replication" later in this chapter.

`--skip-log-warnings`
: This option disables the `--log-warnings` feature so that warning messages are not logged.

`--skip-stack-trace`
: This option prevents the writing of stack traces.

`--slow-query-log[={0|1}]`
: See "Performance optimization."

`--slow-query-log-file=filename`
: See "Performance optimization."

`--sporadic-binlog-dump-fail`
: This option is used by the MySQL test suite for testing and debugging replication.

`--sql_log_bin={0|1}`
: The default value of 1 for this option has clients log to the binary log. A value of 0 disables it.

`--sql_log_off={0|1}`
: The default value of 0 for this option has clients log to the general query log. A value of 1 disables it and general logging is not done for the client.

`--sql_notes={0|1}`
: If this option is set to the default of 1, note-level warning messages are logged. A value of 0 disables it.

`--sql_warnings={0|1}`
: If this option is set to 1, warning messages for single row `INSERT` statements generate an information string. The default value of 0 disables it.

`--sql_quote_show_create={0|1}`
: If this option is set to the default of 1, identifiers in statements will be quoted in the logs. This can be necessary for certain slave servers that may require identifiers to be contained within quotes. A value of 0 disables it.

`--sync_binlog={0|1}`
: If this option is set to a value of 1, the server will synchronize every write to the binary log to the disk. The default value of 0 disables this feature.

Performance optimization

These `mysqld` server options relate to improving server performance. Before changing a server's setting, you should make note of its current setting, and then use the `BENCHMARK( )` function to determine performance before changes are made. After implementing the new server setting, run the `BENCHMARK( )` function again to compare the results. This is just one of many ways in which you might test a server's performance before and after making changes to its settings. The important thing is not to assume that a particular setting will improve performance and to be aware that a change could cause other problems. Test and monitor changes to be sure. For performance options that are specific to InnoDB, see the "InnoDB" subsection of the "Storage engine specific options" section.

`--big-tables`
: This option instructs the server to save temporary results sets to a file to solve problems where results are large and error messages indicate that tables are full.

`--bulk_insert_buffer_size=`*`value`*
: When bulk inserting data into an existing table that already contains data, the MyISAM storage engine uses a special buffer to make the process faster. You can use this option to set the size of that buffer to improve performance. The default value is 8 MB. A value of 0 disables the buffer.

`--concurrent-insert[={0|1|2}]`
: If this option is set to its default of 1, the MyISAM storage engine will allow simultaneous inserting and selecting of data, but only if there are no free spaces on the filesystem within the datafile. A setting of 2 for this option allows concurrent reading and writing despite spaces in the datafile. It just writes the new rows to the end of the datafile if reads are occurring while the server is trying to write. If no concurrent reads are taking place, the server will get a write lock on the table and make use of the blank space. A value of 0 for this option disables concurrent inserting and reading.

`--delayed_insert_limit=`*`value`*
: If an `INSERT` statement is entered with the `DELAYED` parameter, the server delays entering rows if there are `SELECT` statements already running against the table. When the table is free, the server will then insert the delayed rows. This option causes the server to enter a fixed number of rows before rechecking to see whether new `SELECT` statements are queued. If there are, it will delay the inserts again.

`--delayed_insert_timeout=`*`value`*
: When an `INSERT` statement has been issued with the `DELAYED` parameter, the server will wait for the outstanding `SELECT` statements against the table to finish running before executing it. Use this option to set the number of seconds that the server should wait before terminating the `INSERT` statement.

`--delay-key-write[=`*`option`*`]`
: This option instructs the server how to handle key buffers between writes for MyISAM tables. The choices are `OFF`, `ON`, and `ALL`. The `ON` choice delays writes for tables created with `DELAYED KEYS`. The `ALL` choice delays writes for all MyISAM tables. MyISAM tables should not be accessed by another server or clients such as `myisamcheck` when the `ALL` choice is used; it may cause corruption of indexes.

`--delay-key-write-for-all-tables`
: This option instructs the server not to flush key buffers between writes for MyISAM tables. As of version 4.0.3 of MySQL, use `--delay-key-write=ALL` instead.

`--delayed_queue_size=`*`value`*
: When an `INSERT` statement has been entered with the `DELAYED` parameter, the server will wait for the outstanding `SELECT` statements against the table to finish running before executing it. Use this option to set the maximum number of rows that the server should queue from inserts. Any additional rows will not be queued, and the `INSERT` statements will have to wait until the queue is reduced.

`--join_buffer_size=`*`value`*
: This option sets the size of the buffer file to use for joins in which an index is not used. The maximum value for this option is 4 GB, but on 64-bit operating systems, as of version 5.1.23, a larger buffer size may be possible.

`--key_buffer_size=value`
: This option sets the key cache size. This is a buffer used by MyISAM tables for index blocks. The maximum value for this option is 4 GB, but on 64-bit operating systems, as of version 5.1.23, a larger buffer size may be possible. Execute the `SHOW STATUS` statement on the server to see the settings for the key cache.

`--key_cache_age_threshold=value`
: This option sets the point at which a buffer will be switched from what is known as a hot subchain in the key cache to a warm one. Lower values cause the switching to occur faster. The default value is 300. The lowest value allowed is 100.

`--key_cache_block_size=value`
: This option sets the size of blocks in the key cache. The values are in bytes. The default is 1024.

`--key_cache_division_limit=value`
: This option sets the division point between hot and warm subchains in the key cache. The value given represents a percentage of the whole buffer. The default value is 100. A value of 1 to 100 is allowed.

`--large-pages`
: This option enables large pages in memory.

`--log-slow-admin-statements`
: If this option is enabled, administrative SQL statements that take too long to execute will be logged. These include statements such as `ALTER TABLE`, `CHECK TABLE`, and `OPTIMIZE TABLE`.

`--log-slow-queries[=filename]`
: This option instructs the server to log queries that take longer than the number of seconds specified in the value of the `long_query_time` variable. If *`filename`* is specified, entries are recorded in the log file named.

`--log-queries-not-using-indexes`
: When used with the `--log-slow-queries` option, this option causes all queries that do not use indexes to be logged to the slow query log. It is available as of version 4.1 of MySQL.

`--long_query_time=value`
: This option sets the number of seconds that a query can take to execute before it's considered a slow query. If the `--log-slow-queries` option is in use, queries that exceed the number of seconds set by this option will be logged.

`--low-priority-updates`
: This option sets all SQL statements that modify data to a lower priority than `SELECT` statements, by default.

`--max_allowed_packet=value`
: This option sets the maximum size of a packet or a generated string. If using `BLOB` or `TEXT` columns, the variable associated with this option should be at least as large as the largest entry for the column. To determine this, you can execute `SHOW TABLE STATUS LIKE 'table';` on the server and look for the `Max_data_length` field. The maximum size allowed for this option is 1 GB. The `--net_buffer_length` option sets the initial size of buffer packets.

`--max_delayed_threads=`*`value`*
This option sets the maximum number of threads the server can use to handle delayed inserts. See the `--delayed_insert_limit` and `--delayed_insert_timeout` options earlier in this chapter for more information.

`--max_seeks_for_key=`*`value`*
When MySQL searches a table for data based on a `WHERE` clause using an index, it expects to have to search a certain number of rows in the index. You can adjust this expectation with this option. A lower value causes the MySQL optimizer to give preference to indexes over table scans.

`--max_sort_length=`*`value`*
This option sets the maximum number of bytes the server can examine in each field when sorting `BLOB` or `TEXT` columns. Any bytes of data beyond the value set for this option are ignored in sorting. The default is 1024.

`--max_sp_recursion_depth[=`*`value`*`]`
This option sets the maximum depth to which a stored procedure can invoke itself. The default is 0, which disables all recursion, and the maximum depth allowed is 255.

`--max_tmp_tables=`*`value`*
This is a new option that has not yet been implemented. When it is, you will be able to use it to limit the number of temporary tables that a client can have open at one time.

`--max_write_lock_count=`*`value`*
This option limits the number of write locks that may be made without allowing reads to be performed.

`--multi_range_count=`*`value`*
This option sets the maximum number of ranges that may be sent to a table handler at one time for a range select. The default is 256.

`--memlock`
This option is used on filesystems that support `mlockall( )` system calls (e.g., Solaris) to lock the daemon in memory and thereby avoid the use of disk swapping in an attempt to improve performance. Requires the daemon to be started by *root*, which may be a security problem.

MySQL Server and Client

`--optimizer_prune_level[={0|1}]`
This option sets the behavior of the optimizer when it tries to reduce or remove plans that don't seem to be useful. A value of 0 disables heuristics and instructs the optimizer to search as much as possible. The default value of 1 enables heuristics and thereby instructs the optimizer to prune plans.

`--optimizer_search_depth[=`*`value`*`]`
This option sets the maximum depth of searches performed by the query optimizer. A lower number will make for better queries, but it will take longer to perform. A higher number should make queries faster. If the value is set to 0, the server will attempt to decide on the best setting.

`--preload_buffer_size=`*`value`*
This option sets the size of the buffer used to hold preloaded indexes. The default is 32768 (32 KB).

`--query_alloc_block_size=`*`value`*
: This option sets the size of memory blocks that are allocated for use in parsing and executing a statement.

`--query_cache_limit=`*`value`*
: This option sets the maximum size of the query cache in bytes. The default is 1 MB.

`--query_cache_min_res_unit=`*`value`*
: This option sets the minimum size in bytes of blocks used for the query cache. The default is 4096 (4 KB).

`--query_cache_size=`*`value`*
: This option sets the maximum size in bytes of the cache used for query results. The default is 0. Values should be given in multiples of 1024 (1 KB).

`--query_cache_type={0|1|2}`
: This option sets the type of query cache to use on the server. A value of 0 causes the query cache not to be used. The default value of 1 causes all queries to be cached except `SELECT` statements that include the `SQL_NO_CACHE` parameter. A value of 2 means that no queries will be cached except `SELECT` statements that include the `SQL_CACHE` parameter.

`--query_cache_wlock_invalidate[={0|1}]`
: If a table is locked, but the results of querying the same table are already contained in the query cache, the results of a query will be returned if this option is set to 0, the default. Setting it to 1 will disable this feature and users will have to wait for the write lock to be released before reading the table and the related query cache data.

`--query_prealloc_size=`*`value`*
: This option sets the size of the persistent buffer used for parsing and executing statements.

`--range_alloc_block_size=`*`value`*
: This option sets the size of blocks of memory allocated for range queries.

`--read_buffer_size=`*`value`*
: This option sets the size in bytes of the buffer to use for each thread when doing sequential scans. The default value is 131072; the maximum is 2 GB.

`--read_rnd_buffer_size=`*`value`*
: Rows that are sorted by an index are read into a buffer to minimize disk activity. You can set the size of this buffer with this option to a maximum of 2 GB.

`--safemalloc-mem-limit=`*`value`*
: This option is used to simulate a memory shortage when the server has been compiled with the `--with-debug=full` option.

`--shared-memory`
: This option allows shared memory connections by Windows clients locally. It is available as of version 4.1 of MySQL.

`--shared-memory-base-name=`*`name`*
: This option sets the name to use for shared memory connections in Windows. It is available as of version 4.1 of MySQL.

`--skip-concurrent-insert`
: This option prevents simultaneous `SELECT` and `INSERT` statements for MyISAM tables.

`--skip-delay-key-write`
: This option disregards tables marked as `DELAY_KEY_WRITE`. As of version 4.0.3 of MySQL, use `--delay-key-write=OFF` instead.

`--skip-safemalloc`
: This option prevents the server from checking for memory overruns when performing memory allocation and memory freeing activities.

`--skip-thread-priority`
: This option prevents prioritizing of threads.

`--slow-query-log[={0|1}]`
: Slow queries are ones that take more than the number of seconds set by the `--long_query_time` option. A value of 1 for this option enables the logging of slow queries; the default value of 0 disables it. This option is available as of version 5.1.12 of MySQL.

`--slow-query-log-file=`*`filename`*
: This option sets the name of the slow query log file. By default it's *host_name-slow.log*. This option is available as of version 5.1.12 of MySQL.

`--slow_launch_time`
: This option causes a thread's `Slow_launch_threads` status to be updated to reflect whether a thread takes too long to launch.

`--sort_buffer_size=`*`value`*
: This option sets the size of the buffer each thread should use when sorting data for a query. The maximum value for this option is 4 GB, but on 64-bit operating systems, as of version 5.1.23, a larger buffer size may be possible.

`--table_lock_wait_timeout=`*`value`*
: This option sets the number of seconds that the server should wait to get a table lock before it terminates and returns an error. The timeout is related only to connections with active cursors. The default value is 50.

`--table_open_cache=`*`value`*
: This option sets the maximum number of open tables allowed for all threads. Prior to version 5.1.3, this option was called `--table_cache`. Executing the `FLUSH TABLES` statement will close any open tables and reopen any in use.

`--thread_cache_size=`*`value`*
: With this option, you can set the number of threads that the server should cache for reuse. This may lead to quicker connection times for new connections that are made by clients.

`--thread_concurrency=`*`value`*
: The value of the variable associated with this option is used by applications to provide a hint regarding the number of threads that the server should run concurrently. It's used on Solaris systems in conjunction with the `thr_setconcurrency( )` system function.

`--thread_stack=`*`value`*
: This option sets the size of the stack for each thread. The default value is 192 KB.

`--tmp_table_size=`*`value`*
: This option sets the maximum size of internal, in-memory temporary tables. This option is not related to MEMORY tables, though.

`--transaction_alloc_block_size=value`
: The memory pool described under the `--transaction_prealloc_size` option is increased as needed in increments. The amount of increments is drawn from the value of the `transaction_alloc_block_size` server variable. This option can be used to change that variable.

`--transaction_prealloc_size=value`
: A memory pool is used to temporarily store activities related to transactions. The size of that pool expands as needed. Initially, it is set to the size of the value of the server variable `transaction_prealloc_size`. This option can be used to set that variable higher to improve performance.

`--wait_timeout=value`
: This option sets the number of seconds that the server will wait before terminating a nonresponsive connection based on TCP/IP or a socket file. This option is not associated with connections through named pipes or shared memory.

Replication

An alphabetical list follows of `mysqld` server options related to replication. Many also appear earlier in Chapter 8. Although these options can be set at the command line when starting the server, and some can also be set with SQL statements while the server is running, as a general policy the options should be given in the server's options file (e.g., *my.cnf* or *my.ini*, depending on your system). Otherwise, there's a chance that the options may be lost when the server is restarted, in which case replication may fail or at least not function as you want:

`--abort-slave-event-count=value`
: This option is used by the MySQL test suite for testing and debugging replication.

`--disconnect-slave-event-count=value`
: This option is used by the MySQL test suite for testing and debugging replication.

`--init_slave='string'`
: Use this option on the server to specify one or more SQL statements, all combined in a single *`string`*, that are to be executed by the slave each time its SQL thread starts.

`--log-slave-updates`
: This option is used on a slave server to instruct it to write to its own binary log any updates to data made from SQL threads. It requires that the `--log-bin` option be used on the slave. With this method it's possible to have a slave act as master to a slave under it.

`--master-connect-retry=seconds`
: This option sets the number of seconds that a slave thread may sleep before trying to reconnect to the master. The default is 60 seconds. This value is also included in the *master.info* file. If that file exists and is accessible, the value contained in it will override this option.

`--master-host=host`
: This option is superseded by the same information in the *master.info* file and is necessary for replication. It that file doesn't exist or is inaccessible, this option may be used to set the hostname or IP address of the master server.

`--master-info-file=`*`filename`*
: This option sets the name of the master information file. This file is described in detail in Chapter 8 in the section “Replication Process.” By default this file is named *master.info* and is located in the data directory of MySQL.

`--master-password=`*`password`*
: If the *master.info* file doesn't exist or is inaccessible, this option may be used to set the password used by the slave thread for accessing the master server.

`--master-port=`*`port`*
: This option sets the port number on which the master will listen for replication. By default it's 3306. The value for this variable in the *master.info* file, if available, will override this option.

`--master-retry-count=`*`value`*
: This option specifies the number of times the slave should try to connect to the master if attempts fail. The default value is 86400. The interval between retries is set by the option `--master-connect-retry`. Retries are initiated when the slave connection times out for the amount of time set with the `--slave-net-timeout` option.

`--master-ssl`
: This option is similar to `--ssl` in the “Security and connections” section earlier in this chapter, but it applies to a slave's SSL connection with the master server.

`--master-ssl-ca[=`*`value`*`]`
: This option is similar to `--ssl-ca` in the “Security and connections” section earlier in this chapter, but it applies to a slave's SSL connection with the master server.

`--master-ssl-capath[=`*`value`*`]`
: This option is similar to `--ssl-capath` in the “Security and connections” section earlier in this chapter, but it applies to a slave's SSL connection with the master server.

`--master-ssl-cert[=`*`value`*`]`
: This option is similar to `--ssl-cert` in the “Security and connections” section earlier in this chapter, but it applies to a slave's SSL connection with the master server.

`--master-ssl-cipher[=`*`value`*`]`
: This option is similar to `--ssl-cipher` in the “Security and connections” section earlier in this chapter, but it applies to a slave's SSL connection with the master server.

`--master-ssl-key[=`*`value`*`]`
: This option is similar to `--ssl-key` in the “Security and connections” section earlier in this chapter, but it applies to a slave's SSL connection with the master server.

`--master-user=`*`value`*
: This option sets the name of the user account that the slave thread uses to connect to the master server for replication. The user given must have the `REPLICATION SLAVE` privilege on the master. This option is overridden by the *master.info* file.

`--max-binlog-dump-events=`*`value`*
: This option is used by the MySQL test suite for testing and debugging replication.

`--read_only`
: This option prevents users from adding, changing, or deleting data on the server, except for users with `SUPER` privileges. The other exception is that updates from slave threads are allowed. This option does not carry over from a master to its slaves.

It can be set on slaves independently from the master and may be useful to do so to keep slaves synchronized properly.

`--relay-log=`*`filename`*
: This option sets the root name of the relay log file. By default it's *`slave_host_name`*-*relay-bin*. MySQL will rotate the log files and append a suffix to the file name given with this option. The suffix is generally a seven digit number, counting from 0000001.

`--relay-log-index=`*`filename`*
: This option sets the name of the relay log index file. By default it's *`slave_host_name`*-*relay-bin.index*.

`--relay-log-info-file=`*`filename`*
: This option sets the name of the file that the slave will use to record information related to the relay log. By default it's *relay-log.info* and is located in the data directory of MySQL.

`--relay_log_purge[={0|1}]`
: This option is used to make the server automatically purge relay logs when it determines they are no longer necessary. The default value of 1 enables it; a value of 0 disables it.

`--replicate-do-db=`*`database`*
: This option tells the slave thread to limit replication to SQL statements executed against the database given, and only when it is the default database. When the user sets the default database to another database, but executes SQL statements affecting the database given with this option, those statements will not be replicated. Additional databases may be specified with multiple instances of this option.

`--replicate-do-table=`*`database.table`*
: This option tells the slave thread to limit replication to SQL statements executed against the table given. Additional tables may be specified with multiple instances of this option.

`--replicate-ignore-db=`*`database`*
: This option skips replication for SQL statements executed against the database given, but only when it is the default database. So when the user sets the default database to another database, but executes SQL statements affecting the database given with this option, those statements will be replicated. Additional databases may be specified with multiple instances of this option.

`--replicate-ignore-table=`*`database.table`*
: This option omits replication of SQL statements executed against the table given. Additional tables may be specified with multiple instances of this option.

`--replicate-rewrite-db='`*`filename->filename`*`'`
: This option tells the slave to change the database with the first name to have the second name (the name after the ->), but only when the default database on the master is set to the first database.

`--replicate-same-server-id[={0|1}]`
: If this option is set to 1, entries in the binary log with the same `server-id` as the slave will be replicated. This can potentially cause an infinite loop of replication, so it shouldn't be implemented unless necessary and then only for a limited time and purpose. This option is set to 0 by default and is used on the slave server. The option is ignored if `--log-slave-updates` is enabled.

`--replicate-wild-do-table=`*`database.table`*
This option is similar to `--replicate-do-table` except that you may give wildcards (`%` or `_`) for the database and table names. For instance, to match all tables that start with the name *clients*, you would give a value of `clients%`. To literally give a percent sign or an underscore, escape the character with a preceding backslash (i.e., `\%` and `\_`). Additional tables may be specified with multiple instances of this option.

`--replicate-wild-ignore-table=`*`database.table`*
This option is similar to `--replicate-ignore-table` except that you may give wildcards (`%` or `_`) for the database and table names. For instance, to match all tables that start with the name *clients*, you would give a value of `clients%`. To literally give a percent sign or an underscore, escape the character with a preceding backslash (i.e., `\%` and `\_`). Additional tables may be specified with multiple instances of this option.

`--report-host=`*`host`*
Because the master cannot always ascertain the slave's hostname or IP address, use this option to have the slave register with the master and report its hostname or IP address. This information will be returned when `SHOW SLAVE HOSTS` is executed on the master.

`--report-password=`*`value`*
This option sets the password used by the slave to register with the master. If the `--show-slave-auth-info` option is enabled, this information will be returned when `SHOW SLAVE HOSTS` is executed on the master.

`--report-port=`*`value`*
This option sets the port used by the slave to communicate with the master. It should be employed only when a special port is being used or if the server has special tunneling requirements.

`--report-user=`*`value`*
This option sets the username used by the slave to register with the master. If the `--show-slave-auth-info` option is enabled, this information will be returned when `SHOW SLAVE HOSTS` is executed on the master.

`--server-id=`*`value`*
This option ets the local server's server identifier. It must be used on the master as well as each slave, must be unique for each server, and should be set in the options file.

`--show-slave-auth-info`
This option causes the SQL statement `SHOW SLAVE HOSTS` to reveal the slave's username and password if the slave was started with the `--report-user` and the `--report-password` options.

`--slave_compressed_protocol[={0|1}]`
If set to 1, this option instructs the slave to compress data passed between it and the master, if they support compression. The default is 0.

`--slave_load_tmpdir=`*`value`*
This option specifies the directory where the slave stores temporary files used by the `LOAD DATA INFILE` statement.

`--slave-net-timeout=`*`value`*
This option specifies the number of seconds before a slave connection times out and the slave attempts to reconnect. See the options `--master-connect-retry` and `--master-retry-count` earlier in this chapter, as they relate to this option.

`--slave-skip-errors=error_nbr,...|all`
: By default, replication stops on the slave when an error occurs. This option instructs the slave not to terminate replication for specific errors. Error numbers for the errors should be given in a comma-separated list. You may specify all errors by giving the value of `all`. This option generally should not be used, and the value of `all` in particular should probably never be used.

`--sql-slave-skip-counter=number`
: When the slave begins to re-execute commands that the master executed, this option causes the slave to skip the first *number* events from the master's log.

`--skip-slave-start`
: If this option is enabled, the master server won't automatically start the slaves when it's restarted. Instead, you will have to enter the `START SLAVE` statement on each slave to start it.

`--slave_transaction_retries=value`
: This option specifies the number of times the slave should try to execute a transaction before returning an error if the transaction fails because of problems related to InnoDB or NDB settings. For InnoDB, this applies if there is a deadlock or if the transaction takes more time than is allowed by `innodb_lock_wait_timeout`. For NDB, this applies if the transaction takes more time than is allowed by `TransactionDeadlockDetectionTimeout` or `TransactionInactiveTimeout`. The default value of this option is 10.

Storage engine specific options

An alphabetical list follows of `mysqld` server options recognized by particular storage engines (formerly known as table types). The options are grouped into subsections based on the storage engines: "MyISAM," "InnoDB," and "Other storage engine options," which include MEMORY, MERGE, and NDB (MySQL Cluster).

Older versions of MySQL offered BDB options that are not covered in this book because MySQL no longer supports the BDB storage engine. See the documentation on MySQL's web site for information on BDB options if you're still using BDB tables. It's recommended that you migrate those tables to another storage engine. For a list of storage engines and to see their status on your server, enter `SHOW ENGINES`.

Here are a couple of related options that aren't used for a particular storage engine:

`--default-storage-engine=engine`
: This option specifies the default storage engine. MyISAM is the default unless changed with this option. The server variable associated with this option is `storage_engine`. This option is synonymous with the `--default-table-type` option.

`--default-table-type=engine`
: This option is synonymous with `--default-table-engine`.

MyISAM

These options are related to the MyISAM storage engine, which is typically the default storage engine for MySQL. To determine the default storage engine, enter `SHOW VARIABLES LIKE 'storage_engine';` on the server. You can change the default storage engine with the `--default-storage-engine` option:

`--bulk_insert_buffer_size=`*`value`*
: See "Performance optimization" later in this chapter.

`--ft_boolean_syntax=`*`value`*
: This option sets the operators that may be used for FULLTEXT searches of `TEXT` columns in MyISAM tables. The default operators are: `+`, `-`, `>`, `<`, `(`, `)`, `~`, `*`, `:`, `""`, `&`, and `|`.

`--ft_max_word_len=`*`value`*
: This option sets the maximum length of a word for which a FULLTEXT search of a table may be made. After setting this option, rebuild the FULLTEXT index by executing `REPAIR TABLE` *`table`* `QUICK;` on the server.

`--ft_min_word_len=`*`value`*
: Use this option to set the minimum length of a word for which a FULLTEXT search of a table may be made. After setting this option, rebuild the FULLTEXT index by executing `REPAIR TABLE` *`table`* `QUICK;` on the server.

`--ft_query_expansion_limit=`*`value`*
: This option sets the maximum number of matches for FULLTEXT searches that can be made when using the `WITH QUERY EXPANSION` clause.

`--ft_stopword_file=`*`filename`*
: This option specifies a text file containing stopwords, which are words not to be considered in FULLTEXT searches. Comments should not be included in this file, only stopwords. A list of words is built into MySQL by default.

`--keep_files_on_create[={0|1}]`
: If for some reason a file with the prefix *.MYD* or *.MYI* is located in the data directory of MySQL, but wasn't placed there by the server, and a new table is created with the same name as the prefix of the files, MyISAM will overwrite the files. However, if this option is set to 1, the files won't be overwritten and an error will be returned instead. This option was added as of version 5.1.23 of MySQL.

`--myisam_block_size=`*`value`*
: This option sets the block size in bytes for index pages in MyISAM.

`--myisam_data_pointer_size=`*`value`*
: This option sets the default pointer size in bytes for MyISAM tables when tables are created without the `MAX_ROWS` option of the `CREATE TABLE` statement. The default value is 6; valid values range from 2 to 7.

`--myisam_max_extra_sort_file_size=`*`value`*
: This option is deprecated as of version 5.1 of MySQL.

`--myisam_max_sort_file_size=`*`value`*
: This option sets the maximum file size in bytes of the temporary file used by MyISAM when recreating a table's index (i.e., when running the `ALTER TABLE`, `LOAD DATA INFILE`, or `REPAIR TABLE` statements). Any space in excess of this value that may be required will be handled in the key cache. The default value is 2 GB.

`--myisam-recover[=`*`value`*`,...]`
: This option sets the MyISAM storage engine's recovery mode so that all MyISAM tables will be automatically checked and repaired if needed when the server starts. The choices of settings are `BACKUP` (makes backups of recovered tables that were changed), `DEFAULT` (disables this option), `FORCE` (runs recovery regardless of the risk

MySQL Server and Client

of losing data), or `QUICK` (doesn't check rows for tables without any deletions). Multiple choices may be given in a comma-separated list.

`--myisam_repair_threads[={0|1}]`
: With this option enabled, when repairing a table's index each index will be sorted in its own thread. This will potentially increase the speed of the repair process. However, this option is still in beta testing mode. Its default value is 1, enabling the option.

`--myisam_sort_buffer_size=`*`value`*
: This option sets the size of the buffer used for sorting indexes in a MyISAM table. The maximum value for this option is 4 GB, but on 64-bit operating systems, as of version 5.1.23 a larger buffer size may be possible. The variable associated with this option is used when the `ALTER TABLE`, `CREATE INDEX`, or `REPAIR TABLE` statements are executed.

`--myisam_stats_method={nulls_equal|nulls_unequal}`
: When aggregate or statistical functions are used, MyISAM has to decide how to treat NULL values for indexes. If this option is set to `nulls_equal`, all NULL values will be considered equal and their associated columns will be grouped together. If `nulls_unequal` is given, each row will be considered a separate and distinct value and they won't be grouped together.

`--myisam_use_mmap`
: This option instructs MyISAM to use memory mapping on the underlying operating system when reading from and writing to tables.

InnoDB

These options are related to the InnoDB storage engine, a transactional storage engine:

`--innodb`
: This option enables support for the InnoDB storage engine. It is enabled by default. Run the `SHOW STORAGE ENGINES;` statement on the server to see which storage engines are enabled.

`--innodb_additional_mem_pool_size=`*`value`*
: This option sets the size in bytes of the memory pool used by InnoDB for storing the data dictionary and other internal data structure information. The default value is 1 MB. If this option does not allocate enough memory, InnoDB will write warning messages to the error log.

`--innodb_autoextend_increment=`*`value`*
: This option sets the size in megabytes of increments made to the size of a tablespace in InnoDB when it is automatically extended. The default value is 8 (i.e., 8 MB).

`--innodb_autoinc_lock_mode={0|1|2}`
: This option sets the locking mode used when the storage engine generates automatically incremented values. Possible values are 0 (*traditional* mode), 1 (*consecutive* mode), and 2 (*interleaved* mode). The differences are described in the MySQL online manual. In general, processing can get faster under some circumstances as the value of this option gets higher, but results may not always be safe. This option is available as of version 5.1.22 of MySQL.

`--innodb_buffer_pool_awe_mem_mb=value`
: On 32-bit Windows systems, Address Windowing Extensions (AWE) may be available for making use of more than the normal 4 GB memory limit. On such a server, you can use this option to set the amount of AWE memory in megabytes that InnoDB will use for its buffer pool. This option allows for a value of 0 to 63,000. A value of 0 disables it. To take advantage of AWE, you need to recompile MySQL.

`--innodb_buffer_pool_size=value`
: This option sets the size in bytes of the memory buffer used by InnoDB for caching data and indexes.

`--innodb_checksums`
: With this option, which is enabled by default, checksum validation is used on pages read from the filesystem. This provides greater assurance that when data was retrieved there wasn't a problem due to corrupted files or hardware-related trouble. Use the `--skip-innodb-checksums` option to disable it.

`--innodb_commit_concurrency=value`
: This option sets the maximum number of threads that may commit transactions simultaneously. A value of 0 removes the limit on concurrent commits.

`--innodb_data_file_path=path:size...`
: This option allows you to increase the storage space for InnoDB datafiles by specifying names and sizes of datafiles within the directory given with the `--innodb_data_home_dir` option. Each ***size*** is a number followed by `M` for megabytes or `G` for gigabytes. The minimum total of the file sizes should be 10 MB. If no size is given, a 10 MB datafile with autoextending capability will be used by default. For most operating systems, there is a 4 GB maximum limit.

`--innodb_data_home_dir=path`
: This option specifies the base directory for InnoDB datafiles. If not used, the default will be the data directory for MySQL.

`--innodb_doublewrite`
: This option, enabled by default, causes InnoDB to write the data it receives twice. First it writes data to a buffer, then it writes the data to the filesystem, then it compares the data for integrity. To disable this behavior, use the `--skip-innodb_doublewrite` option.

`--innodb_fast_shutdown[={0|1|2}]`
: This option determines the general procedures that InnoDB follows when shutting down the storage engine. If it is set to 0, the process will go much slower (from minutes to hours longer): it will involve a full purge and a merge of the insert buffer. If this option is set to the default of 1, the process is disabled. If it's set to 2, InnoDB will flush its logs and shut down rapidly. When it's restarted, a crash recovery will be conducted. This option is not allowed on NetWare systems.

`--innodb_file_io_threads=value`
: This option sets the number of file I/O threads permitted. The default value is 4. Changing this on Unix-type systems has no effect. On Windows systems, however, performance may be improved with a higher value.

`--innodb_file_per_table`
: InnoDB uses a shared tablespace by default. When this option is enabled, a separate *.idb* file will be created for each new table to be used for data and indexes instead of using the shared tablespace. By default this is disabled.

`--innodb_flush_log_at_trx_commit={0|1|2}`
: This option determines the procedure for flushing and writing to logs along with transaction commits. If it's set to a value of 0, the log buffer is written to the log file and the log is flushed every second, but not at a transaction commit. If it's set to the default of 1, the log buffer is written to the log file and the log is flushed at every transaction commit. If it's set to 2, the log buffer is written to the log file at each transaction commit and the log is flushed every second without reference to the actual commit. It's recommended generally that this option be left at the default value of 1 and that `--sync_binlog` also be set to 1 to enable it.

`--innodb_flush_method={fdatasync | O_DIRECT | O_DSYNC}`
: This option sets the method of synchronizing data and flushing logs with InnoDB. The default value of `fdatasync` instructs InnoDB to use the operating system's `fsync( )` call to synchronize datafiles and log files. The value of `O_DIRECT` has the server use `O_DIRECT` for opening datafiles and `fsync( )` to synchronize datafiles and log files. This value is available only for Linux, FreeBSD, and Solaris systems. `O_DSYNC` has the server use `O_SYNCH` for opening and flushing log files, but uses `fsync( )` to flush datafiles.

`--innodb_force_recovery=`*`level`*
: This option puts InnoDB in crash recovery mode. The allowable values are 1 through 6. Each level includes all previous levels. Level 1 indicates that the server should continue running even if it finds corrupt pages. Level 2 prevents the main thread from running a purge operation if it would cause the server to crash. A value of 3 prevents transaction rollbacks from being run after the recovery is finished. A setting of 4 prevents operations from the insert buffer from running if they would cause the server to crash. Level 5 causes InnoDB not to consider undo logs when starting and to consider all transactions to have been committed. Finally, level 6 instructs the server not to perform a log roll-forward during the recovery.

`--innodb_lock_wait_timeout=`*`value`*
: This option sets the maximum number of seconds that InnoDB can wait to get a lock on a table before it gives up and rolls back a transaction. The default value is 50.

`--innodb_locks_unsafe_for_binlog`
: To achieve something like row-level locking, InnoDB locks the key for a row. This will also generally prevent other users from writing to the space next to the row that has its key locked. Setting this option to a value of 1 disables this extra protection. Setting it to the default value of 0 protects that next key.

`--innodb_log_arch_dir=`*`value`*
: This option sets the file path where completed log files should be archived. Generally, it should be set to the same directory as the option **`--innodb_log_group_home_dir`**. Archiving is generally not used, as it's not needed or used for recovery.

`--innodb_log_archive[={0|1}]`
: A value of 1 instructs InnoDB to archive log files. By default, it's set to 0 because it's no longer used.

`--innodb_log_buffer_size=`*`value`*
: This option sets the size in bytes of InnoDB's log buffer. InnoDB writes from the buffer to the log file. The default value is 1 MB.

`--innodb_log_file_size=`*`value`*
This option sets the size in bytes of the log file in a log group to use with InnoDB. The default value is 5 MB. Larger values for this option make recovery slower. The total of all log files normally cannot be more than 4 GB.

`--innodb_log_files_in_group=`*`value`*
This option determines the number of log files in a log group. The default is 2. Log files are written to in a circular manner.

`--innodb_log_group_home_dir[=`*`path`*`]`
This option sets the file path for InnoDB log files. By default, InnoDB creates two log files in the data directory of MySQL called *ib_logfile0* and *ib_logfile1*.

`--innodb_max_dirty_pages_pct=`*`value`*
In this context, dirty pages are pages that are in the buffer pool but are not yet written to the datafiles. Use this option to set the percentage of dirty pages that may be allowed in the buffer pool. The value given can range from 0 to 100; the default is 90.

`--innodb_max_purge_lag=`*`value`*
This option is related to delays caused by purge operations that are running slowly or are backed up, thus holding up SQL statements that change data. Set the value to the number of such statements that may be delayed during purge operations. The default value of 0 instructs InnoDB not to delay them at all.

`--innodb_mirrored_log_groups=`*`value`*
This option sets the number of mirrored log groups that InnoDB should maintain. By default, this is set to 1 and is usually sufficient.

`--innodb_open_files=`*`value`*
This option sets the maximum number of *.idb* files that may be open at one time. The minimum value is 10; the default is 300. This option applies only when multiple tablespaces are used.

`--innodb-safe-binlog`
This option ensures consistency between the contents of InnoDB tables and the binary log.

`--innodb_status_file`
This option has InnoDB keep a status file of the results of the `SHOW ENGINE INNODB STATUS` statement. It writes to the file occasionally. The file is named *innodb_status.pid* and is usually located in the data directory of MySQL.

`--innodb_support_xa`
This option enables support for a two-phase commit for XA transactions. It's enabled and set to 1 by default. A value of 0 disables it and can sometimes improve performance if the system doesn't use XA transactions.

`--innodb_sync_spin_loops=`*`value`*
This option sets the number of times a thread in InnoDB will wait for a mutex to be free. Once this is exceeded, the thread will be suspended.

`--innodb_table_locks[={0|1}]`
When enabled (i.e., set to 1), this option causes InnoDB to internally lock a table if the `LOCK TABLE` statement is run and `AUTOCOMMIT` is set to 0.

`--innodb_thread_concurrency=`*`value`*
This option sets the maximum number of threads that can concurrently use InnoDB. Additional threads that try to access InnoDB tables are put into wait mode. The value

can be from 0 to 1,000. Before version 5.1.12 of MySQL, any value over 20 was the same as unlimited. A value of 0 disables the waiting behavior and allows unlimited concurrent threads.

`--innodb_thread_sleep_delay=`*`microseconds`*
: This option sets the number of microseconds that a thread may sleep before being put on a queue. The default value is 10,000; 0 disables sleep.

`--skip-innodb`
: This option disables the InnoDB storage engine.

`--skip-innodb-checksums`
: By default, InnoDB uses checksum validation on pages read from the filesystem (see `--innodb-checksums` earlier in this section). This option disables this behavior.

`--skip-innodb-doublewrite`
: By default, InnoDB writes to a buffer before writing to the filesystem (see `--innodb-doublewrite` earlier in this section). This option disables this behavior.

`--timed_mutexes[={0|1}]`
: When this option is set to 1, the server stores the amount of time InnoDB threads waits for mutexes. The default value of 0 disables this option.

Other storage engine options

These options are recognized by storage engines not previously listed. This section includes MEMORY and NDB specific options for the `mysqld` daemon:

`--max_heap_table_size=`*`value`*
: This option sets the maximum number of rows in a MEMORY table. It applies only to tables created or altered after it's set.

`--ndbcluster`
: This option enables support for the NDB Cluster storage engine.

`--ndb-connectstring=`*`string`*
: This option specifies the connect string that the NDB storage engine uses to create its place in a cluster.

`--skip-merge`
: This option disables the MERGE storage engine. It was added in version 5.1.12 of MySQL.

`--skip-ndbcluster`
: This option disables the NDB Cluster storage engine.

mysqld_multi

mysqld_multi

`mysqld_multi [`*`options`*`] {start|stop|report} [`*`server_id`*`]`

This option runs multiple MySQL servers on different socket files and ports. To set up multiple servers, you must create a section for each server in a configuration file (e.g., */etc/my.cnf*). The naming scheme for each section must be `[mysqld`*`n`*`]`, where *`n`* is a different number for each server. You must enter options separately for each server in its own section, even when servers use the same options. At a minimum, each server should use a different socket file or a different TCP/IP port. You should also use different data directories for each server. The directory should be accessible to the operating system user who started the utility. It should not be the *root* user, though, as this would be a security vulnerability. To see an example of how a configuration file might be set up for multiple servers, enter the following from the command line:

```
mysqld_multi --example
```

Once you have configured multiple servers, you can enter something like the following from the command line to start a server:

```
mysqld_multi start 3
```

This line would start server number 3, listed in the configuration file as `[mysqld3]`. By entering **`report`** for the first argument, you can obtain the status on the server. For starting and stopping the server, this script uses the **`mysqladmin`** utility. Here is an alphabetical list of options specific to **`mysqld_multi`** that you can enter from the command line, along with a brief explanation of each:

`--config-file=`*`filename`*
: This option specifies an alternative server configuration file. As of version 5.1.18 of MySQL, though, this option has been deprecated and is treated like **`--defaults-extra-file`**.

`--example`
: This option displays a sample configuration file.

`--help`
: This option displays basic help information.

`--log=`*`filename`*
: This option sets the name of the log file. The default is */tmp/mysqld_multi.log*.

`--mysqladmin=`*`filename`*
: This option points to the executable file of the **`mysqladmin`** utility to invoke.

`--mysqld=`*`filename`*
: This option specifies the MySQL daemon to start, either **`mysqld`** or **`mysqld_safe`**. If this is **`mysqld`**, you should add the **`--pid-file`** option of **`mysqld`** so that each server will have a separate process identifier file. If this option is set to **`mysqld_safe`**, you probably should include the options **`ledir`** and **`mysqld`** as they relate to `mysqld_safe`. You would include them in the options file under the server group for the server started by `mysqld_multi`.

`--no-log`
: This option instructs the utility not to save messages to a log, but to send them to `stdout` instead.

`--password=`*`password`*
: This option provides the password for using **`mysqladmin`**.

`--silent`
: This option disables warning messages from the utility.

`--tcp-ip`
: This option sends this utility's commands to the server using a TCP/IP socket instead of a Unix-domain socket.

`--user=user`
: This option provides the username for using `mysqladmin`. The same user must be used for all servers and must have the `SHUTDOWN` privilege on all of them.

`--version`
: This option displays the version of the utility.

mysqld_safe

mysqld_safe

`mysqld_safe [options]`

`mysqld_safe` is recommended utility for starting the MySQL server because the server is restarted automatically if it dies unexpectedly. The utility is available on Unix and Novell NetWare systems.

Although options may be entered from the command line, they should be included in the options file (e.g., *my.cnf*) under the heading `[mysqld_safe]`. Options specific to `mysqld_safe` should not be passed on the command line because they will be passed to the `mysqld` server, which will try to interpret them. Therefore, options are shown here as they would appear in the configuration file, without initial hyphens. `mysqld_safe` can also accept options for the `mysqld` server, but the configuration file is also better for these because it ensures they will be passed to the daemon when it's reloaded after a crash:

`autoclose`
: On Novell NetWare systems, when `mysqld_safe` closes, the related screen does not close automatically without user interaction. Use this option to have the screen close automatically.

`basedir=path`
: This option is necessary and is used to specify the path to the directory where MySQL files are installed.

`core-file-size=value`
: This option sets the maximum size set for the core file to create if the daemon dies.

`datadir=path`
: This option specifies the directory that contains datafiles (i.e., table files).

`defaults-extra-file=filename`
: This option specifies an additional options file to use after the default file is read. When used at the command line, this has to be the first option, except that `--defaults-file` must precede it if used.

`defaults-file=filename`
: This option specifies the default options file for the server; it can be used to substitute special options for the normal default options files. When used at the command line, this has to be the first option given.

`err-log=filename`
: This option specifies the path to the error log for error messages outside the daemon, such as errors when starting.

`ledir=`*`path`*
: This option is necessary for running `mysqld_safe`. It specifies the path where the daemons may be found.

`log-error[=`*`filename`*`]`
: This option enables logging of error messages and server startup messages, optionally specifying a log file. The default log file is ***host***.*err* in MySQL's data directory, where ***host*** is the host's name.

`mysqld=`*`daemon`*
: This option is required when using a binary distribution and the data directory for MySQL is not in the location originally set by the distribution. With it you specify which daemon to start (i.e., `mysqld`). This daemon program must be in the same directory given with the `ledir` option.

`mysqld-version=[max]`
: This option specifies which daemon to use by providing the suffix of the daemon's name. A value of `max` starts `mysqld-max`, whereas a blank value ensures `mysqld` is started.

`nice=`*`number`*
: This option employs the `nice` utility to give scheduling priority to the value given.

`no-defaults`
: This option instructs the script not to refer to configuration files for options. When used at the command line, this has to be the first option given.

`open-files-limit=`*`number`*
: This option limits the number of files the daemon may open. Only *root* may use this option.

`pid-file=`*`filename`*
: This option specifies the file that will store the server's process identifier.

`port=`*`port`*
: This option specifies the TCP/IP port number to which `mysqld_safe` should listen for incoming connections. Unless started by the *root* filesystem user, the port number should be 1024 or higher.

`skip-kill-mysqld`
: When `mysqld_safe` is started on a Linux system, if this option is not used, any `mysqld` processes that are running will be terminated by it. Use this option to allow existing servers to stay up.

`skip-syslog`
: This option causes the daemon not to log errors to the system's `syslog` facility. The MySQL-specific log will still be written. This option is available as of version 5.1.20 of MySQL. See `syslog` below for more information related to this option.

`socket=`*`filename`*
: This option provides the name of the server's socket file for local connections.

`syslog`
: On operating systems that support the `logger` program, this option instructs the daemon to log error messages to the related `syslog`. This option is available as of version 5.1.20 of MySQL. See `skip-syslog` above for more information related to this option.

`syslog-tag`

When writing error messages to `syslog`, this option marks each message with `mysqld` or `mysqld_safe`, depending on the source of the error. This option is available as of version 5.1.21 of MySQL. See `syslog` and `skip-syslog` previously for more information related to this option.

`timezone=`*`zone`*

This option sets the environment variable `TZ` for the timezone of the server.

`user=`*`user`*

This option specifies the username or user ID number for the user that starts the server.

16
Command-Line Utilities

This chapter describes the utilities that you can use to administer the MySQL server and data. Some interact with the server, and others manipulate MySQL's datafiles directly. Others can be used to make backups of data (e.g., `mysqldump`). The utilities are listed here in alphabetical order.

Some of these utilities are provided with MySQL and are typically installed in a standard directory for executables so that they are automatically on the user's command path. Other utilities have to be downloaded and installed from MySQL AB's site or from a third-party site.

comp_err

`comp_err` *`source destination`*

This utility compiles text files that contain mappings of error codes into a format used by MySQL. This is particularly useful for creating error code messages in spoken languages for which error message files do not already exist. You can also use it to modify error messages to your own wording. To do this, just edit the appropriate *errmsg.txt* file in its default directory. For English messages on Unix systems, the source text file and the compiled system file are found typically in */usr/share/mysql/english*. The following demonstrates how to compile a text file containing error messages in Pig Latin:

```
comp_err /usr/share/mysql/piglatin/errmsg.txt \
         /usr/share/mysql/piglatin/errmsg.sys
```

To make the new set of error messages the default set, add the following line to the MySQL configuration file (e.g., *my.cnf* or *my.ini*, depending on your system) under the `[mysqld]` section:

```
language=/usr/share/mysql/piglatin
```

Notice that only the directory is given and not the filename.

Here is a list of options available for this utility in alphabetical order:

`--charset=`*`path`*`, -C `*`path`*
: This option specifies the path to the character set files. The default directory is */usr/local/mysql/sql/share/charsets*, adjusted for the server's installation location.

`--debug[=`*`options`*`], -# `*`options`*`]`
: This option logs debugging information. The set of options used by default is `'d:t:o,logname'`. See Table 16-1 at the end of the list of options under the `mysqldump` utility for an explanation of these flags and others that may be used.

`--debug-info, -T`
: This option writes debugging information and CPU and memory usage information to the log after the utility ends.

`--header_file=`*`filename`*`, -H `*`filename`*
: This option specifies the error header file. By default, it's *mysqld_error.h*.

`--in_file=`*`filename`*`, -F `*`filename`*
: This option specifies the input file. By default, it's */usr/local/mysql/sql/share/errmsg.txt*, adjusted for the server's installation location.

`--name_file=`*`filename`*`, -N `*`filename`*
: This option specifies the error file. By default, it's *mysqld_ername.h*.

`--out_dir=`*`path`*`, -D `*`path`*
: This option specifies the output directory. By default, it's */usr/local/mysql/sql/share*, adjusted for the server's installation location.

`--out_file=`*`filename`*`, -O `*`filename`*
: This option specifies the output file. By default, it's *errmsg.sys*.

`--statefile=`*`filename`*`, -S `*`filename`*
: This option specifies the SQLSTATE header file to be generated. By default, it's *sql_state.h*.

`--version, -V`
: This option returns the version of the utility.

make_binary_distribution

`make_binary_distribution`

This utility creates a binary distribution of MySQL from the source code. This can be useful, for instance, to a developer who has modified the source code for her needs and wants to make a customized binary version for her associates to use. Executing the script from the directory containing the modified source code generates a GNU zipped TAR file for distribution.

msql2mysql

`msql2mysql `*`program.c`*

This utility converts C API function calls querying the mSQL database, in programs written in C, to the MySQL equivalent functions. The only argument is the name of the source to convert. This utility does not create a copy of the source file. Instead, it converts the given source file itself. Therefore, you should make a backup of the source before issuing the command. This utility isn't always effective in converting all mSQL functions, so manual inspection of the code and testing may be required after a conversion. Note that the `replace` utility is used by `msql2mysql`.

my_print_defaults

`my_print_defaults` *`options filename`*

This utility parses a configuration file, converting key/value pairs into command-line equivalent options. For instance, a line from the *my.cnf* file that reads `basedir=/data/mysql` will be converted to `--basedir=/data/mysql`. To export the MySQL daemon (i.e., *mysqld*) section of *my.cnf* file, enter the following from the command line (the output follows):

```
my_print_defaults --config-file=/etc/my.cnf mysqld
--basedir=/data/mysql
--datadir=/data/mysql
--socket=/tmp/mysql.sock
--tmpdir=/tmp
--log-bin=/data/mysql/logs/log-bin
```

Notice that only the `mysqld` section is parsed and that the header `[mysqld]` and the blank lines are not included in the output. Also, each key/value pair is printed on a separate line. To parse more than one section, you can list additional section names at the end of the command line, separated by spaces.

Here is a list of options available for this utility in alphabetical order:

`--config-file=`*`filename`*`, --defaults-file=`*`filename`*`, -c `*`filename`*
: This option instructs the utility to read only the given configuration or options file (i.e., *my.cnf* or *my.ini*).

`--debug[=`*`options`*`], -# [`*`options`*`]`
: This option logs debugging information. The set of options used by default is `'d:t:o,logname'`. See Table 16-1 at the end of the list of options under the `mysqldump` utility for an explanation of these flags and others that may be used.

`--defaults-extra-file=`*`filename`*`, --extra-file=`*`filename`*`, -e `*`filename`*
: This option instructs the utility to read the given configuration or options file in addition to the default options file (i.e., *my.cnf* or *my.ini*).

`--defaults-group-suffix=`*`suffix`*`, -g `*`suffix`*
: This option instructs the utility to read the options for the groups with the given suffix (e.g., `_clients`).

`--help, -?`
: This option displays basic help information.

`--no-defaults, -n`
: This option indicates that no options file should be used.

`--verbose, -v`
: This option displays more information from the utility.

`--version, -V`
: This option returns the version of the utility.

myisam_ftdump

`myisam_ftdump options table index_nbr`

This utility displays information related to FULLTEXT indexes on MyISAM tables. It must be run from the server. For the table name, you can give either the name of the table or the name of the table's index file with its path (e.g., */data/mysql/clients.MYI*). The third argument for this utility is the index number. To determine the index number, execute `SHOW INDEX FROM table;` for the table you want to examine. In the results, the `Non_unique` field will contain the index numbers:

```
myisam_ftdump --stats /data/mysql/russell_dyer/articles.MYI 1

Total rows: 98
Total words: 38517
Unique words: 9961
Longest word: 33 chars (mysql_opt_use_embedded_connection)
Median length: 7
Average global weight: 3.826532
Most common word: 83 times, weight: -1.710790 (make)
```

Here is a list of options available for this utility in alphabetical order:

`--count, -c`
: This option will display a list of all words found in the specified index of the given table with a count of the number of occurrences of each word, along with its weighting in the index.

`--dump, -d`
: This option is used to dump the index, word weighting, and data offsets.

`--length, -l`
: This option returns the distribution length.

`--stats, -s`
: With this option, you can see some statistical information on the index. If no options are given with the utility, this option is assumed.

`--help, -h, -?`
: This option displays basic help information.

`--verbose, -v`
: This option is meant to display more information, but it seems to have no effect on the results at this time.

myisamchk

`myisamchk options table[.MYI][...]`

This utility checks, repairs, and optimizes MyISAM tables. It works with the table files directly and does not require interaction with the MySQL server. Therefore, it may be necessary to specify the path along with the table or table names in the second argument. Also, tables that are being checked should be locked or the MySQL server daemon should be stopped. This utility works with the index files for the tables, so the suffix *.MYI* may be given for table names to prevent it from attempting to analyze other files. Omitting the suffix (e.g., *work_req* instead of *work_req.**) will have the same effect as giving a specific suffix (*work_req.MYI*). To check all of the tables in a database, use the wildcard (i.e., **.MYI*). Here is a basic example of how you can use `myisamchk` to check one table:

```
myisamchk /data/mysql/workrequests/requests
Checking MyISAM file: /data/mysql/workrequests/requests
Data records:     531   Deleted blocks:       0
myisamchk: warning: 3 clients is using or hasn't closed the table properly
- check file-size
- check key delete-chain
- check record delete-chain
- check index reference
- check data record references index: 1
- check record links
MyISAM-table '/data/mysql/workrequests/requests' is usable but should be
   fixed
```

No options are specified here, so the default of `--check` is used. Notice that `myisamchk` detected a problem with the table. To fix this problem, you can run the utility again, but with the `--recover` option like so:

```
myisamchk --recover /data/mysql/workrequests/requests
- recovering (with sort) MyISAM-table
 '/data/mysql/workrequests/requests'
Data records: 531
- Fixing index 1
```

The following sections list the options available with `myisamchk`.

myisamchk check options

`--check`, `-c`
: This option checks tables for errors.

`--check-only-changed`, `-C`
: This option checks only tables that have changed since the last check.

`--extend-check`, `-e`
: This option checks tables thoroughly. Use it only in extreme cases.

`--fast`, `-F`
: Use this option to have the utility check only tables that haven't been closed properly.

`--force`, `-f`
: This option repairs tables that report errors during check mode. It restarts the utility with the `--recover` option if any errors occur.

`--information`, `-i`
: This option displays statistical information about tables being checked.

`--medium-check`, `-m`
: This option checks tables more thoroughly than `--check`, but not as thoroughly as `--extend-check`.

`--read-only`, `-T`
: This option tells the utility not to mark tables with status information so that tables may be used by the utility during its check. Tables are not marked as checked when using this option.

`--update-state, -U`
: This option has the utility update tables to indicate when they were checked and mark them as crashed if any errors are found.

myisamchk repair options

`--backup, -B`
: This option makes copies of datafiles (*table.MYD*), naming them *table-date-time.BAK*.

`--character-sets-dir=`*`path`*
: This option sets the directory where character sets are located.

`--correct-checksum`
: This option corrects a table's checksum information.

`--data-file-length=`*`number`*`, -D `*`number`*
: This option sets the maximum length of a datafile for rebuilding a full datafile.

`--extend-check, -e`
: This option instructs the utility to attempt to recover all rows, including intentionally deleted ones.

`--force, -f`
: This option instructs the utility to ignore error messages and to overwrite temporary files.

`--keys-used=`*`bitfield`*`, -k `*`bitfield`*
: This option instructs the utility to have MyISAM updates use only specific keys for faster data inserts.

`--max-record-length=`*`number`*
: This option tells the utility to skip rows larger than the length specified if there is not enough memory.

`--no-symlinks, -l`
: This option instructs the utility not to follow symbolic links at the filesystem level.

`--parallel-recover, -p`
: This option is the same as the `--recover` option, but it creates all keys in parallel using different threads.

`--quick, -q`
: This option repairs only indexes, not datafiles, of uncorrupted tables.

`-qq`
: This option repairs only indexes and updates datafiles only when duplicates are found.

`--recover, -r`
: Use this option to recover a table that has been corrupted. You might also try increasing the variable `sort_buffer_size` with this option. If this option does not work, try `--safe-recover`.

`--safe-recover, -o`
: Use this option if `--recover` fails. It also repairs rows that the `--sort-recover` option cannot handle (e.g., duplicate values for unique keys).

`--set-character-set=`*`set`*
: This option specifies the character set to use.

`--set-collation=set`
: This option specifies the collation to use with the utility when sorting table indexes. Execute `SHOW COLLATION;` on the server to retrieve a list of collations that may be used with this option.

`--sort-recover, -n`
: This option instructs the utility to use the sort buffer regardless of whether the temporary file would be too large based on default limits.

`--tmpdir=path, -t path`
: This option specifies the directory used by the utility for temporary files. Multiple directories may be given in a colon-separated list on Unix systems and a semicolon-separated list on Windows systems. By default, this utility uses the value for the environmental variable `TMPDIR`.

`--unpack, -u`
: This option unpacks tables that were packed with the `myisampack` utility.

Other myisamchk options

`--analyze, -a`
: This option optimizes the use of keys in tables. It can help with some joins. Use the `--description` and the `--verbose` options to show the calculated distribution.

`--block-search=offset, -b offset`
: This option searches for a row based on a given offset.

`--description, -d`
: This option displays information about the table.

`--set-auto-increment[=value], -A [value]`
: This option sets the value of an auto-increment column for the next row created. If no value is given, the next value above the highest value found for the column is used.

`--sort-index, -S`
: This option sorts indexes.

`--sort-records=index, -R index`
: This option sorts rows based on the index given.

Global myisamchk options

`--debug[=options], -# [options]`
: This option logs debugging information. The set of options used by default is `'d:t:o,logname'`. See Table 16-1 at the end of the list of options under the `mysqldump` utility for an explanation of these flags and others that may be used.

`--character-sets-dir=path`
: This option specifies the directory containing character sets.

`--help, -?`
: This option displays basic help information.

`--silent, -s`
: This option displays only print error messages. With `-ss` even less information will be displayed.

`--sort-index, -S`
: This option sorts indexes.

`--sort-records=value, -R value`
: This option sorts records based on the index given.

`--tmpdir=path, -t path`
: This option sets the path for temporary files. Additional paths may be given in a colon-separated list.

`--verbose, -v`
: This option displays more information. Additional vs (e.g., -vv) will provide more information.

`--version, -V`
: This option displays the version of the utility.

`--wait, -w`
: This option instructs the utility to wait before proceeding if the table is locked.

myisamlog

`myisamlog options [filename [table ...]]`

This utility scans and extracts information from the *myisam.log* file, which logs debugging messages for the MyISAM table handler. The name of the log file may be given. Also, the command can list specific tables to limit scanning to these tables. To activate the log, add the following line to the MySQL server configuration file (e.g., *my.cnf*) under the `[server]` section or the `[mysqld]` section:

```
log-isam=/data/mysql/logs/myisam.log
```

Here is a list of options available for this utility in alphabetical order:

`-?, -I`
: This option displays basic help information.

`-c number`
: This option limits the output to *number* commands.

`-D`
: Use this option with a server that was compiled with debugging in effect.

`-F path`
: This option provides the file path to use. The path should end with a trailing slash.

`-f files`
: This option sets the maximum number of open files allowed.

`-i`
: This option displays additional information.

`-o offset`
: This option specifies where in the log to begin the scan.

`-P`
: This option displays information about processes.

`-p number`
: This option removes the given number of components from the front of the path.

`-R`
: This option displays the current record position.

-r
: This option displays recovery activities.

-u
: This option displays update activities.

-V
: This option displays the version of the utility.

-v
: This option displays more information. Additional vs (e.g., -vv) will increase the amount of information.

-w
: This option displays file write activities.

myisampack

`myisampack` *`options /path/table`*`[.MYI]`

This utility creates compressed, read-only tables in order to reduce table sizes and to increase retrieval speed. For the table, give the path and table name. Optionally, you can include the *.MYI* file extension with the table name. When reading compressed tables, MySQL decompresses the data in memory. To decompress tables packed with `myisampack`, use `myisamchk` with the `--unpack` option.

Tables that are compressed and later decompressed should be reindexed using `myisamchk`.

A sample run of this utility is:

```
myisamchk --verbose /data/mysql/testing/courses.MYI
```

Here is a list of options available for this utility in alphabetical order:

`--backup`, `-b`
: This option has the utility create a backup of the given table (*table.OLD*).

`--character-sets-dir=`*`filepath`*
: This option specifies the directory containing the character sets the utility should use for sorting data.

`--debug[=`*`options`*`]`, `-# [`*`options`*`]`
: This option logs debugging information. The set of options used by default is `'d:t:o,logname'`. See Table 16-1 at the end of the list of options under the `mysqldump` utility for an explanation of these flags and others that may be used.

`--force`, `-f`
: This option forces a compressed table to be created even if the results are larger than the original, and to overwrite a temporary table (*table.TMD*) if it exists.

`--help`, `-?`
: This option displays basic help information.

`--join=`*`table`*, `-j` *`table`*
: This option instructs the utility to join the tables given into one compressed table. The table structures must be identical.

`--packlength=`*`bytes`*, `-p` *`bytes`*
: This option sets the size of the pointers for records to the number of bytes given (1, 2, or 3).

`--silent`, `-s`
: This option suppresses all information except error messages.

`--tmp_dir=`*`path`*, `-T` *`path`*
: This option specifies the directory in which to write temporary tables.

`--test`, `-t`
: This option has the utility test the compression process without actually compressing the table.

`--verbose`, `-v`
: This option displays information about the compression process.

`--version`, `-V`
: This option displays the version of the utility.

`--wait`, `-w`
: This option instructs the utility to wait before compressing if the table is locked by another client or utility.

mysql_convert_table_format

`mysql_convert_table_format` *`options database`*

This utility converts all tables in a given database from one storage engine to another. By default it converts them to MyISAM. The program requires that Perl and the Perl DBI module and `DBD::mysql` be installed on the system where it's executed.

mysql_convert_table_format options

`--force`
: This option instructs the utility to keep running despite errors.

`--host=`*`host`*, `-h` *`host`*
: This option specifies the host on which to connect and to convert tables.

`--help`, `-?`
: This option displays help information about the utility.

`--password=`*`password`*, `-p` *`password`*
: This option provides the password of the user logging into the server.

`--port=`*`port`*
: This option specifies the port on which to connect to the server. The default is 3306.

`--socket=`*`filename`*, `-S` *`filename`*
: This option provides the name of the server's socket file.

`--type=`*`engine`*
: This option specifies the storage engine to which to convert tables. If not given, MyISAM is assumed.

`--user=`*`user`*, `-u` *`user`*
: This option provides the username for logging into the server.

`--verbose`
: This option displays more information from the utility.

`--version`
: This option returns the version of the utility.

mysql_find_rows

`mysql_find_rows` *`options filename`*

This utility searches a text file containing SQL statements (e.g., a dump file generated by `mysqldump`) for a given pattern and prints the SQL statements it finds. Multiple files may be specified in a comma-separated list:

```
mysql_find_rows --regexp='Graham Greene' < backup.sql > greene_sql_
   statements.txt
```

In this example, the utility will search the dump file *backup.sql* (the redirect for the input is optional) for occurrences of the name of the writer *Graham Greene*. It will write the results—the SQL statements it finds that contain that text—to the *greene_sql_statements.txt* file because of the redirect (i.e., >). Otherwise, the results would be displayed on the screen. When creating a dump file that you want to search with this utility, you may want to avoid the `--extended-insert` option (or use `--skip-opt` to disable it) because that option leaves a single `INSERT` statement in the dump file for all rows in the entire table. Your search with this utility would then show all rows for the table, as it returns the whole SQL statement containing the search pattern.

mysql_find_rows options

`--help`
: This option displays help information about the utility.

`--regexp=`*`pattern`*
: This option specifies the pattern on which the utility is to search the given text file. The pattern is usually entered between quotes. If the option is not given, then the utility will search for `SET` and `USE` statements.

`--rows=`*`number`*
: This option limits the number of rows of the results. It will return the first rows that it finds, up to the number given.

`--skip-use-db`
: This option instructs the utility not to search for `USE` statements, which it searches for by default.

`--start_row=`*`number`*
: This option returns rows starting after the given number of rows.

mysql_fix_extensions

`mysql_fix_extensions` *`path`*

This utility converts the file extensions of the names of MyISAM table files from uppercase to lowercase. The names of MyISAM table files typically end with *.frm*, *.MYD*, and *.MYI*. This utility changes the names of the last two types to *.myd* and *.myi*, respectively. This utility may be necessary when moving database files from servers running on an operating system that is case-insensitive (e.g., Windows) to one that is case-sensitive (e.g., Linux). You need to give the path to the directory for the data, that is, the directory where the database subdirectories are located.

mysql_fix_privilege_tables

`mysql_fix_privilege_tables`

At various points in time, the user security database `mysql` underwent some changes: the complexity of the passwords was changed, more privileges were added, etc. To make upgrading an existing database easier, you can use this utility to implement the changes between versions. Be sure to restart the MySQL server when you are finished running this utility for the changes to take effect. As of version 5.0.19 of MySQL, this utility has been replaced by `mysql_upgrade`. It performs the same functions and has other capabilities.

The only options for the program are `--password`, in which the *root* password is given, and `--verbose` to display more information when running the program.

This program is not available on Windows systems. However, there is an SQL file, *mysql_fix_privilege_tables.sql*, that may be run with the `mysql` client as *root* to perform the same tasks. The SQL file is located either in the *scripts* or the *share* directory where MySQL is installed.

mysql_setpermission

`mysql_setpermission` *`options`*

This utility is an interactive Perl program that allows an administrator to set user privileges. To run the program, you would typically give the `--user` option with the administrative username so you can set privileges. A text menu of options will be displayed for a variety of user administration tasks, including setting the password and privileges for an existing user and creating a new user. The program requires that Perl and the Perl DBI module be installed on the system where it's executed.

mysql_setpermission options

`--host`
: This option specifies the name or IP address of the server for connection.

`--help`
: This option displays help information about the utility.

`--password=`*`password`*
: This option provides the password of the administrative user with which the utility is to log into the server, not the user for which to change privileges.

`--port=`*`port`*
: This option specifies the port number to use for connecting to the server.

`--user=`*`user`*
: This option provides the administrative username for logging into the server, not the user for which to change privileges.

`--socket=`*`filename`*
: This option provides the name of the server's socket file.

mysql_tableinfo

`mysql_tableinfo options new_database [existing_database [existing_table]]`

This utility creates a table containing information about existing tables in a database. You have to specify the database that will contain the newly created metadata tables, and the utility will create the database if it does not exist. If given the name of an existing database, it will use its metadata as its basis. If also given a table name, it will refer to its metadata.

The utility will create four tables in the database: `db`, `col`, `idx`, and `tbl`. This last table may be named `tbl_status` instead. It uses the `SHOW COLUMNS`, `SHOW DATABASES`, `SHOW INDEXES`, `SHOW TABLES`, and `SHOW TABLE STATUS` statements to get metadata information. The user given must have the necessary privileges for these statements.

mysql_tableinfo options

`--clear`
: This option drops all four tables to be created by the utility if they exist, before creating new ones and populating them.

`--clear-only`
: This option drops all four tables to be created by the utility if they exist, but doesn't create new ones—the utility will exit when it's finished deleting the tables.

`--col`
: This option puts column metadata into the `col` table.

`--help, -?, -I`
: This option displays help information about the utility.

`--host=host, -h host`
: This option specifies the host on which to obtain metadata information and to create tables.

`--idx`
: This option puts index metadata into the `idx` table.

`--password=password, -p password`
: This option provides the password of the user logging into the server.

`--port=port, -P port`
: This option specifies the port on which to connect to the server. The default is 3306.

`--prefix=string`
: This option adds a prefix to the names of the tables that the utility creates (e.g., `metadata_db` instead of `db`).

`--quiet, -q`
: This option suppresses all messages except for error messages.

`--socket=filename, -S filename`
: This option provides the name of the server's socket file.

`--tbl-status`
: This option takes metadata from the `SHOW TABLE STATUS` statement instead of `SHOW TABLES`. The result is more metadata but a slower process.

`--user=user, -u user`
: This option provides the username for logging into the server.

mysql_upgrade

`mysql_upgrade` *`options`*

Use this utility after upgrading to a new version of MySQL. It checks all tables for version incompatibilities or problems, and attempts to repair or correct tables if possible. It also updates tables in the `mysql` database for new privileges and other factors available in the newer version of MySQL. Tables that are checked are tagged for the new version so they won't be checked twice. The utility notes the version number in the *mysql_upgrade_info* file located in the data directory for MySQL. This utility replaces the `mysql_fix_privilege_tables` utility because it performs the same function and more.

mysql_upgrade options

`--basedir=`*`path`*
: This option specifies the base directory of the MySQL server.

`--datadir=`*`path`*
: This option specifies the data directory of the MySQL server.

`--debug-check`
: This option writes debugging information to the log when the utility ends. It's available as of version 5.1.21 of MySQL.

`--debug-info`, `-T`
: This option writes debugging information and CPU and memory usage information to the log after the utility ends.

`--force`
: This option forces the utility to check tables despite the *mysql_upgrade_info* file indicating that the tables are marked the same as the version noted in that file.

`--help`, `-?`, `-I`
: This option displays help information about the utility.

`--password=`*`password`*, `-p` *`password`*
: This option provides the password of the user logging into the server.

`--user=`*`user`*, `-u` *`user`*
: This option provides the username for logging into the server. If the option is not given, the *root* user is assumed by default.

`--verbose`
: This option displays more information from the utility.

mysql_waitpid

`mysql_waitpid` *`options PID wait_time`*

This utility uses the Unix system `kill` command to terminate the process identified by a given process identification number, and to wait for termination for the time given in seconds. The process identified and the seconds given must be positive integers. It returns 0 on success or if the process didn't exist. It returns 1 after timeout.

The only options available for this utility are for help (`--help, -?, -I`), the version number (`--version, -V`), and verbosity (`--verbose, -v`).

mysql_zap

`mysql_zap [options] pattern`

Use this utility to kill processes based on a given pattern.

mysql_zap options

`--help, -?, -I`
: This option displays help information about the utility.

`-f`
: This option forces the utility to kill the processes without confirming the action with the user first.

`-signal`
: This option specifies the type of kill: `TERM` (or signal 15) or `KILL` (signal 9). You can give either the name or the number for the kill type. Notice that there is only one dash, not two with this option, and it must be entered before the other options.

`-t`
: This option tests the patterns given without killing the processes.

mysqlaccess

`mysqlaccess [host [user [database]]] [options]`

This utility checks the privileges that a user has for a specific host and database. One use is to run it as a preliminary tool to check for user permissions before proceeding with a customized program that uses one of the APIs.

If MySQL was not installed in the default location for the version you're using, you'll have to set the variable `MYSQL` in the `mysqlaccess` script. Change it with a plain text editor. Look for the following line (near the beginning) and change the file path to where the `mysql` client is located:

```
$MYSQL = '/usr/local/mysql/bin/mysql';  # path to mysql executable
```

With regard to the syntax, the hostname is the first argument and is optional. If not given, *localhost* is assumed. The username given in the second argument is the name of the user for which the utility is checking privileges. The third argument is the database against which to check privileges. The fourth argument involves several possible options, one of which could be the username by which the utility will access the server to gather information on the user named in the second argument. Here is an example of how you might use this utility:

```
mysqlaccess localhost marie workrequests -U russell -P
```

In this example, I give the utility the hostname, then the user I'm inquiring about, then the database name for which I want user privilege information. The `-U` option specifies the username with which to access the server to gather information. This user has full access to the `mysql` database. The `-P` instructs the utility to prompt me for a password.

Here are the results of the preceding inquiry:

```
Access-rights
for USER 'marie', from HOST 'localhost', to DB 'ANY_NEW_DB'
```

```
          +-----------------+---+ +-----------------+---+
          | Select_priv     | Y | | Shutdown_priv   | N |
          | Insert_priv     | N | | Process_priv    | N |
          | Update_priv     | N | | File_priv       | N |
          | Delete_priv     | N | | Grant_priv      | N |
          | Create_priv     | N | | References_priv | N |
          | Drop_priv       | N | | Index_priv      | N |
          | Reload_priv     | N | | Alter_priv      | N |
          +-----------------+---+ +-----------------+---+
NOTE:    A password is required for user 'reader' :-(
The following rules are used:
db    : 'No matching rule'
host  : 'Not processed: host-field is not empty in db-table.'
user:'localhost','marie','6ffa06534985249d','Y','N','N','N',
'N','N','N','N','N','N','N','N','N','N'
```

First, a table is presented that displays the privileges for the combination of the database named, the host given, and the user. This user has only `SELECT` privileges.

Additionally, the results are given in raw form for each component. This user's privileges are the same for all databases and hosts (i.e., there are no entries in the `db` or the `host` tables in the `mysql` database), so there aren't any results for those particular components. For the user component, the command displays details without labels, but they are presented in the order that they are found in the `user` table in the `mysql` database. The third field is the password in the encrypted format in which it is stored. The Ys and Ns are the settings for each user privilege.

Here is a list of options available for this utility in alphabetical order:

`--brief`, `-b`
: This option provides a brief display of results from an inquiry.

`--commit`
: This option copies grant rules from temporary tables to the grant tables.

`--copy`
: This option reloads temporary tables with original data from the grant tables so that privileges take effect.

`--db=`*`database`*, `-d` *`database`*
: This option explicitly specifies the database against which to query the user privileges.

`--debug=`*`level`*
: This option sets the debugging level. The choices are from 0 to 3.

`--help`, `-?`
: This option displays basic help information.

`--host=`*`host`*, `-h` *`host`*
: This option specifies the host on which to obtain privilege information. The localhost is the default.

`--howto`
: This option displays basic examples of usage with sample results.

`--old-server`
: This option stipulates that the server to which the utility is connecting is running an older version of MySQL (prior to 3.21), requiring a different method with regard to `WHERE` clauses in SQL statements.

`--password=`*`password`*, `-p` *`password`*
: This option provides the password of the user logging into the server, not the user on which to check for privileges.

`--plan`
: This option displays plans for further development of the utility by its developers.

`--preview`
: This option displays the differences in temporary grant tables before they are committed.

`--relnotes`
: This option displays notes on each release of the utility.

`--rhost=`*`host`*, `-H` *`host`*
: If the utility is not being run on the same server as the MySQL server that's being queried, use this option to specify the address of the MySQL server to query.

`--rollback`
: This option undoes the last change to user privileges.

`--spassword=`*`password`*, `-P` *`password`*
: This option provides the password when using a superuser.

`--superuser=`*`user`*, `-U` *`user`*
: This option provides a superuser's username.

`--table`, `-t`
: This option displays data in an ASCII table format.

`--user=`*`user`*, `-u` *`user`*
: This option provides the username for logging into the server, not the user on which to check for privileges.

`--version`, `-v`
: This option displays the version of the utility.

mysqladmin

`mysqladmin [`*`options`*`]` *`command`* `[`*`command_options`*`]`

This utility allows you to perform MySQL server administration tasks from the command line. You can use it to check the server's status and settings, flush tables, change passwords, shut down the server, and perform a few other administrative functions. This utility interacts with the MySQL server.

Here is an alphabetical list of options that you can give as the first argument to the utility:

`--character-sets-dir=`*`path`*
: This option specifies the directory that contains character sets.

`--compress`, `-C`
: This option compresses data passed between the utility and the server, if compression is supported.

`--connect_timeout=`*`number`*
: This option sets the number of seconds a connection may be idle before it will time out.

`--count=`*`number`*, `-c` *`number`*
: This option specifies the number of iterations of commands to perform in conjunction with the `--sleep` option.

`--debug=`*`options filename`*, `-#` *`options`*, *`filename`*
: This option logs debugging information. The set of options used by default is `'d:t:o,logname'`. See Table 16-1 at the end of the list of options under the `mysqldump` utility for an explanation of these flags and others that may be used.

`--debug-check`
: This option writes debugging information to the log when the utility ends. It's available as of version 5.1.21 of MySQL.

`--debug-info`
: This option adds debugging information and CPU and memory usage information to the log when the utility ends. It's available as of version 5.1.21 of MySQL.

`--default-character-sets-dir=`*`path`*
: This option specifies the directory that contains the default character sets.

`--force`, `-f`
: This option forces execution of the `DROP DATABASE` statement and others despite error messages.

`--help`, `-?`
: This option displays basic help information.

`--host=`*`host`*, `-h` *`host`*
: This option specifies the name or IP address of the server for connection.

`--no-beep`
: This option instructs the utility not to emit a warning sound for errors. It was added as of version 5.1.17 of MySQL.

`--password[=`*`password`*`]`, `-p[`*`password`*`]`
: This option provides the password to give to the server. No spaces are allowed between the `-p` and the password. If a password is not given, the user will be prompted for one.

`--port=`*`port`*, `-P` *`port`*
: This option specifies the port on which to connect to the server. The default is 3306.

`--relative`, `-r`
: This option displays the differences between values with each iteration of commands issued with the `--sleep` option.

`--shutdown_timeout=`*`number`*
: This option sets the number of seconds the client should wait before shutting down.

`--silent`, `-s`
: This option tells the utility to exit without error messages if a connection to the server cannot be established.

`--sleep=`*`seconds`*, *`-i seconds`*
: This option specifies the number of seconds to wait between the repeated execution of commands. The number of iterations is set by the `--count` option.

`--socket=`*`filename`*, `-S` *`filename`*
: This option provides the name of the server's socket file.

`--ssl`
: This option specifies that secure SSL connections should be used. It requires the server to have SSL enabled.

`--ssl-ca=`*`pem_file`*
: This option specifies the name of the file (i.e., the *pem* file) containing a list of trusted SSL CAs.

`--ssl-capath=`*`path`*
: This option specifies the path to the trusted certificates file (i.e., the *pem* file).

`--ssl-cert=`*`filename`*
: This option specifies the name of the SSL certificate file to use for SSL connections.

`--ssl-cipher=`*`ciphers`*
: This option gives a list of ciphers that may be used for SSL encryption.

`--ssl-key=`*`filename`*
: This option specifies the SSL key file to use for secure connections.

`--ssl-verify-server-cert`
: This option verifies the client's certificate against the server's certificate for the client at startup. It is available as of version 5.1.11 of MySQL.

`--start-slave`
: This option is issued on a slave server to start replication.

`--stop-slave`
: This option is issued on a slave server to stop replication.

`--user=`*`user`*, `-u` *`user`*
: This option specifies a MySQL user other than the current filesystem user.

`--verbose`, `-v`
: This option displays more information.

`--version`, `-V`
: This option displays the version of the utility.

`--vertical`, `-E`
: This option displays output in a vertical format with a separate line for each column of data.

`--wait[=`*`number`*`]`, `-w [`*`number`*`]`
: This option instructs the utility to wait until it can connect to the server. It will retry once unless the number of times it is to retry is given with this option.

mysqladmin commands

The main focus of `mysqladmin` is the commands that perform administrative tasks. Commands are given as the second argument. You can issue one or more commands on the same line. Here is an alphabetical list of commands (with options for some) and an explanation of each:

`create` *`database`*
: This command creates the new database specified.

`debug`
: This command enables debugging of the utility. It writes debugging information to the error log.

`drop` *`database`*
: This command deletes the database specified.

`extended-status`
: This command displays the MySQL server's extended status information.

`flush-hosts`
: This command flushes all cached hosts.

`flush-logs`
: This command flushes all logs.

`flush-privileges`
: This command reloads the grant tables.

`flush-status`
: This command flushes status variables.

`flush-tables`
: This command has the utility flush all tables.

`flush-threads`
: This command flushes the thread cache.

`kill` *`id`*
: This command kills the server thread specified by an identifier. Additional threads may be given in a comma-separated list.

`old-password` *`password`*
: This command changes the password of the user currently connected to the server through the utility to the password given, but in the older encryption method prior to version 4.1 of MySQL.

`password` *`password`*
: This command changes the user's password to the given ***`password`***. Only the password for the user connecting to the server can be changed.

`ping`
: This command determines whether the server is running.

`processlist`
: This command displays a list of active server threads. With the **`--verbose`** option, more information is provided on each thread.

`refresh`
: This command flushes all tables and reloads log files.

`reload`
: This command reloads the grant tables.

`shutdown`
: This command shuts down the MySQL server.

`start-slave`
: This command starts a replication slave server.

`status`
: This command displays the server's status.

`stop-slave`
: This command stops a replication slave server.

`variables`
: This command displays the variables and the values of the server.

`version`
: This command displays the version of the utility.

mysqlbinlog

`mysqlbinlog [`*`options`*`]` *`filename`*

This utility formats the display of the binary log for a MySQL server. Customized applications can also use it for monitoring server activities. The path to the log file to format is given as the second argument for the utility. Additional log files may be given either with filesystem wildcards or by listing them individually, separated by spaces.

Here is an alphabetical list of the options, along with a brief explanation of each:

`--base64-output`
: This option is used to write binary log entries using base-64 encoding. This is used for debugging and should not be used in production. It's available as of version 5.1.5 of MySQL.

`--character-sets-dir=`*`path`*
: This option specifies the directory containing character sets.

`--database=`*`database`*, `-d` *`database`*
: This option displays information regarding only the database given.

`--debug[=`*`options`*`]`, `-# [`*`options`*`]`
: This option logs debugging information, along with various settings (e.g., `'d:t:o,logname'`).

`--debug-check`
: This option writes debugging information to the log when the utility ends. It's available as of version 5.1.21 of MySQL.

`--debug-info`
: This option writes debugging information and CPU and memory usage information to the log after the utility ends.

`--disable-log-bin`, `-D`
: This option disables binary logging.

`--force-read`, `-f`
: This option forces the reading of unknown log information.

`--hexdump`, `-H`
: This option dumps the log in hexadecimal format.

`--help`, `-?`
: This option displays basic help information.

`--host=`*`host`*, `-h` *`host`*
: This option specifies the hostname or IP address of a remote server containing the log file to format.

Command-Line Utilities

`--local-load=`*`path`*, `-l` *`path`*
: This option specifies the local directory in which temporary files are to be prepared for `LOAD DATA INFILE` statements.

`--offset=`*`number`*, `-o` *`number`*
: This option skips *`number`* entries at the start of the log file before starting the display.

`--open_files_limit`
: This option sets the maximum number of open files allowed. The default is 64.

`--password=`*`password`*, `-p` *`password`*
: This option provides the password to the remote server that is being accessed.

`--port=`*`port`*, `-P` *`port`*
: This option specifies the port to use for connecting to a remote server.

`--position=`*`number`*, `-j` *`number`*
: This option sets the number of bytes to skip at the beginning of the log file. It is deprecated; use `--start-position` instead.

`--protocol=`*`protocol`*
: This option specifies the protocol to use when connecting to the server. The choices are `TCP`, `SOCKET`, `PIPE`, and `MEMORY`.

`--read-from-remote-server`, `-R`
: This option reads the binary log from a remote server instead of the local machine. You will need to include the necessary options for connecting to a remote server: `--host`, `--password`, and `--user`. You might also need to include `--port`, `--protocol`, and `--socket`.

`--result-file=`*`filename`*, `-r` *`filename`*
: This option redirects the results of the utility to a given file.

`--server-id=`*`identifier`*
: This option returns entries from the binary log that were generated by a connection matching the given process identifier number. This option is available as of version 5.1.4 of MySQL.

`--set-charset=`*`character_set`*
: This option adds a `SET NAMES` statement to the results to indicate the character set used. It is available as of version 5.1.12 of MySQL.

`--skip-write-binlog`
: This option disables the `--write-binlog` option, which is enabled by default. Otherwise, `ANALYZE TABLE`, `OPTIMIZE TABLE`, and `REPAIR TABLE` statements executed by the utility will be written to the binary log. It's available as of version 5.1.18 of MySQL.

`--short-form`, `-s`
: This option changes the output to a shorter format.

`--socket=`*`filename`*, `-S` *`filename`*
: This option provides the name of the server's socket file for Unix systems, piped name for Windows systems.

`--start-datetime=`*`datetime`*
: This option begins reading the log from the first event recorded with a date and time equal to or greater than the one given. The time can be in `DATETIME` or `TIMESTAMP` format. Use the time zone of the server.

`--start-position=number`
: This option sets the position to start reading the log file.

`--stop-datetime=datetime`
: This option instructs the utility to stop reading the log at the first event recorded with a date and time equal to or greater than the one given. The time can be in `DATETIME` or `TIMESTAMP` format. Use the time zone of the server.

`--stop-position=number`
: This option sets the position to stop reading the log file.

`--table=table, -t table`
: This option obtains information on the table named.

`--to-last-log, -t`
: This option instructs the utility to continue on in sequence reading through all binary logs, starting with the one given until the last log file is processed.

`--user=user, -u user`
: This option specifies the username to use when connecting to a remote server.

`--version, -V`
: This option displays the version of the utility.

`--write-binlog`
: With this option, `ANALYZE TABLE`, `OPTIMIZE TABLE`, and `REPAIR TABLE` statements executed by the utility will be written to the binary log. It's available as of version 5.1.18 of MySQL and is enabled by default. To disable it, use `--skip-write-binlog`.

mysqlbug

`mysqlbug`

This is a script you can use to report bugs to MySQL AB developers. Executed at the command line of the server, this script gathers information on the version of MySQL and related libraries installed, the operating system, as well as how MySQL was compiled.

To run the utility, simply type the command without any options or arguments. After a few moments, a text editor (e.g., Emacs) will be started with a form for reporting the bug. Several of the details will be filled in with information gathered by the script. You can modify this information, and you are expected to answer questions about the bug discovered. This includes a description of how to reproduce the problem or what circumstances occurred that may have caused or contributed to the problem. If you discovered a workaround solution, report this as well. The report created (saved in the */tmp* directory on Unix systems) should be emailed to *dev-bugs@mysql.com*. Go to *http://bugs.mysql.com* to report bugs online.

mysqlcheck

`mysqlcheck [options] database [table]`

This utility checks, repairs, and optimizes MyISAM tables. It works in part on tables for other storage engines as well. It uses the `ANALYZE TABLE`, `CHECK TABLE`, `OPTIMIZE TABLE`, and `REPAIR TABLE` statements. Therefore, if the storage engine supports any of these statements, the operations that can be performed by supported statements can be done using this utility. For MyISAM tables, this utility is similar in use and purpose to `myisamchk`. Instead of working with the table files directly as `myisamchk` does, though, this utility interacts with the MySQL server.

The name of the database containing the tables to check is given as the second argument to the utility. The table to check is given as the third argument. Additional tables may be given in a space-separated list.

Here is a list of options that you can give and a brief explanation of each:

`--all-databases`, `-A`
: This option checks all databases.

`--all-in-1`, `-1`
: This option executes all queries for all tables in each database in one statement rather than as separate queries for each table.

`--analyze`, `-a`
: This option analyzes tables.

`--auto-repair`
: This option automatically repairs any corrupted tables found.

`--character-sets-dir=`*`path`*
: This option specifies the directory containing character sets.

`--check`, `-c`
: This option checks tables for errors.

`--check-only-changed`, `-C`
: This option checks only tables that have changed since the last check, as well as tables that were not closed properly.

`--compress`
: This option compresses data passed between the utility and the server, if compression is supported.

`--databases` *`databases`*, `-B` *`databases`*
: This option specifies more than one database for checking. To specify tables along with databases with this option, use the `--tables` option.

`--debug[=`*`options`*`]`, `-# [`*`options`*`]`
: This option logs debugging information. The set of options used by default is `'d:t:o,logname'`. See Table 16-1 at the end of the list of options under the `mysqldump` utility for an explanation of these flags and others that may be used.

`--debug-check`
: This option writes debugging information to the log when the utility ends. It's available as of version 5.1.21 of MySQL.

`--debug-info`
: This option writes debugging information and CPU and memory usage information to the log after the utility ends.

`--default-character-set=`*`set`*
: This option specifies the default character set. Enter `SHOW CHARACTER SET;` on the server for a list of character sets available.

`--extended, -e`
: This option ensures consistency of data when checking tables. When repairing tables with this option, the utility will attempt to recover all rows, including intentionally deleted ones.

`--fast, -F`
: This option checks only tables that were improperly closed.

`--fix-db-names`
: This option converts the names of databases that contain characters no longer permitted by MySQL as of version 5.1. It's available as of version 5.1.7 of MySQL.

`--fix-table-names`
: This option converts the names of tables that contain characters no longer permitted by MySQL as of version 5.1. It's available as of version 5.1.7.

`--force, -f`
: This option forces processing of tables regardless of SQL errors encountered.

`--help, -?`
: This option displays basic help information.

`--host=host, -h host`
: This option specifies the name or IP address of the server for connection.

`--medium-check, -m`
: This option is more thorough than `--check` but less thorough than `--extended`.

`--optimize, -o`
: This option optimizes tables.

`--password[=`*`password`*`], -p[`*`password`*`]`
: This option provides the password to pass to the server. A space is not permitted after `-p` if the password is given.

`--port=`*`port`*`, -P `*`port`*
: This option specifies the port to use for connecting to the server. The default is 3306.

`--protocol=`*`protocol`*
: This option specifies the protocol to use when connecting to the server. The choices are `TCP`, `SOCKET`, `PIPE`, and `MEMORY`.

`--quick, -q`
: This option checks tables faster by not scanning rows for incorrect links. When used to repair tables, it has the utility repair only the index tree. This option is the fastest method.

`--repair, -r`
: This option repairs tables. Note that it can't repair unique keys containing duplicates.

`--silent, -s`
: This option suppresses all messages except for error messages.

`--socket=`*`filename`*`, -S `*`filename`*
: This option provides the name of the server's socket file.

`--ssl`
: This option specifies that secure SSL connections should be used. It requires the server to have SSL enabled. If this option is enabled on the utility by default, use `--skip-ssl` to disable it.

`--ssl-ca=pem_file`
: This option specifies the name of the file (i.e., the *pem* file) containing a list of trusted SSL CAs.

`--ssl-capath=path`
: This option specifies the path to the trusted certificates file (i.e., the *pem* file).

`--ssl-cert=filename`
: This option specifies the name of the SSL certificate file to use for SSL connections.

`--ssl-cipher=ciphers`
: This option gives a list of ciphers that may be used for SSL encryption.

`--ssl-key=filename`
: This option specifies the SSL key file to use for secure connections.

`--ssl-verify-server-cert`
: This option verifies the client's certificate against the server's certificate for the client at startup. It is available as of version 5.1.11 of MySQL.

`--tables`
: This option specifies table names when using the `--databases` option.

`--use-frm`
: This option uses the table structure in the *.frm* file for repairing a corrupted index.

`--user=user`, `-u user`
: This option specifies the username for connecting to the server.

`--verbose`, `-v`
: This option displays more information.

`--version`, `-V`
: This option displays the version of the utility.

mysqldump

```
mysqldump [options] --all-databases
mysqldump [options] --databases database [database ...]
mysqldump [options] database [table]
```

This utility exports MySQL data and table structures. Typically, you use it to make backups of databases or to copy databases from one server to another. You can run it on an active server. For consistency of data between tables, the tables should be locked (see the `--lock-tables` option) or the `mysqld` daemon should be shutdown.

There are three syntaxes for this utility. The first method shown makes a backup of all databases for the server. The second method backs up specific databases, named in a space-separated list, including all tables in each database. The third method backs up specific tables of a specific database.

Here is an example using the first method, backing up all databases on the server:

```
mysqldump --host=russell.dyerhouse.com --user=russell --password \
   --lock-tables --all-databases > /tmp/workrequests.sql
```

Because the backup is being run from a remote server (i.e., not the localhost), the `--host` option is given with a domain name address for the host. An IP address could be given instead. Making a backup remotely like this will work only if the host grants the necessary privileges to user *russell* with the host from which `mysqldump` is running. The example redirects the results with a greater-than sign to a text file.

To make a backup of a specific database, use the second syntax for this utility. Enter something like the following from the command line:

```
mysqldump -u russell -p --lock-tables workrequests > /tmp/workrequests.sql
```

In this example, the username is given with the `-u` option. The `-p` option tells the utility to prompt the user for a password. These shorter options are interchangeable with their longer, more verbose ones, but the verbose ones are becoming the norm and should be used. The `--lock-tables` option has the server lock the tables, make the backup, and then unlock them when it's finished. Next, we specify the database to back up (`workrequests`). Finally, using the redirect (the greater-than sign), the output is saved to the filename given.

The `--lock-tables` option is generally not necessary because the `--opt` option is a default option and includes locking tables. In fact, if you're making a backup and you do not have the `LOCK TABLES` privilege, you will receive an error when running `mysqldump` because of `--opt`. In such a situation, you'll need to include the `--skip-opt` option to specifically disable `--opt` and thereby not attempt to lock the tables.

If you want to back up specific tables and not an entire database, you can use the third syntax shown at the start of this section for this utility. It's not a very verbose syntax: you simply give the name of the database followed by one or more tables. You don't identify them individually as a database versus tables; you just put them in the proper order without the `--all-database` option. Here's an example of this syntax:

```
mysqldump -u russell -p workrequests work_req clients >
   /tmp/workreq_clients_tables.sql
```

In this example, the database is `workrequests` and the tables to be backed up are `work_req` and `clients`. Their table structures and data will be copied into the text file *workreq_clients_tables.sql*.

The backup or dump file created by `mysqldump` will be in the text file format. It generally will contain a `CREATE TABLE` statement for each table in the database. If you want to eliminate the `CREATE TABLE` statements, add the `--no-create-info`. If they are not included in the dump file generated on your server, add the `--create-options` option and run `mysqldump` again. The dump files will also generally contain a separate `INSERT` statement for each row of data. To back up the data faster, you can add the `--extended-insert` option so that only one `INSERT` with multiple values will be generated for each table instead of separate `INSERT` statements for each row of data.

To restore the data from a dump file created by `mysqldump`, you can use the *mysql* client. To restore the file created by the preceding statement, you can enter the following from the command line:

```
mysql -u russell -p < /tmp/workrequests.sql
```

This example redirects the `stdin` by means of the less-than sign. This instructs the *mysql* client to take input from the file given. It will execute the series of SQL statements contained in the dump file. You won't be placed into monitor mode; you will remain at the command line until it's finished.

You can determine the contents of the dump file by the options you choose. Following is an alphabetical list of options, along with a brief explanation of each. For some options, there is a shorter, less verbose version (i.e., `-u` for `--user`). These shorter options are interchangeable with their longer, more verbose ones, but the verbose ones are becoming the norm and should be used.

mysqldump options

`--add-drop-database`
: This option adds a `DROP DATABASE` statement followed by a `CREATE DATABASE` statement to the export file for each database, thus replacing the existing database and data if restored.

`--add-drop-table`
: This option adds a `DROP TABLE` statement to the export file before each set of `INSERT` statements for each table.

`--add-locks`
: This option adds a `LOCK` statement before each set of `INSERT` statements and an `UNLOCK` after each set.

`--all`, `-a`
: This option includes all MySQL-specific statements in the export file. This option is deprecated as of version 4.1.2 of MySQL. It is replaced with the `--create-options` option.

`--all-databases`, `-A`
: This option exports all databases.

`--all-tablespaces`, `-Y`
: This option is used with MySQL Cluster so that the utility will include the necessary SQL statements related to the NDB storage engine. This option is available as of version 5.1.6 of MySQL.

`--allow-keywords`
: This option makes keywords allowable for column names by including the table name and a dot before such column names in the export file.

`--character-sets-dir=`*`path`*
: This option specifies the directory containing character sets.

`--comments[=0|1]`, `-i`
: If this option is set to a value of 1 (the default), any comments from a table's schema will be included in the export file. If it is set to 0, they won't be included. To disable this option since it's the default, use the `--skip-comments` option.

`--compact`
: This option omits comments from the dump file to make the file more compact. It also calls the `--skip-add-drop-table`, `--skip-add-locks`, `--skip-disable-keys`, and `--skip-set-charset` options. Don't confuse this option with `--compress`. Before version 5.1.2 of MySQL, this option did not work with databases that contained views.

`--compatible=`*`type`*
: This option makes the export file's contents compatible with other database systems. The choices currently are: `ansi`, `mysql323`, `msyql40`, `postgresql`, `oracle`, `mssql`, `db2`, `maxdb` (or `sapdb` for older versions), `no_key_options`, `no_table_options`, and

`no_field_options`. More than one type may be given in a comma-separated list. This option is used with version 4.1.0 of MySQL or higher.

`--complete-insert`, `-c`
: This option generates complete `INSERT` statements in the export file.

`--compress`, `-C`
: This option compresses data passed between the utility and the server, if compression is supported.

`--create-options`
: This option includes all MySQL-specific statements (e.g., `CREATE TABLE`) in the export file. It's synonymous with the `--all` option.

`--databases`, `-B`
: This option names more than one database to export. Table names may not be given with this option unless using the `--tables` option.

`--debug[=`*`options`*`]`, `-#[`*`options`*`]`
: This option logs debugging information. The set of options used by default is `'d:t:o,logname'`. See Table 16-1 at the end of the list of options for this utility for an explanation of these flags and others that may be used. Here is an example of how you might use this option:

```
mysqldump -u russell -p --debug='d:f:i:o,/tmp/mysql_debug.log'
   workrequests > /tmp/workrequests.sql
```

`--debug-check`
: This option writes debugging information to the log when the utility ends. It's available as of version 5.1.21 of MySQL.

`--debug-info`
: This option writes debugging information and CPU and memory usage information to the log after the utility ends.

`--default-character-set=`*`set`*
: This option specifies the default character set for the utility to use. Execute `SHOW CHARACTER SET` from MySQL on the server to get a list of possibilities. By default, recent versions of the utility use UTF-8. Previous versions used Latin 1.

`--delayed-insert`
: This option adds the `DELAYED` keyword to `INSERT` statements in the export file. In older versions of `mysqldump`, this option was `--delayed`.

`--delete-master-logs`
: This option instructs the utility to lock all tables on all servers and then to delete the binary logs of a master replication server after completing the export. Using this option also invokes the `--master-data` option.

`--disable-keys`, `-K`
: For MyISAM tables, this option adds an `ALTER TABLE...DISABLE KEYS` statement to the export file before each set of `INSERT` statements, and an `ALTER TABLE...ENABLE KEYS` statement after each set to optimize later restoration.

`--events`, `-E`
: This option includes events from the databases. It is available as of version 5.1.8 of MySQL.

`--extended-insert, -e`
: This option bundles `INSERT` statements together for each table in the export file to make the export faster. Otherwise, a separate `INSERT` statement for each row of each table will be placed in the dump file.

`--fields-enclosed-by=`*`characters`*
: Use this option with the `--tab` option to specify the characters that start and end fields in the data text file.

`--fields-escaped-by=`*`character`*
: Use this option with the `--tab` option to specify the character that escapes special characters in the data text file. A backslash is the default.

`--fields-optionally-enclosed-by=`*`characters`*
: Use this option with the `--tab` option to specify the characters that can be used when necessary to start and end fields in the data text file.

`--fields-terminated-by=`*`character`*
: Use this option with the `--tab` option to specify the characters that end fields in the data text file.

`--first-slave`
: This option locks all tables on all servers. It has been deprecated and replaced with `--lock-all-tables`.

`--flush-logs, -F`
: This option flushes all logs. It requires the user to have `RELOAD` privilege on the server.

`--flush-privileges`
: This option flushes all privileges. It was added as of version 5.1.12.

`--force, -f`
: This option instructs the utility to continue processing data despite errors. This is useful in completing dumps for irrelevant errors such as ones related to views that no longer exist.

`--help, -?`
: This option displays basic help information.

`--hex-blob`
: This option uses hexadecimal equivalents for `BINARY`, `BIT`, `BLOB`, and `VARBINARY` columns.

`--host=`*`host`*`, -h `*`host`*
: This option specifies the name or IP address of the server for connection. The localhost is the default. The user and host combination and related privileges will need to be set on the server.

`--ignore-table=`*`database.table`*
: This option instructs the utility not to export the given table of the given database. For more than one table, enter this option multiple times with one database and table combination in each.

`--insert-ignore`
: This option adds the `IGNORE` keyword to `INSERT` statements in the dump file.

`--lines-terminated-by=`*`character`*
: Use this option with the `--tab` option to specify the character that ends records in the data text file.

`--lock-tables, -l`
: This option instructs the utility to get a `READ LOCK` on all tables of each database before exporting data, but not on all databases at the same time. It locks a database when it's dumping and releases the lock before locking and dumping the next database. This option is typically used with MyISAM tables. For transactional storage engines, use **`--single-transaction`** instead.

`--lock-all-tables, -x`
: This option locks all tables on all servers. It replaces **`--first-slave`**, which has been deprecated.

`--log-error=`*`logfile`*
: This option writes errors and warning messages to the file named. The file path may be included. This option is available as of version 5.1.18 of MySQL.

`--master-data=`*`value`*
: This option is used with replication. It writes the name of the current binary log file and server's position in the log file to the dump file. It requires the `RELOAD` privilege. It will typically disable **`--lock-tables`** and **`--lock-all-tables`**.

`--no-autocommit`
: This option adds `SET AUTOCOMMIT=0;` before each `INSERT` statement, and a `COMMIT;` statement after each `INSERT` statement.

`--no-create-db, -n`
: This option instructs the utility not to add `CREATE DATABASE` statements to the export file when the **`--all-databases`** option or the **`--databases`** option is used.

`--no-create-info, -t`
: This option instructs the utility not to add `CREATE TABLE` statements to the export file.

`--no-data, -d`
: This option exports only database and table schema, not data.

`--opt`
: This option is a combination of several commonly used options: **`--add-drop-table`**, **`--add-locks`**, **`--create-options`** (or **`--all`** before version 4.1.2), **`--disable-keys`**, **`--extended-insert`**, **`--lock-tables`**, **`--quick`**, and **`--set-charset`**. As of version 4.1 of MySQL, the **`--opt`** option is enabled by default. Use **`--skip-opt`** to disable it for users with limited access.

`--order-by-primary`
: This option sorts rows of tables by their primary key or first index. It slows down the backup process, though.

`--password[=`*`password`*`], -p[`*`password`*`]`
: This option provides the password to pass to the server. A space is not permitted after `-p` if the password is given. If the password is not given when using the `-p` option, the user will be prompted for one.

`--`*`port=port`*`, -P` *`port`*
: This option specifies the port number to use for connecting to the server. A space is expected before the port number when using the `-P` form of the option.

`--protocol=`*`protocol`*
: This option is used to specify the type of protocol to use for connecting to the server. The choices are `TCP`, `SOCKET`, `PIPE`, and `MEMORY`.

`--quick`, `-q`
: This option instructs the utility not to buffer data into a complete results set before exporting. Instead, it exports data one row at a time directly to the export file.

`--quote-names`, `-Q`
: This option places the names of databases, tables, and columns within backticks (`). This is the default option. If the server is running in `ANSI_QUOTES` SQL mode, double quotes will be used instead. This option is enabled by default. Use `--skip-quote-names` to disable it.

`--replace`
: This option puts `REPLACE` statements into the dump file instead of `INSERT` statements. It was added as of version 5.1.3 of MySQL.

`--result-file=`*`filename`*, `-r` *`filename`*, `> filename`
: This option provides the path and the name of the file to which data should be exported. Use the `--result-file` option on Windows systems to prevent newline characters (`\n`) from being converted to carriage return and newline characters (`\r\n`).

`--routines`, `-R`
: This option dumps stored procedures and functions. It was added as of version 5.1.2 of MySQL. It requires the `SELECT` privilege in the `proc` table of the `mysql` database. The statements written to the dump file related to these routines do not include timestamps, so the current time will be used when restoring instead.

`--set-charset`
: This option adds the `SET NAMES` statement to the dump file. It's enabled by default. Use `--skip-set-charset` to disable it.

`--single-transaction`
: This option executes a `BEGIN` statement before exporting to help achieve data consistency with the backup. It's effective only on transactional storage engines. It should not be used with MySQL Cluster.

`--skip-comments`
: This option instructs the utility not to export any comments from a table's schema to the export file. It disables the `--comments` option.

`--skip-opt`
: This option disables the `--opt` option.

`--skip-quote-names`
: This option disables the `--quote-names` option.

`--ssl`
: This option specifies that secure SSL connections should be used. It requires the server to have SSL enabled. If this option is enabled on the utility by default, use `--skip-ssl` to disable it.

`--ssl-ca=`*`pem_file`*
: This option specifies the name of the file (i.e., the *pem* file) containing a list of trusted SSL CAs.

`--ssl-capath=`*`path`*
: This option specifies the path to the trusted certificates file (i.e., the *pem* file).

`--ssl-cert=`*`filename`*
: This option specifies the name of the SSL certificate file to use for SSL connections.

`--ssl-cipher=`*`ciphers`*
: This option gives a list of ciphers that may be used for SSL encryption.

`--ssl-key=`*`filename`*
: This option specifies the SSL key file to use for secure connections.

`--ssl-verify-server-cert`
: This option verifies the client's certificate against the server's certificate for the client at startup. It is available as of version 5.1.11 of MySQL.

`--socket=`*`filename`*, `-S` *`filename`*
: This option provides the name of the server's socket file on a Unix-type system or the named pipe on Windows systems.

`--tab=`*`path`*, `-T` *`path`*
: This option creates two separate export files: one for the table schema (e.g., ***table**.sql*) and another for the data (e.g., ***table**.txt*). The data text file will contain data in a tab-separated format. This option requires `FILE` privilege, and the MySQL server must have write permission for the directory it is to write the exported file.

`--tables`
: This option specifies tables to dump. All names after the `--tables` option are treated as table names and not as database names.

`--triggers`
: This option includes triggers in dump files. It is the default. Use `--skip-triggers` to disable it.

`--tz-utc`
: This option adds `SET TIME_ZONE='+00:00';` to the dump file so that the dump files may be restored on a server in a different time zone and not cause inconsistencies with `TIMESTAMP` columns. This option is available as of version 5.1.2 of MySQL and is enabled by default. Use `--skip-tz-utc` to disable it.

`--user=`*`user`*, `-u` *`user`*
: This option specifies the username for connecting to the server. A space is expected after the `-u` option. If the `-u` version of this option is used and the username is not given, the current system user is assumed.

`--verbose`, `-v`
: This option displays more information.

`--version`, `-V`
: This option displays the version of the utility and exits.

`--where='`*`condition`*`'`, `-w '`*`condition`*`'`
: This option sets a `WHERE` condition for selecting rows from tables to be exported. For instance, suppose that we want to back up the `clients` table with only the clients who are located in New Orleans. We could run the utility like so:

```
mysqldump -u russell -p /
   --where="client_city='New Orleans'" workrequests clients > /tmp/
     workreq_clients_neworleans.sql
```

`--xml`, `-X`
: This option exports databases in XML format.

Command-Line Utilities

mysqldump --debug options

Table 16-1 lists the debugging, tracing, and profiling flags used with the `--debug` option for several MySQL-related utilities. The format is generally `--debug='flag:flag:flag'`. When a particular option needs more details, follow the flag with a comma and the details or extra settings in a comma-separated list: `--debug='flag:flag,setting,setting:flag'`. An alternative to the `--debug='flag:flag:flag'` syntax is `--#flag:flag:flag`. This syntax lacks the equals sign or quotes; the space afterward marks the end of the flags and settings.

Table 16-1. Debugging options

Flag	Description
d	Logs the DBUG macros. To log only certain macros, give the d flag followed by the specific macro keywords.
D	Used to specify a delay after each line in the debugging log. After the flag and a comma, give the number of tenths of a second to delay (e.g., `D,10` for a 1 second delay).
`f`	Limits debugging, tracing, and profiling to particular functions. The `f` flag with no functions listed results in all functions being filtered out of the log.
F	Names the source filename for debugging and tracing output.
`i`	Specifies the process identifier (PID) or thread identifier for each line of debugging and tracing output that is logged.
g	Enables profiling. A file named *dbugmon.out* may be used to provide details for profiling. A list of functions to profile may be given after this flag. If none are specified, all functions will be included.
L	Includes the source file's line number in each line of the debugging and tracing log.
n	Logs the nesting depth of each function for debugging and tracing.
N	Includes a line number in each line of the log.
o	Redirects debugging information to a given file, rather than `stderr`. The filename is given after the flag, separated from it by a comma (e.g., `o,/tmp/mysql_debug.log`).
O	This is the same as the o flag, but the log file is flushed between each write, and possibly opened and closed each time.
p	Limits debugging to given processes. Each process has to be specified with the `DBUG_PROCESS` macro.
P	Writes the current process name for each line to the debugging and tracing logs.
`r`	Resets the previous state's function nesting level.
S	Used with `safemalloc` to locate memory leaks. Will run until nonzero is returned.
`t`	Enables call and exit trace logging. A numeric maximum trace level may be given after the flag, separated from it by a comma.

mysqldumpslow

`mysqldumpslow [options] [filename]`

Use this utility to display a summary of the slow query log. The name of the log file may be given in the second argument. Otherwise, the utility will look to the server's configuration file (i.e., *my.cnf* or *my.ini*, depending on your system) for this information. The following options can narrow the summary or change what is displayed.

mysqldumpslow options

`-a`
: This option instructs the utility not to combine queries with similar SQL statements.

`--debug`, `-d`
: This option enables debugging mode.

`-g` *`expression`*
: This option extracts information on queries that meet the given expression.

`-h` *`host`*
: This option specifies the host's name for which the utility is to scan. By default, log files are named with the server's hostname as the filename's prefix.

`--help`
: This option displays help information on the utility.

`-i` *`host`*
: This option specifies the hostname of the server.

`-l`
: With this option, the lock time is added to the execution time for the utility's summary.

`-n` *`number`*
: This option sets the minimum number of occurrences for reporting.

`-r`
: This option reverses the order of sorts for reporting.

`-s` *`type`*
: This option specifies the type of queries on which to report. The choices are `al` for average lock time, `ar` for average rows, `at` for average execution time, `l` for lock time, `r` for rows, and `t` for execution time.

`-t`
: This option sets the number of queries on which to display.

`--verbose`, `-v`
: This option displays more information.

mysqlhotcopy

`mysqlhotcopy` *`database`* `[`*`path`*`]`

Use this utility to make backup copies of databases while the server is active. It works only on MyISAM and ISAM tables. It makes a simple copy of each database directory and each table file. This results in a separate directory for each database and usually three files for each table: one for the schema, another for the data, and a third for the index. It places a read lock on all of the tables in the database while copying them. Here is an example of how you can copy a database with `mysqlhotcopy`:

```
mysqlhotcopy -u russell -p password workrequests /tmp/backup
```

Note that unlike other MySQL utilities, there is a space between the `-p` and the password. Next, specify the database (`workrequests`). Finally, give the path to write the backup directories. To restore databases or tables that were copied by `mysqlhotcopy`, just copy the table files to be restored to their original data directories.

mysqlhotcopy options

`--addtodest`
: This option instructs the utility not to abort the session or to rename the backup directory, but to add new files to the directory.

`--allowold`
: This option renames any existing backup directory with an *_old* suffix so that the copying may be completed. If the new copy is successful, the old directory is deleted. If it's unsuccessful, the old directory is restored.

`--checkpoint=`*`database.table`*
: This option saves logging information to the named database and table.

`--chroot=`*`path`*
: This option is used to specify the base directory of the `chroot` in which the *mysqld* daemon is located, which should have the same directory of the `--chroot` option.

`--debug`
: This option is used to enable debugging information.

`--dryrun`, `-n`
: This option has the utility test the backup process without actually making a copy.

`--flushlog`
: This option flushes logs after all tables are locked.

`--help`, `-?`
: This option displays basic help information.

`--host=`*`host`*, `-h` *`host`*
: This option specifies the name or IP address of the server for connection.

`--keepold`
: This option instructs the utility when using the `--allowold` option not to delete the old directory if the copying is successful.

`--method=`*`method`*
: This option sets the method used by the utility for copying files. The choices are `cp` or `scp`.

`--noindices`
: This option copies only the headers of index files. Indexes may be rebuilt when restoring copies.

`--password=password`, `-ppassword`
: This option provides the password to pass to the server. A space is permitted after the `-p` option, before the password.

`--port=`*`port`*, `-P` *`port`*
: This option specifies the port number to use for connecting to the server.

`--quiet`, `-q`
: This option suppresses all messages except for error messages.

`--record_log_pos=`*`database.table`*
: This option is used to specify the database and table to record the log position and status of the master and slave servers when using replication.

`--regexp=`*`expression`*
: This option provides a regular expression for determining which databases to copy based on the name.

`--resetmaster`
: This option executes a `RESET MASTER` statement after tables are locked.

`--resetslave`
: This option executes a `RESET SLAVE` statement after tables are locked.

`--socket=`*`filename`*, `-S` *`filename`*
: This option provides the name of the server's socket file.

`--sufix=`*`string`*
: This option specifies the suffix for the copies of databases. The default is `_copy`.

`--tmpdir=`*`path`*
: This option specifies the temporary directory to use. The default is */tmp*.

`--user=`*`user`*, `-u` *`suser`*
: This option specifies the username for connecting to the server.

mysqlimport

```
mysqlimport [options] database filename[ ...]
```

Use this to import data and table structures from a text file given as the third argument into a database named in the second argument. This utility interacts with the server and uses the `LOAD DATA INFILE` statement. The root name of the text file being imported must be the same as the table name. Additional text files may be given in a space-separated list. Options may be given on the command line as the first argument of the utility, or they may be provided in the server's configuration file (e.g., *my.cnf*) under the heading `[client]` or `[mysqlimport]`. When included in the configuration file, options appear without the leading double dashes. Here is an alphabetical list of options you can give for the first argument, along with an explanation of each.

mysqlimport options

`--character-sets-dir=`*`path`*
: This option specifies the directory containing character sets.

`--columns=`*`columns`*, `-c` *`columns`*
: This option identifies the order of fields in the text file as they relate to the columns in the table. Columns are given in a comma-separated list.

`--compress`, `-C`
: This option compresses data passed between the utility and the server, if compression is supported.

`--debug[=`*`options`*`]`, `-#` `[`*`options`*`]`
: This option logs debugging information. The set of options used by default is `'d:t:o,logname'`. See Table 16-1 at the end of the list of the `mysqldump` utility options earlier in this chapter for an explanation of these flags and others that may be used.

`--debug-check`
: This option writes debugging information to the log when the utility ends. It's available as of version 5.1.21 of MySQL.

`--debug-info`
: This option writes debugging information and CPU and memory usage information to the log after the utility ends.

`--default-character-set=`*`set`*
: This option specifies the default character set.

`--defaults-extra-file=`*`filename`*
: This option takes additional options from the text file named.

`--defaults-file=`*`filename`*
: This option instructs the utility to accept options only from the text file named.

`--delete`, `-d`
: This option deletes all data from each target table before importing data from the text file.

`--fields-enclosed-by=`*`characters`*
: This option identifies the characters that indicate the start and end of fields in the text file being imported.

`--fields-escaped-by=`*`character`*
: This option identifies the character that will escape special characters in the text file being imported. A backslash is the default.

`--fields-optionally-enclosed-by=`*`characters`*
: This option identifies the characters that indicate the start and end of fields in the text file being imported.

`--fields-terminated-by=`*`character`*
: This option identifies the character that indicates the end of fields in the text file being imported.

`--force`, `-f`
: This option instructs the utility to continue importing data despite errors encountered.

`--help`, `-?`
: This option displays basic help information.

`--host=`*`host`*, `-h` *`host`*
: This option specifies the name or IP address of the server for connection.

`--ignore`, `-i`
: This option instructs the utility to ignore error messages regarding rows containing duplicate keys and thereby not to replace such rows with imported data.

`--ignore-lines=`*`number`*
: This option instructs the utility to ignore the first number of lines specified. It's useful in skipping headings in the text file being imported.

`--lines-terminated-by=`*`character`*
: This option identifies the character that indicates the end of records in the text file being imported.

`--local`, `-L`
: This option tells the utility that the text file to import is located locally on the client and not on the server, which is the default assumption.

`--lock-tables`, `-l`
: This option locks all tables before importing data.

`--low-priority`
: This option has the utility use the `LOW PRIORITY` keyword when importing data.

`--no-defaults`
: This option tells the utility not to accept options from a configuration file.

`--password[=`*`password`*`]`, `-p[`*`password`*`]`
: This option provides the password to pass to the server. A space is not permitted after the `-p` option if the password is given. If the password is not given, the user will be prompted for one.

`--port=`*`port`*, `-P` *`port`*
: This option specifies the port number to use for connecting to the server.

`--print-defaults`
: This option displays related options found in the server's configuration files.

`--protocol=`*`protocol`*
: This option is used to specify the protocol to use when connecting to the server. The choices are `TCP`, `SOCKET`, `PIPE`, and `MEMORY`.

`--replace`, `-r`
: This option replaces rows that contain duplicate keys with the imported data.

`--silent`, `-s`
: This option suppress all messages except for error messages.

`--socket=`*`filename`*, `-S` *`filename`*
: This option provides the name of the server's socket file.

`--ssl`
: This option specifies that secure SSL connections should be used. It requires the server to have SSL enabled. If this option is enabled on the utility by default, use `--skip-ssl` to disable it.

`--ssl-ca=`*`pem_file`*
: This option specifies the name of the file (i.e., the *pem* file) containing a list of trusted SSL CAs.

`--ssl-capath=`*`path`*
: This option specifies the path to the trusted certificates file (i.e., the *pem* file).

`--ssl-cert=`*`filename`*
: This option specifies the name of the SSL certificate file to use for SSL connections.

`--ssl-cipher=`*`ciphers`*
: This option gives a list of ciphers that may be used for SSL encryption.

`--ssl-key=`*`filename`*
: This option specifies the SSL key file to use for secure connections.

`--ssl-verify-server-cert`
: This option verifies the client's certificate against the server's certificate for the client at startup. It is available as of version 5.1.11 of MySQL.

`--user=`*`user`*, `-u` *`user`*
: This option specifies the username for connecting to the server.

`--verbose`, `-v`
: This option displays more information.

`--version`, `-V`
: This option displays the version of the utility.

mysqlshow

`mysqlshow [options] [database [table [column]]]`

Use this utility to obtain a list of databases, tables, or descriptions of tables. It interacts with the server and uses the `SHOW DATABASES`, `SHOW TABLES`, and `SHOW TABLE` statements. If no database name is given for the second argument, all database names will be listed. If a database name is given along with a table name, the table named will be described. To limit information to specific columns, list the columns desired in the fourth argument:

```
mysqlshow --user=russell -ppassword workrequests work_req
```

The results of this command will be the same as entering the following SQL statement from the *mysql* client:

```
SHOW TABLE workrequests.work_req;
```

Here is an alphabetical list of options that you can give as part of the first argument of the utility, along with a brief explanation of each.

mysqlshow options

`--character-sets-dir=path`
: This option specifies the directory containing character sets.

`--compress, -C`
: This option compresses data passed between the utility and the server, if compression is supported.

`--count`
: This option returns the number of rows for the given table.

`--debug[=options], -# [options]`
: This option logs debugging information. The set of options used by default is `'d:t:o,logname'`. See Table 16-1 at the end of the list the `mysqldump` utility options earlier in this chapter for an explanation of these flags and others that may be used.

`--debug-check`
: This option writes debugging information to the log when the utility ends. It's available as of version 5.1.21 of MySQL.

`--debug-info`
: This option writes debugging information and CPU and memory usage information to the log after the utility ends.

`--default-character-set=set`
: This option specifies the default character set.

`--help, -?`
: This option displays basic help information.

`--host=host, -h host`
: This option specifies the name or IP address of the server for connection.

`--keys, -k`
: This option displays table indexes.

`--password[=password]`, `-p[password]`
: This option provides the password to pass to the server. A space is not permitted after the `-p` option if the password is given. If the password is not given, the user will be prompted for one.

`--port=port`, `-P port`
: This option specifies the port number to use for connecting to the server.

`--protocol=protocol`
: This option specifies the protocol to use when connecting to the server. The choices are `TCP`, `SOCKET`, `PIPE`, and `MEMORY`.

`--show-table-type`, `-t`
: This option adds a column to the results to indicate the type of table: a base table or a view.

`--socket=filename`, `-S filename`
: This option provides the name of the server's socket file.

`--ssl`
: This option specifies that secure SSL connections should be used. It requires the server to have SSL enabled. If this option is enabled on the utility by default, use `--skip-ssl` to disable it.

`--ssl-ca=pem_file`
: This option specifies the name of the file (i.e., the *pem* file) containing a list of trusted SSL CAs.

`--ssl-capath=path`
: This option specifies the path to the trusted certificates file (i.e., the *pem* file).

`--ssl-cert=filename`
: This option specifies the name of the SSL certificate file to use for SSL connections.

`--ssl-cipher=ciphers`
: This option gives a list of ciphers that may be used for SSL encryption.

`--ssl-key=filename`
: This option specifies the SSL key file to use for secure connections.

`--ssl-verify-server-cert`
: This option verifies the client's certificate against the server's certificate for the client at startup. It is available as of version 5.1.11 of MySQL.

`--status`, `-i`
: This option displays additional information regarding tables.

`--user=user`, `-u user`
: This option specifies the username for connecting to the server.

`--verbose`, `-v`
: This option displays more information.

`--version`, `-V`
: This option displays the version of the utility.

mysqlslap

`mysqlslap [options] database`

This utility is used to emulate a load of multiple clients on the server to check the timing of the system. It's available as of version 5.1.4 of MySQL.

mysqlslap options

`--auto-generate-sql, -a`
: If you do not want to use or have a file containing SQL statements for testing the server, nor do you want to manually supply SQL statements from the command line, you can use this option to instruct the utility to automatically generate SQL to emulate a client load.

`--compress, -C`
: This option compresses data passed between the utility and the server, if compression is supported.

`--concurrency=number, -c number`
: Use this option to specify the number of clients to simulate.

`--create=value`
: This option is used to specify a file or string to use for creating a table for use in testing.

`--create-schema=value`
: This option is used to specify a file or string containing a table schema to use for creating a table for use in testing.

`--csv[=filename]`
: This option returns data in a comma-separated value format. It will export the data to the standard output, unless a filename is given. Then it will save the information to that file.

`--debug[=options], -# [options]`
: This option logs debugging information. The set of options used by default is `'d:t:o,logname'`. See Table 16-1 at the end of the list of the `mysqldump` utility options earlier in this chapter for an explanation of these flags and others that may be used.

`--debug-check`
: This option writes debugging information to the log when the utility ends. It's available as of version 5.1.21 of MySQL.

`--debug-info, -T`
: This option writes debugging information and CPU and memory usage information to the log after the utility ends.

`--delimiter=string, -F string`
: Use this option to specify the delimiter used in the SQL file given.

`--engine=engine, -e engine`
: Use this option to specify the storage engine to use for the test table.

`--host=host, -h host`
: This option specifies the host on which to connect to the server.

`--help, -?`
: This option displays help information about the utility.

`--iterations=number`, `-i number`
: This option is used to specify the number of times to run the client load emulation tests.

`--number-char-cols=number`, `-x number`
: When specifying `--auto-generate-sql`, use this option to specify the number of `VARCHAR` columns to use.

`--number-int-cols=number`, `-y number`
: When specifying `--auto-generate-sql`, use this option to specify the number of `INT` columns to use.

`--number-of-queries=number`
: This option is used to specify the number of queries for each client.

`--only-print`
: This option instructs the utility not to run the tests on the server, but to display only what would have been done based on the options given.

`--password=password`, `-p password`
: This option provides the password of the user logging into the server.

`--port=port`
: This option specifies the port on which to connect to the server. The default is 3306.

`--preserve-schema`
: This option preserves the schema used when the utility was run.

`--protocol=protocol`
: This specifies the protocol to use when connecting to the server. The choices are `TCP`, `SOCKET`, `PIPE`, and `MEMORY`.

`--query=value`, `-q value`
: This option is used to give the string or to specify the file to use that contains the `SELECT` statement for querying the server for testing.

`--silent`, `-s`
: This option displays no messages.

`--socket=filename`, `-S filename`
: This option provides the name of the server's socket file for Unix-type systems or the named pipe for Windows systems.

`--ssl`
: This option specifies that secure SSL connections should be used. It requires the server to have SSL enabled. If this option is enabled on the utility by default, use `--skip-ssl` to disable it.

`--ssl-ca=pem_file`
: This option specifies the name of the file (i.e., the *pem* file) containing a list of trusted SSL CAs.

`--ssl-capath=path`
: This option specifies the path to the trusted certificates file (i.e., the *pem* file).

`--ssl-cert=filename`
: This option specifies the name of the SSL certificate file to use for SSL connections.

`--ssl-cipher=ciphers`
: This option gives a list of ciphers that may be used for SSL encryption

`--ssl-key=`*`filename`*
: This option specifies the SSL key file to use for secure connections.

`--ssl-verify-server-cert`
: This option verifies the client's certificate against the server's certificate for the client at startup. It is available as of version 5.1.11 of MySQL.

`--use-threads`
: On Unix-type systems, the `mysqlap` utility uses `fork( )`. This option will instruct the server to use `pthread( )` instead. On Windows systems threads are used by default.

`--user=`*`user`*, `-u` *`user`*
: This option provides the username for logging into the server.

`--verbose`
: This option displays more information from the utility.

`--version`
: This option returns the version of the utility.

perror

`perror [`*`options`*`]` *`code`*

This utility displays descriptions of system error codes that MySQL receives. Multiple error codes may be given in a space-separated list as the second argument. The only options available are for help (`--help`), the version number (`--version`), and verbosity (`--verbose`). As of recent versions of MySQL, the `--ndb` option has been added to get MySQL Cluster error messages.

replace

`replace` *`options filename`*

This program searches and replaces text in a simple text file, such as a dump file. Give the text to be replaced followed by the replacement text. Multiple pairs of such text can be given in a space-separated list. A double-dash (`--`) is used to mark the end of text replacement pairs, after which you list the names of files on which to perform the replacement in a space-separated list.

The only options available for this utility are for help (`-?` or `-I`), silent mode (`-s`), the version number (`-v`), and verbosity (`-V`). You can also specify `-#` followed by a space and flags for debugging. See the explanation of `--debug` under `mysqldump` earlier in this chapter for options that may be given with this flag.

The strings for which the utility is to search may include a few regular expression parameters: `\^` to indicate the start of a line; `\$` for the end of a line; and `\b` for a space.

resolveip

`resolveip [`*`options`*`]` *`host ...`*

This is a simple network program that translates a hostname to its related IP address. If an IP address is given, it returns all domains associated with the address. It has nothing to do with MySQL per se, but it is included in the normal distribution package.

resolve_stack_dump

`resolve_stack_dump` *`options symbols_filename`* [*`numeric_dump_file`*]

This utility resolves addresses and other numeric data into a stack to symbol names. The symbols file given should be the output of executing the following at the command line:

```
nm --numeric-sort mysqld
```

The numeric file named should be the numeric stack from `mysqld`.

Instead of following the basic syntax, you can specify the symbols file with the `--symbols-file` option. You can also specify the numeric dump file with the `--numeric-dump-file` option. For both options, the option is followed by an equals sign and the filename.

IV

APIs and Connectors

This part of the book is a complete reference to database interaction using the most popular languages used with MySQL. Libraries have been created for each language that allow you to connect to a MySQL database and issue SQL statements against it. These permit MySQL to be a backend to other programs or web sites and to hide SQL behind domain-specific, friendly interfaces.

17
C API

This chapter covers the C API provided by MySQL. The first part provides a basic tutorial on how to connect to MySQL and how to query MySQL with C and the C API. Following the tutorial is an alphabetical listing of MySQL functions in the C API with explanations and, in most cases, examples. At the end of this chapter is a listing of special data types for the C API. For the examples in this chapter, I have used a database for a fictitious computer support business. The database contains one table with client work requests (`workreq`) and another with client contact information (`clients`).

Using C with MySQL

This section presents the basic tasks you need to use the C API.

Connecting to MySQL

When writing a C program to interact with MySQL, you first need to prepare variables that will store data necessary for a MySQL connection and query results, and then you need to establish a connection to MySQL. To do this easily, you need to include a couple of C header files (as shown in the code example): *stdio.h* for basic C functions and variables, and *mysql.h* for special MySQL functions and definitions. These two files come with C and MySQL, respectively; you shouldn't have to download them from the Web if both were installed properly:

```
#include <stdio.h>
#include "/usr/include/mysql/mysql.h"
int main(int argc, char *argv[  ])
{
        MYSQL *mysql;
        MYSQL_RES *result;
        MYSQL_ROW row;
```

Because *stdio.h* is surrounded by < and > symbols, C is instructed to look for it in the default location for C header files (e.g., */usr/include*), or in the user's path. Because *mysql.h* may not be in the default locations, the absolute path is given with the aid of double quotes. An alternative here would be <*mysql/mysql.h*> because the header file is in a subdirectory of the default directory.

Within the standard `main` function just shown, variables needed for the connection to MySQL are prepared. The first line creates a pointer to the `MYSQL` structure stored in the `mysql` variable. The next line defines and names a results set based on the definitions for `MYSQL_RES` in *mysql.h*. The results are stored in the `result` array, which will be an array of rows from MySQL. The third line of `main` uses the definition for `MYSQL_ROW` to establish the `row` variable, which will be used later to contain an array of columns from MySQL.

Having included the header files and set the initial variables, we can now set up an object in memory for interacting with the MySQL server using `mysql_init( )`:

```
if(mysql_init(mysql) == NULL)
  {
     fprintf(stderr, "Cannot initialize MySQL");
     return 1;
  }
```

The `if` statement here is testing whether a MySQL object can be initialized. If the initialization fails, a message is printed and the program ends. The `mysql_init( )` function initializes the MySQL object using the `MYSQL` structure declared at the beginning of the main function, called `mysql` by convention. If C is successful in initializing the object, it will go on to attempt to establish a connection to MySQL:

```
if(!mysql_real_connect(mysql, "localhost",
   "user", "password", "db1", 0, NULL, 0))
{
   fprintf(stderr, "%d: %s \n",
      mysql_errno(mysql), mysql_error(mysql));
   return 1;
}
```

The elements of the `mysql_real_connect( )` function here are fairly obvious: first, the MySQL object is referenced; next, the hostname or IP address; then, the username and password; and finally, the database to use. The three remaining items are the port number, the Unix socket filename, and a client flag, if any. Passing zeros and NULL tells the function to use the defaults for these. If the program cannot connect, it is to print the error message generated by the server to the standard error stream, along with the MySQL error number (hence the `%d` format instruction for displaying digits or a number), and finally a string (`%s`) containing the MySQL error message and then a line feed or a newline (`\n`). The actual values to plug into the format follow, separated by commas.

The program so far only makes a connection to MySQL. Now let's look at how you can add code to the program to run an SQL statement with the C API.

Querying MySQL

If the MySQL connection portion of the program is successful, the program can query the MySQL server with a query function such as mysql_query( ):

```
if(mysql_query(mysql, "SELECT col1, col2 FROM table1"))
{
   fprintf(stderr, "%d:  %s\n",
   mysql_errno(mysql), mysql_error(mysql));
}
else
{
   result = mysql_store_result(mysql);
   while(row = mysql_fetch_row(result))
     { printf("\%d - \%s \n", row[0], row[1]); }
   mysql_free_result(result);
}
   mysql_close(mysql);
   return 0;
}
```

Incidentally, this excerpt is using mysql_query( ), but you could use the mysql_real_query( ) function instead. The main difference between the two is that mysql_real_query( ) allows the retrieval of binary data, which may not be necessary but is safer to use. mysql_query( ) returns zero if it's successful and nonzero if it's not successful. So, if the preceding SQL statement does not succeed in selecting data from MySQL, an error message will be printed. However, if the query is successful, the else statement will be executed because the if statement will have received a value of 0 from mysql_query( ). In the else statement block, the first line captures the results of the query and stores them in memory with the use of the mysql_store_result( ) function. Later, the memory will be freed when mysql_free_result( ) is issued with the variable name result given.

Before letting go of the data, though, we must loop through each row of the results set and display the results from each row for the user. We'll do this with a while statement and the mysql_fetch_row( ) function. This function retrieves one row of the results at a time and, in this particular example program, stores each row in the row variable. Then the printf statement prints to the screen the value of each field in the format shown. Notice that each field is extracted by typical array syntax (i.e., array [*n*]). The formatting instructions for printf are enclosed within double quotes, the same method we used with the fprintf in the if statement earlier in this section. Once C has gone through each row of the results, it will stop processing and then free up the buffer of the data, concluding the else statement. This brief program ends with a mysql_close( ) call to finish the MySQL session and to disconnect from MySQL. The final closing curly brace ends the main function.

To compile the program with the GNU C Compiler (*gcc*), you can enter something like the following from the command line:

```
gcc -o mysql_c_prog mysql_c_prog.c \
   -I/usr/include/mysql -L/usr/lib/mysql -lmysqlclient -lm -lz
```

Notice that the paths to the MySQL header file and the MySQL data directory are given as well, and the name of the client library, *mysqlclient*, is also given. These paths may be different on your system. When the compiler attempts to compile the program (here, *mysql_c_prog.c*), it will check for syntax errors in the code. If it finds any, it will fail to compile and will display error messages. If it's successful, the resulting compiled program (*mysql_c_prog*) may be executed.

Functions in Alphabetical Order

The bulk of this chapter consists of a list of C API functions in alphabetical order. Each function is given with its syntax and an explanation. For almost all functions, an example program or excerpt is provided to show how you can use the function. To save space, almost all of the excerpts are shown without the lines of code necessary to start a C program and to connect to MySQL, nor those necessary to close the connection and to end the program. For an example of how you would write opening and closing lines, see the tutorial in the previous section. The examples in this section tend to be more succinct and won't usually include typical error checking. It's assumed that the reader has a basic understanding of C. For the syntax of each function, the data type expected is given before each parameter or argument.

mysql_affected_rows( )

`my_ulonglong mysql_affected_rows(MYSQL *mysql)`

This function returns the number of rows affected by the most recent query for the current session. This function is meaningful only for `INSERT`, `UPDATE`, and `DELETE` statements. For SQL statements that don't affect rows (e.g., `SELECT`), this function will return 0. For errors, it will return –1. Here is an example:

```
...
mysql_query(mysql,"UPDATE workreq
                   SET tech_person_id = '1015'
                   WHERE tech_person_id = '1012'");
my_ulonglong chg = mysql_affected_rows(mysql);
printf("Number of requests reassigned: %ul \n", chg);
...
```

In this example, an `UPDATE` statement is issued and the number of rows changed is extracted with the function and stored in the `chg` variable, which is then printed. For `REPLACE` statements, rows that are replaced are counted twice: once for the deletion and once for the insertion.

mysql_autocommit( )

`my_bool mysql_autocommit(MYSQL *mysql, my_bool mode)`

Use this function to turn on or off autocommit mode. A value of 1 for the second argument of this function turns on the server's autocommit mode. A value of 0 turns it off. The `autocommit` causes the server to update the database after each `INSERT`, `UPDATE`, or

DELETE statement, essentially running each in its own transaction. The default is on. Here is an example:

```
...
mysql_autocommit(mysql, 0);
...
```

mysql_change_user( )

```
my_bool mysql_change_user(MYSQL *mysql, const char *user,
                          const char *password, const char *database)
```

Use this function to change the current user for the MySQL session to the one given as the second argument. The password of the new user is given in the third argument. Since this function will end the current session if successful, it will need to reset the default database. Therefore, a database that it should use for the new connection is to be given as the fourth argument. Here is an example:

```
...
mysql_real_connect(mysql,"localhost","hui","shorty","test","3306",NULL,0);
mysql_select_db(mysql,"workrequests");
...
mysql_change_user(mysql,"russell","password","workrequests");
mysql_query(mysql, "UPDATE workreq
                    SET tech_person_id = '1015'
                    WHERE tech_person_id = '1012'");
...
```

In this example, the program begins with one user for running SQL statements, which are replaced with ellipses. However, for changing a sensitive data column (i.e., the person assigned to perform the work requests), the user is changed to one who has been given the proper authorization to access.

mysql_character_set_name( )

```
const char *mysql_character_set_name(MYSQL *mysql)
```

This function returns the name of the default character set in use by the MySQL server. Here is an example:

```
...
MYSQL *mysql;
const char *char_set;
mysql = mysql_init(NULL);
mysql_real_connect(mysql,"localhost","russell","my_pwd","test","3306",
   NULL,0);
char_set = mysql_character_set_name(mysql);
printf("Character Set: %s \n", char_set);
...
```

To get just the character set name, it's not necessary to select a database. Here are what the results of running this program might look like:

```
Character Set: latin1
```

mysql_close( )

```
void mysql_close(MYSQL *mysql)
```

Use this function to close the connection to the MySQL server. It also deallocates the connection handle pointed to by `MYSQL` if the handle was allocated automatically by `mysql_init( )` or `mysql_connect( )`. It does not return a value. Here is an example:

```
...
mysql_connect(mysql,"localhost","ricky","adams");
...
mysql_close(mysql);
...
```

mysql_commit( )

```
my_bool mysql_commit(MYSQL *mysql)
```

Use this function to commit the current transaction. After this function is executed, `INSERT`, `UPDATE`, and `DELETE` statements are written to the database, and you cannot use the `mysql_rollback( )` function to undo them. The function returns 0 if successful, a non-zero value if unsuccessful. If `mysql_autocommit(mysql, 1)` is used previously, this function does nothing and the return of the function is not relevant. Here is an example:

```
mysql_commit(mysql);
```

mysql_connect( )

```
MYSQL *mysql_connect(MYSQL *mysql, const char *host,
                     const char *user, cont char *password)
```

This function is deprecated in favor of `mysql_real_connect( )`, described later in this chapter.

mysql_create_db( )

```
int mysql_create_db(MYSQL *mysql, const char *database)
```

This function can be used to create a new database on the MySQL server, with the new database name given as the second argument. However, this function has been deprecated. Instead, a `CREATE DATABASE` statement should be given with `mysql_query( )` or `mysql_real_query( )`.

mysql_data_seek( )

```
void mysql_data_seek(MYSQL_RES *result, my_ulonglong offset)
```

Use this function in conjunction with `mysql_store_result( )` and a fetch function such as `mysql_fetch_row( )` to change the current row being fetched to the one specified in the second argument of this function. Here is an example:

```
...
mysql_query(mysql, "SELECT client_id, client_name
                    FROM clients ORDER BY start_date");
result = mysql_store_result(mysql);
```

```
    num_rows = mysql_num_rows(result);
    mysql_data_seek(result, (num_rows - 8));
    while((row = mysql_fetch_row(result)) != NULL)
      { printf("%s (%s) \n", row[1], row[0]); }
    ...
```

This program excerpt retrieves a list of client names along with their respective IDs. Using the `mysql_data_seek( )` function in conjunction with `mysql_fetch_row( )` and a `while` statement, the last eight clients who started with the company will be displayed.

mysql_debug( )

`void mysql_debug(const char *debug)`

Use this function to set debugging if the client was compiled with debugging. The set of options used by default is '`d:t:o,logname`'. See Table 16-1 at the end of the list of options for the `mysqldump` utility in Chapter 16 for an explanation of these flags and others that may be used. Here is an example:

```
...
mysql_debug("d:t:o,filename");
...
```

The filename given could include the path to the log file where debugging information is to be written.

mysql_drop_db( )

`int mysql_drop_db(MYSQL *mysql, const char *database)`

This function may be used to delete the database named in the second argument of the function from the MySQL server. It returns 0 if successful and a nonzero value if not. However, this function has been deprecated. Use `mysql_query( )` or `mysql_real_query( )` with a `DROP DATABASE` statement instead. Here is an example:

```
...
mysql_real_connect(mysql,host,user,password,NULL,0,NULL,0);
...
mysql_drop_db(mysql, "db5");
...
```

This returns a nonzero value if it fails, so a program that uses it should include error checking for the function.

mysql_dump_debug_info( )

`int mysql_dump_debug_info(MYSQL *mysql)`

Use this function to write debugging information about the current connection to the MySQL server's log file. It returns 0 if successful and a nonzero value if not. The user must have administrative privileges. Here is an example:

```
...
if(!mysql_dump_debug_info(mysql))
```

```
    { printf("Debugging Info. Written. \n"); }
...
```

mysql_eof( )

```
my_bool mysql_eof(MYSQL *result)
```

Use this function to determine whether the last row of the results set has been fetched. It returns 0 until end of file is reached and a nonzero value at end of file. This function has been deprecated. Use `mysql_errno( )` and `mysql_error( )`, or `mysql_more_results( )`, instead to check for an error indicating that the last row has been reached.

mysql_errno( )

```
unsigned int mysql_errno(MYSQL *mysql)
```

This function returns the error number for the last function that was run if it failed to execute. If the last function executed was successful, a value of 0 is returned by this function. Here is an example:

```
...
if(mysql_real_connect(mysql,host,"goofy",
                      password,database,0,NULL,0) == NULL)
  {
   printf("Error %d \n", mysql_errno(mysql));
   return 1;
  }
...
```

The program here is attempting to connect to the MySQL server for a user who is not in the `mysql` database.

mysql_error( )

```
char *mysql_error(MYSQL *mysql)
```

This function returns the error message for the last function that was run if it failed to execute. If the last function executed was successful, an empty string is returned by this function. Here is an example:

```
...
if(!mysql_real_connect(mysql,host,"goofy",
                       password,database,0,NULL,0))
  {
   printf("Error Message: %s \n", mysql_error(mysql));
   return 1;
  }
...
```

The program here is attempting to connect to the MySQL server with a user who is not in the `mysql` database.

mysql_escape_string( )

```
unsigned int mysql_escape_string(char *destination,
                                 const char *source,
                                 unsigned int length)
```

This function returns a string given as the second argument with special characters escaped by adding backslashes in front of them. However, this function is a security problem and has been deprecated. Use the `mysql_real_escape_string( )` function instead; it does this job properly and safely.

mysql_fetch_field( )

```
MYSQL_FIELD *mysql_fetch_field(MYSQL_RES *result)
```

This function returns a `MYSQL_FIELD` structure that provides information on a given field of a results set. If you use it in conjunction with a loop statement, you can extract information on each field. Here is an example:

```
...
MYSQL_FIELD *field;
...
mysql_query(mysql, "SELECT * FROM clients LIMIT 1");
result = mysql_store_result(mysql);
while((field = mysql_fetch_field(result)) != NULL)
   { printf("%s \n", field->name);  }
...
```

The wildcard in the `SELECT` statement selects all columns in the table. The loop therefore lists the name of each column. The other possibilities are `field->table` for the table name and `field->def` for the default value of the column.

mysql_fetch_field_direct( )

```
MYSQL_FIELD *mysql_fetch_field_direct(MYSQL_RES *result,
                                      unsigned int field_nbr)
```

This function returns a `MYSQL_FIELD` structure that provides information on a given field of a results set referred to in the first argument of the function. The particular field is given as the second argument. Here is an example:

```
...
MYSQL_FIELD *field;
...
mysql_query(mysql, "SELECT * FROM clients LIMIT 1");
result =  mysql_store_result(mysql);
field =  mysql_fetch_field_direct(result, 0);
printf("%s \n", field->name);
...
```

This function is similar to `mysql_fetch_field( )` except that information on just one specified field can be obtained. In the example here, the name of the first field (0 being the first) will be displayed.

mysql_fetch_fields( )

```
MYSQL_FIELD *mysql_fetch_fields(MYSQL_RES *result)
```

This function returns an array of information about the fields in a results set. Here is an example:

```
...
mysql_query(mysql, "SELECT * FROM clients");
result = mysql_store_result(mysql);
num_fields = mysql_field_count(mysql);
MYSQL_FIELD *field;
field = mysql_fetch_fields(result);
for(i = 0; i < num_fields; i++)
   { printf("%u.%s \n", i, &field[i].name); }
...
```

In addition to the `.name` key to extract the column name, a program can specify `.table` for the table name and `.def` for the default value of the column.

mysql_fetch_lengths( )

```
unsigned long *mysql_fetch_lengths(MYSQL *result)
```

This function returns the length of each column within a particular row of a results set. The values returned can vary for each row fetched, depending on the data contained in the columns. Here is an example:

```
...
mysql_query(mysql, "SELECT * FROM clients");
result = mysql_store_result(mysql);
row = mysql_fetch_row(result);
unsigned int num_fields = mysql_num_fields(result);
unsigned long *lengths = mysql_fetch_lengths(result);
for(i = 0; i < num_fields; i++)
   {
    field = mysql_fetch_field(result);
    printf("%s %lu \n", field->name, lengths[i]);
   }
...
```

This example retrieves one row of the results and checks the lengths of the fields in that row. To retrieve each field, the `SELECT` statement would need to be altered and a `while` statement would be wrapped around the `for` statement to loop through each row.

mysql_fetch_row( )

```
MYSQL_ROW mysql_fetch_row(MYSQL_RES *result)
```

Use this function to retrieve the next row of a results set. When there are no more rows to retrieve, the function returns NULL. Here is a fairly complete example using this function:

```
#include <stdio.h>
#include <stdlib.h>
#include <mysql/mysql.h>
```

```
int main( )
{
   MYSQL *mysql;
   MYSQL_RES *result;
   MYSQL_ROW row;
   MYSQL_FIELD *field;
   int i, num_fields;
   mysql = mysql_init(NULL);
   mysql_real_connect(mysql,"localhost","user","password",
                           "workrequests",0,NULL,0);
   mysql_query(mysql,"SELECT * FROM users");
   result = mysql_store_result(mysql);
   num_fields = mysql_field_count(mysql);
   while((row = mysql_fetch_row(result)) != NULL)
     {
      for(i = 0; i < num_fields; i++)
        {
         field = mysql_fetch_field_direct(result, i);
         printf("%s: %s, ", field->name, row[i]);
        }
      printf("\n");
     }
   mysql_free_result(result);
   mysql_close(mysql);
   return 0;
  }
```

Although this example is a complete program, it's missing the usual error checking methods.

mysql_field_count( )

`unsigned int mysql_field_count(MYSQL *mysql)`

This function returns the number of columns in a results set. You can also use it to test whether there was an error in a SELECT query. A SELECT query will return at least one blank field when there is an error, resulting in a value of 0 for the function. Here is an example:

```
...
if(!result)
   {
    if(mysql_field_count(mysql) == 0)
       {
        printf("Error \n");
        return 1;
       }
   }
...
```

See the entry for the mysql_fetch_row( ) function earlier in this section for another example involving this function.

mysql_field_seek( )

```
MYSQL_FIELD_OFFSET mysql_field_seek(MYSQL_RES *result,
                                    MYSQL_FIELD_OFFSET offset)
```

Use this function in conjunction with `mysql_fetch_field( )` to change the current field being fetched to the one specified in the second argument of this function. The function returns the offset of the field that was current before the function was invoked. A reference to the results set must be passed as the first argument. Here is an example:

```
...
mysql_query(mysql, sql_stmnt);
MYSQL_FIELD_OFFSET offset = 2;
mysql_field_seek(result, offset);
while((field = mysql_fetch_field(result)) != NULL)
   {
    printf("%d: %s \n", mysql_field_tell(result), field->name);
   }
...
```

Using `mysql_field_seek( )` here and an offset of 2, the first two rows of the results set are skipped. The `mysql_field_tell( )` function is used to ascertain the index of the field being displayed within each loop of the `while` statement. The `mysql_field_seek( )` function will return the offset prior to invoking the function. If you change the `mysql_field_seek( )` call in the program to the following, the `old_offset` variable would contain a value of 0, the starting point for a row:

```
...
MYSQL_FIELD_OFFSET old_offset = mysql_field_seek(result, offset);
...
```

You can use this for recording a point in a results set before moving the pointer. The program can later return to that point using the old offset.

mysql_field_tell( )

```
MYSQL_FIELD_OFFSET mysql_field_tell(MYSQL_RES *result)
```

This function returns the value of the field pointer for the current row in use by a fetch function such as `mysql_fetch_field( )`. The field pointer starts at 0 for the first field when a row is retrieved and advances by one as each field is retrieved in sequential order. See `mysql_field_seek( )` earlier in this section for an example of this function.

mysql_free_result( )

```
void mysql_free_result(MYSQL_RES *result)
```

Use this to free memory allocated by a function such as `mysql_store_result( )` in which a `MYSQL_RES` element was employed to store a results set. Here is an example:

```
...
result = mysql_query(mysql, sql_stmnt);
...
mysql_free_result(result);
...
```

Not freeing allocated memory or attempting to access allocated memory after it's freed can cause problems.

mysql_get_client_info( )

```
char *mysql_get_client_info(void)
```

This function returns the client library version. Here is an example:

```
...
const char *info;
info = mysql_get_client_info( );
printf("Client Library Version: %s \n", info);
...
```

mysql_get_character_set_info( )

```
void mysql_get_character_set_info(MYSQL *mysql, MY_CHARSET_INFO *cs)
```

This function returns the default character set information for the database given. It uses the `MY_CHARSET_INFO` structure, so the information may be retrieved with extensions like so:

```
...
if (!mysql_set_character_set(mysql, "utf8"))
{
 MY_CHARSET_INFO ch_set;
 mysql_get_character_set_info(mysql, &ch_set);
 printf("Character Set: %s\n", ch_set.name);
 printf("Collation: %s\n", ch_set.csname);
 printf("Minimum Length for Multibyte Character: %d\n", ch_set.mbminlen);
 printf("Maximum Length for Multibyte Character: %d\n", ch_set.mbmaxlen);
 printf("Comment: %s\n", ch_set.comment);
 printf("Directory: %s\n", ch_set.dir);
}
...
```

Here are the results of this code excerpt:

```
Character Set: utf8_general_ci
Collation: utf8
Minimum Length for Multibyte Character: 1
Maximum Length for Multibyte Character: 3
Comment: UTF-8 Unicode
Directory: (null)
```

mysql_get_client_version( )

```
unsigned long *mysql_get_client_version(void)
```

This function returns the client library version in a numeric format. For example, for version 4.1.7, the function will return 40107. Here is an example:

```
...
unsigned long version;
version = mysql_get_client_version( );
```

```
printf("Client Version: %d \n", version);
...
```

mysql_get_host_info( )

```
char *mysql_get_host_info(MYSQL *mysql)
```

This function returns the hostname and the connection type for the current connection. Here is an example:

```
...
MYSQL *mysql;
mysql = mysql_init(NULL);
mysql_real_connect(mysql,"localhost","marie","password",
                   NULL,0,NULL,0);
printf("Host Info: %s \n", mysql_get_host_info(mysql));
mysql_close(mysql);
...
```

The results of this program excerpt will look something like the following:

```
Host Info: Localhost via UNIX socket
```

mysql_get_proto_info( )

```
unsigned int mysql_get_proto_info(MYSQL *mysql)
```

This function returns the protocol version for the current connection. Here is an example:

```
...
MYSQL *mysql;
mysql = mysql_init(NULL);
mysql_real_connect(mysql,"localhost","root","password",
                   NULL,0,NULL,0);
printf("Protocol: %u \n", mysql_get_proto_info(mysql));
mysql_close(mysql);
...
```

mysql_get_server_info( )

```
char *mysql_get_server_info(MYSQL *mysql)
```

This function returns a string containing the version of MySQL running on the server for the current connection. Here is an example:

```
...
MYSQL *mysql;
mysql = mysql_init(NULL);
mysql_real_connect(mysql,"localhost","root","password",
                   NULL,0,NULL,0);
printf("Server Version: %s \n", mysql_get_server_info(mysql));
mysql_close(mysql);
...
```

mysql_get_server_version( )

`unsigned long mysql_get_server_version(MYSQL *mysql)`

This function returns the version of the server for the current connection in a numeric format. For example, for version 4.1.7, the function will return 40107. Here is an example:

```
...
MYSQL *mysql;
mysql = mysql_init(NULL);
mysql_real_connect(mysql,"localhost","root","password",
NULL,0,NULL,0);
printf("Server Version: %ul \n",
        mysql_get_server_version(mysql));
mysql_close(mysql);
...
```

mysql_get_ssl_cipher( )

`const char *mysql_get_ssl_cipher(MYSQL *mysql)`

This function returns a string with the name of the SSL cipher that was used for the connection given. NULL is returned if there was no cipher used. This function was added as of version 5.1.11 of MySQL. Here is an example:

```
...
const char *cipher_name;
cipher_name = mysql_get_ssl_cipher( );
printf("Name of Cipher: %s \n", cipher_name);
...
```

mysql_hex_string( )

`unsigned long mysql_hex_string(char *to, const char *from, unsigned long length)`

This function translates a hexadecimal string to a format that can be used in an SQL statement. The hexadecimal string is to be given in the *from* position or variable of the function. The results are saved to the *to* variable named, and terminated with a NULL byte. The *length* is the length of bytes of the *from* value. The *to* variable needs to be the *length* times 2 plus 1 in length.

mysql_info( )

`char *mysql_info(MYSQL *mysql)`

This function returns a string containing information provided by MySQL when certain SQL statements are executed. This function works with only five types of SQL statements: `INSERT INTO...SELECT...`, `INSERT INTO... VALUES...`, `LOAD DATA INFILE`, `ALTER TABLE`, and `UPDATE`. For all other statements, this function typically returns NULL. Here is an example:

```
...
mysql_query(mysql, "UPDATE clients
                    SET telephone_areacode = '985'
```

```
                          WHERE city = 'Hammond'");
printf("Query Info: %s \n", mysql_info(mysql));
...
```

The results of this program excerpt will look like the following:

```
Query Info: Rows matched: 3  Changed: 3  Warnings: 0
```

mysql_init( )

`MYSQL *mysql_init(MYSQL *mysql)`

This function optionally allocates, and then initializes, a `MYSQL` object suitable for connecting to a database server and subsequently performing many of the other operations described in this chapter. If the function's parameter is NULL, the library allocates a new object from the heap; otherwise, the user's pointed-to local `MYSQL` object is initialized.

The return value is a pointer to the object, however obtained, and a NULL indicates a failure of allocation or initialization. Calling `mysql_close( )` with this pointer not only releases the connection-related resources, but also frees the object itself if the library had allocated it in the first place.

It's generally safer to allow the library to allocate this object rather than to do so yourself. It avoids hard-to-debug complications that can arise if certain compiler options are not in effect while building the *application* as they were when building the *library*.

Although this function prepares a handle for a database connection, no connection is attempted. Here is an example:

```
...
MYSQL *mysql;
if(mysql_init(mysql) == NULL)
      {
        printf("Could not initialize MySQL object. \n");
        return 1;
      }
...
```

mysql_insert_id( )

`my_ulonglong mysql_insert_id(MYSQL *mysql)`

This function returns the identification number issued to the primary key of the last record inserted using `INSERT` in MySQL for the current connection. This works provided the column utilizes `AUTO_INCREMENT` and the value was not manually set. Otherwise, a value of 0 is returned. Here is an example:

```
...
const char *sql_stmnt =  "INSERT INTO workreq
                          (req_date, client_id, description)
                          VALUES(NOW( ), '1000', 'Net Problem')";
mysql_query(mysql, sql_stmnt);
my_ulonglong wr_id = mysql_insert_id(mysql);
printf("Work Request ID: %ld \n", wr_id);
...
```

mysql_kill( )

`int mysql_kill(MYSQL *mysql, unsigned long identifier)`

Use this function to terminate a thread on the server. The thread identifier is passed as the second argument to the function. If you're attempting to kill the current connection, you can use the `mysql_thread_id( )` function with the session handle. Here is an example:

```
...
if(!mysql_kill(mysql, mysql_thread_id(mysql)))
   { printf("Terminated Current Thread. \n"); }
...
```

To kill a thread other than the current one, you can use the `mysql_list_processes( )` function to list all threads to determine which one to terminate.

mysql_library_end( )

`void mysql_library_end(void)`

Use this function to close the MySQL library after disconnecting from the server. It can free memory and can be used with either the normal client library or the embedded server library. It's used in conjunction with `mysql_library_init( )`.

mysql_library_init( )

`int mysql_library_init(int argc, char **argv, char **groups)`

Use this function to initialize the MySQL library and any related libraries and systems before making any other MySQL function calls. It can be used with both the normal client library or the embedded server library. This function is used within a multithreaded environment. Otherwise, it's not necessary and `mysql_init( )` is sufficient. When finished, use `mysql_library_end( )` to close the library. This function returns zero if successful, nonzero if not.

Here is an example:

```
...
static char *server_args[] = {
  "--datadir='/data'",
  "--key_buffer_size=32M"
};
static char *server_groups[] = {
  "embedded",
  "server",
  (char *)NULL
};
int main(int argc, char *argv[  ]) {
  if(mysql_library_init(sizeof(server_args) / sizeof(char *),
                        server_args, server_groups)) {
    fprintf(stderr, "Cannot initialize MySQL library \n");
    return 1;
  }
...
mysql_library_end();
```

```
    ...
    }
```

mysql_list_dbs( )

```
MYSQL_RES *mysql_list_dbs(MYSQL *mysql, const char *wild)
```

This function returns a results set containing a list of databases found for the current connection. An expression may be given to select databases whose names match a certain pattern. The % or _ characters may be used as wildcards. If NULL is given for the second argument, the names of all databases on the server will be selected in the results set. Here is an example:

```
...
MYSQL_RES *result;
MYSQL_ROW row;
...
result = mysql_list_dbs(mysql, NULL);
while((row = mysql_fetch_row(result)) != NULL)
   { printf("%s \n", row[0]);  }
mysql_free_result(result);
...
```

This excerpt extracts a list of databases from the server using the `mysql_list_dbs( )` function and stores the results. Using the `mysql_fetch_row( )` function, each row of the results set is stored temporarily for printing. To extract a list of databases with "work" in the name, replace NULL with `"%work%"`. As with all results sets, release the resources with `mysql_free_result( )` when finished.

mysql_list_fields( )

```
MYSQL_RES *mysql_list_fields(MYSQL *mysql, const char *table,
                             const char *wild)
```

This function returns a results set containing a list of fields found for the table given as the second argument of the function. An expression may be given as the third argument to select fields whose names match a certain pattern. The % or may be used as wildcards. If NULL is given for the third argument, all fields for the table are returned. The results set must be freed when finished.

Here is an example:

```
...
result = mysql_list_fields(mysql, "stores", "s%");
num_rows = mysql_num_rows(result);
printf("Rows: %d \n", num_rows);
while((row = mysql_fetch_row(result)) != NULL)
   {
    for(i = 0; i < num_rows; i++)
      { printf("%s \n", row[i]); }
   }
mysql_free_result(result);
...
```

mysql_list_processes( )

```
MYSQL_RES *mysql_list_processes(MYSQL *mysql)
```

This function returns a results set containing a list of MySQL server processes or server threads found for the handle given as the argument of the function.

Here is an example:

```
...
result = mysql_list_processes(mysql);
while((row = mysql_fetch_row(result)) != NULL)
  {
   printf("Thread ID: %s \n", row[0]);
   printf("User: %s, Host: %s \n", row[1], row[2]);
   printf("Database: %s, Command: %s \n", row[3], row[4]);
   printf("Time: %s, State: %s, Info: %s \n\n",
          row[5],row[6],row[7]);
  }
mysql_free_result(result);
...
```

Using the `mysql_fetch_row( )` function, each row of the results set is read and each field is displayed with its related label. The results are the same as the `SHOW PROCESSES` query in MySQL. It's important to run the `mysql_free_result( )` function when finished with a results set, as shown here.

mysql_list_tables( )

```
MYSQL_RES *mysql_list_tables(MYSQL *mysql,
                             const char *expression)
```

This function returns a results set containing a list of tables in the currently selected database. An expression may be given as the second argument of the function to select tables whose names match a certain pattern. The `%` or `_` may be used as wildcards. If NULL is given for the second argument, all tables in the database will be returned. Here is an example:

```
...
MYSQL_RES *result;
MYSQL_ROW row;
...
result = mysql_list_tables(mysql, "w%");
while((row = mysql_fetch_row(result)) != NULL)
   { printf("%s \n", row[0]);  }
mysql_free_result(result);
...
```

This excerpt extracts a list of tables beginning with the letter "w" using the `mysql_list_tables( )` function and stores the results in the `result` variable. Using the `mysql_fetch_row( )` function, each row of the results set is stored temporarily in the `row` variable for printing.

mysql_more_results( )

```
my_bool mysql_more_result(MYSQL *mysql)
```

Use this function to determine whether more results remain in a results set when using the `mysql_next_result( )` function to retrieve data. It returns 1 if there are more results, and 0 if not.

mysql_next_result( )

```
int mysql_next_result(MYSQL *mysql)
```

Use this function to read the next row of data from a results set. It returns 0 if successful and if there are more results to retrieve, and –1 if it was successful in retrieving data, but there are no further rows to retrieve. It returns an error (or a value greater than 0) if it's unsuccessful because the results set was not loaded with the data. You can use the `mysql_more_results( )` function to check for more results before invoking this function.

mysql_num_fields( )

```
unsigned int mysql_num_fields(MYSQL_RES *result)
```

This function returns the number of fields in each row of a results set. It is similar to `mysql_field_count( )` except that that function operates on the `MYSQL` handle and not the results set. Here is an example:

```
...
unsigned int num_fields = mysql_num_fields(result);
...
```

See `mysql_fetch_lengths( )` earlier in this section for a more elaborate example that uses this function.

mysql_num_rows( )

```
int mysql_num_rows(MYSQL_RES *result)
```

This function returns the number of rows in the results set when issued after the `mysql_store_result( )` function. When issued after `mysql_use_result( )`, it returns the number of rows already fetched. Here is an example:

```
...
my_ulonglong num_rows = mysql_num_rows(result);
...
```

See `mysql_list_fields( )` earlier in this section for a more elaborate example that uses this function.

mysql_options( )

```
int mysql_options(MYSQL *mysql, enum mysql_option option,
                  const char *value)
```

Use this function to set connection options before a connection has been established using a function such as `mysql_real_connect( )` or `mysql_connect( )`. This function may be used multiple times to set additional options before connecting. For the second argument of the function, you may give specific options for the connection. You may give a value associated with the chosen option for the third argument. Here is an example:

```
...
mysql = mysql_init(NULL);
mysql_options(mysql, MYSQL_OPT_COMPRESS, NULL);
mysql_real_connect(mysql,host,user,password,NULL,0,NULL,0);
...
```

The options permitted for the second argument of the function follow, along with the type of variable or value for the third argument in parentheses and a brief explanation of each:

`MYSQL_OPT_CONNECT_TIMEOUT` *(unsigned int *)*
: This option sets the number of seconds for connection timeout.

`MYSQL_OPT_READ_TIMEOUT` *(unsigned int *)*
: This option sets the timeout for reads from a Windows MySQL server.

`MYSQL_OPT_WRITE_TIMEOUT` *(unsigned int *)*
: This option sets the timeout for writes to a Windows MySQL server.

`MYSQL_OPT_COMPRESS (NULL)`
: This option compresses communications between the client and server if supported by both.

`MYSQL_OPT_LOCAL_INFILE` *(pointer to unsigned integer)*
: This option runs on a file pointed to in the argument. If the pointer is NULL, the `LOAD LOCAL INFILE` statement is run when connecting.

`MYSQL_OPT_NAMED_PIPE (NULL)`
: This option instructs the client to use named pipes for connecting to a Windows NT MySQL server.

`MYSQL_INIT_COMMAND` *(char *)*
: This option instructs the server on connecting to execute an initial SQL statement given as the third argument to the function.

`MYSQL_READ_DEFAULT_FILE` *(char *)*
: This option instructs the server to read a configuration text file named in the third argument of the function instead of the default *my.cnf* configuration file for the client.

`MYSQL_READ_DEFAULT_GROUP` *(char *)*
: This option instructs the server to read a server section or group (e.g., `[special_client]`) from either the default *my.cnf* configuration file or the one specified by the `MYSQL_READ_DEFAULT_FILE` option to this function.

`MYSQL_OPT_PROTOCOL` *(unsigned int *)*
: This option specifies the default protocol for communicating with the server.

`MYSQL_SHARED_MEMORY_BASE_NAME` *(char *)*
: This option names the shared memory object for connecting to the server.

mysql_ping( )

```
int mysql_ping(MYSQL *mysql)
```

Use this function to determine whether the current MYSQL connection is still open. If it's not open, the function attempts to reestablish the connection. If the connection is open or is reestablished, zero is returned. Otherwise, a nonzero value is returned. Here is an example:

```
...
MYSQL *mysql;
int main( )
{
...
   test_connection( );
   mysql_close(mysql);
   test_connection( );
}
test_connection( )
{
   int live;
   live = mysql_ping(mysql);
   if(live){ printf("Connection not alive. \n");  }
   else { printf("Connection alive. \n"); }
}
```

This excerpt employs a user function to test for a MySQL connection.

mysql_query( )

`int mysql_query(MYSQL *mysql, const char *query)`

Use this function to execute the SQL query given as the second argument of the function. Only one SQL statement may be given. For queries containing binary data, use the `mysql_real_query( )` function instead. This function will return zero if successful, and a nonzero value if not. Here is an example:

```
...
MYSQL *mysql;
MYSQL_RES *result;
MYSQL_ROW row;
MYSQL_FIELD *field;
int i, num_fields;
...
mysql = mysql_init(NULL);
mysql_real_connect(mysql,host,user,password,database,0,NULL,0);
const char *sql_stmnt = "SELECT * FROM workreq";
mysql_query(mysql, sql_stmnt, bytes);
result = mysql_store_result(mysql);
num_fields = mysql_field_count(mysql);
while((row = mysql_fetch_row(result)) != NULL)
  {
   for(i = 0; i < num_fields; i++)
     { printf("%s, ", row[i]); }
   printf("\n");
  }
mysql_free_result(result);
mysql_close(mysql);
...
```

Although this example is fairly complete, the lines declaring the variables containing the connection information are not shown. See the example for the `msyql_real_connect( )` function next for those details. The SQL statement in the example is given through a variable, but it could be given within the function if enclosed in double quotes. The results of the query are stored in the `result` variable by way of the `mysql_store_result( )` function. Incidentally, it's important to free the memory allocated for the results with the `mysql_free_result( )` function when finished.

mysql_real_connect( )

```
MYSQL *mysql_real_connect(MYSQL *mysql, const char *host,
                          const char *user, const char *password,
                          const char *user, const char *password,
                          const char *database, uint port,
                          const char *user, const char *password,
                          const char *database, uint port,
                          const char *unix_socket, uint flag)
```

Use this to establish a connection to a MySQL server. The `MYSQL` structure created by `mysql_init( )` is given as the first argument to the function. The hostname, username, and user's password for connecting to the server are given next. The name of the database is given as the fifth argument. The port, the socket file path and name for Unix systems, and any client flags are given as the sixth, seventh, and eighth arguments, respectively. For any parameter requiring a *char* pointer, a value of NULL may be given to instruct the server to use the default setting. For `unsigned int` variables, a value of 0 may be given to rely on the default value. Here is an example:

```
#include <stdio.h>
#include <stdlib.h>
#include <mysql/mysql.h>
int main(void)
{
  MYSQL *mysql;
  MYSQL_RES *result;
  MYSQL_ROW row;
  MYSQL_FIELD *field;
  const char *host = "localhost";
  const char *user = "root";
  const char *password = "my_password";
  const char *database = "workrequests";
  unsigned int port = 3306;
  const char *socket = NULL;
  unsigned long flag = 0;
  int i, num_fields;
  mysql = mysql_init(NULL);
  mysql_real_connect(mysql,host,user,password,database,
                     port,socket,flag);
  const char *sql_stmnt = "SELECT * FROM stores";
  ulong bytes = strlen(sql_stmnt);
  mysql_real_query(mysql, sql_stmnt, bytes);
  result = mysql_store_result(mysql);
  num_fields = mysql_field_count(mysql);
  while((row = mysql_fetch_row(result)) != NULL)
     {
```

```
        for(i = 0; i < num_fields; i++)
          { printf("%s, ", row[i]); }
        printf("\n");
      }
    mysql_free_result(result);
    mysql_close(mysql);
    return 0;
}
```

This example is fairly complete. Each variable is declared at the beginning based on the type called for by the function, along with its respective values. Without having to disconnect and reconnect, you can change the database using the `mysql_select_db( )` function.

mysql_real_escape_string( )

```
unsigned long mysql_real_escape_string(MYSQL *mysql,
                                       char *result_string,
                                       char *result_string,
                                       char *original_string,
                                       char *result_string,
                                       char *original_string,
                                       unsigned long src length)
```

This function writes a string given as the third argument to a string named in the second argument, but with special characters escaped by adding backslashes in front of them. The number of bytes to be copied from the source string is given for the fourth argument. When declaring the two strings, the destination string must be twice the size of the source string, plus one byte. Here is an example:

```
...
const char client_name[  ] = "O'Reilly Media";
ulong bytes = strlen(client_name);
char client_name_esc[(2 * bytes)+1];
mysql_real_escape_string(mysql, client_name_esc,
                         client_name, bytes);
char *sql_stmnt;
sprintf(sql_stmnt, "INSERT INTO clients (client_name)
                    VALUES('%s')", client_name_esc);
mysql_real_query(mysql, sql_stmnt, strlen(sql_stmnt));
...
```

After establishing the initial variable for storing the client's name, the C function `strlen( )` is used to determine the number of bytes contained in the string. Next, the second variable to hold the client's name is declared with a size twice the size of the first variable, plus one byte. The `mysql_real_escape_string( )` function is run with both variables and the size of the first. In this example, the function will place a backslash in front of the apostrophe in the client's name so as not to cause an error when the query is run later. Using the C function `sprintf( )`, the escaped client name is inserted into the SQL statement given. Finally, the SQL statement is run with `mysql_real_query( )`.

mysql_real_query( )

```
int mysql_real_query(MYSQL *mysql, const char *query,
                     unsigned int length)
```

Use this function to execute the SQL query given as the second argument of the function. Only one SQL statement may be given. Unlike `mysql_query( )`, this function can execute queries containing binary data. Because of this feature, the number of bytes contained in the query needs to be given for the third argument. This can be determined with the C function `strlen( )`. The function will return zero if successful, and a nonzero value if not. Here is an example:

```
...
mysql = mysql_init(NULL);
mysql_real_connect(mysql,host,user,password,database,port,socket,flag);
const char *sql_stmnt = "SELECT * FROM stores";
ulong bytes = strlen(sql_stmnt);
mysql_real_query(mysql, sql_stmnt, bytes);
result = mysql_store_result(mysql);
num_fields = mysql_field_count(mysql);
while((row = mysql_fetch_row(result)) != NULL)
  {
   for(i = 0; i < num_fields; i++)
     { printf("%s, ", row[i]); }
   printf("\n");
  }
...
```

In this example, the number of bytes of the variable containing the SQL statement is determined with the C function `strlen( )` and is stored in a separate variable called `bytes`. In turn, the `bytes` variable is given as the third argument to the `mysql_real_query( )` function. As an alternative, `strnlen(sql_stmnt)` could be given as the third argument instead.

mysql_reload( )

```
int mysql_reload(MYSQL *mysql)
```

This function instructs the MySQL server to reload the grants table. It returns zero if successful and a nonzero value if not. This function has been deprecated. Use `mysql_query( )` or `mysql_real_query( )` with a `FLUSH PRIVILEGES` statement instead.

mysql_refresh( )

```
int mysql_refresh(MYSQL *mysql, unsigned int options)
```

Use this function to flush caches and tables. It can also be used to reset a replication server. It returns a value of zero if successful, and nonzero if not. The `RELOAD` privilege is required to use it. Several options may be given: `REFRESH_GRANT`, `REFRESH_LOG`, `REFRESH_TABLES`, `REFRESH_HOSTS`, `REFRESH_MASTER`, `REFRESH_SLAVE`, `REFRESH_STATUS`, and `REFRESH_THREADS`. There are four possible errors that are returned: `CR_COMMANDS_OUT_OF_SYNC`, `CR_SERVER_GONE_ERROR`, `CR_SERVER_LOST`, or `CR_UNKNOWN_ERROR`. Here is an example:

```
...
mysql_refresh(MYSQL mysql, unsigned int REFRESH_TABLES);
...
```

mysql_rollback( )

```
my_bool mysql_rollback(MYSQL *mysql)
```

Use this function to roll back or reverse the current transaction. This will not work if the `mysql_commit( )` function has already been called for the transaction. The function returns zero if successful, and a nonzero value if not.

mysql_row_seek( )

```
MYSQL_ROW_OFFSET mysql_row_seek(MYSQL *result,
                                MYSQL_ROW_OFFSET offset)
```

Use this function to move the pointer of a results set to the row given as the second argument of the function. The pointer given must use the `MYSQL_ROW_OFFSET` structure. Use a function such as `mysql_row_tell( )` to determine the offset in the proper format. Here is an example:

```
...
 MYSQL_ROW_OFFSET special_location;
 while((row = mysql_fetch_row(result)) != NULL)
   {
    if(strcmp(row[1], "1000") == 0)
      {
       special_location = mysql_row_tell(result);
       continue;
      }
    if(!mysql_more_results(mysql))
      {
       mysql_row_seek(result, special_location);
       printf("%s (%s) \n", row[1], row[0]);
       break;
      }
    printf("%s (%s) \n", row[1], row[0]);
   }
...
```

In this example, a list of clients is retrieved, but the developer wants the row with a client identification number of 1000 to be displayed last. So, an `if` statement is used to check for the special record. When it finds the row it's looking for, the `mysql_row_tell( )` function is used to make a note of the point in the results set in which it was found. The remainder of the `while` statement in which the row is to be printed is then skipped. Using the `mysql_more_results( )` function, another `if` statement watches for the end of the results set. If it determines that there are no more rows in the results set to print, it will move the pointer back to the special client using the `mysql_row_seek( )` function and the pointer saved with `mysql_row_tell( )`, print out that particular row's data, and then end the `while` statement with `break`.

mysql_row_tell( )

```
MYSQL_ROW_OFFSET mysql_row_tell(MYSQL_RES *result)
```

This function returns the pointer for the current position in a results set generated from the `mysql_store_result( )` function. The value obtained can be used with mysql_row_seek( ) for changing the pointer while fetching rows. See the mysql_row_seek( ) function earlier in this section for an example of its use.

mysql_select_db( )

```
int mysql_select_db(MYSQL *mysql, const char *database)
```

Use this function to select a different database for the current connection. The name of the new database to use is given as the second argument of the function. It returns zero if successful, and a nonzero value if not. Here is an example:

```
...
mysql = mysql_init(NULL);
mysql_real_connect(mysql,"localhost","ricky","adams",NULL,NULL,NULL,0);
mysql_select_db(mysql,"workrequests");
...
```

mysql_set_character_set( )

```
int mysql_set_character_set(MYSQL *mysql, const char *char_set)
```

Use this function to set the default character set of a connection to the character set given. It returns zero if successful, and a nonzero value if not. Here is an example:

```
...
if (!mysql_set_character_set(mysql, 'utf8'))
{
  printf("Character Set: %s", mysql_character_set_name(mysql));
}
...
```

mysql_set_local_infile_default( )

```
void mysql_set_local_infile_default(MYSQL *mysql)
```

Use this function to set the handler for `LOAD LOCAL DATA INFILE` functions to the defaults necessary for internal use of the C client library. It is normally called automatically by the C library.

mysql_set_local_infile_handler( )

```
void mysql_set_local_infile_handler(MYSQL *mysql,
   int (*local_infile_init)(void **, const char *, void *),
   int (*local_infile_read)(void *, char *, unsigned int),
   void (*local_infile_end)(void *),
   int (*local_infile_error)(void *, char*, unsigned int),
   void *userdata)
```

Use this function to enable callbacks that you will use with the `LOAD DATA LOCAL INFILE` statement. The callback functions must be created first:

```
...
int local_infile_init(void **ptr, const char *file_name, void *user_info);
int local_infile_read(void *ptr, char *buffer, unsigned int buffer_len);
void local_infile_end(void *ptr);
```

CAPI

```
int local_infile_error(void *ptr, char *error_msg, unsigned int
   error_msg_len);
...
```

mysql_set_server_option( )

```
int mysql_set_server_option(MYSQL *mysql,
                            enum mysql_set_option option)
```

Use this function to enable or disable a server option. The only options currently available are MYSQL_OPTION_MULTI_STATEMENTS_ON and MYSQL_OPTION_MULTI_STATEMENTS_OFF, to enable and disable multiple SQL statements, respectively. It returns 0 if successful, and a nonzero value if not.

mysql_shutdown( )

```
int mysql_shutdown(MYSQL *mysql)
```

Use this function to shut down the MySQL server. It returns zero if successful, and a nonzero value if not. Here is an example:

```
...
if(!mysql_ping(mysql))
  {
   mysql_shutdown(mysql);
   printf("Shutting down server \n");
   if(mysql_ping(mysql))
     { printf("MySQL server is down.\n"); }
   }
...
```

The mysql_ping( ) function here checks whether the server is alive. Recall that a zero, not a TRUE, return signifies a live server.

mysql_sqlstate( )

```
const char *mysql_sqlstate(MYSQL *mysql)
```

This function returns the SQLSTATE error code for the last error that occurred for the current connection. The string will contain five characters and is terminated with a NULL character. A lack of error is signified by 00000 and unmapped errors by HY000.

mysql_ssl_set( )

```
my_bool mysql_ssl_set(MYSQL *mysql,
                      const char *key_path,
                      const char *cert_path, const char *ca_path,
                      const char *pem_path, const char *cipher)
```

This function makes a secure connection with SSL. OpenSSL must be enabled in order to use it. Call it before calling mysql_real_connect( ). This function returns zero unless there is a problem, in which case an error will be returned when mysql_real_connect( ) is called. The *key_path* is the path to the key to be used; *cert_path* is the path to the certificate file; *ca_path* is the file path of the certificate authority file; *pem_path* is the directory with trusted SSL CA certificates, which are in the *pem* format; and finally, ***cipher*** contains a list of ciphers permitted for SSL encryption. You can give NULL for parameters that don't apply.

mysql_stat( )

```
char * mysql_stat(MYSQL *mysql)
```

This function returns a character string containing information about the status of the MySQL server for the current connection. Here is an example:

```
...
printf("Server Status \n %s \n", mysql_stat(mysql));
...
```

mysql_store_result( )

```
MYSQL_RES *mysql_store_result(MYSQL *mysql)
```

Use this function to read and store all of a results set in a `MYSQL_RES` structure. When finished with these results, it's necessary to use the `mysql_free_result( )` function to free the memory allocated for storing the results set. The function returns NULL if it's unsuccessful or if the query is not the type that would return any results (e.g., an `UPDATE` statement). Here is an example:

```
...
mysql = mysql_init(NULL);
mysql_real_connect(mysql,"localhost","user","password",
                   "workrequests",0,NULL,0);
mysql_query(mysql,"SELECT * FROM users");
result = mysql_store_result(mysql);
num_fields = mysql_field_count(mysql);
while((row = mysql_fetch_row(result)) != NULL)
   {
    for(i = 0; i < num_fields; i++)
      {
       field = mysql_fetch_field_direct(result, i);
       printf("%s: %s, ", field->name, row[i]);
      }
     printf("\n");
   }
mysql_free_result(result);
...
```

See the example for the `mysql_fetch_row( )` function earlier in this chapter for an alternative method.

mysql_thread_end( )

```
void mysql_thread_end(void)
```

Use this function before calling free memory used by `mysql_thread_init( )`. It returns nothing. It isn't automatically called. Here is an example:

```
...
if(mysql_thread_safe( ))
   { printf("Safe Environment \n"); }
```

```
else{ printf("Unsafe Environment \n"); }
...
```

mysql_thread_id( )

```
unsigned long mysql_thread_id(MYSQL *mysql)
```

This function returns the thread identifier number for the current connection to MySQL. Thread identifiers can change if a connection is closed or restarted. Here is an example:

```
...
int thread = mysql_thread_id(mysql);
printf("Thread ID: %d \n", thread);
...
```

mysql_thread_init( )

```
my_bool mysql_thread_init(void)
```

Use this function to initialize thread specific variables. It's automatically called by `mysql_connect( )`, `mysql_init( )`, `mysql_library_init( )`, and `mysql_server_init( )`. It returns zero if successful, and nonzero if not.

mysql_thread_safe( )

```
unsigned int mysql_thread_safe(void)
```

Use this function to determine whether the MySQL client library is safe for a threaded environment. It returns 1 if safe, 0 if not. Here is an example:

```
...
if(mysql_thread_safe( ))
   { printf("Safe Environment \n"); }
else{ printf("Unsafe Environment \n"); }
...
```

mysql_use_result( )

```
MYSQL_RES *mysql_use_result(MYSQL *mysql)
```

Use this function to read the results of a query, one row at a time. This works in a way similar to the `mysql_store_result( )` function, except that function retrieves all of the data at once and stores it for later use. The `mysql_use_result( )` function is best used when a results set would be large and speed of processing is a concern. With this function, processing may be started sooner without having to wait for all of the data to be retrieved. One drawback to this function is that other queries cannot be run while the results from the first query are in use. Also, functions such as `mysql_data_seek( )` cannot be used and the return value from running `mysql_num_rows( )` is altered, because the complete size of the results set is unknown. Here is an example:

```
...
mysql_query(mysql, "SELECT * FROM clients");
result = mysql_use_result(mysql);
num_fields = mysql_field_count(mysql);
```

```
while((row = mysql_fetch_row(result)) != NULL)
   {
    for(i = 0; i < num_fields; i++)
      {
       field = mysql_fetch_field_direct(result, i);
       printf("%s: %s, ", field->name, row[i]);
      }
   printf("\n");
}
mysql_free_result(result);
...
```

See the example for the mysql_fetch_row( ) function earlier in this chapter for an alternative method.

mysql_warning_count( )

```
unsigned int mysql_warning_count(MYSQL *mysql)
```

This function returns the number of warning messages encountered from the previous query. This can be useful, for instance, when performing multiple INSERT statements with the IGNORE flag. Here is an example:

```
...
MYSQL *mysql;
mysql = mysql_init(NULL);
mysql_real_connect(mysql,"localhost","root","password",
                   "workrequests",0,NULL,0);
...
unsigned int warnings = mysql_warning_count(mysql);
printf("Number of Warnings: %d \n", warnings);
...
```

C API Datatypes

Here is a list of C API data types from the *mysql.h* header file:

MYSQL
: A database handle structure created by mysql_init( ) and released with mysql_close( ).

MYSQL_RES
: A structure for a results set from an SQL query. This structure is used by fetch functions and is released with mysql_free_result( ).

MYSQL_ROW
: A structure for holding a row of data from a results set. The data is retrieved from this structure by the mysql_fetch_row( ) function.

MYSQL_FIELD
: A structure for holding an array of information about a field of a results set. The array may be set with the mysql_fetch_field( ) function. The elements include name, table, and def for the default value.

MYSQL_FIELD_OFFSET
: Used for recording a pointer location for a results set. The offset value can be retrieved by the mysql_row_tell( ) function and deployed with mysql_row_seek( ).

my_ulonglong
: A variable type for storing the number of rows for functions such as mysql_affected_rows( ), mysql_num_rows( ), and mysql_insert_id( ). To print the value of a variable using this type, copy the value to another variable that uses the *unsigned long* type.

18 Perl API

The easiest method of connecting to MySQL with the programming language Perl is to use the Perl DBI module, which is part of the core Perl installation. You can download both Perl and the DBI module from CPAN (*http://www.cpan.org*). I wrote this chapter with the assumption that the reader has Perl installed along with *DBI.pm* and that the reader has a basic knowledge of Perl. Its focus, therefore, is on how to connect to MySQL, run SQL statements, and effectively retrieve data from MySQL using Perl and DBI. This chapter begins with a tutorial on using Perl with MySQL. That's followed by a list of Perl DBI methods and functions used with MySQL, with the syntax and descriptions of each and examples for most. The examples here use the scenario of a bookstore's inventory.

Using Perl DBI with MySQL

This section presents basic tasks that you can perform with Perl DBI. It's meant as a simple tutorial for getting started with the Perl DBI and MySQL.

Connecting to MySQL

To interface with MySQL, first you must call the DBI module and then connect to MySQL. To make a connection to the `bookstore` database using the Perl DBI, only the following lines are needed in a Perl program:

```
#!/usr/bin/perl -w
use strict;

use DBI;

my $dbh = DBI->connect ("DBI:mysql:bookstore:localhost","russell",
   "my_pwd1234")
         or die "Could not connect to database: "
         . DBI->errstr;
```

The first two lines start Perl and set a useful condition for reducing programming errors (`use strict`). The third line calls the DBI module. The next statement (spread over more than one line here) sets up a database handle that specifies the database engine (`mysql`), the name of the database (`bookstore`), the hostname (`localhost`), the username, and the password. Incidentally, the name of the database handle doesn't have to be called `$dbh`—anything will do. Next, the `or` operator provides alternate instructions to be performed if the connection fails. That is, the program will terminate (`die`) and then display the message in quotes along with whatever error message is generated by the driver using the `errstr` method from the DBI—the dot (`.`) merges them together.

Executing an SQL Statement

Making a connection to MySQL does little good unless an SQL statement is executed. Any SQL statement that can be entered from the *mysql* client can be executed through the API. Continuing the previous example and using a fictitious database of a bookstore, let's look at how an SQL statement that retrieves a list of books and their authors from a table containing that information might look:

```
my $sql_stmnt = "SELECT title, author FROM books";

my $sth = $dbh->prepare($sql_stmnt);

$sth->execute();
```

The first line sets up a variable (`$sql_stmnt`) to store the SQL statement. The next line puts together the database handle created earlier and the SQL statement to form the SQL statement handle (`$sth`). Finally, the third line executes the statement handle in the notational method of the DBI module.

Capturing Data

Having connected to MySQL and invoked an SQL statement, what remains is to capture the data results and to display them. MySQL returns the requested data to Perl in columns and rows, as it would with the *mysql* client, but without table formatting. In Perl, MySQL returns rows one at a time and they are usually processed by a loop in Perl. Each row is returned as an array, one element per column in the row. For each array, each element can be parsed into variables for printing and manipulation before receiving or processing the next row. You can do this with a `while` statement like so:

```
while (my($title, $author) = $sth->fetchrow_array()) {
   print "$title ($author) \n";
}
```

At the core of this piece of code is the `fetchrow_array( )` method belonging to the DBI module. As its name suggests, it fetches each row or array of columns, one array at a time. The `while` statement executes its block of code repeatedly so long as there are arrays to process. The value of each element of each array is stored in the two variables $title and $author—and overwritten with each loop. Then the variables are printed to the screen with a newline character after each pair.

Disconnecting from MySQL

Once there is no longer a need to maintain a connection to the MySQL database, it should be terminated. If the connection stays idle for too long, MySQL will eventually break the connection on its own. To minimize the drain on system resources, however, it's a good practice to have programs end their sessions like so:

```
$sth->finish();
$dbh->disconnect();

exit();
```

This first line closes the SQL statement handle. As long as the connection to MySQL is not broken, as it will be in the second line, more SQL statement handles could be issued, prepared, and executed without having to reconnect to MySQL. The last line of code here ends the Perl program.

Temporarily Storing Results

Perhaps a method of retrieving data from MySQL that's cleaner than the one just explained involves capturing all of the data in memory for later use in a program, thus allowing the connection to MySQL to end before processing and displaying the data. Putting MySQL on hold while processing each row as shown earlier can slow down a program, especially when dealing with large amounts of data. It's sometimes better to create a complex data structure (an array of arrays) and then leave the data structure in memory, just passing around a reference number to its location in memory. To do this, instead of using `fetchrow_array( )`, you'd use the `fetchall_arrayref( )` method. As the method's name indicates, it fetches all of the data at once, puts it into an array (an array of rows of data), and returns the array's starting location in memory. Here is a Perl program that uses `fetchall_arrayref( )`:

```
#!/usr/bin/perl -w
use strict;
use DBI;

# Connect to MySQL and execute SQL statement
my $dbh = DBI->connect("DBI:mysql:bookstore:localhost",
                       "username","password")
          || die "Could not connect to database: "
          . DBI->errstr;

my $sql_stmnt = "SELECT title, author
                 FROM books";
my $sth = $dbh->prepare($sql_stmnt);
$sth->execute();

# Retrieve reference number to results
my $books = $sth->fetchall_arrayref();
```

```
$sth->finish();
$dbh->disconnect();

# Loop through array containing rows (arrays)

foreach my $book (@$books){
   # Parse each row and display
   my ($title, $author) = @$book;
   print "$title by $author\n";
}

exit();
```

Instead of embedding the fetch method within a flow control statement, the results of the SQL statement using `fetchall_arrayref( )` are stored in memory. A reference number to the location of those results is stored in the `$books` variable and the connection to MySQL is then closed. A `foreach` statement is employed to extract each reference to each array (i.e., each row, each `$book`) of the complex array. Each record's array is parsed into separate variables (`$title` and `$author`). The values of the variables are displayed using `print`. Incidentally, to learn more about references, see Randal Schwartz's book, *Intermediate Perl* (O'Reilly).

This kind of batch processing of an SQL statement has the added advantage of allowing multiple SQL statements to be performed without them tripping over each other, while still performing complex queries. For instance, suppose that we want to get a list of books written by Henry James, ordered by title, then by publisher, and then by year. This is easy enough in MySQL. Suppose that we also want the inventory count of each title, bookstore by bookstore, with some address information to be displayed between the listing for each store. This becomes a little complicated. One way to do this is to use a `SELECT` statement that retrieves a list of store locations and their relevant information (i.e., their addresses and telephone numbers) and to save a reference to the data in memory. Next, we could issue another SQL statement to retrieve the book inventory data, and then close the MySQL connection. With a flow control statement, we could then print a store header followed by the store's relevant inventory information for each book before moving on to the next store. It would basically look like this:

```
...  # Start program and connect to MySQL

# Retrieve list of stores
my $sql_stmnt = "SELECT store_id, store_name,
                 address, city, state, telephone
                 FROM stores";
my $sth = $dbh->prepare($sql_stmnt);
$sth->execute();
my $stores = $sth->fetchall_arrayref();
$sth->finish();

# Retrieve list of books
my $sql_stmnt = "SELECT title, publisher,
                 pub_year, store_id, quantity
                 FROM books
                 JOIN inventory USING(book_id)
```

```
                 WHERE author = 'Henry James'
                 ORDER BY title, publisher, pub_year";
my $sth = $dbh->prepare($sql_stmnt);
$sth->execute();
my $books = $sth->fetchall_arrayref();
$sth->finish();
$dbh->disconnect();

foreach my $store (@$stores){

   my ($store_id, $store_name, $address,
       $city, $state, $telephone) = @$store;

   print "$store_name\n
          $address\n$city, $state\n
          $telephone\n\n";

   foreach my $book (@$books){

     my ($title, $publisher,
         $pub_year, $store, $qty) = @$book;

     if($store ne $store_id) { next; }

     print "$title ($publisher $pub_year) $qty\n";
   }
}

exit();
```

To save space, I left out the opening lines for the program because they are the same as in the previous program. In the first SQL statement here, we're selecting the store information. With the `fetchall_arrayref( )` method, we're storing the reference for the data in `$stores`. If we were to print out this variable, we would see only a long number and not the actual data. Although an SQL statement may retrieve many rows of data, all of the data will be stored in memory. Therefore, we can issue `finish( )`, and as long as we don't disconnect from MySQL, we can issue another SQL statement. The next SQL statement selects the book inventory information. In the `SELECT` statement we're hardcoding in the author's name. We really should replace that with a variable (e.g., `$author`) and allow the user to set the variable earlier in the program. Once the book inventory information has been collected, the connection to MySQL is terminated and we can begin displaying the data with the use of flow control statements.

The first `foreach` statement loops through the data of each store and prints the address information. Within each loop is another `foreach` loop for processing all of the titles for the particular store. Notice the `if` statement for the book inventory loop. The first record or array for the first store is read and the basic store information is displayed. Then the first array for the inventory is retrieved from its complex array and the elements parsed into variables. If `store` (which is the `store_id`) doesn't match the one that it's on, Perl moves on to the next record. The result is that a store header is displayed and all of the inventory information requested is displayed for the store before Perl goes on to the next store's data.

You can accomplish this task in many ways—some simpler and some tighter—but this gives you a general idea of how to perform it, without keeping the connection to MySQL open while processing data. For more details on using the Perl DBI with MySQL, see Alligator Descartes and Tim Bunce's book, *Programming the Perl DBI* (O'Reilly).

Perl DBI Reference

The following is a list of DBI methods and functions in alphabetical order. The syntax and an explanation of each as well as examples for most are provided. However, to save space, the examples are only excerpts and are missing some components, such as the calling of the DBI module and the creation of a database handle. Also, to focus on the particular method or function described, we'll use a very simple table containing a list of books and the names of their authors with the same `SELECT` statement. See the previous section (the tutorial) for an example of a complete, albeit simple, Perl DBI program. In addition to passing parameters, you can affect the behavior of several methods by setting global values called *attributes*. See the end of this chapter for a list of attributes.

---

available_drivers( )

`DBI->available_drivers([`*`nowarn`*`])`

This function returns a list of available DBD drivers. You can suppress any warning messages by providing the text *`nowarn`* as an argument. Here is an example:

```
...
my @drivers = DBI->available_drivers();

foreach my $driver(@drivers) {
   print "$driver \n";
}
```

---

begin_work( )

`$dbh->begin_work( )`

This funciton is used for transactions with a database. It temporarily turns `AutoCommit` off until `commit( )` or `rollback( )` is run. There are no arguments to this database handle method. In MySQL, this is similar to executing the SQL statement `BEGIN` or `BEGIN WORK`. It will only be effective with a transactional storage engine like InnoDB. At the time of this writing, there is a bug in this function: it returns an error if `AUTOCOMMIT` is already set. The error begins, *Transactions not supported by database....*

bind_col( )

`$sth->bind_col(`*`index`*`, \$`*`variable`*`[, \%`*`attri`*`|`*`type`*`])`

This funciton associates or binds a column from a statement handle to a given variable. The values are updated when the related row is retrieved using a fetch method, without extra copying of data. Here is an example:

```
...
my $sql_stmnt = "SELECT title, author FROM books";
my $sth = $dbh->prepare($sql_stmnt);
$sth->execute();

$sth->bind_col(1, \$title);
$sth->bind_col(2, \$author);

while($sth->fetch()) {
   print "$title by $author \n";
}
```

In this example, we're specifying that the first (1) column be bound to the variable `$title` and the second to `$author`. A separate statement has to be issued for each bind. To bind multiple columns in one statement, use `bind_columns( )`.

To specify the column data type to use for the variable—this can potentially change the data—give the desired SQL standard type as the third argument:

```
...
my $sql_stmnt = "SELECT title, author FROM books";
my $sth = $dbh->prepare($sql_stmnt);
$sth->execute();

$sth->bind_col(1, \$title, { TYPE=>SQL_VARCHAR } );
$sth->bind_col(2, \$author, { TYPE=>SQL_VARCHAR } );

while($sth->fetch()) {
   print "$title by $author \n";
}
```

To get a list of SQL standard data types available on your server, run this program:

```
#!/usr/bin/perl -w
use DBI;

foreach (@{ $DBI::EXPORT_TAGS{sql_types} }) {
   printf "%s=%d\n", $_, &{"DBI::$_"};
}
```

bind_columns( )

`$sth->bind_columns(@`*`variables`*`)`

This function associates or binds columns from a statement handle to a given list of variables (*`@variables`*). The values are updated when the related row is retrieved using a fetch method without extra copying of data. The number of variables given must match the number of columns selected and the columns are assigned to variables in the order the columns are returned. Here is an example:

```
...
my $sql_stmnt = "SELECT title, author FROM books";
my $sth = $dbh->prepare($sql_stmnt);
$sth->execute();

$sth->bind_columns(\$title, \$author);

while($sth->fetch()) {
   print "$title by $author \n";
}
```

bind_param( )

`$sth->param(`*`index`*`, `*`values`*`[, \`*`%attr`*`|`*`type`*`])`

This function associates or binds a value in an SQL statement to a placeholder. Placeholders are indicated by ? in SQL statements and are numbered in the order they appear in the statement, starting with 1. The first argument indicates which placeholder to replace with a given value, i.e., the second argument. The data type may be specified as a third argument. Here is an example:

```
...
my $sql_stmnt = "SELECT title, publisher
                 FROM books WHERE author = ?
                 AND status = ?";
my $sth = $dbh->prepare($sql_stmnt);
$sth->bind_param(1, $author);
$sth->bind_param(2, $status);
$sth->execute();
while(my ($title,$publisher) = $sth->fetchrow_array()) {
   print "$title ($publisher) \n";
}
```

In this example, a placeholder (a question mark) is given in the SQL statement and is replaced with the actual value of `$author` using `bind_param( )`. This must be done before the `execute( )` is issued.

bind_param_array( )

`$sth->bind_param_array(`*`index`*`, {`*`array_ref`*`|`*`string`*`}[, \`*`%attri`*`|`*`type`*`])`

This function associates or binds an array of values in an SQL statement within a `prepare( )` using placeholders. The first argument indicates which placeholder to replace with the array of given values, i.e., the second argument. The values are updated when the related row is retrieved using a fetch method. Attributes may be added or the data type given as a third argument. Here is an example:

```
...
my @old_names = ('Graham Green', 'Virginia Wolf');
my @new_names = ('Graham Greene', 'Virginia Woolf');

my $sql_stmnt = "UPDATE books
                 SET author = ?,
                 status = ?
                 WHERE author = ?";
```

```
my $sth = $dbh->prepare($sql_stmnt);

$sth->bind_param_array(1,\@new_names);
$sth->bind_param_array(2, 'active');
$sth->bind_param_array(3, \@old_names);

$sth->execute_array(undef);

$sth->finish();
```

Notice in this example that the first array contains all of the new author names, the corrected ones. It's not a pairing or a grouping by row. Instead, it's all of the values to be used for the first placeholder in the SQL statement. The second array bound contains the old names in the same order to be used in the `WHERE` clause. Incidentally, the backslash before each array shown here is necessary because an array reference must be given. The second `bind_param_array( )` set in the example uses just a string (i.e., `'active'`). That value will be used for all rows updated.

bind_param_inout( )

`$sth->bind_param_inout(`*`index`*`, \$`*`value`*`, `*`max_length`*`[, \%`*`attri`*`|`*`type`*`])`

This function associates or binds a value in an SQL statement using a placeholder. The first argument indicates which placeholder to replace with a given value, i.e., the second argument. It must be given as a reference (a variable preceded by a backslash). The values are updated when the related row is retrieved using a fetch method. The maximum length of a value is given in the third argument. Attributes may be added or the data type may be given as a fourth argument. This function is generally used with stored procedures.

can( )

`$handle->can($`*`method_name`*`)`

This function returns true if the method named is implemented by the driver. You can use this method within a program to determine whether a method for a handle is available. In the following example, after starting the program and setting the database and statement handles, we use the `can( )` method:

```
...
my @methods = qw(fetchrow_array fetchrow_arrays);

foreach $method(@methods) {
  if($sth->can($method)) { print "\$sth->$method is implemented.\n"; }
  else { print "\$sth->$method is not implemented.\n\n"; }
}
```

Here are the results from running this part of the program. Notice that the second, fictitious method named is not available:

```
$sth->fetchrow_array is implemented.
$sth->fetchrow_arrays is not implemented.
```

clone( )

`$dbh->clone([\%attri])`

Use this function to create a new database handle by reusing the parameters of the database handle calling the method. Additional attributes may be given with the method. Their values will replace any existing values. Any attributes given in the original database handle will be used in the new handle. Here is an example:

```
my $dbh1 = $dbh->clone({AutoCommit=>1});
```

The value of this method is that you can create a second MySQL session with it without having to restate the parameters from earlier. You can also use it if the `disconnect( )` has already been issued for the original database handle.

column_info( )

`$dbh->column_info($catalog, $database, $table, $column)`

This function returns a statement handle for fetching information about columns in a table. Here is an example:

```
...
my $sth = $dbh->column_info(undef, 'bookstore', 'books', '%');
my $col_info = $sth->fetchall_arrayref();

foreach my $info(@$col_info) {
   foreach (@$info) {
      if($_) { print $_ . "|"; }
   }
   print "\n";
}
```

This program excerpt will produce a list of columns in the `books` table of the `bookstore` database. Here are a couple of lines of the program results:

```
bookstore|books|book_id|4|INT|11|10|4|1|NO|1|int(11)|
bookstore|books|title|12|VARCHAR|50|1|12|2|YES|varchar(50)|
...
```

The values of the fields in order are: `TABLE_CAT` (usually empty), `TABLE_SCHEM`, `TABLE_NAME`, `COLUMN_NAME`, `DATA_TYPE`, `TYPE_NAME`, `COLUMN_SIZE`, `BUFFER_LENGTH`, `DECIMAL_DIGITS`, `NUM_PREC_RADIX`, `NULLABLE`, `REMARKS`, `COLUMN_DEF`, `SQL_DATA_TYPE`, `SQL_DATETIME_SUB`, `CHAR_OCTET_LENGTH`, `ORDINAL_POSITION`, and `IS_NULLABLE`.

commit( )

`$dbh->commit( )`

This function commits or makes permanent changes to a database for transactional tables (e.g., InnoDB). It's disregarded if `AutoCommit` is already enabled; a warning message saying "*Commit ineffective while AutoCommit is on*" will be issued.

connect( )

```
DBI->connect(DBI:server:database[:host:port],
             username, password[, \%attri])
```

Use this method to establish a connection to MySQL and to select the default database. The first argument is a list of required values separated by colons: the module (`DBI`), the driver (`mysql`) for a MySQL server, and the database name. The hostname or IP address and port number are optional. The second argument is the username and the third is the user's password. You can substitute any of these settings or values with variables—just be sure to enclose each argument containing variables with double quotes so that the values will be interpolated. Finally, you may give attributes in the fourth argument. Here is an example:

```
my $dbh = DBI->connect('DBI:mysql:bookstore:localhost',
   'paola','caporalle1017', {AutoCommit=>0});
```

In this excerpt, Perl is connecting to the MySQL server with the username *paola* and the password *caporalle1017*, with the database `bookstore`. The attribute `AutoCommit` is set to off so that changes to the data may be undone using `rollback( )`. See the end of this chapter for a list of attributes.

If you don't specify the username or the user's password (i.e., if `undef` is given instead), the value of the environment variables, `DBI_USER` and `DBI_PASS`, will be used if they are defined.

connect_cached( )

```
DBI->connect_cached(DBI:server:database[:host:port],
                    username, password[, \%attri])
```

This method is similar to `connect( )`, except that the database handle is stored in a hash with the given parameters. This allows the database handle to be reused if `connect_cached( )` is called again. You can access and eliminate a cache with the `CachedKids` attribute. This method can cause problems with a database system by inadvertently opening too many connections.

data_diff( )

```
DBI::data_diff(string, string[, length])
```

This function returns the results of both `data_string_desc( )` and `data_string_diff( )`, describing the difference between the two given strings. It returns an empty string if the strings given are identical. Here is an example:

```
...
my $previous_author = 'Graham Greene';

my $sql_stmnt = "SELECT book_id, author
                 FROM books
                 WHERE author LIKE 'Graham%'
                 LIMIT 1";
my $sth = $dbh->prepare($sql_stmnt);
$sth->execute();
```

```
while( my($book_id,$author) = $sth->fetchrow_array()) {
   my $diff = DBI->data_diff($previous_author, $author);
   if($diff) {
      print "$previous_author <=> $author\n$diff \n";
      $previous_author = $author;
   }
}
```

Here are the results of running this program:

```
Graham Green <=> Graham Greene
a: UTF8 off, ASCII, 3 characters 3 bytes
b: UTF8 off, ASCII, 12 characters 12 bytes
Strings differ at index 0: a[0]=D, b[0]=G
```

data_sources( )

`DBI->data_sources([`*`driver`*`, \%`*`attri`*`])`

This function returns a list of databases associated with a given driver. If none is specified, the driver named in the environment variable `DBI_DRIVER` is used. Attributes may be given as a second argument. Here is an example:

```
...
my @drivers = DBI->available_drivers();
      || die "No drivers found.";
foreach my $driver(@drivers) {
   my @sources = DBI->data_sources($driver);
   foreach my $source(@sources) {
      print "$driver:  $source\n";
   }
}
```

data_string_desc( )

`DBI::data_string_desc(`*`string`*`)`

This function returns a description of a given string:

```
...
print DBI->data_string_desc('Graham Greene');
```

Here are the results:

```
UTF8 off, ASCII, 3 characters 3 bytes
```

data_string_diff( )

`DBI::data_string_diff(`*`string`*`[, `*`length`*`])`

This function returns a description of the difference between two given strings. It returns an empty string if the strings given are identical. Here is an example:

```
...
my $diff = DBI->data_string_diff($previous_author, $author);
...
```

Using the example shown in data_diff( ) earlier in this section, but using this function instead, here are the results of running this program:

```
(Graham Green, Graham Greene)
Strings differ at index 0: a[0]=D, b[0]=G
```

disconnect( )

`$dbh->disconnect( )`

This function disconnects a Perl program from a database; it ends a MySQL session. There are no arguments for this function. Depending on your system, it may or may not commit or roll back any open transactions started by the database handle. To be sure, intentionally commit or roll back open transactions before disconnecting. Also, be sure to close any open statement handles by executing finish( ) for each statement handle before disconnecting, like so:

```
$sth->finish();
$dbh->disconnect();
```

do( )

`$dbh->do($sql_stmnt[, \%attri, @values])`

This function executes an SQL statement without having to use the prepare( ) method. It returns the number of rows changed. The first argument contains an SQL statement. If placeholders are used in the SQL statement, their values are provided in a comma-separated list or in an array in the third argument. Statement handle attributes may be given for the second argument. You would use this method only with SQL statements that do not return data values (e.g., use with UPDATE, not SELECT). Here is an example:

```
...
my $sql_stmnt = "UPDATE books SET publisher = ?
                 WHERE publisher = ?";

my @values = ('Oxford Univ. Press', 'OUP');

$dbh->do($sql_stmnt, undef, @values);

$dbh->disconnect();
```

In this example, the initials of a particular publisher are changed to the publisher's name. The SQL statement is executed without a prepare( ) or an execute( )—that is, without a statement handle. Therefore, a finish( ) isn't required, just a disconnect( ). If you want to know the number of rows changed, change the example like so:

```
...
my $rows_changed = $dbh->do($sql_stmnt, undef, @values);
print "Rows Changed: $rows_changed";
```

dump_results( )

`$sth->dump_results(length, row_delimiter, column_delimiter, filehandle})`

This function displays the results of a statement using the `neat_list( )` function on each row for the statement handle given. The first argument is the maximum length of each column's display. For columns containing more characters than the maximum length, the excess will be omitted and ellipses will be presented in its place. The default length is 35 characters. For the second argument, the delimiter for each row may be given—the default is `\n`. The delimiter for columns may also be changed from the default of a comma and a space in the third argument. In the last argument of the function, a file handle that specifies where to direct the results of the function may be given. If one is not specified, `stdout` is used. Here is an example:

```
...
my $sql_stmnt = "SELECT title, authors
                 FROM books
                 WHERE author= 'Henry James' LIMIT 3";
my $sth = $dbh->prepare($sql_stmnt);
$sth->execute();
$results = $sth->dump_results(10, "\n", '|');
...
```

The results of this program would look like this:

```
'The Boston...'|'Henry James'
'The Muse'|'Henry James'
'Washington...'|'Henry James'
3 rows
```

err( )

$handle->err( )

This function returns any error codes from the last driver method call. Here is an example:

```
...
my $dbh = DBI->connect('DBI:mysql:bookstore:localhost','russell',
   'wrong_password')
          || die DBI->err();
```

Notice the `err( )` method is added to the end of the database handle as part of the `die` function from Perl. Here are the results of executing this `connect( )` with the wrong password:

```
DBI connect('bookstore:localhost','russell',...) failed:
1045 at ./dbi_test_program.plx line 8...
```

Notice that the function `err( )` only returns the error code 1045 from the MySQL server. The rest of the text is from Perl in general.

errstr( )

$handle->errstr( )

This function returns any error messages from the last driver method called.

```
...
my $dbh = DBI->connect('DBI:mysql:bookstore:localhost','username',
   'wrong_password')
          || die DBI->errstr;
```

Notice the errstr( ) method is added to the end of the database handle as part of the die function from Perl. Here are the results of executing this connect( ) with the wrong password:

```
DBI connect('bookstore:localhost','russell',...) failed:
Access denied for user 'russell'@'localhost' (using password: YES)
at ./dbi_test_program.plx line 8...
```

Notice that the error message does not display the password given.

execute( )

$sth->execute([*@values*])

This function executes a statement handle that has been processed with the prepare( ) method. A value of undef is returned if there's an error. It returns true if successful, even when the results set is blank or zero. For statements other than SELECT statements, the number of rows affected is returned. Here is an example:

```
...
my $dbh = DBI->connect ("$data_source","$user","$pwd")

my $pub_year = '1961';
my $genre = 'novel';

my $sql_stmnt = "SELECT title, author
                 FROM books
                 WHERE pub_year = '$pub_year'
                 AND genre = '$genre'";
my $sth = $dbh->prepare($sql_stmnt);

my $rows_chg = $sth->execute();

while( my($title,$author) = $sth->fetchrow_array()) {
   print "$title by $author \n";
}
```

You can use placeholders in the SQL statement (e.g., for $pub_year and $genre) by giving the values with execute( ):

```
. . .
my @values = ('1961','novel');

my $sql_stmnt = "SELECT title, author
                 FROM books
                 WHERE pub_year = ?
                 AND genre = ?";
my $sth = $dbh->prepare($sql_stmnt);

$sth->execute(@values);

while( my($title,$author) = $sth->fetchrow_array()) {
   print "$title by $author \n";
}
```

You don't have to put values into an array for use with this method. You can put the strings inside the parentheses of the function (e.g., $sth->execute($pub_year,$genre);).

execute_array( )

`$sth->execute_array(\%attri[, @values)`

Use this function to execute a prepared statement multiple times, once for each set of values given either as the second argument of the method or from previous uses of the `bind_param_array( )` method. If you use the `bind_param_array( )` method, you won't provide the array values with this `execute_array( )` method. For an example of this statement's use with the `bind_param_array( )` method, see that description earlier in this chapter. Here is an example without that method:

```
...
my @old_names = ('Graham Green', 'Virginia Wolf');
my @new_names = ('Graham Greene', 'Virginia Woolf');

my $sql_stmnt = "UPDATE books
                 SET author = ?,
                 status = ?
                 WHERE author = ?";

my $sth = $dbh->prepare($sql_stmnt);

my ($tuple, $rows_chg) = $sth->execute_array(undef, \@new_names, 'active',
   \@old_names);

$sth->finish();
```

Notice that we are able to capture the number of rows changed by the SQL statement. Since we didn't specify any attributes, the `$tuple` variable will be empty. A tuple is an ordered list of values or objects.

execute_for_fetch( )

`execute_for_fetch($fetch[, \@status)`

Use this method to execute multiple statements given as the argument of the method, as a `sub` method. You may give a reference to a subroutine that returns an array of arrays of data. Or you may give the array of arrays as shown in the following example. Tuple status may be given as an array reference for the second argument:

```
...
my @engl = ('one','two','three');
my @ital = ('uno','due','tre');
my @germ = ('eins','zwei','drei');

my @count_values =(\@engl, \@ital, \@germ);

my $sth = $dbh->prepare("INSERT INTO count_three
                        (col1, col2, col3)
                        VALUES (?,?,?)");
my ($rc) = $sth->execute_for_fetch( sub { shift @count_values }, undef);
```

The value of `$rc` is 3. Since the tuple's status is undefined in this example, there is none. However, if you were to give one with the method, you could capture the tuple status as well (e.g., `my ($tuple,$rc) = $sth->execute_for_fetch(...);`). Here are the contents of the test table after running this Perl program:

```
SELECT * FROM count_three;

+------+------+-------+
| col1 | col2 | col3  |
+------+------+-------+
| one  | two  | three |
| uno  | due  | tre   |
| eins | zwei | drei  |
+------+------+-------+
```

fetch( )

`$sth->fetch( )`

This function returns a reference to an array of one row from the results of a statement handle. It's similar to `fetchrow_array( )` except that it requires the use of `bind_col( )` or `bind_columns( )` for setting variables to values fetched. There are no arguments for this function. Here is an example:

```
...
my $sql_stmnt = "SELECT title, author FROM books";
my $sth = $dbh->prepare($sql_stmnt);
$sth->execute();
my ($title, $author);

$sth->bind_columns(\$title, \$author);

while( $sth->fetchrow_array()) {
   print "$title by $author \n";
}
...
```

fetchall_arrayref( )

`$sth->fetchall_arrayref( )`

This function captures the results of a statement and returns a reference to the data. The results are a complex data structure: an array of references, with each reference to an array for each row of data retrieved. You can finish the statement handle after executing this method, since the results are stored in memory. Here is an example:

```
...
my $sql_stmnt = "SELECT title, author FROM books";
my $sth = $dbh->prepare($sql_stmnt);
$sth->execute();
my $books = $sth->fetchall_arrayref();
$sth->finish();

foreach my $book (@$books) {
   my ($title, $author) = @$book;
   print "$title by $author \n";
}
$sth->finish();
```

Notice that after fetchall_arrayref( ) is called, finish( ) is used before the data is parsed. Using foreach, first the array reference is dereferenced (i.e., @$books) and the reference to each array containing a row from the results is stored in a variable ($book). Then that array reference is deferenced (@$book) to parse the fields into variables for use.

fetchall_hashref( )

$sth->fetchall_hashref(*key_column*)

This method captures the result of an SQL statement and returns a reference to the data. The result is a complex data structure: it returns a reference to a hash using the name of the key column given as its key and the value of the key column given as its value. Each key column value is then used as the key to another hash with a reference to yet another hash for each. This final hash has the column names from the SQL statement as its keys and the values of each row of data retrieved as their respective hash values. The unraveling of such a hash reference may become clearer if you study the following code excerpt:

```
...
my $sql_stmnt = "SELECT book_id, title, author
                 FROM books";
my $sth = $dbh->prepare($sql_stmnt);
$sth->execute();

my $books = $sth->fetchall_hashref('book_id');

$sth->finish();

foreach my $book(keys %$books) {
   my $book_id = $books->{$book}->{'book_id'};
   my $title = $books->{$book}->{'title'};
   my $author = $books->{$book}->{'author'};
   print "$title ($book_id) by $author\n";
}
```

Notice for the SQL statement we are able to select more than two columns—that's because this is not a simple hash, but rather a hash of hashes (a key/value pairing is created ultimately from the column names and their respective values). Notice also with the fetchall_hashref( ) that the primary key column of book_id is given within quotes, as a string. Since this is a hash, a column with unique values is given. Looking at the foreach, we use keys to extract just the keys to the dereferenced hash reference. We don't need the values (which are the hashes for each row of data from the results set) at this point: we'll get to that value within the code block of the foreach statement. Each key is then stored in the variable $book. Using that key, we can extract the hashes that are referenced by an object oriented method: $hash_ref->{$key_col}->{'col_name'}. It might help a bit if I show you the preceding code but with the keys and values of the first hash and with more verbose results. We'll have to use a while statement with the each function:

```
...
while( my ($book_key,$book_values) = each(%$books)) {
   my $book_id = $books->{$book_key}->{'book_id'};
   my $title = $books->{$book_key}->{'title'};
   my $author = $books->{$book_key}->{'author'};
   print "$books\->$book_key\->$book_values\->\n
```

```
            {book_id->'$book_id',title->'$title',author->'$author'}\n\n";
    }
```

Here are two lines of the results of the program. You can see the two hashes mentioned earlier. After the first hash, notice the value of book_id is the key to the hash for the row of data. The book_id is also included in the final hash:

```
HASH(0x81e09e4)->1000->HASH(0x81e0b10)->
{book_id->'1000', title->'Mrs. Dalloway', author->'Virginia Woolf'}

HASH(0x81e09e4)->1001->HASH(0x81e0a20)->
{book_id->'1001', title->'The End of the Affair', author->'Graham Greene'}
```

fetchrow_array( )

$sth->fetchrow_array( )

This statement handle method returns one row, the next from the results of an SQL statement in the form of an array, each of whose element is a field of data. Null values retrieved are returned as undefined. An empty value is returned when there is an error or when there are no more rows remaining in the results set. Therefore, if used in a flow control statement such as while, the empty value returned will end the loop statement. Here is an example:

```
...
my $sql_stmnt = "SELECT title, author FROM books";
my $sth = $dbh->prepare($sql_stmnt);
$sth->execute();

while (my ($title, $author) = $sth->fetchrow_array(){
   print "$title by $author \n";
}

$sth->finish();
```

If you know that the SQL statement will return only one row, you won't need the while statement. Instead, you can save the values directly into a tight list of variables:

```
...
my $sql_stmnt = "SELECT title, author
                 FROM books LIMIT 1";
my $sth = $dbh->prepare($sql_stmnt);
$sth->execute();

my ($title, $author) = $sth->fetchrow_array();

print "$title by $author \n";
...
```

fetchrow_arrayref( )

$sth->fetchrow_arrayref( )

This function returns a reference to a place in memory containing an array of one row, the next row from the results of a statement handle. There are no arguments for this function. Null values retrieved are returned as undefined. An empty value is returned when there is an error or when there are no more rows remaining in the results set. Therefore, if used in a flow control statement such as `while`, the empty value returned will end the loop statement. Here is an example:

```
...
my $sql_stmnt = "SELECT title, author FROM books";
my $sth = $dbh->prepare($sql_stmnt);
$sth->execute();

while (my $book = $sth->fetchrow_arrayref()) {
   my ($title, $author) = @$book;
   print "$title by $author \n";
}

$sth->finish();
```

Notice that `fetchrow_arrayref( )` is reused at the beginning of each pass through the `while` statement. This is because a reference to one row is retrieved at a time. The same reference is used for each row retrieved: the array is replaced with each loop. If you want to use array references, you might want to use `fetchall_arrayref( )` instead.

fetchrow_hashref( )

`$sth->fetchrow_hashref([name] )`

This function returns a reference to a place in memory containing a hash of keys and values for one row from the results of a statement handle. The optional argument of this method is to give the statement handle *name* attribute: `NAME` (the default), `NAME_lc`, or `NAME_uc`. See the end of this chapter for a description of these attributes. The *name* must be given within quotes if given as a string. Null values retrieved by this method are returned as undefined. An empty value is returned when there is an error or when there are no more rows remaining in the results set. Therefore, if used in a flow control statement such as `while`, the empty value returned will end the loop statement. Here is an example:

```
...
my $sql_stmnt = "SELECT title, author FROM books";
my $sth = $dbh->prepare($sql_stmnt);
$sth->execute();

while (my $book_ref = $sth->fetchrow_hashref('NAME_uc')) {
   print "$book_ref->{'TITLE'} by $book_ref->{'AUTHOR'} \n";
}

$sth->finish();
```

Notice that the *name* given here with this method instructs the hash to use all uppercase letters for the key names. Therefore, when calling the particular data, the column names are given in all uppercase letters. If no parameter was given, we could use the column names as they are in the table. The `fetchrow_hashref( )` method is much simpler than `fetchall_hashref( )`, but you can't close the statement handle until you're finished processing the results. Therefore, you may want to consider using `fetchall_hashref( )` instead.

finish( )

$sth->finish( )

This method ends a statement handle given that was established by the `prepare( )` method. There are no arguments to the method. It can sometimes help to free system resources. It should be issued only when the statement handle is not going to be reused or is to be replaced. Here is an example:

```
...

my $sql_stmnt = "REPLACE INTO books (title, author)
                 VALUES(?,?)";
my $sth = $dbh->prepare($sql_stmnt);

while( my ($title,$author) = each(%books) ) {
   $sth->execute($title,$author);
}

$sth->finish();
$dbh->disconnect();
```

Since we're reusing the statement handle here (assuming `%books` defined earlier in the program has plenty of data), we especially don't need to call the `finish( )` method after each execution of the SQL statement. Although a statement handle may have been closed with `finish( )`, more statement handles may be created and executed as long as the database handle has not been closed using `disconnect( )`.

foreign_key_info( )

$dbh*->foreign_key_info(*$pk_catalog, *$pk_database*, *$pk_table*,
                         $fk_catalog, *$fk_database*, *$fk_table*[, \%*attri*])

This function returns a statement handle for fetching information about foreign keys in a given table. It's still fairly new and does not seem to be well integrated into MySQL yet.

func( )

$handle->func(@*arguments*, *function_name*)

This function calls private nonportable and nonstandard methods for handles. The name of the function is given as the last argument. Any arguments for the function specified are given first. You can give certain private built-in functions: `_ListDBs` with the hostname and optionally the port as the first parameter (use `data_sources( )` instead); `_ListTables` (deprecated; use `tables( )` instead); `_CreateDB` with the database name as the first parameter; and `_DropDB` with the database name as the first parameter. Here is an example:

```
...
my @tables = $dbh->func('_ListTables');

foreach my $table(@tables) {
   print $table, "\n";
}
```

As this syntax indicates, you can create your own private DBI functions with this method. It's not well supported in MySQL, though.

get_info( )

$dbh->get_info(*type*)

This function returns information about the database handle for the numeric code type (based on SQL standards) given as an argument to the method. Information can include the driver and the capabilities of the data source. The function returns `undef` for an unknown type. Here is an example:

```
...
use DBI::Const::GetInfoType;
...

if($dbh->get_info($GetInfoType{SQL_DBMS_VER}) lt '5.0') {
   print "Old version of MySQL. Upgrade!"
};
```

To see a list of other parameters available and their values on your server, run the following from your server:

```
...
use DBI;
use DBI::Const::GetInfoType;
...
while( my ($key,$value) = each(%GetInfoType) ) {
   my $info = $dbh->get_info( $GetInfoType{"$key"} );
   print "$key\->$info \n";
}
```

installed_drivers( )

DBI->installed_drivers([*nowarn*])

This function returns a hash listing driver names and handles loaded for the current process. These are only the drivers that are loaded for the program that's running, not all that are available and installed. For information on those, use `available_drivers( )`. Here is an example:

```
...
my %drivers = DBI->installed_drivers();

while( my ($key,$values) = each(%drivers)) {
   print "$key -> $values \n";
}
```

installed_versions( )

DBI->installed_versions( )

This function returns a list of installed drivers. There are no arguments to this method. Although it can be used from within a program, it works easily and best from the command line. Enter the following from the command line of the server:

```
perl -MDBI -e 'DBI->installed_versions'
```

last_insert_id( )

`$dbh->last_insert_id($catalog, $database, $table, $column[, \%attr])`

This function returns the value stored in the row identification column of the most recent row inserted for the current MySQL session, provided the identification number was incremented using `AUTO_INCREMENT` in MySQL. It works like the `LAST_INSERT_ID( )` function in MySQL. No arguments for this function are necessary with MySQL: if given, their values are ignored, although `undef` is required at a minimum. Other systems may require other options. This function doesn't work with MySQL before version 1.45 of DBI. It returns undefined if it cannot retrieve the number (which must be retrieved after the insert, and before another statement in MySQL) or if the driver does not support this function.

Here is an example:

```
...
my $sth = $dbh->prepare("INSERT INTO books (title, author)
                         VALUES (?,?)");
$sth->execute($title,$author);

my $book_id = $dbh->last_insert_id(undef,undef,undef,undef,undef);

print "New Book ID: $book_id \n";
$sth->finish();
```

looks_like_number( )

`DBI->looks_like_number(@array)`

This method is used for testing a given array to determine whether each element seems to be a number or not. It returns 1 for each element in an array that appears to be a number; 0 for those that do not. It returns undefined if the element is empty or undefined. Here is an example:

```
...
my $sql_stmnt = "SELECT book_id, title, author, isbn
                 FROM books LIMIT 1";
my $sth = $dbh->prepare($sql_stmnt);
$sth->execute();
my (@book) = $sth->fetchrow_array();

my @num_assessment = DBI->looks_like_number(@book);
my $cnt = 0;

foreach (@num_assessment) {
   if($_) { print "Array Element $cnt looks like a number.\n" };
   ++$cnt;
}
```

The results of this code will show that elements 1 and 4 appear to be numbers.

neat( )

`DBI::neat(string[, length])`

This function returns a string given as the first argument, placed in quotes, for an optional maximum length given as the second argument. It will not escape quotes within the string. If given a numeric value instead of a string, it will not return the results within quotes. It will return NULL values as undefined. Here is an example:

```
...
my $test = "This is Russell's test!";
print "Test: " . DBI::neat($test, 24) . "\n";
```

Here are the results:

```
Test: 'This is Russell's t...'
```

Notice that the results are in single quotes, that the text was truncated even though the maximum length given was enough to just encompass the string. If a value of 25—one more than needed—had been given, then the full text would have been displayed without ellipses. To neaten a list of strings, use the `neat_list( )` function.

neat_list( )

`DBI::neat_list(\@`*`strings`*`[, `*`length`*`, `*`delimiter`*`])`

This function returns a list of strings given as the first argument, placed in quotes, each truncated to an optional maximum length given as the second argument. An optional third argument can specify a delimiter to place between the elements of the list or the array given in the first argument. A comma and a space will be used by default if no delimiter is specified. Here is an example:

```
...
my @test = ("This is a test.", "Another test");
print "Test: " . DBI::neat_list(\@test, 12, '|');
```

Here are the results:

```
Test: 'This is...'|'Another...'
```

parse_dsn( )

`DBI->parse_dsn($`*`data_source_name`*`)`

This function returns the components of the DBI Data Source Name (DSN) values: the scheme (`dbi`); the driver (`$ENV{DBI_DRIVER}`); an optional attribute string; a reference to a hash with the attribute names and values; and the DBI DSN string. Here is an example:

```
...
use DBI;
my $dsn = "DBI:mysql:database=bookstore;host=localhost;port=3306";
my $dbh = DBI->connect ($dsn,$user,$pwd) or die DBI->errstr;

my ($scheme, $driver, $attr_string, $attr_hash, $driver_dsn) =
   DBI->parse_dsn($dsn);
print "DSN: ($scheme, $driver, $attr_string, $attr_hash, $driver_dsn) \n";
```

Here are the results:

```
DSN: (dbi, mysql, , , database=bookstore;host=localhost;port=3306)
```

parse_trace_flag( )

$handle*->parse_trace_flag(*$settings)

This function returns a bit flag for a trace flag name given as an argument. To parse a list of trace flags, see `parse_trace_flags( )` next.

parse_trace_flags( )

$handle*->parse_trace_flags(*$settings)

Use this function to parse a string given as an argument that contains a list of trace settings. These settings are either trace flag names or integers representing trace levels.

ping( )

$dbh->ping( )

Use this function to determine whether a MySQL server is still running and the database connection is still available. There are no arguments for this method. Here is an example:

```
...
$sth->finish();

my $alive = $dbh->ping();
if($alive) { print "MySQL connection is still alive.\n"}
else{ print "MySQL connection is not alive.\n"}

$dbh->disconnect();

if($dbh->ping()) { print "MySQL connection is still alive.\n"}
else{ print "MySQL connection is not alive.\n"}

...
```

The results will show that the connection is alive after the `finish( )` is called, but not after `disconnect( )`.

prepare( )

$sth = *$dbh*->prepare(*statement*[, \%*attr*])

This function creates a statement handle by preparing an SQL statement given as the first argument for subsequent execution with `execute( )`. It returns a reference to the statement handle. The second argument is a hash of attributes and is optional. A prepared statement or a statement handle may be used multiple times until the `disconnect( )` is issued or until the statement handle value is overwritten by another call to `prepare( )` for the same statement handle variable. More than one statement handle can be prepared if different variables are used for storing the handle references. Here is an example:

```
my $dbh = DBI->connect ("$dsn","$user","$pwd")
my $sql_stmnt = "SELECT title, author FROM books";
my $sth = $dbh->prepare($sql_stmnt, {RaiseError => 1, ChopBlanks => 1});
```

Warning messages are enabled here and trailing spaces of fixed-width character columns are trimmed. See the end of this chapter for a list of attributes.

prepare_cached( )

`$dbh->prepare_cached($sql_standard[, \%attr, $active])`

This function creates a statement handle like `prepare( )` does, but it stores the resulting statement handle in a hash. Attributes for the statement handle may be given in the second argument in the form of a hash. The third argument of the method changes the behavior of the handle if an active statement handle is already in the cache. Table 18-1 lists the four choices for this argument.

The statement handle that this method generates is used in basically the same way as the statement handle generated by `prepare( )`. However, it can potentially cause system problems if not used properly. Therefore, use `prepare( )` instead.

Table 18-1. Active argument for prepare_cached( )

Active value	Result
0	Warning messages will be issued, and `finish( )` for the statement handle will be employed.
1	No warning will be displayed, but `finish( )` will be executed.
2	Disables checking for an active handle.
3	Causes the new statement handle to replace the active one.

primary_key( )

`$dbh->primary_key($catalog, $database, $table)`

This function is meant to return a list of primary key column names for a given table. If there are no primary keys, it will return an empty list. This method does not yet seem to be supported in MySQL.

primary_key_info( )

`$dbh->primary_key_info($catalog, $database, $table)`

This function is meant to return a statement handle for fetching information about primary key columns for a table. The values are part of a hash for the statement handle: `TABLE_CAT`, `TABLE_SCHEM`, `TABLE_NAME`, and `KEY_SEQ`. If there is no primary key for the table given, it returns no rows. This method does not yet seem to be supported in MySQL.

private_attribute_info( )

`$handle->private_attribute_info($settings)`

This function is meant to return a reference to a hash containing the private attributes available for the handle from which it is called. There are no parameters of this method, and it does not yet seem to be supported in MySQL.

quote( )

```
$dbh->quote(string[, data_type)
```

Use this method to escape special characters contained in a given string. It's useful in SQL statements, particularly for unknown user input that might contain metacharacters that would cause undesirable behavior in MySQL. You can specify the data type as a second parameter. Don't use this method with bind values and placeholders. Here is an example:

```
...
my $comment = shift;
my $quoted_comment = $dbh->quote($comment);

my $sql_stmnt = "UPDATE books SET comment = ?";
my $sth = $dbh->prepare($sql_stmnt);
$sth->execute($quoted_comment);

print "Original: $comment \n Quoted: $quoted_comment \n";
```

Here are the command line results:

```
Original: Henry James' book "The Muse" is wonderful!
Quoted: 'Henry James\' book \"The Muse\" is wonderful!'
```

quote_identifier( )

```
$dbh->quote_identifier({$name|$catalog, $database[, $table, \%attri]})
```

Use this function to escape special characters of an identifier (e.g., a database, table, or column name) for use in an SQL statement. You can provide only the first parameter (a string containing an identifier name), or you can provide the catalog name (`undef` is acceptable with MySQL), a database name, a table name, and optionally provide database attributes. Here is an example:

```
my $col1 = $dbh->quote_identifier('author');
my $col2 = $dbh->quote_identifier('title');
my $table = $dbh->quote_identifier('books');

my $sql_stmnt = "SELECT $col1, $col2 FROM $table";
print $sql_stmnt;
```

Here is the resulting SQL statement:

```
SELECT `author`, `title` FROM `books`
```

rollback( )

```
$dbh->rollback( )
```

Use this function to undo a transaction that has not yet been committed. This can only be used with transactional (e.g., InnoDB or BDB) tables. It requires that the database handle was created with the `AutoCommit` attribute set to false or 0, and that the changes were not committed using the `commit( )` function or by any other method that might unintentionally commit a transaction.

rows( )

`$sth->rows( )`

This function returns the number of rows affected by the last statement handle executed. It works with UPDATE, INSERT, and DELETE dependably. It doesn't work effectively with SELECT statements unless all rows in a table are selected. If the number of rows is unknown, –1 is returned. There are no arguments to this method. Here is an example:

```
...
my $sql_stmnt = "UPDATE books SET author = 'Robert B. Parker'
                 WHERE author = 'Robert Parker'";
my $sth = $dbh->prepare($sql_stmnt);
$sth->execute();
my $change_count = $sth->rows();
print "$change_count rows were changed.";
```

This program displays the following when run:

```
2 rows were changed
```

selectall_arrayref( )

`$dbh->selectall_arrayref($statement[, \%attri][, @bind_values])`

This function returns a reference to an array, which is the results set of the SQL statement executed. For each row of the results, another reference to an array is returned for each row of data. An optional second argument can specify any of the attributes allowed for the statement handle. If placeholders are used in the SQL statement, their values may be given as an array for the final argument. This method combines `prepare( )`, `execute( )`, and `fetchall_arrayref( )`. Here is an example showing how it might be dereferenced:

```
my $sql_stmnt = "SELECT title, author
                 FROM books WHERE book_id = ?";
my $books = $dbh->selectall_arrayref($sql_stmnt, undef, '1234');

foreach my $book (@$books) {
   my ($title, $author) = @$book;
   print "$title by $author \n";
}
```

Notice that the `prepare( )` method isn't called to prepare the SQL statement or to create a statement handle. This means that `finish( )` doesn't need to be called. However, instead of giving an SQL statement, you can give a statement handle. Since the result is an array reference, it must be deferenced in order to extract the data (i.e., the `@$books`). Using the `foreach` Perl function, each element of the array is extracted (the array reference for each row), which is then deferenced within the code block (`@$book`). From this, the values for the individual fields can be parsed and saved to variables.

selectall_hashref( )

`$dbh->selectall_hashref($statement, $key_field[, \%attri][, @bind_values])`

This function returns a reference to a hash of references to hashes, one for each row from the results of an SQL statement given. This method combines `prepare( )`, `execute( )`, and fetchall_hashref( ). A unique key field must be given for the second argument. This will be used for the key of the main hash of rows from the results set. An optional third argument can specify any of the attributes allowed for a statement handle. If placeholders are used in the SQL statement, their values must be given as an array for the final argument.

Here is an example:

```
...
my $sql_stmnt = "SELECT rec_id, title, author
                 FROM books";

my $books = $dbh->selectall_hashref($sql_stmnt, 'book_id');

foreach my $book_id (keys %$books) {
   print "$books->{$book_id}{title}
          by $books->{$book_id}{author} \n";
}
```

Notice that the prepare( ) method isn't called to prepare the SQL statement or to create a statement handle. This means that finish( ) doesn't need to be called. However, instead of giving an SQL statement, you can give a statement handle. Since the result is a hash reference, it must be deferenced in order to extract the data (i.e., the %$books). Using the foreach and the keys Perl functions, each key of the hash is extracted (the hash reference for each row), which is then deferenced within the code block (%$book). From this, the values for the individual fields can be extracted by the object oriented method.

selectcol_arrayref( )

$dbh*->selectcol_arrayref(*$sql_statement[, \%*attri*][, *@bind_values*])

This returns a reference to an array containing a value in the first column of each row selected. The SQL statement is given as the first argument of the function. This can be particularly useful if the first column is a key field. This function performs prepare( ) and execute( ) on the SQL statement. Here is an example:

```
...
my $sql_stmnt = "SELECT * FROM books";

my $book = $dbh->selectcol_arrayref($sql_stmnt);

foreach my $author_id (@$book){
   print "$author_id \n";
}
```

The prepare( ) method isn't called to create a statement handle if the SQL statement is given with this method, making finish( ) unnecessary. However, a statement handle could be given instead. Since the result is an array reference, it must be deferenced to extract the data (i.e., @$book). Using foreach, each element of the array is extracted, one element per row of the results set, and the value of each temporarily stored in a variable here ($author_id, the first column of the table).

selectrow_array( )

`$dbh->selectrow_array($sql_statement[, \%attri, @values])`

This function returns one row from the results of an SQL statement in the form of an array, where each column returned is represented by an element of the array, in order. This method combines `prepare( )`, `execute( )`, and `fetchrow_array( )`. No statement handle is created, so `finish( )` is unnecessary. An optional second argument can specify any of the attributes allowed for a statement handle. If placeholders are used in the SQL statement, their values must be given as an array for the third argument. Here is an example:

```
...
my $sql_stmnt = "SELECT title, author
                 FROM books WHERE book_id = ?";

my ($title, $author) = $dbh->selectrow_array($sql_stmnt, undef, '1234');

print "$title by $author \n";
```

No attributes are given for the SQL statement in this example, so `undef` is used for the second argument. The third argument provides the `book_id` value for the placeholder in the SQL statement. Notice that this `select_` type of database handle method does not require the use of a control statement to parse the data because it retrieves only one row of data. The `prepare( )` method isn't called to create a statement handle if the SQL statement is given (as it is here), which means `finish( )` is unnecessary. However, a statement handle could be given instead.

selectrow_arrayref( )

`$dbh->selectrow_arrayref($sql_statement[, \%attri][, @values])`

This function returns a reference to an array of one row from the results of an SQL statement given. This method combines `prepare( )`, `execute( )`, and `fetchrow_arrayref( )`. An optional second argument can specify any of the attributes allowed for a statement handle. If placeholders are used in the SQL statement, their values must be given as an array for the third argument. Here is an example:

```
...
my $sql_stmnt = "SELECT title, author
                 FROM books WHERE book_id = ?";

my $book = $dbh->selectrow_arrayref($sql_stmnt, undef, '1234');

my ($title, $author) = @$book;
print "$title by $author \n";
```

The `prepare( )` method isn't called to create a statement handle if the SQL statement is given (as it is here), which means `finish( )` is unnecessary. However, a statement handle could be given instead.

selectrow_hashref( )

`$dbh->selectrow_hashref($sql_statement[, \%attri, @values])`

This function returns a reference to a hash of one row from the results of an SQL statement given. This method combines `prepare( )`, `execute( )`, and `fetchrow_hashref( )`. However, a statement handle could be given. Attributes that may be given for a statement handle may be provided in a hash for the second argument of this method. If placeholders are used in the SQL statement, their values may be given as an array for the third argument.

Here is an example:

```
...
my $sql_stmnt = "SELECT title, author
                 FROM books WHERE book_id = ?";

my $book_ref = $dbh->selectrow_hashref($sql_stmnt, undef, '1234');

print "$book_ref->{title} by $book_ref->{author} \n";
```

Notice that this method captures the names of the columns as the keys to the values in the hash generated. Notice also that because only one row is captured, a control statement is unnecessary.

set_err( )

$handle*->set_err(*$err, *$errstr*[, *$state*[, *$method*[, *$return_value*]]])

This function sets the values for `err`, `errstr`, and `state` for the handle. The *method* (e.g., `RaiseError`) can be changed as well. It returns `undef` unless a different return value is given as the fifth argument to this method. You can use this manually to return an error message to a user. Here is an example:

```
...
my $book_id = shift;
my $books = &get_data_ref($book_id)
   or print "Error: " . DBI->err . DBI->errstr;
...

sub get_data_ref {
  my $book_id = shift;

  if($book_id =~ m/\D/g) {
     return $dbh->DBI::set_err(500, "\nYou entered '$book_id'.\nBad Book
        ID!");
     last;
  }
  ...
}
```

Notice in the subroutine that if it is given a book identifier that contains any nonnumeric characters, it does not proceed and instead returns the error as set by `set_err`. The line of code at the top of the excerpt that calls the subroutine will display the results if true, or display the error number and string. Here are the results of the program when a user enters a book ID that contains a letter:

```
Error: 500
You entered '100g'?
Bad Book ID!
```

state( )

$handle->state( )

This method returns the error code of an error in a five-character format, in the SQLSTATE format. It doesn't seem to be supported in MySQL yet, so it returns either an empty value or, for a general error, S1000. Here is an example:

```
$state = $dbh->state();
print "SQLSTATE: $state";
```

statistics_info( )

$dbh*->statistics_info(*$catalog, *$database*, *$table*, *unique_only*, *quick*)

This method is meant to return an active statement handle that can be used to retrieve statistical information about a given table and its indexes. It's experimental at the time of this writing and its syntax, results, and usage may change. The *unique_only* argument may be set to 1 or 0 to indicate whether or not information only on unique indexes should be retrieved. If *quick* is set to 1, then some information is not returned unless it can be retrieved quickly.

swap_inner_handle( )

$handle*->swap_inner_handle(*$handle)

This method is used to swap handles. However, it's better to create new handles or use some other method within your program. Both the handle that calls the method and the other handle given for the parameter of this method must be of the same type and have the same parent (i.e., $dbh is parent of both $sth1 and $sth2).

table_info( )

$dbh*->table_info(*$catalog, *$database*, *$table*, *$type*[, \%*attri*])

This function returns a statement handle for fetching information about the tables in a given database. In MySQL, any parameters given are ignored, the values from the database handle are used instead, and a list of tables and views for the database is returned. Here is an example:

```
...
my $dbinfo = $dbh->table_info();

while( my($qualifier,$owner,$name,$type,$remarks) =
         $dbinfo->fetchrow_array()) {
   foreach ($qualifier,$owner,$name,$type,$remarks) {
      $_ = '' unless defined $_;
   }
   print "$qualifier $owner $name $type $remarks \n";
}
```

tables( )

$dbh*->tables(*$catalog, *$database*, *$table*, *$type*)

This function returns an array containing a list of tables and views for a database handle. In MySQL, the parameters are ignored and the values are drawn from the database handle. Here is an example:

```
my @tables = $dbh->tables();

foreach $table(@tables) {
   print "$table \n";
}
```

take_imp_data( )

$dbh*->take_imp_data(*$catalog, *$database*, *$table*)

This method severs the database handle that calls it from the API connection data. It returns a binary string of implementation data from the driver about the connection that was severed. This method can cause problems and shouldn't typically be used. It's primarily used when programming a multithreaded connection pool.

trace( )

$handle->trace(*level*[, *log*]) |
DBI->trace( )

This method sets the trace level for a handle. A level of 0 disables tracing; level 1 traces the execution of the database handle; level 2 provides more details including parameter values. If a filename is given as the second argument, trace information will be appended to that log file instead of `stderr`. If `DBI->trace( )` syntax is used instead of a statement handle, it will set the trace level globally. It will return the trace settings it had before it was called as well.

trace_msg( )

$handle->trace_msg(*message*[, *minimum_level*]) |
DBI->trace_msg( )

This function adds text given in the first argument to trace data. A minimum trace level (see the `trace( )` method discussed previously) required for the message to be used may be specified as a second argument. The `DBI->trace_msg( )` syntax uses the given message globally.

type_info( )

$dbh*->type_info([*$data_type])

This function returns a hash containing information on a given data type. If no data type is given, or if `SQL_ALL_TYPES` is given, all will be returned in the hash. The following example shows how this method might be used and lists all the possible results:

```
...
my $dbinfo = $dbh->type_info();

while(my($key, $value) = each(%$dbinfo)){
   print "$key => $value\n";
}
```

type_info_all( )

$dbh->type_info_all( )

This function returns a reference to an array of all data types supported by the driver. The following program excerpt shows how it may be used and shows the results of the method:

```
my @dbinfo = $dbh->type_info_all();
my $dbinfo_hashref = $dbinfo[0];

while( my($key,$value) = each(%$dbinfo_hashref)){
   print "$key => @$value\n";
}
```

Attributes for Handles

This section lists the attribute keys and values that can be given in many Perl DBI methods, as indicated in the previous section with *%attri* in each method's syntax. The basic syntax to set an attribute is ***$handle->attribute=>'setting'***. Attribute key/value pairs are separated by commas and are all contained within a pair of curly braces. For example, to instruct DBI not to return error messages for a database handle, you would do the following when it's created:

```
my $dbh = DBI->connect('DBI:mysql:bookstore:localhost',
   'paola','caporalle1017', {RaiseError=>0});
```

To retrieve a setting, use ***$handle->{attribute}***. This can be stored to a variable or printed:

```
print "dbh->{RaiseError=>" . $dbh->{RaiseError} . "}";
```

If you try this simple line of code, keep in mind that an attribute set to 0 will return an empty value.

Attributes for All Handles

You can use the following attributes with both database handles and statement handles:

`Active (boolean, read-only)`
: This attribute indicates that the handle is active. In the case of a database handle, it indicates that the connection is open. The `disconnect( )` method sets this attribute to 0 in a database handle; `finish( )` sets it to 0 in a statement handle.

`ActiveKids (integer, read-only)`
: This attribute provides the number of active handles under the handle that employed the attribute. If called by a driver handle, the number of database handles will be returned. If called by a database handle, the number of active statement handles will be returned.

`CacheKids (hash ref)`
: This attribute returns a reference to a hash containing child handles for a driver or for a database handle that was created by the `connect_cached( )` or `prepare_cached( )` methods, respectively.

`ChildHandles (array ref)`
: This attribute returns a reference to an array to all accessible handles created by the handle that called this method. These are weak references and the referenced arrays may not be dependably available.

`ChopBlanks (boolean, inherited)`
: This attribute trims trailing spaces from fixed-width character fields (i.e., `CHAR` fields of results sets).

`CompatMode (boolean, inherited)`
: This attribute makes emulation layers compatible with a driver handle. It is not normally used in applications.

`ErrCount (unsigned integer)`
: This attribute keeps a count of the number of errors logged by `set_err( )`.

`Executed (boolean)`
: This attribute determines whether a handle or one of its children has been executed.

`FetchHashKeyName (string, inherited)`
: This attribute instructs `fetchrow_hashref( )` calls to convert column names to either all lowercase (`NAME_lc`) or all uppercase (`NAME_uc`) letters. The default is `NAME`, which indicates no conversion should be performed.

`HandleError (code ref, inherited)`
: This attribute customizes the response to an error caused by the handle. You could use this attribute to run a subroutine in the event of an error:

```
$dbh->{HandleError=> \&my_sub_routine });
```

`HandleSetErr (code ref, inherited)`
: This attribute customizes the settings for `err`, `errstr`, and `state` values of an error caused by the handle. It's similar to the `HandleError` attribute, but it relates to `set_err( )`.

`InactiveDestroy (boolean)`
: This attribute prevents the server from destroying a handle that is out of scope, unless it is closed intentionally with a function such as `finish( )` or `disconnect( )`.

`Kids (integer, read-only)`
: This attribute provides the number of all handles (active and inactive) under the handle that employed the attribute. If it's called by a database handle, the

number of statement handles will be returned. If it's called by a driver handle, the number of database handles will be returned.

`LongReadLen (unsigned integer, inherited)`
: This attribute sets the maximum length of data retrieved from long data type columns (i.e., `BLOB` and `TEXT`).

`LongTruncOK (boolean, inherited)`
: If this attribute is set to true, it may prevent a fetch method from failing if a column's data length exceeds the maximum length set by the `LongReadLen` attribute.

`PrintError (boolean, inherited)`
: If this attribute is set to 1, error codes and error messages associated with the handle will be logged. If it's set to 0, they won't be logged.

`PrintWarn (boolean, inherited)`
: Setting this attribute to 1 will instruct DBI to log warning messages for the handle. Setting it to 0 will instruct it not to log them.

`private_*`
: This attribute stores information on the handle as a private attribute with a customized name starting with `private_`.

`Profile (inherited)`
: This attribute enables the logging of method call timing statistics.

`RaiseError (boolean, inherited)`
: This attribute instructs DBI to raises exceptions when errors are associated with the handle. By default it's set to 0. If set to 1, any DBI error will cause the program to die. If you set this attribute to true, you should also set `PrintError` to true.

`ReadOnly (boolean, inherited)`
: Setting this attribute on a handle to true indicates that all actions with the handle afterward will be read-only activities—data won't be changed using the handle.

`ShowErrorStatement (boolean, inherited)`
: If set to true, this attribute specifies that the SQL statement text of a statement handle should be appended to error messages stemming from the `PrintError`, `PrintWarn`, and `RaiseError` attributes being set to true.

`Taint (boolean, inherited)`
: This attribute combines `TaintIn` and `TaintOut` attributes. Whatever value you set with this attribute will be set for the other two attributes.

`TaintIn (boolean, inherited)`
: This attribute instructs DBI to check whether method calls are tainted, when Perl is running in taint mode.

`TaintOut (boolean, inherited)`
: This attribute instructs DBI to assume that data fetched is tainted, when Perl is running in taint mode.

`TraceLevel (integer, inherited)`
: This attribute sets trace levels and flags for a handle. It's an alternative to the `trace( )` method.

`Type (scalar, read-only)`
: This attribute is used to determine the type of handle. It returns `dr` for a driver handle, `db` for a database handle, and `st` for a statement handle.

`Warn (boolean, inherited)`
: This attribute enables or disables warning messages for poor database procedures.

Attributes Only for Database Handles

`AutoCommit (boolean)`
: This attribute allows the `rollback( )` function to be used if the attribute is set to 0. At the time of this writing, a bug sometimes produces an error when using this attribute.

`Driver (handle)`
: This attribute provides the name of the parent driver: `$dbh->{Driver}->{Name}`.

`Name (string)`
: This attribute provides the name of the database for the database handle.

`RowCacheSize (integer)`
: This attribute is used to suggest a cache size for rows generated for `SELECT` statements. If it's 0, DBI automatically determines the cache size. A value of 1 disables local row caching.

`Statement (string, read-only)`
: This attribute provides the last SQL statement prepared with the database handle, regardless of whether it succeeded.

`Username (string)`
: This attribute provides the name of the user for the database handle.

Attributes Only for Statement Handles

`CursorName (string, read-only)`
: This attribute returns the name of the cursor for the statement handle.

`Database (dbh, read-only)`
: This attribute returns the database handle of the statement handle.

`NAME (array-ref, read-only)`
: This attribute contains a reference to an array containing the names of the columns of the SQL statement from the statement handle.

`NAME_hash (hash-ref, read-only)`
: This attribute returns a reference to a hash containing column name information.

`NAME_lc (array-ref, read-only)`
: This attribute returns a reference to an array containing column name information. The keys are the column names in lowercase letters.

`NAME_lc_hash (hash-ref, read-only)`
: This attribute returns a reference to a hash containing column name information. The keys are the column names in lowercase letters.

`NAME_uc (array-ref, read-only)`
: This attribute returns a reference to an array containing column name information. The keys are the column names in uppercase letters.

`NAME_uc_hash (hash-ref, read-only)`
: This attribute returns a reference to a hash containing column name information. The keys are the column names in uppercase letters.

`NULLABLE (array-ref, read-only)`
: This attribute returns a reference to an array indicating whether each column in the SQL statement of the handle may contain a NULL value.

`NUM_OF_FIELDS (integer, read-only)`
: This attribute returns the number of columns in the SQL statement of the handle.

`NUM_OF_PARAMS (integer, read-only)`
: This attribute returns the number of placeholders in the SQL statement of the handle.

`ParamArrays (hash ref, read-only)`
: This attribute returns a reference to a hash containing the names of placeholders as keys and their associated values for calls made to `bind_param_array( )` and `execute_array( )`.

`ParamTypes (hash ref, read-only)`
: This attribute returns a reference to a hash containing information about placeholders that are bound by calls made to `bind_param( )`. The placeholder names are used as the keys of the hash.

`ParamValues (hash ref, read-only)`
: This attribute returns a reference to a hash of bound parameters and their values.

`RowsInCache (integer, read-only)`
: This attribute returns the number of unfetched rows in the cache if the driver supports row-level caching.

`Statement (string, read-only)`
: This attribute is the SQL statement passed to `prepare( )`.

`TYPE (array-ref, read-only)`
: This attribute contains a reference to an array of codes for international standard values for data types (e.g., 1 for `SQL_CHAR`, 4 for `SQL_INTEGER`).

`PRECISION (array-ref, read-only)`
: This attribute contains a reference to an array containing the length of columns (as set in the table definition) in the SQL statement of the handle.

`SCALE (array-ref, read-only)`
This attribute contains a reference to an array containing the number of decimal places for columns in the SQL statement of the handle.

DBI Dynamic Attributes

These attributes are related to the last handle used, regardless of the type of handle. The syntax of each of these is `$DBI::`*`attribute`*:

`err`
This attribute is synonymous with *`$handle`*`->err`.

`errstr`
This attribute is synonymous with *`$handle`*`->errstr`.

`lasth`
This attribute returns the handle used by the last method call.

`rows`
This attribute is synonymous with *`$handle`*`->rows`.

`state`
This attribute is synonymous with *`$handle`*`->state`.

19
PHP API

One of the most popular programming language and database engine combinations for the Web is PHP with MySQL. This combination works well for many reasons, but primarily because of the speed, stability, and simplicity of both applications. The first part of this chapter provides a basic tutorial on how to connect to and query MySQL with PHP. Following the tutorial is a reference of PHP MySQL functions in alphabetical order. For the examples in this chapter, I use the database of a fictitious computer support business. This database contains one table with client work requests (`workreq`) and another with client contact information (`clients`).

Using PHP with MySQL

This section presents the basic tasks you need to query a MySQL database from PHP. Prior to PHP 5, MySQL was enabled by default. As of PHP 5, it's not enabled and the MySQL library is not packaged with PHP. To enable MySQL with PHP, you need to configure PHP with the `--with-mysql[=`*`/path_to_mysql`*`]` option.

Connecting to MySQL

For a PHP script to interface with MySQL, the script must first make a connection to MySQL, thus establishing a MySQL session. To connect to the fictitious database `workrequests`, a PHP script might begin like this:

```
<?php

$host = 'localhost';
$user = 'russell';
$pw = 'dyer';
$db = 'workrequests';

mysql_connect($host, $user, $pw)
   or die(mysql_error);
```

```
mysql_select_db($db);

?>
```

This excerpt of PHP code starts by establishing the variables with information necessary for connecting to MySQL and the database. After that, PHP connects to MySQL by giving the host and user variables. If it's unsuccessful, the script dies with an error message. If the connection is successful, the `workrequests` database is selected for use. Each PHP script example in this chapter begins with an excerpt of code like this one.

Querying MySQL

In the fictitious database is a table called `workreq` that contains information on client work requests. To retrieve a list of work requests and some basic information on clients, a PHP script begins by connecting to MySQL, as shown in the previous script excerpt. That is followed by the start of a web page and then the invocation of an SQL statement to retrieve and display the data. You can achieve this with code such as the following:

```
... // Connect to MySQL

<html>
<body>
<h2>Work Requests</h2>

<?php
$sql_stmnt = "SELECT wrid, client_name,
              wr_date, description
              FROM workreq, clients
              WHERE status = 'done'
              AND workreq.clientid = clients.clientid";

$results = mysql_query($sql_stmnt)
           or die('Invalid query: ' . mysql_error());

while($row = mysql_fetch_row($results)) {
   list($wrid, $client_name, $wr_date, $description) = $row;
   print "<a href='detail.php?wrid=$wrid'>$client_name -
          $desription ($wr_date)</a><br/>";
}

mysql_close( );
?>
</body>
</html>
```

After connecting to MySQL (substituted with ellipses here) and starting the web page, a variable (`$sql_stmnt`) containing the SQL statement is created. Then the database is queried with the SQL statement, and a reference to the results set is stored in a variable (`$results`). The query is followed by an `or` statement, a common PHP syntax for error checking. The `print` statement executes only if no results are found.

Assuming PHP was successful in querying the database, a `while` statement is used to loop through each row of data retrieved from MySQL. With each pass, using the `mysql_fetch_row( )` function, PHP will temporarily store the fields of data for each row in an array (`$row`). Within the code block of the `while` statement, the PHP `list( )` function parses the elements of the `$row` array into their respective variables. The variables here are named to match their column counterparts. This is not necessary, though—they can be named anything. The array could even be used as it is and the appropriate sequence number referenced to retrieve data. For instance, for the date of the work request, `$row[2]` could be used because it's the third in the sequence (0 is first). Naming the variables as they are here, though, makes it easier to read the code and easier for others to follow later.

The second line of code within the `while` statement displays the data in the format required for the web page. The data is wrapped in a hyperlink with a reference to another PHP script (`details.php`), which will retrieve all of the details for the particular work request selected by a user. That work request will be identified by the work request number (i.e., `wrid`), which is a key column for the `details.php` PHP script. Typically, the value for `wrid` will automatically be placed in a variable by the same name (`$wrid`) regardless of what the variable is named in this script. It's based on the name given in the hyperlink or anchor tag. This will happen if the *php.ini* configuration file has `register_globals` set to *on*, something that is not the case in recent versions of PHP. On Unix and Linux systems, this file is located in the */etc* directory. On a Windows system, it's usually found in the *c:\windows* directory. If not, the value can be referenced using the `$_GET` associative array, which is describe in PHP's online documentation (*http://www.php.net*).

The output of this script is a line for each incomplete work request found in the database. Each line will be linked to another script that presumably can provide details on the work request selected. In this simple example, only a few of the many PHP MySQL functions are used to display data. In the next section of this chapter, each function is described with script excerpts that show how they are used.

PHP MySQL Functions in Alphabetical Order

The rest of this chapter contains a list of PHP MySQL functions in alphabetical order. Each function is given with its syntax and an explanation. An example script, or script excerpt, is provided to show how you can use the function. To save space, almost all of the script excerpts are shown without the lines of code necessary to start a PHP script and to connect to MySQL, and without the lines that should follow to close the connection and to end the script. For an example showing how to write these opening and closing lines, see the tutorial in the previous section.

mysql_affected_rows( )

```
int mysql_affected_rows([connection])
```

This function returns the number of rows affected by a previous SQL statement that modified rows of data for the current MySQL session. The function returns –1 if the previous statement failed. It works only after INSERT, UPDATE, and DELETE statements. See mysql_num_rows( ) later in this section for the number of rows returned by a SELECT statement. The connection identifier may be given as an argument to retrieve the number of rows affected by a different connection. Here is an example:

```
...
$sql_stmnt = "UPDATE workreq
              SET due_date = ADDDATE(due_date, INTERVAL 1 DAY)
              WHERE due_date = '2004-07-28'";
mysql_query($sql_stmnt);
$updated = mysql_affected_rows( );
print "Number of Rows Updated:  $updated \n";
...
```

This script changes the due dates for all work requests by one day.

mysql_change_user( )

`int mysql_change_user(`*`user, password`*`[, `*`database, connection`*`])`

This function can be used to change the username for a MySQL connection. The new username is given as the first argument and the password for that user as the second. A different database from the one in use may be given as a third argument. You can change the user information for a different MySQL connection by specifying it as the fourth argument. If the function is successful, it returns true; if it's unsuccessful, it returns false. This function is no longer available as of version 4 of PHP. Instead, you should establish a new connection with a different user by using the mysql_connect( ) function.

mysql_client_encoding( )

`string mysql_client_encoding([`*`connection`*`])`

This function returns the name of the default character set for the current MySQL connection or, if *connection* is supplied, for that connection. Here is an example:

```
...
$info = mysql_client_encoding( );
print "Encoding in Use: $info \n";
...
```

Here are the results of this script on my server:

```
Encoding in Use:  latin1
```

mysql_close( )

`bool mysql_close([`*`connection`*`])`

This function closes the current or last MySQL connection, or a given connection. The function returns true if it's successful, and false if it's unsuccessful. This function will not close persistent connections started with mysql_pconnect( ). Here is an example:

```
...
$connection = mysql_connect('localhost', 'ricky', 'adams');
mysql_select_db('workrequests', $connection);
```

```
...
mysql_close($connection);
...
```

If a script has opened only one connection to MySQL, it's not necessary to specify the connection link to close as shown here.

mysql_connect( )

```
mysql_connect(server[:port|socket], user, password[,
              new_link, flags])
```

Use this function to start a MySQL connection. The first argument of the function is the server name. If none is specified, *localhost* is assumed. A port may be specified with the server name (separated by a colon) or a socket along with its path. If no port is given, port 3306 is assumed. The username is to be given as the second argument and the user's password as the third. If a connection is attempted that uses the same parameters as a previous one, the existing connection will be used and a new connection link will not be created unless *`new_link`* is specified as the fourth argument of this function. As an optional fifth argument, client flags may be given for the MySQL constants `MYSQL_CLIENT_COMPRESS`, `MYSQL_CLIENT_IGNORE_SPACE`, `MYSQL_CLIENT_INTERACTIVE`, and `MYSQL_CLIENT_SSL`. The function returns a connection identifier if successful; it returns false if it's unsuccessful. Use `mysql_close( )` to close a connection created by `mysql_connect( )`. Here is an example:

```
#!/usr/bin/php -q
<?
   mysql_connect('localhost', 'ricky', 'adams');
   mysql_select_db('workrequests');
...
```

To be able to identify the connection link later, especially when a script will be using more than one link, capture the results of `mysql_connect( )`. Here is a complete script that sets up two connections to MySQL and captures the resource identification number for each link:

```
#!/usr/bin/php -q
<?
$user1 = 'elvis';
$user2 = 'fats';
$connection1 = mysql_connect('localhost', $user1, 'ganslmeier123');
$connection2 = mysql_connect('localhost', $user2, 'holzolling456');
mysql_select_db('workrequests', $connection1);
mysql_select_db('workrequests', $connection2);
counter($connection1,$user1);
counter($connection2,$user2);
function counter($connection,$user) {
   $sql_stmnt = "SELECT * FROM workreq";
   $results = mysql_query($sql_stmnt, $connection);
   if(mysql_errno($connection)){
      print "Could not SELECT with $connection for $user. \n";
      return;
   }
   $count = mysql_num_rows($results);
   print "Number of Rows Found with $connection for $user:
```

```
            $count. \n";
}
mysql_close($connection1);
mysql_close($connection2);
?>
```

In this example, two links are established with different usernames. The `counter( )` subroutine is called twice, once with each connection identifier and username passed to the user-defined function. For the first connection, the user *elvis* does not have `SELECT` privileges, so the SQL statement is unsuccessful. An error is generated and the number of rows is not determined due to the `return` ending the function call. For the second connection, the user *fats* has the necessary privileges, so the function is completed successfully. Here is the output from running this script on my server:

```
Could not SELECT with Resource id #1 for elvis.
Number of Rows Found with Resource id #2 for fats:  528.
```

mysql_create_db( )

`resource mysql_create_db(`*`database`*`[, `*`connection`*`])`

Use this function to create a database in MySQL for the current connection. The name of the database to create is given as the first argument of the function. A different MySQL connection identifier may be given as a second argument. The function returns true if it's successful, false if unsuccessful. This function is deprecated; use the `mysql_query( )` function with the `CREATE DATABASE` statement instead. Still, here is an example:

```
...
mysql_create_db('new_db');
$databases = mysql_list_dbs( );
while($db = mysql_fetch_row($databases)) {
   print $db[0] . "\n";
}
...
```

This script will create a new database and then display a list of databases to allow the user to confirm that it was successful.

mysql_data_seek( )

`bool mysql_data_seek(`*`connection`*`, `*`row`*`)`

Use this function in conjunction with the `mysql_fetch_row( )` function to change the current row being fetched to the one specified in the second argument. The connection identifier is given as the first argument. The function returns true if it's successful; false if it's unsuccessful. Here is an example:

```
...
$sql_stmnt = "SELECT wrid, clientid, description
              FROM workreq";
$results = mysql_query($sql_stmnt);
$count = mysql_num_rows($results);
if ($count > 6) mysql_data_seek($results, $count - 6);
$row = mysql_fetch_row($results);
```

```
while($row = mysql_fetch_object($results)) {
  print "WR-" . $row->wrid . " Client-" . $row->clientid .
        " - " . $row->description .  "\n";
}
...
```

In this script excerpt, the SQL statement is selecting the work request identification numbers for all rows in the table. The results set is stored in `$results`. Using the `mysql_num_rows( )` function, the number of rows is determined and placed in the `$count` variable. To be able to display only the last five work requests, the script calls `mysql_data_seek( )`. The results set is given as the first argument. In order to get the first row of a results set, the offset would be set to 0—so if a results set contains only one row, the row count of 1 minus 1 would need to be given as the second argument of `mysql_data_seek( )`. For the example here, to get the last five records of the results set, the number of rows is reduced by six to move the pointer to the row before the fifth-to-last row. Here is the last line of the output of this script:

```
WR-5755 Client-1000 - Can't connect to network.
```

mysql_db_name( )

`string mysql_db_name(`*`databases, number`*`)`

This function returns the name of the database from the results of the `mysql_list_dbs( )` function, which returns a pointer to a results set containing the names of databases for a MySQL server. The reference to the list of databases is given as the first argument. A number identifying the row to retrieve from the list is given as the second argument. Here is an example:

```
...
$databases = mysql_list_dbs( );
$dbs = mysql_num_rows($databases);
for($index = 0; $index < $dbs; $index++) {
    print mysql_db_name($databases, $index) . "\n";
}
...
```

In this script excerpt, a results set containing a list of databases is retrieved and stored in the `$databases` variable using the `mysql_list_dbs( )` function. That results set is analyzed by `mysql_num_rows( )` to determine the number of records (i.e., the number of database names) that it contains. Using a `for` statement and the number of databases (`$dbs`), the script loops through the results set contained in `$databases`. With each pass, `mysql_db_name( )` extracts the name of each database by changing the second argument of the function as the value of `$index` increments from 0 to the value of `$dbs`.

mysql_db_query( )

`resource mysql_db_query(`*`database, sql_statement`*`[, `*`connection`*`])`

This function can be used to query the database given—for the current MySQL connection, unless another is specified—and to execute the SQL statement given as the second argument. If there isn't currently a connection to the server, it will attempt to establish one. For SQL statements that would not return a results set (e.g., `UPDATE` statements), the function will return true if it's successful and false if it's unsuccessful. This function is deprecated, so use `mysql_query( )` instead. Here is an example:

```
...
$sql_stmnt = "SELECT wrid, clientid, description
              FROM workreq";
$results = mysql_db_query('workrequests', $sql_stmnt);
while($row = mysql_fetch_object($results)) {
  print "WR-" . $row->wrid . ",
         Client-" . $row->clientid . " " .
         $row->description . "\n";
}
...
```

Basically, using `mysql_db_query( )` eliminates the need to use `mysql_select_db( )` and `mysql_query( )`.

mysql_drop_db( )

`bool mysql_drop_db(`*`database`*`[, `*`connection`*`])`

Use this function to delete the database given from the MySQL server. A different connection identifier may be given as a second argument. This function returns true if it's successful, and false if it's unsuccessful. This function has been deprecated; use the `mysql_query( )` function with a `DROP DATABASE` statement instead. Here is an example:

```
...
mysql_dropdb('old_db');
...
```

mysql_errno( )

`int mysql_errno([`*`connection`*`])`

This function returns the error code number for the last MySQL statement issued. The function returns 0 if there was no error. Another MySQL connection identifier may be given as an argument for the function. Here is an example:

```
...
$sql_stmnt = "SELECT * FROM workreqs";
$results = mysql_db_query('workrequests', $sql_stmnt)
           or die (mysql_errno( ) . " " . mysql_error( ) . "\n");
$count = mysql_num_rows($results);
print "Number of Rows Found:  $count \n";
...
```

I've intentionally typed the name of the table incorrectly in the preceding SQL statement. It should read *workreq* and not *workreqs*. Here is the result of this script:

```
1146 Table 'workrequests.workreqs' doesn't exist
```

Notice that the error number code is given by `mysql_errno( )` and the message that follows it is given by `mysql_error( )`, which provides an error message rather than a code.

mysql_error( )

`string mysql_error([connection])`

This function returns the error message for the last MySQL statement issued. It returns nothing if there was no error. Another MySQL connection identifier may be given as an argument for the function. See `mysql_errno( )` earlier in this section for an example of how `mysql_error( )` may be used.

mysql_escape_string( )

`string mysql_escape_string(string)`

This function returns the string given with special characters preceded by backslashes so that they are protected from being interpreted by the SQL interpreter. This function is used in conjunction with `mysql_query( )` to help make SQL statements safe. However, it is deprecated, so use `mysql_real_escape_string( )` instead. Here is an example:

```
...
$clientid = '1000';
$description = "Can't connect to network.";
$description = mysql_escape_string($description);
$sql_stmnt = "INSERT INTO workreq
              (date, clientid, description)
              VALUES(NOW( ), '$clientid', '$description')";
mysql_query($sql_stmnt);
...
```

The string contained in the `$description` variable contains an apostrophe, which would normally cause the SQL statement to fail because the related value in the SQL statement is surrounded by single quotes. Without `mysql_escape_string( )`, an apostrophe would be mistaken for a single quote, which has special meaning in MySQL.

mysql_fetch_array( )

`array mysql_fetch_array(results[, type])`

This function returns an array containing a row of data from an SQL query results set. Data is also stored in an associative array containing the field names as the keys for the values. Field names are derived from either column names or aliases. To choose whether only an array or only an associative array is returned, or both are returned, you may give one of the following as a second argument to the function, respectively: `MYSQL_NUM`, `MYSQL_ASSOC`, or `MYSQL_BOTH`. This function is typically used with a loop statement to work through a results set containing multiple rows of data. When there are no more rows to return, it returns false, which typically triggers the end of the loop. Here is an example:

```
...
$sql_stmnt = "SELECT wrid, clientid, description
              FROM workreq";
$results = mysql_query($sql_stmnt);
while($row = mysql_fetch_array($results)) {
  print "WR-" . $row[0] . ", Client-" .
        $row['clientid'] . " " . $row['description'] . "\n";
}
...
```

Notice that both methods of extracting data from the row fetched are used here: the work request number is retrieved using a standard array data retrieval method (i.e., placing the index number of the array element in square brackets); and the other pieces of data are retrieved using the associative array method (i.e., placing the field name and the key name in brackets).

mysql_fetch_assoc( )

`array mysql_fetch_assoc(`*`results`*`)`

This function returns an associative array containing a row of data from an SQL query results set. Field names of the results set are used as the keys for the values. Field names are derived from column names unless an alias is employed in the SQL statement. This function is typically used with a loop statement to work through a results set containing multiple rows of data. When there are no more rows to return, it returns false, which will end a loop statement. This function is synonymous with `mysql_fetch_array( )` using `MYSQL_ASSOC` as its second argument. Here is an example:

```
...
$sql_stmnt = "SELECT wr_id, client_id, description
              FROM workreq";
$results = mysql_query($sql_stmnt);
while($row = mysql_fetch_assoc($results)) {
  print "WR-" . $row['wr_id'] . ", Client-" .
        $row['client_id'] . " " . $row['description'] . "\n";
}
...
```

This loop is identical to the one for `mysql_fetch_array( )` except that, with the `mysql_fetch_assoc( )` function, the index for a standard array cannot be used to get the work request number—so the `wr_id` key for the associative array stored in `$row` has to be used instead.

mysql_fetch_field( )

`object mysql_fetch_field(`*`results`*`[, `*`offset`*`])`

This function returns an object containing information about a field from a results set given. Information is given on the first field of a results set waiting to be returned; the function can be called repeatedly to report on each field of a `SELECT` statement. A number may be given as the second argument to skip one or more fields. The elements of the object are as follows: `name` for column name; `table` for table name; `max_length` for the maximum length of the column; `not_null`, which has a value of 1 if the column cannot have a NULL value; `primary_key`, which has a value of 1 if the column is a primary key column; `unique_key`, which returns 1 if it's a unique key; `multiple_key`, which returns 1 if it's not unique; `numeric`, which returns 1 if it's a numeric data type; `blob`, which returns 1 if it's a `BLOB` data type; `type`, which returns the data type; `unsigned`, which returns 1 if the column is unsigned; and `zerofill`, which returns 1 if it's a zero-fill column. Here is an example:

```
...
$sql_stmnt = "SELECT * FROM workreq LIMIT 1";
$results = mysql_query($sql_stmnt);
```

```
$num_fields = mysql_num_fields($results);
for ($index = 0; $index < $num_fields; $index++) {
  $info = mysql_fetch_field($results, $index);
  print "$info->name  ($info->type $info->max_length) \n";
}
...
```

Here, all of the columns for one record are selected and placed in `$results`. The number of fields is determined by `mysql_num_fields( )` for the `for` statement that follows. The `for` statement loops through each field of the results set and uses `mysql_fetch_field( )` to return the field information in the form of an object. Then the example prints out the name of the field, the data type, and the maximum length. Here are the first few lines of the output from this script:

```
wr_id  (int 4)
wr_date  (date 10)
clientid  (string 4)
...
```

mysql_fetch_lengths( )

`array mysql_fetch_lengths(`*`results`*`)`

This function returns an array containing the length of each field of a results set from a MySQL query. Here is an example:

```
...
$sql_stmnt = "SELECT wr_id, description, instructions
              FROM workreq";
$results = mysql_query($sql_stmnt);
while($row = mysql_fetch_object($results)) {
  $length = mysql_fetch_lengths($results);
  print "$row->wr_id: description: $length[1],
         instructions: $length[2] \n";
}
...
```

In this example, each work request number is selected, along with the brief description and the lengthy instructions. Looping through each row that is retrieved as an object with `mysql_fetch_object( )` and a `while` statement, the code determines the length of the data for all three fields with `mysql_fetch_lengths( )` and places them in an array. Within the statement block of the `while` statement, the value of the `wr_id` field is extracted, and the lengths of the `description` field and the `instructions` field are pulled out of the `$length` array using the relative index number for each. Here are a few lines of output from this script:

```
...
5753: description: 26, instructions: 254
5754: description: 25, instructions: 156
5755: description: 25, instructions: 170
```

mysql_fetch_object( )

`object mysql_fetch_object(result)`

This function returns a row of data as an object from the results set given. The function returns false if there are no more rows to return. The field names of the results set are used to retrieve data from the object returned. Here is an example:

```
...
$sql_stmnt = "SELECT count(wrid) AS wr_count, client_name
              FROM workreq, clients
              WHERE status <> 'done'
              AND workreq.clientid = clients.clientid
              GROUP BY workreq.clientid
              ORDER BY wr_count DESC";
$results = mysql_query($sql_stmnt);
while($row = mysql_fetch_object($results)) {
  print $row->client_name . " " . $row->wr_count . "\n";
}
...
```

This script is written to generate a list of clients that have outstanding work requests and to give a count of the number of requests for each, in descending order. Within the `while` statement that follows, each row of the results set is processed with `mysql_fetch_object( )`. The value of each element of the object created for each row is displayed by calls using the field names, not the column names. For instance, to get the data from the field with the number of work requests, you use the `wr_count` alias. Here are a few lines from the output of this script:

```
...
Bracey Logistics 3
Neumeyer Consultants  2
Farber Investments 4
```

mysql_fetch_row( )

`array mysql_fetch_row(results)`

This function returns an array containing a row of data from a results set given. This function is typically used in conjunction with a loop statement to retrieve each row of data in a results set. Each loop retrieves the next row. Individual fields appear in the array in the order they appeared in the `SELECT` statement, and can be retrieved by an array index. The loop ends when rows are used up because the function returns NULL. Here is an example:

```
...
$sql_stmnt = "SELECT wr_id, client_name, description
              FROM workreq, clients
              WHERE workreq.clientid = clients.clientid";
$results = mysql_query($sql_stmnt);
while($row = mysql_fetch_row($results)) {
  print "WR-$row[0]: $row[1] - $row[2] \n";
}
...
```

To get the data for each element of the `$row` array created by `mysql_fetch_row( )`, you must know the number corresponding to each element. The index of the elements begins with 0, so `$row[0]` is the first element and, in this case, the work request number because *wr_id* was the first field requested by the `SELECT` statement. Here's one line of the output from this script:

```
WR-5755: Farber Investments - Can't connect to Internet.
```

mysql_field_flags( )

`string mysql_field_flags(`*`results, offset`*`)`

This function returns the field flags for a field of a results set given. See `mysql_fetch_field( )` earlier in this chapter for a description of the flags. Specify the desired field through the offset in the second argument. Here is an example:

```
...
$sql_stmnt = "SELECT * FROM workreq LIMIT 1";
$results = mysql_query($sql_stmnt);
$num_fields = mysql_num_fields($results);
for ($index = 0; $index < $num_fields; $index++) {
  $field_name = mysql_field_name($results, $index);
  $flags = explode(' ', mysql_field_flags($results, $index));
  print "$field_name \n";
  print_r($flags);
  print "\n\n";
}
...
```

After retrieving one row as a sampler—using a `for` statement and the number of fields in the results set—this example determines the field name with `mysql_field_name( )` and the flags for each field using `mysql_field_flags( )`. The `mysql_field_flags( )` function assembles the flags into an array in which the data is separated by spaces. By using the `explode( )` PHP function, you can retrieve the elements of the array without having to know the number of elements, and they are stored in `$flags`. Next, `print_r( )` displays the field name and prints out the flags. Here is the output of the script for the first field:

```
wrid
Array
(
    [0] => not_null
    [1] => primary_key
    [2] => auto_increment
)
```

mysql_field_len( )

`int mysql_field_len(`*`results, index`*`)`

This function returns the length from a field of the results set given. Specify the desired field via the index in the second argument. Here is an example:

```
...
$sql_stmnt = "SELECT * FROM workreq LIMIT 1";
$results = mysql_query($sql_stmnt);
```

```
$num_fields = mysql_num_fields($results);
for ($index = 0; $index < $num_fields; $index++) {
  $field_name = mysql_field_name($results, $index);
  print "$field_name - " .
         mysql_field_len($results, $index) . "\n";
}
...
```

Here, one row has been retrieved from a table and `mysql_num_fields( )` determines the number of fields in the results set. With a `for` statement, each field is processed to determine its name using `mysql_field_name( )` and the length of each field is ascertained with `mysql_field_len( )`. Here are a few lines of the output of this script:

```
wrid - 9
wr_date - 10
clientid - 4
...
```

mysql_field_name( )

`string mysql_field_name(`*`results, index`*`)`

This function returns the name of a field from the results set given. To specify a particular field, the index of the field in the results set is given as the second argument—0 being the first field. Here is an example:

```
...
$sql_stmnt = "SELECT * FROM workreq LIMIT 1";
$results = mysql_query($sql_stmnt);
$num_fields = mysql_num_fields($results);
for ($index = 0; $index < $num_fields; $index++) {
  $field_name = mysql_field_name($results, $index);
  print $field_name . "\n";
}
...
```

The SQL statement here selects one row from the table. Then `mysql_num_fields( )` examines the results of the query and determines the number of fields. The loop processes each field, starting with field 0 using the `mysql_field_name( )` function to extract each field name. The second argument is changed as the `$index` variable is incremented with each loop.

mysql_field_seek( )

`bool mysql_field_seek(`*`results, index`*`)`

Use this function to change the pointer to a different field from the results set given. The amount by which to offset the pointer is given as the second argument. Here is an example:

```
...
$sql_stmnt = "SELECT * FROM workreq LIMIT 1";
$results = mysql_db_query('workrequests', $sql_stmnt,
                          $connection);
$num_fields = mysql_num_fields($results);
mysql_field_seek($results, $num_fields - 3);
```

```
for ($index = 0; $index < 3; $index++) {
  $field = mysql_fetch_field($results, $index);
  print "$field->name \n";
}
...
```

This example determines the number of fields and their values, and then gives the result as the second argument of the `mysql_field_seek( )` function to choose the last three fields of the results set. The `for` statement prints out the field names of the last three fields using `mysql_fetch_field( )`.

mysql_field_table( )

`string mysql_field_table(`*`results, index`*`)`

This function returns the name of the table that contains a particular field from the results set given. An offset for the field is given as the second argument. This is useful for a results set derived from an SQL statement involving multiple tables. Here is an example:

```
...
$sql_stmnt = "SELECT wrid, client_name, description
              FROM workreq, clients
              WHERE workreq.clientid = clients.clientid";
$results = mysql_query($sql_stmnt);
$num_fields = mysql_num_fields($results);
for ($index = 0; $index < $num_fields; $index++) {
  $table = mysql_field_table($results, $index);
  $field = mysql_field_name($results, $index);
  print "$table.$field  \n";
}
...
```

The SQL statement here selects columns from two different tables. Using `mysql_field_table( )` inside of the `for` statement, the code determines the name of the table from which each field comes. The `mysql_field_name( )` function gets the field's name. Here are the results of this script:

```
workreq.wrid
clients.client_name
workreq.description
```

mysql_field_type( )

`string mysql_field_type(`*`results, index`*`)`

This function returns the column data type for a field from the results set given. To specify a particular field, give an offset as the second argument. Here is an example:

```
...
$sql_stmnt = "SELECT * FROM workreq LIMIT 1";
$results = mysql_query($sql_stmnt);
$num_fields = mysql_num_fields($results);
for ($index = 0; $index < $num_fields; $index++) {
  $name = mysql_field_name($results, $index);
  $type = mysql_field_type($results, $index);
  print "$name - $type \n";
```

```
    }
    ...
```

In this example, after one row of data is selected as a sample, `mysql_num_fields( )` determines the number of rows in the results set so that a counter limit may be set up (`$num_fields`) in the `for` statement that follows. Within the `for` statement, the name of the field is extracted using `mysql_field_name( )` and the data type using `mysql_field_type( )`. Here are a few lines of the output of this script:

```
wrid - int
wr_date - date
clientid - string
...
```

mysql_free_result( )

`bool mysql_free_result(results)`

Use this function to free the memory containing the results set given. The function returns true if it's successful, and false if it's unsuccessful. Here is an example:

```
...
mysql_free_result($results);
mysql_close( );
?>
```

There's not much to this function. It merely flushes out the data for the location in memory referenced by the variable given.

mysql_get_client_info( )

`string mysql_get_client_info( )`

This function returns the library version of the MySQL client for the current connection. Here is an example:

```
...
$info = mysql_get_client_info( );
print "Client Version:  $info \n";
...
```

Here are the results of this script on one of my computers:

```
Client Version:  3.23.40
```

mysql_get_host_info( )

`string mysql_get_host_info([connection])`

This function returns information on the host for the current connection to MySQL. You may give an identifier to retrieve information on a host for a different connection. Here is an example:

```
...
$info = mysql_get_client_info( );
print "Connection Info:  $info \n";
...
```

Here are the results of this script when you run it on the host containing the server:

```
Connection Info:  127.0.0.1 via TCP/IP
```

mysql_get_proto_info( )

`int mysql_get_proto_info([connection])`

This function returns the protocol version for the current connection to MySQL. You may give an identifier to retrieve the protocol version for a different connection. Here is an example:

```
...
$info = mysql_get_proto_info( );
print "Protocol Version:  $info \n";
...
```

Here are the results of running this script:

```
Protocol Version:  10
```

mysql_get_server_info( )

`string mysql_get_server_info([connection])`

This function returns the MySQL server version for the current connection to MySQL. You may give an identifier to retrieve the server version for a different connection. Here is an example:

```
...
$info = mysql_get_server_info( );
print "MySQL Server Version:  $info \n";
...
```

Here are the results of running this script:

```
MySQL Server Version:  4.1.1-alpha-standard
```

mysql_info( )

`string mysql_info([connection])`

This function returns information on the last query for the current connection to MySQL. You may give an identifier to retrieve information on a query for a different connection. Here is an example:

```
...
$sql_stmnt = "SELECT * FROM workreq";
$results = mysql_query($sql_stmnt);
print mysql_info( );
...
```

Here are the results of running this script:

```
String format: 528 rows in set
```

mysql_insert_id( )

`int mysql_insert_id([connection])`

This function returns the identification number of the primary key of the last record inserted using `INSERT` for the current connection, provided the column utilizes `AUTO_INCREMENT` and the value was not manually set. Otherwise, it returns 0. Here is an example:

```
...
$sql_stmnt = "INSERT INTO workreq
              (date, clientid, description)
              VALUES(NOW( ), '1000', 'Network Problem')";
mysql_query($sql_stmnt);
$wrid = mysql_insert_id( );
print "Work Request ID:  $wrid \n";
...
```

Here is the output of this script:

```
Work Request ID:  5755
```

mysql_list_dbs( )

`resource mysql_list_dbs([connection])`

This function returns a pointer to a results set containing the names of databases hosted by the MySQL server. The `mysql_db_name( )` function or any function that extracts data from a results set may be used to retrieve individual database names. Here is an example:

```
...
$databases = mysql_list_dbs( );
$dbs = mysql_num_rows($databases);
for($index = 0; $index < $dbs; $index++) {
    print mysql_db_name($databases, $index) . "\n";
}
...
```

mysql_list_fields( )

`resource mysql_list_fields(database, table[, connection])`

This function returns a results set containing information about the columns of a table given for a database specified. The `mysql_field_flags( )`, `mysql_field_len( )`, `mysql_field_name( )`, and `mysql_field_type( )` functions can be used to extract information from the results set. An identifier may be given as a third argument to the function to retrieve information for a different MySQL connection. This function is deprecated, though. Use the `mysql_query( )` function with the `SHOW COLUMNS` statement instead. Here is an example:

```
...
$fields = mysql_list_fields('workrequests', 'workreq');
$num_fields = mysql_num_fields($fields);
for ($index = 0; $index < $num_fields; $index++) {
  print mysql_field_name($fields, $index) . "\n";
```

```
}
...
```

After connecting to MySQL, in the first line the example uses `mysql_list_fields( )` to retrieve a list of column names from the database and table given as arguments. To assist the `for` statement that follows, the `mysql_num_fields( )` function determines the number of fields in the results set, returning a field for each column. Then PHP loops through the `for` statement for all the fields and displays the name of each column using `mysql_field_name( )`. Here are a few lines from the output of this script:

```
wrid
wr_date
clientid
...
```

mysql_list_processes( )

`resource mysql_list_processes([connection])`

This function returns a results set containing information on the server threads for the current connection: the connection identifier, the hostname, the database name, and the command. You may give an identifier to retrieve information for a different connection. Here is an example:

```
...
$processes = mysql_list_processes($connection);
while ($row = mysql_fetch_array($processes)){
   print "$row['Id'], $row['Host'],
          $row['db'], $row['Command']";
}
...
```

mysql_list_tables( )

`resource mysql_list_tables(database[, connection])`

This function returns a results set containing a list of tables for *database*. You may give an identifier as a second argument to retrieve information for a different connection. The `mysql_tablename( )` function can be used to extract the names of the tables from the results set of this function. This function is deprecated, though. Use the `mysql_query( )` function with the `SHOW TABLES` statement instead. Here is an example:

```
...
$tables = mysql_list_tables('workrequests');
$num_tables = mysql_num_rows($tables);
for($index = 0; $index < $num_tables ; $index++) {
    print mysql_tablename($tables, $index) . "\n";
}
...
```

The first line shown here gives the database name as an argument for the `mysql_list_tables( )` function. The results are stored in the `$tables` variable. Next, the number of rows and the number of tables found are determined and stored in `$num_tables`. Using a `for` statement to loop through the list of tables in the results set, each table name is printed out with the assistance of `mysql_tablename( )`. The second argument of `mysql_tablename( )` is adjusted incrementally by using the `$index` variable, which will increase from 0 to the value of the `$num_tables` variable.

mysql_num_fields( )

`int mysql_num_fields(results)`

This function returns the number of fields of the results set given. Here is an example:

```
...
$fields = mysql_list_fields('workrequests', 'workreq');
$num_fields = mysql_num_fields($fields);
for ($index = 0; $index < $num_fields; $index++) {
  print mysql_field_name($fields, $index) . "\n";
}
...
```

As this example shows, `mysql_num_fields( )` can be useful in conjunction with other functions. Here, a list of fields for a table is retrieved using `mysql_list_fields( )`. In order to help the code display the names of the fields using a `for` statement, we need to determine the number of fields. The `mysql_num_fields( )` function is handy for figuring out this bit of information.

mysql_num_rows( )

`int mysql_num_rows(results)`

This function returns the number of rows in the results set given, generated by issuing a `SELECT` statement. For other types of SQL statements that don't return a results set, use `mysql_affected_rows( )`. Here is an example:

```
...
$sql_stmnt = "SELECT * FROM workreq";
$results = mysql_query($sql_stmnt);
$count = mysql_num_rows($results);
print "Number of Rows Found:  $count \n";
...
```

mysql_pconnect( )

`resource mysql_pconnect(server[:port|socket], user, password[, flags])`

Use this function to open a persistent connection to MySQL. The connection will not end with the closing of the PHP script that opened the connection, and it cannot be closed with `mysql_close( )`. The first argument of the function is the server name. If none is specified, *localhost* is assumed. A port may be specified with the server name (separated by a colon) or a socket along with its path. If no port is given, port 3306 is assumed. The username is given as the second argument and the user's password as the third. If you attempt a connection that uses the same parameters as a previous one, it uses the existing connection instead of creating a new connection. As an optional fourth argument, you can give client flags for the MySQL constants `MYSQL_CLIENT_COMPRESS`, `MYSQL_CLIENT_IGNORE_SPACE`, `MYSQL_CLIENT_INTERACTIVE`, and `MYSQL_CLIENT_SSL`. The function returns a connection identifier if it's successful; it returns false if it's unsuccessful.

Here is an example:

```
mysql_pconnect('localhost', 'russell', 'dyer');
```

mysql_ping( )

`bool mysql_ping([connection])`

Use this function to determine whether the current MySQL connection is still open. If it's not open, the function attempts to reestablish the connection. If the connection is open or reopened, the function returns true. If the connection is not open and cannot be reestablished, it returns false. You may give an identifier to ping a different connection. Here is an example:

```
...
$ping = mysql_ping($connection);
print "Info:  $ping \n";
...
```

This function is available as of version 4.3 of PHP.

mysql_query( )

`resource mysql_query(sql_statement[, connection])`

Use this function to execute an SQL statement given. You may give an identifier as a second argument to query through a different connection. The function returns false if the query is unsuccessful. For SQL statements not designed to return a results set (e.g., `INSERT`), the function returns trueif successful. If not successful, it returns a reference to a results set. Here is an example:

```
...
$sql_stmnt = "SELECT wrid, client_name, description
              FROM workreq, clients
              WHERE workreq.clientid = clients.clientid";
$results = mysql_query($sql_stmnt, $connection);
while($row = mysql_fetch_row($results)) {
  print "WR-$row[0]: $row[1] - $row[2] \n";
}
...
```

Here's one line from the output of this script:

```
WR-5755: Farber Investments - Can't connect to network.
```

mysql_real_escape_string( )

`string mysql_real_escape_string(string[, link])`

This function returns the string given with special characters preceded by backslashes so that they are protected from being interpreted by the SQL interpreter. Use this in conjunction with the `mysql_query( )` function to make SQL statements safe. This function does not escape `%` or `_` characters, but it does take into account the character set of the connection. A different connection may be specified as the second argument to the function. This function is similar to `mysql_escape_string( )`, but it escapes a string based on the character set for the current connection.

mysql_result( )

`string mysql_result(`*`results`*`, `*`row`*`[, `*`field|offset`*`])`

This function returns the data from one field of a *row* from ***results***. Normally, this statement returns the next row and can be reused to retrieve results sequentially. As a third argument, you can give either a field name (i.e., the column or alias name) or an offset to change the pointer for the function. This function is typically used in conjunction with a loop statement to process each field of a results set. Here is an example:

```
...
$sql_stmnt = "SELECT client_name FROM clients";
$results = mysql_query($sql_stmnt);
$num_rows = mysql_num_rows($results);
for ($index = 0; $index < $num_rows; $index++) {
   print mysql_result($results, $index) . "\n";
}
...
```

This script queries the database for a list of client names. Using the `mysql_num_row( )` function, the number of rows contained in the results set is determined. Using that bit of data, a `for` statement is constructed to loop through the results set using `mysql_result( )` to extract one field of data per row. Otherwise, a function such as `mysql_fetch_array( )` would have to be used in conjunction with the usual method of retrieving data from an array (e.g., `$row[0]`).

mysql_select_db( )

`bool mysql_select_db(`*`database`*`[, `*`connection`*`])`

This function sets the database to be used by the current MySQL connection, but you also can use it to set the database for another connection by supplying it as a second argument. The function returns true if it's successful, and false if it's unsuccessful. Here is an example:

```
...
$connection = mysql_connect('localhost','tina','muller');
mysql_select_db('workrequests', $connection);
...
```

mysql_set_charset( )

`bool mysql_set_charset(`*`char_set`*`[, `*`connection`*`])`

This function sets the default character set for the current connection to MySQL, or for a connection given with the function. For a list of acceptable character set names that may be given as an argument to this function, execute `SHOW CHARACTER SET;` from the `mysql` client. Here is an example:

```
...
mysql_set_charset('utf8', $connection);
...
```

mysql_stat( )

`string mysql_stat([connection])`

This function returns the status of the server for the current MySQL connection, but you also can use it to get the status for another connection. The function returns—as a space-separated list—the flush tables, open tables, queries, queries per second, threads, and uptime for the server. This function is available as of version 4.3 of PHP. Here is an example:

```
...
$connection = mysql_connect('localhost',
                            'jacinta', 'richardson');
$info = explode(' ', mysql_stat($connection));
print_r($info);
...
```

The `explode( )` PHP function lists the elements of the space-separated values contained in the associative array generated by `mysql_stat( )` along with their respective keys.

mysql_tablename( )

`string mysql_tablename(results, index)`

This function returns the table name for a particular table in the results set given by `mysql_list_tables( )`. You can specify an index to retrieve a particular element of the results set. This function is deprecated, though. Use the `mysql_query( )` function with the `SHOW TABLES` statement instead. Here is an example:

```
...
$tables = mysql_list_tables('workrequests');
$tbs = mysql_num_rows($tables);
for($index = 0; $index < $tbs; $index++) {
    print mysql_tablename($tables, $index) . "\n";
}
...
```

mysql_thread_id( )

`int mysql_thread_id([connection])`

This function returns the thread identification number for the current MySQL connection. You may give an identifier for another connection. This function is available as of version 4.3 of PHP. Here is an example:

```
...
$connection = mysql_connect('127.0.0.1', 'russell', 'spenser');
$info = mysql_thread_id($connection);
print "Thread ID:  $info \n";
...
```

mysql_unbuffered_query( )

`resource mysql_unbuffered_query(`*`sql_statement`*`[, `*`connection`*`])`

Use this function to execute an SQL statement given without buffering the results so that you can retrieve the data without having to wait for the results set to be completed. You may give an identifier as a second argument to interface with a different connection. The function returns false if the query is unsuccessful. For SQL statements that do not return a results set based on their nature (e.g., `INSERT`), the function returns true when successful. Use this function with care because an enormous results set could overwhelm the program's allocated memory. Here is an example:

```
...
$sql_stmnt = "SELECT wrid, client_name, description
              FROM workreq, clients
              WHERE workreq.clientid = clients.clientid";
$results = mysql_unbuffered_query($sql_stmnt, $connection);
while($row = mysql_fetch_row($results)) {
  print "WR-$row[0]: $row[1] - $row[2] \n";
}
...
```

There's no difference in the syntax of `mysql_unbuffered_query( )` and `mysql_query( )`, nor in the handling of the results. The only differences in this function are the speed for large databases and the fact that functions such as `mysql_num_row( )` and `mysql_data_seek( )` cannot be used, because the results set is not buffered and therefore cannot be analyzed by these functions.

V

Appendixes

This part of the book contains quick-reference information that applies to many of the chapters and is often desired in a compact format by a programmer or administrator.

A
Data Types

When a table is created using the `CREATE TABLE` statement, every column in a table must be declared as one of the data types supported by MySQL. A column in a table can be added or changed using the `ALTER TABLE` statement. Data types can be organized in three basic groups: numeric, date and time, and string. This appendix provides a listing of data types along with their limitations.

Numeric Data Types

Standard SQL numeric data types are allowed: accurate numeric data types (i.e., `BIGINT`, `DECIMAL`, `INTEGER`, `MEDIUMINT`, `NUMERIC`, `SMALLINT`, and `TINYINT`) and approximate numeric data types (i.e., `DOUBLE` and `FLOAT`). For all numeric data types, you can use the `UNSIGNED` and `ZEROFILL` flags depending on your needs. If `UNSIGNED` is omitted, `SIGNED` is assumed. A numeric data type has different allowable ranges based on whether it's `SIGNED` or `UNSIGNED`. The `ZEROFILL` flag instructs MySQL to pad the unused spaces to the left of a number with zeros. For example, a column with a data type set to `INT(10)` using `ZEROFILL` will display the number 5 as 0000000005. If the `ZEROFILL` flag is used, `UNSIGNED` is assumed for the column. When subtracting values where one is `UNSIGNED`, the results will become `UNSIGNED`.

For several of the numeric data types, you can specify a width for displaying. This number cannot exceed 255. The display width is a factor only when `ZEROFILL` is used for the column. You may also specify the number of digits allowed for the decimals, including the decimal point.

Approximate numeric data types store floating-point numbers such as fractions where an approximation must be made. For instance, an accurate number, per se, cannot be stored for 1/3 because the decimal point for 3 continues on endlessly. MySQL provides two approximate numeric data types: `FLOAT` and `DOUBLE` with their synonyms.

Following is a list of numeric data types. They're not organized alphabetically; instead, they're organized in ascending order based on the size of numeric values they can contain, with the column data types that may be used for approximate numbers listed last.

BIT

BIT[(*width*)]

This is a bit-field data column type. With this column you can specify the maximum number of bits. It accepts 1 to 64. If no width is given, 1 bit is assumed. You can use this column to store binary data (i.e., data composed of 1s and 0s). You can also use this column in conjunction with functions like `BIN( )`. Here is an example with a column that has a data type of `BIT(8)`:

```
SELECT server_id
FROM servers
WHERE status = BIT(4);
```

This statement will return rows where the `status` column has a value of `00000100`, which is the binary equivalent of 4.

TINYINT

TINYINT[(*width*)] [UNSIGNED] [ZEROFILL]

This data column type can be used for tiny integers. The signed range can be from –128 to 127; unsigned can be from 0 to 255. The default if no width is given is 4. This column type can be useful for a simple logical column. For example, `TINYINT(1)` can be used for a column in which you only want a value of 1 or 0, `yes` or `no`. You could just as easily use `BOOLEAN`, though.

BOOL, BOOLEAN

BOOL

This data column type, `BOOL`, is synonymous with `BOOLEAN` and `TINYINT(1)`. In fact, if you set a column to this type and then use the `DESCRIBE` statement to see the description of the column, it will show it as a `TINYINT(1)`. It can be useful for a simple logical column in which you want only a true or false value. For example, if a column labeled `active` was a `BOOLEAN` type, you could do something like the following:

```
SELECT client_name AS 'Client',
IF(active, 'Active', 'Inactive') AS Status
FROM clients;
```

This statement will show each client name in the table with the words `Active` or `Inactive` next to each name. This works because the `IF( )` function checks for a value of 1 or 0 for the value given; it returns the second parameter given if the value is 1, the third parameter if the value is 0.

SMALLINT

`SMALLINT[(width)] [UNSIGNED] [ZEROFILL]`

Use this data column type for small integer values. The signed range can be from –32,768 to 32,767; unsigned can be from 0 to 65,535. The default if no width is given is 6.

MEDIUMINT

`MEDIUMINT[(width)] [UNSIGNED] [ZEROFILL]`

This data column type is for integer values of medium size. The signed range can be from –8,388,608 to 8,388,607; unsigned can be from 0 to 16,777,215. The default if no width is given is 9.

INT, INTEGER

`INT[(width)] [UNSIGNED] [ZEROFILL]`

This is probably the most common numeric data column type used. The signed range can be from –2,147,483,648 to 2,147,483,647; unsigned can be from 0 to 4,294,967,295. The default if no width is given is 11. `INTEGER` is a synonym for this data type.

BIGINT, SERIAL

`BIGINT[(width)] [UNSIGNED] [ZEROFILL]`

This data column type is for integer values of a large size. The signed range can be from –9,223,372,036,854,775,808 to 9,223,372,036,854,775,807; unsigned can be from 0 to 18,446,744,073,709,551,615. The default if no width is given is 20. `SERIAL` is a synonym for this data type, but with specific column options: `BIGINT`, `UNSIGNED`, `NOT NULL`, `AUTO_INCREMENT`, and `UNIQUE`.

FLOAT

`FLOAT[(width, decimals)|(bit_precision)] [UNSIGNED] [ZEROFILL]`

You can specify a level of precision for this data type. It may be from 0 to 24 for single-precision floating-point numbers, and from 25 to 53 for double-precision floating-point numbers. To make it ODBC-compatible, you can use the second syntax that specifies the precision only in bits. If you don't give a precision with `FLOAT`, a single-precision floating point is assumed. If the SQL mode for the server has the `REAL_AS_FLOAT` option enabled, `REAL` is a synonym for `FLOAT`. This is set with the `--sql-mode` option when starting the server.

DOUBLE, DOUBLE PRECISION

`DOUBLE[(width, decimals)] [UNSIGNED] [ZEROFILL]`

Use this data column type for approximate, floating-point numbers. The width given is the maximum width of the total digits—on both sides of the decimal place, not including the decimal point. The decimals given are the number of decimals allowed and the number for which it zero-fills. For example, a column type setting of `DOUBLE(4,2)` that is given a value of 123.4 will return a warning and store the value as 99.99, the maximum amount given the width. If the same column is given a value of 12.3, it won't generate any warnings and it will store the value as 12.30.

The signed range of values can be from –1.7976931348623157E+308 to –2.2250738585072014E–308; the unsigned range from 2.2250738585072014E–308 to 1.7976931348623157E+308. Usually these limits aren't possible due to the hardware and operating system limits of the server. The accuracy of this data type is up to about 15 decimal places.

With this data type, if `UNSIGNED` is specified, negative values are not allowed. If the SQL mode for the server does not have the `REAL_AS_FLOAT` option enabled, `REAL` is a synonym for `DOUBLE`.

DEC, DECIMAL, FIXED, NUMERIC

`DECIMAL[(`*`width`*`[, `*`decimals`*`])] [UNSIGNED] [ZEROFILL]`

This data column type is similar to `FLOAT`, but it's used for accurate, fixed-point numbers. When calculating with a `DECIMAL` column, it has a 65-digit level of precision. The width given is the maximum width of the total digits—on both sides of the decimal place, not including the decimal point or the negative sign if a negative number. The decimals given are the number of decimals allowed and the number for which it zero-fills. For example, a column type setting of `DECIMAL(4,2)` that is given a value of 123.4 will return a warning and store the value as 99.99, the maximum amount given the width. If the same column is given a value of 12.3, it won't generate any warnings and will store the value as 12.30. If `UNSIGNED` is used with `DECIMAL`, negative values are not allowed.

MySQL stores numbers in `DECIMAL` columns as strings. Therefore, numbers outside the maximum numeric range for this data type may be stored in a `DECIMAL` column. This data type may be retrieved and displayed as a string, but in a numeric context (i.e., as part of a calculation), it cannot exceed the values shown in the table.

Date and Time Data Types

There are a few column data types for storing date and time values. They are listed in Table A-1. The table also lists the valid ranges for each data type. If a value that is not permitted or that is outside the acceptable range for the data type is inserted, zeros are used instead. You can override this feature by starting the server with `--sql-mode='ALLOW_INVALID_DATES`. As of version 5.0.2 of MySQL, warnings are generated when inserting invalid dates or times. For dates that are inserted with only 2 digits for the year, values from 00 to 69 are assumed to be in the 21st century. For years from 70 to 99, they are assumed to be in the 20th century.

Table A-1. Date and time data types

Data type	Format	Range
`DATE`	`yyyy-mm-dd`	1000-01-01 to 9999-12-31
`DATETIME`	`yyyy-mm-dd hh:mm:ss`	1000-01-01 00:00:00 to 9999-12-31 00:00:00

Data type	Format	Range
TIMESTAMP	yyyy-mm-dd hh:mm:ss	1970-01-01 00:00:00 to 2037-12-31 23:59:59
TIME	hh:mm:ss	–838:59:59 to 838:59:59
YEAR[(2|4)]	yy or yyyy	1970 to 2069, or 1901 to 2155

Times values may be given either as a string or numerically. To give them as a string, you can enter a value as `d hh:mm:ss.f`. In this format, `d` stands for the number of days, and has an allowable range of 0 to 34. The `f` stands for a fractional number of seconds. This value will not be stored, though. The ability to store fractional seconds is expected to be added in future releases of MySQL. You don't have to specify values for all elements of a time. Instead, you can enter a time value using one of these formats: `hh:mm:ss.f`, `hh:mm:ss`, `hh:mm`, or just `ss`. If you want to include the number of days, you can use these formats: `d hh:mm:ss`, `d hh:mm`, or `d hh`. You can also drop the colons and just enter `hhmmss`, but you can't add minutes onto the end of that format. The data type `TIMESTAMP` stores the date and time as the number of seconds since the epoch (its earliest date allowed), but it displays this number with the format `yyyy-mm-dd hh:mm:ss`. MySQL will automatically convert a date or time to its numeric date equivalent when it is used in a numeric context, and it will convert a numeric date to a date or time. If it isn't given a date, MySQL will use a default of the current date—this is the primary difference between this column data type and `DATETIME`.

String Data Types

There are several column data types for storing strings. String data types are case-sensitive, so lowercase and uppercase letters remain unchanged when stored or retrieved. For a few of the string data types, you may specify a maximum column width. If a string is entered in a column that exceeds the width set for the column, the string will be right-truncated when stored. Binary strings are case-sensitive.

Following is a list of string data types. They're not organized alphabetically; instead, they're organized in ascending order based on the size of string values they can contain. This list also includes the width in characters or bytes for each data type.

CHAR

```
CHAR(width) [BINARY|ASCII|UNICODE] [CHARACTER SET character_set]
   [COLLATE collation]
```

The `CHAR` data type is a fixed-width column, padded with spaces to the right as needed. The spaces are not included in the results when queried. This column may be from 0 to 255 characters wide. The default if no width is given is 1. This type is synonymous with `CHARACTER`. You can also use `NATIONAL CHARACTER` or `NCHAR` to indicate that a predefined national character set is to be used. Columns are right-padded with spaces when stored. `FULLTEXT` indexing and searching may be performed on a `CHAR` column with a MyISAM table.

As of version 4.1 of MySQL, you can specify the ASCII attribute for use with the CHAR data type. This will set the column to the latin1 character set. Also as of version 4.1 of MySQL, you can specify the UNICODE attribute, which will set the column to the ucs2 character set.

VARCHAR

VARCHAR(*width*) [BINARY]

The VARCHAR data type adjusts its width and does not pad the strings stored. Any trailing spaces contained in a string that is stored are removed. This column may be from 0 to 65,535 characters wide. The type of character set given can affect the number of characters given, as some require more than one byte per character (e.g., UTF-8). The default if no width is given is 1. This type is synonymous with CHARACTER VARYING. You can also use NATIONAL VARCHAR to indicate that a predefined national character set is to be used. FULLTEXT indexing and searching may be performed on a VARCHAR column with a MyISAM table.

BINARY

BINARY(*width*)

This data type stores data as binary strings, not as character strings like CHAR does. The width given is for the maximum width in bytes—this value must be specified. This data type replaces CHAR BINARY. Before version 4.1.2 of MySQL, if you added the BINARY flag after CHAR, it instructed MySQL to treat the values as byte strings for sorting and comparing. If a BINARY column is used in an expression, all elements of the expression are treated as binary.

VARBINARY

VARBINARY(*width*) [CHARACTER SET *character_set*] [COLLATE *collation*]

This data type stores data as binary strings, not as character strings like VARCHAR. The width given is for the maximum width in bytes—this value must be specified. If you want to use a character set for the column other than the default for the table, you can give one for the column. Values are sorted based on the collation of the character set for the column. This data type replaces VARCHAR BINARY. Before version 4.1.2 of MySQL, if you added the BINARY flag after VARCHAR, it instructed MySQL to treat the values as byte strings for sorting and comparing. All elements of the expression are then treated as binary.

TINYBLOB

TINYBLOB

This column data type allows for the storage of binary data. The maximum width is 255 bytes.

TINYTEXT

TINYTEXT[CHARACTER SET *character_set*] [COLLATE *collation*]

This column data type allows for the storage of text data. The maximum width is 255 bytes. If you want to use a character set for the column other than the default for the table, you can give one for the column. Values are sorted based on the collation of the character set for the column.

BLOB

`BLOB[(`*`width`*`)]`

This column data type allows for the storage of a large amount of binary data. You may give a width with this data type; the maximum is 65,535 bytes. If you attempt to store a value in a `BLOB` column that is larger than its limit, unless the server is set to SQL strict mode, the data will be truncated and a warning message will be generated. If strict mode is on, the data will be rejected and an error will be returned. A `BLOB` column cannot have a default value. For sorting data, the value given for the system variable `max_sort_length` will be used. Only the number of bytes specified by that variable for each column will be included in sorts.

TEXT

`TEXT[(`*`width`*`)] [CHARACTER SET `*`character_set`*`] [COLLATE `*`collation`*`]`

This column data type allows for the storage of a large amount of text data. You may give a width with this data type; the maximum is 65,535 bytes. If you attempt to store a value in a `TEXT` column that is larger than its limit, unless the server is set to SQL strict mode, the data will be truncated and a warning message will be generated. If strict mode is on, the data will be rejected and an error will be returned. A `TEXT` column cannot have a default value. For sorting data, the value given for the system variable `max_sort_length` will be used. Only the number of bytes specified by that variable for each column will be included in sorts. `FULLTEXT` indexing and searching may be performed on a `TEXT` column with a MyISAM table, but not on a `BLOB` column. If you want to use a character set for the column other than the default for the table, you can give one for the column. Values are sorted based on the collation of the character set for the column.

MEDIUMBLOB

`MEDIUMBLOB`

This column data type allows for the storage of a large amount of binary data. The maximum width is 16,777,215 bytes.

MEDIUMTEXT

`MEDIUMTEXT [CHARACTER SET `*`character_set`*`] [COLLATE `*`collation`*`]`

This column data type allows for the storage of a large amount of text data. The maximum width is 16,777,215 bytes. If you want to use a character set for the column other than the default for the table, you can give one for the column. Values are sorted based on the collation of the character set for the column.

LONGBLOB

```
LONGBLOB
```

This column data type allows for the storage of a large amount of binary data. The maximum width is 4 GB.

LONGTEXT

```
LONGTEXT [CHARACTER SET character_set] [COLLATE collation]
```

This column data type allows for the storage of a large amount of text data. The maximum width is 4 GB. If you want to use a character set for the column other than the default for the table, you can give one for the column. Values are sorted based on the collation of the character set for the column.

ENUM

```
ENUM('value', ...) [CHARACTER SET character_set] [COLLATE collation]
```

An `ENUM` column is one in which all possible choices are enumerated (e.g., `ENUM('yes', 'no', 'maybe')`). It's possible for it to contain a blank value (i.e., '') and NULL. If an `ENUM` column is set up to allow NULL values, NULL will be the default value. If an `ENUM` column is set up with `NOT NULL`, NULL isn't allowed and the default value becomes the first element given.

MySQL stores a numeric index of the enumerated values in the column, 1 being the first value. The values can be retrieved when the column is used in a numeric context (e.g., `SELECT col1 + 0 FROM table1;`). The reverse may be performed when entering data into a column (e.g., `UPDATE table1 SET col1 = 3;` to set the value to the third element). The column values are sorted in ascending order based on the numeric index, not on their corresponding enumerated values. If you want to use a character set for the column other than the default for the table, you can give one for the column. Values are sorted based on the collation of the character set for the column.

SET

```
SET('value', ...) [CHARACTER SET character_set] [COLLATE collation]
```

The `SET` data type is similar to `ENUM`, except that a `SET` column can hold multiple values (e.g., `UPDATE table1 SET col1 = 'a, b';`). For this data type, values may be filtered with the `FIND_IN_SET( )` function. If you want to use a character set for the column other than the default for the table, you can give one for the column. Values are sorted based on the collation of the character set for the column.

B
Operators

Operators are used in mathematical or logical operations. An operator is typically placed between two values (i.e., numbers, strings, columns, or expressions) that you want to compare or evaluate. There are four types of operators: arithmetic, relational, logical, and bitwise. This appendix provides a listing of operators grouped into these four types. This appendix also includes a list of special pattern-matching characters and constructs for regular expressions.

Arithmetic Operators

The arithmetic operators in MySQL work only on numbers, not on strings. However, MySQL will convert a string into a number when in a numeric context if it can. If it can't convert a particular string, it will return 0. Table B-1 lists the arithmetic operators allowed.

The minus sign may be used for subtracting numbers or for setting a number to a negative. The `DIV` operator converts values to integers and returns only integers. It doesn't round fractions that would be returned, but rather truncates them.

Table B-1. Arithmetic operators

Operator	Use
+	Addition
-	Subtraction and negation
*	Multiplication
/	Division
DIV	Division of integers
%	Modulo division

Relational Operators

Relational operators are used for comparing numbers and strings. If a string is compared to a number, MySQL will try to convert the string to a number. If a `TIMESTAMP` column is compared to a string or a number, MySQL will attempt to convert the string or number to a timestamp value. If it's unsuccessful at converting the other value to a timestamp, it will convert the `TIMESTAMP` column's value to a string or a number. `TIME` and `DATE` columns are compared to other values as strings. Table B-2 lists the logical and relational operators allowed in MySQL.

The minus sign may be used for subtracting numbers or for setting a number to a negative. The equals sign is used to compare two values. If one value is NULL, though, NULL will be returned. The `<=>` operator is used to compare values for equality; it's NULL-safe. For example, an SQL statement containing something like `IF(col1 <=> col2)`, where the values of both are NULL, will return 1 and not NULL.

Table B-2. Relational operators

Operator	Use
`<`	Less than
`>`	Greater than
`<=`	Less than or equal to
`>=`	Greater than or equal to
`expression` `BETWEEN n AND n`	Between first and second number
`expression` `NOT BETWEEN n AND n`	Not between first and second number
`IN (...)`	In a set
`NOT IN (...)`	Not in a set
`=`	Equal to
`<=>`	Equal to (for comparing NULL values)
`LIKE`	Matches a pattern
`SOUNDS LIKE`	Matches a sound pattern (see `SOUNDEX( )` function described in Chapter 11)
`NOT LIKE`	Doesn't match a pattern
`REGEXP`, `RLIKE`	Matches a regular expression
`NOT REGEXP`	Doesn't match a regular expression
`!=`	Not equal to
`<>`	Not equal to
`NOT`, `!`	Negates
`IS NULL`	NULL
`IS NOT NULL`	Not NULL

Logical Operators

Logical operators are used for evaluating values or expressions for true, false, or unknown. Table B-3 lists allowable logical operators.

The operators IS and IS NOT are added in version 5.0.2 of MySQL. A boolean value of TRUE, FALSE, or UNKNOWN should immediately follow these operators.

Table B-3. Logical operators

Operator	Use
AND	Logical AND
&&	Logical AND
IS *boolean*	Logical equal
IS NOT *boolean*	Logical equal
OR	Logical OR
||	Logical OR
NOT	Logical NOT
!	Logical NOT
XOR	Logical XOR

Bitwise Operators

Bitwise operators are used for comparing numbers based on their binary digits. These operators are listed in Table B-4.

The tilde (~) may be used to invert the bits of a value.

Table B-4. Bitwise operators

Operator	Use
|	OR
^	XOR
&	AND
<<	Shift bits to left
>>	Shift bits to right
~	NOT or invert bits

Regular Expressions

When using the operators REGEXP, RLIKE, and NOT REGEXP, you may need special characters and parameters to be able to search for data based on regular expressions. Table B-5 lists the special characters, and Table B-6 shows special constructs that may be used. In keeping with convention, patterns to match are given within quotes.

As an example of a regular expression used with a SELECT statement, suppose that we want to find the name of a particular student in a college's database, but we can't quite remember his last name. All we remember is that it's something like *Smith*, but it could be *Smithfield* or maybe *Smyth*. We could run an SQL statement like the following to get a list of possibilities:

```
SELECT student_id,
CONCAT(name_first, SPACE(1), name_last) AS Student
FROM students
WHERE name_last REGEXP 'Smith.*|Smyth';
```

As an example using a pattern-matching construct, suppose that we suspect there are a few student records in which the name columns contain numeric characters. Suppose also that there are some student records in which the social_security column contains characters other than numbers or dashes. We could search for them by executing an SQL statement like the following:

```
SELECT student_id, soc_sec,
CONCAT(name_first, SPACE(1), name_last) AS Student
FROM students
WHERE CONCAT(name_first, name_last) REGEXP '[[:digit:]]+'
OR soc_sec REGEXP '[[:alpha:]]+';
```

As an example of a construct using a character name, suppose that the column containing Social Security tax identification numbers (i.e., soc_sec) shouldn't contain the usual hyphen separator (i.e., 443-78-8391). We could enter an SQL statement like the following to find records with hyphens in that column:

```
SELECT student_id, soc_sec,
CONCAT(name_first, SPACE(1), name_last) AS Student
FROM students
WHERE soc_sec REGEXP '[[.hyphen.]]+';
```

To find any rows that do not specifically meet the format for the Social Security number (i.e., *nnn-nn-nnnn*), we could use this longer but more specific regular expression:

```
SELECT student_id, soc_sec,
CONCAT(name_first, SPACE(1), name_last) AS Student
FROM students
WHERE soc_sec NOT REGEXP
'[[:digit:]]{3}[[.hyphen.]]{1}[[:digit:]]{2}[[.hyphen.]]{1}[[:digit:]]{4}';
```

Notice that this statement uses the curly braces after each construct to specify the exact number of characters or digits permitted.

Table B-5. Pattern-matching characters

Character	Use
^	Matches the beginning of the string.
$	Matches the beginning of the string.
.	Matches any character, space, or line ending.
*	Matches zero or more of the characters immediately preceding.

Character	Use
+	Matches one or more of the characters immediately preceding.
?	Matches zero or one of the characters immediately preceding.
|	An OR operator; matches the characters before or after it (e.g., 'Russell|Rusty').
(*characters*)*	Matches zero or more occurrences of the sequence of characters given in parentheses.
{*number*}	Specifies the number of occurrences of the previous pattern given.
{*number*,*number*}	Specifies the minimum number of occurrences of the previous pattern given, followed by the maximum number of occurrences. If only the minimum number is omitted, 0 is assumed. If just the maximum number is omitted, unlimited is assumed.
[*x*-*x*]	Specifies a range of characters in alphabetical order (e.g., '[a-g]' for the first seven lowercase letters), or numbers in numeric sequence (e.g., '[0-9]' for all numbers).

Table B-6. Pattern-matching constructs

Construct	Use
[.*character*.]	Matches the given character or character name (e.g., backslash, carriage return, newline, tab).
[=*character*=]	Matches characters of the same class as the character given.
[[:<:]]	Matches the beginning of a word.
[[:>:]]	Matches the end of a word.
[:alnum:]	Matches alphanumeric characters.
[:alpha:]	Matches alphabetical characters.
[:blank:]	Matches a blank or whitespace characters.
[:cntrl:]	Matches control characters.
[:digit:]	Matches digits.
[:lower:]	Matches lowercase alphabetical characters.
[:print:]	Matches graphic and space characters.
[:punct:]	Matches punctuation characters.
[:space:]	Matches space, carriage return, newline, and tab characters.
[:upper:]	Matches uppercase alphabetical characters.
[:xdigit:]	Matches hexadecimal characters.

C
Server and Environment Variables

The MySQL server and many of its clients and utilities use several environment variables provided by the operating system. For some programs, the user can override some of these variables by command-line options or values set in an options file (i.e., *my.cnf* or *my.ini*, depending on your system). Table C-1 lists the variables used.

Table C-1. Variables and their uses

Variable	Use
`CC`	C compiler
`CXX`	C++ compiler
`CFLAGS`	C compiler flags
`CXXFLAGS`	C++ compiler flags
`DBI_USER`	Default username for Perl DBI applications
`DBI_TRACE`	Perl DBI trace options
`HOME`	Default path for *mysql* client program history file
`LD_RUN_PATH`	Path for *libmysqlclient.so* file
`MYSQL_DEBUG`	Debug trace options
`MYSQL_GROUP_SUFFIX`	Relates to the value given with the `--defaults-group-suffix` option for a program like the *mysql* client
`MYSQL_HISTFILE`	Default path for the *mysql* client program history file
`MYSQL_HOME`	Contains the path for the server's options file (e.g., *my.cnf*); available as of version 5.0.3 of MySQL
`MYSQL_HOST`	Default host for *mysql* client program
`MYSQL_PS1`	Command-line prompt for the first line of a statement for the *mysql* client program
`MYSQL_PWD`	Default password for connecting to the server
`MYSQL_TCP_PORT`	Default TCP/IP port number
`MYSQL_UNIX_PORT`	Default Unix socket filename

Variable	Use
PATH	Path for the MySQL programs
TMPDIR	Path for a temporary directory
TZ	Timezone of the server
UMASK_DIR	Permissions settings for creating directories
UMASK	Permissions settings for creating files
USER	Default username for connecting to the server running on MS Windows or Novell NetWare

Index

Symbols

A

We'd like to hear your suggestions for improving our indexes. Send email to *index@oreilly.com*.

B

C

D

F

G

H

I

J

K

L

M

N

O

P

Q

R

S

T

V

W

X

Y

About the Author

Russell J.T. Dyer, a freelance writer specializing in MySQL database software, is the editor of the MySQL Knowledge Base (*http://www.mysql.com/network/knowledgebase.html*). He is the author of the first edition of *MySQL in a Nutshell* (*http://www.oreilly.com/catalog/mysqlian/*) and has writen articles for many publications: DevZone (a MySQL publication), *Linux Journal*, ONlamp.com, *The Perl Journal*, Red Hat Magazine, *Sys Admin* magazine, TechRepublic, Unix Review, and XML.com. He has also finished his first novel, *In Search of Kafka*. More information on Russell, along with a list of his published articles and links to them, can be found on his web site at *http://russell.dyerhouse.com*.

Colophon

The animal on the cover of *MySQL in a Nutshell*, Second Edition, is the pied kingfisher (*Ceryle rudis*). At 80 grams and 28 centimeters in length, the pied kingfisher is the largest bird in the world capable of a true hover in still air. Like most kingfishers, it hunts small fish from a perch or by hovering over open water. But unlike others, the pied kingfisher often travels up to three miles from land. While the closely related giant kingfisher relies heavily on shoreline perching places, the pied kingfisher can hover above choppy water and swallow its prey on the fly. For this adaptive skill, the pied kingfisher is considered the most advanced of the 87 kingfisher species.

Pied kingfishers are common and widespread across much of Africa, the Middle East, and Southeast Asia, and are easily distinguishable from other kingfishers by their unique black and white markings. Never far from water, pied kingfishers breed in burrows excavated into riverbanks. These birds form family groups, with the previous season's offspring often helping to raise their parents' next brood. Additional male helpers may also contribute food depending on their availability. If food is scarce, the breeding male feeds its mate, while helpers feed both parents and chicks after hatching. Helpers may thus increase their chances of mating with a nesting female the following year.

Although kingfishers are known for their fishing skills, many kingfishers don't eat fish at all; among those that do, less than half of all dives are successful. Kingfishers are apparently blind under water, so their survival depends on perfect aim from above. They are able to judge both the size and depth of fish swimming below—the two greatest factors in determining a likely and rewarding catch. The instant a kingfisher hits water, opaque, protective third eyelids called nicitating membranes cover the eyes. More than a few hungry kingfishers have been seen emerging with stones in their bills. Still, among piscivorous birds, the kingfisher has earned its name justly.

The cover image is a 19th-century engraving from the Dover Pictorial Archive. The cover font is Adobe ITC Garamond. The text font is Linotype Birka; the heading font is Adobe Myriad Condensed; and the code font is LucasFont's TheSansMonoCondensed.

Related Titles from O'Reilly

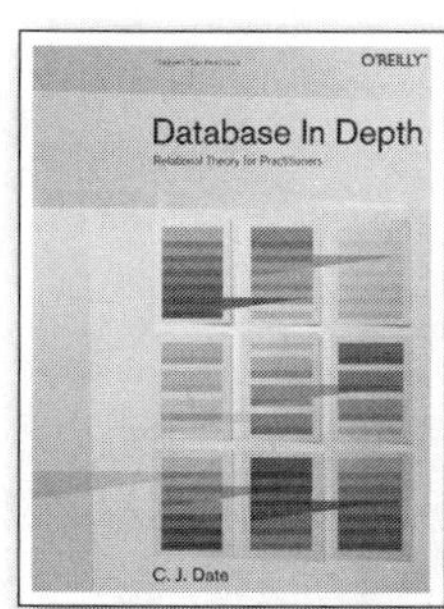

Database

The Art of SQL

Database in Depth

FileMaker Pro 9: The Missing Manual

Head First SQL

High Performance MySQL

Learning MySQL

Learning PHP and MySQL, *2nd Edition*

Learning SQL

Learning SQL on SQL Server 2005

Managing & Using MySQL, *2nd Edition*

MySQL Cookbook, *2nd Edition*

MySQL in a Nutshell

MySQL Pocket Reference, *2nd Edition*

MySQL Reference Manual

MySQL Stored Procedure Programming

Oracle Essentials, 4th *Edition*

Oracle PL/SQL Best Practices, *2nd Edition*

Oracle PL/SQL Language Pocket Reference, *4th Edition*

Practical PostgreSQL

Programming SQL Server 2005

The Relational Database Dictionary

SQL Cookbook

SQL in a Nutshell, *2nd Edition*

SQL Pocket Guide, *2nd Edition*

SQL Tuning

Understanding MySQL Internals